The Nondramatic Works of John Ford

medieval & renaissance texts & studies

VOLUME 85

RENAISSANCE ENGLISH TEXT SOCIETY
SEVENTH SERIES
Vol. XV (1990)

The Nondramatic Works of John Ford

edited by

L. E. STOCK
GILLES D. MONSARRAT
JUDITH M. KENNEDY
DENNIS DANIELSON

Medieval & Renaissance Texts & Studies
in conjunction with
Renaissance English Text Society
Binghamton, New York
1991

© Copyright 1991
Center for Medieval and Early Renaissance Studies
State University of New York at Binghamton

Library of Congress Cataloging-in-Publication Data

Ford, John, 1586–ca. 1640.
   [Selections. 1991]
   The nondramatic works of John Ford / edited by L.E. Stock ... [et al.].
     p. cm. — (Medieval & Renaissance texts & studies : v. 85)
(The Renaissance English Text Society ; 7th ser., vol. 15.)
   Includes index.
   ISBN 0-86698-097-0
   1. Stock, Leo Edward, 1927– . II. Title. III. Series. IV. Series: Renaissance English
Text Society (Series) ; vol. 15.
PR2522.S77 1991
821'.3–dc20   91-27571
                                                                                   CIP

This book is made to last.
It is set in Goudy Light, smythe-sewn
and printed on acid-free paper
to library specifications

Printed in the United States of America

Editors

General Editor: L. E. Stock
University of Ottawa

Editors: Gilles D. Monsarrat
Université de Bourgogne

Judith M. Kennedy
St. Thomas University

Dennis Danielson
University of British Columbia

Editorial Assistant: Marta Straznicky
Queen's University

RETS *Editorial Committee*

A. R. Braunmuller
Suzanne Gossett
W. Speed Hill, Chair

Contents

List of Title and MS Pages	viii
Preface	ix
Short-Titles	xv
Honor Triumphant	3
edited by Judith M. Kennedy	
Fames Memoriall, or The Earle of Devonshire Deceased	63
edited by L. E. Stock	
Christes Bloodie Sweat	135
edited by Dennis Danielson	
The Golden Meane	217
edited by Gilles D. Monsarrat and L. E. Stock	
A Line of Life	279
edited by Gilles D. Monsarrat and L. E. Stock	
Shorter Pieces	331
edited by L. E. Stock	
Textual Notes	365
Commentary	384
Glossary	435
Index	446
The Renaissance English Text Society	458

List of Title and MS Pages

I. *Honor Triumphant*

    Title page (1606), The Pierpont Morgan Library, New York. PML 17622. By permission. — 1

II. *Fames Memoriall*

    Title page (1606), The Bodleian Library, Mason. H.89. By Permission. — 61

    The Bodleian Library, Malone. 238(10), fols. v^v–1^r. By permission. — 84

III. *Christes Bloodie Sweat*

    Title page (1613), The Bodleian Library, Malone. 297 (3). By permission. — 133

IV. *The Golden Meane*

    Title page (1613), The Bodleian Library, 8° S. 14(3) Art. By permission. — 215

    Title page (1614), The Bodleian Library, Antiq. G.e.1.(3). By permission. — 230

    Title page (1638), The Bodleian Library, Vet. A2.f.293. By permission. — 230

V. *A Line of Life*

    Title page (1620), The Bodleian Library, 8° L.78. Th.(3). By permission. — 277

    The British Library, Lansdowne MS. 350, fols. *4^v–1^r. By permission. — 298

VI. *Shorter Pieces*

    "A Contract of Love and Trueth," The British Library, Egerton MS. 2725, fols. 134^v–135^r. By permission. — 361

Preface

The present edition brings together for the first time all the nondramatic works that can be ascribed either definitely or with some probability to John Ford. The majority of them have either been out of print since the seventeenth century or been reprinted only in inadequate, sometimes incomplete nineteenth-century editions. In some cases problems of attribution delayed the acceptance of works into the Ford canon.

Henry Weber, the first editor of Ford's works, was aware of *Fames Memoriall* but not of the other nondramatic works, observing that "our author did not again seek the favour of the public in print till twenty-three years after this first attempt" (1:x). He did not, however, see fit to publish the poem.

William Gifford edited Ford's work sixteen years later, and although he despised Weber as possessing "no knowledge whatever" and being "secure in ignorance" (1:li–lii), nevertheless followed him in his error: "that he published nothing we are warranted to conclude ...," again citing a gap of twenty-three years. He based his belief on Ford's assertion in the Dedication to *The Lovers Melancholy* that this was the "first piece that ever courted Reader." That this statement refers to Ford as a writer of plays, he seems to suggest by inserting "dramatic" in brackets before "piece" (1:xii), but the only longer nondramatic piece he prints, or seems aware of, is *Fames Memoriall* with Ford's lines in memory of Ben Jonson, which he adds at the end of his second volume. He approves of the poem to Jonson as "a warm and cordial tribute," but dismisses the few other shorter poems he knew. "Two or three smaller pieces, of a complimentary kind, might be added; but they are not worth the labour of transcribing" (1:lxxix).

We must wait for Alexander Dyce's edition for the appearance of more nondramatic works. Dyce reprinted and expanded the Gifford edition in 1869 (reprinted 1895). He added *Honor Triumphant* and *A Line of Life*, as well as three short poems at the end of his third volume: the verses on Barnabe Barnes's *Foure Bookes of Offices*, the Memorial to Sir Thomas Overbury, and the lines on Shirley's *The Wedding*. Finding later that he had forgotten the verses on Brome's *The Northern Lasse*, he had them fitted into a blank page after his introduction in volume 1. Only three acknowledged shorter poems remain, as Dyce in the same place declares he now believes the lines on the *Foure Bookes of Offices* "are from the pen of the poet's cousin."¹ Although published over a century ago and more complete than its predecessors, Dyce's edition contains only three of the five longer nondramatic works now generally accepted as Ford's and five of the approximately fifteen shorter poems.[2]

The works here brought together have few claims to independent importance: they are the efforts of a young man beginning his career, uncertainly feeling his way, and trying his hand at various popular forms. The importance of these early works depends on their author's place as one of the greatest of Stuart dramatists and their usefulness in the reappraisal and understanding of Ford's plays themselves. Critics no longer dismiss Ford as decadent, and this reappraisal has taken into account the nondramatic works, not simply for parallels of phrase and expression, but for the articulation of values, especially in the moral and religious works, that reappear again and again in the plays.[3]

That these works have been increasingly discussed and held to be of importance in the understanding of Ford the dramatist and that these works have been largely unobtainable for the modern reader would seem sufficient justification for the present volume.

Editorial Practice

—i/j, u/v, w/vv, and long s have been modernized, except in Latin, where consonantal i is retained.

—word spacing has been regularized throughout, including separation of some linked words.

—lower case initial letters after a full stop and at the beginning of lines of verse have been capitalized.

—wrong font, wrong case, and turned letters have been silently changed and abbreviations silently expanded.

---

[1] G-D, 1:ix. Dyce's forgetfulness was not confined to this instance. In his edition of Webster (1830; revised 1857) he had printed Ford's verses on the *Duchess of Malfi*. In both editions a note identifies the writer as the dramatist.

[2] The later editions of Bang (1908) and De Vocht (1927) contained only plays, although De Vocht announced in his volume a third and final Ford volume which was to include *Fames Memoriall, Honor Triumphant*, and *A Line of Life*.

[3] See, for example, the work of Oliver and Leech, the extended study of Ford's moral position by Stavig, and more recently the books of Huebert and Farr.

—digraphs have been preserved, but purely typographical ligatures ignored.
—indentation of verse lines (e.g., of a concluding couplet for a stanza) has been normalized.
—square brackets signal adoption of non-copy-text readings, authority for which is documented in Textual Notes.
—catch-words are ignored.
—when a word is broken across a page break, the hyphen is ignored and the vertical bar referencing that break to the appropriate signature or foliation has been placed after the entire word.
—the original typography of initial ornamental capitals has been regularized to the form: initial full cap plus small caps.

Acknowledgments

A short history of the present edition will allow me to acknowledge my debts for help generously given and gratefully received.

The original impetus for my work on the nondramatic Ford was provided years ago by Wolfgang Clemen, to whom my grateful thanks are due for many kindnesses during my years in Munich. During the same period I received much valuable help and advice from two of Professor Clemen's younger colleagues at the Lugwig-Maximilians University, Werner von Koppenfels and Manfred Pfister, and later from Hans Walter Gabler, who generously made computing facilities available to me.

My initial work was confined to editions of *The Golden Meane* and *A Line of Life*. Shortly after their completion, I learned that Gilles Monsarrat of the University of Dijon had also edited these two works independently. This knowledge led to an exchange first of letters and then of texts and to the first of many pleasant and productive visits to Dijon in the course of the following years.

There is no one to whom the new edition owes more than to Professor Monsarrat. My own debt is immense, not only on the works on which his name appears, but for his generous help and advice on all aspects of the volume. Neither my debt nor my gratitude can be exaggerated.

At first it seemed that, since our independent approaches to the editing of *The Golden Meane* and *A Line of Life* were in many respects different, new editions combining elements from both introductions and commentary notes should be prepared for publication. This was then done.

It soon, however, became obvious to us that having gone this far, it would be better to push on toward a complete edition of the nondramatic works, as the remaining works were written during the same period and often closely connected in thought and language. Not to have done so would have left the reader constantly frustrated by innumerable references to works not easily available.

With this decision, Professor Monsarrat kindly agreed to take over responsibility for putting *The Golden Meane* and *A Line of Life* in final form for publication, while I edited *Fames Memoriall* and *Shorter Pieces* and took on the task of finding editors for the remaining works and co-ordinating all our efforts.

To edit *Honor Triumphant* we were fortunate to obtain Judith Kennedy of St. Thomas University, already an experienced editor of English Renaissance texts. To edit *Christes Bloodie Sweat* we secured Dennis Danielson, then my colleague at the University of Ottawa and now at the University of British Columbia, whose interest in and work on seventeenth-century theology equipped him admirably for this task. Working with both our new editors was a pleasure; no general editor could have asked for more goodwill and ready co-operation.

For a number of reasons, not least because of other academic commitments and duties on the part of all of us, the edition has moved rather slowly towards completion. In these circumstances, more than the usual thanks are due for the patience, understanding and continuing support from my Dean at the University of Ottawa, Marcel Hamelin, and three chairmen of the English Department, David Jeffrey, John Hill, and Frank Tierney.

This support included generous grants of leave, financial assistance, technical and secretarial facilities, and, most especially supplying a series of research and editorial assistants. Three in particular must be singled out, Klaus Jochum, for excellent work on the earlier texts over a period of several years, Anne Le Dressay for a shorter period, and finally Marta Straznicky, with whose most capable assistance the work was delivered to the publisher.

That publisher, the Renaissance English Text Society, has supported the continuing work on the nondramatic Ford under three presidents, David Bevington, W. Speed Hill, and Arthur Kinney. While thanks are due to each, special recognition must be given to W. Speed Hill, chair of the RETS Editorial Committee for the volume, who, together with Suzanne Gossett and A. R. Braunmuller, worked closely with us, going over texts and introductions in very considerable detail. Their generosity with their time,

PREFACE   xiii

despite the many other demands upon them, has strengthened our work greatly.

Frederick Burelbach, whose unpublished Harvard thesis-edition of the nondramatic works almost twenty-five years ago was a pioneering effort to which all subsequent Ford editions are indebted, generously supplied me with his complete Ford research, including important work done after the completion of his thesis-edition.

Many other scholars have kindly helped with suggestions for solving particular problems. Two that come especially to mind are Ronald Huebert and Colin Gibson. My friend Colin Wells looked over and improved my Latin translations.

In the course of preparing my own editions and collecting texts, I visited many libraries in England and the United States and found help and courtesy everywhere. My greatest debts, however, are to the two libraries where most of the work was done: to the Shakespeare Bibliotek in Munich and its Librarian, Ingeborg Boltz, and to the Bodleian, especially to the ever-helpful staff of Duke Humfrey's Library.

L. E. Stock
Oxford
January, 1989

Short-Titles

The abbreviated titles used for Ford's works are as follows:

BH	*The Broken Heart* (1633)
CBS	*Christes Bloodie Sweat* (1613)
FCN	*The Fancies, Chast and Noble* (1638)
FM	*Fames Memoriall* (1606)
GM	*The Golden Meane* (1613)
HT	*Honor Triumphant* (1606)
LL	*A Line of Life* (1620)
LM	*The Lovers Melancholy* (1629)
LS	*Loves Sacrifice* (1633)
LT	*The Ladies Triall* (1639)
MM	*The Monarchs Meeting* (published with HT; lacks separate title page)
PW	*Perkin Warbeck* (1634)
Q	*The Queen* (1653)
SP	*Shorter Pieces* (this edition)
TP	*'Tis Pitty Shee's a Whore* (1633)
WE	*The Witch of Edmonton* (1621)
Akrigg	G. P. V. Akrigg, *Shakespeare and the Earl of Southampton* (Cambridge, Mass., 1968).
Anderson	Donald K. Anderson, Jr., *John Ford* (New York, 1972).
Arber	Edward Arber, *A Transcript of the Registers of the Company of Stationers of London; 1554-1640*, 5 vols. (1875-94).
Bang-De Vocht	*John Ford's Dramatic Works*, ed. W. Bang, Materialien zur Kunde des älteren Englischen Dramas, vol. 23 (Louvain, 1908), and H. De Vocht, *Materials for the Study of the Old English Drama*, n.s., vol. 1 (Louvain, 1927); reprinted in one volume (Vaduz, 1963).
Bestiary	*The Book of Beasts: Being a Translation from a Latin Bestiary of the Twelfth Century*, ed. T. H. White (London, 1954).

Burelbach	Frederick M. Burelbach, Jr., "The Nondramatic Works of John Ford: A Transcript and Reprint with a Critical Introduction," unpublished Ph.D. dissertation, Harvard University, 1965.
Castiglione	Baldassare Castiglione, *The Book of the Courtier*, trans. Sir Thomas Hoby (1561); ed. W. D. Drayton Henderson (London, 1928; reprinted, 1948).
Chaucer	*The Works of Geoffrey Chaucer*, 2d ed., ed. F. N. Robinson (London, 1957).
Cockeram	Henry Cockeram, *The English Dictionarie of 1623*, with a prefatory note by Chauncey B. Tinker (New York, 1930).
Coleridge	Hartley Coleridge, *The Dramatic Works of Massinger and Ford* (London, 1840).
Common Prayer	*The Book of Common Prayer 1559: The Elizabethan Prayer Book*, ed. John E. Booty (Charlottesville, 1976).
Cooper	Thomas Cooper, *Thesaurus Lingæ Romanæ et Britannicæ 1565*, Scolar Press Facsimile (Menston, England, 1969).
Davies	*The Complete Works of John Davies of Hereford*, ed. A. B. Grosart, 2 vols. (Edinburgh, 1878).
Davril	Robert Davril, *Le Drame de John Ford* (Paris, 1954).
DNB	*Dictionary of National Biography*, ed. Leslie Stephen, 63 vols. (London, 1887).
Erasmus	*Opera Omnia*, 10 vols. (Leiden, 1703–6; facsimile reprint, London, 1962).
Falls	Cyril Falls, *Mountjoy: Elizabethan General* (London, 1955).
Farr	Dorothy M. Farr, *John Ford and the Caroline Theatre* (London, 1979).
GB	*The Geneva Bible, A facsimile of the 1560 edition*, ed. Lloyd E. Berry (Madison, 1969).
G-D	*The Works of John Ford*, ed. William Gifford with additions by Alexander Dyce, 3 vols. (London, 1869; reprinted, 1895).

Gifford	William Gifford, ed., *The Dramatic Works of John Ford*, 2 vols. (London, 1827).
Harington	Sir John Harington, *Nugæ Antiquæ*, ed. T. Park, 2 vols. (London, 1804).
Haslewood	Joseph Haslewood, ed., *Fames Memoriall* (London, 1819).
Heywood, *Gunaikeion*	Thomas Heywood, *Gunaikeion: or nine bookes of various history, concerninge women* (1624).
Hill	*The Lover's Melancholy*, ed. R. F. Hill, The Revels Plays (Manchester, 1985).
Holinshed	Raphael Holinshed, *Holinshed's Chronicles of England, Scotland, and Ireland*, 6 vols. (London, 1807–8).
Huebert	Ronald Huebert, *John Ford: Baroque English Dramatist* (London, 1977).
Jones	Frederick M. Jones, *Mountjoy: The Last Elizabethan Deputy* (Dublin, 1958).
Leech	Clifford Leech, *John Ford and the Drama of His Time* (London, 1957).
Lyly	*The Complete Works of John Lyly*, ed. R. W. Bond, 3 vols. (Oxford, 1902; reprinted 1967).
Martz	Louis L. Martz, *The Poetry of Meditation: A Study in English Religious Literature of the Seventeenth Century*, rev. ed. (New Haven, 1962).
Merchant	David C. Merchant, "An Edition of 'Honor Triumphant' and 'The Monarchs' Meeting'," unpublished M.A. thesis, University of Birmingham, 1970.
Nashe	*The Works of Thomas Nashe*, ed. R. B. McKerrow, revised by F. P. Wilson, 5 vols. (Oxford, 1904–10; reprinted, 1958).
Norman	Colin J. Norman, "A Critical Edition of *The Golden Mean* and *A Line of Life* by John Ford," unpublished Ph.D. thesis, University of London, 1968.
ODEP	*Oxford Dictionary of English Proverbs*, 3d ed., revised by F. P. Wilson (Oxford, 1970).
OED	*Oxford English Dictionary*, ed. James A. H. Murray et al., 13 vols. (Oxford, 1933).

Oliver	H. J. Oliver, *The Problem of John Ford* (Melbourne, 1955).
Onions	C. T. Onions, *A Shakespeare Glossary*, 2d ed. (Oxford, 1919; reprinted, 1953).
Plutarch, *Lives*	*Plutarch's Lives: Englished by Sir Thomas North*, 10 vols. (London, 1899–1908).
Roper	*'Tis Pity She's a Whore*, ed. Derek Roper, The Revels Plays (London, 1975).
Sargeaunt	M. Joan Sargeaunt, *John Ford* (Oxford, 1935).
Sensabaugh	G. F. Sensabaugh, *The Tragic Muse of John Ford* (Stanford, 1944).
Shakespeare, *Works*	*The Complete Works*, ed. Peter Alexander (London and Glasgow, 1951; reprinted, 1980).
Sherman	S. P. Sherman, "Forde's Contribution to the Decadence of the Drama," in *John Fordes Dramatische Werke*, ed. W. Bang (Louvain, 1908).
Sidney, *Poems*	*Poems*, ed. William A. Ringler, Jr. (Oxford, 1962).
Sidney, *Prose Works*	*The Prose Works of Sir Philip Sidney*, ed. Albert Feuillerat, 4 vols. (Cambridge, 1912–26; reprinted, 1962).
Smith	Charles G. Smith, *Shakespeare's Proverb Lore: His Use of the "Sententiae" of Leonard Culman and Publilius Syrus* (Cambridge, Mass., 1963).
Spencer	*The Broken Heart*, ed. T. J. B. Spencer, The Revels Plays (Manchester, 1980).
Spenser, *Works*	*Works: A Variorum Edition*, ed. E. A. Greenlaw, F. M. Padelford, C. G. Osgood, et al., 10 vols. (Baltimore, 1932–49).
Stavig	Mark Stavig, *John Ford and the Traditional Moral Order* (Madison, 1968).
STC	A. W. Pollard and G. R. Redgrave, *A Short-Title Catalogue of bookes printed in England, Scotland, and Ireland 1475–1640*, 2d ed., revised and enlarged, begun by W. A. Jackson and F. S. Ferguson, completed by Katharine F. Pantzer, 2 vols. (London, 1976–86).
Tasso	Ercole and Torquato Tasso, *Of mariage and

	wiving, trans. R. T[ofte?] (London, 1599; STC 23690).
Tilley	Morris P. Tilley, *A Dictionary of the Proverbs in England in the Sixteenth and Seventeenth Centuries* (Ann Arbor, 1950; reprinted, New York, 1984).
Tucker	Kenneth Tucker, *A Bibliography of Writings by and about John Ford and Cyril Tourneur* (Boston, 1977).
Ure	*Perkin Warbeck*, ed. Peter Ure, The Revels Plays (London, 1968).
Weber	Henry Weber, *The Dramatic Works of John Ford*, 2 vols. (Edinburgh, 1811).

HONOR TRIVMPHANT.

OR
The Peeres Chal-
lenge, by Armes defensible, at Tilt,
Turney, and Barriers.

In Honor of all faire Ladies, and in defence of these foure positions following.

1. *Knights in Ladies seruice haue no free-will.*
2. *Beauty is the mainteiner of valour.*
3. *Faire Lady was neuer false.*
4. *Perfect Louers are onely wise.*

Mainteined by Arguments.

ALSO
The Monarches meeting:
OR
The King of Denmarkes welcome
into England.

Tam Mercurio, quam Marti.

AT LONDON
Printed for *Francis Burton*.
1606.

Title page (1606), The Pierpont Morgan Library,
New York. PML 17622. By permission.

Honor Triumphant
Occasion

Christian IV, King of Denmark and brother-in-law to James I, visited England from 17 July to 11 August 1606. His visit was eagerly awaited, splendidly celebrated, and abundantly recorded. Ford was one of several writers who rushed into print on the occasion, and his *Honor Triumphant. Or The Peeres Challenge ... Also The Monarches meeting: Or The King of Denmarkes welcome into England* was entered in the Stationers' Register on 25 July. The connection of the poems of *The Monarches meeting* with the royal visit is obvious; background for the connection of *Honor Triumphant. Or the Peeres Challenge* with the occasion is provided by letters of William Drummond of Hawthornden written while he was staying at court at Greenwich, where his father was gentleman-usher to King James (DNB). The two letters directly concerned with the challenge, dated 1 and 28 June, read as follows:

> *The Challenge of the Knights Errant.*
> *To the Right Honourable, the Earl of—*

> Knowing the Delight your Lordship was wont to take in the Sports of Court, whether as Beholder or Actor, I thought I should not importune your Honour in sending you the Challenge of the Errant Knights, proclaimed with Sound of Trumpet before the Palace-Gate of Greenwich.

>> *To all Honourable Men of Arms and Knights*
>> *Adventurers of Hereditary Note and Exemplary*
>> *Nobleness, that for most maintainable Actions*
>> *do weild their Swords or Launces in the Quest*
>> *of Glory.*

> Right Brave and Chevalrous, wheresoever through the World, we Four Knights Errant, denominated of the *Fortunate Island*, Servants of the Destinies; Awaken your sleeping Courages with *Mavortial* Greetings. Know ye that our Sovereign Lady and Mistris, Mother of the Fates and Empress of high Achievements, revolving of late the

Adamantine Leafs of her eternal Volumes; and finding in them that the Triumphal Times were now at hand, wherein the marvellous Adventures of the *Lucent Pillar* should be revealed to the Wonder of Times and Men, (as *Merlin*, Secretary to her most inward Designs, did long since prophecy) hath therefore (most deeply weighing with herself how necessary it is that sound Opinions should prepare the Way to so unheard of a Marvel) been pleased to command us her voluntary, but ever most humble Votaries, solemnly to publish and maintain by all the allowed Ways of Knightly Arguing these Four indisputable Propositions following.

1. *That in Service of Ladies no Knight hath free Will.*
2. *That it is Beauty maintaineth the World in Valour.*
3. *That no fair Lady was ever false.*
4. *That none can be perfectly wise but Lovers.*

Against which, or any of which, if any of you shall dare to argue at Point of Launce and Sword in honourable Lists, before rarest Beauty and best Judgments: Then again know you, that we the said Four Champions shall, by the high Sufferance of Heaven, and Virtue of our Knightly Valour, be ready, at the Valley of *Mirefleure*, constantly to answer and make perfect our imposed Undertakings, against all such of you as shall within Fourty Days after the first publick Intimation of our universal Challenge, arrive to attend the glorious Issue of the thrice famous Adventure of *the Lucent Pillar*, in which Prizes are reserved and ordained (by the happy Fate of our Country and Crown) for Three several succeeding Days of Trial at Tilt, Tourney and at Barriers.

The Maintainers of the Four Positions are,

The Earl of *Lenox*, the First.
The Earl of *Arundel*, the Second.
The Earl of *Pembroke*, the Third.
The Earl of *Montgomery*, the Fourth.

The King of *Denmark* is expected here daily, for whose Entertainment this Challenge appeareth to be given forth; who, if his Courage answer his Fame, will not be an idle On-looker to such Pastimes, which I would wish your Lordship to see, at least *in speculo constellato*.

Greenwich, June 1. 1606.
To the Right Honourable—

It was not in my Default, but of the Matter it self, that I wrote unto your Lordship the Event of the Challenge of the *Errant Knights*. A Gentleman told me he heard of it in the Court of *France*. It is answered, but in Words, yet well to this Purpose.

To the Errant Knights of the Fortunate Islands, Servant Men to the Destinies, awaking our ever awake Courages, with their Mavortial Greetings.

Most tonitruous, astonishing Chevaliers, Re-know ye, that we of Hereditary and Fee-simple Blood, and undegenerating Valour to *Doucel del Phoebus, Amadis de Gaul, Palmerin de Oliva,* and *Ascuper le Huge,* rather by the Bounds of your Challenge, than by the Show of your Meanings, have ecchoed in the Vault of our Understanding, the Volley of your Desires; and do allow you this for Answer. We confidently entertain your Challenge with your Circumstance proposed already, seeing the Event in the Cause; for old defended Virtue of Women is expired; and Men overcome with Women, are made less than themselves, and far inferior to the Valour of uneffeminate Knights. We are sorry, that any in the Shape or Apparel of Valour, should either be so short of Experience, or so unable to bring to their Wills their Knowledges, as to undertake the long forsaken Cause of a Sex, that have spent all their Virtue, which is sullied by Falshood, to the Abuse of their own Defenders; at the first, their Minds drew Wrath and Judgment, and now their Bodies draw Passion into a blind Adventure. Wherefore, we deny your Assertions, being assured of these Truths which tread down your Fancies; and these ours, in Peace and Pity, we offer to your Second Considerations; which, otherwise, if you believe not, will prove themselves Masters of you and yours.

1. *That a Man at the Years of Discretion, hath his Love in his own Hands.*
2. *That Beauty melteth Valour, and maketh the Tongue far readier than the Sword.*
3. *That fairest Ladies are falsest, having fairest Occasions.*
4. *That to Love, and to be Wise, were ever two Men's Parts.*

Against you, arm'd with the Truth of these, we shall come with sharp Arguments, not doubting to beat Falshood into her Darkness, unable to endure the Beams of the *Lucent Pillar;* the Mystery whereof ye vaunt we honour. Expect us therefore, if your rash Heat consume not before Performance.

The King, not without Laughter, can see, read the Challenge, and put the Noblemen Defenders in Expectation to be answered, but the Answerers have not appeared.

Greenwich, June 28, 1606.[1]

The jesting tone and controversial contradictions of this challenge and its answer give added point to Ford's debating method in *Honor Triumphant* of asserting an extreme position and then countering imagined objections.

It is tempting to suppose that the affair of the four Knights Errant was pursued at the tilts of 5 August, in which both King Christian and Prince Henry participated and where the "Earl of Arundell ranne with his Majestie of Denmarke, and brake three staves a peece, to the great joy of all the beholders," and that perhaps Ford's verbal jousting was part of the "other delightfull sport" in which the evening was spent "till time of night called them to rest."[2] However, Drummond does not mention the challenge in his letter of 6 August that describes the tilting; nor does he have anything to say of the evening's entertainment, omissions that suggest there was nothing in fact to report.

Six items connected with the visit, including *Honor Triumphant*, were entered in the Stationers' Register between 25 July and 19 August,[3] and all appeared in print expeditiously. Two other notable memorials of the visit are Ben Jonson's brief "The Entertainment of the Two Kings at Theobalds"[4] (the earl of Salisbury's estate in Hertfordshire) and Sir John Harington's outrageously funny account of the drunken cavortings during

---

[1] *The Works of William Drummond of Hawthornden* (Edinburgh, 1711), 231-32, 233. Both letters are reprinted in J. Nichols, *Progresses ... of King James the First* (London, 1828), 2: 49-50, 51-52. Drummond's other four letters relating to the royal visit, of 18 July and 3, 6, and 12 August, are reprinted by Nichols, 2:53, 73, 88, and 90, respectively. Nichols's choice of material relating to the royal visit is very full; see 2:49-95. Neither he nor Sidney Lee in the *DNB* identifies the earl to whom Drummond is writing; possibly he was the head of the senior branch of the family, the Drummonds of Stobhall, recently created earl of Perth. Another version of the challenge (dated 1612) is found in Harleian MS. 4888, no. 20.

[2] H. Roberts, *Englands Farewell to Christian the fourth, famous King of Denmarke* (London, 1606), B4^{r-v}. Stow's *Chronicle* also records that Christian "ranne at Tilt against the Duke of Lenox, the Earles of Arundell and Southampton, and the Lord Compton" (Nichols, 2:88).

[3] Arber, 3:142^{r-v}.

[4] *Ben Jonson*, ed. C. H. Herford and P. and E. Simpson (Oxford, 1925-52), 7:145-50. Printed in Nichols, 2:70-71.

the feasting there.⁵ Of the items entered in the Stationers' Register, two are by Henry Roberts: the *Kinge of Denmarkes entertainement at Tilberie Hope* (entered 30 July; STC 21085) and *Englandes farewell to CHRISTIAN the FFOURTHE ... With a relacon of ... shewes and seuerall pastymes ...* (entered 19 August; STC 21079). These amount to detailed journalistic coverage of the days' events. The *entertainement* takes the story to 31 July, as its title page advertises:

> The Most royall and Honourable entertainement, of the famous and renowmed King, Christiern the fourth, King of Denmarke, &c. who with a Fleete of gallant ships, arrived on Thursday the 16. [17] day of July 1606. In Tylbery-Hope, neere Gravesend. With a relation of his meeting, by our royall King, the Prince and Nobles of our realme: the pleasures sundry times shewed, for his gracious welcome, and most famous and admirable entertainement at Theobalds. With the royall passage on Thursday the 31. of July, thorough the Citty of London, and honorable shewes there presented them, and maner of their passing.

Englandes farewell, after some pious musings on the political utility of Christian love (puns always intended), picks up the story on 1 August and carries it to the embarking of the Danish king at Gravesend 11 August. The pamphlet ends with an unintentionally amusing comment on the extraordinary measures King Christian took to control drunkenness among his attendants.⁶

The Kinge of Denmarkes welcomme, entered on 8 August, is the anonymous "discourse from a Gentleman to a friend of his in the northerne parts" (STC 5194). It takes the story only to 6 August, and, as Nichols notes, "contains the substance of what is related by Robarts" (2:54). It does, however, add a few interesting details, including the texts of the "Welcome Song" at Theobalds⁷ and of the "most excellent song sung dialogue wise"

---

⁵ Harington, 1:348-54; printed in Nichols, 2:72-74. Another dramatist and poet who contributed to the occasion was John Marston, who composed in Latin an address of welcome and speeches for Concordia, Londinum, and Neptunus to accompany the pageant presented in Cheapside during the kings' progress on 31 July. This "Argument of the Spectacle" was printed in the nineteenth century by Grosart and Bullen and re-edited from manuscript by Arnold Davenport in *The Poems of John Marston* (Liverpool, 1961), 183-88.

⁶ STC 21085; STC 21079. Both pamphlets are printed in Nichols, 2:54-69 and 75-85.

⁷ Reprinted by Herford and Simpson, *Ben Jonson*, 10:401-2.

in the pastoral entertainment in the Fleet during the progress through the city of London.[8]

One Latin item, a sermon given by Thomas Playfere (STC 20008) on the Sunday before the conclusion of the riotous four-day visit to Theobalds, is entered on 29 July. As Roberts puts it, "On Sunday they rest from their pleasures, giving the honor of that day to him that sanctified the same, and hearing learned Sermons" (C2ᵛ).

Also entered on 29 July is the only item in the group besides Ford's that is a work of the literary poetic imagination. It is John Davies of Hereford's *Bien Venu. Greate Britaines Welcome to Hir Greate Friendes, and Deere Brethren the Danes* (STC 6329), sixty stanzas of *ottava rima*, with a dedicatory sonnet to the earl of Montgomery and Sir James Hay.[9] A rather dull poem, with a strained reaching for an ecstatic and religious tone, it contains an extended passage whose references to the challenge have some interest for Ford's work.

> Yee noble Blouds to Honours Taske assign'd,
> Let now your mounting Spirits make you mount,
> Such Pegasses as may out-fly the winde,
> And shiver Staves, at Tilt (beyond your wont)
> That Times to come in Poets Staves, may finde,
> Yee did great *Arthurs* Minions farre surmount:
>   Proclame a Chalenge through the world to make,
>   Your valours knowne, for Kingly honors sake.
>
> Yee read of many Chalenges proclaim'd,
> By Keysors past, that present Time admires;
> And how the Victors have their Daughters claim'd
> As the proposed Prizes by their Sires:
> Out-run those Runners, sith their fame is maim'd
> That runne but through effeminate desires:
>   Runne yee for glorie, and your Soveraignes grace,
>   So shall your fames runne farre beyond your Race.

---

[8] Described by Drummond of Hawthornden in his letter of 3 August (*Works*, 232; Nichols, 2:73).

[9] *Bien Venu* has been reprinted in *The Complete Works of John Davies of Hereford*, ed. A. B. Grosart (Edinburgh, 1878), and, together with a Danish trans. of the 1607 German trans. of Henry Roberts's two pamphlets, at Copenhagen in 1957, to commemorate the Danish visit of Queen Elizabeth II in May of that year.

If Pompe to Prowesse ere were kindly knit,
Now to your Prowesse add ye pompe, sans pride:
And to your pompe the richest show of wit,
For, oft such showes, do showes more simple hide,
And to the Showers glorie gaine by it,
That els perhaps (in gold) might not be eyde:
    As Heaven hath Starres her face to beautifie,
    So be you Starres, to make Earths Heavenly.

And like the Starres opposed, and dispos'd,
Produce ye wonders, mankinde to amaze:
Let *Denmarke* see great Brittaine, with her clos'd,
Makes the World stand in wonderment at gaze;
Sith of their Mould it sees halfe-Gods compos'd,
That doe the memorie of others raze:
    The manner of your motions fetch from thence,
    From whence the Starres derive their influence.

So shall they be all glorious, like the Sunne,
That runnes oblikelie to the Heavens Race:
So, though your deeds for Pompe, and praise be donne,
It is dispenc't with, by the Heavenly grace:
Sith Princes they alow a Race to runne,
As may, with pompe, devide them from the Base:
    „The Time, and Place, and Persons may be such,
    „That Pompe may show her *All*, yet not too much.

For, Charge is measur'd by Hability,
Not by the Cost, what ere the Charges are;
Showes most majestick, fit most Majestie;
Which is in Earth, where Kings as one appeare:
Uniting so their Raies of Roialty,
Which needs must make it great, as it is rare:
    Then spare no Cost, sith Gold for glori's made,
    And glory now is got, which cannot fade.

For, Honors Chalenge now is on her wings,
Flying (from Hence) through all the Continent;
Lighting no where but in the Courts of Kings:
Inciting all (in earnest meriment)
To prove their force, by Armes, which glorie brings

>   Against the bravest *British* hardiment:
>   If therefore now ye shrinke (sith gold is deere)
>   Y'are farre from Glorie, sith ye are so neere.
>
>   If many Worlds ye seek, or Ages live,
>   Perhaps ye should not find occasion such,
>   As now rich *Opportunity* doth give
>   To make you *Fame-full* though it empt your Pouche:
>   Two Kings thus met, make Kingdomes richly thrive,
>   Though it unlines their Purse with wearing much:
>   Then, sith but seld, or ne're Kings consort thus,
>   Be glorious now, or still inglorious.
>
>   Get Phænix-feathers to adorne your Crests,
>   Wherein imparadize the Soule of Wit
>   With such device as onelie Wit disgests;
>   Yet fills him head-full with receiving it:
>   Your Launces tip with Diamonds; your Rests
>   Of Rubies make, this pretious time to fit:
>   Arme ye in gold, that golden worlds may view,
>   Great *Britain*'s metamorphos'd to Peru.
>   (sigs. A4ᵛ–B2ʳ)

Davies wishes in part to counter objections to the heavy expenditures involved in the celebrations (a dissonant note perennially recurrent among the joyful strains of royal and state occasions), but he also glances at the other aspect of the Danish visit that appears to have shocked the more staid elements of English society:

>   Then let thy Conduits runne with rarest wines,
>   That all may freely drinke all health to thee:
>   And to those Kings, their Heires, and their Assignes,
>   By whom thou art, or maist the better bee:
>   Yet, O beware of Drunkards fowle designes,
>   Take healthes, while thou from surfet maist be free:
>   „For 'tis no glorie, but a foule reproach,
>   „To take (like Tuns) the wine that Shame doth broch:
>   (sig. C1ʳ)

Of course, the Danes had been "traduced and taxed of ... heavy-headed revel" even before James ascended the English throne with his Danish queen, and Anne's pleasure-loving extravagance was already causing grumblings in the early years of the reign. However, posterity must be grateful to her for her encouragement of Ben Jonson and Inigo Jones. The brilliant combination of art and poetry in courtly revel was spectacularly demonstrated at the beginning of 1606 in *Hymenaei; or, The Solemnities of Masque and Barriers*, a "sport" of dazzling splendor, where (as John Pory reports) the men and women "were so rich in jewels ... as was most glorious. I think they hired and borrowed all the principal jewels and ropes of perle both in court or citty."[10] The earl of Arundel and the earl and countess of Montgomery were among the masquers, and the duke of Lennox was "chieftain" of one of the sets of combatants in the barriers during the festivities, which celebrated the marriage of the earl of Essex and Lady Frances, daughter of the earl of Suffolk. The king and queen, and James's close kinsmen Lennox, were in their thirties, but other favorites such as Arundel and the Herbert brothers were in their late teens or early twenties and very much involved in the rituals of courtship as well as courtliness. The glamour of such entertainments as *Hymenaei*, with their amatory and chivalric associations and atmosphere of youthful ardor, must have been exhilarating to a young man of wit and sensibility such as John Ford. Of the Inns not of the court, a clerk not a knight, he had no gold to pour out in metamorphosing England to Peru, but he could respond to the mercurial rather than *"Mavortial"* challenge to "imparadize the Soule of Wit" by adding his "richest show" to the pomp "in earnest meriment."[11]

It appears, however, that Ford's contribution was not an official or integral part of the courtly entertainment of tilting on 5 August, in contrast to Ben Jonson's official text for the great house entertainment at Theobalds or Marston's for the civic pageantry on the entry into London. Ford's declamations might well have accompanied the martial exercises, in the manner of the learned disputations which were part of Essex's Accession Day celebrations in 1595,[12] but in August 1606 not even the challenge and its answer seem to have figured in the order of the evening. In fact, the entertainment on 5 August seems to have been low-key, a far cry from

---

[10] Quoted in S. Orgel and R. Strong, *Inigo Jones* (London, Berkeley, and Los Angeles, 1973), 1:106.

[11] See Davies, quoted above, 9.

[12] Alan Young, *Tudor and Jacobean Tournaments* (London, 1987), 172. (I am grateful to Professor Young for lending me a copy of his book before it was generally available.)

(for instance) the splendid festivities at the marriage of the princesses of Savoy to the dukes of Mantua and Modena in 1608, where surely room could have been found for Ford's witty addresses among the "cartels; poesies; devises; festins; bals; balets à pied & à cheval; combats d'animaux; feux de joye" that accompanied the tilts and tournaments.[13] Perhaps for Christian's visit the courtly functions as well as the civic pageants were curtailed through lack of adequate time for preparation,[14] or perhaps the court had already been sufficiently entertained by the challenge, which was promulgated before 1 June, and by Ford's statement of "reasons for the defence," which was entered on the Stationers' Register nearly two weeks before the tilts took place. Nevertheless, it is to be hoped that the most excellent ladies, the countesses of Pembroke and Montgomery, to whom Ford dedicates his *jeu d'esprit*, enjoyed it; surely his colleagues at the Middle Temple did.

The Work

The challenge of the Knights Errant and its answer give Ford the framework for his display of wit and partly dictate the manner and tone as well as the theme. The courtly mode of the challenge is fashionably archaic in its revival of medieval chivalry and romance, but the tone is closer to Ariosto than to Malory or Spenser. The answer contests the exalted praise of ladies in the challenge with the assertion that "old defended Virtue of Women is expired" and a litany of familiar antifeminist charges. Both praise and blame in their exaggerated language invited the king's laughter. In expanding on this courtly game, Ford had been set his theme in the four propositions (see p. 2 above), given the context of courtly chivalric romance, invited to pursue two popular debates of the day (on love and beauty, and the nature of women), and directed toward a jesting treatment of his material. The form he chooses is that of the declamatory paradox,

---

[13] Marc Vulson de la Colombière, *Le vray theatre d'honneur*, 1:304. The description ends on a charmingly romantic note, saying that "le Soleil se couchant" ("the Sun [was] going to bed") and night was always favorable to lovers: "Tellement qu'on peut dire qu'un Dieu les ayant engagez au combat, une Deesse les en retira" ("So that one could say that a God having enlisted them in battle, a Goddess withdrew them from it") (1:360).

[14] David M. Bergeron, *English Civic Pageantry 1588–1642* (Columbia, South Carolina, 1971), 91.

well suited "to exercise yong wittes in difficult matters. Wherein is no offence to Gods honour, the estate of Princes or private mens honest actions: but pleasant recreation to beguile the iniquity of time," and particularly appropriate for budding lawyers to stretch their wits, as knights must exercise "in the most common and vulgare actes of Armes."[15] Ford's method follows the established patterns of academic rhetoric and logic, particularly those for sophistical disputation. The popularity of this sort of exercise is attested by John Donne's essays in the form, probably written a dozen or more years earlier at Lincoln's Inn when he (like Ford in 1606) was little more than twenty.[16] Even before 1606, however, paradox could seem outdated, as Desdemona implies in scorning "old fond paradoxes to make fools laugh" (Othello, 2.1.138–39).

However, one of the benefits of writing extended paradoxical declamations is that the practitioner is forced "to seeke diligentlie and laboriously, for sound reasons, proofes, authorities, histories, and very darke or hidden memories" ([Lando], sig. A4ᵛ): in other words, to use all the resources of his schooling in invention. The literary context within which Ford discovers his material shows a mixture of long tradition and fashionable modernity akin to the spirit informing the late Elizabethan and early Jacobean tournament. In a sense the old and traditional was also the fashionably new, as turn-of-the-century editions of Chaucer and Castiglione indicate, but the young Ford's taste seems also to turn to the slightly old but continuing fashion for romance and to translations both old and new, particularly from Italian. The proper way to pursue "the sovereign life of Love, which is the true beginning Of all honor,"[17] had been a popular subject of debate and discussion in the courts of Europe at least since Andreas was chaplain to Marie de Champagne; and as in Andreas's codification of the art, devotion was always likely to reverse itself to misogyny. The medieval tradition of courtly love was fashionably and authoritatively at hand in Speght's two recent editions of Chaucer's works (1598 and 1602), with all the accretions of "the Renaissance Chaucer." There Ford would find not only the famous lovers Troylus and Cresseida (with Henryson's grim poem on her fate), and Chaucer's many other explorations of love and sex in The Canterbury Tales and the shorter love poems, but also debates on love

---

[15] [Ortensio Lando], The Defence of Contraries (1593; STC 6467), title page; sig. A4ʳ.
[16] John Donne, Paradoxes and Problems, ed. Helen Peters (Oxford, 1980), xxvi–xxvii.
[17] James I. Wimsatt, Chaucer and the Poems of 'CH' (Totowa, New Jersey, 1982), 11.

such as "The Cuckoo and the Nightingale" and such jesting and bawdy variations on courtly ritual as the late "The Court of Love" or the scurrilous ballade "O mossie Quince." In this context the mild bawdiness in Ford's poems "Love once was free from love," "Wise seeming Censors," and "Love is that tickling blood" is decorous.

The authority on courtly behavior was Castiglione. Ford could have used Hoby's 1561 English translation of *Il Cortegiano*, reprinted as recently as 1603, or John Wolfe's parallel Italian, French, and English texts edition of 1588, or even Bartholomew Clerke's Latin version of 1571, which reached its fifth edition in 1603. Ford does not borrow the dialogue form of *The Courtier*, but he retains a tone of serio-comic debate. *The Courtier* was also a suitable exemplar for the style Ford aimed at: as Hoskins recommends, "a kind of diligent negligence," whose "life" and "very strength and sinews" is "made up by pithy sayings, similitudes, conceits, allusions to some known history, or other commonplace; such as are in the *Courtier* and the second book of Cicero *De Oratore*."[18] Ford's playful use of Neoplatonic theories of love and beauty depends on the ideas given widest currency by Castiglione.

Most of the popular and influential prose works on such topics were, like *The Courtier* and Guazzo's *Civile Conversation* (1586), translations. The subjects of the first three days' discourses of another, Annibale Romei's *The Courtiers Academie* (1598)—"Of Beautie," "Of humane Love," and "Of Honour"—anticipate Ford's argument; the work was dedicated by its translator to the much admired subject of Ford's *Fames Memoriall*, Mountjoy. The fashionable appeal of these discourses even led to the 1598 translation of the *Hecatonphila* of the fifteenth-century architect L. B. Alberti, an elegant piece on the art of love composed on the occasion of the marriage of the duke of Ferrara's son. Besides "Triumphs, Tilts, Maskes, Barriers," there were "stately Tragedies, and queint conceited Comedies" and "civill discourse and familiar conference liberally passed between the Lords and Ladies." Among the latter was this discourse. Nothing in the 1598 edition tells the reader that the work had been written more than a hundred years earlier; its interests and style seem thoroughly consonant with contemporary tastes.

A more recent manifestation of continuing interest in popular Neoplatonic philosophy was Tommaso Buoni's *Problemes of Beautie and all humane affections*, translated by Samson Lennard, who dates his dedicato-

---

[18] *Directions for Speech and Style*, ed. H. H. Hudson (Princeton, 1935), 7.

ry epistle "30. April 1606." Ford may have read it before writing his tract in July, but even if he did not, its similar concerns show how close Ford was to contemporary taste. His argument that the wisdom of lovers leads to divine considerations is set out in Buoni's prefatory "Discourse" on beauty that shines through everything and "manifesteth her sparkling lustres, not only to things earthly, but heavenly. So that ascending even from the lowest things that are, unto the highest, we do still discover the greater wonders of this so great a God, communicated to us by the Archfigure of al beautie.... And therefore to conclude, let ingenious men convert their studies to the contemplation of the Beauty of Gods creatures, and thereby learn to direct their loves, to the love of that chiefe, and supreme fayre" (sigs. B7^r and B12^v; cf. *HT*, 653-72). The "Problemes," brief essays on such topics as "Wherefore doeth Beauty shine especially in women," "Why is Beauty worthy of Love?" and "Why is Beauty enjoyed, least esteemed?" canvass many of Ford's opinions and arguments.

Much of the fun of Ford's performance arises from its exploitation of the clash between an exalted ideal of love and feminine beauty, and a jaundiced view of female depravity. The opposed positions, and the frequent artificiality of their opposition, are particularly clear in the 1599 translation, probably by Robert Tofte, *Of Mariage and Wiving. An excellent, pleasant, and Philosphicall Controversie, betweene the two famous Tassi now living, the one Hercules the Philosopher, the other, Torquato the Poet*. Ercole musters the ancients and the church fathers in a long and only moderately amusing definition of "the fountaine and originall of all evill"—woman (sig. G1^v); the Wife of Bath would have pushed him into the fire by page two. He even manages to quote Petrarch in the antifeminist cause. His poetic kinsman, however, gently points out how his works (as a newly married lover) differ from his speeches: "you ... by the one, would make some proofe of the excellencie of your sharpe wit, and by the other, manifest unto the world your constancie in love, whereby as in the first you are to bee counted wittie, so in the last you are worthie to be commended for your wisdome" (sig. H1^r). Torquato suggests some "eloquent gentlewoman" will refute Ercole's objections and allegations with her reasons and arguments, but mostly expects him to "be utterly confounded by her admirable bewtie, which is such a silent kinde of eloquence, as it is of farre more force and power to persuade every way, then any other painted or passionate Rhetoricque whatsoever" (sig. H1^v). Torquato's argument that "because Chastitie is the bewtie of the soule, there is reason that a faire soule be resident ... in a faire bodie: that very same beautie which we see in sweete Gentlewomens faces, being no other thing, then the right glittering luster, and glorious brightnes of a victorious and triumphant soule" (sig. H4ʳ) suggests the language as well as the substance of Ford's poetic summation of his position on the relationship of constancy and beauty (*HT*, 590-97).

Eloquent beauty was not, however, enough to silence the antifeminists—or those who thought they could find an audience and make a little money by exercising their pens on this fascinating topic. Two examples of "Pamphlets against the dignitie of the female sex" (*HT*, 75-76) may serve: in 1603 Thomas Dekker published an amusing version of *Les Quinze Joyes de Mariage* titled *The Batchelars Banquet* (probably translated, according to the revised STC, not by Dekker but by Tofte); and early in 1606 Barnaby Rich denominated many of his *Faultes faults and nothing else but faultes* as follies of the Amorist: "And call you this love? I, it is love sir reverence, I have heard of many that were mad for love, yet I never heard of any that were wise in love. I have read of Conquerers whom Love have made effeminate, but I never heard of any whom Love hath made truly valiant, I know where wise-men have beene besotted by fancie, but I could never learne where fancie made a wise man" (sig. F4ᵛ). Rich is copious in his description of harlots and evil women. (Feminists will be happy to note that seven years later he published *The excellency of good women*.) There was of course a vast literature on the feminist question.[19]

Elizabethan prose fiction was even more preoccupied with the merits of women, the problems of love, and the rituals of courtship than the drama, poetry, and pamphlets of the time. Romantic plots provided a framework for witty and stylistic display in works more often addressed to gentlemen readers than to gentlewomen. Ford's familiarity with the genre is clear in his easy reference to Robert Greene's *Ciceronis Amor: Tullies Love* (see *HT*, 166-69). But the work that provides the most illuminating background for his efforts in *Honor Triumphant* is the greatest of the Elizabethan prose romances, Sidney's *Arcadia*, particularly the early chapters

---

[19] An excellent survey is L. B. Wright, *Middle-Class Culture in Elizabethan England* (Chapel Hill, 1935; reprint, Ithaca, 1958); see esp. 466-67. Useful bibliographies may also be found in Carroll Camden, *The Elizabethan Woman* (New York and London, 1952); Ruth Kelso, *Doctrine for the Lady of the Renaissance* (Urbana, 1956); Linda Woodbridge, *Women and the English Renaissance* (Urbana, 1984). For a historian's view, Keith Wrightson's *English Society 1580-1680* (London, 1982) may be preferred to Lawrence Stone's influential interpretations.

which describe how Pyrocles and Musidorus succumb to love. Two major episodes, where Musidorus not yet in love confronts Pyrocles transformed into an Amazon and where Pyrocles discovers his lovelorn friend transformed into the shepherd Dorus, are separated by Phalantus's challenge, triumph, and tournament of beauty in defense of Artesia. The whole sequence closely parallels Ford's performance in its linking of the chivalric and the amatory, its problematic arguments, and its union of jest and earnest.

One indication of Ford's admiration for Sidney may be his attachment to antimetabole, "a sentence inversed or turned back." As Hoskins says, "Our learned knight skipped often into this figure ... yet he concealed the particularity of his affection by this, sometimes by not turning the words wholly back as they lay" (p. 15). So too Ford varies the figure, as in "ladies are moulded of this temper, and tempered in the mould of love" (*HT*, 208-9). Quite probably Ford saw a manuscript of the *Directions for Speech and Style* of his more eminent senior fellow Templar: he would surely have agreed that "*a Sir Philip Sidney*" is a suitable synecdoche for "an eloquent, learned, valiant gent[leman]" (11).

Certainly the ideal of such a gentleman fired Ford's imagination, as he shows in eulogizing Mountjoy. In *Fames Memoriall*, he celebrates Mountjoy's valor and learning, love and loyalty, in the spirit of the tributes to Astrophel published eleven years earlier in Spenser's *Complaints*, inspired by the truth to his poetic vision of the courtier rather than by "Mercenary hopes or servile flattery" (*FM*, Ep. Ded. 06 25-26).

A number of critics have seen this late Elizabethan aristocratic temper as characteristic of Ford's plays as well. S. P. Sherman calls him " by nature a follower of the courtly, aristocratic, and romantic tradition ... saturated with the language and sentiments of the *Fairy Queen*, the *Euphues*, the *Arcadia* and the *Astrophel and Stella*" (23:viii-ix). Robert Davril sees *Honor Triumphant* evolving naturally from *Fames Memoriall*, and in its concentration on "amour chevaleresque, amour courtois" both revealing his youthful aspirations and looking forward to the preoccupations of his later drama (81-82). Clifford Leech insists on the importance of Ford's "cult of aristocracy" in *Christes Bloodie Sweat* as well as in *Fames Memoriall* and *Honor Triumphant*, and finds in the plays a similar aristocratic tendency towards "exaltation of the exceptional human being"; *Honor Triumphant* in particular anticipates the fascination with "the court and the courtly ideal" which permeates Ford's drama (19, 26, 21). Mark Stavig recognizes that "Ford's early non-dramatic work is filled with the same themes—love, honor, resolution, ambition—that pervade his plays," and sees the subjects of *Fames Memoriall* and *Honor Triumphant* as "congenial to his aristocratic and ambitious temperament" (xix, 3). Robert Ornstein characterizes Ford's plays as aristocratic rather than popular entertainment, citing *Honor Triumphant* in discussing Ford's ideals of love, his attempts to recapture the meaning of honor "as a guide to the conduct of life," and his projection of "the aristocratic values of his age into a storied or aesthetically distanced past."[20]

There is less critical unanimity regarding the tone and intention of *Honor Triumphant*. Sherman and Stavig represent the extremes. To Sherman, Ford was "fervently romantic": "what is truly unique in his genius is his serious application of romantic ideals to real life." For him, *Honor Triumphant* is given significance by "the warmth and sincerity with which Forde espouses the romantic point of view; the style is affected, but not the sentiments." Ford's earnest commitment to the ideals of "his romantic Platonizing predecessors" leads Sherman to find the drama of Ford's plays in "the romantic individualism of passion" (viii-ix, xix). Stavig, however, takes *Honor Triumphant* to be a satire and proposes as "the most plausible interpretation, that Ford was being ironic and was poking fun at the arguments he seems to be praising." This view of Ford's ironic detachment colors Stavig's interpretation of the plays as well: "Never does Ford get involved in elaborate speculation about anything. To Ford, man soaring to involved justifications of self is man corrupted by a deceiving intellect. In *Honor Triumphant* he is already poking fun at the pretense of so much Platonic theorizing about love." Stavig's analysis of the humor arising from what he considers Ford's ironic use of biblical language, mythological reference, and a Swiftian persona is provocative but not finally persuasive. *Honor Triumphant* could be reasonably described as "a witty *jeu d'esprit* on a topical subject," but the "picture of a sardonic, analytic, mocking Ford in *Honor Triumphant*" is very difficult to recognize (7, 187, 19).

Most critics have perceived the paradoxical union of jest and earnest in *Honor Triumphant*; how they interpret it is often influenced by their reactions to the artifice of Ford's style. Davril chooses to see the jest as not part of Ford's intention: the answer to the challenge is the work of "un anonyme farceur," but Ford himself "prit même la chose fort sérieusement." Not surprisingly, this attitude leads Davril to find "d'étranges discordances"

---

[20] *The Moral Vision of Jacobean Tragedy* (Madison, 1960), 200-201.

in *Honor Triumphant* between the ideal and the sensual, a clash which he hears at the heart of Ford's tragedies (80-81). Alienated by the work, H. J. Oliver makes no attempt to reconcile its paradoxes: "Ford has flashes of what may be humour ... but if parts are written with the tongue in the cheek, others are at least half-serious and correspondingly duller" (11-12). Donald Anderson is even more frankly antagonistic: "With its labored rhetoric and facile argumentation, *Honor Triumphant* strives for cleverness rather than conviction ..."; it is a "display of verbal and logical ingenuity," "a defense for courtly charades," and "an attempt at sophistication by a young writer seeking recognition." He admits that "some of the ideas and some of the language remind us of Ford's plays, most of which center on love," but mentions only two examples: Giovanni's speech on mind and body in 2.5 of *'Tis Pity She's a Whore*, and Ithocles' insistence on the divinity of beauty in 4.1 of *The Broken Heart* (21-23, 32). Dorothy Farr echoes Anderson, but suggests that Ford in *Honor Triumphant* insincerely adopts "the ideas of a coterie which he was to humour for artistic purposes of his own in mature work for the theatre" (9), a long way from Leech's reading of *Honor Triumphant* as an enthusiastic endorsement of the aristocratic code. Leech acknowledges "the affected language and extravagant argument" of *Honor Triumphant*, but he also commends Ford's "evident enjoyment of his literary task. He is almost aware of the thing's absurdity, but its attraction is stronger" (24, 21). The pull of contrary positions is also recognized by Derek Roper, who finds Ford's arguments "though sometimes paradoxical or facetious" yet "for the most part earnest" (xxi).

The range of possible reactions to Ford's tone in *Honor Triumphant* is reflected in varying interpretations of the plays. The most frequently cited example of a dramatic parallel to *Honor Triumphant* is Giovanni's speech demonstrating that his and Annabella's love must be virtuous. Ornstein condemns it as "high-spirited casuistry for casuistry's sake, an egotistic display of shallow wit," and yet (five pages later) praises Giovanni's almost immediately succeeding description of Annabella for "sweetness and affection," "fresh beauty and meaning," "a love of the flesh that touches the spiritual, an ardor that is unsullied by the courtly sensual wit of Suckling and Carew" (205, 210). Ornstein's contradictory responses to the scene mirror those aroused by *Honor Triumphant*; and in fact, such contradiction is inherent in the paradoxical nature of the subject itself: woman, beauty, and love. Where there is ambivalence, a style "like to a bold sharp sophister" is appropriate, and *Hero and Leander* provides a better guide to the tone of *Honor Triumphant*'s eroticism than, say, Spenser's *Fowre Hymnes*, in that it points forward to the "blend of erotic and religious feeling" that, according to Ronald Huebert, makes Ford a distinctively baroque dramatist (38).

Yet although the arguments are strong for perceiving in Ford a baroque sensibility, in *Honor Triumphant* the older strains of courtly behavior as transmitted by Castiglione and Sidney prevail. A fuller examination of the range of virtuous love and sinful desire could hardly be imagined than *Astrophel and Stella* and *The Countess of Pembroke's Arcadia*, which comprise a complete handbook of the contradictions of love, the intellectual debates arising from them, and the rhetoric appropriate to the aristocratic lover. If these fictions suggest that Ford's approach might be merely frivolous, then the exalted Neoplatonism of Castiglione should be remembered. But *The Courtier* contains almost a whole book on jests, as well as Bembo's discourse on love—itself brought to an end with a jest. The youthful Ford may have been over-ambitious in hoping that he was sufficiently "wittie and eloquent" to "plainely shew that women are as full of vertues as men be," but few would deny that in his plays he later achieved this proof, showing that women are often "a great deale more" "full of vertues": for, as Lady Emilia says, "vertue is the female, and vice the male" (Castiglione, 183).

The Text

Honor Triumphant was entered in the Stationer's Register to Francis Burton on 25 July 1606:

> ffrauncis Burton Entered for his Copie under the handes of Master GABRIELL POWELL and the wardens A booke called *Honour triumphant or the peares Challenge by Armes to be defended against all Commers &c.* Also *the Monarchies meeting or the kinge of Denmarkes welcome into England/* .... vj^d

The title page of the 1606 edition is reproduced above (p. 1).

Collation: 4°: A-F^4 [$3 signed (-A1, A2)], 24 leaves, unnumbered [pp. 1-48]

Contents: A1 blank, A2^r title, A2^v list of challengers and positions, A3 dedicatory epistle, A4^r to the reader, A4^v blank, B1^r-E3^v *Honor tryumphant*, E4^r-F3^v *The Monarchs meeting*, F4 blank

RT [within rules]: A3ᵛ-A4ʳ *The Epistle Dedicatorie.* | To every sundry
opinioned | *Reader.*
B1ᵛ-C1ʳ *Knights* [roman k, B2ᵛ] *in Ladies seruice* | *haue no free-will.*
C2ʳ *of Valour.*
C2ᵛ-D1ʳ *Beautie is the Maintainer* | *of Valour.*
D2ʳ *neuer false.*
D2ᵛ-D4ᵛ *Faire Ladie* [*Ladye*, D3ᵛ] *was* | *neuer false.*
E1ᵛ-E3ʳ *Perfect Louers are* | *Onely wise.*
E3ᵛ *Perfect Louers are onely wise.*
E4ᵛ-F3ʳ *The Monarches* [*Monarchs*, F1ᵛ, F2ᵛ] *meeting, or* | *The King
of Denmarkes welcome.*
F3ᵛ *The King of Denmarkes welcome.*

Catchwords: A-B, [none] B-C, shall C-D, first D-E, TO E-F, Like

There are three known copies of the 1606 edition:

[A] Pierpont Morgan Library (W 3 17622 C). A large copy, with all
signatures, catchwords, and top rules intact. A1 is torn, with only a
stub remaining.

[B] British Library (C.33.d.25). Lacks A1 and F4; A2 and A3 have been
repaired. Some signatures have been shaved; the catchwords of D2ʳ
and D3ᵛ are shaved but legible. On the lower part of F3ᵛ, in a seven-
teenth-century hand, are written the following verses:

> Forde can afforde much flatterring praise to women,
>   w ch they cannot afforde for to performe;
>   perfidious are they? most vntrue to men
>   farr gone in ill, and never to returne
>
>   Dust is lighter then ~~the~~ a feather
>   and the wynde more lighte then either
>   yet womans fickle mynde
>   more lighte then feather dust or
>   (wynde
>
>   A woman is a needfull evill
>   a seen [page cut]

The last couplet could perhaps be completed "a seeming good, a very devill."

[C] Folger Shakespeare Library (STC 11160). So closely shaved that most signatures and catchwords are missing, some bottom lines are barely legible, and the last line of D4^v "of hornes." is missing. Unfortunately, this is the copy reproduced in the University Microfilm series.

Press variants indicate only one fully corrected forme. The first reading below is that of the corrected state and has been silently adopted.

SHEET B OUTER FORME   Corrected: A
                       Uncorrected: BC

sig.	1^r	(13)	*Neoterickes*] *Neotorickes*
	2^v	(80)	redemption] redemptions
		(82)	not,] ~ ∧
		(91)	opinion,] ~ ∧
		(95)	in-|sufferable] in | sufferable
	3^r	(103)	*dispositions:*] ~,
		(104)	Apostataes] Apostates
		(109)	acceptance] acceprance
		(113)	Poet,] ~ ∧
		(116)	deseruing] deseruiug
	4^v	(180)	*fauour,*] ~ ∧
		(183)	*dallie*] *dailie*
		(186)	*beautie*] *beutie*

There are two other variants among copies on this forme: a damaged "t" on 2^v has slipped further in copy A and looks like a comma; on 3^r the period following "preserve" (113) is visible only in copy B. Although "beautie" is the most common spelling throughout, "beutie" and "bewty" also occur, often on the same page as "beautie" or "beauty," perhaps indicating that the corrector had a preference for the form with "a" not entirely shared by the compositor.

Single variants occur on five other formes, but only one is clearly a correction. The other four are differences in punctuation resulting from type slippage or variations in inking. The correction occurs on E3^r, where in B *"perfect"* is emended to *"perfectly"*, the space between *"wise"* and *"Lovers"* being reduced to accommodate *"ly"* added at the end of the line.

A period for a comma three lines above has not been emended; nor has the reading "*convinction*" on the second line of the page been altered. (On the editorial emendation of *convinction* to *conjunction*, see below, 392-93.) The variants are as follows: in each case the first listed reading has been adopted.

Sheet B Inner forme
  sig. 3ᵛ (137) lover.] AB, ~ ᴀ C
Sheet C Inner forme
  sig. 4ʳ (351) liking.] C, ~ ᴀ AB
Sheet D Outer forme
  sig. 4ᵛ (601) what,] AC, ~ ᴀ B
Sheet D Inner forme
  sig. 1ᵛ (432) hand-maid] B, hand maid AC
Sheet E Outer forme
  sig. 3ʳ (729) *perfectly*] B, *perfect* AC

One other variant has often been commented on: on A3ᵛ the dedication in A and C is signed "I. F.", but in B the signature "Iohn Forde" appears. F. M. Burelbach comments that the copy "appears to have been sophisticated" (188n). The variation seems to be the product of late tampering and without authority. It has not been adopted in this edition.

Editorial emendations are as follows:

HT 60 the] tbe 06
  500 cooled.] ~ᴀ 06
  506 *Bewty*)] ~ᴀ 06
  529 so obstinate] to obstinate 06
  582 Women!] ~. 06
  707 *conjunction*] *conuinction* 06
  726 brier,] ~. 06
MM 120 Danes)] ~ᴀ 06
  181 lowd,] ~. 06

Honor Triumphant appeared in two nineteenth-century editions. In 1843 the Shakespeare Society published *Honour Triumphant and A Line of Life: Two Tracts by John Forde, the Dramatist, Unknown to the Editor of his Works, and Now First Reprinted from the Original Copies Published in 1606 and 1620*. The copy of *Honor Triumphant* used was probably that now in the British Library. No conclusions can be drawn from the punctuation, which is freely altered, or from the spelling, which erratically follows the original, but the dedication is signed "John Forde," the reading at sig. E3ʳ (729) is *"perfectly"* (see above, 23), and the editor's only two noted departures from his text indicate that he was using a copy with the uncorrected state of the outer forme of sheet B. These two are the correction of "redemptions" and "dailie" to "redemption" and "dallie" (*HT*, 80, 183). The editor silently corrects "acceprance" to "acceptance" (*HT*, 109), but leaves the misspellings of "neotorickes" for "Neoterickes" and "apostates" for "Apostataes" (*HT*, 13, 104).

In 1869 (reprinted 1895) Dyce added *Honor Triumphant* to the third volume of his revision of Gifford's edition of Ford's works, an edition that has no authority, being a modernized reprint from the Shakespeare Society text, as Dyce notes (3:336). Dependence on that text introduces further errors. For example, when the Shakespeare Society text prints "distust" for "distast" (*Ep. Ded.* 9), Dyce emends to "distrust."

In this century there have been two unpublished editions of *Honor Triumphant*. In his Harvard dissertation of 1965 "The Nondramatic Works of John Ford: A Transcript and Reprint With a Critical Introduction," F. M. Burelbach gives a transcript of the British Library copy, with variants in the Folger and Pierpont Morgan copies noted at the foot of the page. In his Birmingham MA thesis of 1970, "An Edition of 'Honour Triumphant' and 'The Monarch's Meeting'," D. C. Merchant gives a modernized text based on the British Library copy and provides lists of press variants and editorial emendations in an appendix.

HONOR TRIUMPHANT.

OR
The Peeres Challenge, by Armes defensible, at Tilt, *Turney, and Barriers.*

In Honor of all faire Ladies, and in defence of these foure positions following.

1. *Knights in Ladies service have no free-will.*
2. *Beauty is the mainteiner of valour.*
3. *Faire Lady was never false.*
4. *Perfect Lovers are onely wise.*

Mainteined by Arguments.

ALSO
The Monarches meeting:
OR
The King of Denmarkes *welcome* into England.

Tam Mercurio, quam Marti.

AT LONDON
Printed for *Francis Burton.*
1606.

To the most noble Lord, the Duke
of *Lennox* his grace.

First Position.
*Knights in Ladies service have
no free-will.*

To the Right Honorable the
Earle of *Arundel.*

Second Position.
Beauty is the mainteiner of valour.

To the Right Honorable the
Earle of *Pembrooke.*

Third Position.
Faire Ladie was never false.

To the Right Honorable the
Earle of *Mountgomery.*

Fourth Position.
Perfect lovers are onely wise.

To the Rightly Honourable, and *truely worthy Ladies, the Countesse* of *Pembrooke*, and the Countesse of *Mountgomerie*.

MOST EXCELLENT LADIES. Where perfect honour is ennobled with accomplisht perfection, Beauty is not scant: which evermore is the glorious shrine of honourable favour: else had I misconceited mine owne hopes, and beene gravelled in mine own conceipts: but my strong confidence, is my confident warrant: neither can ye distast that, which explanes, but what is done for you, what is done by yours. If the pleasure ye shall take in the Defenders, who are yours, by the defence, which is for you, be great: then the acceptance cannot be lesse, in reading the reasons for that defence: especially being to you devoted: and onely to you devoted. What defects and weakely mainteyning arguments, in the arguments there are, your protection shal wipe off, and the trueth it selfe (which needes no lustre) chiefly privilege. I affect no singularity, I boast no affectation: yet can I not freeze in the one, when I am temperately heated with the other. To whom (noble Countesses) | should I dedicate the ornaments of love, and beauty? but to the beautifullest ornaments, worthy to be beloved. Neither doubt I, but as these endeavours were willingly intended, so will they as gratefully bee accepted. Otherwise (as I hope, as I feare not) I will be an alien to mine owne issue: as unworthy to be christened for mine, since dis-esteemed in being mine. Others, who oppose themselves, if not by *Mercury* perswaded, I referre to be by *Mars* enforced. So adventuring at once all my deserts, in your like or dislike: I rest.

Devoted to your ho-
nourable virtues,

I. F.

To every sundry opinioned *Reader.*

A4ʳ

READER,

I intend not to make any tedious Apologie: if thou be my friend,
5 thou wilt censure friendly: if a stranger, indifferently: if an enemie,
I esteeme thee not. Then thus:

>   *I write not to content each cavelling braine,*
>   *But eyes of noblest spirits: he that loves mee*
>   *Will thanke my labours, and commend my veyne,*
> 10 *For any others envy, least it moves mee.*
>   "He that will storme at every wrongfull hate,
>   "*Must not referre it to desert, but fate.*
>
>   *Let Ladies smile upon my lines, I care not*
>   *For idle faults in graver Censors eye:*
> 15 *On whose opinion (truth it is) I dare not,*
>   *The merit of my studies to rely.*
>   *Heere is the comfort, which doth cheere despaire,*
>   *I shall be lik't not of the grave, but faire.*

Meritum rependant venustæ.

Honor tryumphant.

B1r

TO THE RIGHT NO-
ble Lord, the Duke of
Lennox his Grace.

5   First Position.

Knights in Ladies service have
no free-will.

Right Noble Lord,

How certaine it is, both by the tradition of ancient and moderne
10 judgements avowed, that *everie man is not borne for himselfe;* the com-
munitie of the sawe, and the authoritie of reason shall bee a Priviledge
sufficient; but how much mistaken both the Philosophers of old and
later *Neoterickes* have been, their owne ignorance makes manifest: *A
man* (say they) *is partly borne for his Countrey, partly for his Parents, part-*
15 *ly for his friends, nothing or (if any thing yet) least and lastly for himselfe.*
True, yet had the sensible touch of passion toucht them with the
feeling of a passionate sence; how much more and more truely might
they have affirmed, that *the chiefest creation of man was (next his owne
soule) to doe homage to the excellent frame of beautie, a woman*: A wom-
20 an? the art of nature, | the lively perfection of heavens Architecture: B1v
for though

> *Man be the little world where wonder lyes;*
> yet *Women are Saints above earth's Paradise.*

For what is he, who is so absolute a Lord of himselfe? so power-
full in his owne power? so free of his owne affections? as being en-
snared in the pleasing servitude of a gracious beautie, can or durst
to undertake any occasion of remisnesse, but his own hart wil be
the first guilty accuser of his owne folly, and his sincere repentance
doe pennance in the language of griefe, in the griefe of despaire.
Againe, what is he then, that being free from this captived happinesse
of love, as it were disdaining to stoope to the bondage of beautie,
will not at length feele the miserie of his scorne, and be scorned in
the wracke of his miserie? besides, may hee not be desperate of his
owne merit, to thinke himselfe the onely exiled abject, banished from
out the acceptance of a Ladies favour, as also his owne unworthinesse,
which cannot deserve so delicious a blessing? say then such a one
be entertained, as a happie servant to a more glorious mistresse: how
soone, how much is his owne free rule of himselfe indeered to the
commaund of a precious Goddesse, neither then hath he, neither is
it meet he should have any more domination over his owne affec-
tions. *Mars* throwes downe his weapons, and *Venus* leads him cap-
tive, the lustre of her eyes, and the glorie of her worth are of such
unresistable a force, as the weakenesse of his manhood, or the apt-
nesse of his frailtie, are neither able to endure the ones reflection,
or withstand the others temptation: how then? must he yeeld? true:
not to captivitie, | but freedome; *for to bee captived to beautie, is to* B2^r
bee free to vertue: who would not put of an armour of hard steele
and turne from his enemies, to be enchained in pleasure, and turne
to a lady in a bed of soft down? *foolish hardinesse, is hardened foolish-*
nesse, when securest love is the loveliest securitie.

   Love once was free from love, and had a will
  To play the wanton wag, he strooke full many,
  And tooke delight soft thoughts of ease to kill:
  Yet he himselfe was never spoyld of any.
   Love carelesse would go walke, when by a grove
  Love saw a Nymph, when straight Love fell in love.

   Cupid *with* Psiches *fell in love, whose beauty*
  Dazled the lustre of his wandring eye:
  Forcing his heart devote obsequious duty,

> 60 *Unto the wonder of her diety.*
>   *Herein was* Cupid *blind, who els could see*
>   *Love now captiv'd his heart, which earst was free.*
>
>   *Love hath no power ere he gaine his rest,*
>   *But to impawne, sweare, promise, and protest;*
> 65 *Alas, what is it then that men in bed*
>   *Will not vow, urge, to gain a maidenhead:*
>   *Which being got, they ever after stand*
>   *Devoted to their Ladies deere commaund.*

Then what man of reason is he, who would be so unreasonable in his owne desires, to wish himselfe obstinatly foolish; or thinke himselfe foolishlie wise: by containing his owne dissolute infranchisment, in the | boundlesse limitts of his owne frantick wilfulnesse? such and of such nature are they, who in the rancorous spleenes of an unprevailing rancour, durst not onelie in the mallice of their tongues to speake, but in the venome of their hearts, to copy out whole pamphlets against the dignitie of the female sex: either without respect that they themselves came from a woman, or without regard that a woman wrought the peace for their weak-ballac't soules: (*oh but say such*) had not a woman beene the tempter and efficient of our fall, we had not needed a redemption: alas sillie betrayers of your owne follie? wretched blasphemers against the perfection of nature? can ye not, or will yee not understand that the blessing of this fall, is salvation? assurance of heaven? certainty of joyes? yes it is doubtlesly probable that women are, *Natures pride, Vertues ornaments, Angels on earth, worthy to be served, Saints in heaven, Memorable to be registred.*

> *Ne ii sunt amore digni,*
> *Quos indignos reiicit amor.*

Would any man live happie in content of mind? fortunate in prosperitie of content? singular in the repute of account? blessed in beeing inriched with earths rarest blessing? let him then ennoble his deserts, by deserving to be beloved: of whome? of popular opinion, or unstable vulgar dependances? no, but of love it selfe *a woman.* Would any be miserable? let him be excluded from the favour of beauty; and it is a misery incomparable, a torment unspeakable, a death, yea

a hell insufferable. How then comes it to passe that some vaine op-
pugners of love thinke? that by serving of a ladie, | they themselves B3ʳ
both honour in their love, and ought to be honoured for loving of
their beloved? it is easily answered, by the imperfection of their man-
hood, and pride of their grosse erronious folly. For this in the rules
of affection is text, *Whosoever truely love, and are truly of their ladies
beloved, ought in their service to employ their endevours;* more for the honour
and deserving *the continuance of their ladies good will, than any way to
respect the* Free-will *of their owne heedlesse dispositions*: else are they de-
generate Bastards, and Apostataes, revolting from the principals, and
principall rules of sincere devotion. It is not ynough for any man
that hath by long suit, tedious imprecations, jeopardous hazard, toyle
of bodie, griefe of mind, pitifull laments, obsequious fawnings, desper-
ate passions, and passionate despaire; at length for a meed or requitall
to his unrest, gained the favourable acceptance, of his most and best
desired ladie: it is not I say then ynough, for such a man to thinke,
that by his pennance in obtayning, he hath performed a Knights service
having obtained: but he must thenceforth, as much employ his in-
dustrie to preserve. For well sayd the Poet, whosoever sayd it,

Non minor est virtus quam quærere parta tueri.

Perfect service, and serviceable loyaltie, is seene more cleerely in
deserving love and maintaining it, than in attempting or laboring
for it. How can any one be sayd truely to serve, when he more respects
the libertie of his owne affections, than the imposition of Ladies com-
mand? to attaine happinesse, and then neglect it, is but an unhappie
negligence, a negligent unhappinesse: it is an unthankfull ingrati-
tude, than which | nothing can be to heaven more hainous, and in B3ᵛ
the regard of men more detestable. Herein are certaine chuffes differ-
ing from the glorious nature of gentilitie; who having stumbled upon
the raritie of beautie, are cloyed in their owne delicacies: not prizing
the invaluable jewell of what they possesse, not esteeming the bene-
fit of their precious felicitie: but like swine touze pearle without
respect, when as generous spirits glorie in their ample fortune: and
subject themselves to their chiefest glorie, for to be a deserving ser-
vant to a deserved ladie, is liberally to enjoy heaven on earth. If there-
fore the scope of mortalitie consist in the fruition of imparadised con-

tent, or a contented paradise? how requisite is it, that Knights (for under these titles of honour, doe I conclude true lovers) should loose the freedome of their owne wils, to be serviceable to the wils of their choycest ladies? who can serve two Masters? who can be a master of himselfe, when he is a servant to his ladie? but either he scornes the humilitie due to her, or affects a singularitie to himselfe, if the one, he is no servant; if the other, an unfit lover. Why? for because a true lover must frame his actions to the behestes of his ladie, and magnifying her worthinesse. Hence is it sayd, and truely sayd, *Knights in ladies service have no free-will*: that is, they ought not to be their owne, nor subject to their owne pleasure, unlesse to please themselves in the recreation which tendeth to their ladies honour. How pithily sayd a wise man,

Non amare decet, at amari præstat.

To love, is common to sensualitie; but to be beloved, is the crown of desert; they best deserve to be beloved, who deserve love; and they principally deserve | love, who can moderate their private affection, and levell the scope of desert, to the executing their ladies commaund, and adorne their names by martiall feates of armes. As for instance, *Paris* defended *Hellen* with the losse of his life: *Troylus* would fight for *Cresseida*: *Æneas* wonne *Lavinia* with the dint of his weapon, and sweat of bloud: *Pælops* hazarded his life for *Hippodamia,* yea what better example than of late in our owne territorie? that noble untimelie cropt spirit of honour, our english *Hector,* who car'd not to undergoe any gust of spleene, and censure, for his never-sufficiently admired *Opia,* a perfect *Penelope* to her ancient knight *Ulisses,* he an unfained *Ulisses* to her, for whose sake neither the wiles of *Circes,* or inchauntments of *Syrens,* or brunt of warrs, could force or intice to forgetfulnes. But examples may seeme rather tedious than convenient, I leave the certainty of them to their authours, with this proviso, that *what is manifest, needs no commentarie.* Now then considering the perfections of ladies, have been both in former and moderne ages, so resonant through every climate of the world: what dull spirit? what leaden apprehension hath he? that would be more curious, to undertake the yoake of their service, then forward to participate their beauties. *Lentulus* the Roman warrior, after all his conquests abroad, was willingly captiv'd and conquered at home; insomuch as at the first veiw of *Terentia*, hee fear'd not to say, *Non bellum, non fortuna*: Fate cannot limitt, warre cannot subdue the efficatie of love.

> *The fleeting pashions of disloyall minds,*
> *Proceeds from wrong directed scope of lust,*
> *Inconstant chaunge beseems grosse-feeding hindes,*
> *In whose deserts is neither faith, or trust.*
>   *When noble spirits in the bonds of dutie,*
>   *Pay tribute to the excellence of beautie.*
>
> *For gentle temper of a freer blood,*
> *Counts bondage to a ladie willing pleasure,*
> *Adoring service of best worthy good:*
> *And deeme their toile for favour, pleasing leasure:*
>   *Not reckoning commaund, servilitie,*
>   *But true performance, true nobilitie.*
>
> *To talke, converse, or dallie, is not love:*
> *But amorous wantonnesse of idle play,*
> *Brunts of defence doth firme affection prove,*
> *Who would not fight when beautie is the prey?*
>   *Then who is he who would not think hee's free,*
>   *When hee's inthral'd to loves captivitie?*

Loves captivitie is freedoms infranchisement, and whosoever is a prisoner, to the merrit of fairnesse, is absolutely naturalized a denizen to happines. To conclude (for in knowen verities many proofes are needlesse) a true, and truely loving knights libertie, ought to be inchained, to the disposure of his ladie: her will must be to him a law, and that law, not penall, but irrefragable. The sincerity of his tryed affection, must bee an obstacle to wilfulnes, with due consideration, that although he be bound to undergoe her pleasure, so he shall undertake no *shame* that may displease. For from *the faire proceeds nothing but what is faire*. Ladies are mild, and fearefull to impose dangers: wise, and will prevent them: especially such daungers, as either may threaten inglorious dishonour, or likely perill to their beloved. Timorous they are of the worst, carefull (and in that care ambitious) for the best. Nature made them Females, vertuously kinde, women, angelically vertuous: horror befits not their sex, or unthankefulnesse their beauties: for although warre defends the right of love, yet love cannot brooke the severitie of warre.

Dalliance in chambers, harmelesse play and sport,
Doe with the sweetes of love, much better sort.

Since then ladies are moulded of this temper, and tempered in the mould of love, mildnesse, and kindnesse: what is that Knight that would not be their captive? insomuch as the bluntest cynicke, must in reason avow, that it is most reason, that *Knights in Ladies service have no Free-will.*

TO THE RIGHT
Honourable the Earle
of Arundel.

Second Position.

Beautie is the Maintainer of Valour.

Right Honourable.

It is no prejudice to the precious claritie of knowledge, even in undoubted truthes, to make truth more doubtles, for in matters of wrong, arguments doe confound sence, when in explanation of right, they doe senceably approove it. Tis good; *Mysterie in demonstration, is a confused nicenesse.* So knowne is the certainty of this Position, *Et domi, et foris,* that whosoever would seeme ignorantly strange, would but bewray his strangely rude ignorance in seeming so. *Beautie* (say we) *is the maintayner of Valour*: Who is so blunt as knowes it not? who is so blockish as will not (and may with justice) defend it? an instance even in the entrance shall bee no absurditie. In the infancie of the Romane Empire, (as *Plutarch* to the purpose rehearseth) the Romanes violently seazed upon the *Sabines* | ladies: by violence they wonne them, by valour they justified their winning; insomuch as ever after betwixt these warlike Nations began both increase of hatred, and defiance of hostilitie. In which times *Kissing* had his first originall, devised by the *Sabine* ladies, as an earnest-peny of desart, to the guerdon of the Romanes desperate toyle. For although in the eyes of some more Stoicall censures, *Kissing* seems but a needlesse ceremonie, yet in the feeling of love, it is the first tast of love, the first certaintie of hope, the first hope of obtaining, the first obtaining of favour, the first favour of graunt, the first graunt of assurance, the first and principallest assurance of affection; the first shadow of the substance of after contented happinesse, happy pleasure, pleasing heaven; but to our matter. Men for the most part (some more heroycall inclinations by nature excepted) are in the frailtie of their humanitie, so fearefull of harmes, and so desirous of the preservative of life: as although not the discouragement of cowardise, yet proper instinct of mortalitie, will deter them from wilfull, and imminent running into perill. Some againe are of that frozen and cold temperature of disposition, as according to the proverbe, they esteeme it provident safetie, to *sleepe in a whole skinne.* Of this imbecilitie are many, who have only enjoyed, the lazie softnesse of vitious ease; and never felt, at least never conceited the touch of any miserie, no not of gentilitie. The selfe alone meanes therefore, that were to bee ordayned, for a provocation, and incitement to livelyhood of manhood was, the quintessence, raritie, yea rare quintessence of divine astonishment, *Beautie*: upon whose al-perfection, the greedy eye of | desire (even in spirits of clay and mud) being fixt, hath stir'd up such a ravishment of possession, as they now esteeme all dangers weake; nay, all impossibilities facilities, to possesse it. That Cardinall-vertue of invincible *fortitude,* had long since ben level'd with *cowardise,* had not beauty the *alarum* to *magnanimitie,* rent the distrust of weaknes and strengthened it with contempt of precedencie; æmulation of desert. Say then, how probable is it? how indubitate hereditary is the dependance of Valor, to the merit of *beauty? Beautie!* which prickes on the slowest, encourageth the faint-harted, sharpens the dull, commaundeth the stowtest, recreateth the wearie, and guerdoneth the deserving. *Beautie!* the largesse of the Gods; the comfort of men; the bounty of heaven; the prize of earth; the paradise of glory; the *Via lactea* to felicitie; the wonder of it selfe, *beautie.* This is that *Achilles* impenetrable shield, which everie *Ulisses* pleads for, every *Ajax* fights for; this is that golden fleece, which the *Argonautes* sued to find, which *Jason* toyling enjoied. This is that famoused *Trophey,* which *Philip* would have his sonne *Alexander* in the games of *Olympus* to wrastle for. How much are they deceived (I mean these fainter bloods) who vainly imagine, that souldiers fight for spoile only; Generals hazard their

persons for greedines; Sea-men traffique for avarice: Knights wander for prey, or that any jeopards his life, chiefely for lucre. Does not the marchant venture ship-wrack to returne with a present, that may purchase his Ladies liking? and in her liking his owne blisse?
does not the souldier fight abroad to preserve his ladie in safety at home? does not the generall commaund, that hee may returne with victorie gracious | in his Ladies eyes? does not the Knight errant attempt threatnings of horrour? adventures of dread? thunder of death it selfe? onely to rumour his fame in the eares of his ladie? does he not range for the succour of beautie? for the freedome of beautie? for the joy of beautie? and all spoyle that the souldier bleedes for, all the greedinesse that commaunders sweat for, all the avarice that the Marchant trades for, all the prey that the Knight adventures for, all the benefite that everie one and all of these hope, wish, pray, contend for, is the fruition of *Beautie:* than which nothing can be more gratefull, nothing is so acceptable.

Valour. *Through streames of blood and massacres of death,*
   I spend the troubles of a glorious breath.
   In feates of armes and lifes dread desperation,
   I touze to gaine me Fame *and* Reputation.
   All that I strive for, is to comprehend
   Honour; *to honour all my labours tend.*

Honour. Valour *doth aime at me, I aime at* Beautie,
   And make my greatnes greater by my dutie.
   Valour *doth fight for me, when all my prize*
   Consist's in favour of sweet Beauties *eies.*
   Honour *sustaineth* Valour: *when againe*
   Beautie *feedes* Honour: *and in that them twaine.*

Beautie. *Mean-bred deserts who covet much ambition,*
   Having attain'd it, ever grow ambitious:
   Soring to gaine my love, in whose tuition
   Their greatnes is advaunst, and made propitious:
   I strengthen cowards, and exalt the spirits
   Of weaknesse, I maintaine proud chivalrie:
   In me the drifts of Honour *pledge their merits:*

> *To guerdon and discerne* worthes *dignitie:*
> *And but for me they brunts of hazard loath:*
> Honour *payes* Valour: Beutie *rules them both.*

The whole scope that *Valour,* and men of valiant courage ayme their drifts at, is for the most part a *famous name,* and reputed *Honour:* but the marke which honour directs his levell to, is to participate the delightfull sweets of sweetest *Beautie,* which in al succeeding posterities, hath been of so powerfull and powerfully respected awe, that for the hopes, which men have evermore conceived of enjoying it, they have with accoutrements of defence been prest, for feare of losing, to preserve it. *Beautie!* why it is the life of *magnanimitie,* it is the perfect sparke, whose lustre reflecteth boldnesse to the timorous. *Beautie!* what is it? what can it else be? but the modell of all *fortitude,* for this proofe (unlesse I be mistaken as I am not) did the antiquaries of the elder world, such as were *Martialists,* attribute all worship unto *Pallas,* all adoration to *Bellona,* reverencing her as the Goddesse of armes, yet shee a woman. Fayre she was, els in vaine would shee strive with *Venus* for the golden ball: valiant she was, els with foolish superstition, did the ancient best *Warriors* adore her, and the younger *Sophyes* allow her, yes, yes, she was wise, beautifull, and valiant, including this morrall, that as shee had courage, so was shee a woman, whose force was not more fierce to terrifie, but her *Beutie* was as piercing to wound. Did they applaud her martiall disposition? true, but they did reverence | her amiable looks, most certain it is, the valiant may and do contend with the valiant, but *Beautie* hath the maistery of both.

Audentes forma cogit audaces.

Love breaths more resolution into the forwardnes of the resolved; for never have we read, never heard of any undaunted Champion, who being free in his owne affections, did strive so much by perillous exployts, to adorne the rumour of fame; but if he after were blest, by being an entertained servant to some worthy ladie, those daungers which before seemed dangers, he would now deeme easie, and all easy atchivements, toyes, onely that should then bee most honorable, which threatned most terror. *Hercules* valued the swimming over the Sea, to breed wonder in *Deianeira,* not for that he desired to doe it, but because she should admire, and commend the deed. Why do spruce courtiers, practize courtlike activitie? but to breed delight to their Ladyes. Why doe men in generall contend to exceed in braverie? but to be noted the bravest of their ladies. Why doe cormorants hoord treasure? but to attract some ladies liking. Why do poore men toyle? great men traverse? but all to one end, to share *Beautie.* Why doe Kings and greatest Princes, thirst to enlarge their empires and dominions? but to be noted for more eminent, and more to be loved for that eminence of their ladies. Let us looke into all the devoyres of mankind, and they all tend to the content of *Beautie:* Men to honour men, is rather a bootlesse feare, then in regardfull love; but for men to bee honoured of ladies, is the scope of all felicitie. Men in kindnesse are mutually lambs, but | in corrivall-shipp of love, C4ᵛ Lyons. Should I fight for my friend, I might be appeazed in my choller, but for my lady, I am inexorable.

Chalibs mihi circa pectus.

The teares of widows, the cries of babes, the condolement of Parents, the intreaties of Children, the wounds of the maimed, the wracke of the oppressed, cannot move pity in a steeled hart, which fights for report in the honor of his lady. It is said of the *Turks* they traine their youth in discipline of warre, with intent of cruelty, beleeve it I cannot be perswaded, that being so absolute warriors, they shuld so wholy be murtherous tyrants, except to returne with triumph in the sight of their ladies. *Tamburlaine,* the scourge of God, and savadgest monster of his time; never made a slaughter upon any of his conquered captives, but the principallest he ever sent as slaves to his queene *Zenocrate,* intending that as she was the deity, who infus'd strength into his armes: so shee should be the whole glory of his tryumph.

Pax ruat in bellum, sociumque in prælia fœdus:
Causa subit; nulla fronte regendus Amor.

How requisite it is then for a kingdom, which would be fortifyed with choyce of magnanimous spirits, to be also inriched with the ornament of *Beauty:* the expediency in occasions of necessity makes evident. I have often marvailed why the Romanes (famous for their loves) going to battaile against a world of so many nations, as they did, for more suerty of victory, had not carried their ladies with them: that by the sight of them their enfeebled strength, might (like the head of *Hydra*) doubly have renued. Doubtles had *Julius Cæsar,* at his | first arrivall for the conquest of *Britane,* brought with him Cleopatra, he would never have twise suffered so shamefull a repulse. What infinite examples might here be alledged, for the probation, that *Beauty* hath evermore instigated audacity to the dullest? finally in the apprehension of common reason, let every man examine himselfe, whether it be not the immediat norisher of al *fortitude?* It is, it hath been, and ever wilbe the nurse, and foode of heroicall chivalry, for valor not seasoned with the hopes of love, is an irresolute valour. A souldier, and libertine, is an unarmed souldier? *Beauty* is the spur to *Honor; Honor* the serviceable attendant on *Beauty,* yet will some home-bred poring Academicke say, it is the only means to make a warrior a flat coward: for *Beauty* allures to delights, delights to ease, ease consequently the fosterer to discouraged pusillanimity: but let such an unexperienced plodder knowe, it is as difficult for him to censure of courage, as it is easy for the couragious to scorne his censure, or indeed rather pittie his ridiculous folly in censuring, as *Hanniball* did *Phormio,* when he would read him a lecture of war, who had ever bin trained in the wars: as if a mild lover may not dally at home in a cabinet, yet the selfe same be a severe souldier in the field. Let therfore every man of reason, be reasonable in understanding, and where he cannot contradict, confesse that *the truth is greatest and chiefly prevaileth,* principally when armes will justifie, what arguments confirme, and arguments againe reciprocally corroborate what armes (on the behalfe of justice) doth maintaine, and rightly maintaine, that merely of it selfe, *Beauty is the maintainer of Valour.*

TO THE RIGHT HONO-
rable the Earle of *Pembroke.*

Third Position.

Faire Ladie was never false.

Right Honorable

The temperature of the mind follows the temperature of the bodie. Which certaine axiome (sayes that sage Prince of Philosophers *Aristotle*) is ever more infallible. Then doe not I a little marvell, what arrogant spleen of malediction with teeth of juyceles envie, durst to detract from the worthines of *Beauty?* terming it a particular blessing, bestowed for a more general curse. Terming it fickle, deceitfull, inconstant, when if the sawes of authority be authenticall, nothing can be more precious, nothing in it selfe so vertuous. *Faire Ladie was never false?* Oh sayes some curious impostor, *Euge hominem?* a goodly theame? much witt no doubt expected? few proofes produced? who will not sweare the contrary? who will not beleeve the contrarie as his Creed? vaine fondlings, as many as so beleeve, doubtlesse shall be so deceived; and doe penance for their errour in the gall of their distrust. For if *the temperature of the mind, follow the temperature of the bodie?* (text it is) then without controversie, as the outward shape is more singular, so the inward vertues must be most exquisite. Nature is but the hand-mayd to heaven. *Beautie* is the rarest workemanship of Natures power. So questionlesse where the hand-maid of heaven hath imparted her art, the blessings of the Gods are plentifully abounding. Neither will they make | that lame, which nature hath framed perfect. For why? can falshood lye hidden under the raritie of fairnesse? no more than vice can lurke under the plumes of vertue; which is meerely impossible. Beautie is but a faire Inne to lodge more fairer guests within. It is but the lively colour of an excellent tasting wine. It is the greatest *good* in it selfe, that heart of humanitie can wish for. If *deformitie* be the dreg's and scum of earths disgrace? if it be (as it is) the curse of the Parents transgression, layd upon the child? then contrarily, must *beautie* be the immediate testimonie of heavens favor? why were people in times past, called Giants and Monsters? but for the ugly appearance of their shapes. Neither were they in body so mishapen, as in conditions odious. So then even in them it is manifestly verified, that foulest enormities harbour in fowlest formes, then it followes, that *firmest vertues, are shrowded in the fairest complexions.* Some indeed oppose an argument, that *Beauty* of it selfe is a great *good:* but the abuse most wretched and common. Yea, so common, that the very face of *beautie* is a presumption: yea more, a warrant of *inconstancie;* to such is easily replyed. Such abuse proceeds not from *perfect beautie,* but from the adulterate counterfeit of *beautie, art.* Of this nature are those that being intemperately wanton, strive with artificiall cunning, to cover the defects of *nature.* For *true beautie,* as it is of it selfe a *good,* so is it in it selfe simple, innocent, and harmelesse. Into which no thought of unkindnesse, can penetrate: and being once subject to love, can never, will never be tempted to loosnesse. O strange sayes one! oh heresie cries another; palpably false! falsely absurd; do not Poets the pillars of your folly affirme, that *Venus* forsooth your only Deity of your passions, the queen of your thoughtts, the boast and goddesse | of your loves, was absolutely false to her husband? else had *Cupid* been unborne; *Æneas* unbegotten. And yet *lady was never faire and false!* was not *Helen* of *Greece* made a Trojan stale; a scorne to posterities, whose verie name is ominous to cuckolds. Do not all chronicles of antiquity shew? not only that the *faire,* but the *fairest* have prooved *lightest?* and yet *faire ladie was never false.* True, the Poets say so, who being themselves lasciviously addicted, thought it great inhumanity, at least injurie, that *Beautie* shuld be ingrost to the proper use of one alone man. Besides if Poets are to be credited, *Venus* was a Goddesse, not framed by *nature,* but yssuing from the Gods, and therfore above humane apprehension. Poets speak truth to warrant their writs, and so was *Venus faire,* they devise fictions to approove their wits; so was she *immodest*: with this Caveat, that she was *Venus,* was a troth; that she was trothles, a fiction. Also *Helen* was counted *faire,* because many affected her, procur'd by her enticing wantones, inviting allurements. Curteous I thinke she was, and therfore beloved, *faire* never, for then not *fickle*. Indeed I acknowledge, old writers being themselves past the youth of love, and sunke into dotage, have inveighed against the dignity of that sex, not upon knowledg, but mere supposition, deming that because the worst are haunted of the worst for their lewdnes, condemne the *fairest* for being *faire,* as the principall inchantment. Now so much difference is there, betwixt the wanton and the *faire,* as the *wanton* may be beloved, but the *faire,* wil not be *wanton*. It is to be supposed, that such as inclined to the loose ficklenesse of change, are not of that excellent temper, of true bewty, because then they knowing their own merit, (as women of that nature do) wold be by how much the more noted, by so much the more tender of the preservation of | their honors report. And somewhat precizely (pardon troth) prize their own value: *Scire tuum nihil est nisi te scire hoc sciat alter.* To be *faire,* and not admired is as a hidden minerall: yet to be admired, and not preserve that admiration, is an unvalued indignity. But as ladies are *fair,* so are they *wise,* and as they are both *faire* and *wise; constant*. Alas, most know, and many fele, that *bewty* is not easily woed to love; many bitter conflicts, of oppressed griefs, are to be indured, ere they are won to listen to affection. And at length being persuaded, they were not so obdurat before to be sued to, as they are now most *constant* in their loves: most sincerely firme to their choice. Experience teacheth it, that stele is not soon hot, yet being once fired, is lesse easily cooled. An example or two, shal warrant the credit of the rest: who could bee more industrious to his ladie, than *Theseus* was in gaining *Ariadne?* who being conquered, was ever most fast to him: though injuriously; yea, perfidiously forsaken of him. *Portia* so inderely reverenced *Cato,* as she would for his preservation swallow coles. *Alcest* wold die for *Admetus*. And *Penelope* (the mirror of the *Greeke* matrons, both for *constancy* and *Bewty*) wold never falsify her faith to *Ulisses*. I my self shuld account such proofs inconvenient, did not the proofe of my defence, rely upon former instances compared both with present and latter times. *Diana* renowned for *beauty,* was more renowned for *chastity,* insomuch as singularly, and truly *fairest* ladies contended to be her nymphs, if trust to writers may be attributed: *rara præclara*: according to the proverbe, that the *fairest* are the *fairest*, that is the best and best to be estemed. what is more to be urged for the ratifying our maintenance: but the *exterior beauty, is assurance of the interior quality*. To answere to every vain objection, that some more nice wits, only seeming witty in censure and | misconstruction, is not here intended, as *fronti nulla fides*: the *ficklenes* of *Cresseida*: the *mutability* of some *Lais*: let it suffice, they are fictions and nugatory invectives, of deservingly abused poets: or repulsed *Annalogers,* ridiculous in the understanding of the wise: contemptible, in the perseverance of understanding. It is even as impossible for *ladies* of *quaintest formes,* to incline to thoughts of trothles *impudency*, as for monsters of *deformity*, to produce effects of *vertue*. Needs there any other demonstration, then the admirable (almost incredible) ornament of chastity? *Lucrece* the Roman dame, the paragon of those times, the mirror of those daies, for ravishing perfection of *beauty*: harmeles, unspotted *Lucrece*? who did withstand lust to the eternizing her honor, and monumented her rape with extremity of death. Who is he [so] obstinate in his errour? so wilful in his madnes? so mad in his erronius wilfulnes? as would not even in the glas of *Lucresias* perseverance (even to the uttermost extinct of life) se the wonder of *bewty*, matched with the individuat adjunct unsoyled *constancy.*

Constantia est gemella venustatis individua.

Three particularities there are, that stand firme for this position: *examples,* already alledged: *approbation of judgment* newly rehearsed: and *ground of troth* now to be verefi'de. verefi'de said I? the self assurance of the subject, is a testimony most probable, if *vice* be the nourisher of *vice, vertue* must be the effect of *vertue*. That is sincerely a *vertue,* which is a *good,* and that *good* is *Beauty,* so herein *fictions* comprehend *truth,* as *forma bonum*: yet ere I wade further, and be gravel'd in the ouze, and quicksand of my own intention, I am for the clearing of such, as may misconceite my drift, to make an Apology for my defence: neither by my just justification, of an apparant verity, the *wanton* shall taxe my indevours, as ridiculous: knowing | their own imperfections, nor challenge this, as a due belonging to the encouragment of their lenity. I confesse (and blush that occasion should be ministred of confession) that many there are, whose bewitching lookes, drawe youth into folly, and age into dotage, rather madnes: too many there are, whose smooth *counterfeit,* in the indiscretion of virility, may passe for *Beauty*: when the counterfeiters, are so mutable, as they are neither ever their own, or ever certaine any on's. Yea, even in *great* personages, this loosnesse is an imboldning, to the *meaner*: rather a president to the *worst* of offending: the greatnes of their estates (I speake of some that have beene) bolstereth out the community, of licentious immodesty, whose shames were they enameled in the tableture of their foreheads, it would be a hideous visour, to more deformed complections, more enormious conditions. Such there are, who under the abhomination of luxury, (nicely termed kindnes) import the pretexted glosse of *beauties* name, to such are also mercenarye slaves, intimated servants, against whom, although my purpose is not to inveigh, yet doe I here exclude them from out the assotiation of the *faire*: let those be *false, beautifull* they are not. In them the *temperature of the body, follows the temperature of the mind*: not the *temperature of the mind, the temperature of the body*: Of whom the philosopher insisteth. As I said before, so I here avow that the error of their enchanting amyablenes bewitcheth their adherents, who being ensnared in the nets of their *lasciviousnes,* esteeme that prime *beauty* which they themselves deliciously enjoy. For as the *loose* have no substance, but fading *art* to attract, so the excellently *faire,* have no *falshood* to be soyled; no cunning to beguile; no visor to delude. They are doves without gals; swans without spots; fawnes without spleene: they are *simple,* and will not | be trained; *faire* and cannot be tempted: they are the pure colour of *white,* without staine, whose delicate eares, by prophaned tongues may bee enforced to heare ill, but whose unmoved breasts, by the fond cannot be enflamed to consent to il. Herein are the *bewtiful* said to be Angels on earth, for that as they exceed others in wonder of *beauty;* so they excell all other in graces of *vertue*: it shall not be amisse, to answere to the malevolent will of some witty malevolent detractors.

Adverse.

Women! ô *they are fickle falling starres:*
Tydes in their ebbes, Moones ever in the wayne,

Frost in the thawe, faint hearted in the wars
Of constancy, yet constant in disdaine.
Women! ô they are creatures most unholly:
Borne for a scourge to men, and curbe to folly.
Mulieri ne credas, ne mortuæ quidem.

Proofe.

Women! why they are fixed lamps of heaven,
Shining bright lustre to the hearts of men.
Firme diamonds, and faire, bright lookes, hearts even:
Constant in scorne of motions, where and when
Princes for ladies praise have fell at odds,
They are of men ador'd, belov'd of Gods:
The highest blessing, that to earth's uncommon,
Is mans perfection, soule of life, a woman.
Diis compares fœminae.

Every *faire* lady is *lovely*, but every *lovely* ladye is not *faire*: so then the *lovely* may be *fickle*, but the *faire* cannot be *inconstant*: what should I more say, and yet what have I saide that is inough? what, that can bee too much? and yet is not to much? since the only experience of the subject, commendeth his own worthines. To such then as credit it, I wish them a faire lady: to misbelevers and infidels in *love* this curse: may their ladies be foule, and so be loathsome, yet *false*, and repay them with the common crest of hornes.

TO THE RIGHT
Honourable the Earle of *Mountgomery*.

The fourth and last Position.

Perfect lovers are onely wise.

Right Honourable,

Perspicax est amatorum vigilans ocellus, prævidet adversa, studet horis convenientibus. A perfect lover is never lesse idle, then when he is idle: never more busied, then when least seriously imployed.

> *Wise seeming* Censors *count that labour vaine,*
> *Which is devoted to the hopes of love,*
> *When they themselves, themselves much vainer prove,*
> *By holding Lovers labours in disdaine:*
> *They have forgot the wiles which made them tremble,*
> *In heat of youth, when youth their bloods did move,*
> *What wit they use'd, what teares they did dissemble.*

> *Their now waxt shallow apprehensions, then*
> *Were quick to see the worst, wise to prevent it:*
> *How they pleas'd fancie, how they might content it,*
> *How much their hearts differ'd from hearts of men:*
> *How provident they were to fawne, to flatter,*
> *To sweare, vow, urge their griefe and to lament it:*
> *Alas who would not doo't in such a matter.*

> *Love makes men wise, 'tis not a feeling kisse,*
> *That's the true sport, ther's sport more sweet then this:*

> *To which, ere lovers throughly doe attaine,*
> *They must attend, doe service, grieve, and faine.*
> *For this with Ladies honours best doth fit,*
> *Not to be conquered by* Desire, *but* Witt.

In all ages, both past and present, never have there beene more witty pollicies, more politicke circumventions broached then in speedie obtaining of delatorie love: which is in it selfe so urgent, so impatient of delayes, as the soundest sleights, quaintest devises, have beene studied for accomplishing, of rest to unrest, ease to disquiet, remedy to desperation. Three things triall hath taught to be expedient for mastery in love. After choice, *Patience* to indure reproofes, *Witt* to procure content, *Boldnesse* to attempt at opportunities. Vaine is *patience* without *hope: hope* desperate without *meanes: meanes,* when occasion proffers her forelock, and women toleration: *hinderance,* without *boldnesse.* Yet *boldnesse* without *witte,* is to no use, neither without *witte* shall *time* be ever found when to be *bold.* In a perfect lover therefore, all these three are judicially cohered. Also if a curious surveior will upon this approve, that lovers have beene witty, yet disallow any wisedom in this witt, by distinguishing a different discrepancie betwixt witt and wisdome, since the one tendeth onely to folly of humanity, the other to consideration of divinity, I will answer, that perfect *Lovers,* even in this respect are perfectly *wise,* as with ease thus: being overcome with the affection, of some excellently deserving beauty, with admiration of | the singular perfection thereof, with what curious workmanship it is framed, with what glorye of Majesty it is endowed: it is an immediate occasion, to bring them in serious conceit, of weighing the wonders of the heavens in compacting such admirable quintessence, in so precious a forme, by which they will deeply revolve the dignitye of GOD in that mould, and truely acknowledge the weakenesse of their owne nature, in comparison of *Beauty.* This is the ready and directest course, to force men to consider their owne frailty, and magnifie the omnipotency of their creator, in fashioning both. So as *Love* is the onely line which leadeth man to the font of *Wisedome*; that is, to the gloryfying of heavens power, and confessing mans imbecillity. Who then can deny? who will not allowe? that *Perfect Lovers are onely wise*? onely wise! true, for men devoted to contemplation of Theologie, are withdrawne from the absolute, and due reverence (somtime) of him to whome they chiefly owe all due reverence, by humane affaires: when *Lovers* have evermore the *Idea* of *Beauty* in their imaginations, and therefore hourely do adore their makers Architecture. *Perfect Lovers are onely wise*: now againe to humanity: the dullest wit, the most unseasoned capacity, being once salted with the tast of love, sharpens his dulnesse, and seasons his capacity, to study any slieght, any device for setting a period to his desires. Insomuch, as no time shall ever present any oportunity of study, but all invention is used, all conceiptes imployed, for the fruition of his beloved: who beeing injoyed, yet his wittes are never idle, but industrious for conservation of what hee injoyes, as loath to impart from that | which with so much vigilancie he not easily obtained. As hitherto I have proceeded with demonstration of examples: so now (to the purpose) will I inferre an instance, to the more effectuall proofe of this. The Greekes after the discursion of *Helen,* preparing an expedition against *Troy,* both for acquittance of their injury, and recovery of their false (never truly faire) Queene, stood not in more need of *Achilles* for his courage, then of *Ulisses* for his counsaile: who being then newly married, to his perfectly faire *Penelope,* was upon good cause (moved in the tendernesse of his love) unwilling to that action: but excuse could not prevaile, except pollicie could finde excuse: he feares much, but loves more, which love even at an instant ripens his invention: *Love* ripeneth his *invention,* he faines madnesse, and for *madnesse to advise in sober actions, would prove but a mad advise, an unadvised madnesse*: but he was discovered and went. Secondly, what undoubted wisedom in him, did charme his eares, against the incantations of the Syrens: the devoute affection which he bore to his *Penelope,* quickning his apprehension. Was ever man a truer lover? and ever man more truly wise? It is infallibly certaine, certainly infallible, *perfect lovers are onely wise.* Now it may be cavelled, that that cannot be, for how can *Lovers* be *wise,* when *Love* it selfe is both *vaine, idle,* and *foolish*? a toye? a meere conceit of fancie? But how vaine, foolish, idle, and fantasticall are they that so conceive? *Love* is the onely band, the alone obligation, that traffiques betwixt earthly creatures and heavenly Angels, that unites woman to man, yea man to man, nay man to himselfe, and himselfe to *God. Love*

705 is the dignity of mans worth, not a *blind Cupid,* a sensuall lust, as
Poets faine: but an earnest and reasonable | *desire of good,* as authorities E3r
confirme. It is an *entire [conjunction]* of soules together.

>*Mutua sors animi, pia commutatio mentis,*
>   *sub fido fidum est pectore pignus* Amor.
>710 *Quid magis est placidum? nihil est fœlicius illo;*
>   *Pax jucunda, manus splendida, tuta quies.*
>*Fulget in auricoma nitido cum robore forma:*
>   *Ipsa sua splendens gaudet* Amore Venus.

>Love *is that tickling blood, which softly creepes,*
>715 *Into the pleasures of a quiet brest:*
>*Presenting pretty dreames in slumbring sleepes,*
>*And in a Ladies boosome takes his rest.*
>   Love *bath's him in the channell of delight,*
>   *Which lovers sigh for, and wish they also might.*

>720 *Of twenty thousand 't is the* wittiest *passion,*
>Wise, *in foreseeing of ensuing care:*
>*Makes lovers provident, yeelds consolation,*
>*And checks the bad from ill, if so they dare.*
>   *Love is that fountaine, where the springs do lye,*
>725   *Whence sweetest waters run, yet never drie.*

>*Love is that harmlesse* prick, *in pleasant brier,*
>*Which doth most please the sent, and breed* desire.

Thus much for satisfaction of the *witty.* Now briefly followes for
a conclusion to the *wise. Lovers are perfectly wise, and simply perfect:*
730 indeed absolutely perfect, insomuch as nothing is more expedient to
the full accomplishment of a wise man, then to be a Lover. Now
would any man seeme to oppose himselfe, to the adverse maintain-
ing of what hath already been prooved? it will | be evident, he shall E3v
more toyle his braines to affirme an untroth, then the praise or com-
735 mendation hee expects, with a generall *Plaudite* will countervaile. If
any champion will likewise be desperate hardy, to undertake a disal-
lowance, of these challenged positions, question-lesse he neede not
doubt, but he shall not soner be armed, but as soone foyled, and in

the vulgar confession of shame, acknowledge his deerely bought wilfulnesse. But I leave that to triall. I heere meane to be a pen man, no champion.

Conclusion.

WOULD any man be gracious in a Ladies favour? let him then subject himselfe to her wil. Would any be valiant and renowned for chivalry? let him serve under the colours of beauty. Would any strive to be blessed in having a Lady truly constant? let him choose her truly faire. Would any be *perfectly wise*? let him be *perfectly loving.* Would any be happy? couragious? singular? or provident? let him be a lover. In that life consisteth all happinesse, all courage, all glory, all wisdome. But as for such, who doe *frigescere ad ignem,* I do desist to inveigh against their cold spirits: onely in this, I hate them, that I pitty them.

> *He who will strive to please each curious eye,*
> *Must freeze in silence. But I care not I,*
> *Let better favours favour mine indevour,*
> *The vulgar tauntings shall affright me never.*
> *May it please you, to whom it is intended.*

Then

T'is glory to deserve, though not commended.

Non omnibus studeo:
non malevolis.

FINIS.

THE
Monarchs meeting,
Or
The King of *Denmarkes* welcome,
into England.

    Now had the harvest of the yeare brought forth,
        The blessed frute of long expected hope,
    And leveld with the toile of labours worth,
        The crop of fatnesse, to the trad's-mans scope.

    Now were the blossomes ripened to the hand,
        Of well deserving sweat: when all anon,
    The mighty ruler of a peacefull land,
        Began to take his wisht progression.

    Calme was the sea, and gentle gustes did blow,
        A whistling gale unto the flagges of peace:
    Full were the streames, and smooth soft tides did flow,
        And gave assurance of contented ease.

    When on the bubbling beauty of fayre *Thames*,
        (Urg'd by the princely love of amitie)
    A *Christian* King, in state, and majestie,
        Was entertain'd with sundry showes of games.

    The silver Christall streame, was proud to beare,
        The burthen of a person, each way graced,
    With all the rites of humane *Love* and *Feare*,
        In whose high lookes, *honour* was lively placed.

    Much welcome was the tydings of this newes,
        Unto the royall eare of worthy *James*:

> Preparing with all speed, that speed might use,
>   With his owne presence to ennoble *Thames*.
>
> Looke how did *Jove* salute the minor Gods,
>   Inviting all in heaven at a feast,
> Where no more awe was reverenc'd, no odds,
>   Betwixt his proper person and the rest.
>
> So did these Princes meet, in whose first meeting,
>   *Joy* was aboundant in the truce of *love:*
> Each inter-changing a concordant greeting,
>   Which in the peeres of both did comfort move.
>
> Ambitious was the river of this honour,
>   Knowing the value of the weight she bore:
> Grac'd that such favour *Kings* bestow'd upon her,
>   Bearing a richer burthen nere before.
>
> Kings met, and Kings saluted one another,
>   Eyther rejoycing in the others sight:
> Princes with Princes, brother joy'd with brother,
>   Each solacing the other with delight.
>
> A goodly view of Majestie it was,
>   To see such intimated league betwixt them:
> They striv'd in kindnesse how they might surpasse,
>   Sporting the season which the tide prefixt them.
>
> Like to a Prince in every point aright,
>   He came, and like a Prince was entertained:
> With all the tipes of dignity bedight,
>   With all the friendship, friendship could have claimed.
>
> O what a gladsome sight of joy it is?
>   When monarches so are linkt in amitie?
> How strengthened are those Empires with safe blisse,
>   Where two such Princes joyne in unitie?
>
> Great both are in dominions, yet more great,
>   In being vertuously religious:
> Fresh blooming piety doth praise beget,

In godly zeale. Let *tyrants be litigious?*

What *He* amongst the stoutest of contempt?
   Full in command? and fuller in disdaine?
Durst any threats of en'mity attempt?
65   Or to oppose himselfe against those twaine?

Those twaine! so firmly are they matcht together,
   So everlastingly affectionate.
So individually combin'd together,
   As they love none of both, who do one hate.

70 Power with power, realme with realme united,
   hearts joyn'd with hearts, and hand imbrac'd in hand:
Should all the world of nations be excited,
   Yet all the world could scarse those two withstand.

Nor is it faining shew of smooth pretext,
75   But doubtlesse troth of love which brought him hither:
Let none with such suspition be perplext,
   For then they never had thus come together.

Nor can it be suppos'd, a Prince so mighty,
   so worthy in himselfe, so absolute:
80 Who hath so large a rule, a charge so weighty,
   would leave his countrie, but for meere repute.

Puissant is the *Danish* King, and strong,
   In all the sinews of approved force:
Valiant, and able, for to right the wrong,
85   That should proceed from any eager course.

It is no common thing seene every day,
   Scarce in an age, to see so great a state:
From out his countries boundes to come away,
   For visitation of an neighbouring mate.

90 It is no common honour, that is done
   Unto our happy land by his arriving:
Much *worth* thereby, and *glory* have we won,
   Our home-bred hearts, with stranger loves reviving.

Two Kings in *England* have beene rarely seene,
    Two Kings for singularitie renowned:
The like before hath hardly ever beene,
    for never were two with more honour crowned.

This may we boast, and after times report,
How much the King of *Denmarke* grac'd our age:
A King of so much eminence, such port,
By his arrivall did his love ingage.

England with *Denmarke, Denmarke* eke with us,
Are firmely now in league, conjoyned in one:
Seaven Kingdomes now againe united thus
Are strength'ned, so as stronger can be none.
    Then as a certaine and welwishing greeting,
    We thus applaud the monarchs happy meeting.

HAYLE Princely stemme of great magnificence?
Issue of royall blood, who dost commence
True instance of thy fast undoubted love,
And by thy comming certainely approve
The pledge of peace, thus low in humblest heart
Regreetes unto thy truce doe we impart.
With fit applause our thankes devoutly running,
Gives welcome to the honour of thy comming.
Time cannot rase, nor amity surcease
Betwixt our realme and thine a long liv'd peace.
Whiles thoughts are undefil'd, and credit true,
From age to age this league will still renue.
And thou thy selfe (great King of Danes) wilt joy,
Counting the hazards which thou didst imploy
Daungers of thankes: by tasting approbation
Of spotlesse friendship with our willing nation.
We are not subtile French, *to fawne and flatter:*
Nor Spaniards *hot in shew, yet cold in matter.*
Trothlesse Italian *fleeting* Irish *wiles,*
(Whose trust when most protesting most beguiles)
We deeme dishonour. Germaine policies,

Or everchanging Indian *fopperies*
130 *We spurne. Know we are* English *hating wrongs,*
Bearing our thoughts decipher'd in our tongs.
Rather the sunne may in his courses alter,
Then we in true-meant trust *our promise faulter:*
Which of our chiefest emulating foes
135 *Can justly taxe us? but we ever chose*
To die with fame, then live with infamy,
Purchas'd with disesteemed trechery.
What needs an instance? rumor will avow,
We have our troth ingraven in our brow.
140 "Who are in nature, false yet free in name,
"Are servile slaves to feare, and fooles to shame.
What more? we are thy friends, and thou art our,
Thy love is ours, and our force thy power.
Long may this happy thred of faith be woven,
145 *And nere have dissolution but with heaven.*
Fatall and joyous doth the knot begin,
Then who doth breake it first, commits first sin.
Lo then great monarch, with what words of zeale,
Thy comming wee imbrace, and hopes reveale
150 *Of linkt conjunction: prest to gratifie*
That love, which thou with love dost ratifie.
Here speakes the clamour of a publicke voyce,
Which speaking, all do publikely rejoyce
Thy safe arrivall: England *thankes the honour,*
155 *Which by thy presence thou bestowest upon her.*
Sounding lowd Ecchoes of thy Kingly fame,
And making trophees, to adorne thy name.
    The Clarions breath thy welcome, Bells do ring,
    Praise shoutes, whiles all thy friends thus sweetly sing.

160 # The applause Song for the King of Denmarkes *arrivall*.

       IN the most happy season of the yeare,
         When fayrest sun-shine glistered on the earth,
       The royall King of *Denmarke* did appeare,
165   And tun'd the hearts of *England* full with mirth:
       In goodly majesty, and princely cheere,
         Even in the fullest crop of harvest's birth:
           When birdes with pleasant notes did sweetly sing,
           To give a hearty welcome to the King.
170   Prettily, prettily,
            With musick sweet,
            Did *Philomele* merily,
              and joyfully,
                and ever prettily,
175   The noble King of *Denmarke* greet.
       Welcome to *England,* Prince of high degree,
       And all our song shall ever welcome be.

       Our King himselfe rejoyced in his sight,
       His presence to the Court did breed delight,
180   Blithe was the country, and the Citty proud.
       Cornets with trumpets, shrill did blow, and lowd,
         To welcome to our land,
         With hearty greeting:
         (By our Kings command)
185   The Monarches meeting.
           Which we fulfilling,
            With love and mindes willing,
              Joyn'd together,
              Welcome hither,

190   Friendly,
                        and ever
                          kindly,
    The *Danish* King, a Prince of high degree,
    For all our song shall ever *welcome* bee.
195   To *welcome* all our notes, and love doth tend,
    In that sence we began, with that we end.

Cantibus et carmine.

FINIS.

FAMES MEMORIALL,

OR
The Earle of Deuonshire
Deceased:

With his honourable life, peacefull end, and solemne Funerall.

———————— *quis talia fando,*
Mirmydonum, Dolopúmue, aut duri miles Vlissi
Temperet à lachrimis? ————

AT LONDON
Printed for *Christopher Purset*, dwelling at the signe of
the *Mary Magdalens* head neer Staple Inne
in *Holborne*, 1606.

Title page (1606), The Bodleian Library, Mason. H.89. By permission.

Fames Memoriall, or The Earle of Devonshire Deceased

Devonshire

Charles Brooke Blount, the eighth Lord Mountjoy and first earl of Devonshire,[1] was descended from an ancient and noble family, fallen upon hard times, that can be traced in English history back to William the Conqueror, when the three sons of Rudolph count of Guisnes in Picardy fought at Hastings. Two of them, Sir Robert Le Blount and Sir William Le Blount, were leading officers and received English lands as a reward for their services. Efforts to trace the family back to Harold V of Denmark and even the Roman Flavii are well documented (see Jones 15-20).

The name Mountjoy, by which the subject of Ford's poem is generally known, came into the family by marriage in 1357. A particularly gallant ancestor was the Sir Walter Blount, celebrated by Shakespeare in *1 Henry IV*, 5.3, who fell at Shrewsbury in 1403. Other Blounts served in high positions at court and began the family tradition of patronizing learning. The father of Ford's subject, the sixth Lord Mountjoy, however, lost heavily in mining ventures and, it is said, alchemy. His elder brother William, the seventh Lord Mountjoy, was something of a wastrel.

Ford's Mountjoy was born in 1563; the exact date and place of birth are unknown (Falls 18-19). He seems to have been determined from youth to restore the family fortunes, for when his parents wished to have his picture painted, as Fynes Moryson tells us, "he chose to be drawne with a Trowell in his hand, and this Mot; *Ad reaedificandum antiquum Domum*, To rebuild the ancient house" (2.1.1, p. 45). The young man studied, briefly it seems, at Oxford. Moryson continues: "he came young and not well grounded from Oxford university" but through his own study became learned in languages and military theory. "But his chiefe delight was in the study of Divinity" (2.1.1, p. 47).

---

[1] There are two modern biographies: Falls and Jones. Especially useful early sources are Robert Naunton's *Fragmenta Regalia* (London, 1641; Wing N 249) for his earlier life and Fynes Moryson's *An Itinerary* (London, 1617; STC 18205) for the years following his appointment as lord deputy.

When he was about twenty years old, Blount had the good fortune to be noticed by Queen Elizabeth. He had gone to Whitehall "to see the fashion of the Court." She noticed the good-looking young man, "browne-haired, of a sweet face, and of a most neat composure, tall in his person," and asked who he was:

> Thus enquirie, with the eye of hir Majesty fixed upon him, as she was wont to doe, and to daunt men she knew not, stirred the bloud of this young Gentleman, in somuch as his colour went and came, which the Queene observing, called unto him, and gave him her hand to kisse, encouraging him with gracious words, and new lookes, and so diverting her speech to the Lords and Ladyes, she sayd that she no sooner observed him, but she knew there was in him some Noble bloud, with some other expressions of pitty towards his house, And then againe demanding his name, she sayd, faile you not to come to the Court, and I will bethinke my selfe, how to do you good; And this was his inlet, and beginning of his grace. (Naunton, 36)

So indeed were courtiers made and favorites chosen. The future Mountjoy now joined the gilded circle of young men whose careers depended entirely on pleasing the queen, where rewards and advancement were balanced by the restrictions of the court and by Elizabeth's reluctance to allow her favorites to risk themselves in the wars.

The first ten years of Charles Blount's life as a courtier were thus frustrating and his military experience severely limited. He served intermittently in the Netherlands, was wounded, knighted by Leicester, and finally called home in October 1587 by a letter in the queen's own hand. The next year he fought as a volunteer against the Armada. When the company of which he was nominally commander was tranferred from the Netherlands to Brittany to fight the invading Spaniards, Blount, it is said, had "twice, or thrice, stolen away" without permission to join it but seems to have missed most of the fighting. Again he was called home and reprimanded. "You will never leave," Elizabeth is reported to have told him, "till you are knock't over the head, as that inconsiderate fellow *Sidney* was, you shall goe when I send you, in the meane time, see that you lodge in the Court [which was then at Whitehall] where you may follow your Booke, read, and discourse of the warres" (Naunton, 19–20).

There were, however, compensations for enforced idleness. In 1584 Blount was elected to Parliament. After his service against the Armada, he was made Keeper of the New Forest and, in 1594, governor of Portsmouth.

Further, despite his absence from the theater of war, the queen gave orders that he be paid the same wages as the officers at the front (Falls, 34-35). In the same year the death of his brother brought him the title of Lord Mountjoy.

In time military opportunity would present itself. Although expressly forbidden to join the Cadiz expedition in 1596, where glory was to be obtained, the next year brought his surprising appointment as lieutenant general of the expedition fitted out to attack the Spanish coast and the Azores. This appointment, over the heads of a number of far more experienced soldiers, was at the insistence of Elizabeth and caused much ill feeling. Despite high hopes, the expedition failed through a combination of bad luck and Essex's poor leadership. There was relatively little fighting, and Mountjoy was unable to distinguish himself.

The defeat and near destruction of the English army in August of 1598 by the Irish rebel Tyrone turned the attention of queen and council to Ireland. Years of neglect and mismanagement culminating in this defeat had drastically reduced the territory under English control. No longer could half-measures be tolerated; a major effort was decided upon. Mountjoy was favored by the queen and nominated for the post of lord deputy. In the end, after much discussion, the post went to Essex, who had strongly objected to Mountjoy's appointment on the ground of his limited military experience and because he "was too much given to Bookishness."[2]

The story of Essex's failure to restore the English position in Ireland is well known: how, with the largest army ever sent into that kingdom, he spent the summer of 1599 in fruitless progresses through the southern and central regions; how, when he finally turned north to face Tyrone, the season was late and his army much weakened; how, eventually, he conferred privately with the arch-rebel and concluded a shameful truce; how, finally, in flat disobedience to his orders, he left his army and returned to England to imprisonment, rebellion, and death.

Now at last came the opportunity that was to earn Mountjoy his place in history. He appeared strangely reluctant to take the command. Whether this was because of the seeming hopelessness of the task, for reasons of health, or as a subtle attempt to obtain the reappointment of his friend

---

[2] Camden, *History of the Most Renowned and Victorious Princess Elizabeth, Late Queen of England* (London, 1688; Wing, 363), 567. For a discussion of Essex's motive in opposing his friend and accepting an appointment he himself seemed not to want, see Jones, 44-46.

Essex by his own refusal is impossible to say. Falls suggests a reluctance to leave his lover Penelope Devereux (112 and see below).

Here is not the place to describe the Irish campaigns of Mountjoy.[3] For our purposes a résumé of his methods will suffice. The new commander immediately seized the initiative. Beginning with a series of minor actions designed to restore the fighting ability and morale of his troops, he soon began to move decisively into enemy territory, where gradually a string of forts was constructed and regularly provisioned. English sea power was used to establish and supply coastal bases. His marches were swift and secret, avoiding ambushes, in which the Irish were at their best, and attempting to draw his foe instead into open battle. Rebel lands were systematically laid waste, crops burnt, and livestock driven off. Contrary to custom, Mountjoy campaigned in winter.

All these were elements in a carefully-conceived and successful plan to use the English advantages to the full and to deprive the rebels of their formerly secure bases and sources of supply. His attacks left the Irish with the choice of fighting in the open to defend their farms or of seeing them destroyed and facing starvation. In all this Mountjoy showed himself the perfect professional in whose plans, unlike those of Essex, impulse and emotion played no part. His own officers were often unaware of his intentions, but his personal engagement, despite bouts of illness, was unceasing.

By these means, the Irish rebels had been greatly weakened by the time their Spanish allies landed in force in the southern port of Kinsale. Mountjoy rose to the occasion, showing not only his wonted coolness and calculation but the willingness to take considerable, if calculated, risks. He marched south immediately with what few soldiers were at hand to establish a blockade of the port while summoning reinforcements from the north and from England. As these slowly arrived, he tightened the siege despite appalling winter weather, shortage of supplies, and sickness among his troops.

Tyrone was now again faced with hard alternatives: to come to the aid of the Spaniards and fight in the open, or to watch the destruction both of his allies and of his own hopes. Reluctantly, pushed on by his associates

---

[3] The best account is in Falls, chaps. 10–14. Moryson, who was Mountjoy's secretary, gives a detailed and largely eyewitness account in Part 2 of *An Itinerary*; Camden, a summary in Book 4, 550–54, 637–46, and 655–58.

and the demands of the Spaniards, he marched south with a large force until he was in a position to besiege the besiegers, and Mountjoy was caught between the Spaniards in Kinsale and the Irish to the north. Refusing to retreat or remain in his position in the face of superior numbers, Mountyjoy attacked. Leaving a force to contain the Spaniards, he turned on the Irish, routed them, and returned to his siege lines before the Spaniards could take advantage of his absence. Kinsale surrendered shortly thereafter, and its garrison returned to Spain.

The magnitude of Mountjoy's victory and the poor showing of the rebels seriously diminished the prestige of Tyrone. The pacification of rebel districts continued, and the Irish leader was soon little more than a hunted criminal with a small band of followers.

Mountjoy had never been vindictive and had never sought the destruction of his foes. Fire and sword had always been carefully calculated instruments of his policy of making Ireland not a sullen conquered country held down by a large army of occupation, but a reasonably contented part of Elizabeth's dominions. To this end, he had always rewarded the loyal Irish and allowed rebel chiefs generous terms when they submitted. He now tried to get the queen's agreement to terms of submission that Tyrone would accept. Elizabeth was reluctant but eventually agreed, and Tyrone came to Dublin to make his submission to the lord deputy in person. At this moment news of the queen's death reached Mountjoy. If true, all would have to wait until the new ruler's pleasure was known. However, the news was not official, so Mountjoy swore the messenger to secrecy and received Tyrone's submission on the dead queen's terms. When the official confirmation of her death arrived, Tyrone is reported to have wept; had he held out a week longer, he might have expected more generous treatment from King James.

From James, Mountjoy reaped much reward. Immediately he was made privy councillor. It was arranged that Mountjoy would return to England with the title lord lieutenant, whence he could continue to manage Irish affairs through a new lord deputy responsible to him. In addition, he was to receive two-thirds of the Irish vice-regal emoluments. By June 1603 he was back in London, where honors, grants, and titles were heaped upon him, culminating in his creation as earl of Devonshire (Falls, 210, 219, *et passim*). Fewer than three years of life remained to him.

He became, next to his friend Cecil, the most powerful of James's ministers, responsible especially for military matters, but also increasingly for civil. Thus he was both commander of the forces raised to put down any rebellion that might follow the Gunpowder Plot and a member of the committee investigating the plot. Despite periods of ill health, he continued to be active in Irish affairs. Under his rule Ireland was so peaceful that the armed forces for the whole kingdom could be reduced to some eleven hundred men.

The end came suddenly. In late March 1606, he was, according to Moryson, surprised with a burning fever. After making his will he assured his friends, in Moryson's account, "Let death looke never so ugly, he would meet him smiling which he nobly performed, for I never saw a brave spirit part more mildely from the old mansion, than his did, departing most peaceably after nine daies of sicknesse, upon the third of Aprill in the beginning of the yeere 1606" (2.3.2, p. 296).

He was buried in state in Westminster Abbey; no trace of his tomb remains. As he died without legitimate issue, his title became dormant, and thus "he who had raised his house to the highest glory, became the instrument of its extinction" (Jones 182).

Mountjoy and Essex

The complex relationship of Mountjoy and Essex concerns us only as it relates to an understanding of Ford's poem. After early jealousy on the part of Essex and a duel in which Essex was wounded,[4] the two men became friends and political allies. Mounjoy served under Essex in the Azores expedition, and by the late 1590s was, with Southampton, leader of the Essex party at court. In the period between Essex's precipitous return from Ireland and his rebellion and death, Mountjoy was closely involved in the sometimes questionable attempts to restore the fallen favorite. These involved a secret correspondence with James of Scotland, whose claims the Essex party supported, and a plan by which Mountjoy, once in command of the army in Ireland, would return with over four thousand men to support the restoration of Essex. While Mountjoy repeatedly proclaimed his loyalty to Elizabeth, these actions nevertheless placed that loyalty in a doubtful light.

Once in Ireland, Mountjoy's caution and common sense regained the

---

[4] The story of Essex's remark on seeing the young Charles Blount wearing the queen's favor ("Now I perceive every fool must have a favour") is told by Naunton, 52-53.

upper hand, and he backed away from the foolhardy projects being considered by Essex and Southampton. Still, Essex's rebellion, trial, confession, and execution gave Mountjoy cause for alarm. In carefully-worded letters to Elizabeth and Cecil he pledged his renewed loyalty. With a compassion encouraged by his military successes in Ireland and their need of him, they subtly let him know that they knew the whole story but chose to accept his protestations and to overlook the past.[5]

Mountjoy and Penelope

It is impossible to establish with certainty the beginning of the relationship between Mountjoy and Penelope Devereux. In his biography of Archbishop Laud, Peter Heylyn wrote that "some assurance passed between them of a future marriage." Since the young Charles Blount was, at the time, merely a younger son without title or fortune, Penelope was married in 1581 to Lord Rich, "a man of independent Fortune ... otherwise of an uncourtly disposition."[6] Penelope's celebrated relationship to Philip Sidney and her inspiration of *Astrophel and Stella* do not concern us here. Sidney himself married in 1583 and died in 1586. Whatever the accuracy of Heylyn's account, it is at least certain that during the course of the 1580s Mountjoy and Penelope became lovers. By 1590 George Peele was able to hint at the relationship with the inevitable pun

> Comes Sir *Charles Blount*, in *Or* and *Azure* dight,
> Rich in his colours, richer in his thoughts,
> Rich in his Fortune, Honor, Armes, and Arte.[7]

The relationship between the lovers was open and tolerated, with whatever reluctance, by Lord Rich. Lady Rich bore Mountjoy five children out of wedlock in addition to those she bore her husband. Finally, in

---

[5] On the relationship of Essex and Mountjoy after the former's fall from royal favor, see Falls, 110–16, Jones, 93–102, and Akrigg, 96–104.

[6] Peter Heylyn, *Cyprianus Anglicus* (London, 1668; Wing, 1699), 57. For her lover's statement that she was married "against her will unto one against whom she did protest at the very solemnity," see Falls, 59. See also Maud Rawson, *Penelope Rich and her Circle* (London, 1911).

[7] George Peele, "The Sixth Couple" (sig. B1ʳ) in *Polyhymnia* (London, 1590; STC 19546).

November 1605, Lord and Lady Rich were divorced, and Mountjoy, now earl of Devonshire, persuaded his chaplain William Laud, the future archbishop, to perform the marriage by which Penelope became countess of Devonshire. The ceremony took place on St. Stephen's Day, 26 December 1605.

A controversy arose at once whether or not Penelope was free to marry. Was her divorce *a menso et thoro* or *a vinculo matrimonii*? Unfortunately, the matter was far from clear in post-Reformation England, and precedents and authorities could be cited for both positions.[8] Laud seems also to have been motivated by the couple's intention to marry before Penelope was forced to wed Lord Rich: this did not amount to a pre-contract *in furo judicii* but sufficed *in foro conscientiae*.[9] He may also have been motivated by the desire to please his powerful patron.

Devonshire defended himself with a tract justifying his marriage, a remarkably learned effort replete with citations from Scripture and the Fathers.[10]

Ford's Historical Perspective

Ford was clearly aware of the events of Mountjoy's life that were common knowledge when he wrote his elegy. That he chose to ignore much of this biographical material and in places falsify it is more a matter of style than ignorance (see below, 73-74). Some comment, however, is required regarding Ford's treatment of Mountjoy's relationships with Essex and with Penelope Devereux, Lady Rich.

Concerning Essex, Ford's praise of the dead earl and defense of his character are manifestations of the continuing popularity of Essex in the years following his execution. With the accession of King James, whom the Essex party had always supported, Essex's reputation underwent a belated rehabilitation. James showed marked favor to many belonging to that party; the prompt release and restoration of the condemned Southampton is perhaps the most striking example. Essex's enemies, notably Ralegh, were

---

[8] For the historical and canonical background, see George Elliot Howard, *A History of Matrimonial Institutions* (Chicago, 1904), 2:53 ff.

[9] Heylyn, 57-58. See also William Hutton, *William Laud* (London, 1895), 8 and note.

[10] A manuscript copy is in the Bodleian (MS. Tanner 278); it is printed in Rawson, 320-42.

disgraced, and the executed traitor of 1601 now became the subject of exaggerated praise.[11]

The common defense was that the actions of Essex, which were hardly to be denied, were purposely misinterpreted by his foes, and thus his loyalty to the queen and his attempt to remove his enemies from court were branded treason. The underlying motive for this misinterpretation was envy of Essex's greatness. Thus Pricket asks, "But Envie, why dids't thou againe conspire?...." (sig. B3ᵛ). This is exactly Ford's explanation when he speaks of "Renowned *Devoreux*, whose aukward fate, / Was misconceited by fowle envies hate" (347-48). It is too simple to argue that since Ford was dedicating his poem to Essex's sister, he was forced to praise the dead earl. There is no reason to believe that the young poet did not share the widely-held view favorable to Essex, or indeed that choosing Mountjoy as a hero to elegize would not imply a favorable view of his hero's friend. Ford repeated the claim seven years later that Essex was "cast downe by envie" (*The Golden Meane*, 122). Another seven years was to pass before there was evidence of Ford modifying this opinion in *A Line of Life*, where he speaks of the earl's over-confidence; but here again he speaks of those who "flattered and envyed his Greatnesse" (549-57).

The Work

An elegy of formidable length (1162 lines), *Fames Memoriall, or the Earle of Devonshire Deceased*, is written mainly in rime royal. It is divided as follows: 131 stanzas (917 lines); nine short epitaphs or *Tombes* of varying form and length; twenty more stanzas (140 lines). The first and longest section is further subdivided. The initial eight stanzas (48 lines) serve as a prologue, introducing the personified character of Fame who "Sores now aloft triumphant" (10). The qualities worthy of fame are alluded to ("hauty fame adornes nobility" [26]) and reference is made to the Nine Worthies who are now surpassed by Mountjoy. Finally Fame

> Imprints in Canons of eternall glorye,
> Worth's monumentall rites, great *Mountjoyes* story.
> (55-56)

---

[11] See, for example, Robert Pricket, *Honors Fame in Triumph Riding, Or The Life and Death of the Late Honorable Earle of Essex* (London, 1604; STC 20339), ed. A. Grosart (Manchester, 1881).

Thus Ford justifies his title and prepares not only for the biography to follow but for Mountjoy's promotion to the rank of a tenth worthy. The six following stanzas are in general praise of the great man; the biography begins with the fifteenth (99). Mountjoy's youth, his education, his coming to court, and his service in the Low Countries are all alluded to. A long section (344-504) is devoted to the Irish wars, ending with his triumphant return and creation as earl of Devonshire.

Here follows a section (505-630) on the newly-created peer's service in time of peace with an attempt to illustrate his greatness of character in five stanzas each beginning "True virtue grac'd his mind." Ford then turns his attention to Penelope and the disputed marriage for fifty-six lines (631-86). He returns to further praise of Devonshire's service and character in lines 687-917, which lead up to the nine *Tombes*. Each of these is given a separate page with the title "His Tombe. | The Epitaph." Each is bordered and, in the printed edition, given an ornament. The form varies, with differing combinations of rhyming lines within stanzas, and the stanzas themselves of varying length. Thus *Tombes* 1, 2, and 9 have ten lines each, with a division of 4-4-2; and *Tombes* 3 and 4, fourteen lines (4-4-4-2) with the stanza line length varied to form urn shapes, apparent only in the manuscript, where they are outlined in ink. In *Tombes* 5 and 6 the first two lines are divided to achieve pyramid forms, and *Tombes* 7 and 8 each have ten lines divided 8-2.

The last section of the poem (1023-1162), having connected the nine *Tombes* with the Nine Worthies, declares that "*Devonshire* in himselfe all nine contain'd" (1029). It is Ford's own extended equivalent to the epitaphs, now without biographical reference, both mourning Mountjoy's death and celebrating his apotheosis. The repeated images of the last stanzas (for example, five lines beginning with "Above" in the last stanza) parallel the soaring of Fame in the first stanzas.

Ford's poem is followed in the manuscript and the printed copy by an "Anagramma ex Camdeno"; the printed copy has in addition, after the epistle dedicatory, an acrostic verse that with some effort manages the name PE|NE|LO|PE| |CONTE|S| |OF| |DEVO|N|SH|IRE,[12] and two commendatory verses.

---

[12] Complicated acrostics, though seldom so desperately complicated as this one, were not unknown. Thomas Heywood's, attached to his elegy on the death of Prince Henry (London, 1613; STC 13323), runs simultaneously the names of C A R O L U S in the odd numbered lines and J A C O B U S in the even.

The literary weaknesses of *Fames Memoriall* are manifold and manifest. Its chief stylistic device is iterated hyperbole: exaggeration piled upon exaggeration. Rather than itemize these faults however, we should consider the circumstances of its composition to determine what Ford was trying to do, however ineptly. When Mountjoy died on 3 April 1606, Ford was nearing his twentieth birthday (we do not know the exact date of his birth, but it was presumably shortly before he was baptized 17 April 1586). He had for over three years been a student at the Middle Temple, where he was admitted 16 November 1602. In the epistle dedicatory he speaks of his "weake talent" and "unfeathered Muse" and of "studyes much differente" at the Inns of Court. Almost certainly the poem was one of his first attempts at extended verse writing. He was, further, under the influence of Barnabe Barnes; the older poet seems to have become his friend and mentor, and his stylistic influence was not a happy one.

Nevertheless, there is clearly more than a literary judgement in the attacks of the early critics. Gifford wondered "why he came forward in so inauspicious a cause."[13] Dyce remarked that Penelope seemed to have thought "her private engagement of a more binding character than her vow at the altar; and the usual consequences followed" (3.281n). Clearly Ford's early attempt to defend two adulterers who attempted to marry and, as many thought, were disgraced, could be seen as a foretaste of the "immoral" and "decadent" dramas to follow.

As unfair as the attacks of Ford's early critics is the comparison of this fledgling effort with Samuel Daniel's *Funerall Poeme*. An older and more experienced poet, Daniel had enjoyed the patronage of his subject for over a decade. Whatever their relative success or failure, the two men were not trying to write the same type of poem. Drawing on his knowledge and experience, Daniel wrote a subtle and accurate account of an extraordinary human being. Ford wrote an impersonal elegy about a public hero he had never known and about whom he seemed to have little information.

In a poem as long as *Fames Memoriall*, there was ample room for at least some of the dramatic events of his subject's life. Surely these would have appealed to one later to become famous as a dramatic writer. Why, for example, is there no mention of Mountjoy's military adventures before his Irish campaigns except for a fleeting reference, completely without

---

[13] G–D, 1:ix.

detail, to the "wars of *Belgia*" (309)? Why is no single action in Ireland mentioned, not even Mountjoy's overwhelming victory at Kinsale?

Ford's lack of such reference cannot be ascribed completely to ignorance of his subject. Kinsale was the last great victory of Elizabeth's reign, and the young Ford could no more have been ignorant of it than the young Tennyson of Waterloo. Rather, Ford omitted detail and particular reference in a deliberate attempt to portray a hero in the classical pattern. A hero has such-and-such virtues: a hero acts in this and that way. Since Mountjoy was a hero, these virtues and ways of acting are simply applied to him, without example, by way of affirmation, buttressed by repetition and hyperbole.

An example of this method is found in the five stanzas beginning "True virtue grac'd his mind" (575-609). The first four are devoted to the four cardinal virtues; each ends with two proverbial lines in which the particular virtue treated is again named. Everything said in these stanzas applies equally to any person possessing these virtues. The fifth stanza then affirms that "Since all these vertues were in him combin'd / Truth will avow true vertue grac'd his mind" (608-9).

Awareness of Ford's intention also helps to explain things that appear to be simply historical errors. In the section on the start of the Irish campaign, Mountjoy is pictured as determined to conquer or die (360-61); he is "Incenc'st with rage" (372). All this has nothing to do with the historical Mountjoy, cool, reserved, calculating, and seemingly passionless: the intellectual who had learned the art of war in his library. But for Ford the wrath of the hero before battle is an essential part of his heroic picture; if Mountjoy did not act in that way, he *should* have.

To understand Ford's intention is not to suggest that it was the best way for an inexperienced young poet to attempt his elegy, still less to attempt it at such length. *Fames Memoriall* remains an ambitious but finally inauspicious beginning for one who was later to achieve greatness in quite a different genre.

Literary Context

Even if Mountjoy had been a man of less talent and literary interest, the patronage system of the time and his position as courtier, soldier, and finally (as earl of Devonshire) statesman, would have made him the object of a flood of dedications. In fact Mountjoy was known to his contemporaries as a man of bookish nature, a collector, and an avid reader who assembled an impressive library, a man ideally suited by his nature and training to exercise the function of patron.

Mountjoy's most generous and most important instance of patronage was toward Samuel Daniel, who, as early as 1595, expressed his gratitude in *The Civil Wars*.[14] The close relationship between the two men continued until Mountjoy's death in 1606. However, there is no record, and no reason to assume, that Ford had any contact with Mountjoy. Indeed, the evidence of the epistle dedicatory points to the contrary. Over two dozen surviving dedications to Mountjoy by contemporary writers are listed by Williams,[15] including Bacon, Bastard, Breton, Du Vair, Greene, Markham, and Nashe.

Of the longer poems written to commemorate Mountjoy's death, three survive. They are *Fames Memoriall*, Daniel's *A Funerall Poeme upon the Death of the late noble Earle of Devonshire* (STC 6256), and the anonymous *In honorable memory of the Right noble Earle of Devonshire late deceased*. This last poem, eighty lines of iambic pentameter, is prefixed to John Coprario's *Funeral Teares*, a cycle of seven short lyrics set to music by Coprario in which Penelope is shown lamenting the loss of her husband.[16] It may well be by Ford and is included in this edition.[17]

Very different is Daniel's *Funerall Poeme*, some 450 lines of iambic pentameter. It is, in comparison to Ford's work, a thoughtful piece, with an evaluation of the dead man's character obviously based on a long and close association. Unlike Ford, Daniel makes no attempt to condemn or defend the marriage:

> Summon detraction, to object the worst
> That may be told, and utter all it can.

---

[14] In *The First Fowre Bookes of the Civile Wars* (London, 1595), B2ʳ:
And thou *Charles Mountjoy* borne the worldes' delight,
That hast receiv'd into thy quiet shore
Me tempest-driven fortune-tossed wight ...

For an account of the relationship, see Joan Rees, *Samuel Daniel* (Liverpool, 1964), especially chaps. 4 and 6.

[15] Franklin B. Williams, Jr., *Index of Dedications and Commendatory Verses in English Books before 1641* (London, 1966).

[16] London, 1606; STC 5679. There are copies in the British Library and the Bodleian. See also Richard McGrady, "Coperario's *Funeral Teares*," *The Music Review* 38.3 (August, 1977): 163-76. *Funeral Teares* was recorded in 1981 on Oiseau-Lyre (DSLO 576).

[17] See SP, II.

> It cannot find a blemish to b'inforst,
> Against him, other, then he was a man,
> And built of flesh and blood, and did live here
> Within the region of infirmity. (331-36)[18]

Daniel tells us of his patron's habit of marking his books and of his reluctance to take the Irish command, and he describes the deathbed scene. His use of biographical facts is much greater than Ford's in a poem only one-third as long.

The Critics

Unfortunately, the most important opinion of *Fames Memoriall*, that of the lady to whom it was dedicated, we shall never learn. Penelope Devereux, later Lady Rich, and finally dowager countess of Devonshire, was no stranger to poets or poetry: she had been, over thirty years earlier, Sidney's "Stella."

Of the later editors of *Fames Memoriall*, the opinion of Joseph Haslewood is the most positive. For him *Fames Memoriall* is a "gem," and his edition's purpose was to remedy its exclusion from Weber's edition of Ford's works. This exclusion came, he believed, only from Weber's ignorance of the work. "Indeed there is little reason to suppose, he could have omitted an article so reputable to the rising talents of the author, had he been acquainted with its merits"(4).

From this modest apogee, the reputation of the work declined rapidly. Gifford dismisses the work as "the holiday task of an ambitious school-boy" (1:1xv), and having aimed a blow at Haslewood for supporting Weber, returns to the subject of *Fames Memoriall*, its repetitions and wearisome vexations, as, for example, when Ford, "after dragging his reader through a hundred seven-line stanzas demands 'What more yet unremembered can I say?'" The conclusion is "a childish rant, which can only excite pity by its hopeless imbecility" (1:1xxviii).

Dyce continues in the same vein. When he comes to the marriage of the newly created earl of Devonshire with Lady Rich, he remarks, "It is distressing to pursue his history" (4:279n). Influenced by moral as well as

---

[18] *A Funerall Poeme* is reprinted in vol. 1 of Grosart's edition of Daniel; his line numbering is inexact, but given for convenience.

literary considerations, neither Gifford nor Dyce can accept Devonshire's marriage or Ford's outspoken defense of it.

The twentieth century has viewed *Fames Memoriall* more calmly, if less enthusiastically. For Sherman, writing in 1916, *Fames Memoriall* was "a barely tolerable performance inspired by a youthful enthusiasm and a desire to make himself known as a poet in polite society" (vi). It yielded, as did *Honor Triumphant* of the same year, "to closer scrutiny extremely suggestive hints on the sources of Ford's ideas and culture, on the native bias of his character, and on his peculiar conception of tragedy" (ix). For Sargeaunt, the verses were "wearisome in style" but "of value as reflecting the thought and feeling of the very young man (Ford must have been about twenty years old at this time) who wrote them" (5). Davril accepts the poem as "un hommage véritable, une admiration sincère pour celui qui, en dépit d'une liaison tapageuse demeurait un des premiers gentilshommes d'Angleterre"(76). The literary quality of the work he finds quite médiocre:

> Qui reconnaîtrait pourtant dans ce poème insipide les qualités du dramaturge? Aussi ne voulons-nous retenir de cette première tentative que le jeune enthousiasme qui ose s'affirmer avec assez d'audace pour faire échec aux préjugés, et soutenir la grandeur et la pureté des sentiments en dépit des lois et des institutions humaines. (79)

Oliver finds the poem "of no great literary merit"; its occasional successful epigram cannot save it from "overwhelming monotony" (9–11). Leech saw in *Fames Memoriall* "nothing of the later Ford," but acknowledged that "in the direction of its feeling it gives a hint of its writer's future" (20). Chiefly concerned as he is with the morality of Ford's defense of Devonshire's marriage and its historical circumstances, Stavig contents himself with the judgement that it "is of very uneven quality" (3). Finally, Huebert acknowledges that the early works in general "show little promise, and no dramatic subtlety at all. One can hardly say that the author of *Fames Memoriall* (1606) develops or matures into the dramatist of the 1630s, because there is little in *Fames Memoriall* worth developing or capable of maturing"; for him, Ford is "a sincere but tedious young versifier" (195).

The Texts

There are two authoritative forms of the text of *Fames Memoriall*. The first is the quarto printed in 1606. It was not entered in the Stationers' Register.

FAMES MEMORIALL, | [rule] OR | The Earle of Devonshire | *Deceased*: | [rule] | With his honourable life, peacefull end, | and Solemne Funerall. | [rule] | —— *quis talia fando* | *Mirmydonûm, Dolopûmue, aut duri miles Vlissi* | *Temperet à lacrimis?*—— | [The arms of the Blount family] | [rule] | AT LONDON | Printed for *Christopher Purfet*, dwelling at the signe of | the *Mary Magdalens* head neer Staple Inne | *in Holborne*, 1606.

A1^v shows the crest of the Blount family; A2–A3 the epistle dedicatory with the signature IO: FORDE. The acrostic is printed on A3^v and the commendatory verses on A4. The poem itself begins on B1^r under the title "THE | EARLE of *Devonshire* deceased." The running title "*The Earle of Devonshire* (verso) *Deceased*. (recto) begins on B1^v–B2^r and carries on, with minor variations suggesting that several skeleton forms were used, to the end of the poem on G4. Where the seven-line stanzas break off on F1^r for the insertion of the nine "Tombe" epitaphs, each of which is given a page, the Blount crest is repeated in the space thus made available. Camden's anagram (G4^v) is headed and followed by ornaments. STC lists it as 11158.

The second is a manuscript (17 cm x 12 cm) prepared for presentation to the widowed countess, as Edmond Malone noted.[19] It is inscribed in a neat secretary hand with italic used chiefly for title page, titles, epistle dedicatory, and the "Tombe" epitaphs. The leaves are numbered i–v and 1–31. Leaf iii, originally blank, has a note by Malone ("E. M. 1779") and a further undated note by him. The title page is on leaf iv and reads:

[rule] | Fames Memoriall. | or | The Earle of Devonshire | deceased | [short rule] | [rule]——quis talia fando | Mirmidonum, Dolopumue, aut duri miles Vlissi | temperet a lachrimis——| [rule]

There is no date given, but 1606 can be safely assumed. The acrostic and commendatory verses are lacking, but Camden's anagram is on the last leaf (31). The most important differences are in the epistle dedicatory, in the inclusion of three additional stanzas, and changes in the verses immediately preceding them.

---

[19] Opposite the title page of his copy, Malone wrote: "Of this poem I have the original copy in manuscript. When I purchased it, it was a gift, and appeared to have been the very copy that was presented by the author, John Ford, to the Countess of Devonshire. It is now boxed up with Ford's Plays" (Bodleian MS. Malone 319).

Purchased by Malone and acquired by the Bodleian in 1821, the manuscript was discovered there by Rachel Poole.[20] Bertram Lloyd, who rediscovered it in 1925,[21] argued that it was a holograph; he reasoned that a twenty-year-old law student would not have wasted money hiring a copyist and that no one but the author would have "struggled without the hope of worldly gain." In 1935 Sargeaunt agreed (6), but twenty years later Oliver demurred (9), pointing out several obvious errors that one could expect from a copyist but not from an author. More recently, G. D. Monsarrat has argued that the manuscript is indeed scribal, that neither it nor the quarto can be considered uniquely authoritative, and that "the choice of each reading must be made on its own merits."[22]

The most substantial differences between the manuscript and the printed text relate directly to Penelope, countess of Devonshire: changes in the epistle dedicatory, changes in certain lines in the section directly related to her, and the omission in the printed edition of three stanzas directly addressed to her in the manuscript.

In the epistle dedicatory of the manuscript, Ford says:

> yet ere I committed it to the presse (for fame undivulged is an hidden Minerall) being unknowne unto you, I might have beene imputed as much impudent, as fond: if I had not first presented it to your milder view: Earnest to understand whether your acceptation and liking may priviledge the passe under your honorable conduct ...

In the printed edition this is replaced by:

> Let not therfore (worthy Countesse) my rasher presumption, seeme presumpuous folly, in the eyes of your discreeter judgement, in that without your privitie (being a meere straunger alltogether unknowne unto you) I have thus adventured, to shelter my lines, under the well-guided conduct of your Honorable name: grounding my boldnes upon this assurance, that true gentility is ever accompanyd (especially in your sex, more specially in your selfe) with her inseparable adjunct, singular Humanity, principally towards those, whom neither Merce-

---

[20] *Notes and Queries*, no. 79 (2 July 1887): 3-4.
[21] "An Inedited Manuscript of Ford's *Fames Memoriall*," *Review of English Studies* 1 (1925): 93-95.
[22] "Printed Texts and Presentation Manuscripts: The Case of John Ford's *Fame's Memorial* and *A Line of Life*," *The Library*, 6th Ser., 2.1 (March 1980): 80-85.

nary hopes or servile flattery, have induced to speake but with the Priviledge of troth.

The last sentence of the printed text adds "Thus (*Madame*) presuming on your acceptance." The printed text makes no mention of the poem's having been submitted to Penelope's "milder view" for approval. The acceptance is rather presumed on the basis of the recipient's virtues overlooking the poet's boldness in dedicating to her without her "privitie."

The changes in the sections directly related to Penelope are the rewriting of lines 646, 648, 649, and 651, and in a number of individual words in the printed text. "Unjust disgrace" (652) becomes, for example, "A sad disgrace"; "povertie" (655) becomes "worldly cares." Three stanzas (659-79) that follow directly are omitted from the printed text: they not only concern Penelope but are directly addressed to her. Both Rachel Poole and Bertram Lloyd concluded that prudence led to the omission.[23]

Their surmises appear now far less likely than when they were advanced, for the exercise of prudence presumes a situation where prudence is necessary. Previous generations accepted at face value, and sometimes with Victorian relish, that the lovers were guilty, their marriage invalid, and that after attempting it they were disgraced, banished from court, and ended their days in public obloquy (see Jones, 179-82). In his 1955 biography of Mountjoy, Cyril Falls investigates in considerable detail the validity of the marriage and the reaction to it (220-32), concluding that "the King was in fact offended, that Charles and Penelope were blamed and perhaps by some treated coldly, but that the suggestion of their being sent to Coventry is almost certainly exaggerated"(227).

This is borne out by the records of Devonshire's activities in the three months between the wedding ceremony and his death. Within a month (21 January 1606) he was appointed to a committee to consider laws for the preservation of religion; in February he was concerned with attainders in connection with the Gunpowder Plot; in March he could not attend the Lords because he was in attendance on the king. "Whatever small degree of truth may have been embedded in the story that Charles and Penelope were given the cold shoulder after their marriage at Wanstead, this does not apply to her after her lord's death. She was daily visited by the greatest in the land" (Falls, 238). It was at this moment that Ford wrote his elegy.

---

[23] See Poole, 4, and Lloyd, 94, 95.

There is no reason to doubt that Penelope received the manuscript. The special form of the epistle dedicatory establishes it as a presentation copy far better than Malone's noting that it had gilt edges when he purchased it (see note 19 above). There is no reason to believe Ford went to all this trouble and expense without seeing that it was delivered.

Looking at the text itself, there is nothing in the three omitted stanzas more outspoken than in the stanzas surrounding them. If they were omitted for the sake of prudence, then the effort was patently incompetent. Nor does the revision of lines and phrases suggest any effort to tone down the assertions of the manuscript.

That Ford himself wished, or was asked, to remove the three stanzas in which Penelope is directly addressed and to rewrite the epistle dedicatory to involve the widowed countess less directly is entirely possible. The grounds could have been simply a sense of delicacy, a feeling of propriety, or a realization that the stanzas, especially the second, were exaggerated and inaccurate.[24]

Fames Memoriall was not reprinted until 1819. When Henry Weber brought out his two-volume *The Dramatic Works of John Ford* (Edinburgh, 1811), its omission prompted Joseph Haslewood to publish it eight years later. It was included by Gifford (1827) and by Dyce (1869), who revised Gifford's edition (reprinted by A. H. Bullen in 1895). None of these editors was aware of the manuscript.

In 1965, the unpublished Harvard doctoral dissertation of Frederick M. Burelbach, Jr., "The Nondramatic Works of John Ford," included *Fames Memoriall*. The poem was presented with manuscript and quarto on facing pages. The quarto, based on the Huntington Library copy, was collated with eight other copies. No commentary was supplied but there is a long general introduction.

---

[24] Hartley Coleridge suggested in 1839 the possibility that the story of Mountjoy and Penelope served as the basis for the Orgilus-Penthea plot in *The Broken Heart* (1vi) and Sherman pointed out the resemblances between the two pairs of lovers (*PMLA* 17 [1909]: 274–85); in each case the couples love and plan to marry but are separated. Penelope was forced to marry Lord Rich; Penthea must wed Bassanes. But Penelope lived openly with Mountjoy while married to Rich, bore her lover five children out of wedlock, and eventually married him. Penthea rejects a liaison with Orgilus after her marriage, goes mad, and dies. Her character bears no resemblance to that of Penelope, nor does that or Orgilus to Mountjoy. *Fames Memoriall* is a source for *BH* only in the basic situation of enforced marriage.

The present edition is based on collation of the following copies of the printed text of 1606: Oxford, Bodleian Library (2 copies); London, British Library; London, Lambeth Palace Library; Cambridge, England, King's College Library; Chatsworth, Library of the Duke of Devonshire; Washington, D. C., The Folger Shakespeare Library; Cambridge, Massachusetts, Harvard University Library (former W. A. White copy); Princeton, New Jersey, Princeton University Library (Robert Taylor Collection); San Marino, California, Henry Huntington Library.

Collation of these copies reveals press-variants in only outer B Forme (B1^r, B2^v, B3^r, B4^v). The uncorrected copies are the two in the Bodley and the copies at Lambeth and Chatsworth. The last lacks G2, G3, G4, thus ending after the last of the *Tombes*. The corrected copies are those of the British Library, Folger, Huntington, King's College, Harvard, and Princeton. Of the corrected copies, King's College lacks B4 and F1, and the rebound Folger copy has A4 misplaced between A1 and A2. Corrections in outer B are as follows:

		UNCORRECTED COPIES	CORRECTED COPIES
B1^r	3	worth	*worth*
	12	bright	bright,
	18	sea and land:	Sea and Land:
	20	spirits	Spirits
B2^v	78	he	He
	87	commentaryes ... cote,	Commentaryes ... cote
	92	peere	Peere
B3^r	133	For nobles none but court should entertain.	For court should none but nobles entertain.
B4^v	199	houres	howres
	204	reachiug ... brooke,	reaching ... brooke
	213	buck ... bore	Buck ... Bore
	214	sty ... race,	Sty ... race;
	215	grace,	grace:
	217	and fame	and fames

IN THE CORRECTED COPIES
- 92   "Ritch" in Huntingtion, King's College, and Princeton copies.
- 214* all copies have "but" instead of "out" except Huntingtion, which agrees with MS.

IN ALL COPIES
- 243   all copies have "sacrisise" for "sacrifice".
- 271* all copies have "gate" instead of "gall" except Huntington and King's College, which agree with MS (also necessary for rhyme).
- 853* all copies have "night no might" instead of "night no night", which agrees with MS.
- 1095 all copies have "greedines" instead of "greediness" except Huntington.

All corrections listed in the second column have been adopted, as have those asterisked above.

    The epistle dedicatory of the manuscript appears in brackets after that of the printed copy; the stanzas that appear only in the manuscript are inserted in the proper place in brackets and here printed for the first time. The list of variants includes individual lines and words which vary from the printed copy. Where the manuscript reading seems to make better sense it has been adopted and placed in brackets in the text. The spelling, punctuation, and capitalization of the manuscript have been noted or adopted only where they are of significance. In general, the manuscript punctuation is very light and the capitalization very irregular. Rebinding has buried some line endings; cutting has removed others and completely eliminated line 14.

The Earle of Devonshire
Deceased.

Minerall being vnknowne vnto you, I might
haue beene imputed as much impudent as fond
if I had not first presented it to yo.r milder
view. Earnest to vnderstand whether your
acceptation and liking may priuiledge the
passe vnder your honorable conduct: w.ch if
it may, I shall deeme my willing paines, ...
though hitherto confined to the Inns of Court
a Studie different ynoughe guerdoned, and
myne vnfeathered Muse ricklie graced w.th
Plumes of soe worthie a Protectresse.

The honourer and Lover of
Your Noble perfections
John Ford.

T. H.

Earle of Devonshire.
Deceased.

Swift tyme hee spedie pursuant of Fate
Sommons to glorious vertues Damnizd
The lasting volume whose noates tounge encreas'd
in Paragon characters immortalizd.
Whose noates spent inhearst, hath forme of spirits
breath'd to vnfayn'ted truth springs from y.e same
to gather forth towring daughter Fame.

Fame her who long rough'sey imparciall trohant
From the blinded backe of healthy might
Soared more aloft tryumphant top and towne
My valiant pursewer, yeer then the last
And by her more mere froome so much more bright
Whose fame's active behaviour to Triumphe w...

Which liue with thoughts prophane sheld in vain.

FAMES MEMORIALL,

OR

The Earle of Devonshire *Deceased*:

With his honourable life, peacefull end,
and solemne Funerall.

quis talia fando
Mirmydonûm, Dolopûmue, aut duri miles Ulissi
Temperet à lachrimis?

AT LONDON

Printed for *Christopher Purset,* dwelling at the signe of
the *Mary Magdalens* head neer Staple Inne
in Holborne, 1606.

To the Rightly right Honorable Lady, the Lady *Penelope*, Countesse of *Devonshire*.

A2ʳ

MOST NOBLE LADY, had the blessings whilom bestowed, and too soon deprived, beene as permanent, as they were glorious: the world had not then had such a generall cause of just sorrow to bewaile, nor I of perticular griefe to inscribe, the present losse of so worthy a lord: but a most sad trueth it is, *Fate may be lamented, never recalled*: upon which infallible axiome, desperate of all possibility, either of regaining the same, or hoping his peere: as much as in the reache of my weake talent lay (unusuall to this stile) I have endevored to register his memory, whose memory will grace my labors. To you, | (excel- lent Lady) it was intended, to you it is addressed: not doubting, but whatsoever hath beene of him sayd, and trewly saide, your honourable favour, will allow the favourable protection of your expressest patronage, who whiles he lived endowed you and justly endowed you, with all the principalles of his sincerest hart, and best fortunes. Let not therfore (worthy Countesse) my rasher presumption, seeme presumpuous folly, in the eyes of your discreeter judgement, in that without your privitie (being a meere straunger alltogether unknowne unto you) I have thus adventured, to shelter my lines, under the well-guided conduct of your Honorable name: grounding my boldnes upon this assurance, that true gentility is ever accompanyd (especially in your sex, more specially in your selfe) with her inseparable adjunct, singular Humanity, principally towards those, whom neither Mercenary hopes or servile flattery, have induced to speake but with the Priviledge of troth. And as for such, who misdeeme virtue without cause, innocency shall pitty them, though not eagerly with mortall | hate: yet simply with naked truth to which envy is ever opposite.

A2ᵛ

A3ʳ

30 Thus (*Madame*) presuming on your acceptance, I will in the meane
while, thinke my willing paynes (hitherto
confined to the Innes of Courte studyes
much differente) highlie guerdoned,
and mine unfeathered Muse (as
35   soone dead as borne) ritchly
graced, under the plumes
of so worthy a pro-
tectresse.

The honourer and lover of your
40   noble perfections,
Jo: FORDE.

[To the rightlie right honorable Ladie the ladie Penelope Countess of Devonsheire.

 Most noble ladie. had the blessings latelie bestowed, and too soone deprived, beene as permanent, as they were glorious, the world had not then had such generall cause of sorrow to bewayle, nor I of perticuler greife to inscribe the present losse of soe worthie a Lord: But a most sad truth it is, "fate may be lamented, never recal'd," upon which infallable axiome, desperate of all possibilitie, either of regaining the same, or finding the like; asmuch as in the reach of my talent lay (unusuall to this stile) I have indevoured to register his memory, whose memory will grace my labours. To you (Excellent Ladie) it was intended, to you it is addressed, not doubting but whatsoever hath beene of him said, and truely said, your honorable favour will allow the favourable protection of your expressest patronage, who whiles hee lived indued you with all the principalls of his heart and fortunes; yet ere I committed it to the presse (for fame undivulged is an hidden | Minerall) being unknowne unto you, I might have beene imputed as much impudent, as fond: if I had not first presented it to your milder view: Earnest to understand whether your acceptation and liking may priviledge the passe under your honorable conduct: which if it may, I shall deeme my willing paines, (though hitherto confined to the Inns of Court a studie different) highlie guerdoned; and myne unfeathered Muse richlie graced with the Plumes of soe worthie a protectresse.

The honourer and lover of
Your Noble perfections

John Ford.]

To eache affected Reader.

PErverse construction of a plaine intent,
NEither is scorn'd, respected, or dispis'd:
LOsing of their sleight loves, who never meant,
PEculiar knowledge, willingly is pris'd,
5   **CONTE**nted happinesse, **S**ecured peace,
   OF selfe content is ever happiest ease.

DEVOtion to the carelesse is meer folly,
No **SH**allow envy of malicious **IRE**,
Can move my resolution, grounded wholly
10 On hopes of better judgement, I desire
   The favour of my favourers, not any
   Unwilling eyes, I strive not to please many.

Non omnibus studeo,
non malevolis.

To Master *John Forde* of the Middle Temple, upon his *Fames Memoriall,* this Madrigall.

If that renowmed Lord (whose powerfull fame,
   in strength of wars, and calmes of peace exceeded)
20   hath after death purchas'd so great a name,
   that it must prosper as it hath proceeded:
Then must in time those spightfull plants be weeded;
   which living yet, him living would have choaked:
   and those sweet wittes touch'd with a sacred flame
25   of his ritch virtues, shall advance the same.
But thou (by those deserts in him provoked
   that song his honours which so much exceeded;

    whose pleasant pen in sacred water soaked
       of *Castaly* did register his worth)
30 Reapest much part of honour for thy pen,
       through him: faire mirror of our Englishmen,
    whom with due dignity thy *Muse* set fourth.

              B<small>AR</small>: B<small>ARNES</small>.

In eundem.

35 *Vivit, in æternum vivet* Dux *inclitus armis,*
    Mountjoyus: vivet Forde *Poema tuum,*
Maior uterque suo genio. Vi carminis Heros,
    Materiæ fœlix nobilis autor ope,

              T. P.

The EARLE of Devonshire deceased.

    SWIFT Time the speedy pursevant of heaven,
    Sommons to glorious virtues canoniz'd,
    The lasting volume where *worth* roves uneven
    In brazen characters immortaliz'd;
5   Where merit lives imbrac't, base scorne despis'd:
       Linckt to untainted Truth sprong from the same,
       Begets his eaglet-towring daughter Fame.

    Fame, she who long coucht her emperiall crowne,
    Within the blinded darke of swarthy night,
10 Sores now aloft triumphant up and downe,
    With radiant splendour gayer then the light,
    And by how much more known so much more bright,
       Proclaimes aloud defiance to disdaine,
       Which hir with thoughts prophane shold entertain.

15 Nor doth she lacky in this vale of mud,
    This razed world, but still in state arise,
    Lifting her plumed crest from out the flood
    Of Sea and Land: whiles she with wonder flies
    About the circle of the toplesse skyes:
20   And Spirits most heroicke doth enflame,
       With adoration of hir sacred name.

    Base *Feare* the onely monument of slaves,
    Progenitor to shame, skorne to gentilitye,
    Herauld to usher pesants to their graves,
25 Becomes abjected thoughts of faint servility,
    Whiles hauty fame adornes nobility:

  Planting hir gorgeous throne upon the crest,
  Of honour casked in a royall breast.

This makes grosse dregges of soules admire the verse
30 Of shrill strayn'd Artsmen whose Ambrosiack quills
Whiles they desert's *Encomions* sweet rehearse,
The world with wonder and amazement fills,
Affrighted with the threats of horrid ills:
  Astonishing the chaffe of pampered men,
35 With high rear'd accents of their golden pen.

O that some sacred poet now surviv'd,
Som *Homer* to new mourn *Achilles* losse,
Our deare *Achilles* losse, of life depriv'd,
Who living, life in dangers death did tosse,
40 Not daunted with this hazard or that crosse:
  O that he liv'd with scholyes most devine,
  To cote and add one worthy to the nine.

The nine had past for saints, had not our time
Obscur'd the beames of their bright splendent prayse,
45 By a more noble worthy whose sublime
Invicted spirit in most hard assayes,
Still added reverent statues to his daies,
  Surmounting all the nine in worth as far,
  As *Sol* the tincture of the meanest star.

50 Now hovering fame hath vail'd hir false recluse,
Makes reputation and beleefe her warrant,
Wonder and trueth hir convoy to traduce
Hir train of shouts accomplishing hir errant,
Venting concealed virtue now apparant:
55 Imprints in Canons of eternall glorye,
  Worth's monumentall rites, great *Mountjoyes* story.

Great M O U N T J O Y ! were that name sincerely scand,
Mysterious Hieroglificks would explane,
Each letter's allegory, grace the hand,
60 By whom the sence shold learnedly be drawn

To stop the dull conceits of wits prophane:
  Diving into the depth of hidden art,
  To give but due to eache deserving part.

That is with homage to adore thy name,
As a ritch relique of memoriall,
A trophey consecrated unto fame,
Adding within our hearts historiall,
High Epithetes past hyperbolicall.
  Yet all to meane to ballance equall forrage,
  And sympathize in joincture with thy courage.

Live, ô live yee whom poets deck with lyes,
Raising your deeds to fames which never end,
Our Patriot staynes your fictions, no disguise
Of painted prayse his glory shall extend,
His owne great valour his deserts commend:
  Such is his sounding notice all do know it,
  No poet can grace him, he every poet.

None him, He all can grace, his very story
Gives lawrell to the Writer, crownes of bay,
The title of his name attributes glory,
The subject doth the Authors skill bewray,
Inlarging still his theame and scope to say:
  Nor is one found amongst a world of men,
  Who [can perfect] his actions with his pen.

Had he himselfe like *Julius Cæsar* wrote,
Whiles as he liv'd his owne acts commendation,
In fluent Commentaryes us'd to cote
Eche hazards conquest by a trew probation,
Exemplify'd with termes of arts relation:
  Then had he wingd in height of fame for ever,
  His fame his name (as now) been razed never.

Goe yet ritch-stiled Peere and overtake,
(Thy selfe shalt priviledge thy selfe by merit)
Thy soules-united *Essex* for whose sake,

Thou didst advance thy love, which did inherit
The deere reversion of his elate spirit:
   Then go great *Montjoy* lustre of this age,
   Pace still thy name in pompous equipage.

When first his birth [produc't] this prime of hope,
An impe of promise mild proclivitie;
Gratious aspects even in his Horoscope,
Prædominated his nativity,
Alotting in his [urne] nobility:
   That being nobly borne he might persever,
   Inthro'nd by fame nobilitated ever.

Now when his infant yeares waxt mellow ripe,
[Ballanc't] in pithy scales of youths discretion;
As past the childish feare, feare of a stripe,
Or schools correct with deeper [gravd] impression,
He scorn'd the mimick thoughts of base condition:
   By earnest documents foreshowing wholy,
   His just contempt of unreguarded folly.

For having suckt the rudiments of learning,
Grammars Elixar juice and quintessence,
He soon approv'd his judgement by discerning,
Applying with industrious diligence,
To follow studies of more consequence:
   Then by a syllogistick kind of warre,
   He ruminates on thoughts which nobler are.

He learnes sharp-witted logick to confute
With quick distinctions, sleights of Sophistry,
Inritching his ritche knowledge doth it sute,
And sounds the depth of quaint philosophye,
Himselfe the mirror of morality:
   And proves by instance *Aristotle* lyes,
   Who yong mens aptnesse to the same denies.

He studies it, yet is himselfe the subject,
Subject of civill virtues, chiefe of good,

Arts pith and natures dearling, honours object
130 As noble by his wit as by his blood,
Honour and wisedome on his forehead stood:
    Thus now to court he goes there to remain,
    For court should none but nobles entertain.

Noble he was, witnesse his elate spirit
135 Whose unappalled stomak scorn'd compare,
Noble he was, witnesse his peerlesse merite,
Which stain'd competitours, witnesse his rare
Renown'd examples do the same declare:
    Noble he was, in that he could not brooke
140   To have his equall, or for sword or booke.

O had his auncestors but heretofore
Dream't such a sonn should spring from out their lyne,
They might have truely griev'd, and evermore
Have blusht to thinke on it, that one divine
145 Shold be their offspring, deeming it a signe
    Of a lesse glorious happinesse for them,
    Better might they have drawn their race from him.

Then happy they that are or shalbe ever,
Deducted from the issue of this bloud,
150 Immortall be this name, worn-wasted never,
The Index to trew fame, happy the good
Allyed in him by kin or Brotherhood:
    Such his desert nor time nor malice term'd it,
    His youth first promis'd and his yeares confirm'd it.

155 For being now appendant to the court,
His presence was the court to draw it to him
The saints of that smooth Paradise resort
With pleasure to behold, beholding woo him,
And what their favours can, they vow to do him:
160   Yea he rejoyc'd the earths great deity,
    That such a subject grac'd hir empery.

Here he began to tast the fragrant smack,

> The *catapotion* of heart-easing love,
> Here he perseverd to assault the wrack,
165 Of supple passion, proving to disprove,
> That any soyle firm-setled thoughts should move:
>> Here was he first who taught what should be done,
>> How Ladyes shold be lov'd, serv'd, [woo'd] and woon.

> In this secured solace of sweet peace
170 He nurc't his yonger joyes, not wholy bent
> To wanton, sicke, lascivious, [amour's] ease
> But to more primer passions of content,
> Of civill mirth and jocond merriment:
>> Mirth in his looks, and virtue in his toung
175 Fresh as the balme, smooth as the Mermaides song.

> Activity abroad, daliance in chambers,
> Becomes a perfect courtier, such was he,
> What mayden breast so nice, as locks of amber
> Could not inchant with loves captivity?
180 Free spirits soone are caught when slaves go free:
>> What uncontrouled soule is so precise,
>> As may, yet will not tast earths paradise?

> *Mountjoy* (the mounting joy of heavens perfection)
> Was all a man should be in such an age,
185 Nor voyd of lov's sence, nor yoakt in subjection
> Of servile passion, theame for every stage,
> Honour for him did honours pawne ingage:
>> Be witnesse slanders selfe, who must avow
>> Virtue adornd his mind, triumph his brow.

190 Nor did the pleasure of these courtly sports,
> Indeer him to the softnesse of such ease;
> His ever-mounting thought far more imports,
> The thirst of fame such form'd *Ideas* please,
> The resty delicates of sweet disease:
195 To run a race at tilt, to catch the ring,
>> Did greater glory to his projects bring.

Let smooth-chind Amorists be cloyde in play,
And surfet on the bane of hatefull leisure,
Let idle howres follies youth betray,
Unto the idle shame of boundlesse pleasure,
Such petty apes of silke want reasons measure:
    Great *Mountjoy* saw such loosnes of the witty
    Which seing did not more disdain then pity.

No, his deep-reaching spirit could not brooke
The fond addiction to such vanity,
Reguardfull of his honor he forsooke,
The smicker use of court-humanity,
Of rurall clownage or urbanity:
    He lov'd the worthy and endevoring prov'd,
    How of the worthy he might be belov'd.

Now he delights to see the faulcon sore,
About the top of heaven: then to chase,
The nimble Buck, or hunt the bristled Bore
From [out] the Sty of terror, now the race;
Barriers and sports of honorable grace:
    Not games of thriftlesse prodigality,
    But plots of fame and fames eternity.

For after toyes of courtshippe he assaies,
Which way to manage an untamed horse,
When, how, to spur, and rayn, to stop, and raise,
Close sitting, voltage of a manlike force,
When in career to meet with gallant course:
    As Centaures were both horse and [man]: so he
    Seemd on the horse nor could discerned be.

Such private exercise which limn'd the way
To publique reputation was his scope;
Ech howr grac'd howr, and each day grac'd day
With further expectation of great hope
Nor did his youth his noble levels stoppe:
    He aymd at high designes, and so attaynd
    The high assigns to which his spirit aymd.

Lo heere the pith of valour moulded fast,
In curious workmanship of natures art:
Lo here the monuments which ever last,
To all succeeding ages of desert,
Noble in all, and all in every part:
  Records of fame, and characters of brasse,
  Containing acts, such acts conceit do passe.

Triumphant soule of such a princelike Lord,
O I coulde dry the fountaines of myne eyes,
Upon thy coffins hearse and every word,
Which sorow shold out-sigh or grief implies,
I could resolve two drops of sacrifice:
  And spend them on the evergaping womb
  Of the unseason'd earth, thy sacred tombe.

The sweetest cygnet of thy comforts heaven,
Thy lifes last paradise, thy hearts first love
Could not bemoan the losse of thee bereven
With more sweet-piercing plaints then I have strove,
To volly my discomforts yet approve
  (Deer creature) thy [too] deerly bought distresse,
  By vulgar censures base unhappinesse.

But ah be still thy selfe, let not defame,
Of the rude *Chaos* aggravate thy woes
The multitudes blind slander is no shame;
Rusticity his joy by malice knowes,
The better best in judging better showes:
  Let grosse uncivill hinds reguardlesse sleepe,
  Remember thou thy losse, remembring weepe.

So mayst thou knightly youth who wert his friend,
Companion to his chamber and his bed,
His lov's much largesse did to thee extend,
And made the rumor of thy name be spred,
Even to thy native West wher thou wert bred:
  Ah do not him forget who honourd thee
  With perfect rites of mutuall amitie.

Nor canst thou stop the floodgates of thine eyes, 7ᵛ
Great Peer of worth and state, who griev'd thy thrall,
For Peerlesse *Essex* strife who sought to rise,
270 In vertuous honour which procur'd thy fall
Devonshire bewayld thy dangers bitter gall:
    Then in requitall of much more then this
    Sigh thou for him, still love, and cherish his.

As much grave patron of sage wisedoms lore, C2ʳ
275 Mayst thou lament thy friendes untimely race,
Who ever favour'd thee cause thou hast bore,
(Whiles he was *Ireland's* viceroy) thy great place,
Of treasurer in most respected grace:
    His death deserves thy teares to solemnize
280   His ceremonious funerall obsequies.

Ye safe secured fathers of wise peace,
Just senators and magistrates in aw,
Wealthy home-breaders which ingrosse your ease,
Ye learned legists of contentious law,
285 Ye rulers all who him victorious saw:
    Feare ye like strokes as him of life deprives,
    He was a brazen wall to guard your lives.

Double toung-oyled courtiers whose neat phrases, 8ʳ
Do modell foorth your wittes maturity,
290 In honied speeches and sick-thoughted graces,
Cloking your soules in sins obscurity,
Yet fan your lightnesse in security,
    Weep on his reverent coarse: for such as he
    Now is, (not as he was) your selves shall be.

295 But ô forsaken souldiers ye have lost,
The *Atlas* of your hopes, your staffe, your stay,
The staffe and stay of your ambitious boast,
Who guerdon'd you with services due [pay],
On him the burthen of your treasure lay:
300   Reason commands your sorow for whose sake,
    Himselfe all toile of paines would undertake.

Like *Mars* in arms triumphant ye have seene, C2ᵛ
This warlike champion whose undanted mind
Was never yet appall'd but still hath been,
305 Steeled against the worst, nor hath declin'd
To dull distrust but evermore enshrind
    In goodly views of horror ready prest,
    To purchase glory by his hands unrest.

Witnesse (ye wars of *Belgia*) who tell, 8ᵛ
310 Of his eternall fame, heroique spirit,
Incomparable height which did excell,
The common height of common stomacks merit,
He lineally did thirst of worth inherit:
    A chronicle of lasting memory,
315   A president of matchlesse souldery.

Let every private action of desert,
Be theames for other pen's to labour in,
My quill shall onely knowne reports insert:
Who publicke credence and belief may win
320 Not to be taxt with fictions, Ideots sin:
    Time cannot wrong nor envy shall not wound,
    The lawfull right of his due praises sound.

O who will lend me som deep-moving stile?
Or add unto my bluntnesse quick conceit?
325 What gentle goddesse wil vouchsafe a smile
To mine unpolisht muse? what tempting bait
Of formall grace upon my lynes will wayte?
    What power divine of some more angell woman,
    Will make me thinke my verses more then common?

330 Flint-hearted *Lycia* may with mild aspect, C3ʳ/9ʳ
Cast up the sigh of some fore-matched skorn
And in the mixture of disdayns neglect,
My death-bewayling scope of griefe adorne,
Reviving dulnesse of a wit forlorne:
335   Amongst the fansies of hir rivall lover,
    Some groane with this deere nobles funerall cover.

No, beauty full of change, forbeare thy care,
An Angell more celestiall payes hir vowes,
Upon her lord deceasd who did not spare,
To gratifie the frontyres of hir brows,
With as much pleasure as content allowes:
    Thou Lady on my lines cast favors glory,
    Whiles I inscribe great *Mountjoys* Irish story.

When fickle chance and deaths blindfold decree,
From the tribunall seat of awfull state,
Had hurried downe in black calamity
Renowned *Devoreux*, whose aukward fate,
Was misconceited by fowle envies hate:
    Back was he cal'd from *Ireland* to come home,
    And noble *Mountjoy* must supply his roome.

Looke how two heart-united brothers part,
The one to slaughter, th'other to distrust,
Yet sorowing each with other pawns his hart
As being loath to goe, yet go they must,
Either to horror and a death unjust:
    So *Essex* parts with *Mountjoy*, [either] mourning
    The losse of others sight as nere returning.

So *Mountjoy* parts with *Essex*, and now flies
Upon the wings of griefes to tents of terror;
Or els to vaunt his name above the skies,
Or leave his livelesse carkasse as a mirror
Of monumented feare to friends of error:
    Vowing revenge should on that land extend,
    Which wrought the downfal of his worthiest friend.

Unblessed soyle (quoth he), rebellious nation,
Which hast with trechery sent troups to death,
Butcher of valiant bloods, earths reprobation,
Heavens curse and natures monster, drawing breath,
By others wracks (as triall witnesseth):
    Since by the meanes of thee my friend hath dy'd,
    Mine arme shall scourge the loosenessse of thy pride.

Incenc'st with rage and treble-girt with force
Of Justice, force and valour on he goes,
With sword and fire voyd of a smooth remorse,
He greets the strength of his half-conquered foes,
And on them yoakes of bondage doth impose:
    Or all must yeeld to mercy, or els flie,
    Yet flying all must fight, and fighting die.

But ô far be it from the height of fame,
To triumph on submission, he would not
Not tyrant-like in bloodshed boast agayne,
He hated it as to his worth a blot,
By lenitie more honour hath he got.
    He was as by his favorites appear'd,
    More fear'd then lov'd, yet much more lov'd then feard.

Destruction to the stiffneck't rebells stoute,
(Stout in their headlong miseries) was bent,
Ruine unto the false inconstant route;
But favour to the willing still he meant,
A perfect noble mind's trew document:
    A rule infallible experience bred,
    To strive for conquest, spare the conquered.

What myriades of hosts could not constraine,
He by his courteous mildnesse brought to passe
What all devoyr of mercie could not traine,
By his victorious power enforced was,
Both words of milk, and thunderbolts of brasse
    Attended on the pleasure of his nod,
    They deemd him for a humane demy-god.

And thou *Tyrone* the idole most adored,
Amongst the superstitious mutiners,
Whose deepe ambitious reach was still implored,
To raise more millions of treacherers,
Of homicidiall cruell slaughterers:
    Even thou thy selfe, when any traitor spake
    Of *Mountjoy*, at that very name didst quake.

That verie name did prostitute the heart
Of mischief-breeding counsailes in the dust;
In hearing of that name they felt the smart,
410 Of vanquisht dread as augur to distrust,
Which was by feare inthral'd, by doubt discust:
   Mountjoy a name importing threats of thunder,
   Frustrating hopes of life, and life asunder.

Mountjoy a name of grim severity,
415 *Mountjoy* a name of meeknes, peace and love,
Mountjoy a name to rayne temerity,
Mountjoy a name which vertue did approve,
Mountjoy a name which joy did ever moove:
   Mountjoy a charter of invicted fame,
420   Yet *Mountjoy* was far greater then his name.

His name which stretcht beyond the boundlesse limits,
Of all the oceans empire and made knowne
His hauty chivalry in forraine climates,
Which by the trumpe of glore was lowdly blowne,
425 In courtes of greatest princes of renowne:
   Each palace with an eccho speaking shrill,
   Resounded his fayre deeds of honour still.

The wily Irish whose inveterate hate,
Unto the lawes of Justice nere would bow,
430 Whose sleightes no powr of power could abate,
Or ever undermine before till now,
With gentle menace of a pliant brow:
   This man more then a man, this god in arms,
   United, ceasing plots of further harmes.

435 Now they began to see, and seeing feele
The sweet of concord, bitternesse of warre,
The sharpe reproofe of double-edged steele,
The peace of peace, how wretched brawlers are
How blessed the secure, content doth farre
440   Exceed contention, better shun wars toile,
   Then ever live in faction by the spoile.

The sonne against the Father long oppos'd,
The Unkle with the nephew at debate,
The friend with troupes of foe-like friends inclos'd.
Brother with brother set in mortall hate,
Kin which with Kin did kindred violate:
    Duty, alliance, frindship, blood, and love:
    All striving, he to concord all did move.

Peeres in defiance of each others greatnesse,
Nobles complotting nobles speedy fall,
He reconcil'd, and made them tast the sweetnes,
Of happy league and freed them from the gall
Of steepe destructions, ruine, ruines thrall:
    Tygers and lions, bores, and raging Bulles,
    Hath he atton'd with Leopards and Wolves.

A land of penury, scarcity, and want
He hath inritcht with plenty, ease and store;
A land where humain reason was most scant
He hath endow'd with wisdomes sacred lore,
Accosting it more fertile then before:
    A land of Barbarous inhumanitye
    He hath reduc't to blessed piety.

Now had he ripened all his hopes at full,
Imparadiz'd his soule in deare content
And wrought the nature of a people dull
To what his glory aym'd at when he meante,
To set a period to his banishment:
    And greete his native soyle with much desire
    To get a guerdon'd favour for his hyre.

Now did he feed his laboures with delight
Of viewing his diviner soveraigne,
Presenting conquests of well mastred spight
Unto her gracious love, and thence obtaine,
Hir willing acceptation as a gaine
    Of reward after toyle, and glad hir yeares,
    In strengthning hir dominions, chasing feares.

But ô ere he could apprehend that joye
She flew from earth to bewtifye the heaven,
Eliza dy'de, death's javelin did destroy
480 The ever boast of England; fate had weaven
The twist of life, and hir of life bereaven.
    She dy'de and left the worlde in tears of terror
    To weepe hir losse and woonder at her mirror.

Never it was her hap to see that land
485 Which long had boyld in stern rebellious treason
To be subdu'de unto her mild commaund
And vaunt the Trophey of that peacefull season,
Malice did ever blind their sences reason:
    She dy'de ere rumour could that ease relate,
490   The newes was happy, but for hir [too] late,

[Too] late for her and for our Lord [too] late,
Hir death for him too soon, but shorte anon
Distrust was turnd to trust, for in greate state
England's *Mæcenas* in succession
495 Was soone made know'n by Proclamation
    And undertooke the Burthen of the crowne
    Advauncing merit low disgrace threw downe.

As Cæsar led his captive slaves to Rome
To grace his triumph, magnify his fame
500 So now did *Mountjoy* with Tyrone come home
Victorious, welcome, adding to his name
(By favour of our King who gave the same)
    A Style of honour to his blood innated
    Devonshieres ennobled Earle was created.

505 In Robes of peace, accoutrements of rest
He was advanc't a Counsayllour and joy'd
The soft fruition of a graver breast
Not with the Brunt of warrefare more annoyde
Nor with the dint of hazard overcloyde
510   But sate with judgment to discerne of lawes
    Which he had guarded with his swordes applause.

In him was England two fould fortunate
He was her champion and her Senator
Both to defend her good, and moderate,
515 To fight both for her safety, and confer,
Both to encourage subjects and deter
    Revollters from offending, both in one
    And one in both himselfe he was alone.

Thus loving all he liv'd belov'd of all,   13ᵛ
520 Save some whome emulation did enrage
To spit the venom of their rancour's gall,
Which dropt upon themselves and made the stage
A publique Theater for follyes badge
    Their shame will still outlive theyr memory
525   Onely remembered in infamy.

Such poorer in desert then ritch in woorth,   D2ᵛ
Are but as shadowes which appear but are not,
Such but disgorge lanck indiscretion forth,
Of needlesse repetitions which declare not
530 Trew grounds, when for the trueth it self they care not,
    Yet hold themselves abusd and highly scorne,
    To brooke the chance to which themselves ar born.

Go weake betraiers of your witlesse madnesse!
Your malice will revert upon your breasts,
535 Not lookes of graver nicenesse, nicer sadnesse,
Can shadow imputations of unrests,
His greater spirit at your fondnesse jests:
    You vex your selves, not him, and make men gaze,
    At your own wrongs which your own tongues do blaze.

540 Sinck blind detraction into lowest earth,   14ʳ
[Lett] ballad-rimers tyre their galled wits,
Scornes to their patrones making juycelesse mirth,
To grosse attentors by their hired writs,
Dispraise with such poore hackneys better fits:
545   Well may such envy those heroyicke deeds,
    There apprehensions leane conceit exceeds.

Fame-royallized *Devonshire* setled now,
In well-deserved place of eminence,
The expectance of his wisedom doth allow,
550 By cancelling affayres of consequence,
And by endevours of sage diligence:
    Approves his greatnesse, largesse to applie
    The fruits of dear-experienc't pollicy.

Not puft with weening self-affected pride,
555 Common to upstart honours counterfeite,
But favouring the worthy he suppli'd,
Deserts necessities, and made the height
Of his advancement on their needs to waite:
    "True noblenes with breth sucks noble spirits
560   "When bastard broods conceite but bastard merits.

Men rais'd to flote of fortune from the mud,
Of low dejection and at length grown great,
Forget that they are men, and scorn the blood
Of meane allyance, boasting in the seat
565 Of empire which ambition doth beget:
    Such not esteeme desert but sensuall vaunts,
    Of parasites and fawning sycophaunts.

Be tyrants kings to such servility?
And peasants servile to such currs of shame?
570 *Devonshire* the issue of nobility,
Avoyded rumor of such foule defame,
True virtue grac'd his mind, applause his name:
    Applause his name, which whiles the heavens divine
    Containe their lights, upon the earth will shine.

575 True virtue grac'd his mind be witnesse ever,
The provident forecare of wise discretion,
His wary prudence which did still endevor
To hold him from the wrack of spights impression,
From faith approv'd he never made digression:
580   "That is true prudence when devoyd of feare,
    "A man untoucht himselfe upright doth beare.

Trew vertue grac'd his mind in which was grounded
The modest essence of firme Temperaunce
Which never was with fortunes chaunge confounded
585 Or troubled with the Crosse of fickle chaunce,
Distrust his spirit never could enhaunce:
    That man is perfect temperate whose life
    Can never be disturb'd but free from strife.

Trew virtue grac'd his mind, witnesse his courage
590 His resolution-armed Fortitude,
Witnesse his stomack's prime which striv'd to forrage
Extreames even by extremityes subdu'de,
Slaves with the eys of pitty he review'd:
    He who can Conquer miseryes in neede
595   Enjoyes the height of fortitude indeede.

Trew virtue grac'd his minde, witnesse at last
His sober cariage, twixt the scales of measure
Who when he was in awe of Justice plac't
Studyed how to the meanest to doe pleasure,
600 So rare a guift in such a man's a treasure:
    Sincerest Justice is not to decerne
    But to defend, ayde, further and confirme.

True virtue grac'd his mind, witnesse all these
Which in his person were essenciall,
605 Ready to helpe the poore, the great to please
In rites of honour, neither greate or small
Would he prefer, but merit paiz'd them all:
    Since all these vertues were in him combin'd
    Truth will avow true vertue grac'd his mind:

610 Not in the wrack of Prodigality
Nor thriftlesse riot of respectlesse meane
Did he extend his liberalitye
But to his honors credit, where was seen
Apparent worthinesse, he still hath been
615   A Patron to the learned and a propp,
    To favour studyes now dispised cropp.

Thou marrow of our English poesy
Thou life and blood of verse canst record this,
The Bounty of his zeale can gratifye
620   Thy labour's of endeavors: what was his
He graunted to thy muses happiest blisse,
    A liberall *Mæcenas* to rewarde thee
    A Lord of speciall favour to reguard thee.

By firm allegiance, courtesie, and kindnesse,
625   Unto his prince, his peeres, his frindes, indeer'd:
By sterne constraint, meek scorne, and willing blindnes,
Of all his foes, backbiters, grudgers, fear'd,
He in his life-time evermore appeard;
    Peace, pitty, love, with mildnesse, ease, and rest,
630   Rul'd, forgave, joyde, his soule, his wrongs, his breast.

Linck't, in the gracefull bonds of dearest life
Unjustly term'd disgracefull he enjoyd,
Contents aboundance, happinesse was rife
Pleasure secure, no troubled thought annoyd
635   His [comforts] sweetes, toyle was in toyle destroyd:
    Maugre the throat of malice, spight of spight
    He liv'd united to his hearts delighte.

His hearts delight who was that glorious starre
Which bewtified the value of our lande,
640   The lightes of whose perfections brighter are
Then all the lampes, which in the lustre stand
Of heavens forehead, by discretion scan'd,
    Wits ornament, earth's love, loves Paradise
    A Saint divine, a bewty fairly wise.

645   A bewtye fayrely-wise, wisely discreete
In wincking mildely at the toong of rumour,
A saint, meerely divine, divinely sweete,
In banishing the pride of idle humour
Not relishing the vanity of tumour:
650   More then, a female of so high a race;
    With meekenesse bearing sorrows sad disgrace.

A sad disgrace? ô that the eyes of sence
Should prye into the nature of the worst
Poore fortunes envy, greatnesse eminence,
Because themselves in worldly cares are nurc't.
Deluding types of honour as accurst
    When they themselves ar most accurst of all
    Who being lowest lower cannot fall.

[Lyve thou untoucht forever above fame!
More happie that thou canst not be more haplesse!
"The wordes of malice are an usuall game,
Whose mouth is lawlesse, whose invention saplesse,
Their breast of hony tornes to poison paplesse,
    Still be thine eares to sufferance tun'd readie
    In mynde resolv'd, in resolution stedie.

What hee amongst the proudest of contempt
Whiles as thy sunshine lasted, did not bend
Unto thy presence? flattery redempt
With service on their service did attend?
All stryving to admire, protest, comend,
    Which now by imputation black as hell
    They seeme to derrogate from dooing well.

Thy virtue caus'd thy honor to support thee
In noble contract of undoubted merit,
His knowledge to his Credence did report thee
A creature of a more then female sperit,
Concord of musick did thy soule inherit,
    Courtiers but Counterfeit thy Rarity
    For thy perfections brook't no parity.]

Even as a quire of modell-tuning birds,
Chirping their layes in natures pliant straine,
Even so these courtiers flow'd in termes of words,
Untill the Nightingale in sweet complaine,
Did urge the rest as ravisht to refraine:
    So this heart-stealing goddesse charm'd their eares,
    To heare her fluent wit, they blush at theirs.

  Let merit take hir due, unfeed I write,
  Compel'd by instance of apparent right,
  Nor choa'kt with private hopes doe I indite,
690 But led by trueth as knowne as is the light,
  By proofe as cleere as day, as day as bright:
    I reck not taunting mocks, but pity rather
    The foolish offspring of so vaine a father.

  Devonshire I write of thee a theam of wonder
695 Wonder unto posterity succeeding,
  A stile importing fame as lowde as thunder,
  Sounding throughout the world: the times yet breding
  Shall deifie thee by thy stories reading:
    Making large statues to honorifie
700 Thy name, memorialls rites to glorifie.

  As oft as *James* the monarch of our peace,
  Shall be in after chronicles recited,
  In that to heav'ns applause and subjects ease
  England and *Scotland* he in one united,
705 A sight with which true *Britains* were delighted:
    So oft shalt thou eternall favour gaine,
    Who recollected'st *Ireland* to them twaine.

  A worke of thankes in strengthening the force
  Of such an entire Empire now secure,
710 A world within it selfe which whiles the course
  Of heaven continueth lasting wil endure
  Fearlesse of forraign power, strong and sure
    A bulwarke intermur'd with walls of Brasse,
    A like can never bee, nor ever was.

715 Twas the Puissant vigour of thine arme,
  T'was the well-labouring project of thy braine
  Which did allay the further feare of harme,
  Inriching *Brittayn* with this happy gaine
  Of blessed peace which now it doth retaine,
720 It was thy warye resolution brought it,
    It was thy ready pollicy that wrought it.

Thou wer't a *Phœnix*, such a bird is rare
Rare in this wodden age of avarice,
When thirst of gold, not Fame, may best compare,
725 With those of choycest worth, "rich men are wise,
"Honest, if honesty consist in vice
　　"Strong purses have strong frinds, he hath most praise
　　"Who hath most wealth: ô blindnesse of our dayes!

Dye thoughtes of such corruption, we intend 18^v
730 To shew the substance not the shadowed gloze,
The prayse we speake of doth itselfe commend
And need's no ornament unlike to those
Who by *preconion's* virtue doth impose
　　A taske upon our quill, not what we would,
735 　　Doe wee inferr but what in right we should.

He whom we treat of was a president,
Both for the valiant and judicious,
Both *Mercury* and *Mars* were resident
In him at once, sweet words delicious,
740 And horryd battaile were to him auspicious:
　　Both armes and arguments to force or traine,
　　To win by mildnesse, or by threats constraine.

Two speciall beauties chiefly did adorne E2^r
His faire unblemisht soule and spotlesse mind,
745 To god religious he himselfe hath borne,
With zealous reverence in zeale enshrind,
And to his prince still loyall ever kind:
　　At [th'ons] monarchick government he trembled,
　　'Cause it the others deity resembled.

750 Devout in fervency of ardent love 19^r
Unto the value of salvation,
The due respect of sov'raignty did move,
Unto his princes throne an intimation
Of feare, not mask't in smooth dissimulation:
755 　　He of his race hereafter may be voucht,
　　That he was sound in both, in both untoucht.

What more yet unremembred can I say,
And yet what have I sayd that might suffice?
He was the trophey of a greater day,
Then time would ever limit to our eyes,
He was a peere of best approved guise:
   He was the best, the most, most best of all,
   Heaven's pride, earths joy, we may him justly call.

Heavens pride? for heaven into him infus'd,
The quintessence of ripe perfection,
No guift on him bestow'd he hath abus'd,
But betterd by his better lifes direction,
Keping [Contempt] of virtue in subjection:
   A penitentiall contrite votary,
   To sanctimonious taintlesse purity.

Earth's joy, for in the earth he liv'd renown'd
By all the excellency of natures art
With all the boast and pith of honor crown'd
That royalty to merit could impart,
The wreathe of joyes was set beneath his hart:
   The light of worth's delight, the Pharaos tower
   Which was refulgent by his Lordly power.

Thus in the jollity of humane pleasure
Advaunc't to steps of state and high degree,
Beloved and ador'd in equall measure
Of greatest and the meanest, fates decree
Bent power against his power, for (aye me)
   (Fye on that for) whiles he in glory stood,
   Of worldly pompe cold droop't his noble blood.

O what *Heraclitus* would spare his eyes
To show'r teares in showers and distill
The liquid of a greev'd hearts sacrifice
Which will consume itselfe, what dolefull knell
Of pearcing grones will sigh the worst of ill:
   The worst of ill, the worst of cruell fate,
   Could spit even in the bitternesse of hate.

All yee who hitherto have read his story,
Just Panegyrickes of Heroyque deedes,
Prepare your eyes to weep, your harts to sory
The wracke of darknesse which from death proceedes,
The murther of delight which murther breedes,
   Loe heere an alteration briefly chaung'd
   Now all but joy, now from all joy estrang'd.

O Coward times why doe you keepe your dayes?
O Orbes of heaven why doe you runne your course?
O seas why doe not floods your waves uprayse
And ne're reflow agayne with moderate sourse?
O Sun why dost not quench thy beames hot force?
   O why doe all things certaine setled tarye,
   Save men's short lives who still unconstant vary?

Instance unpartiall death, deafe sorrow's subject
Pleasures abater, fickle youth's dispiser
Headstrong in malice, inaffected object
To every sence, the subtile slye inticer
To guilded hopes, the heaven's wil's revisor:
   Instance his triumph, instance his sure dart
   Which misseth none, hits home still to the hart.

Now had the season enterteyn'd the spring
And giv'n a welcome to the dayes of mirth,
When sweet harmonious birds began to sing
With pleasant roundelayes which grac'd the earth,
By long expectance of the blossoms birth,
   When at the dawne of Floraes trimmed pride
   Ere shee perfum'd the ayr, greate *Devonshiere* died.

He dy'de, a sullyde word, a [word] of ruth:
For ever be it stamp't in misery:
Feareful unto the old, hated of youth,
Markt with the fingar of calamity:
Blotted from light of day, nights Herauldry,
   He dy'de, briefe accents but enduring woe
   The letters for whole dates of griefes may goe.

Torment of mischiefe how thou grat'st my breast,
Mischiefe of torment how thou rackst my soule,
Unhappy cares how is your heart distrest,
830 Wretched unhappiness which dost controwle
The blisse of comfort, and alike enroule
    Sad fortune in the dust, break life asunder,
    Death is lifes miracle, scorns thanklesse wonder.

Wonder ô wonder of short breathed error,
835 A relique consecrated to defame,
A curb unto the wise, to fools a terror;
A terror of contempt, feare hate and shame,
A black oblivionizing of worths name:
    A razer out of memory, the merit
840   Of many noble peers and peerlesse spirit.

Who dy'd? not he whose mungrell baser thought
Was steeped in the puddle of servility,
Not he who daies of easie softnesse sought,
But threats of horror fitting his nobility,
845 To coronize high-soar'd gentility:
    Who di'd? a man? nay more a perfect saint
    Leaving the world in tears of sad complaint.

Life? ah no life but soone extinguisht tapers,
Tapers? no tapers, but a burnt out light,
850 Light? ah no light but exhalacions vapors,
Vapours? no vapoures but il-blinded sight,
Sight? ah no sight but hel's eternall night.
    [Ah] night no night but picture of an elfe,
    Ah elfe? no elfe but very death it selfe.

855 Then life is death, and death the farthest goale
Of transitory frailty to conclude
The freedom of the while-imprisond soule,
And stop the streames of heat by death subdu'd
To wan and chilly cold, fates hand is rude:
860   None favouring the limit of an howr,
    But doth all sort of states alike devour.

Devour thou them and surfet on the baite
Of thine insatiate rapine! exercise
The utmost of thy vengeaunce nor delay it!
Let meagre gluttony yet tyrannise,
To use extreames! thy power we despise:
    Kill whom thou darst, since *Devonshire* did depart,
    We scorn the malice of thine envious dart.

Sleep still in rest, honor thy bones enshrine,
(Victorious lord) sweet peace attend thy grave,
Mount thy best part with angels wings divine
About the throne of *Jove* in quires to crave
By madrigalls the joyes that thou wouldst have.
    So ever shall while dates of times remaine
    The heavens thy soule, the earth thy fame containe.

If to be learned in the Arts of skill
If to be bewtifi'de with choyce of nature,
If to be guiltlesse from the soyle of ill
(Save soyle of [slaunder]) if the perfect feature,
Consist in being heaven's [quaint] architecture
    Then ever shall while dates of times remayne,
    The heavens thy soule, the earth thy fame contayne.

If to be fear'd and lov'd be humane glory,
If to be dow'd with plenty of desert,
If to be chronicled in honours story:
If youth which grave discretion did convert
It selfe in commendation may insert:
    Then ever shall while dates of times remaine,
    The heavens thy soule, the earth thy fame containe.

If wisedom stand in checking rasher follie,
If virtue do depend on perfect zeale,
He in the one was wise, in th'other holy;
If to reguard the prosperous common weale,
Be shewes of commendation to reveale.
    Then ever shall while dates of times remaine,
    The heavens thy soule, the earth thy fame containe.

If to be virtuous, zealous, valiant, wise,
Learned, respective of his countries good,
Upright, in case of conscience precise,
900 Just, bounteous, pitifull, noble by blood,
Be to deserve the name of lively-hood.
    Then ever shall while dates of times remaine,
    The heavens thy soule, the earth thy fame contayne.

For thou wast all of these, too high for earth,
905 Therefore more fit for heaven where thou rainest,
The angells joy'd thy soules delightfull mirth,
And therefore fetcht thee hence, whereby thou gainest
The fruit of paradize where thou remainest:
    And ever shalt remaine from us bereaven,
910   Great as thou wast on earth, more great in heaven.

But ô give leave ere I forbeare my pen,
Thy worth in what I may t'exemplifie,
And set thee as a president to men,
The due of thy desert to amplifie,
915 And thy humanity to deifie:
    Of thy much merit to cast up the summe,
    Thus be thy epitaph, and here thy tombe.

His Tombe.

The Epitaph.

The course of time hath finisht now his breath,
Whom brunt of war could never force to death:
920 *Whose thirst of worth the world could not suffice,*
Within a bredth of earth contented lyes.

Betwixt the gods and men doubly devided,
His soule with them, his fame with us abided;
In this his life and death was countervaild,
925 *He justly liv'd belov'd, he dy'd bewaild.*

        And so his happy memorie,
        Shall last to all posterity.

His Tombe.

The Epitaph.

      Day weareth day, howre [consumeth] howr,
      Years years, and age doth age devour;
930 *The man who now beholds the sun,*
      Ere it decline his life is done.

      So by this great Lord doth appeare,
      Whose honoured bones ly buried here;
      Whose bones though they interred lye,
935 *His glorious name will never dye:*

                But live in praise,
                To after daies.

His Tombe.

The Epitaph.

Here lies he dead who living liv'd in Fame,
Consumd in body, fresh reviv'd in name;
His worthy deeds exceeded tearme of date,
Alike his praise will never stoope to fate.

For who is he that can suppose,
That stones, great Devonshire *could enclose;*
Whose noble acts renowned were,
Whiles as he lived every where:

England *rejoyced in his valours due,*
Which Ireland *felt, and feeling did it rue:*
But now by destiny heere sleeps he dead,
Whiles as his glory through the world is spred.

Urging the greate in emulation,
Of his true honours commendation.

His Tombe.

The Epitaph.

No one exceeds in all, yet amongst many,
Yea amongst all he could do more then any;
Though more then mortall virtue grac'd his mind,
He was unto a mortall end confin'd:

And forc'd to yeeld unto deaths force,
Who in his shaft hath no remorse:
Princes, beggars, great and small,
He spareth none, he killeth all,

So did he rob high Devonshire *of his breath,*
Whose worth in spight of death will out live death;
Advantage such his merit doth retaine,
He in his name will live renewd againe.

And so though death his life deprive,
His life in death will new revive.

His Tombe.

The Epitaph.

> *By*
> *cruell dint of*
> *death's respectlesse dart,*
> Greate Devonshires *soule*
> *did from his bodye parte:*
> *And left his carkasse in this earthly slime,*
> *Whiles his fames essence to the skies did clime:*
> *Roaving abroade, to fill the latter dayes*
> *With woonder of his JUST deserved prayse:*
> *So that eache AGE will in the time to come,*
> *Admire his worthinesse, and mourne his TOMBE:*
>
> *Which they shall ever count a shrine,*
> *Of some deceased saint divine.*

His Tombe.

The Epitaph.

Lo
here I
reste, who
living was adored,
With all the honour
Love could have implored:
What earthly pomp might beautify my name,
In pryde of glorie I enjoyde the same:
A Champion ever readye to defende her,
A Senatoure preste always to commend her:
Though with my harts delight my life [was] gract't,
Yet I in peace of death was [cropt] at last:

And now entombed here I lie,
A mirror in eternity.

His Tombe.

The Epitaph.

O what soere thou be that passest by,
Looke on this hearse and weepe thy eye-lids dry,
The monument of worth, the angells pleasure,
Which hordeth glories ritch invalued treasure:
The reliques of a saint, an earthly creature,
Clad in the perfect mould of angell feature:
Who lives even after life, now being dead,
Welcome to heaven in earth canonized.

        The shoutes of fame,
        Echoe his name.

His Tombe.

The Epitaph.

In blessed peace and soule-united rest,
Here sleeps the carkasse of a peer most blest;
1005 *Whose downfall all the plots of cursed fight*
Could not procure, or terrifie his might:
But evermore he tam'd the pride of folly,
And castigated drifts of slaves unholy,
Yet death at last with force of vigor grim,
1010 *When he had conquered many, conquered him.*

And here amongst the quiet numbers,
Of happy soules he sweetly slumbers.

His Tombe.

The Epitaph.

The boast of Brittaine *and the life of state,*
The pith of valour, noblenesse innate,
1015 *Foes scourge, friends hopes, sustainer of the poore,*
Whom most men did imbrace, all men adore.

Fautor of learning, quintessence of arts,
Honours true livelihood, monarch of harts,
The sacred ofspring of a virtuous womb,
1020 *Lyes here enshrined in this hallowed Tombe.*

From out whose Phoenix *dust ariseth,*
Renowne, *which earths whole globe inticeth.*

Loe heer nine tombes, on every tombe engrav'd,
Nine Epitaphs shewing that worthyes nine
For each peculiar [one] a Toomb hath crav'd;
That their deserts who while [they] liv'd did shine
Might now be monumented in their shrine,
    Yet all those nine no glory hence have gain'd
    For *Devonshire* in himselfe all nine contain'd.

The nine poore figures of a following substance
Did but present an after ages mirrour
Who should more fame then they deserv'd advance
And manifest the truth of that times error,
Including *Devonshiere* earth's admired terrour,
    For all the Poets who have sung of them
    Have but in mistery adored him.

O now droppe eye-balls into sinck of mudd!
Be harsh the tunes of my unfeathered muse!
Sorrow suck upp my griefes! consume the blud,
Of my youths mirth! let meager death infuse,
The soule of sadnesse to untimely newes!
    Dead is the hight of glory, dead is all
    The pride of earth which was angelicall.

Ah that the goddesse whome in heart I serve
(Though never mine) bright *Lycia* the cruell
The cruell-subtile would the name deserve
Of lesser wise! and not abuse the Jewell
Of witt, which adds unto my flame more fuell,
    Hir thoughts to elder merits are confin'd
    Not to the solace of my yonger mind.

Bee't so? yet on the theame of this Ile spend
The residue of plaintes and ever mourne
The losse of this greate lord, till travayles send
More comfort to my wretched hart forlorne,
Who since at home disgrac'd abroade is borne
    To sigh the remnant of my wearied breath
    In lamentation of his haplesse death,

Sheath up the sword of war, for *Mars* is dead
Seale up the smoothed lippes of Eloquence,
For flowing *Mercury* is buried,
Droope wisedome, *Numas* grave intelligence
Is vanisht, *Affrican's* stout eminence,
   In Devonshire lyes obscur'd, for he alone
   Exceeded all, they all dide in him one.

Charles the greate is dead who farre excelled
Charles whome former times did call the great
Charles who whilome whils on earth he dweled,
Adorn'd the exaltation of his seat
By the alarum of deaths grim retreate,
   Is mustered to the camp from whence he came
   Cherub's, and *Seraphims* of datelesse fame.

O that a man should ever be created
To eternize his glory heere on earth:
Yet have his pompe of glory soone abated,
Even at the present issue of his birth
And loose the Trophey of that instant mirth:
   Heere is the guerdon'd meede of victory
   No sooner to atchieve, assoone to dy.

Is death the rewarde of a glorious deede?
Is death the fee of valour? is desert
Repayd with death? shall honours gayne Proceed
By losse of life? ô then a cowards heart
Of earthly comfort hath the better part:
   Then better live in peace and live, then trye
   The brunt of conquest and reguardlesse dye.

Dye thoughtes of such disgrace, dye thirst of state,
Dye thoughts of empty ayr'd ambition
Dye thoughtes of soring [majestie] elate
Dye inclination to conscript condition
Dye pride of Empyre, sov'raignetyes commission,
   All that in soule of life may bee estem'd
   Oh dye, [fate] cannot be with bribes redeem'd.

>   Dye portly hunger of eternity
>   Dye hott desires of unbounded pleasure,
> 1095 Dye greedines of false prosperity,
>   Dye giddie solace of ill suted leisure,
>   Dye hopes of hoorded canker-eaten treasure:
>   Ambition, Empire, glory, hopes and joy
>   For ever dye, for death will all destroye.
>
> 1100 For death will all destroy as he hath donn,
>   In seising to his strong remorslesse gripe
>   All triumphs Noble *Devonshiere* ever wonn,
>   Plucking the blossomes of his youth unripe
>   And make them yeeld unto his thanklesse gripe:
> 1105   But, ah why should we task his dart uneven
>   Who took from earth what was more fit for heaven.
>
>   He was more fitte for heaven then to survive
>   Amongst the chaffe of this unseason'd age,
>   Where new fantastick joyes doe seek to thrive
> 1110 By following sensuall toyes of follyes rage,
>   Making the glosse of vice true vertues badge:
>   He saw that shame which misery begun it,
>   Seing he did it scorne and scorning shun it.
>
>   Hence sprung the venom of impoysoned hate,
> 1115 Poore malediction's sting, who did despise
>   Bright honor's stamp, which in his bosome sate,
>   For that he could not brooke to temporise
>   With humours masked in those times disguise:
>   But let dogs barke: his soules above theyr anger
> 1120   They cannot wound his worth with envies slander.
>
>   He sleepes secured and in blessed slumber's
>   Of peacefull rest he carelesse rests in peace,
>   Singing lowd antheames with the sacred numbers
>   Of happy saints, whose notes do never cease
> 1125 But evermore renewing fresh increase.
>   Whiles he doth sing and angels pleasure take,
>   We mourne his death and sorry for his sake.

Not for his sake but for our haplesse owne,
Who had so rich a prise and did not know it,
Jewell's being had for Jewel's are not know'n,
For men in happy fortune doe foreslow it,
The value when 'tis lost doth chiefly shew it,
 So wretched is our blindnesse, and so hatefull,
 As for the guifts we have we are ungratefull.

Even as a poring scholler who hath read
Some Cosmographick Booke, and finds the prayse
Of some delitious land deciphered
Cast's sundry plots how by what meanes and wayes,
He may pertake those pleasures, months and dayes,
 Being spent he goes and ravisht with the mayne
 Of such [delights], he nere returnes agayne.

So *Devonshiere* by the Bookes of inspiration
Contemplating the joyes of heavens content
In serious thoughts of meditation
Which he in perfect zeal had long time spent
Thirsting to be immortall hence he went,
 He thither comes and glorying [in that spheare]
 Unmindfull of this home, he triumphes there.

Long may he triumph over topping cloudes,
Of our all-desperate mouldes vexation,
Pittying the sorrow which our danger crowds
With joylesse taste of true joyes desolation,
Whiles he enjoyes his soules high delectation:
 Long may he live whom death now cannot move
 His fame below, his spirit wings above.

Above the reach of humane witts conceite
Above the censure of depraved spight
Above earths paradizes counterfeyt
Above imagination of delight,
Above all thoughts to think or pens to write:
 Ther doth he datelesse dayes of comfort spend,
 Renowned in his life, blest in his end.

Anagramma ex Camdeno.

CAROLUS BLUNTUS.

Bonus, ut sol clarus.

In life upright and therefore rightly *good*,
Whose glory shind on earth and thence a *Sunn*
By his renowne *as cleere* hee's understood,
Whose light did set when as his life was done:
   Bright as the sun, good ever to advance,
   The soule of merit spurning ignorance.

Good in the virtue of his powerfull arme,
Which broughte more peace to peace, chac't feares of harm,
And whiles he liv'd a wonder maz'd the light,
Two suns appeard at once, at once as bright:
   For when he dyde and left his fame behind,
   One *Sunn* remaynd, the truest *Sun* declin'd.

      Dignum laude virum,
      Musa vetat mori.

Title page (1613), The Bodleian Library, Malone. 297 (3). By permission.

Christes Bloodie Sweat
Authorship and Dedication

Because the epistle dedicatory of *Christes Bloodie Sweat* was signed only "I. F.," the poem was first attributed to Joseph Fletcher. Alexander B. Grosart included it in his edition of the poems of Fletcher (1869; see below, 151–52), and it was presumably excluded from Gifford and Dyce for the same reason. Later it was listed in the original STC (1926) and in countless library catalogues as Fletcher's. The Revised STC continues to list 11076 under Fletcher but acknowledges that "the attribution ... is dubious" and the poem is "more likely by John Ford" (1:490). More recent scholars, however, have indeed established *Christes Bloodie Sweat* as Ford's. In 1934 Joan Sargeaunt drew attention to Joseph Hunter's mid-nineteenth-century attribution of the poem to Ford and pointed to stylistic and thematic parallels between *Christes Bloodie Sweat* and other of Ford's works, including *'Tis Pity She's a Whore* and *Fames Memoriall*.[1] In 1971 Gilles D. Monsarrat pointed to further parallels, in particular between *Christes Bloodie Sweat* and *The Golden Mean*, both of which appeared in 1613 and therefore especially invite comparison.[2] Monsarrat sums up the case:

> If we remember that the epistle dedicatory of *Christes Bloodie Sweat* is signed "I. F.," that there is no other writer to whom evidence points for authorship, that the poem affords many parallel passages with Ford's poems, prose pamphlets, and plays, and that the evidence presented in this note supplements Miss Sargeaunt's arguments, it seems that there is very small reason to doubt that Ford wrote *Christes Bloodie Sweat* himself. (25)

The poem's major parallels with Ford's other works are cited in the Commentary.[3]

---

[1] "Writings Ascribed to John Ford by Joseph Hunter in *Chorus Vatum*," *Review of English Studies* 10 (1934): 165–76.

[2] "John Ford's Authorship of *Christes Bloodie Sweat*," *English Language Notes* 9.1 (September 1971): 20–25.

[3] On the relation of CBS to Ford's other works, see Sargeaunt, 8–11, especially on how CBS undermines the view that Ford is "an apostle of free love" (10). See also the Introduction to GM, below, and Monsarrat, "The Unity of John Ford: *'Tis Pity She's a Whore* and *Christ's Bloody Sweat*," *Studies in Philology* 77.3 (1980): 247–70.

Ford dedicated *Christes Bloodie Sweat* to William Herbert, third earl of Pembroke (1580-1630), student of Samuel Daniel, nephew of Sir Philip Sidney, friend of John Donne, kinsman to George Herbert, and such a patron of letters that John Aubrey called him "the greatest Mecænas to learned men of any peer of his time or since ... very generous and open handed."[4] It is not known whether Ford's dedicating his poem to Pembroke in fact led to Ford's receiving any patronage. But the dedication might well have impressed its subject as having been written with care and conviction. Pembroke is addressed as "One of his Majesties most Honorable privie Counsaile," which he in fact became in September 1611, less than two years before the publication of *Christes Bloodie Sweat* (DNB). And in order to praise Pembroke's virtue and nobility, Ford risks damning the greater part of the peerage of his day, remarking that "Vertues" and "Noblenesse" "in this age, doe so seldome meete in one, as most usually to bee Great, and to bee Good, is required a double person." Such strong language may explain why Ford signed the dedication with no more than his initials.

The high moral tone of the dedication carries over into Ford's preface to the reader, where he introduces a theme he will return to in the poem itself (31-42) and that his reader will find recurring in poets such as George Herbert, namely that of poetry's being freed from serving the lustful and the false to serving spiritual truth. Herbert writes, "Who sayes that fictions onely and false hair / Become a verse? Is there in truth no beautie?"[5] Ford puts forward *Christes Bloodie Sweat* as his own proof that verse *"may deliver good matter,"* although he apologizes for its not always achieving a *"fit harmonie of words."* He does, nevertheless, express the desire *"that many should take comfort"* in his efforts; and in his last sentence he requests *"that faults in Printing may be charitably corrected"* and *"that the sence of the matter may be wisely ... construed."* Ford's modern editor and reader can take comfort in knowing that Ford himself has thus sanctioned both of their respective tasks.

---

[4] *Aubrey's Natural History of Wiltshire* (1847; rpt. Newton Abbot, Devon, 1969), 77.
[5] "Jordan (1)," *The Works of George Herbert*, ed. F. E. Hutchinson (Oxford, 1953), 56. See also Martz on Southwell, 283-84.

Title, Style, Method, Theology

The title *Christes Bloodie Sweat: or The Sonne of God in His Agonie* echoes the Litany from *The Book of Common Prayer*:

> By thine agony and bloody sweat, by thy cross and passion, by thy precious death and burial, by thy glorious resurrection and ascension, and by the coming of the Holy Ghost.
> Good Lord deliver us.[6]

The language and subject of this part of the Litany as well as of Ford's title derive from the account of Christ's Passion, just prior to his betrayal, in Luke 22:44: "But being in an agonie, he prayed more earnestly: and his sweate was like droppes of blood, trickling downe to the grounde" (GB). Late in the sixteenth century, the recusant poet Robert Southwell (1561?-1595), wrote a poem also entitled "Christs bloody sweat."[7] In Ford's time the twenty-four lines of this poem existed only in manuscript, so it is unlikely that Ford borrowed his title or subject from Southwell. Nevertheless, the existence of the earlier poem, together with other instances of Roman Catholic meditations upon Christ's agony,[8] demonstrates that the title and the subject of *Christes Bloodie Sweat* were the common property of all Christians, regardless of ecclesiastical loyalties.

Another poem that invites comparison with *Christes Bloodie Sweat* is

---

[6] *Common Prayer*, 69.

[7] *The Poems of Robert Southwell, S. J.*, ed. James H. McDonald and Nancy Pollard Brown (Oxford, 1967), 18-19; and see Commentary note to 277-82.

[8] See, for example, *the Rosary of our Savyour Jesu Gyveng thankes and prayse to his holy name by maner of meditacion and prayer* [1520?] (STC 14571), chap. iv, which praises Christ thus for his sufferings in Gethsemane:

> For thy blessed prayer in the gardeyn / at the mount of Olovet / whiche thre tymes thou dyd offre unto thy eternall father in hevyn / with great payne and agony: wherin it dyd appere / that thou was very man / sayeng by premedytacion in thy soule / all the great and unportable paynes / whiche it was thy blessed wyll to suffre for the raunsome of mankynde. And this blessed lorde / tastyng of all these paynes afore by consyderacion / thy humanyte was cast in suche feare / drede / and agony / that thy precious swette / with thy most precious blode / for payne dyd issue out of thy body / tricclying downe of thy swete body / and in great droppes fallyng on the grounde in great plentie.

The Countesse of Penbrook's Passion, composed by Nicholas Breton some time during the last decade of the sixteenth century[9] and dedicated, as the title indicates, to Mary Sidney Herbert, to whose son, as just mentioned, Ford dedicated *Christes Bloodie Sweat*. Like Ford's poem, *The Countesse of Penbrook's Passion* is a meditation on the sufferings of Christ and an attempt to make them personally present and efficacious. Though only about a third the length of Ford's poem, Breton's poem is written in the same stanza.

This "Venus and Adonis" stanza (so named after Shakespeare's poem)[10] consists of six iambic pentameter lines rhyming *ababcc*. *Christes Bloodie Sweat* has 318 such stanzas, for a total of 1,908 lines. The stanza, like rhyme royal, from which it differs only by omitting a third *b*-rhymed line, is well suited to a long narrative or semi-narrative poem in that it creates a "focus" on units larger than the couplet or the quatrain even while containing these units. At the same time the stanzas create discrete parcels of syntax, meaning, and thought that give the reader a sense of moving through the poem itself step by step. The couplet, as it so often does in a sonnet or at the end of a scene in a play, sums up or comments on the lines that precede it.

Ford seeks to balance this sense of the discreteness of each stanza by means of the frequent use of anadiplosis linking the last line of one stanza to the first line of the next (for example, at 12-13, 18-19, 78-79, 120-21, 192-93, 264-65, and so on). At other times Ford uses iteration in the first or last lines of consecutive stanzas to create a strong sense of continuity (for example, "Here saw he ...": 295, 307, 313, 325, 337, 343, 361, 379, 391, 397; "The only wordes he used": 684, 690, 696, 702; and so on). And sometimes he simply repeats the entire last line of a stanza, making it the first line of the next one (for example, 1518-19, 1524-25, 1530-31, 1536-37, and 1542-43).

Critical response to *Christes Bloodie Sweat* has been limited in both

---

[9] *The Works in Verse and Prose of Nicholas Breton*, ed. Alexander B. Grosart, 2 vols., (1879; rpt. New York, 1966). In his headnote to *The Countesse of Penbrook's Passion* in vol. 1 Grosart debunks the notion that the countess herself wrote the poem. (See also *DNB*, "Herbert, Mary.") The poem had, in 1862, been published with the attribution to the countess and with the non-authorial title "A Poem on our Saviour's Passion." The erroneous title and attribution are nevertheless repeated by Davril (86n) when he cites the poem as an earlier example of the passion genre that Ford would (according to Davril) undoubtedly have known. The errors are simply repeated again by Anderson, 24.

[10] See Paul Fussell, *Poetic Meter and Poetic Form*, rev. ed. (New York, 1979), 142.

quantity and enthusiasm, although stylistic variations such as those just mentioned, together with the poem's use of dialogue, enjambment, and metrical variation, lead H. J. Oliver to compare it favorably with *Fames Memoriall*: "In short, you could say of *Christes Bloodie Sweat*, as you could not say of *Fames Memoriall*, that the author is beginning to be interesting as a poet" (14). Similarly restrained approbation is expressed by Derek Roper, who says the poem passes "from a satirical survey of society to a rather confused but sometimes powerful presentation of Christian (some would say Calvinist) doctrine."[11] Joan Sargeaunt, by contrast, simply calls it "a religious poem ... of no very great poetic merit" (9).

Although *Christes Bloodie Sweat* does have its weaknesses, its poetic merits can be seen more clearly if we compare it briefly with Breton's *The Countesse of Penbrook's Passion*, mentioned above. Granted that a sustained religious meditation on physical sufferings is not attractive to most modern tastes, religious or nonreligious, how well do the two poets, Ford and Breton, perform their poetic duties? Compare the opening stanzas of the two poems:

Breton:

>   Where shall I finde that melancholy muse
>   That never hard of any thinge but mone?
>   And reade the passiones that her pen doth use,
>   When she and sorrow sadlye sitt alone;
>   To tell the world more then the world can tell?
>   What fits, inded most fitlye figure hell.

Ford:

>   Downe from the throane of everlasting grace,
>   Where Host's of *Angells* guard eternall soules
>   The great *Vice-gerent* of his Fathers place,
>   Gods sonne discendes, from far above the *Poles*:
>   And gently yet againe attempt's to winne,
>   The Monarchy of hearts usurp't by sinne.

From Breton's stanza one can scarcely tell what his poem is going to be about. The rhetorical question is abstract in its diction, merely conventional

---

[11] Roper, xxi–xxii. See also Stavig, 24.

in its tone, and stylistically self-conscious in its word-play and alliteration. By contrast, Ford's language, beginning with the opening trochee, is emphatic and direct; the concrete "throane," "sonne," and "hearts" forcefully counterpoint the more abstract rhyming words "grace," "soules," "winne," "sinne," which thematically both frame the stanza and introduce the subject of the entire poem, as does also the language of monarchy and usurpation at the macrocosmic and microcosmic levels.

Early in both poems we find stanzas exemplifying the "wasted youth" topos.

Breton:

> My infant's yeares myspente in childishe toyes,
> My riper age in rules of litle reasone;
> My better yeares in all mistaken joyes,
> My present time,—Oh most unhapie seasone!—
>   In fruiteles labours and in ruthles love:
>   Oh what a horror hath my harte to prove.
>
> I sighe to se my infancie myspent,
> I morne to finde my youthfull life misled;
> I weepe to feele my further discontent,
> I dye to trye how love is livinge dead;
>   I sighe, I morne, I weepe, I livinge dye,
>   And yett must live to shew more miserye.
>
>   (stanzas 11-12)

Ford:

> Thou (quoth it [God's voice]) that hast spent thy best of dayes,
> In [thriftlesse] rimes (sweete baytes to poyson Youth)
> Led with the wanton hopes of laude and praise,
> Vaine shadowes of delight, seales of untruth,
>   Now I impose new taskes uppon thy Pen,
>   To shew my sorrowes to the eyes of Men.
>
>   (lines 31-36)

In Breton's stanzas, even while purportedly addressing himself to the lofty task of displaying Christ's passion, the poet is conspicuous for his self-absorption. Ford, however, by using dialogue, avoids the danger of self-indulgence that lurks in confession. That he has misspent his youth is here not his own confession, but a charge uttered by the voice of God himself. Even the conventional "Pen" is *Ford's* pen, one that must move under the weight of directly apprehended obligation—unlike the "pen" of Breton's opening stanza, which belongs to a lugubrious muse whose whereabouts and voice the poet has not yet been able to discern.

Both poems, finally, figure Christ as the Pelican.

Breton:

> Am I not one of that unhapie broode,
> The pellican doth figure in her neste?
> When I muste live but by his only bloode:
> In whose sweet love, my life doth only rest.
> > O wretched bird, but I more wretched creature
> > To figure such a birde in such a nature.
>
> (stanza 54)

Ford:

> This was that Pellican indeed, retyr'd
> Into the desert of a troubled breast,
> Who for to pay the ransome long desir'd,
> Consum'd himselfe to give his people rest:
> > A Pellican indeed, that with her bloud
> > Pulls out her heart, to give her Chickens food.
>
> (lines 271–76; see also Commentary)

Again Breton obscures the image he presents amid mists of self-indulgence. If it is the redemptive Passion of Christ, the suffering of the pelican, that is being expounded, why "unhapie broode" and "I more wretched creature"? Furthermore, the figure of the pelican in Breton is not so much presented as merely referred to *qua* figure. Ford, by contrast, baldly declares the identification—"This was that Pellican"—and carries on to fuse, rather than merely to connect, the image with the thing imaged. In his stanza the particular is made to comment economically and without indulgence upon the general, rather than the other way around. And this melding of abstract and concrete is effected not only by diction but also by syntax, as in the parallelism of the biblical (and male) "to give his people rest" with the homely (and female) "to give her Chickens food." Sargeaunt may be right that the poetic merits of *Christes Bloodie Sweat* are not "very great." Yet it does have merits that a modern lack of enthusiasm for the passion genre should not cause us to overlook.

The most important structural principle of Ford's poem is what Louis L. Martz has called the "Method of Meditation" (25). Martz's "central definition" of this method is drawn from a mainly Roman Catholic, Counter-Reformation tradition of piety summed up in the writings of François de Sales, who declares that

> when we thinke of heavenly things, not to learne but to love them, that is called to meditate: and the exercise thereof Meditation: in which our mynd, not as a flie, by a simple musing nor yet as a locust, to eat and be filled, but as a sacred Bee flies amongst the flowres of holy mysteries, to extract from them the honie of Divine Love.... So that meditation is an attentive thought iterated, or voluntarily intertained in the mynd, to excitate the will to holy affections and resolutions.[12]

No one would accuse Ford in his poem of almost two thousand lines of not iterating an attentive thought or of losing any opportunity to excite his and his reader's wills to holy affections and resolutions.

But a further aspect of meditation needs emphasis. Admittedly, the very idea of a long poem on Christ's bloody sweat may strike the modern reader as peculiar. We somehow do not feel it quite polite to spend hours concentrating our thoughts on "blood and guts," at least not as a religious exercise. Yet it is precisely this sort of concreteness and physicality that is of the essence in the tradition of meditation in which Ford participates. In his *Spiritual Exercises* (1548) Ignatius Loyola mandates as a prelude to meditation the imagining of a setting with physical, visible details that can facilitate higher meditations on that truth which itself is invisible:

> St. Ignatius directs that one must also use the image-forming faculty to provide a concrete and vivid setting for a meditation on invisible things; for example, in meditation upon sins, he says, "the composition will be to see with the eyes of the imagination and to consider that my soul is imprisoned in this corruptible body, and my whole self in this vale of misery, as it were in exile among brute beasts."[13]

Or as Luis de la Puente puts it in his *Meditations*:

---

[12] *A Treatise of the Love of God* (Douay, 1630), 324–25, quoted in Martz, 15.
[13] Martz, 28, quoting from *The Text of the Spiritual Exercises of Saint Ignatius*, 4th ed. (Westminister, MD, 1943), 20–21.

If I am to thinke upon hell, I will imagine some place like an obscure, straight, horrible dungeon full of fier, and the soules therin burning in the middest of those flames. And if I am to meditate [on] the birth of Christ, I will forme the figure of some open place without shelter, and a childe wrapped in swaddling cloutes, layed in a manger: and so in the rest.[14]

Thus the "concrete" imagining of Christ's bloody sweat is a prelude to a more abstract consideration of Christ's sufferings generally and of their meaning.

Yet another characteristic of the sort of meditation Martz describes is "the preparatory prayer," "a simple, short request for grace in the proper performance of the exercise"(27); in this regard Ford presents us with something of a deviation from the meditative norm. For Ford does not pray for God's help in pursuing his chosen course of meditation; rather, the meditations seem to choose him, and it is God's voice, not his, that is first to speak.[15] Using the present tense, the first four stanzas of *Christes Bloodie Sweat* establish the general scene of Christ's passion; then stanza five (though its syntax is ambiguous) introduces the voice of God, which initiates—indeed *has initiated*—the meditations and their purpose (31-96). The poet's role is to respond, to obey (97), not himself to initiate the meditation. His role vis-à-vis God is passive; his spirit, "ravish't" (25); the point here is clearly theological as well as literary. As does Ignatius, Ford requires divine grace in order to be able to perform his meditation properly. But, perhaps in keeping with his basic Protestantism, that grace for Ford must be *prevenient*—it must be the grace that precedes every human effort or merit, the grace that comes to him who is so incapacitated by sin that he cannot in his own strength even request grace.[16]

---

[14] *Meditations upon the Mysteries of our Holie Faith* [trans. John Heigham], 2 vols. (St. Omer, 1619), 1:23.

[15] Although Martz emphasizes the *active* character of meditation in "The Action of the Self: Devotional Poetry in the Seventeenth Century" (in *Metaphysical Poetry*, ed. Malcolm Bradbury and David Palmer, Stratford-Upon-Avon Studies 11 [New York, 1970], 101-21), Ford's "passivity" in *CBS* supports Anthony Low's suggestion that in our definition of devotional poetry "there is no good reason to exclude . . . forms that are passive rather than active"; see *Love's Architecture: Devotional Modes in Seventeenth-Century English Poetry* (New York, 1978), 7.

[16] See, for example, *The Writings of James Arminius*, trans. James Nichols and W. R. Bagnall, (1853; rpt. Grand Rapids, 1956) 2:472: "That I may not be said, like Pelagius, to practice delusion with regard to the word 'grace,' I mean by it that which is the grace of

Ford does ultimately offer up a prayer, but it follows, not precedes, his long course of meditation. As the meditation of the first four stanzas leads the poet before the "mercie-seat" (26-27), so the scenes presented by the entire sweep of the poem will, with the moving of God's Spirit, be matter for further meditation: Ford beseeches

> that thy Spirit may be strong,
> To move my heart, and gently to commit
> To meditations, all the lines I writ.
>
> (1816-18)

Repentance follows, not precedes, such meditations:

> let thy wounds deface
> The wounds of mine infection, now *begin*
> Throughly to wash me from mine odious sin.
>
> (1822-24; italics added)

In this way the process of meditation becomes the process of the speaker's own soul, its movement towards repentance. And finally—beyond, yet integral with that individual movement—is the poem's public, evangelical purpose, which seeks the reader's participation in the process of the poem. Within the poem, indeed, that purpose is mandated by Christ himself:

> May bee, some wandring eye that shall survey
> This wonder of my *Sweat*, in those thy numbers,
> Will take a truce with time, and shake away
> From off his Soule, the lusts wherein it slumbers:
> Then hast thou hid a multitude of sin,
> If all thy paines, one Soule from ruine win.
>
> (1873-78)

The method of meditation as practiced in Ford's long poem, then, involves a repeated fixing of the eye upon the sufferings of Christ, usually followed by a more discursive and abstract meditation upon the scene

---

Christ and which belongs to regeneration. I affirm, therefore, that this grace is simply and absolutely necessary for the illumination of the mind, the due ordering of the affections, and the inclination of the will to that which is good.... This grace [*praevenit*] goes before, accompanies, and follows; it excites, assists, operates that we will, and co-operates lest we will in vain."

depicted. Ford's description of those sufferings begins with Christ's own first-person account (31-96), continues with the poet's third-person narrative of the scene in Gethsemane, and ends with the thematic core of the poem, the "sweate of blood" (216). The poet then states directly that the result of the scene he has described—of one's gazing on "those faire signes" —should be "An holy meditation" (219-20). Ford keeps coming back to the concrete details of his subject before venturing once more into homily, repeatedly reestablishing a single focus that both gives the poem a coherent structure and creates its main effect. At its best, *Christes Bloodie Sweat* displays (to use Martz's words again) a "habit of feeling theological issues as part of a concrete, dramatic scene" (29-30). As Ford himself puts it:

> Tis not enough to read the Bible over,
> Here to fold downe a leafe, and there to quote it,
> Now to behold the Lord in blood, then hover
> And range: but freely in thy heart to note it:
>   For where the *Word* doth tel us *Christ* did bleed,
>   And sweat, there must our thoghts both drink and feed.
>   (1147-52)

Ford's language here of drinking and feeding, which clearly refers to the elements of Holy Communion and to the Church's symbolic participation in the body and blood of Christ, leads us on to consider briefly the hermeneutics and theology that Ford employs in *Christes Bloodie Sweat*. But to describe Ford's hermeneutical method is simply to re-describe his meditative method from a slightly different angle. Focusing on the concrete details of Christ's suffering involves Ford in an account of the *literal* meaning of Scripture; his more abstract meditations upon those concrete details lead him into the realm of *spiritual* interpretation of the literal text. The famous "fourfold" method that grew out of this basic distinction between literal and spiritual readings is described by Thomas Aquinas:

> That first signification whereby words signify things belongs to the first sense, the historical or literal. That signification whereby things signified by words have themselves also a signification is called the spiritual sense, which is based on the literal, and presupposes it. Now this spiritual sense has a threefold division.... So far as the things of the Old Law signify the things of the New Law, there is the allegorical sense; so far as the things done in Christ, or so far as the things which signify Christ, are types of what we ought to do, there is the

moral sense. But so far as they signify what relates to eternal glory, there is the anagogical sense.[17]

Although Protestant teaching declared that the scriptural text had but one meaning, that single meaning was nevertheless seen as comprehending both the literal and the spiritual. As Martin Luther put it:

> The Holy Spirit is the plainest writer and speaker in heaven and earth, and therefore his words cannot have more than one, and that the very simplest, sense, which we call the literal, ordinary, natural, sense. That the things indicated by the simple sense of his simple words should signify something further and different, and therefore one thing should always signify another, is more a question of words or of language. For the same is true of all other things outside the Scriptures, since all of God's works and creatures are living signs and words of God, as St. Augustine and all the teachers declare.[18]

Christes Bloodie Sweat is thus a single extended, detailed, spiritual (or allegorical) interpretation of the literal substance of Christ's agony. At its most self-conscious, moreover, its method is to treat Christ's bloody sweat as both *signifier* and *signified*. For example, Ford's metaphor in 541–46 presupposes a typological backdrop in which events in the Old Testament prefigure events in the New, in which, thus, Christ's sweat is *signified*:

> *Christs bloody* sweate, was that distilling river,
> The comfortable *Jordan*, whose faire streames
> Did cleanse the *Syrian Naaman*, and deliver
> His bodie from the leprosies extreames:
>
> (541–44)

But the spiritual interpretation immediately follows:

> We all are *Naamans* leprous, but more foule,
> Till in his bloody sweate he purge our soule.
>
> (545–46)

---

[17] *Summa theologiæ*, Part 1, Q. i, Art. 10; (London: Burns, Oates, & Washbourne [n.d.]).

[18] Luther, *Answer to Goat Esmer*, *Works of Martin Luther* (Philadelphia, 1930), 3:350. On Luther's and other Reformers' views regarding allegory, typology, and the single sense of Scripture, see especially Barbara Kiefer Lewalski, *Protestant Poetics and the Seventeenth-Century Religious Lyric* (Princeton, 1979), 110–23. See also Ira Clark, *Christ Revealed: The History of the Neotypological Lyric in the English Renaissance* (Gainesville, 1982), 10–16.

And so again the literal—the actual sweat of Christ—is also a *signifier* of the process that the sinner must undergo if he or she is to acquire spiritual health.[19]

In this way Ford clearly seeks to build his meditation upon the established foundations of the typological method. And thus the Jordan, the Red Sea (1709), and various other natural sources of liquid, together with the blood of Christ or the waters of baptism which they signify, provide a series of liquid symbols and metaphors that Ford can develop further in connection with his central object, the agony of Christ, meditation on which eventuates in yet a further liquid, the sinner's tears of repentance (1141-46).

The blood and sacrifice of Christ were necessary because man is a sinner and stands in violation of God's holy law, and Ford's presentation of the doctrine of the substitutionary atonement is quite orthodox: Christ

> must feele, the curse and scourging rod,
> Of our and his (through us) offended God.
>
> No sacrifice or incense could appease,
> Or reconcile the Majestie above:
> No Customary *Rites*, no *Tribute* please,
> No law redeeme the breach of his deare love:
>   His most just justice, would no mercy give,
>   But God as man must die, that men may live.
>
> (101-8)

As Milton, later in the century, has God say of man:

> Die he or justice must; unless for him
> Some other able, and as willing, pay
> The rigid satisfaction, death for death.
>
> (*Paradise Lost* 3.210-12)

All human beings are sinners; sin brings death; but Christ, himself sinless, offers to die to release humankind from their condemnation. And in so doing he does not cancel justice, but satisfies it. As Ford says,

---

[19] On typology's being modified to include, as things signified, not only Christ but also events in the lives of his followers, see Lewalski, *Protestant Poetics*, 128-40.

> Not that his death could abrogate the will
> Of his great Father, for he aym'd not to it;
> But that, in death, he wholly might fulfill
> The eternall Justice, as hee came to doe it:
>   Who as hee, death from men for sin required,
>   Had in his Sons death, more than death desired.
>   (1681–86)

In another respect, however, Ford's doctrine of the atonement presents a problem for interpretation. At times, Ford sounds as if he holds to the Calvinist view of a strict, "double" predestination, namely, that both the elect and the reprobate are predestined by the will of God to their respective destinies. As Calvin puts it, "whom God passeth over, he rejecteth: and for none other cause, but for that he will exclude them from the inheritance which he doth predestinate to his children."[20] Similarly, Ford allegorizes the children of Israel and the "Hoast of *Egypt*" as types respectively of the elect and the reprobate. God's light serves to blind the eyes of the latter and procure for them "certaine death" (1716); for "all such as are despis'd / Are darkned" (1720–21). God thus is seen as actively despising the reprobate. Furthermore, in at least one place Ford endorses the doctrine of "limited atonement": "neither did the *Death* or *Bloodie sweat* / Of *Christ*, extend to soules ordain'd to Hell" (1687–88).[21] And yet elsewhere, Ford asserts that Christ "dy'd ... That *every one* might be redeem'd from hell" (1800; italics added).

Manifestly, Ford is a poet, not a theologian, and *Christes Bloodie Sweat* neither is nor pretends to be a work of systematic theology. Its emphasis is devotional and meditative; and if one reads it, one will do so in order not to gain any fresh theological insights, but to catch an otherwise unobtainable glimpse of a devotional and meditative side to Ford's poetry.

---

[20] *The Institution of Christian Religion*, trans. Thomas Norton (1561; London, 1599; STC 4423), 3.23.1.

[21] Although this doctrine is one of the so-called "five points" of Calvinism asserted at the Synod of Dort in 1618–19, recent scholarship suggests that it was not Calvin but rather some of his followers, such as Theodore Beza, who were responsible for the doctrine. See Brian G. Armstrong, *Calvinism and the Amyraut Heresy* (Madison, 1969), 38–42; and R. T. Kendall, *Calvin and English Calvinism to 1649* (Oxford, 1979), 145–46, 149. I discuss these and related issues in *Milton's Good God: A Study in Literary Theodicy* (Cambridge and New York, 1982), chap. 3.

The Text

Christes Bloodie Sweat was published in 1613, being entered in the Stationers' Register to Ralph Blower on 22 May of that year, as follows:

Raffe Blore   Entred for his copie under the handes of master Mason. and master Warden Harison a booke Called. *CHRISTes bloody sweatt* . vj^d

(Arber, 3:524)

There was an apparent re-issue in 1616 with a cancel title page identical to the title-page of 1613 (reproduced on 133) except for the imprint, which reads:

LONDON | Printed by R. B. and are to be | sold by *Henry Bell*, at his shop | *without Bishopsgate.* | 1616.

The titles are numbered in the STC 11076 and 11077 respectively.

In spite of the slightly differing title pages, however, all extant copies of the text belong to the same impression, and I shall here treat them as variant states of a single edition (13).

Collation: 4°: A-I^4 [$3 signed (-A1, A2)], 36 leaves, pp. [8] 1-64 (misprinting 32 as "23", 58 as "59", 59 as "58")

Contents: a1^{r-v} blank, A2^r title, A2^v blank, A3^{r-v} dedicatory epistle, A4^r to the reader, A4^v blank, B1^r-I4^v text

RT [within rules]: A3^v THE EPISTLE [misprinted EFISTLE] DEDICATORIE B1^v-I4^v *Christes Bloudy Sweate.* [printed as *Christes Bloudy sweate.* on B2^r, C1^r, C2^r, D3^r, D4^r, E3^r, E4^r, F1^r, F2^r, G1^r, G2^r, H1^r, H2^r, I1^r, I2^r]

Catchwords: A-B, [none] B-C, Hee C-D, All D-E, Which E-F, A F-G, Weary G-H, Can H-I, Who

There are seven known copies of this edition (the Sydney University copy listed in the rev. STC is only on microfilm):

[A]   British Library, London (11623.bb.14). The printed title page, A2, is missing, and in its place is a pen-and-ink facsimile, dated 1613, that adds "By I. F." after the title.

[B]   British Library, London (C.57.b.39). Lacks A1. Cancel title page dated 1616.

[C]   Bodleian Library, Oxford (Mal.297(3)). Lacks A1. The original title page, A2^r, dated 1613, is intact.

[D] The Wodehouse Library, Dulwich College, London. The title page (1613) is trimmed and attached to a leaf bound but not conjugate with the other sheets. Lacks A1 and, more seriously, I4.
[E] Folger Shakespeare Library, Washington, D.C. (Catalogued by STC number, 11076). 1613 title page. Lacks A1.
[F] University of Illinois Library, Urbana (X821/F6351c). Lacks all of A1-4.
[G] University of Illinois Library, Urbana (X821/F6351c/1616). Cancel title page dated 1616. Lacks A1 and A3.

The state of the variant sheets is as follows. The first reading given is that of the corrected state and has been silently adopted.

SHEET B OUTER FORME   Corrected: *ABCDEF*
                                                 Uncorrected: G

sig.	3^r	(129)	Teares] Cares

SHEET B INNER FORME   Corrected: *ABDEFG*
                                                 Uncorrected: C

sig.	1^v	(39)	Musicke,]~ ₳
		(44)	woes,] ~ ₳
	3^v	(143)	Untrim'd] Untrim₳d

SHEET C OUTER FORME   Corrected: *BCG*
                                                 Uncorrected: *ADEF*

sig.	1^r	(231)	objur'd] obai'd corrected in *D* by means of a pasted-on slip.)
		(235)	hyr'd] heard
sig.	2^v	(332)	intrusted] intrused
	3^r	(350)	trim'd] train'd
		(363)	cunning] turning
		(369 marg)	5.26.] 15.26
	4^v	(446 marg)	2.Tim.] 1.Tim.
		(456 marg)	1.Cor.] 2.Cor.

SHEET C INNER FORME   Corrected: *D* (first stage),
                                                                A (second stage),
                                                                 B and *E* (third stage),
                                                                 C (fourth stage),
                                                                 G (fifth stage)

			Uncorrected: F
sig.	1ᵛ	(259)	the] th DF
		(263 marg)	1.John.] .1John. ABCDEF
		(277)	Phoenix] Phaenix ADF
		(278)	spring] psring F
		(281)	Phoenix] Phaenix ADF
		(285)	of] om F
	4ʳ	(419)	fewer] feuer F
		(428 marg)	24.] 74. ABDEF

SHEET E INNER FORME

Corrected: ABDG
Uncorrected: CEF

sig.	2ʳ	(796)	with] wirh
	3ᵛ	(876)	a] as
		(883)	else] om
	4ʳ	(892)	inforced] iuforced

SHEET F OUTER FORME

Corrected: ABCDFG
Uncorrected: E

sig.	1ʳ	(949)	Sonne] Son
		(959)	bloody] om
		(968)	diet] diets
		(976)	*art*] art
	3ʳ	(1095)	still] om

SHEET G OUTER FORME

Corrected: ACEFG
Uncorrected: BD

sig.	1ʳ	(1218)	not] nor

SHEET H INNER FORME

Corrected: AD
Uncorrected: BCEFG

sig.	1ᵛ	(1465)	immur'd] inur'd

SHEET I INNER FORME

Corrected: ACEFG
Uncorrected: B (D lacks leaf I4)

sig.	4ʳ	(1877 marg)	Jam.5.20.] om

The only other published edition of *Christes Bloodie Sweat* appeared in 1869 in the Fuller Worthies' Library *Poems of Joseph Fletcher*, edited by

Alexander B. Grosart, whose title page indicates that it was "PRINTED FOR PRIVATE CIRCULATION"—"106 *copies only.*" Grosart appears not to have collated copies of *13* and probably based his edition on a single copy. He reproduces the uncorrected substantive readings from both outer C (231, "obai'd" for "objur'd," etc.) and inner H (1465, "inur'd" for "immur'd"), evidence that strongly suggests that his copy-text was other than A, B, C, D, or G. Grosart also could not have used F alone, for it lacks the dedicatory epistle and preface to the reader, which Grosart includes. He must therefore have based his edition on E or else on some other, now-unknown copy. In any case, although Grosart suggests many sensible emendations, he also introduces a large number of new errors, and I have not, in the textual apparatus that follows, noted Grosart's readings unless they seem to represent needed substantive emendation.

F. M. Burelbach's 1965 Harvard dissertation includes a transcript of *Christes Bloodie Sweat* based on A, with variants from B, C, D, and E noted at the foot of the page. Because it *is* a transcript and not actually an edition, it is not cited in the textual apparatus. However, a second unpublished thesis, M. I. Scott's "A Critical Edition of *Christes Bloodie Sweat*" (University of Birmingham, 1967), is noted when its readings reflect substantive emendation, though not when it simply adopts those of Grosart. When citing Grosart or Scott in the apparatus I have silently regularized the orthography of their emendations in conformity with the conventions of the present edition.

The printed text of *Christes Bloodie Sweat* (*13*) poses a number of problems for the editor, many of them soluble only by means of speculation. Some problems relate simply to what a passage means—and to whether emendation would clarify meaning or merely paper over an obscurity inherent in Ford's poetry (see for example 603-6). Others are raised by metrical irregularity (such as in 1374, 1491, 1776). In such cases I have avoided purely speculative emendation and allowed obscurity or irregularity to stand, or else have indicated my conjecture by means of square brackets in the text. Some other problems are attributable simply to compositorial circumstances, such as the crowding of a line leading to shortened spellings or omitted punctuation (for example, 1116). Still others seem to be caused by what we can assume was the reading of copy from manuscript, and in such cases we can often infer emendations *per ductum litterarum.*

These and other conservative emendations, as well as correction of obvious misprints in *13*, have been bracketed in the text, listed among the Textual Notes, and (normally) justified in the Commentary. Especially in matters of punctuation, changes have been avoided unless there seemed compelling reasons for them. I have retained, for example, the frequent use (based presumably on Ford's manuscript practice) of "?" where we would expect "!" However, I have silently supplied capitals at the beginning of lines where they are wanting and periods at the ends of stanzas where no punctuation is provided. I have silently emended the punctuation of marginal biblical citations to make them conform with what appears to be the general usage of 13, namely, book, chapter, and verse, each followed by a period (for example, Esay.53.3.). And I have also silently aligned some marginal notes so as to position them nearer the line in the text that they seem intended to support or illuminate. Otherwise the alignment of marginal references follows as closely as possible that of 13. All such references are to the Geneva Bible; in the few cases in which its numbering of verses differs from that of the Authorized (King James) Version, an explanatory note is provided in the Commentary.

The Commentary for *Christes Bloodie Sweat* follows the principles set down for this edition as a whole, with one addition: where the meaning of a difficult passage in the text of *Christes Bloodie Sweat* is adequately illuminated by the biblical text cited in the margin, I have provided no commentary of my own.

Acknowledgements

I am grateful to the librarians of the British Library, the Bodleian Library, the Wodehouse Library (Dulwich College), The Folger Shakespeare Library, and the library of the University of Illinois (Urbana) for assisting in various ways my attempts at copying and collating the original printed text of *Christes Bloodie Sweat*. I would also like to thank Lorena Henry Larmer, who rendered cheerful and much-needed help in the early stages of editing, and J. A. Lavin, who kindly read and commented on an early draft of the textual introduction. I especially wish to record my gratitude to G. D. Monsarrat and W. Speed Hill for innumerable, painstaking, and invaluable suggestions on all matters pertaining to this edition of *Christes Bloodie Sweat*. But my greatest debt of gratitude is to my colleague L. E. Stock for unfailing encouragement, advice, and generosity throughout this project.

D.D.

CHRISTES BLOODIE SWEAT.

OR

THE SONNE OF GOD IN HIS *AGONIE*.

TO THE RIGHT

HONORABLE, WILLIAM

Earle of PEMBROOKE, &c. One of his
Majesties most Honorable privie Coun-
saile, and Knight of the Noble
Order of the Garter, &c.

RIGHT HONORABLE, as your Titles doe ennoble your Vertues, so (in the Judgement of those that know you) your Vertues doe as much more intitle your Noblenesse: which two, in this age, doe so sel-
10 dome meete in one, as most usually to bee Great, and to bee Good, is required a double person. It is not so (and it is not so reported) in you; being reputed therein to deserve the Honours you possesse, for chiefly loving the desertfull. These assurances, have encouraged mee, to offer to your judicious view, this little labour, which con-
15 taines but a Summarie of the Sonne of Gods sorrowes, Wherein, let mee | crave this favour from your Noble bountie, to measure, with the defect in writing, the sweetnesse of what is written: the effect of that sweetnesse, and the benefit of that effect. And as for mee (my good Lord) I shall take comfort in my paines, if you to whom
20 they are devoted, (beeing wonne hereto by the generall commenda-
tion of your merit) please to allow your Patronage to one, who offers, what hee offers, in the perfect nakednesse of perfect simplicitie. Resting

*A lover of your person, for
your Noble worthinesse.*

J. F.

¶ To such as shall peruse this Booke. A4ʳ

POETRIE *is so every way made the Herauld of wantonnesse, as there is not now any thing too uncleane for lascivious rime; which among some (in whose hearts God hath wrought better things) hath bin the cause, why so generall*
5 *an imputation is laid upon this ancient and industrious Arte. And I, to cleere (as I might) verse, from the soyle of this unworthinesse, have herein (at least) proved that it may deliver good matter, with fit harmonie of words, though I have erred in the latter. The way to* Doe well, *is not so doubtfull, as not to be sought; neither so darke, but it may bee found. I confesse, I have,*
10 *touching my perticular, beene long carried with the doubts of* folly, youth, *and* opinion, *and as long miscaried in the darknesse of unhappinesse, both in* invention *and* action. *This was not the path that led to a contented rest, or a respected name. In regarde whereof, I have heere set forth the witnesse that may testifie what I desire to bee. Not that many should know*
15 *it, but that many should take comfort by it. And (kind Reader) this is my request, that faults in Printing may be charitably corrected; that the sence of the matter may be wisely (and herein truely) construed, and so shall yee both approve your owne Judgements, and right the Authour in his hopes.*

Farewell.

CHRISTES
Bloudy Sweat.

DOWNE from the throane of everlasting grace,
Where Host's of *Angells* guard eternall soules
The great *Vice-gerent* of his Fathers place,
Gods sonne discendes, from far above the *Poles*:
    And gently yet againe attempt's to winne,
    The Monarchy of hearts usurp't by sinne.

Deare Ransome where the payment is in bloud,
Deare bloud where every droppe out-values golde,
Deare dropes, in whom lyes more the creatures good,
Then selfe creations treasure can unfolde:
    Deare ransome, deerer bloud, most deerest droppes,
    Whose price is life, which life, death underproppes.

Death underpropp's that life which *Frailty* lost,
All *Frailty* living in the death of one,
Of one, *all one* with all, who freely crost,
The written booke of debt and Hell alone:
    [Ah], t'is a sad and lamentable story,
    To view the passion of the Lord of Glory.

A Lord of *Glory*, *Prince* of Heaven and Peace,
An elder brother of the sonnes of rest,
An Heyre of *promise*, that with large encrease,
A Kingdome and an Empire hath possest:
    Whereby those poore weake soules in earth cast downe,
    Like *Kings* in Heaven, shall all support a Crowne.

Such thoughts as those, whiles in a ravish't spirit,
Faire meditations Summoned to appeare,
Before the *Arke*, and mercie-seat of merrit,

    A sacred flame mixt with an holy feare,
       As if Gods voyce had spoke, seem'd to invite,
30   My heart to prompt, my ready hand to write.

    Thou (quoth it) that hast spent thy best of dayes,
    In [thriftlesse] rimes (sweete baytes to poyson Youth)
    Led with the wanton hopes of laude and praise,
    Vaine shadowes of delight, seales of untruth,
35   Now I impose new taskes uppon thy Pen,
       To shew my sorrowes to the eyes of Men.

    Set then the tenour of thy dolefull song,
    To the deepe accentes of my bloudy sweate?
    Sweete straines of Musicke, sweetly mixt among,
40   The discord of my paines, the pleasure great,
      The comforts lasting that the world hath got,
       By the delightfull sound, of his sad note.

    Here then unclaspe the burthen of my woes,
    My woes, distil'd into a streame of teares,
45   My teares, begetting sighes, which sighes disclose
    A rocke of torment, which affliction beares:
      My griefes, teares, sighes, the rocke, seas, windes unfain'd
      Whence shipwrackt soules, the Land of safety gayn'd.

    For whiles incompast in a fleshly frame,   B2ʳ
50   A cloude of darke mortality I liv'd:
    I liv'd the subject both of scorne and shame,
    Banisht from mirth, of comfortes all depriv'd: Esay.53.3.
      Horrors with scandall, cares with cares did strive,
      And ever as I liv'd, I died alive.

55   Teares in mine eyes, division in my heart,
    Disgrace uppon my name, plaintes in my breast,
    Thirst in my sufferance, hunger in my smart,   Mat.4.2.
    Naked and cold, imprison'd and opprest:
      Troubled within, tempted without, my Head   Luke.9.58.
60   Uncertaine, where to lead me to my bed.

    Poore and forsaken [every] day in daunger

Of wrath and Treason, lesser pris'd then dust,
Of all abhor'd, even to mine owne a stranger,
No man my friend, in any friend no trust: Psal.41.9.
  My miracles tearm'd divilish, and my prayer Mat.12.24.
  Hipocrisie, my sorrowes held dispayer.

This entertaynment in the world I had,
Yet for the world expos'd my selfe to all:
All more then this though this be all to sad,
But hereto did my Fathers will me call:
  Which most above the rest his [will] with paine,
  Did cleave my soule, all woe-begon in twaine.

The charge of whose hot wrath so fearefull was,
As against Nature chang'd my sweate to bloud:
Which trickling downe my cheekes uppon the grasse, Luke.22.44.
Well tould the agony wherein I stood:
  An agony indeed, whose trembling heate,
  Powr'd out the wonder of a bloudy sweate.

Which bloudy Sweate, for that it is a theame, B2ᵛ
(The happie matter of a moving stile)
That now I challenge from thy sacred dreame,
And meditations (in that dreame) the while,
  Thou undertake, to Register that part,
  And with my spirit, I will guide thy heart.

Remember first the sorrowes thou hast past,
The shame thou hast escap't, what thou hast felt,
How I have ever succour'd thee at last,
How gently, with thee and thy sinnes I dealt,
  Thinke on the griefes, have made thy pride decline,
  For by thine owne, thou mayst conceave of mine.

For as the Sunne exceedes the smallest Starre,
In height of glory, in his goulden Spheres:
Whiles as I was with men a man, so farre,
And much more, did my horrors exceed theires:
  But thou begin, and where thy sacred fires
  Waxe dimme, my breath shall quicken thy desires.

Thus then I soone obayd the Heavenly voice,
And wrot; the weight of vengeance now increast,
From God the Father on his sonne, whose choyce
100 Would not from that injunction be releast:
    But he must feele, the curse and scourging rod,
    Of our and his (through us) offended God.

No sacrifice or incense could appease,
Or reconcile the Majestie above:
105 No Customary *Rites*, no *Tribute* please,
No law redeeme the breach of his deare love:
    His most just justice, would no mercy give,
    But God as man must die, that men may live.

The holy and inviolate decree,   Acts.2.23.   B3ʳ
110 In his unchaunging wisdome had appointed,
That the true way to happines should bee
Found out in bloud, and bloud of his annointed:
    Whose pure Vermilion red, did fairely guild,   John.1.29.36.
    Sinn's blacke as night, for whom this lambe was kild.   Reve.
                                                                                                    5.8.9.
115 Meeke and unfriended to the world he came,
Lowly, sad, patient, in his humbled lookes   Zech.9.9.
The Mirror of humility; so tame,   Mat.21.5.
As if his forehead had bin sorrowes bookes: Mat.11.29.
    Thus whiles the Jewes hopes, with ambition wing'd   Mat.12.18.
120   Flew through the earth, their *Saviour* came; un-king'd.   19.20.

Un-king'd good man, so far from any grace
Of earthly majestie, of Crownes of state: Mar.6.2.3.4.5.6.7.
As he was set much lower then the base,   Luke.4.22. to 31.
Beneath the sight of pittie or of hate:
125   Yet this is that *Messiah*, he who brings   John.1.41.
    Life in his death, makes men saints, *Saints as Kings*.

What eye did ever see him laugh? what eares
Have heard him speake the languages of pleasure?
But every eye that saw him, saw his Teares,   John.11.33.35.38.
130 All Eares that heard him, heard him speake in measure: Mar.8.12.
    For still his wordes, with griefe such measure kept,   Luke.19.41.42.
    His speech was sighes, and as he spoke, he wept.

No hand did lend on little Cloth to drye,
The rivers on his cheekes, no thought bewail'd Lam.1.12.
His solitary Cares, but all past by
Those unrespected griefes, his heart assail'd;
    Himselfe he seem'd, as if he meant to crave,
    But of himselfe, to beare him to his grave.

His precious head, crown'd with a goodly fleece, B3ᵛ
Of hayres more precious, then are goulden threedes,
Appeares, but as an *Artist's* Maister peece
Scarce worth to view his lockes him over-spreads Mat.27.29.
    Untrim'd: as if they ought that head no duety,
    So much his dayly woes had chaung'd his beauty.

His face in which the *Rose* did with the lilly, Esay.53.2.
Strive curiously for chaunge in little space,
Through many untaught sighes, appear'd so silly,
As t'was but like the ruins of a face:
    Never was man, so excellently nam'd,
    For shape, whom sadnesse had so soone unfram'd.

And now the fulnesse of the time drew on, John.13.1.
When he should pay the ransome of his death, Gal.4.5.
To make oblation of his bloud alone, Eph.1.10.
Offring the last gaspe of a guiltlesse breath:
    As if his onely arrant from the wombe
    Were but to run a race unto his Tombe.

When with the small remainder of his stocke, Mat.26.37.
A remnant of the worldes un-numbred son's,
A little remnant, a poore simple flocke,
This pastour with those sheepe together run's,
    To sequester them and himselfe apart, Luke.21.37.
    That he might offer upp to God his heart.

Not far from the *Holy Cittie* stood,
The mount of Olivet, at whose steepe *Base* Mat.21.1. et 24.3.
Ceadron the river, with a gentle flood, John.18.1.
Made Musicke to the silence of that place:

      Neere which was *Gethsemane*, whereto [they] say,   Mar.14.32.
      He often came and often us'd to pray.

      Retyr'd from out the clamours of the day,   B4^r
170   Our Saviour with his chosen thither came:
      That with more leysure hee might freely pray,   Luke.22.40.
      Before the houre that must dissolve the frame
         Of his mortallity, the curse and scourge
         He was to beare, from sinners sinne to purge.

175   And feeling now th'approaching horrors neere,
      Of God's inkindled wrath, the time at hand
      Of coming vengeance, trembling in his feare,
      (Which being man he knew not to commaund)   John.8.59.
         His soule was heavy to the death, his heart   Mat.26.38.
180   Through wounded, ere he felt his woundes to smart.

      Burst with the burthen of tormenting anguish,   Esay.53.4.7.
      Wasted with bitter throbbes, his hastning paine
      Did make his Manhood quake, and sadly languish
      In agonyes so heavy to sustaine,
185   As but the Jewish malice was to heady,
         New death's were needlesse, he was dead already.

      In terrors buried quicke, he strove to hast
      To the prepared Sepulcher of shame:
      Dreading the judgment, heaven had over past
190   Uppon his humaine frailty hell to tame:
         His flesh and God-head strove, but he the while,
         Meeke in his suffraunce, did both weepe and smile:

      His God-head smil'd to see his man-hood weepe,
      Remembring what his Godhead had decreed:
195   His man-hood did a sure full reckoning keepe,
      Of every sorrow, that could sorrow breed:
         And faine he would as man from death, be-los'd
         Which on himselfe as God, himselfe impos'd.   John.10.18.

      Father hee pray'd, and lifted up his eyes,   B4^v
200   (For in his eyes he had inthron'd his heart)   Mat.26.39.

Father? ah that those terrors might suffize?
Ah that this deadly banquet might depart?
   In which without thy wrath, I might not sup,
   The health of sicke soules, in a poys'ned Cup.

And if it may be possible? But ôh? Mar.14.36.
Let not my prayers disanull thy will?
If thine eternall counsaile order so,
That I must thy severe decree fulfill?
   Father, so it let bee? though death hath wonne
   Gayne on my flesh, yet O thy will be done. Luke.22.42.
Phil.2.8.

Heere sincking downe, for being sore opprest,
With all the worldes innumerable sinnes,
Assaulted in that conflict, and distrest, Heb.2.9.
An *Angell* comforts him, and he begins Luke.22.43.
   To shake of those his feares in which he stood,
   Which from his passions drew a sweate of blood. Verse.44.ibid.

Deere eye what-soe're thou be that shall peruse,
The burthen of those lamentable lines?
An holy meditation may infuse,
A-mazement to thy soule by those faire signes:
   Heere stay thy wandring gaze, and faintly heare
   (Ere thou read more) thou mayst let fall a teare?

And thinke it not a labour all un-meete,
To spend a sigh on this unhappy view?
Wofull the subject, but the gaine is sweete,
By which all serve no more, but raigne a new:
   For every teare of water thou canst shed?
   The heart of *Christ*, a teare of bloud hath bled.

Hee sweat not droppes of bloud for his owne cause, C1ʳ
For hee unblemish't lambe was innocent: Psal.18.23.
Hee had objur'd no God, hee broke no Lawes, 1.Pet.2.22.
Hee harbourd no deceit, no falshood meant, Esay.53.9.
   Hee never wrong'd his freind by secret stealth,
   Nor by oppression sought to purchase wealth.

235   His tongue for gaine was never hyr'd to lye,
         Or tu'nd to sweare, or flatter, curse, or fawne,
         Lust could not traine his heart, or love his eye,
         No wanton baites of pleasure could impawne
            His chast desire, to forfet to delight
240   The lawelesse issues of a banefull night.

         His meekenes thirsted not revenge, his minde
         Was never set on wrath, no fruitlesse pride
         Travail'd new fashions curiously to finde,   Luke.9.2.3.
         He onely car'd his naked wast to hide:
245   He never sought to be reputed brave,
         So he had clothes, yet clothes could scarcely have.

         He lov'd not sloath (unprofitable rest)
         Which eates, and feedes, and onely feedes and eates:
         Excesse of feeding he hath not profest,
250   To surfet in varietie of Meates:
            His diet was not change, or choyse: his dish
            Some-times a Barly loafe, sometimes a fish.   Mat.14.19.

         No Wines of mixture, or new drinkes to drowne
         His soule he us'd: he was, as Nature made him,
255   A drinker, but no drunkard: to uncrowne   John.4.7.
         His innocence no friendship should perswade him: Mat.11.19.
            His voyce un-fee'd, spoke to a Nation dull,   Luke.4.21.
            And fed the sheepe, but would not share the Wooll. Mar.6.6.

         Hee did not stop his eares against the cryes   C1ᵛ
260   Of harmelesse suters, to doe justice right;
         Hee envi'd not the great, nor did despise
         The broken hearted poore, borne downe by might:
            But without doing evill, all to win   1.John.3.5.
            He lost his life; and yet he knew no sin.   Mat.8.17.

265   He knew no sinne, then needed not to sweat
         The liquid moysture of dissolved bloud,
         For his owne faults, but ours; our faults so great,
         As scant is one amongst a thousand good

And yet that one of thousands, if the letter
Of life were surely scand, might bee much better.

This was that Pellican indeed, retyr'd
Into the desert of a troubled breast,
Who for to pay the ransome long desir'd,
Consum'd himselfe to give his people rest:
    A Pellican indeed, that with her bloud
    Pulls out her heart, to give her Chickens food.

He like the *Phoenix* burning in the Sun,
That from his ashes may spring up a younger,
Doth beate himselfe to death, and will not shun
The fire, that weake men may in him grow stronger:
    A perfect *Phoenix*, that most gladly dyes,
    That many in his only death may rise.   Heb.9.28.

In every sex, and some of all degrees,
He saw the mispent ryot of their Talent:
No sin escapt the eye of his decrees,
But he beheld how apt men were to fall in't:
    For so is prone mortalyty accurst,
    As still it strives to plot and woorke the woorst.

This man of men did in his troubled spirit   C2r
Into a streame of soft compassion melt
His Icye bloud, that frailty might inherit
The sun of comfort, by the griefes he felt:
    Each drop of bloud he shed, he, shed it then   Levi.17.11.
    To wash a severall sin from severall men.   Heb.10.22.

Here saw he Princes in the awfull throne   as hapned by *Herod*.
Of eminencie, how wantonly they strove
For thirst of glory, to protect alone   Mat.2.8.
Religious name, not for religious love: Luke.3.1.
    Graceing the gracelesse, in whom grace was lost, Acts.12.21.22.
    Such Parasites as knew to flatter most.   John.18.22.

For those he sweated bloud: that they whom Heaven
Created gods, on earth, should so prophane

By courses indirect and lawes un-even,   Psal.82.1.6.
Of will and sensuall lust, the law first drawne   Rev.17.2.
305   By that eternall royalty, who stood
To watch their faults: for Kings he sweated bloud.

Here saw he such, who under those were plac't
In seates of greatnesse and commaundes of state:
How fond in their madnesse they did wast   Luke.23.12.
310 Their greatnesse in ambition and debate:
   Ayming not to support, but scorne the good,   Acts.23.4.5.
   By unjust force, for such he sweated bloud.

Here saw he how in *Moses* chayre there raign'd   Mat.7.15.
Scribes cloath'd in wool of Lambes, and speaking well,   Mat.23.2.
315 But Wolves in nature, so coruptly stayn'd,   Mat.7.3.
As if they were but messengers of hell: John.8.44.
   Abusing unlearn'd soules and *Levits* power,   Mat.23.13.
   More ready, then to cherrish, to devoure.   Mar.12.40.

Those whom the breath of God at first inspir'd   C2ᵛ
320 To shine as Lampes, and speake the Heavenly sound,   Mat.5.14.
With *Angels* tongues, were silent, if not hir'd,   Eze.22.25.
More studying with the scriptures to compound   Mat.15.9.
   Their owne traditions, and for those indeed,   Mar.7.7.
   In heavy droppes the sweat of *Christ* did bleed.

325 Here saw he Lawyers soberly engoun'd,   Luke.11.46.52.
Wanting the Robe of Justice: not regarding
The poore mans right, nor where the case was sound,   Luk.18.2.3.
But giving Judgment, as he felt rewarding: Pro.29.4.
   Whose tongue was bought, against that side was weake,
330   Most times as well to hold his peace, as speake:

For them he sweated bloud, and heere he saw
Intrusted jurisdiction over-sway'd   John.12.43.
By partiall favour, above forme of Law,
Cold Conscience, by which Conscience was betray'd:
335   For those condemning, were condemn'd [so] much,   Luke.6.37.
   As they condemn'd, He sweated bloud for such.   Mat.7.1.2.

Heere saw he Souldiers toyling in the heat Luke.3.14.
Of cruelty, not measuring the right,
Why they bore Armes, but to content the great,
And their owne lawlesse hate, prepar'd to fight,
    For prey and spoyle adventuring to rent
    Their lives and soules, for those his bloud Hee spent.

Heere saw he others that did keepe the sword as in Annas
Of office and authority, in peace, and Cayphas
Compacted in a knot, not to accord
Or set at unity strifes, but increase: John.18.13.14.
    Wounding or sparing with a watchfull hand, Pro.29.2.
    As some superiour person should commaund.

For them he sweated bloud: heere with much griefe C3^r
He saw how *Schollers*, trim'd with strength of wit,
Inricht with knowledge, and of men the chiefe, Eccle.10.1.2.
For knowing more then men, with straynes unfit Mat.11.19.
    Did boast their pride, which wisdome disallow'd,
    For being still both needy and yet proud: Pro.14.6.

Schollers he saw, how foolishly they strove,
With tearmes of Art and smooth beguiling rimes,
To paynt the grosenes of unlawfull love, James.3.15.
And prove the sinnes that did corrupt the times, Acts.19.19.
    Mayntayning up-start sectes which all with-stood Mic.2.1.
    Truthes precious light: for those He sweated bloud. Gal.5.20.
1.Tim.1.4.

Heere saw he some, whose servile basenes waited
Uppon such vices as attend the great, as the *Hero-*
Whom Hell with all it's nimble cunning bayted *dians:*
To usher lusts, by many a subtill feat, Mat.22.16.
    Those make good cloathes their God, and pay the fees Luke.7.25.
    Of lewdnes, with faire wordes and supple knees. Mat.11.8.

For those did Jesus sweate in bloud: with those
Heere saw he some, that were in nature skil'd,
Searching the rules of Phisicke, to disclose Mar.5.26.
The treasure that the helpe of Art could yeeld,

How Gold did prompt them, and the thirst of wealth,
To hasten death, or to recover health.

Much mischiefe and abuse he saw in such,
How they would cocker lust, and stir up heat
375 Of wanton bloud, concealing shame too much,
With many sinnes, too many to repeat:
    For those and their iniquities, *Christes* griefe
    Did sweate in bloud, to give their soules reliefe.

Heere saw he men, whose winged vessels brought   C3ᵛ
380 From lands far off, the Marchandize of profit,
How by their factors, all the world was sought,   Rev.18.23.
For Precious wares such as made plenty of it: Hos.12.7.8.
    And yeelded to their greedy hopes such treasure,   Mic.6.10.
    As they had heap't, by subtill weight and measure.   11.12.

385 Thus did they wast the poore, and purchase wealth   1.Cor.6.8.
By falshood in extremityes retyring   1.Thes.4.6.
As they pretend, for benefit of health,
To their full garners: greedily conspiring
    How they might starve the hungry, and still keepe   Reve.18.3.
390   Their gould, for those his bloudy sweate did weepe.   11.

Heere saw he others, curst with large posessions   such as was
Hard Landlords, raysing rentes, who still would grutch   *Achab* to
The bread of honest gayne, by sterne oppressions,   *Naboth.*
Wrangling for earth, till earth they had too much,   1.Kin.21.2.
395   For those the Lord, now being man was driven,   Psal.83.5.
    To sweat in bloud: that those might be forgiven.   Job.9.24.

Heere saw he yet a woorser sort, provoking   Eze.18.12.13.
The wrath of God, who living still in plenty,   et.22.12.13.
And cunning in Arethmeticke, lay soaking
400 The needy: gayning on the hundred twenty: Pro.22.23.
    Unconscionable usurers, not contented   Rom.2.5.
    With ten to one? nor one of ten repented.   2.Pet.3.9.
    James.5.3.

For them he sweated bloud, here saw he Creatures   Gen.6.2.

In face as sweete as Angels, dy'd in grayne,
405 Of natures Art, fayre Miracle of features,
Wonder of beauty, loves delicious trayne,
    Adorn'd with seeming graces that did shine
    So glorious, as they were esteem'd devine.

Women they were, Saintes to behold, in view   C4^r
410 Chast Matrons, but (O frailtyes curst) in triall
More vaine then vanitie, and more untrue   Pro.31.30.
Then falshood: [ ] only cunning in deniall: Pro.7.10.
    In whose deniall vertue was so scant,
    As when they [most] deni'd, they most will graunt.

415 Wordes, wit, and fayrnesse, [ar] the smiling ginnes
Wherewith they catch insnard men: whereto heaven   Eccle.7.28.
Bestow'd for blessings, are but bands to sinnes
Abus'd; whom God made straight, those make [un-]even:
    Of whom the most are worst, the fewer good,   Ibid.30.
420   The good not free, for all he sweated bloud.

No sex was uncorrupt, but all in all,
In every fashion, and in each degree,
Drew comfort from the sower-bitter Gall
Of his afflictions, therein to set free
425   That soules from bondage, and to coole that heate
    Of just damnation, in his bloudy sweate.

The tide of killing Sinnes was swollen high,
And could not be abated to an ebb,   Rom.3.23.24.
Before the blessed Son of God must dye,
430 Undoing by his death the painefull webb,
    The web of endlesse paynes that Sathan lay'd,
    In which the Soules of sinners were betray'd.

Even as a man that treades a wearie pace,
In laborinthes, continually in doubt
435 To find the center of the curious trace,
Once entred, still uncertaine to get out,
    Before some skillfull maister by a twist,
    Doth guide him, in or out, or as he list;

Or as some *Christian* Marchant by a Turke   C4ᵛ
440   Surprisd, and chayn'd, is made a gally-slave,
Whipt every day, and forc't to toyle and worke,
Consum'd with griefe, still living in a grave,
    Untill some one more strong, doth free his payne,
    And set's him in his wonted state agayne:

445   So men, that in a maze of deathfull errour
Did treade the pathes of miseries and woe,   2.Tim.2.26.
Bound by that Turke the *Devill*, slav'd to that terror   Deu.6.21.
Of condemnation, labour'd to and fro:
    Till *Christ* by death, did lead them out of sinne,   Gal.3.26.
450   And free'd them from the bondage they were in.

The Devill could not with his active might   Mat.12.28.29.
Prevaile against the Lord, but he abates
His policy and strength; and skil'd in fight,   Mar.3.27.
Conquer's the sting of *Death*, cast downe hell gates,   Hose.13.14.
455   Triumphes on sinne, kept darke confusion under,   Mat.16.18.
    Breaking the cursed Dragons head a sunder.   1.Cor.15.55.56.
                                                                                    Gen.3.15.

Captivitie, led Captive, doth un-maske
The hideous visor of his dismall smiles,
And all the world shakes off the irkesome taske
460   It had sustayn'd, and see's the deadly guiles,
    The sugred bane, the draught it had suck't up
    Of spiced pleasures in a damned cup.

A damned cup, a cup of Gods fierce wrath,
Of fornications, of consuming wine,   Rev.18.3.
465   A cup, such as restoratives none hath,
But meere consumptions, no way to refine
    New bloud as Cordialls, but to over-cloy
    The Dyet of the *Soule*, and *Soule* destroy.

All those hath *Christes* deere bloudy sweat layd open,   D1ʳ
470   (For even his death was but a sweate in bloud)
Offring to all in heart contrite and broken,
The benefit of life and living foode:
    Not foode not *Manna*, that shall perish, waste,   John.6.31.35.

Or stincke, but bread that shall for ever last.

475 For ever last? O who would spend his dayes,
In transitory follyes of delight?
Such as passe soone away, and soone decayes,
Vanish as soone as thought forgotten quite?
    When they beyond all tearme of time or date
480   Might raigne as *Kings*, but in a happier state?

This did the *Leacher* sleeping in the sheetes
Which reeke with lust, but thinke on, he would weepe;
This did the *Drunkard* reeling in the streetes
(Then only wise when hee doth onlie sleepe)
485   Consider, he might sigh; and not incline
    To vomit out his soule in streames of wine.

This did the *Miscreants* (*Gallants* cald) who boldly,
Teare Godes eternall name, with liberall oathes,
Remember, they would pray, and not so coldly
490 Quench zeale, by warming pride in costly clothes:
    For zeale doth last, when clothes are worne and rotten;
    Men great, once seen in rags, are soone forgotten.

This did the gamsters, spending nightes and dayes,
In loosing what they gaine (such gaine is losse)
495 For-cast, they would repent, and [leave] such playes,
Reputing mony (as it is) but drosse:
    They, whiles other cheate, in hope of slime,
    Ill-gotten thrift, doe cheate their selves of time.

This did the lov-sicke musicke-straining wanton,   D1ᵛ
500 Who leades his life in sonnetting some *Ay-mees*:
Ponder, he'd cease, and then there would be scant one
En-amour'd on so many lisping *Shees*:
    But changing better notes, they would take pittie
    On their owne soules, and sing a sweeter dittie.

505 This did the bloody-minded butcher mildly
Conceive, he would not be so flesht in strife,
He would not over-given be so wildly,

To stabbe, to fight, to scorne the weight of life:
Who seekes a name by murther, and doth prize it,
510   Being termd a true brave *Spirit* hardly buyes it.

This did the mockers of th'elect and holy,
Whom God hath set on earth to do his will,
Regard they could not be so curst in folly,   2.Kin.2.23.
As to persever in their mischiefe still: Acts.2.13.
515   Despising Preachers, and nicke naming those,   Mat.10.22.
With malice, whom the holy ghost [hath] chose.

This did the women of much shame and badnesse,
Who prostitute their bodies [to] disgrace,
In penance, and a feeling tuch of sadnesse
520 But looke into, they would not be so base,
To gaine diseases, but with hearts all rent   Joh.8.11.
Redeeme the unchast houres, they have mispent.

He that doth most addict himselfe to sin,
Did he but bathe his thoughts and once a day
525 Wash, through his earnest meditations, in
The bloody sweat of *Christ*, and truely pray
To be made cleane, by sorrowes strongly urged,
Soone should he hate his faults, and soone be purged.

But this to flesh and frailty is so strange,   D2^r
530 So hard to thinke, so difficult to doe,
As tis almost impossible to change,
From bad to good though God in mercy woe
Mortality, to tast of mercies treasure,
Yet O, tis hard to leave the baites of pleasure.

535 O thou that dalliest in secure content?
And dost not feele the sinnes that over-presse thee?
Thinke on his bloodie sweate and straight repent,
Before a heavier Judgement do distresse thee?
And then alas, in that un-hopefull state,
540   The time is past thou wilt repent too late.

Christs bloody sweate, was that distilling river,

The comfortable *Jordan*, whose faire streames   2.Kin.5.14.
Did cleanse the *Syrian Naaman*, and deliver
His bodie from the leprosies extreames:
545   We all are *Naamans* leprous, but more foule,
    Till in his bloody sweate he purge our soule.

Christs bloody sweate that precious poole is, truely   Joh.5.2.
Bethesda cald, where he that was dis-easd
For eight and thirty yeares, did waite most duly
550 To be put in, thereby to be releasd:
    We all are sicke, and languishingly hover,
    Till in his bloody sweat, we health recover.

Christs bloody sweat, that *Siloam* is, where he
Must strive to wash his eyes, who was borne blind,   Joh.9.7.
555 In which pure laver, he attaind to see
With eyes of body, and with eyes of mind:
    So must we wash, our blindnesse is so great,
    In the fresh fountaine of his bloody sweat.

These are the waters of eternall life,   Esa.12.3.   D2ᵛ
560 And he that drinkes them shall not thirst againe;   John.4.14.
Not springs of *Meribath*, or floods of strife,   Nu.20.13.
To move contentions, or produce disdaine,
    For such as tast this licour, shall possesse
    Sure peace of conscience, perfect happinesse.

565 Doth any love to be in love with beautie?
Come hither, in those drops he shall behold
Water and blood, both in their proper dutie,
So lively as Arts selfe would have extold:
    In curious figures, shadowing delight,
570   Blood like to red, and Water like to white.

Doth any covet time-beguiling song?
Come hither, heare is musicke in this sweate;
Words sung to God, spoke with a zeale so strong,
As that it doth his bloody sweate beget.
575   This must inchant the senses, and impart,
    Not solace to the eare, but to the heart.   Ephe.5.19.

Doth any wish for costly fare or diet?
Come hither, banquet in his sacred passion.
Heres comfort for the soule, and perfect quiet,
Such food as *Christ* himselfe had in like fashion,
   When talking with the woman at the well,
   He eat what no man but himselfe could tell.   Joh.4.32.

Doth any hope for Honor or promotion,
Come hither, let him meditate on this,
And with the sacrifice of true devotion,
Lift up his voice to aske continuing blisse.
   And to him shalbe given with increase,
   A crowne of glory, a firme throane of peace.   1.Pet.5.4.
                                                                          2.Tim.4.8.

Doth any take content in strength and might,   D3^r
Come hither from this bloud recover trust,
And hee shall put the Divels force to flight,
Rebate the dartes of Hell and judge th'unjust: 1.Joh.2.14.
   And beare the Crosse and conquer in like manner,   Jam.4.7.
   Safe Souldiers fighting under *Christ* his banner.

It is an honour in the eyes of men,
If when the King in person is in field,
Some forward spirit desperately then
Assault his foe, and force him for to yeeld.
   For which attempt, if such a one by right,
   Under the standard royall be made *Knight*,

It is an honour, and to times succeeding,
This banneret shall purchase lasting fame:
What honour is it then if one lie bleeding,
Under the wounds of *Christ* and in his name?
   By Christian combat, levell in the dust
   The worlds aspiring sinnes, [denoting] lust.

Hee that doth overcome himselfe and see,
His guerdon by the holy written word,
Is a faire *man* at *armes* more strong then hee,
Who plowes up *Kingdomes* with his threatning sword;

> For greater enemies incampe about,
> *Mans* owne weake heart, then any are without.

> Here lurkes adulteries, fornication, rapes,
> Murthers, false testimonies, slaunders, pride,   Mat.15.19.
615   *Treason,* backe-biting, evill thoughts, escapes,   Mar.7.21.22.
> Thefts, foolishnes, affections fondly ei'de,
>> Uncleannesse, covetousnesse, deceits and all,
>> Which brings the poore captived soule in thrall.

> Turne then thy weapons on thy selfe, O man,   D3ᵛ
620   And fight against those enemies within thee,
> Beat downe thy proper strength, sincerely scan
> The horror of those foes that aime to win thee:
>> Put plates of righteousnes upon thy brest,   Eph.6.14.
>> And have thy feet shod with the Gospels rest.   Vers.15.

625   Gird on thy loines with veritie, and take   Vers.14.
> Salvations helmet to secure thy head,   Vers.17.
> Beare up the shield of faith and hourely shake   Vers.16.
> The spirits sword and on thy watchfull bed   Ibid.
>> Keepe centinell when all thy powers retreat,   Colos.4.2.
630   Then come and bath thee in his *bloody sweat.*

> For as the Hart long hunted on the mountaines,   Psa.42.1.
> Breathlesse doth pant for life but all in vaine,
> Untill revived in the lively fountaines,
> He doth recover strength and breath againe:
635   So we of breath, of life, are all depriv'd,
>> Til in his *bloody sweat* we be reviv'd.

> The curse on man from God when first he fell
> From the free comforts of possessed grace,
> Was danger of a second death and hell
640   Eating his bread with sweate upon his face,   Gen.3.19.
>> Then all his sweate his sorrowes did decree him,
>> This *bloody sweat* should from his sorrowes free him.

> Sweat was ordaind to get us bread, which bread
> *Achab* the king did to *Michaiah* give

645   When to the prison causing to be led,
    He did ordaine the prophet to relieve
      With bread, which shewd his cruell jurisdiction
      In giving bread, but bread twas of *Affliction*.   1.Kin.22.27.

    In sweate we eate our bread, such bread as *David*   D4ʳ
650   A man of God, and chosen to his heart,   1.Sam.13.14.
    Cride out he had, when doubting to be saved
    He bore the weakenesse of the Churches smart:
      Bread twas indeed, so kneaded up in feares,
      As well he witnest twas the *bread of teares*.   Psa.80.5.

655   In sweat we eate our bread, such bread so scant,
    As *Esay* promisd to the faithlesse Jewes,
    Who being pierc't with famine, sterv'd with want,
    Sought stranger gods and did the knowne refuse.
      Such bread is our bread, and be sweated so,
660   Bread of adversitie, and *bread of woe*.   Esa.30.20.

    As then the sweat in getting of our bread,
    Did set before our eyes the curse we live in,
    So may this *bloody sweat* abandon dread,
    In onely which we know we are forgiven:
665   Then let us in those sweates redeeme time past,
      Feeling the first, still have in mind the last.

    And still as often as our heart presents us
    The memory of our unhappy fall,
    By sweating for that bread which discontents us
670   So often, let us call to mind withall
      This sweat of comfort, that doth hourely bleed
      Our wofull soules with *bread of life* to feed.

    Let not the pleasures of uncertaine tast,
    Beguile our palates to deceive our hearts:
675   Let not the momentarie hopes that wast,
    Invite to folly that too soone departs:
      But let us looke on *Christ* the way and dore,   Joh.10.7.9.
      That all must tread as he hath gone before.

	Peeter and *Andrew, James* and *John*, whom first	D4ᵛ
680	The Lord elected to be great on earth,	Mat.4.19.
	From men with men in rancke of men the worst,	
	The meanest in degree of basest birth,	
	When they were cald Gods glory for to see,	
	The only wordes he us'd, were *follow mee.*	

685	*Mathew* surnamed *Levy* who to raise	
	His estate to wealth and Honour sate and tooke	
	Custome, and tallage till his better dayes,	
	Approached when the time was he forsooke	
	Vaine trust, and was God's glory cald to see,	
690	The only wordes *Christ* us'd, were follow mee.	Mar.2.14.

	The rich man that to justifie himselfe,	
	By keeping whole the fire-condemning law,	
	Hee that was sad to leave his worldly pelfe	
	When the trew [mean] to righteousnesse he saw:	
695	To him then cald Gods glory for to see	
	The onely wordes he us'd, were follow mee.	Mar.10.21.

	To him that would be just, but first had rather	Luke.9.61.
	To bid his guestes at home farewell and he,	
	Who chose to lay into his grave his father,	Mat.8.21.
700	Before he ment a *Nazuarite* to be:	
	When they should come Gods glory for to see,	
	The only wordes he us'd, were follow mee.	Ibid.22.

	Phillip when yet redemption was not knowne,	
	To bee on earth found such a saving favour,	
705	As that the Lord did chose him for his owne,	
	By calling him unto the precious savour	
	Of life, to life, Gods glory for to see,	
	Yet all the wordes he us'd, were follow me.	John.1.43.

	Which *follow me,* must not be understood	E1ʳ
710	In fastes of Miracle, or earthly pleasure,	
	Nor striving, as he did in sweating blood,	
	To know no sin, but to attaine the treasure	

        Of never-fading joyes, of true salvation,
        By holding worldly pompe in detestation.   Jo.2.15.16.

715   For he who follows *Christ* must not respect
        Promotion, money, glory, ease, delight:
        But poverty, reproofe, and selfe-neglect,   Ro.13.14.
        Disgrace, teares, hunger, cold, thirst, scorne, despight;   Mat.10.37.
          Friends, father, mother, brethren, children, wife,   Mat.19.29.
720   Must be forgon, yea landes and goods and life.

        His Crosse must be tooke up, and as he was
        In meekenesse, sufferance, patience, and sobrietie,   Luk.9.23.
        Such must we be, thus must we over passe   1.Pet.2.21.22.
        The wars of frayltie, lusts sacietie,
725   We must lay downe our lives, and gaine the crowne
          Of life indeed, as life we do lay downe.   Mat.10.39.

        Unto the simple was the Lord revealed,
        To men obscure, disdained, and unlearned,
        His mercy from the mighty is concealed,   1.Cor.1.27.28.
730   He onely of the poore will be discerned,
          That they who to the world are poore in show, Joh.21.3.4.
          Might teach the world, and greatnesse overthrow. Mat.5.3.

        When to the barre of judgement we shall plead,
        And hold up guiltie hands, and sue for grace,
735   A booke shall be brought foorth thereon to read
        A *miserere mei*, but our case   Psal.51.1.
          Wilbe so hard, our sins will so deprave us,
          As then our booke will come too late to save us.

        For then our booke, the booke that doth containe, El^v
740   The words of life, *Christs bloody sweat* and passion,
        That booke will witnesse how we did disdaine
        His love, and drive us to a desperation,
          And then not every one that cries *Lord, Lord,*
          Shalbe receiv'd, for scorning of his word.   Mat.7.21.

745   Then shall the *Lord* reply, for you I sweated
        Sad drops of blood, and yet you would not love me:

> For you in agonie, my heart was heated,
> My wounds did cry, yet would ye not approve me:
> I know ye not, ye cursed creatures goe   Mat.25.41.
> Where damned soules do feele eternall woe.   Psa.6.8.
>
> Never may day give comfort to your cryes,
> But over-cloud you in perpetuall night:
> Never hence forward may your hopes arise,
> For to behold my life-restoring sight:
> Let death and divels torture you for ever,
> For you shalbe released *never, never.*

Here shall the *wantons* for a downy bed,
Be rackt on pallets of stil-burning steele:
Here shall the *glutton,* that hath dayly fed,
On choice of daintie diet, hourely feele
    Worse meat then toads, and beyond time be drencht
    In flames of fire, that never shalbe quencht.

Each moment shall the *killer,* be tormented
With [stabbes], that shall not so procure his death:
The *drunkard* that would never be contented
With drinking up whole flagons at a breath,
    Shalbe deni'd (as he with thirst is stung)
    A drop of water for to coole his tongue.

The *mony-hoording Miser* in his throat   E2^r
Shall swallow molten lead: the *spruce perfum'd*
Shall smell most loathsome brimstone: he who wrote
Soule-killing rimes, shall living be consum'd
    By such a gnawing worme, that never dies,   Mar.9.44.
    And heare in stead of musicke hellish cries.

No sin that is not washt in true repentance,
Shall scape in every sence to be perplexed:
But every sin and sinner shall have sentence,
To be without all end with horrors vexed.   Rom.6.23.
    And that not for a day, a month, a score
    Of yeares, or terme, or time, but evermore.

For as the God whom such have once offended,
Is infinite in majestie and power:
So shall their tortures be to them extended
Most infinite, and cease not to devoure:
    And after thousand thousand yeares, their sin
    Is no more free then when it did begin.

Loe here the view of soules condemn'd to hell,
Yet here is not the woorst of their indurance,
Their greater torments are for that they fell
From everlasting joyes, and knowne assurance
    Of Gods great glory: which so long remaines:
    As date-lesse as are their all-scorning paines.

Unto the blessed shall he change his voyce,
And with as much grim horror as he spoke,
The curse of wrath: so sweet shalbe the voyce,
That with a gratious mildnesse shall provoke
    Laughter and comfort to the long distrest,
    When he shall call them to his quiet rest.   Luke.6.21.

Come (will *he* say) ye blessed of my Father,
Unto the kingdome he hath chosen for you: Mat.25.34.
Since in the time of frailtie ye had rather
Then serve as worldlings, have the world abhor you:
    You gron'd, and sigh'd, and mortifide the flesh,
    Waiting till I, your sorrowes do refresh.

My *Bloody sweate* won pitie in your eyes,
And you poore soules did love me in my griefes,
My base reproofe you no way did despise.
Hungry, cold, naked, thirstie, your reliefes
    Did cheare my dying heart: for which regard
    Take *life eternall,* for your due reward.

Here shall the *Martyrs* slaine upon the Alter
Of persecution, for his glorious sake
By Bannishment, the sword, the axe, the halter,
The water, racke, the whip, the fierie stake,

815	No longer crie, *how long?* but rest in peace,	Rev.6.10.
	And have such pleasures as shall never cease.	

Here shall the meeke in spirit be exalted,
The naked clothd, in perfect robes of white: Ibid.11.
The poore that felt no tast of sin, be salted
820   With savours of exceeding great delight:
    The hungry fed, the sicke releev'd, the chast
    With honors, that shall never [fail] be grac't.

Those when the Trumpet from the flaming skies,
Shall sound a summons to the day of doome,   Mat.24.31.
825 Heard shrill even from the simple to the wise,   1.The.4.17.
Shall with the Lord of glory fairely come,
    And stand as witnesses, then to provoke   Psa.50.3.
    The Lord to judgment, whiles the heavens smoke.   Joel.2.30.

Here *Dives* from the flames he suffers in,   Luk.16.23.   E3^r
830 Lookes up, and faintly, on the Lords right hand,
(Who comes to pay the wages of his sin)
Beholds poore *Lazarus* in triumph stand
    And then his conscience prompts him, telling how
    As he did once scorne him, he scorns him now.

835 What boots complaints? or whither can he run
To hide him from that presence? all in vaine
He cals to mind the follyes he hath done,
But cannot ransome backe his time againe;
    Justice pronounceth, as it justly fitted:
840   *Sin shewd no pittie, sinne must not be pittied.*

Unto this Audit and severe accompt,
How we have liv'd? what words we spoke, what praier
We made? what thoughts we thought? how wee surmount
In goodnesse? how the poore we did repaire:
845   What can we answer? but in meeke accord
    Confesse us guiltie, and cry mercy Lord?

A sparrow cannot fall unto the ground
Without the providence of God above: Mat.10.29.

	Our haires are numbred, and we shalbe found	Ibid.30.
850	The heires of promise, as we hate or love:	
	The secrets of our hearts are not our owne,	
	Our hearts and secrets then will both be knowne.	1.Cor.4.5.

	Before the issue of which dolefull day,	
	When no excuse will be admitted there,	
855	A time is given, and a tongue to pray,	
	O who will then that precious time deferre?	
	But whiles the sufferance of our God is great,	
	Fly to the safety of his *Bloody sweate*.	

	His *bloody sweate* the comfortable matter,	E3ᵛ
860	That must renew us in the time of need,	
	Both meat and drink: blood, meat, and drink, the water,	
	The last to quicken, and the first to feed:	
	Water the seale of *Baptisme* doth present,	Eph.5.26.
	And *blood* his *supper*: each a sacrament.	John.6.55.

	See here in earnest meditations, now	
865	The mystery of all salvation,	Eph.1.9.10.
	How orderly God hath ordaind, and how	
	He wisely wrought it from the first creation,	
	So good this gracious God is to defend us,	
870	As he fore-thinks the means that must commend us.	

	When *Christ* prepar'd himselfe to die, and beare	
	The wrath of God that we in him might live:	
	The time of his sowre passion drawing neare,	
	In which he was his life for us to give,	
875	Retird alone his father to intreat,	
	His agonies brought forth a bloody sweat.	

	So when upon the crosse he had indur'd	
	The bitter pangs of hell, and breathd the last,	
	Confounding death that had his death procur'd	
880	When all the tide of cruell griefes was past,	
	A souldier with a speare did pierce his side,	
	When blood with water gushing was espied.	Joh.19.34.

Water and blood what could it else intend
Or wher-unto so likened could it be
But to the bloody sweat his soule did send
Before his death, opprest in agonie:
 That as the first before his death diminisht
 Death of the soule, this in his death that finisht.

He di'd indeed not as an actor dies
To die to day, and live againe to morrow,
In shew to please the audience, or disguise
The idle habit of inforced sorrow:
 The Crosse his stage was, and he plaid the part
 Of one that for his friend did pawne his heart.

His heart he pawnd, and yet not for his friend,
For who was friend to him, or who did love him?
But to his deadly foe he did extend,   *Colos.1.21.*
His dearest blood to them that did reprove him,
 For such as tooke his life from him, he gave
 Such life, as by his life they could not have.

Great miracle of love, redemptions wonder,
Where he that should be su'd to, sues to those:
Who would not sue to him, but still kept under
That better part which he in mercy chose:
 Rare president of value, which discovers
 How love is scant, where plenty is of lovers.

If we but looke into the little home,
The home of our owne selves, we may espie
How many pyrates still make haste to come
To wrecke our soules, whom whiles we do defie
 We entertaine, and freely, but unsought,
 Make marchandize of what we never bought.

The pearle and the treasures which the Lord
Did witnesse, were of an unvalued price: *Mat.13.44.45.46.*
Jesus did purchase of his owne accord
To free us from our death deserving vice,

And left us for an heritage, the gaine
Of life immortall ever to remaine.

Hels gaping wombe which every minute sunke   E4ᵛ
920   Millions of soules, and would not be content   Pro.27.20.
With streams of blood, which greedily it drunke,
But still cryde *more,* his mercy did prevent,
    For he shut up the jawes, and did acquit
    The rav'nous gorge of that devouring pit.

925   The ever empty swallow of the grave
And bottomlesse confusion of the deepe
His blood hath made in vaine, and this doth save
From dangers, such as dangers dayly keepe.
    Deaths sting it hath rebated and un-edg'd
930   Such soules as were in sorrowes bondage pledg'd.

What should a sinner doe? or whither flie
To hide him from his shame that ever wakes?
Poore man lesse then a man who cannot die,
Nor cannot live so much his Care mistakes,
935   And still he drawes destruction with his breath,
    As t'is all one to suffer life or death.

Sad thoughts like burning furies still pursue him,
And seeke his life who them alive doth cherrish,
Fond thoughts whose inward eyes no sooner view him
940   But kill that Maister, who once dead, they perish:
    His thoughts do tell his conscience of his thrall,
    His conscience makes him thinke that he must fall.

What shall he crie to mountaines to conceale him?
Or shall he beg, the seas to over-drench him?   Luk.23.30.
945   The mountaines are remov'd and cannot heale him   Psa.139.9.
The Seas are dry, and they cannot entrench him,   Rev.6.14.
    But ever as he hopes the light to shun,
    In groping for the night he findes the sunne.

A Sonne whose glory doth disclose abroade   F1ʳ
950   The secrets of his [hearte], and layes all open,

Lines out the sundry paths that he hath trode,
Unfolds the severall treasons he hath spoken:
    The inside of his bosome is apparant,   1.Joh.3.20.
    And he hath none excuse to pleade his warrant.

955 What can he now resolve, but to retire
Unto the sweat of *Christ,* and cleft in mind,
Humbled in meeke astonishment, desire
Comfort in this his bloody Bath to find:
    Which bloody sweat, when every helpe doth faile
960   To cure the soule, that onely doth availe.

Pure distillations are but vaine receits,
Curious to draine, but comfortlesse in tast,
Compounded Cordials are unwise deceits,
Whose vertue doth but with the present last:
965   *Christs* body is the Limbecke that must yeeld
    Distilled blood, our soules from death to shield.

If pleasures, honors, money, gifts, promotion,
Phisicke, restorative, repasted diet,
Ease, cost, delights, cold heate, prophane devotion,
970 Drinkes, purges, observation, courtly quiet,
    Or one, or all, the soules spots could expell,
    Great Kings had never ran so fast to hell.

The Princes of the *Sodomites,* the chiefes
Of *Aegypt, Achab, Eserod,* and the rest,
975 Had never felt the terrours of their griefes,
If *art* could have a remedy exprest,
    But therefore di'd they, cause they knew no good,
    To purge them in the streame of *Christ his blood.*

The [womane], painting *Jesabel,* the whore
980 Of th'*Israelitish* monarch, could not hide   2.Kin.9.30.
Her sins from God, but as her selfe was poore
In virtue, so she dy'd in naked pride:
    O had she seene *Christs bloody sweat* contriv'd   1.Kin.19.4.5.
    In his *Eliahs* griefe, she might have liv'd.

	But they whom worldly pleasures wrap in woe,	
985		
	Esteemd this sweat a fancie or a fable,	
	Which one day they will find was nothing so,	
	When to recall againe they are not able:	
	And then this blood which hath procurd a crowne	
990	Shalbe a flood, not to refresh but drowne.	

	What is a man but dust made up in forme?	Gen.3.19.
	Fraile, weake, corrupted: keeping time in motion,	
	A ship at sea, ore-turnd with every storme:	
	Eates, sleeps, and dies, unsetled in devotion:	
995	In health unbridled, in his yeares a span,	
	A fading bloome, and such a thing is man.	1.Pet.1.24.

Mans beautie but a frame made up in snow,
Immixt with waxe, which melts with every Sun,
Even so experience teacheth men to know,
1000　　How soone this worke of frailtie is undone:
　　　　　A winters frost, or summers parching heate,
　　　　　Doth soone this pictures ornament defeate.

Yet as a cunning fire-worke lighted glowes,
Spits and with hissing wonders dares the skies,
1005　Till being wasted, downe it fal, and showes
No more, his matter spent it weakely dies,
　　　　And vanisheth to aire and smoke, so men
　　　　In health are strong, but dying vanish then.

	Man as a cunning fire-worke in his power,	F2ʳ
1010	Dares God and heaven, and kicks against the Lord,	Psal.12.4.
	Till all his force be spent, then in an hower	
	Abates, decaies, fals of his owne accord:	
	Being indeed as nothing, in despaire	
	Of doing ill, fumes into smoke and aire.	

1015	But here is not the end of all his ils,	
	His greater soules vexation is behind,	
	A death which both the soule and body kils,	
	To which the miserable are confind:	Rev.14.18.

And then too late they wish to coole the heate,
1020 Of flames and brimstone, in *Christs bloody sweate.*

If one condemnd for some notorious fact,
Labour his pardon, and doth surely thinke
His life is safe: forgets his former act,
Doth revell, sweare, prophane, carouse and drinke,
1025 Whiles thus his jolly time he doth apply,
  One sayes that he within an hower must die;

How cold that newes strikes to his heart? his cheeks
How soone they change their merriment? and he
With what submission pensive, humbly seekes
1030 For grace to alter that unhop't decree?
  How would he promise, beg, protest, or give
  All that he had, or could procure to live.

Such is the case, who till the day draw neare,
Wherein we must surrender up the right
1035 We hold of living: do our soules appeare
Slaves to disorder, servants to delight:
  But when we are arrested to depart,
  Then we can feele the dolours of our heart.

Yet *Christ* is not regarded, who stood up   F2ᵛ
1040 And in the last day of the feast cride out,
Ho come to me, all ye who thirst, and sup   Jo.7.37.38.
Rivers of life, drinke freely round about:
  And if there come a scarcitie of food,   Joh.6.5.
  My flesh shalbe your bread, your drinke my blood.   Ibid.54.

1045 Dull eares who will not listen to this call?
Dull eyes who will not see this fount of ease?
Dull heart that will not shun temptations gall?
Dull soule that will not seeke this God to please?
  Dul eares, dul eyes, dul heart, dul soule, whose strife
1050 Nor heares, nor sees, nor thinks, nor seeks for life.

Life may be freed from everlasting wrath,
Which is prepar'd for those which will not live,

If they but aime to bathe them in the bath
Of *Christ* his blood, which he doth frankly give
   To cleanse and wash away each leprous spot,
   That use of sinne doth feed as sinne begot.

Besieged man-kind when the foe assaults,
Of number-lesse temptations, shrikes or feares,
Mew'd up in care, and yeeldeth to the faults,
Whom as a weighty burthen still he beares:
   And ere he loose the honour of the field,
   Doth like a turne-coat, to his weaknesse yeeld.

Where now is faith? where is that courage now
Which proud mortalitie presumes it hath?
Base servile frailtie doth despairing bow
To weare the fetters of consuming wrath,
   So cowards boast in time of peace, but flie
   When warres increase, and unremembred die.

Others there are, who smooth the front of sin,
And maske his ugly fore-head with the coulour
Of lust ingendred novelties, to win
Grace to their arts by making art seeme fuller:
   And they their foolish wits with pride to prove,
   Will strive forsooth to make a God of love.

They are the divels secretaries right,
Whose rules have drawne whole troopes of soules to hell
That might have else bene sav'd, they day and night
Toyle out their braines, that mischiefe might excell,
   They feele the whips whiles as they kisse the rod,
   By making lust the divell, and the god.

Love is no god, as some of wicked times
(Led with the dreaming dotage of their folly)
Have set him foorth in their lascivious rimes,
Bewitch'd with errors, and conceits unholy:
   It is a raging blood, affections blind,
   Which boiles both in the body and the mind.

But such whose lawfull thoughts, and honest heat,
Doth temperately move with chast desires,
To choose an equall partner, and beget
Like comforts by alike inkindled fires:
    Such find no doubt in union made so even,
    Sweet fruits of succors, and on earth a heaven.

Such find the pastures of their soules and hearts,
Refreshed by the soft distilling dew,
Of *Christs deare bloody sweate*, which still imparts
Plenty of life and joyes so surely trew,
    As like a barren ground they drinke the pleasure,
    Of that inestimable showre of treasure.

If every word we write, and speake, or thought   Mat.12.36. F3ᵛ
We thinke, or [deede] we do, or hower we spend,
Shall one day to a strict account be brought,
When shall be made a whole and finall end,
    Then all in vaine we shall [commend] that wit,
    Which hath in sinne or thought, or spoke, or writ.   Act.8.22.

Those Angels who as Porters guard the gate
Of Gods eternall kingdome, will controule
All entrance there, and curiously debate
Questions of quarrel with the trembling soule,
    And like some churlish officer at court,
    Keepe backe the presse of all the worser sort.

Here now the soule is baffaild whiles they chide,
What are ye? soules opprest: but whither presse ye?
Into the court of God here to abide,
What sicke? yes sicke: whom seeke ye to dresse ye?
    Christ our physition: who hath sent ye to him?   Mar.2.17.
    Our faith: what faith? such faith as comes to woe him.

Woe him for what? for life: where are your seales
Of pietie and truth? lost, lost: O fooles
Get hence? our wounded care appeales   Mat.22.11.
To mercy, promised in the sacred schooles:

To Justice? no to mercy we behave us:
Justice condemns you? yet will mercy save us.

Have you then bathd your sins? in what: in sweat?
What sweat? his bloody sweat: we have not known it:
Ah have you not? no: then you are to great
In sins, sins? sins, and those have overthrowne it:
  Hence soules away, ye are too late deluded,
  Thus are the wicked soules from heaven excluded.

Thus are the wicked soules from heaven excluded,   F4^r
And torturd in the horror of their feares,
Heavens gate is shut, when they would have intruded,
And al because they were too slacke in teares:
  Which are the ready tokens *Christ* hath lent,
  His bloody sweate on earth to represent.

Never was teare from any heart let fall,   Mat.5.4.
In true repentance, but the Lord of grace,
Hath seene and botled up, and kept it all
For such as must his saving health embrace:
  This is a rule in text for certaine given,
  An eye still drie doth seldome come to heaven.

He who can gush out teares as twere a flood,
Of christall sorrows, and a zeale unfained,
Doth purge his faults in *Christ* his sweat of blood,
And with his faults shal never more be stained,
  Stars in their brightnes shal not shine so glorious,
  Nor all the Kings on earth be so victorious.

Tis not enough to reade the Bible over,
Here to fold downe a leafe, and there to quote it,
Now to behold the Lord in blood, then hover
And range: but freely in thy heart to note it:
  For where the *Word* doth tel us *Christ* did bleed,
  And sweat, there must our thoghts both drink and feed.

Did but a King before a publicke view,
Imbrace and kisse his subject, how would fame

1155 Speed such a favour, how would people sue,
To grace their service by his onely name:
   So here doth *Christ* a much more [grace] impart,   Pro.23.26.
   And cryes to all, *My sonne give me thy heart.*

My sonne give me thy heart, and in exchange   F4^v
1160 Take mine, I both will kisse thee and embrace thee: Can.1.1.
What heavenly words are in this voyce? O strange?
See sinner how the God of love doth grace thee,
   My sonne give me thy heart, but give me thine
   And I will sweat in blood, to pawne thee mine.

1165 God knocks, then let us open: let not hell
Barre out the King of mercie: he intreates,
Let not the divell disswade: God comes to dwell
With men, let men him entertaine: he sweates
   For us, let us for him like dutie keepe:
1170   He sweated blood, let us in sorrow weepe.

A man that lives in pleasures, as his dayes
Increase, the dayes past over seeme a dreame:
Stil newer joy, more hope of joy bewrayes,
And as he lives, he lives still in extreame:
1175   He wakes to sleepe, and sleeps in hope to wake:
   So here is all the pleasure he can take.

Is this a life? O what a life is this?
To covet age, which being come is hated:
Whose end is death, which death the utmost is
1180 Of ev'ry lease that in the grave is dated:
   They that enjoy what their owne hearts can crave
   Crave onely time, which brings them to the grave.

And here they die, and dying once die all,
Die al as they unworthily have liv'd,
1185 No part of them survives, but feeles the thral
Of life in death, and death of life depriv'd:
   Thus then the promise of al the worlds desire,
   Beares life to die, then dies [to life intire].

	Weary unrest, and restlesse wearie woe,	G1ʳ
1190	That leads to pleasures in their birth abortive:	
	How much more better were it to forgoe	
	A life so grievous, and a death so sportive?	

  And rest the griefes so numberlesse and great,
  In the sweet slumber of his bloody sweat?

1195 When *Pharaohs* heart was hardned, and deny'd
  Freedome to *Israel*, the Lord to scourge   Exo.7.3.
  Pharaohs ambition and detested pride,   Ibid.19.20.
  Which mercy could not win, nor mildnesse urge:
   Commanded *Aaron* when he toucht the flood,
1200 Th' *Aegyptian* waters all were turnd to blood.

  Water was turnd to blood, but in this sweat
  Here blood is turnd to water: as the first
  Betoken'd plagues for sins, the last doth treat
  Redemption from those sins, who were accurst:
1205   The first his wrath, the last doth shew his love,
   His justice this did, that his mercy prove.

  By blood offences in the written law,
  Unto the law of grace were reconciled;
  By blood offences must redemption draw,   Heb.9.13.14.
1210 From blood; which blood the Gospel now is stiled:
   The law, the blood of Goats and buls desired,
   The Gospel hath the blood of *Christ* required.

  A surety for his friend that is arrested,
  Kept close in prison, bound in yron chaines,
1215 Is hungry, cold, and weary, sicke, and wrested
  To change of inward griefes, and outward paines:
   Deserves from him for whom he [is] asseast,
   If not a full reward, yet thanks at least.

  So he, who in the absence of his friend,   G1ᵛ
1220 Whom malice hath upbraided with abuse,
  Doth undertake his quarrell to defend,
  Clearing the imputation with excuse,

Fights and is wounded; being wounded dyes,
May justly claime the tribute of his eyes.

1225 *Jesus*, the sonne of God was at our sute
Arested, and imprison'd in the frame
Of flesh; was fetter'd, and of no repute,   Joh.1.14.
Tyr'd with his griefes, the by-word of defame,
  All this he was, and did, yet to relieve him,
1230 Wee scarce can in our hearts finde thankes to give him.

Hee undertooke our quarrell with the Devill,
When we were all unable to resist,   Rev.12.7.8.
And in that quarrell to discharge our evill,   Luk.1.71.
Was wounded to the death, yet wee persist
1235   Too obstinate in malice, and forebeare
  Upon his bleeding wounds to shed one teare.

Wee see upon his furrow-[crowned] face
The print of sorrowes stampe, yet not regard him;
Wee see his honour level'd with disgrace,
1240 Yet with our only thankes will not reward him:
  'Tis bad to sin; sin 'tis to be ungratefull,
  Sin is abhorr'd, unthankfulnesse is hatefull.

Goe then Remembrance, tell that Queene of Reason
(Fayre bride to *Christ*) the Soule her lover comes,   Mat.25.1.
1245 Deckt in his wedding robes, and courts the season   Rev.21.9.
With choyce of pleasures, and with many [sums]
  Of sure deserts, invites this wandring Queene,
  To be as true as he to her hath beene.

Ladie (quoth hee) thy fortunes have not won   G2^r
1250 My heart to love, thy beauty cannot force mee
To wanton dotage, what my care hath done,
No time shall alter, no reports divorce mee:
  For to my chaster flames thy zeale gave fuell,
  And I will guard thee, if thou be not cruell.

1255 No dower from thy treasuries I crave,
No wanton dilliance in a bed of lust,

Thy purenesse is the portion I would have,
Artlesse simplicitie and steedy trust: Rom.16.19.
    And if thou prove but constant to implore
    Vertue with goodnesse, I will aske no more.

Heere vowes the soule virginity, and sweares Cant.2.16.
Shee will bee only his, and meanes to doe it,
Untill distracted in her fleshly feares,
She shrinkes from her first troth when she comes to it,
    And like a strumpet false, she heere forswore,
    That plighted promise she had made before.

Simplicitie was woo'd by youthfull lust,
And would not yeeld; young lust did see old sinne,
Old sin assaults simplicitie, whose trust
Thus to make lesse she trimly doth beginne:
    Faire daughter listen, time will come when thou
    Shalt change thy hue, and be as I am now.

Unhealthie, old, forsaken, and despis'd,
I lead a life, who was adored then;
Beautie amidst the croppe is only priz'd,
Faire soules, in youth, are chiefly lik'd of men:
    But when my time did court me I for-went it,
    And lost my daies, and now I doe repent it.

Daughter wilt thou alone live unpossest, G2ᵛ
Of youths best ornaments and natures joyes?
Wilt thou deny to be a mother blest,
In pretty daughters, and more pretty boyes?
    O no, had not our mothers tooke their lot,
    Wee had bene yet unborne and unbegot.

Heaven hath ordained thee to be sweet on earth,
Both love and youth do homage to thine eyes,
And wilt thou curbe thy selfe of pleasures mirth?
By vainely striving how to be precise?
    She that hath fairenesse were as good have none,
    If foolishly she keepe it all for one.

Yet you forsooth young mistresse in the folly,
Of standing on some pleasure threatning text,
Dreame of some great renowne, in being holly,
Reade this, and that, and that, and what is next:
 I know not what, and ever vainly plod,
 In hope to marry with the Sonne of God.

No doubt: come yet, Ile tell a safer way,
If you will needs to that ambition clime,
Do it at last, but spend thy youth in play,
Revell, enjoy the freedome of the time:
 And when y'are old, unfit for sport, bereaven
 Of youth and joyes, then you may think on heaven.

Tush daughter, God respects thee in thine age,   Eze.18.21.22.
As well as in thy prime, and he will beare
With flesh and blood, then seeke not to ingage
Best of delight, before delights do weare:
 And thou to God maist be (my words are truth)
 As welcome in thine age, as in thy youth.

Wonne is the soule with this, or rather lost,   G3^r
Sins sweet temptation hath undon the zone
Of Maiden chastitye, the feeld is lost,
Lust hath prevailde and *Christ* is left alone.
 For now the soule resolves that sports unfold
 Law to the young, repentance fits the old.

Yet thus that kinde good God will not give over,
But once againe by parley doth attempt,
To court this perjur'd dame: and like a lover
Scorn'd of his Lady from all hope exempt,
 Pittyes the shipwracke of her tainted name,
 And yet by Mariage would recure her fame.

I know (quoth *Christ*) I love thee, els I would not,
Have swimd unto thee in a Sea of blood:
More testifie my love thou know'st I could not,
Long have I strove to bring [thy] soule to good:

   And witnesse here this crimson sweat, howe I,
   (O soule of man) doe for thy whoredomes dye.

How often in my bosome did I sue
To have thee lodg'd, how often did I call thee   Luk.13.34.
From strange imbracements; from affections new,
Whose only surfeit did too soone inthrall thee?
  And yet thou would'st not come, till age bereft thee,
  Then I must take thee when all els have left thee:

When yeeres have made thee all unfit for action,
When lust hath suckt thy Marrow drye, and those
With whom thou hadst conspir'd in trothles faction,
Shall shun thy lewdnesse, and deride thy woes:
  To mee thou then wilt come and I must hide
  The knowne defects of thy declined pride:

Call but to minde what 'tis to bee a whoore,   G3ᵛ
A whoore, the worst of creatures, trades her pleasures
With all diseases, lives till she be poore;
Sels all to buy damnation, never measures
  Or shame, or health, but makes her bodies mart
  Her soules confusion; such an one thou art.   Heb.13.4.

And though perhaps temptation might perswade thee,
That even the winter of thine age shall finde,
If thou repent, mercie from him that made thee,
Bee not secure, for thou shalt feele thy minde
  So farre devided, so corruptly bent,
  As then thou canst not if thou wouldst repent.

Redeeme the poore remainder of thy daies,
Deaden the life of thy lascivious lust,
Take pittie on thy selfe, forsake thy waies   Eze.18.31.
Of licorish bondage, hate what is unjust,
  Be trewe to my desires, when sin assaults,
  And Ile forget thy wrongs, forgive thy faults.

Did ever man speake thus! was ever creature
In such a language courted, when the heat

Of wilfull madnesse wrought the soules defeature,
The God that should have punisht, doth intreat:
   Hee in whose power it is to scourge the sinner,
   With words of mildnesse doth assay to win her.   Mat.11.28.

Reade in this morrall, if it may be term'd so,
Christs love, the soules infection, this is willing,
That wilfull, and eschues to be confirm'd so
That from his love she may behold distilling,
   A sweat of blood, as if his blood complaines
   To tell her of the horrors he sustaines.

Guilt reades a lecture of her foule misdeeds,   G4^r
And bids her looke upon this streame of red,
Layes to her view the speaking sweat that bleeds,
When she lyes gasping on her death-full bed:
   And then her conscience, summon'd to the doome
   Of Judgement, hastes unto her toombe.

When now o God (she cries) and have I liv'd,
Ah shall I live no more? Is grace and beautie
Vanisht so soone, of all respect depriv'd?
Must pompe and state renounce her wonted dutie?
   Must my devided soule contemn'd and lost,
   Surrender up my short appalled Ghost?

Inconstant fate, and wilt thou change thy course,
And leave mee to the terrors of my dread?
Can gold prolong no life? Must life by force
Be shadowed with the ruines of the dead?
   'Tis bad to die; but oh, I feele the curse   Joh.8.9.
   Of my owne conscience doth accuse mee worse.   Rom.2.15.

Oh, had I twentie thousand mints of treasure,
Kingdoms to morgage, worlds within my power,
I would give all, but for a little leasure,
A little little minute, one small hower,
   That I might sue for grace, from grace cast downe,
   But oh, I see my [angry] God doth frowne.

	Bee not, O be not mov'd thou glorious sonne,	
	Time was when thou didst sue to mee, I crave	
1395	Thy bountie of thy bloodie sweat; and runne	
	With confident assurance to my grave:	Psal.46.2.

      Bee not, O be not mov'd thou glorious sonne,
      Time was when thou didst sue to mee, I crave
1395 Thy bountie of thy bloodie sweat; and runne
      With confident assurance to my grave: Psal.46.2.
        Thou art my spouse, I am thy bride, esteeme mee,
        None but my Christ, none did but hee redeeme mee.

      Heare I disclaime the follies of my will,   G4ᵛ
1400 Heare I returne the sinnes my frailties gave mee:
      Heare I forsake my heart-inveigling ill,
      Heare fly I to his onlie blood did save me:
        Mercie, O mercie, I commend as even
        My whordomes to the dust, my soule to heaven.

1405 *Christ* is appeas'd, and where the soule is prest
      With sence of knowinge shee hath done amisse,
      Asking for grace, shee is with grace redrest,
      Her case is pittied, shee forgiven is,   Mat.7.7.
        But this so seldome hapneth and so rare,
1410   Scant two such soules amongst a million are.

      Presumption leads the readie path to hell,
      For whilst wee looke on mercie we forget
      The equallnes of *Justice*, and compell
      Our soules to runne into a greater debt,
1415   That God is mercifull 'tis true, so must
        Our bouldnes eke remember hee is just.   Pro.13.10.
                                                                           Rom.11.20.
      Oft hath bin seene a woman who hath lov'd
      Some constant friend who black mischance hath slain
      How looking on his wounds shee hath bin mov'd
1420 To rent her haire and fatallie complaine,
        Cursing her birth and life, refraining food,
        Kissinge the silent murmur of his bloode.

      Weeping uppon his bodie, as if teares
      Could make the gaping windowes that let in
1425 Ungentell Death close up, and then inferres:
      Wrech, wreched villiane! could not such lookes win

Remorce in thy hard hart! with manie words
Which then against the butcher griefe affords.

Can this a woman doe? and should the soule,   H1^r
Behold her lover, Christ slaine, not lamenting,
Or should she entertaine a thought so foule,
As to gaze upon his wounds without repenting:
   Should wanton carnall love so much deplore,
   And shall not true religion doe much more?

A Soule which in the Gospell reads the Storie
Of Christs most bloodie sweat, and deadly wounds,
Cannot, in rules of zeale, but be most sorie,
Whilst sorrow mingled with remorce confounds   Joh.20.11.
   Reason and sence, that spectacle to pittie,
   Whilst both sigh out this lamentable dittie.

And art thou dead! and must mine eyes behold,
The Lord of glorie crucifi'd for mee!
And is he dead, is his sweet bodie cold!
Made earth with earth, and doe I live to see,
   The great acquittance of my debt discharg'd,
   Seal'd with his blood, that I might be inlarg'd.

Unhappie hand that gave the fatall stroke,
Which wrought the subject of my weeping eyes,
But most unhappie mee, who did provoke
With blushlesse sinnes, the cause for which hee dies: Gal.1.4.
   But I, if it were possible, would faine,
   With kissing of his wounds, fetch life againe.

Take heere the tribute of my mourning heart,
A poore weake widowed souls complaints remaining,
Fit earnest of my death-desiring smart,
Smarting in death, and dying in complaining:
   As my offences did my Saviour peirce,   Psal.22.16.
   So with my sorrowes will I decke his hearce.

First, I abjure all sin-contriving thoughts,   H1^v
Heere I renounce each sin-inviting word,

Then ev'ry sin-effecting acte, which dotes
On flesh, I will no more: let Heaven record
   My fast indissoluble vowes, I strive
   For *Christ* alone, his votarie to live.

His wounds shall be my cloyster, heere immur'd,
Ile sequester my solace from the living:
His drops of blood my beads, with which secur'd   1.Pet.2.24.
Ile score the prayers of my heart mis-giving:
   My waxen Taper, whose cleere light applies
   Light to my blindnesse, shall be his faire eyes.

My booke, the Legend of his Storie; Zeale,
The incense I will offer up; Contrition
My penance; the confession I reveale,
My guilt; my Hope the comforts of fruition;
   His spirit my Confessor; Faith the gift,
   Which must absolve mee, and his Love my shrift.

Whiles on the Alter of his Innocence,
Ile lay the poore oblation of my heart:
His Death shall be the Pardon to dispence
With all my sins, set free in every part:
   My teares the holy water, and the fires
   To burne this sacrifice, my chaste desires.

And now, my God, no day shall overslip mee,
But I will meditate on thy great passion;
My selfe-accusing conscience shall so whip mee,
As I will neede no other condemnation:
   Bee thou but pleas'd to pittie those my feares,
   And ev'ry day Ile wet thy tombe with teares.

This, if a man can picke out time to doe,   H2ʳ
His conscience may assure him that he is
A sanctifi'd creature, and cald to
The happie tydings of eternall blisse:
   And thus he may be sure that for *Christs* sake,
   Christs bloodie sweat, he doth indeed pertake.

1495 So is he purg'd with water, fed with blood,
       Regenerate in Baptisme, and made whole
       By eating the Lords Supper, tasting good
       In the repasted diet of his soule:
           Whereby those bloodie streames of sweat did staine
1500   The cheekes of *Christ*, were not all spent in vaine.

       God will not thinke the heavinesse he felt,
       Even to the death, when he was man with us,
       Paynes cast-away: but as in love he dealt
       With soule-endangered men by suffring thus:
1505   Yet will he not repent, when he shall know
           What thankfulnesse in heart we doe bestow.   Psal.50.14.

       The crimson dye of his carnation red,
       Hath washt the soule in puritie of white,   Esay.1.18.
       The conduit of the water that he bled,
1510   Hath dy'd the soule in graine of wisht delight:
           Water hath dy'd, and blood hath washt, 'tis strange,
           But true; his vertue hath procur'd this change.

       Nor is it strange since the most curious eye
       That saw him lead his solitary life,
1515   Whiles he was man on earth, could not espie
       One blemish in his actions, prone to strife,
           But all he spoke, or did, was wonders theame,
           For even the coate he wore was without seame. Joh.19.23.

       For even the coate he wore was without seame,   H2ᵛ
1520   Implying his sinceritie and truth,
       Unmov'd in joy, undaunted in extreame,
       Nor fearing age, nor vainly spending youth:
           Loving where he was hated, ayming still
           To save from death, such as were bent to kill.

1525   To save from death, such as were bent to kill,
       Men, bloodied in the feates of cruell hate,
       Of hatefull crueltie, and to fulfill
       The wrath and measure of a wofull state:

	Yet those with gentle sighes, and teares, his ayme,
1530	Strove from the day of vengeance to reclaime.

	Strove, from the day of vengeance to reclaime,	
	A day of vengeance, when they shall behold	
	His wounds, to whom they gave a deadly maime,	Zech.13.6.
	Crying *Revenge*, and they themselves be sold	
1535	Unto an heavie doome, yet *Christ*, who saw it	
	With meeke perswasions labour'd to withdraw it.	

	With meeke perswasions labour'd to withdraw it,	1.Pet.2.21.
	And taught them by example how to shun	
	Death, whiles they liv'd, who would not over awe it,	
1540	But headlong to their owne destruction run:	
	Yet He, when no invitement could intreat,	
	Wept for their errors in his *bloodie sweat*.	

	Wept for their errors in his *bloodie sweat*,
	His *bloodie sweat*, that crucifi'd delight,
1545	Delight, which all was smoother'd in a heat,
	An heat of passion, an unsollac't sight:
	Unsollac't sight, when hee with griefes repleat,
	Wept for sins error in his *bloodie sweat*.

	Eyes were the Instruments ordayn'd to weepe,	H3ʳ
1550	But eyes in such a case must not suffice;	
	For his whole bodie did due order keepe,	
	It undertooke the office of his eyes,	
	That as his eyes his precious teares did waste,	
	So did his heart, bleede teares of blood as fast.	

	Wherein his sorrowes sadly did abound,
1555	Not measur'd by compulsion, but free will,
	That as his eyes, so might his heart be drown'd,
	Surcharg'd with burthens of amazing ill:
	And if his shedding teares his blood did paine,
1560	His drops of blood, pai'd back his teares againe.

	His eye was but an echo to his heart,
	Which answer'd every accent of his woe,

While both his eye and heart did beare a part,
As said the one, the other echo'd so:
   Was ever man as I am? (quoth his eyes)   Lamen.3.1.
   I am, (alas) his heavie heart replyes.

His Eyes cry out in teares, *O cruell paine!*
O cruell paine his Heart saies! (quoth his Eyes)
And must I then be slaine? I must be slaine
Answeres his Heart, his eyes, *Ah let me die,*
   Me die, his Heart; his Eyes *dye, dye content,*
   I die content, his Heart, thus both consent.

Not like the fawning of some subtile queane,
Some *Dalilah,* that flatters and beguiles,   Judg.16.4.
Knowing Arts rule, how to abuse the meane,
To laugh in teares, and both to weepe in smiles:
   Christ could not doe so, he wept teares in deed,
   Such teares as 'twas all one to weepe or bleed.

He wept not to deceive, but to revive;   H3ᵛ
He bleeded not in shew, but bled in proofe:
Not like the Crocodile, life to deprive,
But gave such life, as nere was; not aloofe:
   He wept, he bled, he bled, he wept a flood,
   Blood in his teares, and water in his blood.

Weeping and bleeding for offending men,
His *bloodie sweat* in agonies so fitted,
As for his enemies he groned then,
So for his owne, and sins by both committed:
   His enemies conceiv'd a fatall loathing,
   His owne perceiving all, conceived nothing.

Those few Apostles who had heard him teach,
And knew him to be Gods begotten sonne,
They 'mongst whom he every day did preach,
Seeing the miracles that he had done:
   Were weake in faith, in understanding dull,
   Poore in their plentie, sterv'd with being full.

Blindnesse so farre their ignorance did tempt,
With weaknesse of beliefe (ambitions feast)
As knowing *Christ* was come, yet still they dreamt
Of pettie Kings, or being Dukes at least:
   Supposing *Christ's* spirituall Kingdomes mirth
   Contain'd a goodly Kingdome here on earth.

And as the Anti-christian throne is now
Propt up with scarlet robes and triple crownes,
To vassaile Princes rights, and to allow
All as it likes, or hates, with smiles or frownes:
   Commanding, forcing, with his proud decree,
   Such did they hope the throne of *Christ* should bee.

For when the Lord had finisht now his errant,
Returning to his Father that had sent him,
Sealing his power with his deaths strict warrant,
When neither Hell nor Sathan could prevent him:
   Yet dreamt they on, and said Lord (as before)   Acts.1.6.
   Wilt thou thy Kingdom now to us restore?

Could this but breed his griefe, when he foresaw
Peters deniall, his Apostles scatter'd?   Luk.22.57.
His owne to feele the rigour of the Law,   Joh.16.32.
Zeale cold, Faith dead, Hope lost, frailtie batter'd:
   Devisions breeding, Kings aspiring great?
   All these, and such like brought his *bloodie sweat*.

For shortly he beheld the comming curse,
Upon the sacred Scriptures Commentaries,
How, though the Jewes were nought, a people worse,
Whose studies are the Devils Seminaries,
   Should make the name of *Jesus,* the disguise   Mat.24.23.24.
   Of countenancing impudence and lyes.

Such, like a nose of waxe, doe wrest the word
To colour sinne, and hellishly pervert
Christs sacred Gospell, whiles with one accord
They boast the glorie of their owne desert:

Damning the simple and the poore in minde,
As serves their lusts, *Blinde guides to lead the blinde.*

All those the Lord foresaw, and gron'd in Spirit,
Sweated in blood, was heavie to the death,
That so his precious passion, blamelesse merit,
Should be abus'd, that he had giv'n his breath,
 His life, his ghost, his soule, yet could not win
 Such wretched creatures, from inchanting sin.

Inchanting sinne, that with it's cunning charmes   H4ᵛ
Luls men in death-full sleepes, and slily makes
Impostum'd ulcers of unsenced harmes,
Rockes them in Lethargies, and never wakes   Prov.2.10.
 Reason, to feele the bane-impotion'd wrath,
 Which by such dead securitie it hath.

This was the cause that from our Saviour drew
A *bloodie sweat*, so grievous to be borne,
As did the eyes of cruell men but view,
How with this bloodie tempest he was worne,
 Humane compassion could not choose but melt,
 To thinke upon the sorrowes which he felt.

No measure did his payned soule acquaint
With ease or respite, no Arithmeticke
Cast up the summe of his unheard complaint,
No heart conceive the dolours that did pricke
 With fiery stings, his manhood, and appall
 His face with streames, which burst in twain his gall.

For as a River running in a round,
Having no vent or sluce to slide away,
Will make, by force, eruptions in the ground,
Drowne all the neighbour-land, and never stay,
 Till with a violent course and headlong rage,
 It slacke his strength, and of it selfe asswage.

Even so the tide of many griefes abounding,
Sweld in the bosome of the Sonne of God,

1665 Still growing to a head, and still confounding
His fraile mortalitie (deepe horrors rod)
   Till bursting foorth with might and furie great,
   It drown'd his bodie in a *bloodie sweat*.

Who ever saw (as often hath beene seene)
1670 A shoure of blood, but thought it did portend
Some doome of Judgement, or some angry teene
Of heavens-incensed King? So heere the end
   Of this strange bloodie raine, doth shew in briefe,
   How shortly *Christ* was to be wrapt in griefe.

11ʳ

1675 The pangs of death, th'ntollerable paines,
Which wofull creatures were to undergoe;
The man *Christ Jesus*, in this sweat sustaines,
Consuming wrath, and soule-devouring woe
   He felt, that he, us men might timely free,
1680   From Gods unchanging, and divine Decree.

Not that his death could abrogate the will
Of his great Father, for he aym'd not to it;
But that, in death, he wholly might fulfill
The eternall Justice, as hee came to doe it:
1685   Who as hee, death from men for sin required,
   Had in his Sons death, more than death desired.

Yet neither did the *Death* or *Bloodie sweat*
Of *Christ,* extend to soules ordain'd to Hell:
But to the chosen, and elect, beget
1690 A double life, although the Scriptures tell
   How this meeke *Lambe of God* did chiefly come
   To call the lost sheepe, and the strayers home.

Mat.9.13.
1.Tim.1.13.

Looke how the blessed doe pertake the good
(Sweete pledge of bountie, precious Seale of Joyes)
1695 Which issues from his *Water* and his *Blood,*
So both alike the *Reprobate* destroyes:
   Gods mercies to the *Righteous,* to his foes
   Are Justice, to augment their endlesse woes.

When *Isack's* seede fled from th'*Egyptian* force,   11ᵛ
And through the Red Sea tooke the readie way,
The waters stood on heapes, and staid their course,
Both waves and windes the passage did obey: Psal.78.13.
    And in those waters safely past on ground,
    In which, whiles *Pharaoh* follow'd, he was drown'd.   Exo.14.28.

Whereby, as water sav'd the Lords Elect,
And led them through the terrors of the deepe,
So water, to them of a dev'lish sect,
Prov'd sodaine death, and never-waking sleepe:
    Christs bloodie sweat is that Red Sea, whose power   1.Cor.10.
    Secures the good, and doth the bad devoure.   1.4.

The Cloude and fierie Piller that gave light
Unto the children, in the desert plaines;
The one by day, the other shin'd by night,
Guiding their journeis, comforting their paines;   Exo.13.21.
    Were to the Hoast of *Egypt*, mistes obscure   Exo.14.20.
    To blind their eyes, and certaine death procure.

Which burning Pillar, and which shining Cloud,
Is *Christ*, unto whose blood such are baptiz'd,   1.Cor.10.4.
As by the Holy Spirit are allow'd,
When otherwise, all such as are despis'd
    Are darkned in the comforts of their sight,
    And loose the glorie of this holy light.

A greater light, more holy and Divine,
Surpassing all the splendour of the Sun,
Could never to the eyes of mortals shine,
Then this most sacred *Blood*, which hath undon,
    And laid to publick view the Mount of Evill,
    Which both was fram'd, and colourd by the Devill.

In after-times, when in the winters cold,   12ʳ
Folkes use to warme them by their nightly fires;
Such Parents as the time of life termes old,
Wasting the season, as the night requires:

In stead of tales, may to their children tell,
What to the *Lord of glorie* once befell.

1735 Once, may they say, (my childe) a time there was,
When men were beasts, so cruelly they liv'd,
As they did nights and dayes in pleasure passe,
Like some of Reason and of Sence depriv'd:
 Not fearing God, or loving man, giv'n ore
1740 To Lust and Will, as beasts could doe no more.

The naughtie Devill slylie did intice,
By sensuall sports and pittilesse deceits,
Our weake fore-fathers to insnaring vice;
Masking his tyrannie with wanton baites:
1745 And wee, in them, did every thing he wil'd us,
 Till the foule feind (my childe) had almost kild us.

But straight, when our good God almightie saw,
How neere unto the Pit-hole wee were brought,
For being not obedient to his Law,
1750 He forthwith of a remedie bethought: Eph.1.9.10.
 And hee, to save us from this wicked Feind,
 His onely *Sonne* into the world did send.

A lovely *Sonne* (my childe) a daintie boy,
Who had a cheeke as red as any cherie,
1755 Sweete babie, was his mothers only joy,
And made her heavie heart full often merie:
 Who, though he were Gods Son, yet like a stranger,
 Hee in a Stable borne was, in a Manger.   Luk.2.7.

And poore, God knowes he was, (my childe) not fine, 12ᵛ
1760 Or like a gentleman in gay attyre:
But simple clothes hee had, which was a signe
How little to be proud, hee did desire:
 Yet if hee would have sought for worldly grace,
 Hee might have gone in silke, and golden lace.

1765 When he was twelve yeeres old (marke this my child)
Hee was a perfect Scholer, and did pose

	Great learned clarkes, and Doctors, but so milde	Luk.2.46.
	As hee would never chide, but rather chose	
	To teach then anger, and one might perswade him	
1770	To doe whats'ever any bodie bad him.	

Thirtie good yeeres and odde, this blessed man,
Liv'd on the earth; in all which time he seem'd
So comfortlesse, with lookes so pale and wan,
As if he had not bin by men esteem'd,
    Full many an hungry meale he made, and lay   Luk.[12.]23.
    Bare-leg'd and bare-foote many a day.

Hee never laugh'd, but he did evermore
Weepe, weepe continually; and (O my child)
Hee never did none harm; he holpt the poore,
Cur'd the diseas'd, and such as were beguild
    With witches, and with wicked things (God blesse us)
    He drove them from us when they would oppres us.

And hee made much of children, and did good
To every one, yet wicked men did strive   Mat.19.14.
To take away his life, and shed his blood,
Whiles yet this blessed *Jesus* was alive:
    And on a time, he was so much dismaid,
    Hee *sweated blood*, as he his prayers said.   Luk.22.44.

But what is worse then this, (hard-hearted Jewes)   13ʳ
Did hang this good good man upon the crosse,
Nayling his feet and hands, and did misuse
This gentle soule, whom they did fiercely tosse
    From post to pillar, and would not be still'd,
    Untill they had this, our *Redeemer* kill'd.

Heere now, may bee, the prettie childe will weepe,
And aske his parents why they us'd him so;
To which they may reply, that God did keepe
His soule alive, though life he did forgoe:
    For *Christ* (my childe) so dy'd, then may they tell,
    That every one might be redeem'd from hell.

Much might be added more, to spend the howers,
In better leasure then an anticke tale;
Teaching the sillie hearers how the powers
Above reserv'd us from the Devils sale:
    Whom had not *Christ* his blood regain'd the [wreath]
    Of life, all us lost, sin had sold to death.

Come then, sad Patron of this *bloodie sweat*,
And with thine everlasting comforts cherish
Unfenced *Faith*, which daily is beset
With treasons, which intice the soule to perish:
    In the delicious *Bath* of *Blood* and *Water*,
    Cleance leporous Soules, and Hels dominion batter.

And here, my God, the glorious Sonne of peace,
I close the musicke of my weeping song;
And further to inlarge, thy sorrowes cease,
Beseeching that thy Spirit may be strong,
    To move my heart, and gently to commit
    To meditations, all the lines I writ.

Let not the frailtie of my youth misled,   Psal.25.7.   13ᵛ
Be once remembred in the day of grace;
Let not the bloodie drops which thou hast bled,
Condemne me guiltie; let thy wounds deface
    The wounds of mine infection, now begin
    Throughly to wash mee from mine odious sin.   Psal.51.2.

The howres and daies which I have spent in vaine,
In fruitlesse studies, and inventive pleasure,
Redeeme, O *Christ*, and call them backe againe,
Doe not, in Judgement, mine offences measure:
    But, in thy mercies, hide my faults; protect
    My sighes, let thy love cover my defect.

Heere, Saviour of the world, worke that I may
Begin to live anew, and in this theame
Of thy sad *bloodie sweat*, learne out the way
Of life indeed, and wake mee from the dreame

1835   Wherein my Soule long slept, and felt the terrour,
        Of double two Apprentiships to errour.

        And now, my God, if I discharged have,
        This imposition of thine heavenly taske,
        Some token of thy being pleas'd I crave,   Jud.6.37.
1840   Some certaine knowledge of thy will I aske:
            For Heaven, and Angels with my soule record,
            I no way have traduc'd the written word.

        No malice to detract from rules of State,
        No singuler conceit to purchace fame,
1845   No pointing at some person, neither hate
        To any private wrongs, have made mee name
            The Plurisies of sin; but as thy *Sweat*
            All sins hath purg'd, all sins I did repeat.

        For which, as first thy Spirit did invite,   14ʳ
1850   In holy raptures to advance my minde,
        From earthly slime, of holy things to write;
        So having written, likewise let mee finde
            Of thy most precious priviledge, some token
            To grace the trueth of all that hath bin spoken.

1855   Heere, in the pensive solace of my Soule,
        Me thought, a soft coole winde did gently breath,
        As if my spirit were now transported whole,
        Unto another life, from carnall death:
            When straight a shining light perfum'd the roome,
1860   Out of which light, a whispring voyce did come.

        Rest there (it said) and toyle thee now no more,
        Knit up the period of thy trembling Stile;
        And learne to live, not as thou didst before,
        But in a smoother course; and I the while,
1865   Will teach thee how thou shalt attaine the place,
            Where quiet soules doe end their happie race.

        For since thou hast with such modest care,
        (Although thy verse doe want the grace of words)

	Limn'd out my wounds, and told them as they are,	
1870	So lively as thy simple skill affords:	Mar.12.43.
	Ile take thy meaning in the better part,	
	And for thine offring will accept thy heart.	

      May bee, some wandring eye that shall survey
      This wonder of my *Sweat*, in those thy numbers,
1875 Will take a truce with time, and shake away
      From off his Soule, the lusts wherein it slumbers:
          Then hast thou hid a multitude of sin,   Jam.5.20.
          If all thy paines, one Soule from ruine win.

      And blessedly hereafter shall succeed,   14^v
1880 Thy studies and thy labours, if thou shunne
      The path that thou hast trode, and wilt take heed
      To undoe the many follies thou hast done:
          For if thou have respect unto my Lawes,
          Before my Father I will plead thy cause.

1885 But thou, marke well these words; *A time shall be*
      When *Reason* shall beate downe the force of might,
      And *Natures Sonnes* shall wish for peace, but see
      Th'effects of blood, and feele the scourge of fight:
          Now unrespected, and not felt: but men
1890   Shall, what they had unprais'd, remember then.

      Happie the soule that sleepes in peace, and thou,
      Provide against such daies, watch, fast, and crave
      A dissolution, and prepare thee how   Phil.2.12.
      Thy conscience may be furnisht for thy grave:
1895   Nor doe repute it for a fabling jeste,
          Which sayes; *Good conscience is a daily feaste.*

      Feast on in that, and henceforth be secure
      In strength of Faith: let all thy cares be eas'd
      By bathing in my *Blood*, and fountaine pure
1900 Of this my *Sweat*, and I in this am pleas'd:
          Rest thou, for loe, the Angels in their rankes
          Waite my returne; thy labour be thy thankes.

Up flew the light, and silence shew'd the voyce
Retir'd to stilnesse; which depriv'd my sence
Of all the glory of that heavenly noyse,
Which with such sweet content departed thence:
   Forthwith, my Soule, her wonted habit tooke,
   And I seal'd up my comforts in a booke.

FINIS.

THE GOLDEN Meane.

Lately written, as occasion serued, to a great LORD.

Discoursing The Noblenesse of perfect Virtue in extreames.

LONDON:
Printed for *Ieffery Chorlton.*
1613.

Title page (1613), The Bodleian Library,
8° S. 14(3) Art. By permission.

The Golden Meane
Authorship and Dedication

First published in 1613, *The Golden Meane* has not appeared in print since 1638;[1] as the pamphlet first appeared without the author's name, it has taken three centuries for scholars to identify John Ford as its author. However, in view of the accumulating evidence, Ford's authorship can now no longer be called into question.

In 1926 A. W. Pollard and G. R. Redgrave's *Short-Title Catalogue* tentatively attributed it to Anthony Stafford (STC 17757); the revised STC merely adds Ford's name ("Attrib. to J. Ford and to A. Stafford").[2] Yet in the 1858 catalogue of Thomas Kerslake, a Bristol bookseller, a copy of the 1614 edition was attributed to "John de la Ford"; this was noted by the antiquary Joseph Hunter.[3] Kerslake's catalogue entry and Hunter's note went unnoticed until Sargeaunt's article on "Writings Ascribed to John Ford by Joseph Hunter in *Chorus Vatum*."[4] She concluded that "any

---

[1] The Shakespeare Society edition does not include GM, but there have been at least four unpublished editions of GM and LL: Frederick M. Burelbach (Ph.D. diss., Harvard University, 1965), Colin J. Norman (Ph.D. thesis, London, 1968), G. D. Monsarrat (thèse complémentaire, Paris IV, 1974, completed 1969), L. E. Stock (Dr. phil., Munich, 1975).

[2] The fact that the two surviving copies of the first edition of GM are bound with Stafford's *Meditations, and Resolutions* (1612), also printed by Humphrey Lownes, was a decisive factor in the attribution to Stafford. This was mentioned by E. N. S. Thompson, *The Seventeenth-Century English Essay*, University of Iowa Studies (Iowa City, 1926), 73 n. 1, and by G. C. Moore Smith, "Anthony Stafford," *Notes and Queries* 152 (1927): 220-21. But the two works are really very different in style, form, and contents. GM does not fit into the sequence of Stafford's works, and whereas Stafford frequently stressed the tensions and oppositions between Stoicism and Christianity, Ford simply dissociated the two, publishing separately, the same year, GM and CBS. Moreover, by 1613, Stafford had been influenced not only by Seneca (like Ford), but also by Lipsius's *Manuductio ad Stoicam philosophiam* (1604) and Epictetus, neither of which influenced GM; for Stafford's sources, see G. D. Monsarrat, *Light from the Porch: Stoicism and English Renaissance Literature* (Paris, 1984), 117-25.

[3] For Kerslake's complete entry, see below Commentary, 419 (on LL, Ep. Ded. 26). The catalogue has usually been dated 1757, by mistake; there is a copy in the Central Library of Bristol. For Hunter, see *Chorus Vatum Anglicanorum* (British Library, Add. MS. 24489), 3, fol. 328^r.

[4] *Review of English Studies*, 10 (1934): 165-76.

future editor of Ford's works should consider the inclusion ... of both *Christes Bloodie Sweat* and *The Golden Meane*," quoting Ford's acknowledgement of his authorship in the dedicatory epistle to *A Line of Life* (1620):

> "In all things, no one thing can more requisitely bee observed to be practised, then The Golden Meane: The exemplification whereof, however heretofore attributed, I dare not so poorely under-value my selfe and labours, as not to call mine." (A5^r; 301, below)

Moreover, as *A Line of Life* builds upon *The Golden Meane*, the two can be considered as two parts of a single work. The basic premises are the same; the argumentation is the same; the particular virtues to be aimed at are the same. *A Line of Life* does not cover the ground already surveyed in *The Golden Meane*: it develops Ford's ideas of conduct. Sargeaunt drew attention to the final paragraph of *The Golden Meane* and the first words of the dedicatory epistle to *A Line of Life*: "to be perfectly Noble because wise," and "WISE, and therein NOBLE"—the same idea in different words. Finally, the end of *A Line of Life* (835-44), summarizing the "miseries" treated in *The Golden Meane* and reaffirming that the good man overcomes all, leads immediately to the general conclusion of both works.[5]

The identity of the dedicatee suggests why it appeared anonymously: the epistle to the earl of Northumberland was almost an act of political defiance. The 1613 title page merely stated that it was "Lately written, as occasion served, to a great LORD," but in 1614 the reader was informed that "*it was formerly written* to the Earle of *Northumberland*." Henry Percy, ninth earl of Northumberland, had been in the Tower since 1605 for alleged complicity in the Gunpowder Plot. His position in relation to James had long been a difficult one as, before Elizabeth's death, Cecil established a secret correspondence with James, using Lord Henry Howard as an ostensible writer of his letters.[6] He unremittingly blackened North-

---

[5] Davril noted three further parallels to the plays (89-90). Oliver wrote that "once one has the clue, one sees parallels between [GM and LL] everywhere, in theme and in treatment" (14). Leech thought Ford's authorship "is not much in doubt" (24). Stavig said that GM "is accepted as Ford's by all post-Sargeaunt Ford scholars. The evidence is impressive" (21). Monsarrat, "John Ford's Authorship of *Christes Bloodie Sweat*," *English Language Notes* 9 (1971): 20-25, showed parallels between the two works published in 1613. Anderson considered that "scholars now generally agree that Ford is the likely author of *The Golden Mean*" (26).

[6] For the background to this correspondence, see D. Mathew, *James I* (London, 1967), 100 ff.

umberland, quoting him as preferring to die rather than see James king of England, and linking the earl in "the diabolical triplicity" with Lord Cobham and Sir Walter Ralegh.[7] D. H. Willson remarks that "without a doubt the King came to England poisoned against them."[8] At first, however, Northumberland prospered; he was made captain of the Band of Gentlemen Pensioners and appears to have been on good terms with the king, like himself a scholar and an intellectual.[9]

Northumberland's fall is traceable to the Gunpowder Plot. Although it is certain he was not one of the conspirators, circumstantial evidence piled up against him. His cousin Thomas Percy was one of the ringleaders and dined with him on the day the plot was discovered (4 November 1605). In the days following, the earl busily occupied himself with his own financial affairs, sending messengers north without including in his instructions orders to capture the conspirators. Most seriously, he had neglected to administer the Oath of Supremacy to his cousin Thomas Percy when admitting him to the Band of Gentlemen Pensioners, although as captain he was strictly bound to do so.[10]

Seizing his chance, Cecil, now earl of Salisbury, had Northumberland placed first in the custody of the archbishop of Canterbury and then in the Tower (27 November 1605). He was tried in June 1607 and sentenced to life imprisonment in the Tower, fined £30,000, removed from all his offices, and declared incapable of holding any of them thereafter.

Thus, in 1613, the earl had been in prison for eight years and was to remain there another eight. During these sixteen years he received only two dedications, Ford's and another in 1620, just before his release.[11] Small wonder Ford wished to remain anonymous. He speaks of "*a due debt of thankfulnesse*" (1613, A5^{r-v}), but why he was thankful to Northumberland is not known, nor is the nature of the "occasion" mentioned on the 1613 title page. There is no record of any reward for the dedication in the

---

[7] See G. P. V. Akrigg, *Jacobean Pageant: The Court of James I* (London, 1962), 37.

[8] *King James VI and I* (1956; London, 1966), 157.

[9] For a discussion of Northumberland's scholarship and library, see G. R. Batho, "The Library of the 'Wizard' Earl: Henry Percy Ninth Earl of Northumberland (1564-1632)," *The Library*, 5th series, 15 (1960): 246-61, and Mathew, *James I*, 120 ff.

[10] For the charges and Northumberland's condemnation, see John Stow, *The Annales* (1615 ed.), 884.

[11] For the other dedication, see STC, 21603.7.

earl's papers.[12] Ford's connection with Northumberland, or rather with his family, continued with the dedication in 1620 of a presentation manuscript of *A Line of Life* to Sir James Hay. This wastrel, who became Viscount Doncaster and earl of Carlisle, had married Lucy Percy, the earl's second daughter, in 1617, but without her father's consent. This did not prevent Hay from using his influence to secure the release of his father-in-law.

Whatever Ford's personal reasons for dedicating *The Golden Meane* to Northumberland, the choice was apposite, as the pamphlet is about "The Noblenesse of perfect Virtue in extreames" (1613, title page). One of the "Sixe Miseries that may befall a Noble man" (431-33, marginal note) is imprisonment, which often happens "to men of great place and qualitie" (1035). Ford shows how a noble and resolute mind can make the most of such a trial and overcome it. The earl was a scholar, and he had an extensive library in the Tower; if he ever read *The Golden Meane* he may have said with Ford: "varietie of bookes are sweet companions, and plenty of noble thoughts happy recreations: If I be a prisoner I will either talke with my Library, or sport with my thoughts, since one being learned, will prove sure instructers, the latter being Noble, worthy delights" (1101-5).

Argument and Style

The Golden Meane is an adaptation of classical, especially Stoic, moral philosophy to the circumstances of Stuart noblemen. It first defines the main characteristics of virtue and then sets forth "the chiefe misfortunes that can, or doe usually happen" (429-30) to noblemen: disfavor (due either to private malice, self-unworthiness, envy, or the sovereign's inconstancy), neglect, forfeiture of estate, banishment, imprisonment, and death. These are the things indifferent of the Stoics and the "outward evils" of Pierre Charron.[13] Virtue provides the "remedies" to these "reputed miseries."

The basic concept of Ford's moral philosophy is resolution; it is on this "plot" that he builds the "excellent frame of the *Golden Meane*" (404). But resolution is only one of a cluster of related concepts: moderation,

---

[12] Information supplied by Dr. G. R. Batho.

[13] See Seneca, *Epist.* 82.10, and Cicero, *De finibus* 3.15.50-51. Charron lists "sicknesse, griefe (I include these two in one), captivitie, banishment, want, infamie, losse of friends, death" (*Of Wisdome*, trans. S. Lennard, ?1611, 3.21, p. 511). Ford does not seem to be indebted to Charron.

temperance, goodness, wisdom, and nobleness. His use of these concepts derives essentially from Cicero and Seneca. In the first book of the *De Officiis* Cicero analyzes the four cardinal virtues, a traditional division to which Ford adheres (822). After speaking of wisdom, justice, and fortitude, Cicero comes to the fourth virtue, which he often calls "temperantia."[14] Three other words are also used to denominate this virtue, "moderatio," "constantia," and "modus," as well as expressions denoting tranquillity of the mind and freedom from passion.[15] Temperance, self-control, constancy, measure, and tranquillity of mind are different facets of a single attitude and virtue. But, as Cicero remarks, the virtues "are all mutually linked and bound together,"[16] and "constantia" is also part of the third cardinal virtue, "fortitudo."[17] For Cicero, these concepts center on the idea of "decorum," the harmonious adaptation to social life. Ford centers these concepts (temperance, moderation, constancy, measure) not on "propriety" but on "resolution." Wanting to describe "perfect Vertue in extremes," he draws the Ciceronian concepts towards Stoicism under the influence of Seneca.

Ford never mentions Seneca in *The Golden Meane* although he repeatedly borrows from the *Epistulae morales*, the *De providentia*, the *De tranquillitate animi*, and the *Consolationes* to Polybius and Marcia. Sometimes he merely borrows a striking simile (32-35, 173-74), a proverbial expression (169-70), or a paradox (23-24); but other borrowings are of greater philosophical significance (104-19, 223-35). Outward things such as wealth, honor, and political power are unreliable; the wise man must remember *"that whatsoever may happen to another, may happen to himselfe"* (114-15), and he must therefore be prepared for whatever may befall him (231-34). Men must learn "to conquer by bearing their destinies" (182).

All the borrowings from Seneca are carefully selected: none has any metaphysical implication incompatible with Christianity. Ford makes almost no mention of fate; only when speaking of death does he insist that what is necessary and fatal must be accepted (987-89). He believes in the action of divine Providence but refers to it only in passing (78-79 and 902; also

---

[14] *De officiis* 1.5.15; 1.27.93,96; 1.28.98; 1.40.143; 3.33.116. See also *Tusc. Disp.*, 3.8.16, 18; 3.17.36.
[15] See *De officiis* 1.5, 27-29, etc., and *Tusc. Disp.* 3.8.
[16] *Tusc. Disp.* 3.8.17; see *De officiis* 2.10.35.
[17] *De officiis* 1.20.67, 21.72, 23.80.

LL, 139). His caution in avoiding these problems is all the more remarkable as he was familiar with the *De constantia* of Justus Lipsius, in which they are treated extensively; but, as Lipsius says, "this place is somewhat slipperie."[18] Ford's reticence cannot be due to any lack of interest, as Fate, Destiny, and Providence are central to several of his dramatic plots; no doubt he felt freer in his plays than in a didactic pamphlet.

Ford's "golden meane"[19] is not derived from the Artistotelian conception of virtue as a mean between two vicious extremes. Rather, it is closely linked with temperance and moderation: "Heere now is a broad path, leading, or more truly teaching the readie course to the excellent meane of *Temperance* and *Moderation*" (576-77). The three concepts are linked in the *De officiis*, and in Seneca, for whom measure ("modus") is a characteristic of what is virtuous and good.[20] Ford never defines "moderation"; he merely states that it is *"the life of Vertue"* (Ep. Ded. 9). Though it is sometimes linked with the "mean" (381-86, 576-77), it is much more often used as the equivalent of "self-control" or "firmness." Ford speaks of "moderation in those sadnesses" (166), of a "steady moderation" (603-4), and of "moderation in extreames" (1256).[21] A wise man should bear his losses "with moderation" because "true valour [is] perfect moderation" (933-34; also 894 and LL, Cor 51-53). Ford's "moderation" is thus very close to "constancy," as is also the case with Cicero.[22] This merging of the virtues into one another is confusing for the reader, but Ford is following Cicero and the Stoic doctrine of the unity of virtue. The idea that temperance, moderation, constancy, and the golden mean should merge into one another, was, in the Renaissance, by no means peculiar to Ford. Here is Virtue's description of herself in a prefatory poem to Lawrence Humphrey's

---

[18] *Two Bookes of Constancie*, trans. J. Stradling (1594), 1.17, p. 41. For Ford's use of Lipsius, see GM, 917, and the Commentary on LL, 18-25.

[19] This is a translation of the Horatian "aurea mediocritas" (*Odes* 2.10.5); the expression was tending to replace the earlier "golden mediocrity." "The golden mean" is found as early as 1563 in the English version of Lawrence Humphrey's *The Nobles* (C2ᵛ and Y8ᵛ where it translates the single Latin word "mediocritas"). "Mean" and "mediocrity" were often coupled together. See also Tilley M.792 and ODEP, 317.

[20] See *Epist.* 66.9 (reading "omnis in modo est virtus"), 76.24; 92.3, 11; *De Vita Beata* 13.5.

[21] The OED ("moderation," 2) quotes Calvin, *Institutes*, trans. Norton (1561): "a pacience and quiete moderation of hart" (1.17.8). This corresponds to the Latin "patientiam placidamque animi moderationem" and to the French "patience et tranquillité."

[22] See *De officiis* 1.5.17; 1.28.98; 1.29.102; *Tusc. Disp.* 3.8.17-18; 4.17.37.

The Nobles (1563):

> That meane am I, whych constant mynds do frame
> Undaunted to eche chaunge that chaunce may bryng
> By just desert to scale the forte of fame.
>
> C2^v

In Thomas Gainsford's *The Rich Cabinet* (1616) the section on temperance is introduced by the following couplet:

> *Nothing too much: mixe water with the wine;*
> *The mean is best, which temperance doth define.*
>
> fol. 143^v

For Thomas Rogers, moderation "bringeth with it another vertue whiche is called Suffering" and teaches us to "beare and forbeare," according to the teaching of Epictetus.[23]

Resolution was one of the most pervasive concepts of Renaissance moral philosophy;[24] it was through resolution, isolated from rationalism and pantheism, that the influence of Stoicism was most widespread. It meant much the same as "constancy," and the two words were frequently coupled together. Resolution, for Ford, is the virtue which enables us to withstand calamities and troubles (76-77, 1056-57) and to face death with equanimity (286-87, 1170). Resolution is a "Castle" (737); it is therefore "setled," "stayed," and "sure," and it gives man a "quiet calme" (172, 286-87, 970). Resolution is not simply strength of character and steadiness, it is also an intellectual virtue which is grounded on knowledge, on a correct assessment of what is good and what is evil: this is why a truly resolved mind is a "prepared" mind (156, 404-5).

With resolution we find not only constancy and steadiness, but also fortitude and courage, valor, sufferance, and perseverance. Moreover, Ford frequently calls resolution virtuous and noble (610, 629, 931). Virtue and

---

[23] *A Philosophicall Discourse, entituled, The Anatomie of the Minde*, 1576, 2.24, "Of Moderation," fol. 129^{r-v}. Moderation is one of the "parts" of temperance.

[24] See, for instance, Sidney, *The Arcadia* (pub. 1590, 1593); Sir William Cornwallis, *Essayes* (1600), essay 1, "Of Resolution"; G. Powel, *The Resolved Christian, Exhorting to Resolution* (1600), *passim*; R. Johnson, *Essaies* (1607 ed.), B1^{r-v}, D1^r, D2^r, D7^v, F7^r, G6^r, G7^r; J. Hall, *Characters of Vertues and Vices* (1608), "Of a Valiant man," "Of a Patient man"; N. Breton, *Characters upon Essaies Morall, And Divine* (1615), 28-30, "Resolution"; T. Gainsford, *The Rich Cabinet* (1616), fol. 130^r-131^v; O. Felltham, *Resolves* (1628 ed.), 4-7, "Of Resolution."

Wisdom on the one hand and nobility on the other are, with resolution, the pillars of Ford's moral philosophy.

The nature and definition of nobility (or "noblenesse") were much discussed in the sixteenth and seventeenth centuries. It was usual to distinguish three kinds: "NOBILITIE *Caelestiall*, which consisteth in RELIGION: Nobility *Philosophicall*, which is got by *Morall vertues*: and Nobilitie *Politicall*."[25] Divine or celestial nobility is usually "left to God and the theologians,"[26] and there are two sources of secular nobility: birth and virtue. The question of the relation between these two is at the heart of all the debates on the subject. Most authors, under the influence of classical moral philosophy, insist on the primacy of virtue and on the superiority of moral nobility over nobility of blood, sometimes asserting that nobility of blood without virtue is "but vanitie."[27] As Barnabe Rich put it:

> *Nobilitie* it selfe (as some would describe it) is a commendation proceeding from the deserts of our ancient Progenitors: but to speake truely, both according to *Divinity* and *Philosophie*, there is no true Nobility, but that which proceedes from vertue.[28]

As Seneca says, "The soul alone renders us noble."[29] Juvenal summed up the doctrine in a line often quoted and paraphrased: "nobilitas sola est atque unica virtus" (8.20).

Ford too derives true nobleness from virtue; he speaks of "a wise man (who is the true Nobleman)."[30] Passages in both *The Golden Meane* and *A Line of Life* underline the primacy of what is inward and what belongs to the mind (GM, 20-23; LL, Cor 27-30). But Ford does not always adhere to this conception; not only does he derive nobility from wisdom, but he also derives wisdom from nobility. The final words of *The Golden Meane* are: "to be truely wise because Noble: to be perfectly Noble because wise" (1329). The two concepts are therefore very close to one another, so close that they sometimes seem to be almost identical. Ford often speaks of

---

[25] Thomas Milles, "Of Nobility Political and Civill," in *The Catalogue of Honor* (1610), B1ʳ.

[26] Ruth Kelso, *The Doctrine of the English Gentleman in the Sixteenth Century* (Urbana, 1929), 21.

[27] R. Barckley, *A Discourse of the Felicitie of Man* (1603 ed.), 266.

[28] B. Rich, *Roome for a Gentleman* (1609), D1ᵛ.

[29] *Epist.* 44.5. See also *De beneficiis*, 3.28.1-2, and Boethius, *Consolatio* 3.6 verse.

[30] GM, 160-61; see also 1280-81, 1306.

"a wise and noble man," but also of "a Wise or a Noble man" (601), as if the two words were interchangeable. When he succumbs to the charms of antimetabole combined with polyptoton he speaks of "the wisely Noble and Nobly wise" (478), thus obscuring even more the distinction between the two. Yet Ford also says that "an Honourable race" (1283) contributes to nobleness, and in the 1614 additions he clearly distinguishes between them:

> To be wise, and to be Noble, are two distinct happinesses; as different and as much divided the one from the other (though some few times they meete in one particular) as *Goodnesse*, and *Greatnesse*, as *Fortune* and *vertue*; as a *King* and a *Tyrant*. There are many *Noble*, which are strangers to *Wisedome*: but not any *Wise*, who is not allyed to *Noblenesse* (1285-90; see also, 30-31, 315-16).

Many who have political nobility are not wise, but all those that are wise possess moral nobility. Reciprocal derivation, identity, and difference: the lack of consistency in Ford's treatment of nobility and wisdom is often misleading for his reader.

When in *The Golden Meane* Ford comes to the last of the six "reputed miseries," death, he soon introduces the idea of an afterlife; if we are tortured by "the weight of our misdeeds" (1199), it is because we are afraid of being "for ever a dying" (1204). Such is the fate of the damned, whose sufferings are vividly described in *Christes Bloodie Sweat* (see 757-74). But death is also "the end of all sorrowes..., if the partie to die be truely reconciled to his God and to his conscience" (1184-85); it is "the quickening to a better life" (1214-15; see also 1171-72 and *LL*, 9-11). Death "is a path to blessednesse, and such as are good will finde it: It is a banquet of all goodnesse, and such as bee blessed have found it" (1239-41). The significant words in this quotation, "good" and "goodness," Ford frequently associates with Christianity. Goodness is the essence of God Himself: "God (whom to call *good* is but an improprietie of description) is not singly *bonus* good, but *Bonitas* goodnesse" (*LL*, 819). But goodness is not identical with wisdom. Though Ford often uses the word "good" without any religious connotations, and even sometimes without distinguishing it from "wise" (536, 799-805, 927; *LL*, 189), the wise man and the good man are several times contrasted in both *The Golden Meane* and *A Line of Life*. Their attitudes toward death are different: "*Death* to a wise man cannot come unlooked for, nor to a good man unwisht for: since the wise, knowing that they must die, know likewise that *resolution* is the best comfort to welcome *death,* and the good being confident of their owne innocencies, desire the change of a better life."[31]

Religion plays a more important part in *A Line of Life* than in *The Golden Meane;* nevertheless, there is a definite Christian background to *The Golden Meane.* Ford shows that wisdom furnishes the remedy for "reputed miseries," but only the good man finds the path to blessedness after death. This path, described in *Christes Bloodie Sweat,* shows how to avoid the true misery of an unending death.

The Golden Meane points to the need for "self-reformation," *Christes Bloodie Sweat* to the need for "true repentance." Reformation and repentance both bring about "another birth": "A remedie against *selfe-unworthinesse,* must be found out in a *selfe-reformation;* which being sincerely performed, the follies of the past times belong not to the reformed."[32] *The Golden Meane* and *Christes Bloodie Sweat* are parallel and complementary, not contradictory.

Though Ford has carefully planned the "disposition" of *The Golden Meane,* the reader may feel confused because the multiplicity of related concepts blurs his meaning. There is, moreover, much uncertainty in the handling of some basic ideas; this has been noted for nobility, but it is also the case with "misery."

Ford states in *The Golden Meane* that disfavor, neglect, forfeiture of estate, banishment, imprisonment, and death are not real miseries. The wise man must "prepare his courage with this resolution, that Miserie is no Miserie; for that is onely a Miserie which is lasting, and thought so: and reputed Miserie is not lasting, because *death* out-weares it; is not thought so, because *death* will finish it" (1251-54; see also 1018-21). A misery is truly such, then, only if it lasts; but there is always death and to men "guided by the refined light of judgement: it is esteemed (as it is) the onely remedie and securest ease against misery" (1165-67). But in the 1614 additions Ford introduces another conception of "miserie": ". . . that which is an accident of change of estate, from better to worse, occasioned by the evill disposition of an unworthines of minde" (414-15). The illustration of this statement equates misery with moral evil (416-28); such a conception,

---

[31] GM, 1168-72; see also 1205-6. The good man is also contrasted with the great man at 321-22, 1285-88, and LL, 531-32.

[32] GM, 529-31. For "reformation," see also 227, 392, 548, 552, 880, 904, 1065, 1142; LL, 153. For "repentance," see CBS, 775, 1129-46. For the religious expression (John 3:3) "another birth," see GM, 549.

which is Stoic, has nothing to do with the *duration* of misery. Sometimes, also, misery is simply used as the equivalent of "misfortune" or "calamity" (4-5).

Another source of confusion is that Ford often sacrifices clarity of expression to stylistic effect. He is particularly fond of figures of repetition. Sometimes he merely repeats the same word, or grammatical homophones, or words derived from the same root (polyptoton): "an idle labour to labour to" (152), "affecting his owne affections" (659). But most of his figures are more complex and involve the repetition of several words. These words are usually repeated in inverse order (antimetabole): "to be truely wise because Noble: to be perfectly Noble because wise" (1329), here combined with homoioteleuton. One of Ford's favorite figures is antimetabole with two nouns linked by the preposition "of" (Davril, 440-41): "they therein chiefly shewe the vertue, of their greatnes, and the greatnesse of their vertue" (79-80; see also 133). At times the reader wanders through a maze of words, wondering whether Ford is trying to lead or to mislead him: "Hee then who now witnesseth by his moderation in those sadnesses, the courage of his Noblenesse, by the Noblenesse of his Wisedome is both perfectly wise in being so couragious, and as perfectly couragious in being so noble."[33] Though Ford's frequently euphuistic style compares favorably with much of the shapeless prose of his contemporaries, his genius was more suited to dramatic verse than to moral prose.

Ford's rhetoric and style are strengthened and enlivened in three ways. First, his prose is studded with proverbial expressions (the title itself) or proverbs.[34] Second, he makes extensive use of imagery. His similes and metaphors are usually common and traditional ("gusts and tides of adversitie," etc.), but occasionally striking and original: "a christning of reputation" (550-51), "the moveable sandes of his Princes favour" (626), "*Bountie* strings up the hearts of the common people" (842-43). A few images are typically Fordian, for instance "float" and "visor,"[35] but the reader of *The Golden Meane* probably best remembers Ford's extended similes: the swollen bladder, the silken cloak, and the most elaborate of all, the journey

---

[33] GM, 165-68. See also 348-50, 729-30, 1242-43, and LL, 47-48, 395-96, 660-61.
[34] See the text and Commentary for Ep. Ded. 15, Text 27-28, 131-32, 141-42, 168-72, 207-8, 231-34, 243-44, 503, 570-71, 593, 626, 671, 718, 722, 795, 798-99, 820-21, 837, 876-77, 930-31, 935-37, 938-39, 1052, 1077-78, 1123-24, 1125-28, 1128-30, 1184, 1220-21.
[35] See the text and Commentary for 48 and 360-61, also LL, 495.

to Constantinople, transposed from Seneca.[36] The building metaphor is recurrent (see 395-97 and Commentary), conveying the idea that the golden mean is not obtained in a day but only reached through constancy and resolution in the path of virtue.

Finally, Ford illustrates his argument with many "examples" from "former times" because they have "force ... to instruct the present" (1022-23). He takes them mostly from antiquity,[37] but also from "our owne moderne Chronicles," sometimes very recent, as in the case of Essex.[38] Some of these examples were famous, like the falls of Sejanus or Wolsey, others unusual, like the stories of Isocacius and Abdolominus (see 84-89, 784-92). The sources of two "examples" show that Ford was already interested in the theater even though, as far as we know, he was not yet writing for the stage: his Diogenes comes from John Lyly's *Campaspe* and his Thomas Mowbray from Shakespeare's *Richard II*.[39]

The Text

There are three early editions of *The Golden Meane*, published in 1613, 1614, and 1638. It was entered in the Stationers' Register on 14 June 1613: "Geffray Charlton. Entred for his copie under th[e h]andes of master. NYD and master Harison warden. A booke Called *'the golden meane'* Lately. *Wrytten as occasion served to A great Lord Discoursinge the noblenes of perfect vertue in extremes* ... vj^d" (Arber, 3:526). The first two editions (STC 17757-58) were printed by Humphrey Lownes.

There are two known copies of the 1613 edition, one in the British Library (lacking the last three ruled or blank leaves G4-6) and one in the Bodleian (lacking C6 and C7); the title page is reproduced above (215).

---

[36] See 4-14, 247-85 (journey), 297-308 (bladder), 826-32 (silken cloak), 917-26, 1207-15.

[37] See 85, 116-19, 134-36, 223-25, 386-87, 501-2, 520-23, 543-47, 616, 787-91, 820-21, 955-56, 960-68, 1022-26, 1107-13, 1243-47.

[38] See 119-23, 516-20, 615, 756-62, 956-57, 996-1004, 1009-18.

[39] See the Commentary on 134-36 (Diogenes) and 996, 999-1000, 1001-4 (Mowbray), also 935-37. For the connection between GM and Ford's plays see Introduction to LL, 286, below.

Collation: 12°: A⁶ B-F¹² G⁶ [$5 signed (-A3, A5, G4, G5)],72 leaves, pp. [12] 1-126 (misprinting 53 as "23," 72 as "48") [6]
Contents: A1ʳ ruled, A1ᵛ blank, A2ʳ ruled, A2ᵛ blank, A3ʳ title, A3ᵛ blank, A4ʳ-A5ᵛ epistle, A6ʳ⁻ᵛ ruled, B1ʳ-G3ᵛ text, G4ʳ⁻ᵛ ruled, G5ʳ-6ᵛ blank
RT [within rules]: A4ᵛ-5ᵛ To the Reader. B1ᵛ-G3ᵛ *The Golden Meane.* [*Mneae* on B-F11ʳ]
Catchwords: A-B, [none] B-C, cannot C-D, doe D-E, iudgement E-F, of F-G, former,

A second edition, "Enlarged by the first Authour," appeared in 1614; almost thirty percent of the text consists of new material. There are five known copies (Bodleian; British Library; Lincoln Cathedral; St Mary's Seminary, New Oscott, Warwickshire; Huntington Library);[40] the title page is reproduced on the overleaf, 230.

Collation: 12°: A-H¹² [$5 signed (-A3)], 96 leaves, pp. [12], 1-177 (misprinting 53 as "35," 82-148 as "88-154," 149 as "136," 150-51 as "156-57," 152-53 as "139-40," 154-55 as "160-61," 156 as "142," 157-77 as "163-83") [3]
Contents: A1ʳ ruled, A1ᵛ blank, A2 ʳ⁻ᵛ ruled, A3ʳ title, A3ᵛ ruled, A4ʳ-5ᵛ epistle, A6ʳ "Benè ... publico.," A6ᵛ ruled, A7ᵛ-H11ʳ text, H11ᵛ-12ᵛ blank
RT: [within rules]: A4ᵛ-5ᵛ The Epistle. A7ᵛ-H11ʳ *The Golden Meane.*
Catchwords: A-B, maruell B-C, know C-D, To D-E, giuen E-F, beare F-G, man G-H, with

The Golden Meane was again published in 1638, with a title page engraved by William Marshall (reproduced on the overleaf, 230), followed by a letterpress title page present in eight of the surviving copies in either of two states (STC 17759 and 17759.5). In three copies (British Library 8404.a.28; Worcester College; Syracuse University) it reads:

[within double rule] THE | GOLDEN | Meane. | [rule] | Enlarged by the | first Author. | [rule] | As it was formerly writ- | ten to the Earle of | *Northumberland.* | [rule] | Discoursing | The Noblenesse of perfect | Vertue in extremes. | [rule] | *The third Edition.* | [rule] | LONDON. | Printed by *J. H.* for *John Benson,* | and are to be sold at his shop in | S. *Dunstans* Church-yard. | 1638.

---

[40] The revised STC (17758) adds a copy at the University of California, Los Angeles, but this is a ghost.

Title page (1614), The Bodleian Library, Antiq. G.e.1.(3). By permission.

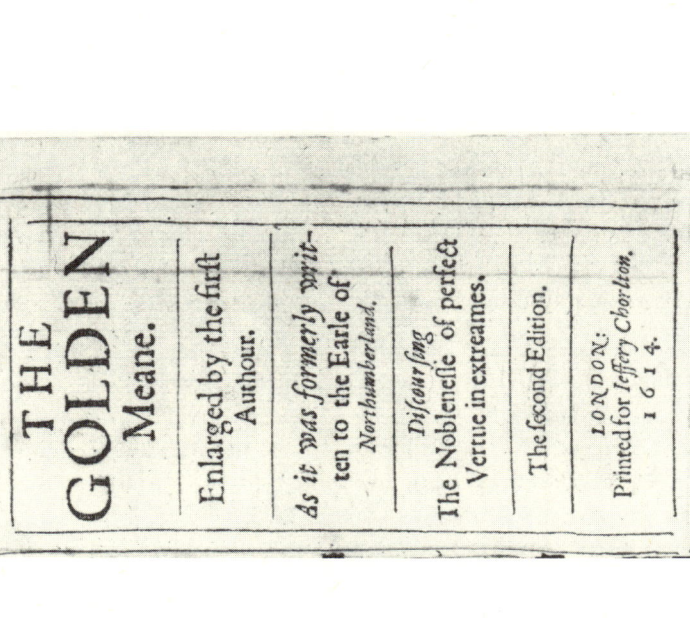

Title page (1638), The Bodleian Library, Vet. A2.f.293. By permission.

In five copies (British Library 8407.a.24; Lambeth; 2 at Cambridge University Library; University of Pennsylvania) *"The third Edition."* has been replaced by fourteen small ornaments. Finally, in four copies (London University; Bodleian; two at Folger) the letterpress title page is missing. The following bibliographical description applies to copies with both the engraved and the letterpress title pages:

Collation: 12°: (engr. tit.+) A-H^{12} [$5 signed (-A1, A3)], 97 leaves, pp. [8], 1-182, [4]

Contents: π1^r engr. tit., π1^v blank, A1^r letterpress title, A1^v *"Fiat 3^a. Editio juxta hoc Exemplar. S A.* BAKER. Ex *aedibus* Lond. Maii *3.* 1638.*,"* A2^r-3^r epistle and *"Benè ... publico."* [A3^r], A3^v blank, A4^r-H10^v text, H11^r same as A1^v, H11^v-12^v blank

RT [within rules]: A2^v-3^r THE EPISTLE | DEDICATORY. A4^v-H10^v The Golden Meane.

Catchwords: A-B, unto B-C, breath; C-D, losse D-E, al- E-F, tie F-G, verthrow: G-H, for

The third edition of *The Golden Meane* was printed the same year as *The Fancies, Chast and Noble* and a year earlier than *The Ladies Triall*, which had been licensed by Herbert on 3 May 1638 and entered in the Stationers' Register on 6 November 1638. Ford was thus still in London and active in 1638. It seems, however, that he was in no way connected with the 1638 edition of *The Golden Meane*, in which his name does not appear. Having acknowledged his authorship of the pamphlet in the preface to *A Line of Life*, there was no reason for him to want the 1638 edition to be anonymous.

This edition was printed by J. Haviland for John Benson who, on 1 August 1636, was allowed by the court of the Stationers' Company to finish printing 1500 copies of *The Golden Meane*, "paying ... upon the finishing of the Impression such fyne as this Co^{rt}. shall thinke fitt."[41] The printing was delayed for some unknown reason, and the payment of Benson's "fyne for the poore for printing ye golden Meane" was recorded only on 19 December 1638 (p. 487).

The 1638 edition is carefully printed, with fewer obvious misprints than the previous ones, but it was set from a copy of the 1614 edition and it is

---

[41] William A. Jackson, ed., *Records of the Court of the Stationers' Company 1602 to 1640* (London, 1957), 285.

therefore without authority. It tends to modernize the vocabulary, spelling, and grammar (91, 667, 732, 746, 917), and it corrects some misprints that had been passed on from the first to the second edition (252, 718) or introduced in 1614 (640). Its pointing is also heavier, particularly with commas.

When comparing the third edition with the first two it is necessary to distinguish between the original 1613 text and the 1614 additions. In the original portion of the text there are ten cases where an identical 1613-1638 reading differs from that of 1614. Nine of these, however, are merely due to a coincidental return in 1638 to the 1613 punctuation.[42] The remaining case is due to 1638 having been set from a copy of 1614 in which the outer forme of sheet D was uncorrected; the third edition thus reprinted an erroneous reading that has been corrected in the surviving copies of 1614 (see 582 and Commentary). Sometimes, when confronted with troublesome readings in its copy, the third edition made an unsatisfactory emendation (changing "aspertion" to "aspersion" at 495) and failed to restore the correct 1613 reading (61). For the original portion of the text, then, 1638 derives from 1614; the first edition was not consulted.

As regards the 1614 additions, the third edition improves the punctuation in several cases (135, 142, 181, 442, 948, 1206) or corrects a minor mistake (388); it also preserves some errors or unsatisfactory passages (381, 393, 731, 845, 942), emends incorrectly (480), and even sometimes corrupts a sound text (474-75, 1102). Finally, the third edition introduces in this part of the text two substantive variants which are difficult to account for: "more" for "much" (446) and "still" for "euer" (543). In neither case is the meaning modified significantly, nor is there any stylistic improvement. The most likely explanation is that these are compositorial lapses due to the compositor's memorizing the meaning rather than the exact wording. If Ford had annotated a copy of 1614 for the third edition, he surely would not have altered just these two words. To sum up, 1638 is essentially a reprint of the second edition; none of its variants have any authority, though some of its emendations should be adopted in a critical edition.[43]

---

[42] There are 89 punctuation differences between 1613 and 1614; it is therefore natural that a few of the many punctuation changes introduced in 1638 should coincide with the 1613 pointing.

[43] For the 1638 edition, all substantive variants have been recorded in the textual notes. Punctuation variants have been recorded only when they have been adopted or when they agree with 1613 against 1614.

The first two editions are both substantive: 1613 in the whole of its text, 1614 in the additions. In its derived sections, the second edition often reprints the first line for line, and sometimes page for page. In the 1613 edition there are twenty lines to the page from B to the end of E, and then nineteen in F and G; in the 1614 edition there are twenty lines to the page for the text proper until the end of F (except on F6^r, which has nineteen), and then nineteen in G and H. The change occurs at the same place in the text; G1^r (1614) corresponds to E12^v-F1^r (1613). In these reprinted pages there is an average of about three changes per page in the accidentals, not counting the punctuation. The frequency of these changes varies considerably; thus there are no changes on three pages (B10^v, F5^v, G9^r), while there are thirteen changes in the accidentals, plus one in the punctuation, on H5^r.

The second edition was not merely "enlarged by the first Authour"; he also occasionally corrected or revised the original portion of the text, in which there are over thirty substantive variants. A few of these are probably compositorial slips, as the difference is only a single letter.[44] However, only Ford can have corrected "*Abdo-hominus*" to "*Abdo-lominus*" (787), unless of course there was a press-correction in the copy used by the 1614 compositor.[45] He was also probably responsible for the change from "*art*" to "*Act*" (922), where the 1613 compositor must have made the common error of reading a "c" as an "r." A compositor might omit a short word ("a," 630; "of," 862) but it is unlikely that he added "themselves" (13), "may" (84), or "more" (1226). Revisions involving several words are certainly authorial: "onely best worthie" instead of "BEST WORthy Reader" (Ep. Ded. 2); "*one day*" for "*once*" (Ep. Ded. 6-7); "(or never surely)" for "surely" (622-23); and "in resolved steadinesse to" in place of "to resolve steadinesse in" (1327). But even most of the minor changes are very probably authorial, as can be seen by examining, for instance, fols. F3^v and F4^r. These two pages reprint the 1613 text line for line except for two different line breaks (out of forty) involving "of" and "it." There are only

---

[44] For one letter changed, added or deleted, see the textual notes for 64, 205, 220, 285, 321, 365, 368, 495, 628, 640, 787, 868, 922, 1026, 1122, 1230.

[45] There are no press-variants in the two surviving copies of 1613. The following misprints, present in both copies, have not been recorded in the textual notes except at 252: "Thereof˄ For" (61), "graue˄ Death" (215), "speker," (223; instead of "speker)" which is given correctly in the catchword), "apporued" (252), "of such as are not truely directed by truest iudgement" is repeated after "truest iudgement" (780), "inward˄" (879; instead of "inward)"), "hearts)" (911; instead of "hearts˄").

five spelling variants and one punctuation change. As the compositor was so faithful to his copy it is logical to conclude that the three important variants are authorial; "mine" (for "of mine"), "later" ("latter"), "it is" ("is it"). Such minor revisions (or corrections) are to be expected of an author preparing the second edition of a text printed a year earlier.

A comparison between the printed text and the manuscript of *A Line of Life* shows that they both derive from a well-punctuated and carefully italicized manuscript (see below, 289, 290) and that Ford, therefore, did not neglect such matters. Though authors naturally concerned themselves with the substantives of their text rather than its accidentals, it is improbable that Ford never altered the spelling, punctuation, word order, or italics of the 1613 printed text when preparing it for the second edition. Some of the changes are no doubt due to the 1614 compositor's zeal or carelessness, but one can find typographical evidence showing that others are probably authorial.

The overwhelming majority of spelling changes are common variants of the period: be (1613) / bee (1614; 124), bee/be (460), either/eyther (688), eyther/either (772). The second edition usually changes the final -y to -ie (misery/miserie), but as this preference for -ie occurs also in the additions set from Ford's manuscript it is impossible to tell which of the two compositors remained closer to his copy. Some of the more interesting spelling changes seem to be authorial. At the beginning of the epistle "*Volumne*" becomes "*Volume*," and this occurs between two substantive changes at lines 2 and 6–7; the lineation was not changed but the already thick blank spaces in the line had to be increased because "n" was taken out. Both the printed text and the manuscript of *Fames Memoriall* (3) spell the word without an "n". Another interesting change is found on fol. F4^r, which has already been described; "atchivements" was changed to "atchievements" in a line where the blank spaces were already very thin in 1613. Because of the extra "e" there is no space between "owne" and "atchievements" in 1614; any compositor would try to avoid this, so he probably added the "e" because it was an authorial correction.

The 1613 edition is well punctuated, and 1614 is identical about twenty-four times out of twenty-five; the changes are either isolated or in clusters. In 236 lines of 1614 text on fols F9^v–G3^v, the second edition reprints 1613 line for line with only six punctuation changes; then, in the next nineteen lines (G3^v–G4^r), there are seven changes and the 1613 lineation is disrupted. The punctuation was adequate in the first edition, but the revision improves it slightly and may be authorial.

There are only four changes in italicization. Three are probably compositorial,[46] but the change from "opinion ... Humour" to *Opinion ... Humour*" (359-60) may well be authorial.

Though 1613 is closer to Ford's manuscript, 1614 was set from a corrected and revised copy of the first edition. There is evidence, though of course no absolute proof, that Ford did not confine his revisions to what we now call substantives. The 1614 edition has therefore been chosen as copy-text for the whole of *The Golden Meane* in order to adopt the authorial revisions and corrections en masse, whatever their extent. As some of the alterations were no doubt made by the 1614 compositor, the punctuation of the first edition has been recorded in the textual notes. The overall soundness of the second edition of the original part is confirmed by the fact that the proportion of misprints and press-variants is smaller than in the additions.[47]

The state of the variant sheets is as follows: the first reading is that of the corrected state and it has been adopted unless otherwise indicated. 1614 additions are asterisked.[48]

SHEET A INNER FORME Corrected: A, B, C, E
                     Uncorrected: D

sig.	5ᵛ	(Ep. Ded. 14)	*principally*] *prrincipally*
	9ᵛ	(43)	passion] passiion
	10ʳ	(46)	imployed] impolyed
	11ᵛ	(67)	complement.] complement ·
	11ᵛ	(70)	weakenesse (lines 8-11 of sig. 11ᵛ have been reset in *ABCE*)] weaknes

---

[46] The/The (1613/1614; 29), *Miserable*/Miserable (twice; 1094), *imprisonment*/imprisonement (1179).

[47] The following misprints have been noted in all the copies of 1614 (for the press-variants, see above). They have been silently corrected and are not recorded in the textual notes except at 252 and 640. The 1614 additions are asterisked. Misprints: compa- pared (6-7), can (59, catchword, hyphen missing), chiose (69), a bandoning (204), a (237, hyphen missing at end of line for "alike"), thcn (241), appourcd (252), iu command (260), *flaot (300), *eae (409), *it it (411), *a a (412), vsurpring (460), madnesse (640), *cf (662), *onely (664), *aud (721), *heads* (722, catchword), *A bundance* (798), aud (880), btweene (904), *ouer (937), vnder (963, hyphen missing), *banshment* (1006), ship, (1130, catchword), rhat (1142), imaginerh (1192).

[48] All known copies have been collated: British Library (A), Bodleian (B), Huntington (C; microfilm), Lincoln Cathedral (D), St Mary's Seminary, New Oscott, Warwickshire (E; microfilm), G. D. Monsarrat (F; see Additional Note, 238).

SHEET B OUTER FORME

?Corrected: AC
?Uncorrected: BDE

*sig.   7ʳ   (180)   tasting] lasting (see Commentary)

SHEET B INNER FORME

Corrected: ACDE
Uncorrected: B

*sig.   3ᵛ   (129)   Such∧ men,] Such, men∧
*4ʳ   (136)   him,] him∧
*4ʳ   (139)   they] thy
*7ᵛ   (189)   vnseemely behauiour (fitly∧∧and] vnsemly behauiour ∧fitly, (and

SHEET C OUTER FORME

Corrected: ABCD
Uncorrected: E

*sig   2ᵛ   (299)   needle,] needle∧
*2ᵛ   (300)   other] ther
*3ʳ   (304)   retayning] retaining
*3ʳ   (305)   decay, then like∧ Bladders,] decay∧ then like, Bladders∧
*4ᵛ   (328)   here] heare
*4ᵛ   (329)   *Steddinesse*] *Steddiuesse*
*4ᵛ   (331)   impossibilitie] Impossibilitie
*5ʳ   (335)   libertie,] libertie∧
*5ʳ   (336)   man?] man.
*5ʳ   (338)   our] ouer
*5ʳ   (339)   mities (catchword)] mities?
*8ᵛ   (387)   com- (line-ending)] com∧
*10ᵛ   (417)   will- (line-ending)] will∧
*11ʳ   (424)   assassination] assasination
*11ʳ   (425)   Such-like] Such∧like (This may not be a correction as the hyphen is very pale in B)
*11ʳ   (427)   misfortunes∧] misfortunes,
*12ᵛ   (449)   and little] and litle
*12ᵛ   (452)   and] And

SHEET D OUTER FORME

Corrected: A C (first stage), D (second stage)
Uncorrected: BE

*sig.	7ʳ	(551)	vnworthie] vuworthie BE
	*7ʳ	(552)	that] that, ABCE

SHEET F OUTER FORME   Corrected: AC
                             Uncorrected: BDE

There are three major variants (by/be, world/word, no/or) and two minor ones (that,/that∧, complement∧/complement,). For the major variants, two of the correct readings are found in A and C ("be", as in 1613; "word", in the additions) and one in B, D, and E ("or", as in 1613). For the two minor variants, A and C agree with 1613. On sig. 3ʳ the line endings of the paragraph from "There may" to "of ruine" are identical with those of 1613 except in the second line. This seems to have been first set as "that, O my estate being" instead of "that ô my estate being for-" in 1613. The addition of a comma entailed the carrying over of "for-" to the next line. The comma was probably then removed during correction, hence the thick spaces around "O". On balance, it thus seems likely that A and C represent the corrected state of the forme and that "no" is an erroneous correction.

sig.	3ʳ	(852)	that∧] that,
	7ʳ	(913)	be the] by the
	9ʳ	(942)	word] world
	10ᵛ	(972)	complement∧] complement,
	11ʳ	(974)	or BDE] no AC (erroneous correction)

SHEET F INNER FORME   Corrected: B E (first stage),
                               D (second stage)
                             Uncorrected: A C

sig.	4ʳ	(872)	bloud;] bloud, ABCE
	10ʳ	(962)	be] de AC

SHEET G INNER FORME   Corrected: A (first stage),
                               DE (second stage), B (third stage)
                             Uncorrected: C

sig.	2ʳ	(1021)	misery] misey AC
	4ʳ	(1055–56)	commendation, in] commendatio, in] ADE commendation in,] C

7ᵛ	(1104)	thoughts,] thoughts‸ C
9ᵛ	(1132)	therefore] thereforo C
9ᵛ	(1132)	know] kuow C

SHEET H INNER FORME   Corrected: *AD*
                       Uncorrected: *BCE*

*sig. 6ʳ (1261)   personages] pesornages

ADDITIONAL NOTE ON COPY F

This copy was sold in June 1991 by E. M. Lawson & Co., East Hagbourne, Oxfordshire. It bears on the title page the signature "Ch: Towneley" in italic; this is (according to Lawson's catalogue) "either Charles or Christopher, both antiquaries." But "Towneley" is also written in secretary on sig. F10ᵛ and the book was most probably first owned by Christopher (1604–1674) rather than by Charles (1737–1805).

In respect of the press variants, F is different from all the other copies in having the inner forme of sheet C in an uncorrected state:

sig.	5ᵛ	(342)	any burthen] any buithen
	8ʳ	(380)	man,] man‸
		(384)	all, the] all‸ the
	10ʳ	(413)	vntruly] vntuly
			Miserable] miserable

The other formes are as follows:
A INNER: corrected; B OUTER: ?uncorrected; B INNER: corrected; C OUTER: uncorrected; D OUTER: uncorrected; F OUTER: uncorrected; F INNER: corrected (first stage); G INNER: corrected (third stage); H INNER: corrected.

THE GOLDEN Meane.

Enlarged by the first Authour.

As it was formerly writ-ten to the Earle of Northumberland.

Discoursing
The Noblenesse of perfect Vertue in extreames.

The second Edition.

LONDON:
Printed for *Jeffery Chorlton.*

1 6 1 4.

TO THE
onely best worthie.

SYR: *(as for any other Nobler titles they are but separable Accidents) if Vertue be not too partially overswayed | by Fortune, I have heere cast into a small Volume a large summe of love. Such a love as is rather warranted by a dutifull observance then any shadow of Complement. I may one day open my selfe, when either Opinion is without eares, or suggestion without eyes. Heere you may view and read Vertue personated in moderation: | heere you may know and prove Moderation to be the life of Vertue. Bee a president to your selfe what you should bee; as you are a president to others of what you are. It sufficeth me that I maske in the true simplenesse of a loyall honesty, and there shall no time steale from my remembrance, wherein I will fayle to witnesse the payment of a due | debt of thankfulnesse to one principally great in being nobly stiled in his owne worthinesse.*

    Benè vixit, qui benè latuit:
             Nam
    Honestè sapit qui non servivit malo publico.

THE GOLDEN Meane.

MEN, as they are all the Sonnes of their Mothers, are all the subjects of miserie; borne to live few dayes in many dangers: whose glory (if they were Monarches of their owne desires) | may be well compared to their shadowes in the Sunne; For, as the bodies shadow is at Morning before us, at Noone beside us, and at Night behinde us; so is earthly glory, at Morning or in the prime before us, in a goodly lustre; at Noone or in the full, besides us, in a violent heate; at Night or in the wane, behinde us, in a neglected pitty. The difference that is, is amongst some, that at Noone, or in the Meridian of their greatnesse, in stead of having their glory beside them, they are themselves beside their | glory. But such undoubtedly, are rather strangers to the bloud of Vertue then any way indued with the spirit of perfect noblenesse. But so unsetled are the grounds of frailties courses, as here is yet not the totall summe of being miserable. If men could as well frame their mindes to their change of fortunes, as their change of misfortunes doth corrupt their mindes, greatnesse would as truly welcome calamitie, as the base doe rejoyce in being great. Hereunto not the outward actions of the bodie, but the inward | temper of the minde must be framed, since the first are but handmaids to the latter. Even as one lying in the bed of visitation and death, doth not therefore die because he is sicke, but because he lives (for the deprivation of life is death, not sicknesse) so the minde of man divided by the consumption and disease of humour, being touched with affliction, is not therefore miserable because it suffers miserie, but because it hath once tasted (and beene lifted up to) happinesse.

The *Golden Meane*, so | aunciently commended, is onely there perfectly observed, where true Wisdome and true Nobilitie are the speciall ornaments of a prepared minde: In which, if those two meete, is figuratively included an allusion to the Sea: which, though clouds raine downe into it waters from above, and waters send flouds here

beneath, yet doth it retaine all, either without losse of saltnesse, or
any shew of overflowing: The minde of a Wise and Noble man is
such, that what or how many gusts and tides of | adversitie assault A9ᵛ
him, they may at all times rather arme, then at any time oppresse
him, since his resolution cannot overflow with the rudenesse of passion;
for that his excellent and refined temperature will ever retaine
the salt of judgement and moderation; the one proving a *Wise*, the
other a *Noble* man.

In sorrowes or adversities nothing is so fearefull as feare it selfe;
which passion of weakenesse is so below the heart of vertue, that
a minde trained up in the exercises of honour, | cannot as much as A10ʳ
let fall one looke to behold it. If it be inquired what it is, or to what
usefull end, either of ease or pollicy, it may be imployed? in the first
will be found little lesse then a desperate basenesse; in the latter nothing
more then an ungrounded desperatenesse. A man in the float of
prosperitie to feare that hee may fall, argues both the distrust of his
owne merit, [and] the danger of his dispostion. A man in the ebbe
of his plenty, to feare a worse mischiefe then that of being poore | A10ᵛ
or despised, argues both his unworthynesse in procuring, and his impatiencie
in bearing his fortune.

Feare with hope, is the readie witnesse of basenes: Feare without
hope, the proclaimer of folly. And if there can be any miserie superlative,
or if it were possible that there could be an extreame in measure,
it is in the feare of those twaine; yet doubtles the heaviest of
the two torments is to feare without hope. Either of which, to a
minde Noble and vertuous, are so much a stranger, as there | cannot A11ʳ
be found an interpretor, who to an honourable resolution can inforce
either the construction or understanding thereof. For it [is] as
meerely impossible for a great and excellent spirit to conceive thoughts
tending to basenesse, as for the base to apprehend the singular designes
belonging to the Nobly-minded. Soone then it is to be observed,
that the distinction betweene a worthy and a servile person, must
be rather found out in the qualitie of their mindes, then the command
of authoritie | and complement. In which it is also further to A11ᵛ
be observed, that in the composition of their mindes, there is as great
and exquisite choise to be made, aswell how as wherein the excellency
of such a composition must be remarked. The servile weakenesse

of such, whose education, nature, experience, and wisdome cannot claime any prioritie in desert, is so great, as it onely shewes that it distateth not calamitie, so long as it is full fed with the happinesse of plenty and ease. In the worthy | and desertfull it is nothing so: A12ʳ
75 for they truely considering the custome and necessitie (as they are men) of feeling change of states, doe ever arme their resolution, before it come, for calamitie, as when it comes, in it, against calamitie; wherein if the great and vertuous accidentally (not to speake of divine providence) fall, they therein chiefly shewe the vertue, of their
80 greatnes, and the greatnesse of their vertue, in that they know they then feele no more then at all times they were ordained | to beare. A12ᵛ
Such referre all accidents of infelicitie, to the incidence of their frailtie; measuring that being Men, they are but the miseries of men that may befall them. It was (not to be tedious in examples) a wonderfull
85 noblenesse and constancy in *Isocacius*, a chiefe man of *Antioch*, who standing at the Barre of judgement, was spoken to by *Posæus* the Soveraigne, who said; *Seest thou not* Isocacius *in what plight thou art?* Isocacius answered him, *I see it* (quoth hee) *and* | *marvell not; for* B1ʳ
since I am my selfe humane, I am come into an humane miserie.
90 Rare and wonderfull was the courage and temperance of this unimited Nobleman: and surely, where the minde is conformable, to remember it is carried in a bodie of Flesh, Discretion is the plotter, and moderation the actor of a notable worke. This worke, as it is to bee continued with singular fortitude, so must there a foun-
95 dation bee layd of an especiall wisedome; for hee who will climbe to the full height | of deserved glory, must ascend by the degrees B1ᵛ
of deserving fore-cast: which fore-cast, is even the ground-worke or basis of *perfect Vertue in extremitie*. It behoveth then a Noble and wise man, so to order the frame of his minde, that in what Sunshine of
100 greatnes soever he be, he may ever expect a storme to overcloud his eminence. And this is to be done by judicially examining, what the greatest temporall blessings approved by the vulgar opinion, in their owne properties are, and how subject | to monthly, daily, hourely B2ʳ
alteration: As what riches are they (as wealth is understood) whom
105 povertie and famine may not suddenly follow? what honour is that (as politique dignitie is understood) whose power, whose largenesse, whose dependences may not be followed by blemish, by envy, or by

extreame contempt? what Kingdome is that (as commaund and worldly governement is understood) to which may not ruine be ordained, depopulation, and mischiefe?

Prosperitie and adversitie | are not by long times often sundred; for sometimes is scant an houres difference betweene a Throne and a Cottage: *whereby all men may know that the condition of every man is changeable; and the wise may know that whatsoever may happen to another, may happen to himselfe.*

In auncient Recordes *Pompey* for wealth, *Sejanus* for Honour, *Ptolomy* for Kingdomes, are memorable: yet was *Pompey* for all his wealth poore, and beg'd. *Sejanus* for all his honour disgraced and executed: *Ptolomy* for all his | Kingdomes forgotten and extinguisht. If we would inquire into our owne moderne Chronicles; we may read of *Woolsey* the Cardinall, abounding in riches and abounding in miserie: ROBERT, Earle of ESSEX, propt up in honours, and cast downe by envie. Many of the *Henries*, Kings of much power and small fortune: other our Histories mention, who might as fitly bee heere induced, but that those being freshest in memorie, and all within the compasse of one age, will sooner stirre up our hearts, | and worke an impression in our beliefes, then others who are with us of lesse credite, because of more antiquitie.

Such men, as guided by the motions which perswade them to shrinke under the weight of their afflictions when they happen, and doe indeed yeeld unto that weaknes, doe but stand in their owne light, and deprive themselves of the best and only means which should shew the strength of their Courage in the Courage of their strength; in which respect the Cynicke Philosopher | told *Alexander*, standing betweene him and the Sunne, that he tooke that from him, that he could not give him, when men so unarmed against the necessitie of their sufferances, neede not an *Alexander* to shadow them from comfort, since their owne childishnesse is so great a discomfort, as that they want no secondarie interruption, from the way to learne and enjoy unhappinesse.

It is too usuall a custome amongst friends in calamitie, (if calamitie may be said to finde friends, as | it seldome doth, rather to disharten the partie grieved then by counsell and encouragement to strengthen him in a forward perseverance in resolution. Doubtlesse such a one as is not deafe to the discord of these passionate repetitions is much nearer to despaire then remedie, into which miserie if he fall he is truly miserable, and more miserable then any ordinarie misfortune that men are subject unto, can make another more resolvedly tempered at any time to feele: for which cause the consideration | what some in former times have beene, is an especiall and sure ground of ease, (if it be rightly applied) to acknowledge what hee himselfe now is, and this is not an idle labour to labour to attaine one direct rule which may leade to that worthie and lasting monument of that perfect vertue we speake of.

Another effectuall consideration to the building of this excellent worke of a resolved and prepared minde, is even in the foundation to be thought on. For if there be no certaintie in Wealth, in Honour, | in Soveraignty (in the fruition of whom, chiefely, if not onely, resteth the Paradise of an earthly Heaven) much lesse assurance may be dream't of in any inferiour pleasures: for which a wise man (who is the true Nobleman) ought thus to resolve, that he is not Lord of his owne minde who is undanted, as long as his fortunes are ministers to his will: but when he is cast down, or rather cast away in his hopes, undone in his expectation, set below his owne heart, unfriended, and the subject of uncomforting pittie: | Hee then who now witnesseth by his moderation in those sadnesses, the courage of his Noblenesse, by the Noblenesse of his Wisedome is both perfectly wise in being so couragious, and as perfectly couragious in being so noble. It was well said of one, that *A calme Sea and a faire Winde proves not a Sailers skill*. A sure Pilot is proved in a doubtfull storme, and a wise noble minde is truly tried in the storme of adversitie, not in the calme of felicitie. Fortune envies nothing more then a setled and | well governed resolution; and such a Marriner deserves remembrance to posteritie, who in Shipwracke dies, imbracing the Maste, rather then hee who faintly for feare of drowning leapes into the Sea.

Can it be imagined that a fellow by law appointed to some severe death should be reputed valiant if when the executioner is to performe the commaund of Justice the wofull prisoner winke in feare to see his owne bloud? Is this praise-worthie when we are more terrified with | the sight of our miseries then with tasting and sustayning them? Surely no; yet such is the madnesse of those who have not learn't to conquere by bearing their destinies, as when the tide of sorrowes rush upon them they doe so impatiently accuse themselves of wretchednesse, as truely they doe nothing else but winke (and herein deserve as much contempt as those that winke) for feare to behold the executions they are to undergoe.

As it oftentimes is seene the onely way to put some notorious foole that esteemes | the perfection of a brave spirit to consist in the B7ᵛ fopperie of unseemely behaviour (fitly and yet more grossely tearmed swaggering) out of his vaine bias is by once daring him in his owne qualitie; so is it with unprosperous passages of infelicitie when it chanceth, if we out-dare it, and strive and strive, and ever as it comes more and more, so lesse and lesse to yeeld unto it, without all peradventure we shall not onely qualifie the hate of adversities worst assault, but purchase that ease and | consolation to our distresses, that B8ʳ wee shall have our mindes becalmed with the blessednesse of content, and rest what Windes of heavinesse so ever rage, or over, or about us. And he who thus prepareth himselfe, is a Noble man, for his courage will argue his Noblenesse: so must hee likewise bee necessarily a wise man, for his moderation will commend his wisedome.

Lastly, if neither the respect of the instabilitie of humane endowments, neither the regard of honor, | being prone to fall, nor the B8ᵛ unstaidnesse of Kingdomes (the Scepter beeing the highest flight of Ambition) cannot imprint in the minde an abandoning of it selfe, by reputing earthly delight and acquisitions to be in their owne nature, as in their owne nature they are, passable and uncertaine; yet may the surenesse of paying a debt (which cannot be excused) to death, be a mayne and singular motive to a noble and wise man, for sufferance of all changes of conditions and estates, with the sweetely-united | blessings, *Judgement* and *Content*. He that remem- B9ʳ bers that he lives a life, cannot but fore-thinke that he must die a death: If hee looke into what life it selfe is, hee shall finde (by experience of the past, and proofe of the present age) that it is none other but a journey to death. If a man examine the scope of his owne desires, they will fall out to be a desiring to hasten to his grave. Death and the grave (two tortures to the memory of worldly foolish men) are the onely principall ends to which the vanitie of | pleasures runne B9ᵛ at: For men in wealth, in honour, in government, desire the time to come; the one in hope of increase of his gaine, the other of his greatnesse, the third of Empyrie. So what else doe they but covet by growing elder in daies, to flie to the full race of their living, which is death? Of this a true Noble-man should not, and a true wise man cannot feare. It was an answere (worthy the speker) of the Philosopher, who hearing of his Sonnes death said: *When I had begotten him I well knew hee | should die*: and who would be so ignorant as not to confesse that whosoever is brought out of the wombe is destined also to the sepulchre of the earth? To a man prepared by the light of the minds vertue, this is ever seeming necessarie, as well willingly to restore that when it is required of him, though it were by death, as to enjoy that which is given him, if it were his life, since one being borne into the one cannot escape the other. The Minde should ever keepe measure, what of necessitie it must suffer let it | not feare: what is doubtfull that it may suffer, let it always looke for: So shall it not be afflicted before afflictions doe come; nor unprovided when they are come.

All men, yea all things, must be freed by an end, though the end bee not alike to all, neither in manner or time; some forgoe their lives in the middle of their time, some in the dawning of their life, some live till they are even weary of living, some dying naturally, some violently, others enforcedly, many (in respect of men) casually, | but all at some time dying. In this kinde then it is questionable, whether it bee more foolish not to know, or more shamefull not to imbrace nature: Hee that lives well needeth not to feare the uglines of death appearing in any forme, or in any disguise; if he first resolve, that whensoever or howsoever hee comes, yet it is but death, and it must come.

Some one that is to travaile of necessity upon the hazard of his life, unto Constantinople by land, being unexperienc't in the | dangers, and the many miseries of his journey, for his better instructions, seekes comfort in the councell of another, who hath bought knowledge of the way with the price of many weary and distressed paces, and being come, learnes this for an approved certainty; that first the journey it selfe is long and tedious, the way troublesome and uneven, the change of ayres infectious and unhealthy, the desarts wast and uncomfortable, directions chargeable and uncertaine, here Theeves

prepared to spoyle, there | Beasts set all on ravine; surety no where, B12r
danger on all hands, and, what is the worst of these adventures, if
hee obtaine the scope of his desires, and arrive even to the furthest
of his journey, yet shall he there finde a Turke that is Emperour, cruell
260 in nature, boundlesse in command, faithlesse of truth, treacherous,
and full of the bloud of Christians: What comfort resteth to bee hoped
for from this afflicted travailer, or what should he doe? To goe is
the hazard of life, to stay the certainty of death: now the Noblenes
| of Wisedome must direct, and the Vertue of Noblenesse incourage B12v
265 his resolution, to resolve a steadines of minde to countermaund the
heavinesse of both fortunes: And it behoves such a man, so travail-
ing, to be prepared, aswell to beare danger when he meetes with
it, as to be instructed before, that there is danger to be met with.
In like manner is every man borne to greatnesse, so likewise borne
270 to journey to death. To which ere he come, (death being the furthest
home of all our travailes) we must | know that wee are to passe C1r
through the miseries of mortallity, and particularly informe our selves
that life it selfe (how short soever) in respect of it's frailty, is long
and tedious, the manner of living troublesome and uneven, the change
275 of estates infectious to the minde, unhealthy to the soule, the wil-
dernesse of opinion and judgement wasted by the cause, and com-
fortlesse in the effects of folly: directions to reformation chargeable,
if we respect our ignorance, uncertaine if wee remember our wilful-
nesse: | Here on the one side are theeves, even our affections, to spoile C1v
280 us of vertue; there on the other side Beasts, which are defects of rea-
son, set on to devoure us; even our manner of living is a baite to
allure us from the surety of life, and when wee are come to the dead-
ly sickenesse that must finish our course, the worst of evill is, that
having past all the quick-sands and perils of life, wee have within
285 us death it selfe in our owne conscience, to bring us to death.

    Nothing is left therefore | to a man borne to live, but a stayed C2r
and a sure resolution to be armed to die. In which hee is to care,
not where hee shall die, or in what manner, or in what estate, but
that hee must die, and in what minde, and in what memorable vertues.
290   Heere, the foundation to the erecting the Master-piece of the *Golden
Meane* being layd now upon these or some other considerations, not
much differing from these; a Noble wise man is then to know his

owne worth, wherby calamity may not | cast him so downe, as that C2ᵛ
he cannot call to minde that he hath beene once happy; as greatnes
might not so lift him up as that he should be secure that hee could
never be unhappie.

For as a Bladder that is blowne up wil (being fast tied) many daies
continue full if laid aside, and not unbound, but with the least pricke
of a needle, how little soever, looseth both his fulnesse and strength;
even so, and none other is it with some, who as long as the float
of their greatnesse lasteth being | never pricked with the sharpe sting C3ʳ
of opposition and change, doe vainely imagine that they are unfit
to enjoy plentie, who cannot support it with a lively and lasting in-
heritance of retayning it: but when a very little alteration of their
pompe waineth their pompe to a decay, then like Bladders, they burst
with venting their owne breath; chiefely for that they were alway
cursed with that mischievous flatteries of themselves that they were
too great to fall. *Securitie* in the possession of Honor | and prosperitie C3ᵛ
is a headlong running to ruine: he who hath in himself worth and
worthinesse will so moderate the course of his resolution and actions
as that his resolutions shall be directed to doe well, as his actions
may prove that he meant well; and then whatsoever the end fall out
to be, repentance cannot buy afterwit too deare, nor after-wit have
cause to repent too late.

It is much needfull that worthie personages having merit to com-
mend their bloud, and birth to make goodly their merit, | should C4ʳ
in such sort bee both knowers and directors of their owne vertues
as neither honourable estimation should so purchase the opinion of
vanitie, to be blowne up with the simplicitie of pride; neither a too
low discent to the weakenesse of servilitie, that they are become the
miracles of [pittie]. He that knowes himselfe, not that he is so much
a great man as a good man; knowes likewise it is a labour of as rare
desert to preserve *Goodnesse*, as to finde it; as on the other part, the
meerely ambitious rather | studie to finde greatnesse, then being found C4ᵛ
and enjoyed to preserve it. Such principles in generall, being by a
discerning judgement contrived, the contriver cannot bee farre from
the [paths] that leade to this *Golden Meane*.

If here it be objected a difficultie in observation of those former
grounds, and the ease of prescribing rules to *Constancie* and *Steddinesse*

much to differ from the narrownesse of using them; it may well be replied that there is perversenesse rather then impossibilitie in much disputation. | For commonly with pleasure men will binde their indeavour to indeavour any course which out of their conceit shall yeeld content to the libertie of their wils; and why then should it bee more hard to restraine that libertie, as wel for the accomplishing a perfect man? In sickenesse and disease of the bodie we are well pleased to observe diet, to abstaine from meates most agreeable to our appetites, and shall it be thought an unreasonable injunction to diet our pleasures and infirmities | for the health of the minde? Ambitious men in compassing the plots of revenge upon others, will tye themselves to many straite inconveniences; so should good men much more allow any burthen (if it be called a burthen to deserve excellent reputation) to worke miracles (above the capacitie of the vulgar) upon themselves, which daily as they should doe, so being truly (as they are truly proved to be) good, they will doe, in the ordinarie progresse of their lives and practise of their behaviours, as wel | for Example as Honours sake.

It is many times seene that those who lead their lives according to the measure of their will and power, doe not measure their will and power according to the frailtie of their lives; yet certainely they lead an evill life who are still beginning to live, for that life is ever unperfect which hath learned but the first onely rule to goodnesse: certaine other, then chiefly begin to live when they are certaine to end the race of so living, by death; and some also | there are, who end their lives before they can well be said to have begun to live.

Most men subject to those unhappinesses, like things floating on the water, doe not goe, but are carried; not the counsell of providence directs [their] steps to goe by the staffe of Discretion, but they are wholly rather carried by the violent streame of *Opinion* and Conceit, precisely termed *Humour*. To unmaske the vizour that hides the deformitie of this customarie vilenesse, much guilt is | to be laid on the change of the times, or indeed on the change of men in the times. For, whiles the World was yet in her infancy, neyther was such plentie of temptation to invite, neyther was vanitie so plentifull to tempt the happinesse of that age to the miseries of this: But as dayes grew more numberles in number, so men in those dayes waxed more ir-

regular in manners: which irregularitie of manners, increased by the deprivation of reason in men of all conditions; in fooles ever; in the wise | often; for even the wise doe themselves, not seldome suffer an C7ᵛ
370 eclipse of reason.

The difference that is, is for that such a defect proceeds rather out of the infirmity of nature, then out of any subjection of the minde: for, where the minde is subjected to the grossenes of errour, there doth the man so for the time (so subjected) forsake the course of
375 Wisedome, which like a fixed Starre should (howsoever the heavens move) be unmoveable, and unmoved in the Center of his place; | C8ʳ and such as so is, is truly said to be true *Noblenesse*, true *Vertue*, true *Wisdome*.

It is one thing to doe well, and another thing to continue to doe
380 well: for it is not enough to be a good man, unlesse he be a good man, still. That to see an Noble man who hath sifted from him the lets and impediments which might hinder his resolution in the attayning and retayning this singuler worke of moderation, knowes that the *Meane* ever in all, the middle betweene all, then leaves to
385 bee the *Meane* when it | begins to incline to the right, or decline C8ᵛ to the left side. In the Historie of the elder Romans *Mutius Scævola* is principally commended for being constant in his paines to the end. A *Mutius Scævola* is every free spirit, and his spirit hath he (at least the praise of it) who persevers in his sufferances, so it be in a case
390 of reputation; otherwise it cannot bee but improperly called the *Meane* unlesse it be also in a noble carriage of extremitie in a good cause, or in such a cause which newnesse and | reformation doth better C9ʳ and make good. Not to exceede in words, let us yet come somewhat more particularly to the matter proposed.

395 Even as one that is to frame a goodly building on a delightfull plot of ground, doth first providently forecast as well of the hazards and hinderances that may come, as the charge which daily must come. Amongst which must principally be considered, the title of the right, and what clayme may be laid thereto, and what meanes may be used
400 | to remove that clayme. Then the necessitie of provision, the casuall C9ᵛ change of weather, the wearinesse of working; for all which, if interaccidents of extremitie should happen, remedies for the same must be thought on. So a man in his minde wisely resolved to the build-

ing of this excellent frame of the *Golden Meane*, on the plot of a pre-
pared resolution, must endeavour to provide cures against the fates
of extremitie: A few of which extremities that doe many times as-
sault the temper of a Noble vertue, | it shall not much differ from
the purpose and present to point at.

But first of all, ere the miseries severally to be
treated of, are set forth; it will be fit to be inquired
what a Miserie is; and how it may be so positively
called. Every misfortune is not a miserie, though the publicke errour
intitle (but untruly) the unfortunate, Miserable. A Miserie is rightly
and properly that which is an accident of change of estate, from bet-
ter to worse, occasioned by the evill disposition of an unworthines
of minde. | This is indeede a *Misery*, into which, whatsoever hee be
that falleth, he cannot accidentally, but willfully, and deservedly come:
although touching the change of estate, it may best be called an *Acci-
dent*, since all estates being temporall and temporary, are by reason
of their mutabilitie, accidentall. In example, as a man who hath com-
mitted some wicked act, as the murther of his Prince, or other sub-
ject, being prompted hereto by no other reason, then his owne private
ambition and revenge, | and afterwards applaudes impenitently his
cursed assassination or villanie. This man is indeede come into a ful-
nesse of miserie. Such-like might be inferred, but for that the judg-
ment of the times misconster miseries in another sence, and the cus-
tomarie misfortunes which betide many men daylie, are clearest in
sight, having onely toucht at this: wee will descend to those.

With men of Honour and Nobilitie, the chiefe
misfortunes that can, or doe usually happen, are
| either *Disfavour, Neglect,* forfeit of *Estate, Ban-
ishment, Imprisonment,* or *Death.* The remedies
against all which, shall easily in particular bee sub-
serted.

Disfavour, often times comes either through *Privie
malice, selfe-unworthynesse, Envie,* or sometimes
through the variablenesse of an unguided Princes inclination: To each
of those, a wise man may, and a good man will, soone apply a medi-
cine, and in that a recovery.

Disfavour is usually knowne, according to the | opinion of the

> What a Miserie is.

> Sixe Miseries that may befall a Noble man.

> 1 *Disfavor.*

multitude, by the name of disgrace; for it is a certaine assurance (as the received vanitie of the common errour reputeth, that how deere so ever a great or worthy person hath beene to the bosomes and counsels of his Soveraigne, yet if in any measure there be but a dayes, or an houres intermission of that royall love, then straight such a favorite is esteemed disgraced; and which is a much stranger madnesse, if the Prince having out of his affection exalted some one or other to place and titles | of Honour, yet if some person be not ever rising to more and more Honors, he is accounted to stand by little and little in the rancke of a disgraced *Courtier*. So that to speake truth, there can be but little hope to attaine the *Meane* by him in his fortunes (and so, neither by consequent in the managing of his owne resolutions) who onely depends upon the suretie of being indeared to his Soveraign, unlesse he firmely rest prepared to entertaine any slacknes of preferment with a wise and discreet content.

To deserve the grace of a Prince is an honorable happinesse; yet is not the losse of it (being once deserved) a misery; especially to wise men, since wise men may bee made subject, but never subjects to miserie: calamitie may exercise, but not oversway their vertues: misfortune may be an usurping tyrant to paine them, but never a received soveraigne to command them: If the Prince his gracious favour be lost through the *privie malice* of some, who fill the eares of Majestie with the discord | of slaunder and untruth, grounded upon the sandie foundation of uncertaine discontent, or dishonourable revenge, then hath a wise Noble man, out of those very wrongs, strong arguments to perswade his reason, that there is much reason why he should bee perswaded to moderation: for being innocent of any voluntarie action or intent that might make his faith questionable, or his service dangerous, or his merit of lesse value then a voyce of generall commendations hath formerly | witnessed, his owne cleerenesse may ever rest upon the unmoved pillars of his owne Noble integritie.

Privie Malice
1. cause of *Disfavour.*

Hee knowes not the way to preferment by his Princes love, who will not know that privie malice doth bend all it's cunning and dishonestie to lay a stumbling blocke in his passage hereunto. Heare is a Conquest well worthie a triumph, if in the height of the favour royall, a man in honour can so dispose of his owne carriage (which

verie fewe can, yet the wisely | Noble and Nobly wise will doe) as D2ᵛ
that in the closet and harbour of his own knowledge he be sure that
there [he] is free of any guilt which the sting of privie malice would
labor to wound him with. This then standing thus, why should any
desertfull vertue storme for the losse of that favour which in his owne
innocence it hath merited to keepe? He is surely happie, and not farre
from a blessing, no not farre from a blessednesse, who can say to
himselfe, *I am true and time shall not blemish me; | I will be in my truth* D3ʳ
approved, and time cannot wrong mee; If I live, my truth shall bring mee
with peace to my death, when I die, my steddinesse shall give immortalitie
to my life. Here, to such a man (that can thus say) is securitie in the
conscience, wisedome in living, noblenesse in death.

Where a man in grace with his Soveraigne fals *Self-unworthines,*
from it by a *selfe-unworthinesse*, it is farre otherwise: 2. cause of
and undoubtedly, whosoever is so impoisoned with *Disfavour.*
the diseases of | his minde, or the infirmitie of his bodie hath great D3ᵛ
and principall causes to move him to seeke for remedy against the
[despection] of the one, and the aspertion of the latter. To this *selfe-*
unworthinesse, eyther in minde or bodie, may be referred *Ambition*,
the Mother of disloyall plots and practises: *Discontent*, the Nurse to
conspiracies; *Covetousnes,* that kindling fires with the fuel of *Monopo-*
lies is inforced to quench them with the teares of disgrace, and that
which soone followes thereon, | Contempt. *Vaine-glory*, or *Pride*, which D4ʳ
whiles with *Pompeys* minde it cannot brooke the title of a superiour,
is with *Pompeys* fortunes cast downe beneath the pittie of their equals.
Faction, which like a foolish Flye in the candle, labors her owne death;
with other diseases, too many to be tediously recited: or to this *self-*
unworthines, thorough the infirmitie of the body, which more espe-
cially consists in action, may be referred Ryot, in al men a madnes,
in Noble men a blemish, and to good Princes most displeasant; or
| Quarrelling, which ever brings danger with too late repentance; D4ᵛ
or wantonnes, the overthrow of many goodly kindreds and families;
or scurrility, with other such like. Since when mention is made of
the unworthinesse of bodie, it is not any defect in Nature, or naturall
proportion, but in manners outwardly acted. For many times it is
commonly seene, that where Nature hath fail'd in some parts of the
outward man, she hath oftentimes supplied those wants with a preg-
nancy of minde.

A president whereof is, | (not to borrow of auncient Histories) D5ʳ
even in the CHRONICLES of our present memories, in the person of
ROBERT, the late Earle of SALISBURIE, a man whose unevennesse of
shape was perfected with the perfect furniture of a reaching and in-
dustrious wit. So was the crookednesse of *Æsope* made straight in
the sweetnesse of his invention. And *Socrates*, that odde man of *Athens*,
is said to have said of himselfe, *that education and Art in him, had changed
the course of Natures unfurnished workmanship.*

Of these, and such imperfections of bodie, it is not here intended, D5ᵛ
but of such as by their owne *selfe-unworthinesse* in bodie, in minde,
and often in both, doe loose the intrest, their Bloud, Birth, and
Noblenesse (being noble indeed by those both) hath in their Princes
opinion.

A remedie against *selfe-unworthinesse*, must be found out in a *selfe-
reformation*; which being sincerely performed, the follies of the past
times belong not to the reformed.

If one should call such a one (as hath beene knowne | for a notori- D6ʳ
ous robber) Theefe, being certainely sorrowfull, penitent, and accompt-
able for all his errours in that kinde, doubtlesse it were much in-
discretion in the Agent to speake so to him, and more in the Patient
to esteeme it as spoken of him, since wise and good men as they
do not repute those things theirs which they have not done, so must
they neither acknowledge for theirs which they now presently doe
not. *Non vocamus ea nostra quæ non ipsi fecimus, at quæ non ipsi facimus*,
as the right sense | of the olde Verse contayneth. D6ᵛ

In reason it cannot but be confessed, that it is much more to bee
wished, to change from *evill to good*, then from *temperance to libertie*.
Marcus Aurelius wil be ever renowmed and more memorable, for his
latter government, then was *Nero* for his first five yeares, yet had the
one by his beginning, purchast a strong beliefe, that hee could not
raigne amisse: as the other, by the disorders of his youth that there
was little hope he could deserve to raigne | at all. It appertaines not D7ʳ
to any man what he hath beene, if he be throughly reformed; since
a new life gives another birth: the leaving of evill, being but a buriall
of evill, and the imbracing of worthinesse, a christning of reputa-
tion: how unworthie soever then a Princes favorite hath beene, yet
his reformation gives praise to his change, and so is still by that to
comfort his fall from greatnes, and esteeme himself fit for that favour,

which though he hath lost, yet he hath again found in his owne
merite.

So then: Hath a great PEERE lost his Princes favour, because he deserved to loose it? let not this deject or cast him downe in minde, since as by a chaunge from good to worser hee forwent his Princes love, or rather his Princes love him; So yet by a change from bad to better, hee still is worthie of a repossession of that love, though hee repossesse it not: And what worth cannot be seene by the publique little eye of the great world, by reason of his beeing clouded from the Sunne of his life and glory, his Prince; let it bee so much the more seene by the private great eye of his owne little world (even himselfe and his owne comforts) and teach him to know the difference betweene a great and a good man, the one preferring vertue onely for greatnesse, the other preferring greatnesse for the greatnesse of vertue onely.

Another cause, which not seldom procureth *dis-favour* from the Prince, is that old enemie to desert *Envie*, who is so auncient a Courtier, and so tried in the passages of all ages, that such a man as is in favour with his Soveraigne, deserving so to be, and imagining himselfe to be without the compasse of *Envie*, is too securely, and in that securitie, too simply armed against his owne ruine.

Envie the 3. cause of *Disfavour*.

Heere now is a broad path, leading, or more truly teaching the readie course to the excellent meane of *Temperance* and *Moderation*. Every man ought to rejoyce and solace himselfe in his owne perfections: for it is as beast-like not to know his proper value at all, as it is divellish to know it too much. *Humble-Pride* is a proud humilitie, and such as exercise it with innocence rather then curiositie, doe but shew the difference betweene a nobly generous, and a basely fantasticall Nature. Whereby then should a man be perswaded that he is an imbracer of vertue, more then in that hee is prosecuted by the restlesse venome of the envious?

Hath this secret mischiefe displaced any desertfull favorite of the benefite of the favour royall? assuredly hee hath little cause to distaste it any thing, or to be moved from the commendation of a resolved minde, that as hee shall by tempering his disgrace with sufferance, increase the honor of his merit, so shall hee give matter still of more envie to the envious, who are oftentimes as much afflicted with the patience, as they are with the prosperitie of the party envied.

It is better to be envied then pittied, pitty proceeding out of a cold charitie | towards the miserable; envie out of a corruption of qualitie against the vertuous. If it be objected that the losse of a Princes favour, through the instigation of some envious opposite, hath most cause to afflict a noble minde, in that his enemie hath prevailed against him; the same reason may be answered with the same reason. That such an enimie cannot be said to prevaile, who fights with the weapons of a dishonourable treachery; and what greater triumph or conquest can a Wise or | a Noble man wish to enjoy, then to torment his adversary with the perfections of his vertue? But in the meane time *envy* overrules? True, and here is an inducement to a steady moderation, in that it is but *envy*. But the Princes favour is by this meanes lost? So is a Noble mans selfe-worthinesse by the same meanes found: and it is a greater blemish to the judgement of a Prince so traduced, not to examine the particulars why hee doth reject a worthy subject, then to the subjects worthinesse, without | particular examinations from his Prince to be rejected. So, neither then should *envy* remove, but for that it is *envy*, confirme and strengthen a noble resolution.

Sometimes the *variablenesse of the Princes inclination*, his addiction to change from royall Vertues to horrible Vices, is the reason of his *disfavour* with those who are of the best desart: Such and of such conditions were in *England*, RICHARD *the second*, in *Rome*, NERO, in *Sicile*, DIONISIUS, and such are for the most part | all Tyrants, who if they exercise not their tirannies over the lives, yet certainly exercise it over the harts of their faithfullest subjects. Such Princes are rather wanton in their favours then judicious, and the weakenesse of vertue is the cause of that deprivation of judgement. How happy is that man who hath lost that grace (with a Prince of that condition) which he may rest confident he never (or never surely) had?

The Princes inconstancy, the last cause of *Disfavour*.

And above many other motives, this is most generall and most effectuall | to rectifie a wise mans minde, for such a one as layes the foundations of his hopes on the moveable sandes of his Princes favour, is like a foolish Marchant that adventures all his substance in a broken vessell: and hee that relyes on the unhappinesse of such favour, must of necessitie banish al Noble resolutions from his dissignes: for it is a headlong folly, and wilfull [distraction] that such a one seekes, if hee doe not as well resolve to endevour to preserve and continue his Princes grace | as to finde and enjoy it.

Now this is a direct, or indeede indirect running away from the maine worke of goodnesse: for to as many vices as the Nature and life of a wicked man may be inclined, to so many must he addresse himselfe to be a bawd, if not an actor in them; and of all unhappines this is the first. Certainly good Clarkes have said, and experience doth witnesse, that an exact Courtier is seldome a good man; for not to speake of generall enormities in particular; Courtiers are most times | given over to those two wonderfull [madnesses], *Pride* and *Riot*, Pride countenancing their Riot, and Riot making glorious their Pride. What a blessing (for it is more then a happinesse) the shunning of those common errours is, the wiseman will acknowledge, and the fortunately Noble may prove.

Princes sometimes are unguided in their dispositions, and then he who is neerest in favor, is in greatest danger of his place, which happening many times, puts him in many | feares, in so much as even the ground worke that beares up his ambition is shaken with every breath of an unpleasant word: And what miserie then can that be, to be out of this miserie; especially when the Prince is of a changeable and devided minde? So that he that will ingeniously looke into the worst of a Princes disfavour (himselfe not detected of unworthines) may likewise ingeniously confesse that there is much gaine in such a losse.

Quinquennium Neronis.

One generall note is ever remarkeable in a | Prince, whose uncertaintie of favour, is curious to please his variablenesse in the change of newe friends; that then the *Ancient Nobilitie* beares alwaies the least sway; for the government of that Princes minde, is so besotted with affecting his owne affections, as hee accounteth those onely worthie of the Noblest titles and preferments, which hee imagineth are (but in themselves else are not) desertfull.

And (most lamentably) are places of Authoritie rent from the | administration of perfect *Wisedome*, and perfect *Noblenesse*, to be conferred on those, who are *onely wise, because thought so, and onely Noble,*

because made so. Wherin the *Noble* indeed are upon very trifles quar-
relled against, that the possession of their Honors and Jurisdictions,
may passe smother away to other upstart favorites: and this cannot
be other then a maine wound, both to *vertue* and the *lovers of vertue*.

That people which is under the commaund of that Prince, who
is alwaies | chosing of new Minions, were without all question be
rather governed by a childe (which is one curse to a bodie politique)
then by such a Soveraigne, as is ever in his approvements childish.
So likewise if a whole Kingdome smart in the inconstancie of an
uncertaine head, how much shall private members of that large com-
pact smart, who are nearest at hand, to receive the whips which such
an inconstancie (upon very causelesse toyes of conceit) is like to afflict
them with, and inflict | upon them? *Sweet is the bread of content, and
the sleepe of securitie is a bread of sweetenesse*: both which (being the
sinewes that knit together the joyntes of life) everie one whose free-
hold of estate relyes upon a *Court nod*, may not seldome misse: for
Distrust must give digestion to his foode, as *Envie* will minister op-
position to his rest. And how then can hee be reputed miserable,
who hath shooke off the yoke of his feare, and with it the feare of
a greater yoke?

Of other miseries, (which are so reputed amongst   *Of Neglect.*
men) that may happen to a Noble person, *Neglect*
is esteemed another, that is, when his service for his countrey, or
advise for the State, or indeavours to content his Soveraigne, are eyther
not commended, or at least not rewarded; heere is required indeed
much vertue to conquer that part of man which is meerely man,
and to stand resolute upon the guard of his owne worthinesse. This
Neglect in a Prince, comes | from an insensible ingratitude, or want
of discerning quicknesse in the faculties of his soule. If from ingrati-
tude, (a sinne hatefull in all men, but in Kings, estates, or gover-
nours horrible) then that fortune, or (if you so please to terme it)
misery of *Neglect* is easie to be borne: for by how much a Prince is
unthankful in rewarding the service of his subject, by so much the
more is he ingaged to all memories of being a dishonorable debtor.

And though a man is bound to pay the best of | his service eyther
to his KING or COUNTRY, in the safetie of the one, and preservation
of the other, and dutie to both, yet so are both his KING and Coun-

try interchangeably bound to favour, cherish, and respect worth in a worthy deserver. But if *Neglect* proceed out of a want of judgement or a decerning Vertue, then hath the neglected much more cause to beare that injury. A man is not to expect thanks from an Oxe, or a Horse, for feeding, littering, dressing and smoothing of him, because it | is an Oxe or a Horse to whom hee doth it. Truely a E5ᵛ governour of people, that can eate, clothe and feede [by] another mans labours, and cannot give acknowledgement at least to him who by the working of his braines, expence of his bloud, and consumption of his estate, or such like services, doth in peace, feede and clothe his King and Country, such a ruler differs in this little from a beast, that hath not reason, or at least the use of reason.

But if *Neglect* come from the unsteddinesse of | the common peo- E6ʳ ple, then it is nothing strange: for as they are wonne in an houre, so are they lost in a minute; and whosoever coveteth popular applause, or depends upon the praises of the vulgar, doth with the dogge in *Æsope, Amittere carnes, captare* [*umbras*]; imbrace clouds, and beget Centaures; and doth justly deserve no commendations at all for so seeking to be commended.

Not without fit cause were the greater number of the ruder, and more ignorant sort in a kingdome called a *beast with many* | *heads*; E6ᵛ many heads they are indeed, and yet but one beast. For that as well in their loves, as in their hatreds, they are not guided by any proportion, no not by any portion at all of reason. *Violence in judgement and wilfulnesse in errour*, like two untamed Heifers, draw them and their best knowledges quite contrarie waies. In so much as often their voyces discent from their meaning, and most often their harts from their voyces. All that they know to doe, is that they know, that they know not what to do; | all what they meane to determine, proves E7ʳ in effect, but determination of meaning nothing at all. They intend (most foolishly) what they never put in action, they many time act (most unsafely) what was never within the compasse of their intention. And are these, things, for *A wise* and *Noble man* to crave helpe from, for building a Castle of defence against the siege of adversities? Or are these fit Instruments that should threaten a man (who hath built indeed a Castle of resolution in his | owne stayed E7ᵛ wisedome) with feare of contempt? they are not; but he truly is prepared against this mischiefe of *neglect*, who wins the multitude without feare to loose them, or looseth them without care to winne them, so that his owne *goodnesse* make him safe against the danger of *Opinion* or *Accusation*.

If yet it be fit to inquire further into the maine construction, what, or of what value and moment this *Neglect* is, experience in others will learne us to be Schoole-masters to | our selves; for let a man be never so [eminent] in authoritie under his PRINCE, let him have what greatnesse he can imagine, and what Adoration and Reverence the humilitie of the publique wonder can give, let his words bee observed as *Oracles*, his commaunds as *Lawes*, his displeasure as *Death*, yet with the flight of a thought if upon some dislike grounded or ungrounded, the King at any time shorten his Royall favour, or the Law in any | poynt take hold on him, whereby he appeares to the judgement of the world to bee entring into the way of miserie, how sensibly and how soone shall he feele an alteration of those large flatteries which the servilitie of the uncertaine people promised?

A witnesse hereof in his time was, and in this time may bee, *John*, that great and last Duke of NORTHUMBERLAND, whose pride and ruine were at once hastened by the too much confidence he had | in the hearts of the Cominaltie; with what speed was hee disgraced of his Soveraigne, forsaken of the Lords, and despised of the multitude, who is onely covetous of any Noveltie, though it be change from the good to the worst? A just man therefore (whose soundnesse of minde like the Centre of the earth stands ever unmoved) by the light of those few precedent reasons may understand how easie it is for the popular judgement as well in distinctions of Miseries as of happinesse to | erre: for as they account estates and conditions miserable, which are not sustained with the vanitie of outward glory, or fulnesse of substance; so doe they likewise reckon that felicity the truest happinesse, whose dignitie and mightinesse is like the blazing Starre, for the present, as strange as fearefull: and for a Wise, a Good, a Noble Spirit to bee dejected with the *neglect* of love in such creatures, would bee strong proofe that hee never had the perfect relish either of perfect | wisedome, perfect goodnesse, or perfect Nobilitie.

Like as hath before beene said of *Neglect*, so much, or more, may be inferred of that misery called the *forfeiture of Estate*, that is, of all such plenty or fulnesse of temporall substance, as with worldly men the name and possession of riches doth include. *Forfeiture of Estate.*

Of all other Miseries this in the judgement of such as are not truly directed by truest judgement, is reputed the most miserable: insomuch | as most men thinke, and so thinking, so resolve, that *Death*, in any forme, is much more tollerable then beggary (for so they terme poverty) by any casualty.

One example or president to both Noble and understanding men, of what commendation the abandoning of rich fortunes [is], being reported by *Quintus Curtius*, may be remembred with immortall glory, of *Abdo-lominus*, a poore man; rich in all plenty, except plenty of riches, to whom *Alexander* of MACEDON, proffering the Kingdome of *Sidon* | to him, who was before but a Gardener, was by him refused, who replied that he would take no care to loose that which hee never cared to enjoy. The Historie is worthy, and the answere full of observation, and will bee ever memorable.

Of all other things, free spirits and wise men should least respect the losse of temporall wealth, which is no part of a man.

The furniture of the minde, is the man himselfe: which if it be apparrelled (as it should be) with ornaments that were never | bound prentice to that thraldome which keepes Creatures of lowe hopes in bondage, is then chiefly free it selfe. *Abundance* was created for use, not for *worship*: it is an excellent *Servant*, but a most evill *Master*. A *wise man* ought to live by it, not for it: since they are neither of the essence of the *soule*, to make it immortall, nor of the *minde*, to give it rest without vexation, nor of the *body* to keep it from putrifaction. *Worldly substance* being in it's nature corruptible, cannot so bewitch a good *man*, that he | should repute it to be other then *worldly substance*, and therefore corruptible.

Riches were fitly by the Philosophers called *bona Fortunæ*, uncertaine endowments; to figure unto us, that as fortune is ever variable, so should her benefits be reputed but unconstant friends: in regard whereof they were excluded from the gifts, as well of the body, as of the minde, that is, neither Health, Beautie or vertues of any sort, did neede the ornament of those gifts of Fortune.

A good man, if of his owne industrie and merit hee hath pur- E12ᵛ
chased unto himselfe wealth, hath little reason to grieve at the losse
of them, since he remaines still as perfect in the cunning of gayning
as when he first began: but another of more aboundance, whose pos-
sessions come to him by inheritance without any care of his owne,
he hath no reason at all to distaste the seizure of his estate, since
he doth forgo but that which hee never laboured for. Truly in respect
of this it behoveth every resolved minde to | beare the courage of F1ʳ
the wise man of GREECE, that said, hee at all times carried all what
was his with him wheresoever he went.

Wisedome, Temperance, Valour, Justice, are the substance and heredi-
tary possessions of a perfectly happie man, and these *riches* cannot
be forfaited, except by a decay of Vertue, they cannot be seized ex-
cept the owner cast them off, they cannot suffer contempt so long
as they be nourished in a Noble minde. Indeed *riches* are to a good
man like a light silken Cloake upon his | backe, who is else provided F1ᵛ
against the extreamitie of cold with warme furres: So he that hath
his owne goodnesse and resolution to warme him in all Winters of
adversitie, needs wealth but as a thinne silken Cloake upon a furred
Gowne, rather to shew the vanitie of his disposition, then any usefull
imployment to the sustenance of life.

If nature be provided for against hunger with meate; against frosts
with apparrell; against contempt with comelinesse, the desire of money
or | large Lordships, argues but the base filthinesse of an unsatisfied F2ʳ
covetousnesse.

In all men the way to *covet is the way to bee poore.* For how can
hee be sayd to be *Rich* who wants? and he certainely wants, who
is ever more desiring. In soules not refined by knowledge, *Covetous-
nesse* is shamefull, but in *Noble men* so shamefull, as what abundance
of Vertue else soever they have, this onely vice drownes it, darkenes
it, makes it *all, nothing. Bountie* strings up the hearts | of the com- F2ᵛ
mon people, which hath both in former and latter times, gained an
inheritance to the memories of some, who cannot and will not die,
though they bee dead. Such [as] love *Riches,* upon no other ground,
then for to be rich, burie themselves alive; and so [burie] themselves,
as that it is impossible they should ever be ranck't amongst others,
that strive to inrich themselves with the possession of the *Golden
Meane,* and to a *Noble* and *Wise man* how great soever the losse of

his estate bee, his estate | cannot be lost, if he have well learned to F3ʳ
beare it with *Constancy* and *Comfort*.

There may be objected, that O my estate being forfeited, mine Heires are beggard, and the antiquitie of my ancestors house made the spectacle of ruine.

This being admitted, it is soone answered, that the houses of most continuance, and personages of Noblest birthes account that antiquity of best estimation which is derived from the longest discent, in which they shall finde, that the first of their honors | were gotten F3ᵛ by him, who was in as low an ebbe of fulnesse, as hee is now at the present: for all greatnes had a beginning, and the beginning of that greatnesse is desert. Am I Noble, let me know that this noblenesse is the least part mine; for my fathers wonne it by their vertue, they had the glory, but I enjoy the Titles. Have I robd mine Heires of those Titles, Honours, or Possessions? let them strive to have more honour in deserving more, that their Successors may as much remember their | vertues, as I have remembred the vertues of my Aunces- F4ʳ tors. Questionlesse howsoever the reputation of a continued Family in ancient Honours, be preferred above any men of later greatnesse, of some whose worth hath raised his house to a noble stile, yet it is in the lawes of reason most reasonable; that hee should deserve more respect, that by his owne atchievements hath purchased dignitie, then others that onely have it by the priviledge of bloud; since the one weares but the shadowes | of his Predecessors triumphes, F4ᵛ the other the substance of his owne.

Povertie is no burthen to them as can sustaine it, is no enemy to such as will imbrace it: He is onely miserable that knowes not to be content with his Fortune, especially if his fall bee procured by his owne errours. Then the surest, the Noblest, the onely meanes to redeeme publique calamitie, is by a publique (and yet inward) profession of sufferance; for in all persons and personages, reformation of folly is a worke of more | praise then the working of folly is a cause F5ʳ of disgrace.

What miserie can it then be, to be eased of that care, which onely brings care in the possession? Of all mischiefes, the greatest mischiefe is to be a rich man, with a rich mans minde. There is no more reason why a meerely covetous man should love Gold, but for that it

is yellow or fayre; Pastures, because they are greene; and so hath the envious much more reason to covet abundance of wealth, because other men should want it. A covetous miser, | is rightly a malicious F5ᵛ
890 consumer, for in heaping for himselfe, he consumes the maintenance of the needy: yet it is to be noted, that plenty is not always to be dispraised, if the having of it doe not procure a scarcitie. But what losse is so great in a worldly estate (considering how weake it is more then in opinion) which a wise man should not beare with moderation?
895 It is a misery to want, but a greater misery to have too much: but for a good man to hugge the love of | abundance, that he should F6ʳ imagine the losse of it, should make him miserable; I must conclude this point, that he hath neither goodnesse nor resolution: if goodnesse, his content should be his best estate; if resolution, his want
900 cannot be esteemed the worst povertie, since extremitie is a singuler Teacher to learne us that we are men, and that there is both a Divine power and a providence above us; the one consisting in being a GOD, the other in having a God-head.

The difference betweene a wise man, reformed F6ᵛ
Of Banishment.
905 by counsell and instruction, and an ignorant man, informed in will and folly, is, that the wise will make good use of all adversitie, when the ignorant thinks all adversitie intollerable.

This is proved in the greatnesse of a Noble courage, when it is enforced to forsake (eyther upon publike disgrace, or some private
910 causes) the comforts of his friends and Country, which men of low hearts doe account a miserie of mischiefes, and reckon that *banishment* | is a bad kinde of torture. F7ʳ

It may not be denied but that such may be the unworthinesse of the action for which a man is banished, that his owne conscience
915 will in all places be a tormentor to his memory, and then the wound which he beares with him can never by chaunge of place or time bee wholy cured. Such a one, another of this latter times, well compared to the wounded Doe in *Virgil,* who (as the Poet sayes) fled over Hils and Mountaines to escape *Lipsius.*
920 death, but | all in vaine, for still in her sides the Bow-mans killing F7ᵛ Arrow stickes. So, those men who have the Arrow of some *mischievous Act,* piercing their afflicted hearts, although they bee banished from the place where they have committed villanie, yet they doe but

goe from it, they cannot forget it. They flie the detraction of their sinne, but cannot shunne it; or if they could shunne the deed (as they cannot) what can that availe when the doer is the man himselfe?

In good men, who | through divers misfortunes are sequestred F8ʳ from their native Countries upon wrongfull or sleight occasions, it is nothing so: for to them if they rightly (as being good they will) instruct themselves in the first rules of wisedome, all Countreyes are a home. A Noble and free resolution is a stranger no where; in which respect, men perfectly wise, are sayd to bee perfectly valiant, since as true wisedome is perfect valour, so is true valour perfect moderation.

The heavens are a covering as well abroad as at home, and the F8ᵛ one and the same Sunne shines in a strange countrey, that shines in our native birth places. It is nothing for a man (if he be *good*) whither he goe, so he beare *himselfe* with *himselfe*. That place is a *home*, where any man lives well: as for instance, how many thousands would range into other Countries, and renounce their owne, so they might be bettered in their estates? and why then may not a *banished man* do the like, onely dispensing | with the word it selfe? Had former times F9ʳ bin so possessed with a love to those Countryes they were borne in, a great part of the world had to this day bin both unpeopled, and unknowne. The discoverers whereof (famous through many ages) cannot bee in their reputation any way blemished, if they be tearmed *banished men*: for so (if yee please) without just offence, they may be called. But saith some, they went voluntarily; I, by compultion: By compultion, it's true he goeth, who goeth not willingly; | other- F9ᵛ wise here is all the difference, *I am an exile, because I must goe; they were exiles because they did goe*: here is likewise the Coherence, as they *went free*, I *goe freely*.

Many men have abandoned their Countries and made themselves voluntary exiles upon a desire and greedy hope of gaine, or better prosperitie: such have bene of the Romans, *Romulus* and *Aeneas*; of the *Patavynes, Antenor*; of the *Britaines* (if the history bee of credite) even our owne *Brute*; yet truely the end of those men was no | way F10ʳ glorious; for they may more rightly be called fugitives and runnagates, then exiles or travailers.

He deserved well of the Common-wealth of *Athens,* who having instituted excellent lawes for the state publique, tooke oath of the Magistrates that his lawes should be dayly and duely practised, till his returne from a journey which hee was to undertake: the Oath being received, the good man freely lived banished from his Country, never returning, that for the safety of his | Country, his lawes might bee kept inviolable: Yet was this wise man so farre in this *banishment* from reproofe, that his action, and memory in his action, will never be forgotten.

Of all accidents that can happen to a prepared minde, this of *banishment* hath little cause to trouble the quiet calme of a steady resolution. It is often seene that sundry persons for rarities sake, for morall instruction in complement or in behaviour, willingly sometimes travaile into forraine lands, and there spend their time for three, | sixe, tenne yeeres or more, with great delight, taking pleasure and content in so growing old: Even so in like manner, let a good man resolve himselfe that this hard word of *banishment* is but a journey of pleasure into some outlanding country, not proposing or limitting to the minde a time of comming backe, but always minding some fit imployment why hee should goe: as if hee were but Ambassador from his owne to some unknowne Prince: and with what dishonor can an Ambassadour be blemished, | who in the service of his Soveraigne leaves his life as a pledge of his dutie? It may be in the bonds of Nature, some man will esteeme it an heavy misfortune to forsake, or (as in the worst sence they terme it) to be thrust from the fruition of the comfort of his Friends, Children, Allyes, and Kinsfolkes: such a thought can no more move the temper of a resolved minde; then it should doe if hee were to leave the world, since in dying, and in being banished, heere is the difference, that the one necessitie | is commanded by an unchangeable decree from Heaven, the other by a severe imposition of man; both being a severation of old friends.

What a madnesse were it in any to repute death (being thereto naturally called) a misery? Even so let him thinke of *Banishment,* and withall, compare the great fortunes that some have attained unto in that estate of exile, with the possibilitie of his owne.

THOMAS MOWBRAY, Duke of *Norffolk* in the Raigne of RICHARD | the second, being by the said King, by reason of the Kings youth and indiscretion, and in regard of some other differences between *Mowbray* and other Princes of the bloud, upon an appeale of Treason, banished; was so farre from being heerewith dejected, that adding practise to the noblenesse of his courage, hee undertooke a glorious warre in the land of *Palestine,* against the common enemie of God and Truth, the *Turke,* and willingly made his bloud a sacrifice to the redemption of his Fame. Happy | man, that sought out Death G1r with victorie, before that Death could make him unhappie by finding him out with overthrow: Happie *banishment*, which hath beene the meanes of such a memorie, and happie cause of *banishment* that was the first occasion to such meanes of being memorable.

In like manner, *Henry* of *Richmond,* being for his interest in the Crowne by that monster of men and Kings, RICHARD *the third,* [banished;] found (by his | even carriage and well tempered modera- G1v tion) such favour and love in the Courts and hearts of forrayne Princes, as that being strengthened with their strengthes, and encouraged by his owne right and vertue, he not onely returned to challenge but to recover his owne, and to purge the Land of so intollerable mischiefe as the governement of that cruell usurper and bloudie King had made it sigh under. Happie *banishment*, in so glorifying that Prince: Happy | Prince, in so disposing that *banishment*: for it is certainely G2r true, that not any accident of misfortune (as the world accounts) but the minde of the patient in suffering, or not suffering, makes it a misery.

If examples be of any force (as they must be) by the president of former times to instruct the present, then may *Pompey* for greatnesse, *Affricanus* for Counsell, *Hannybal* for courage, and *Ovid* for wit, tell us that *banishment* doth not always happen to miserable men, | ex- G2v cept their owne [impatiencie] worke their owne calamitie.

In short, a Wise and Noble man, by what hath beene said, may consider what might more have beene said, to the building in this life this structure of the *Golden Meane,* against the stormes and infelicitie of being a banished man, since a wise man resolved in all trials, is never confined within the limits of place, but upon all necessarie occurrents doth repute himselfe even in his birth to | be the G3r worlds Citizen.

Heere yet followes *Imprisonment*; which often happening to men of great place and qualitie is not thought the least kinde of miserie, which men of such mindes doe with their bodies restraint locke up and imprison all the best faculties of their reason, forcing Reason to be a slave to Fortune, and rewarding the excellent dignitie of the soule, with the corruption of Judgement and Nature. [Of *Imprisonment.*]

Such a man as is kept within the inforcement | of restraint, must imitate that *Dædalus* whom the ancient Poets fayne to have wings, with which he fled from that inaccessible Castle where he was detayned with his Sonne *Icarus* a prisoner. G3ᵛ

The Morall, cannot but give matter of note and application: *Icarus* the sonne, betokens or may betoken the incapacitie of mens bodies, and *Dædalus* the quicknesse of minde, both which being the one with the other imprisoned, the one, which is the bodie, personated in *Icarus*, | for want of moderation fals [in] the attempt of escape: the other, which is the minde, patern'd in *Dædalus,* conquers adversitie by flying from it, in bearing it: *Medio tutissimum iter*; The GOLDEN MEANE *superat ferendo*; triumphs on the rigour of imprisonment by the freedome of a noble minde. G4ʳ

To a man arm'd in his extremities, often trials are but as many often praises, and every triall gives a severall crowne of commendation, in bearing many troubles with one | and the selfe-same resolution. G4ᵛ

What can (if a man rightly consider) be a lesse punishment for *a great* or for any fault at all then *Imprisonment*? in which it is lawfull to use the benefit of all those five sences, wherein hee may take as much comfort, as if he enjoy'd the common ayre. *Imprisonment* gives a faire stoppe, to runne over the whole world of thoughts: it retires the minde to a more serious Meditation of what is most needfull to | be meditated on: it gives large roome to remember all errors that have beene past, and to intend any reformation that is to come: it stops the eare from hearing the clamours of the day, and hinders the eye from seeing the vanities of folly. *Imprisonment* is a contemplative *Philosophie*; it is an armour of proofe against the batterie of carnall *libertie*, it will teach to know what is *good*, it will teach to know G5ʳ

1070 how to be *good*; and being rightly applied, cannot but lend Instruction, | whereby *a wise man* may tread the readie path that leades to G5ᵛ immortalitie.

If the use of *imprisonment* be but onely a little made use of, it will be found that there is no meanes under the ordinances of Heaven 1075 so availeable for a man to consider the miserie of greatnesse, as the feeling the misery (so mistermed) of *imprisonment*.

Men, accompanied with the imployment of worthie thoughts, are never lesse idle then when they are alone, never more | seriously busied G6ʳ then when they are onely busied, (and have time so to be busied) 1080 with remembring that they are men: not that such a remembrance should cast them lower then the consideration of frailetie, but raise them higher then the acting of folly; not to depresse the motions perswading Temperance, but to rectifie the perswasions moving to vertue: Hee is stronger that conquers his owne passions, then hee 1085 that after winning many Countreyes, becomes | a passionate con- G6ᵛ querour.

The life of instruction is reading, and leisure the life of reading, and a retired restraint the life of leisure: which restraint is onely terrible in being called *imprisonment*. One that for a great summe of 1090 money would pledge himselfe to live in a chamber, a yeere or two, or seaven, will not thinke such an indurance a misery, because the hope of gaine doth lessen or rather annihilate the severitie of that injunction.

Miserable men, and Miserable mankinde that will undertake such G7ʳ 1095 an affliction for bettering of their temporall estates, which being imposed for the bettering of the estate of their reason and judgement, they account insufferable. Basenesse of Nature that suffers that for greedinesse, which being had, is not certaine one houre to be possessed, and yet will in the same kinde forgoe that which being once 1100 possest is never lost; O the furniture of the minde, which being indeed | the true lasting and onely best riches! varietie of bookes are G7ᵛ sweet companions, and plenty of noble thoughts happy recreations: If I be a prisoner I will either talke with my Library, or sport with my thoughts, since one being learned, will prove sure instructers, 1105 the latter being Noble, worthy delights.

A man that is restrayned from liberty, hath the liberty of retayning his owne worthinesse, as worthily may be seene in *Massinissa*,

who being made captive to *Scipio*, told him | *thou must* Scipio (quoth   G8ʳ
he) *enjoy the benefit of thy fortune, by taking from me my life, or of thy*
mercy, by loosing my bonds: Take my life thou freest mee from bondes,
free mee from bondes, thou bindest me in bondes of love; but if thou
lettest me live a captive, know *Scipio* I have a heart that did never,
nor ever can feele servile captivitie.

It is certaine that such as see their friends in bondage and in dur-
ance, who have Noble mindes, see them, and see them not: | they   G8ᵛ
see them as men, but not as they are, more then men.

Imprisonment is an excellent preparation to goodnesse, since ever
after, in all fortunes, a man that hath beene a prisoner may know
by himselfe how subject a humane estate is to the brittlenesse of al-
teration; and he that doth not much amend his errors by this kind
of triall, is neyther destined to be an attemptor of any notable ver-
tue, or a desirer of any vertuous note. It is a milde Tutor, to teach
as | well how to governe as how to serve; for he who can serve ad-   G9ʳ
versitie with meekenesse, can guide prosperitie with discretion.

Hee who is a prisoner, hath herein great cause to finde his friend,
for such as are ingaged in a promise of love, that [love] not the per-
son for his fortune, will shew likewise that they feare not his misfor-
tune, because they love his person. The saying is old, and verified
in this age of the World, *that a man may have many friends and yet*
little friendship: | but here a man shall soone be taught to distinguish   G9ᵛ
the difference betweene friendship and friends, although it is not to
be urged that therefore it is fit that every one who would know truely
his friends, should make himselfe, or be made a prisoner; but that
every one being a prisoner should then have fit time to know how
hee is esteemed.

Imprisonment is not of such vertue in it selfe that men should seeke
to be prisoners, thereby to be happy, but being by casualtie | en-   G10ʳ
forced upon any, the use thereof may be so happy, that hee who is
imprisoned may not think himselfe miserable.

Even as hee who being followed by the memory of some evill act,
though he have his body at libertie, yet is still *imprisoned* in the guilt
of his minde. So he that reformeth the crookednesse of his condi-
tion, by the imitation of goodnesse, though his body be imprisoned,
hath by the selfe-same reason the freedome of the minde.

More excellent far it | is, and much more to be wished, to be out   G10ᵛ of the Jayle of *Opinion*, then out of the Jayle of *Indurance*. The minde cannot feele bondage except it bee made servile to much unworthinesse, and then being free, though the body be laden with many heavie chaines, the heart triumpheth over that tiranny which imposeth them, by being lightned from such a burden by a singuler moderation: if I be imprisoned I will expect the worst, which is death, if I die, I will be assured of the | best, which is freedome; freedome as well of my soule from a wearied body as of my body from a wearisome prison.

Imprisonment is a gentle sickenesse, not to kill, but to chasten the patient: and as men naturally proud may be humbled, but will never be humble, so men of a meeke condition may be launced for the recovery of health, but not wounded to the hastening of death: which a Wise and Noble man, well fore-casting, may arme himselfe | against reputed miseries, and amongst them all, against this one of *imprisonment*, that whensoever it should come to him, it should come to him rather to exercise, then to overthrow him.

Finally, amongst such men, whose reason is overswayed by nature, *Death* is reckoned for a misery, and is to them a misery indeede; but to others guided by the refined light of judgement: it is esteemed (as it is) the onely remedie and securest ease against misery. *Of Death.*

Death to a wise man cannot come unlooked for, nor to a good man unwisht for: since the wise, knowing that they must die, know likewise that *resolution* is the best comfort to welcome *death*, and the good being confident of their owne innocencies, desire the change of a better life.

He that will overcome affliction by sufferance, beare calamitie with courage, weary out feare with hope, let him be resolute, that the worst of trials is *death*; and for that be armed | whensoever it shall come, and be ready to imbrace it.

If a Noble or a Wise man, after disfavour of his Prince, neglect of his Countrey, forfeiture of his Estate, banishment from his Friends, imprisonment of his Person, or any other esteemed extreames bee threatned with the losse of his head, or execution in any manner, certainely he hath great cause to rejoyce; for he is not worthy to see any end of his sorrowes, who is not prepared to meet it | with a H1ʳ merrie heart.

The end of all sorrowes is *Death*, if the partie to die be truely reconciled to his God and to his conscience.

But it was once said by a good and a great man, that death was onely feared because we know not what it is, for who hath come from the dead to informe us eyther of the ease in suffering, or of the joy after suffering. To this I should thinke that the verie doubt it selfe is a resolution to the doubt: for who can feare that | which H1ᵛ hee knowes not, yea rather hee will not know death for that he feares it. A man who is to loose one of his hands, no doubt but imagineth the paine in losing, to exceede the paine which at the instant he feeleth, yet having his hand cut off within short time shall forget what that payne was.

By the sight of anothers losse of a member, let us remember that in Death we feele no more paine in being sundred from the use of all our | members, then we should in the losse of one. It is to be H2ʳ confessed that if the weight of our misdeeds torture us when we are to leave the world, and that we have not set the household of our soules and bodies in order, then the cause is otherwise, for he is not to be blamed who is willing to shunne an ending miserie for a miserie that hath none end; and this is not the feare of Death, but the feare of being for ever a dying, which torments the conscience: otherwise Death | in it selfe is peace, rest, ease, joy, like the hope H2ᵛ of good men, the comfort of wise men, the happinesse of Noble men.

The old Poets did fitly fayne *Death* to bee the childe of the Night, and Sleepe to be the Sister of *Death*; wisely including, that as Night and Sleepe wrap up all in stilnesse, so should *Death* more perfectly finish the course of evils, by burying them in a grave, never to arise.

And no doubt, but herein *Death* and Night have much affinitie, that | as the Night is fearefull, because darke; but sweet, because H3ʳ giving rest: So is *Death* in his shadowe (which is the night of opinion) before it comes, full of horrour, but in substance (which is the quickening to a better life) when it comes, full of joyes.

It may be heere objected, that to die for some supposed offence by an enforced Death, is scandalous, and therefore miserable.

But it may be answered, that such an objection | betokens but H3ᵛ
the feare of frailtie. For if it be examined, wee must confesse that
the houre of *death*, even to them that most looke for and desire it,
is uncertaine, and they cannot be so provided at an instant as others
that know the instant when they are to suffer.

Herein men destined to *death* for some offence, are (as it may seeme)
more happie in their end, then they are unhappie in their disorder
of living that hath brought them to that end.

Men, appointed to die, knowing the time certaine have more rea- H4ʳ
son, and no doubt doe accordingly fit themselves to forsake and cast
off all those parts and thoughts that might make them mortall, then
others who onely dreame of a dying time, but not resolving that
they draw neere to the time, are many times suddenly taken in the
fulnesse of their filthinesse, and in the high tide of acting unlawfull
pleasures or abuses: and here surely betweene the manner of dying,
the last | is most fearefull, since the former, knowing the minute H4ᵛ
in which they are to depart from the world, doe by the stroake of
Justice enjoy that benefit which wise and good men doe in mercie
sigh and hope for.

Death is a happie Haven, and men shipwrackt in the Sea of this
earth cannot but covet it: it is a safe Inne and men poasting in the
journeyes of wearinesse cannot but seeke it: It is a path to blessed-
nesse, and such as are good will finde it: It | is a banquet of all good- H5ʳ
nesse, and such as bee blessed have found it.

Hee is unworthie to live that is not worthie enough to die, and
he is not unworthie to die that hath lived worthily. The woman that
demaunded of *Jupiter* that he would give to her two Sonnes the greatest
happinesse that could bee bestowed from heaven on men, had the
same night her sonnes both dead, as if the greatest humane felicitie
were to be freed from being humane.

To conclude (for something hath beene said of this before) he which H5ᵛ
will wisely and nobly practise the observation of the *Golden Meane*,
and shew the greatnesse of Vertue in extreames, must keepe truce
with his passions, and prepare his courage with this resolution, that
Miserie is no Miserie; for that is onely a Miserie which is lasting,
and thought so: and reputed Miserie is not lasting, because *death* out-
weares it; is not thought so, because *death* will finish it: in the resolving
| on the one, Wisedome will prove a Noble minde, in the other H6ʳ

Noblenesse will patterne out a wiseman: for moderation in extreames make perfect both.

After the discourse of these former supposed miseries (contracted within the number of sixe) might likewise bee added certaine other myseries which both might and doe not seldome happen to great personages; as to be deprived of all hope of continuing their families, in seeing an end of | their race and houses in their owne persons. But considering this, this is no miserie, unlesse wee should strive against a power, which would prove madnesse without remedie, and foolishnesse without pittie. So likewise the unevennesse of match amongst great personages with partners, whose wantonnesse is sometimes the cause that many Noble houses runne to decay. But to this as it hath beene said before, those things concerne us not which we our selves doe | not, and the weakenes of frailtie is to be winked at, or being seene not to be noted by the courage of wisdome. Other might be inferred which foolish men thinke miseries, but indeed are not: they may be rather called crosses then miseries, and such a one as can temper himselfe in the former, alreadie spoken of, shall finde those latter, or any such like those, but meere trifles, not worthie of repetition: neyther are they to this worke any way esteemed aunswerable | to have reference.

Other miseries that sometimes happen. H6ᵛ

H7ʳ

H7ᵛ

In the viewe of what hath beene said, under the titles of a Wise and a Noble man, are comprehended all men, of all degrees and fortunes, whose Vertues doe make them wise; as their wisedome doth make them Noble. For wisedome consisteth not onely in gray heads, but in a steadie providence how to doe, and Noblenesse constisteth not onely in an Honourable race; but in a prudent resolution | what to doe.

H8ʳ

To be wise, and to be Noble, are two distinct happinesses; as different and as much divided the one from the other (though some few times they meete in one particular) as *Goodnesse*, and *Greatnesse*, as *Fortune* and *vertue*; as a *King* and a *Tyrant*.

There are many *Noble*, which are strangers to *Wisedome*: but not any *Wise*, who is not allyed to *Noblenesse*. Mens mindes are so wholy now-a-dayes impoysoned with the love | of yeelding to their naturall infirmities as they will not acknowledge *desert*, to have equalitie and partage with *Authoritie*. A rich man purchasing dignitie, is undoubt-

H8ᵛ

edly reputed a *perfect man*; for otherwise (sayes the common deceived opinion) it is impossible (without much merit) that hee could have attained to such an height of respect. And this is surely to be lamented, that vanitie should (not seldome) rise to the titles of *Noble*; while *Wisdome* fals | from the titles, wherein, and whereby, it hath bin once ennobled.

For as every man is a little *Common-wealth* in himselfe, well ordered, if his actions and intents be ordered by a disposition of doing and meaning well: so is every one where libertie of pleasing his owne indiscretion over-maistereth him, a *Common-wealth* turned upside downe, rude, and contemptible. None otherwise is it in a state politicke, grounded by *Noble* and *Wise* men, if the governors | thereof, be therefore indeede *Noble*, because *Wise*; else it cannot be but the ruines of a government, the sicknesse and disease of a state, the calamitie and bondage of a people: and surely the affinitie betweene a morall and a reall Common-wealth, cannot be unnecessarilye applyed, since as in the one, so in the other, there are often references of most likelinesse: as by many eminent monuments of the proofes of Wisemen of former ages, hath and is | sufficiently warranted.

Now as a *Wiseman* will with much patience suffer the losse of hearing, comming by indisposition of health; or of his sight, or of any other weakenesse incident to nature, by which hee shall deserve the commendation of a Noble *spirit*, by not resisting what hee cannot remedy: So much more wil a *Wiseman* patiently undergoe the oppression of any outward misery, which is much lesse then the losse, either of any sence or member, and yet shall heerein | likewise be reputed truely *Noble*.

In a word, everie action, and the minde of every one that hath a minde to act, is limited within the precincts of those two humane blessings, *to wit*, *Wisedome* and *Noblenesse*. Wisedome informes the minde, and NOBLENESSE commends the actions: insomuch as every one who can act wisely, and deliberate Nobly, squaring his resolution in resolved steadinesse to both fortunes, may of merit be inrolled amongst | the memorable: and be remembred by the desertfull to be truely wise because Noble: to be perfectly Noble because wise.

F I N I S.

A LINE OF LIFE.

Pointing at the *Immortalitie* of a Vertuous NAME.

Printed by *W. S.* for *N. Butter*, and are to be sold at his shop neere Saint *Austens* gate.
1620.

Title page (1620), The Bodleian Library,
8° L.78. Th.(3). By permission.

A Line of Life
Occasion

Between 1613 and 1620, the only literary activities of John Ford that we know of were connected with the death of Sir Thomas Overbury in 1613. Overbury was imprisoned in the Tower on 26 April 1613 and died there of poisoning on 14 September. Ford may well have known Overbury personally, but evidence of this is lacking.[1] In 1614, the first edition of Overbury's *Wife* (STC 18903.5) opened with two commendatory poems by John Ford; they disappeared from the second edition published the same year (STC 18904) but this included, among "many witty Characters, and conceited Newes, written by himselfe and other learned Gentlemen his friends," two characters, "A Wise-man" and "A noble Spirit," perhaps also by Ford.[2] If so, they would form a natural link between the end of *The Golden Meane* ("to be perfectly Noble because wise") and the first words of the dedicatory epistle to *A Line of Life* ("WISE, and therein NOBLE").

The following year, on 25 November 1615, Lawrence Lisle, the bookseller who had published *The Wife*, entered in the Stationers' Register "A booke called, *Sir THOMAS OVERBURYes Ghost contayneinge the history of his life and untimely death* by JOHN FFORD gent[leman]." No copy survives, and the book may never have been printed. By the end of November 1615 everyone was awaiting the developments of the Overbury affair. Richard Weston, Mrs. Turner, and Sir Gervase Elwes had all been found guilty and executed; the earl of Somerset had been in the Tower since 2 November, and Frances, his wife, was in custody at Blackfriars awaiting the birth of her child. Making the most of the situation, Lisle entered "*the portra[i]ture of Sir THOMAS OVERBURY*" (STC 18921.3) on 20 January 1616, followed on 28 January by "A booke of Sir THOMAS OVERBURYes *observations of his travelles in Fraunce Germany and the*

---

[1] Overbury became a member of the Middle Temple in 1597 but seems to have left before Ford's admission. However, see Davril, 91.

[2] For the texts of the poems and the characters, see below, 341–44. On Ford's authorship see 339 n. 10, below.

*Lowe Countryes.*³ In 1616, the eighth edition of *The Wife* (STC 18910) contained a poem by Ford in memory of Sir Thomas Overbury.⁴

Two of the "learned Gentlemen" who contributed characters to *The Wife* were Dekker and Webster; their contributions to its successive editions may have brought them into contact with Ford. *The Witch of Edmonton*, the first play with which Ford can be definitely connected, was written by him with Dekker and Rowley, and when *The Duchess of Malfi* was published in 1623, it contained commendatory lines by Ford.⁵

A Line of Life was published in 1620. In dedicating his work to Sir James Hay, whom he did not know personally (see Ep. Ded., 8-9), Ford was seeking the patronage and help of one of James's most influential courtiers. By 1620 he seems to have been a disappointed man. He speaks of "the povertye of [his] uncomforted studies" and complains that he is "farr beneath the happynes of thriving fortunes" (Ep. Ded., 18-19, 21-22). It is difficult to believe that a man of Ford's intellectual ability was not alluding to himself when he wrote the following:

> Certainly (without disparagement to desert in great men) there are many particular persons, fit for publike imployments, whose ablenesse and sufficiencie, is no way inferiour to the prayses of the mightiest, but that they are clouded in their lownesse, and obscured in their privatnesse, but else would and could give testimony to the World, that all fulnesse and perfection is not confined to Eminence and Authoritie. (596-602)

As Ford may have been trying to catch the king's eye, it was advisable to omit from the printed edition of *A Line of Life* anything that might give offense (see below, 285, 292). Though he protests his sincerity, Ford's eulogy of James is pure flattery, and his words are echoed by those of Pelias, a courtier, praising Prince Palador in *The Lovers Melancholy*:

> May it please you grace,
> I think you do contain within yourself
> The great elixir, soul, and quintessence
> Of all divine perfections; are the glory

---

³ The earliest known edition is dated 1626; STC 18903.
⁴ For the text of this poem, see below, 344.
⁵ For the text of these verses, see below, 345.

Of mankind, and the only strict example
For earthly monarchies to square out their lives by.
(2.1.104-9)

In *A Line of Life* Ford calls James I *"this onely patterne"* (815) and adds that he "teacheth by his example, others securely and readily to runne, by his *Line of Life*, to the immortalitie of a vertuous name" (824-26). He must have known that his words were those of a mere Pelias, and he would not have stooped to such flattery had he not been seeking preferment. But it was evidently not forthcoming, and the following year, in 1621, he turned to the stage.

The Work

Like *The Golden Meane*, *A Line of Life* belongs to the vast body of Renaissance didactic prose on matters "moral," "political," and "divine," three adjectives often found on title pages. The genre extends from collections of brief pieces, such as Bacon's *Essayes* (1597), Anthony Stafford's *Meditations, and Resolutions* (1612) or Owen Felltham's first century of *Resolves* (?1623), to formal treatises like Sir Richard Barckley's *Discourse of the Felicitie of Man* (1598). Ford's prose pamphlets are more unified than "dispersed Meditacons" but less ambitious than formal treatises. Educating and guiding the governing class had been a self-appointed task of the early humanists: Sir Thomas Elyot wrote for "governours"; Ford writes for "publike men."

"Resolution" is central to both *A Line of Life* and *The Golden Meane*, and the two pamphlets are very close both in contents and in style.[6] But *A Line of Life* is more than a mere restatement of *The Golden Meane*; it builds from it and "complements rather than repeats the earlier work."[7]

As *The Golden Meane* describes the resolution needed by a nobleman to confront the various miseries that may befall him, it stresses constancy in adversity, a mainly passive virtue. Such a virtue is not absent from *A Line of Life*; men in public places need to be "most constantly armed in the defensive armor of a selfe-worthie resolution" (524-26). But the

---

[6] For instance, Ford shows the dangers of envy for men in public life in GM, 569-610 and LL, 530-43.

[7] Anderson, *John Ford*, 30.

principal purpose of *A Line of Life* is to describe a resolution that leads to action; this active virtue is guided by "goodness," a concept Ford mentioned only briefly in 1613 (see 225-26, above) and which now becomes the core of his argument. Goodness is the *"line of life"*; that is, the "infallible rule, which wee as we are men, and more then men; Christians, and more then Christians, the image of our maker; must take our level by" (77-79).

Like the earlier pamphlet, *A Line of Life* begins with an introductory section. Ford immediately insists on the difference between living and living "well," between *"Life* desired for the only benefit of living" and "a *good Life."* Men who merely live "both dye finally and dye all."[8] That is to say, they undergo the eternal death of damnation, whereas those who "indeavour to live well,... dye to live, and live for ever" (10-11).[9] Thus, at the outset, Ford strikes a religious note which will become clearer and more insistent in his final section.

Between the introductory pages (lines 3-127) and the Corollary, Ford divides his "demonstration" into what he calls the three "branches" of resolution. The first sets out man's "proper dutie" as he is simply a man; the second shows how he should discharge his duties as a "public man"; and the third declares that the "good man" acts virtuously towards his fellow creatures, not because of public obligations but simply because he is truly good. However, this division into different "branches" is somewhat misleading, because goodness is really essential to each of them and is not confined to the third.

Each human being must see to it that reason governs his *"little world"* so as to counteract the "proclivitie of corrupted Nature" and its "frailtie"; men's first duty to themselves is to be "Commanders of their owne infirmities" (290-91). If a man learns "to rejoyce in true goodnesse" (223), he will be able to withstand temptations and prefer the solitary path of virtue to the madness of the multitude. Without this inner virtue no one can assume the office of a public man and resist the snares of flattery or the assaults of envy; "A PUBLIKE MAN hath not more neede to be *Bonus Civis,* a good *Statist,* then *Bonus Vir,* good in himselfe" (379-80). Public men must stand "on the guard of their owne Pietie and Wisedome" (610-11).

---

[8] In CBS, Ford writes that those who live only for pleasures finally come to the grave, "And here they die, and dying once die all" (1183). See also GM, 1203-4.

[9] See also 25-26, 61-63, 112-13, 265-66 (compare CBS, 810).

Finally, the good man "doth (beside the care he hath of himselfe in particular) attend all his drifts and actions, to bee a servant for others, for the good of others, as if it were his owne" (648-50). He desires "to doe good to all" (665)[10] and wants to "make all like unto himselfe, that is, Good Men" (692-93). Such a man is generous, helps those that are in distress, and upholds learning and justice.

Ford's "good man" is possessed of the virtues set forth in *The Golden Meane*. Like a Stoic wise man, "hee loves *Vertue* for it selfe" (659-60); "his owne solace is to him, as an inexpugnable castle of strength" (735-36);[11] Socrates, for instance, confronted his unjust accusers with the "noble constancie and resolution of a wise man" (750-51). Ford wonders whether Socrates, "a meere morrall man" (744) and not a Christian, may be called a "good man"; he answers in the negative, whereas in *The Golden Meane* he unreservedly called him "a good and a great man" (1186). Socrates, he now argues, was "inlightned with the only beames of nature" (752), but the good man of *A Line of Life* is "inspired with a farre richer and diviner knowledge then humanitie" (754-55). Goodness is really the nature of God himself (819-20); Ford had called Christ "this good good man" in *Christes Bloodie Sweat* (1790). The best human example of goodness is James I, "knowne to be, JAMES THE GOOD" (812-13) because he is "not onely a *good King*, but a *good man*" (823-24). Though James is presented as the model of goodness, the emphasis on Christianity makes for a more universal conception of virtue than in *The Golden Meane,* which was concerned only with the miseries that befall men of honor and nobility. In the Corollary, Ford states that "A *good Man* is the man, that even the greatest or lowest should both *bee,* and resolve *to be*" (Cor. 49-50).

In *A Line of Life,* Ford crowns the Stoic resolution of *The Golden Meane* with the Christian goodness of *Christes Bloodie Sweat*. However, just as in *The Golden Meane* he never clearly defines the various virtues he mentions, so in *A Line of Life* he does not analyze the precise relationship between "resolution" and "goodness," content with the idea that virtuous resolution is necessary to achieve goodness and that true goodness is Christian and not philosophical. The contrast between classical wisdom and Christian goodness was hardly original, and Ford may have remembered Justus Lipsius: "It is a plausible kind of praise to be called a learned

---

[10] Christ "did good / To every one" (CBS, 1783-84).
[11] See also the Stoic statement at Cor. 27-30.

man: but better to be called a wise man; and best of all to have the title of a good man."[12]

While Ford's method in *A Line of Life* is essentially the same as in *The Golden Meane*, there are differences. He illustrates his argument with *exempla*, but those he takes from antiquity are mostly short;[13] indeed he insists that there is no need "to search histories of other times" (308), preferring to dwell on examples "chancing within the compasse of twentie yeares" (545-46). Simply as a man, Lord Harington (d. 1614) is praised for his "rare and admirable course of life" (314-15). But Sir Walter Ralegh (d. 1618) was subject to "many changes of *resolution*" and was "so unsteddie, that his too much apprehension was the foile of his judgement" (338-41); yet he redeemed himself at the hour of death and "his *Wisdome* and *Courage* appeared ... in his last demeanour" (346-47). For public men, Ford gives three negative precedents to show how they can fall from greatness: the earl of Essex (d. 1601) in England, Charles duke of Biron (d. 1602) in France, and Johan van Oldenbarnevelt (d. 1619) in the Netherlands. All lacked the virtuous resolution that could have kept them in the path of goodness. The good man himself "cannot be more expressly exemplified in any president or myrrour" than in James I (778).

In *The Golden Mean*, Ford had borrowed silently from Seneca, indicating only one of his sources in a marginal note ("*Lipsius*," 918). His method is rather different in *A Line of Life*. He now repeatedly cites various classical authors in the margin, so that his argument derives authority from Aristotle, Aristophanes, St. Augustine, Cicero, Diogenes Laertius, Dio Cassius, Horace, Isocrates, Juvenal, Plato, Pliny the Elder, Plutarch, Quintilian, Seneca, and Velleius Paterculus. His debt to Seneca is less extensive than in *The Golden Meane*, but the Roman philosopher retains pride of place as the first two "branches" of resolution are both concluded with long quotations from the *Epistulae* which "comprehend" (354) and "knit up" (630) what has been said. But Ford uses Seneca very freely. At 356-60 he quotes with approval part of a passage in which Seneca gives the arguments of those who advocate a life of pleasure, because of its shortness; but these,

---

[12] *Of Constancie* 2.4, trans. Stradling (1594), 68. For a borrowing from Lipsius, see 18-25 and Commentary.

[13] See 182-84, 300-307, 721-22, 807, Cor. 42-45. But the examples of Epaminondas (292-300), Achilles (616-23), Socrates (744-56) and Demosthenes (Cor. 31-42) are fairly lengthy.

Seneca adds, must be rejected as carefully as Ulysses shunned the voices of the sirens.[14]

Though Ford (apparently) acknowledges his debts to Seneca, he silently borrows some of his marginal notes, in particular a cluster of references (to Plato, Aristotle, and Isocrates) that conflates two series of citations in James's *Basilikon Doron*, the only modern work to be honored with a marginal reference in *A Line of Life*.[15] In a paragraph about his son's "companie and servants" James advises the young prince as follows: "see that they be indued with such honest qualitites, as are meete for such offices, as yee ordain them to serve in; ... And shortlie, followe good king *Davids* counsel in the choise of your servants, by setting your eies upon the faithful and upright of the land to dwel with you" (64–65). And a little further on he tells Henry to choose "men of knowne wisdome, honestie, and good conscience" for "the offices of the crowne and estate" (68). Ford uses James's references to Plato, Artistotle, and Isocrates in his section on public men for a paragraph about the "choice of men in Office in the Commonwealth" (373–74). Aware of his debt and hoping that the royal eyes might read *A Line of Life*, Ford was careful to explain that he did not want "to dive into the depth of *Policie*, or to set downe any positive rules, what a right *Statesman* should be" (387–89). James had asserted that, "having learned both the theoricke and practicke" of government, he himself was more qualified to give "particular precepts" than "any simple schoole-man, that onely knowes matters of kingdomes by contemplation" ("To the Reader," sig. B1^{r-v}). Ford was therefore chary of appearing as foolish as Phormio, who lectured on the art of war in front of Hannibal (389–92).

The main features of Ford's style did not change from *The Golden Meane* to *A Line of Life*. He is as fond of figures of repetition (occasionally sacrificing clarity to stylistic effect), and he still uses antimetabole with two nouns linked by the preposition "of ": "the *greatnesse of his goodnesse*; ... the *goodnesse of his greatnesse*" (784–85). He makes extensive use of similes and metaphors, among which is again found building imagery;[16] there are now fewer extended similes: the most "lively and remarkeable" of these, the ship of life, is silently pilfered from Lipsius (18–25; see also 616–29).

---

[14] At 633–40 Ford adapts and conflates several fragments of the same letter (see Commentary).

[15] See 372–78 and Commentary. Ford acknowledges his debt to *Basilikon Doron* at 771 and probably borrowed the references he gives at 27–28 (see Commentary).

[16] See 53–56, 607–10, and GM, 395–97, Commentary.

Critics have not been kind to Ford's two pamphlets,[17] and it is fair to say that the ideas expressed are neither original nor always thought out or connected with sufficient care. What remains most vividly in the mind of Ford's reader is his insistence on resolution and a few of his extended similes. Yet the pamphlets do enable us to understand better the plays that have kept his name alive. The connection between the prose pamphlets and the plays is twofold. We find, first of all, a common texture of characteristic words, phrases, images, and incidental thoughts, many of which have been cross-referenced in the commentary. Moreover, Ford's prose usage can warn editors of the plays against unnecessary emendations.[18]

But the link between the nondramatic and the dramatic works of Ford is richer than such verbal parallels and can often reach the very meaning of a play.[19] As Clifford Leech has written, "we may find in each of his plays something of all the strains of his non-dramatic writings," but "it is *The Golden Meane* and *A Line of Life* that are most significant for *The Broken Heart* and *Perkin Warbeck*" (26). The concept of "resolution," with its associated virtues, is central to both plays. *Perkin Warbeck* is closest to *The Golden Meane*: both the protagonist of the play and the noblemen of the pamphlet have to confront external "miseries" which can only be overcome with "resolution." Perkin "persevers in his sufferances" (GM, 389) and when the time comes he is "armed to die" (GM, 287, and PW, 5.3.214). He is almost resolution incarnate. The main characters of *The Broken Heart*—Calantha, Penthea, Ithocles, Orgilus, Bassanes—do not contend so much with external misfortunes as with the demands of their own "commanding love." Yet their resolution enables them to preserve their Spartan constancy in spite of their wasting passions. Death is endured with a stoical dignity that can neither heal nor conceal a broken heart.

---

[17] Oliver: "commonplace in thought" (20). Leech: "The thought is unremarkable ... neither pamphlet is a work of distinction" (25-26). Stavig: "the stock concepts of Christian humanism" (21).

[18] For example, neither "this armes" (BH, 5.2.109) nor "this lousie close-stoole Empricks" (LM, 4.2.1-2) should be emended to "his" or "these"; see GM, 307 and Commentary.

[19] See Anderson, 27, 32, 81-85 (on PW); T. Orbison, *The Tragic Vision of John Ford* (Salzburg, 1974) 150-77 (on PW); Monsarrat, *Light from the Porch*, 239-52 (on BH and PW).

The Text

There are two authoritative texts of A Line of Life, a printed text and a manuscript. The printed text is a duodecimo published in 1620 (STC 11162). It was entered in the Stationers' Register on 10 October 1620: "Master. Butter. Entred for his Copie vnder the handes of Master Doctor GOAD, and Master Lownes warden, A booke Called The lyne of life, written by J. FORDE ... vj^d" (Arber, 4:41). The printer was William Stansby.

Only two copies are extant, one in the Bodleian Library and one in the British Library, the latter imperfect and lacking leaves D1 and G6 (blank); the title page is reproduced above, 277.

Collation: 12°: A^6 B-F^{12} G^6 [$5 signed (-A1, A5, G5)], 72 leaves, pp. [12] 1-129 (misprinting 78-79 as "76-77", 82-83 as "80-81", 86-87 as "84-85", 90-91 as "88-89", 94-95 as "92-93", 97-129 as "95-127") [3]
Contents: A1^r title, A1^v blank, A2^r-5^v epistle, A6^r "Æstatis ... FORD.", A6^v blank, B1^r-G5^r text, G5^v-6^v blank
RT [within rules]: B1^v-G5^r LINEA VITÆ. | A Line of Life.
Catchwords: A-B, [none] B-C, son C-D, leanes D-E, spo- E-F, Man F-G, tion

The manuscript of A Line of Life is the third item in British Library, Lansdowne MS 350.[20] When the Lansdowne manuscripts were purchased in 1807, A Line of Life was already part of the miscellaneous volume in which it is found today. The other items have no connection with Ford's pamphlet and must have all been bound together during the eighteenth century.[21]

A Line of Life occupies folios 138-78, according to the most recent pencilled numbering.[22] The first three folios (blank, title, epistle; now

---

[20] It is mentioned in Index of English Literary Manuscripts, ed. Peter Beal, 2.2.90 (FoJ 3).

[21] The volume includes a catalogue of Roman Catholic martyrs (fols. 1-32); a Latin commentary on the Articles of the Church of England, by A. Pritchard, 1699 (fols. 33-137); a transcription of Thomas James's apology for John Wycliffe (fols. 179-236), by John Lewis, the author of a Life of Wycliffe (London, 1720). A fragment of the Golden Legend, originally fol. 1 of the volume, has been removed and transferred to another volume.

[22] The oldest foliation for the volume is in ink and the leaves of A Line of Life are numbered from 142 to 182; under this there is a pencilled foliation from 139-179. These two foliations have been crossed out.

numbered 138-40) were not originally numbered, while the following folios, with the text proper, were numbered 1-38 (now numbered 141-78).[23] The leaves measure about 145mm x 187mm; there is one watermark, of the bunch of grapes variety, very similar to Heawood 2094.[24] Prior to 1965 the manuscript was in poor condition and several leaves were loose. The volume was rebound in that year and there are now six gatherings, mounted on guards, but these gatherings are not identical with the original ones, as is clear from an examination of the watermarks.[25] These always occur on the inner side of a leaf, in a medial position, and each watermark is therefore divided between two leaves. The pattern of the watermarks indicates that the original make-up of the manuscript was as follows: 4 [first leaf missing] -8-8-8-8-8 [last two leaves missing]. Instead of the present 41 leaves there must have been originally at least 44 leaves.

The missing leaf of the first gathering was most probably blank, as were the last two leaves of the final gathering. The printed text contains "The Corollarie," which occupies eleven pages (F12^r-G5^r). This portion of the text is not present in the manuscript and was probably never part of it. A page of the manuscript corresponds to about a page and a half of the printed text; the two leaves missing from the end of the gathering could not, therefore, have included the Corollary. An entire gathering may have been lost, but this is unlikely considering the condition of the manuscript. The last page of the manuscript (fol. 38^v) is blank, though ruled, suggesting that the manuscript is complete; however, it lacks a "Finis" at the end of the text. Probably copying from an autograph in which "Finis" was placed after the Corollary, the scribe apparently forgot to supply it at the end of the manuscript. As the Corollary adds little to the basic argument, Ford may have decided to omit it in the copy dedicated to Hay.

The manuscript is a presentation copy written in a neat, professional-looking secretary script, with occasional use of italic. It is not in Ford's hand, as the copyist had no Greek, which is omitted from the marginal

---

[23] In this edition, the original numbering has been indicated; the preliminary leaves have been given an asterisk followed by the number.

[24] E. Heawood, *Watermarks Mainly of the 17th and 18th Centuries* (Hilversum, 1950).

[25] The present gatherings are 4-6-10-6-10-6. The final leaf of the last gathering (fol. 179) belongs to the next manuscript; it is different paper with a different watermark. But, except for the first gathering, the two central leaves of the present gatherings coincide with the central leaves of the original gatherings; it is some of the outer leaves (fols. 141, 148, 157, 164, and 173) that were misplaced when the volume was rebound.

notes (747, 771-72), and small Latin, as he wrote "alieneus" for "aheneus" in a quotation from Horace (739; see also 437 and Commentary). It is possibly by the same scribe who, fifteen years earlier, had prepared the manuscript of *Fames Memoriall*, but the evidence is inconclusive.[26]

The texts of manuscript and the printed text are very close to one another. For example, Ford normally used the inflection -(e)s in the third person singular. Except for "hath" and "doth," the -th inflection occurs only five times in both texts (131, 706-7, 708, 824) and in one or the other in another four cases (36, 210, 426, 674). Instead of "doth" at 426 (as in all other cases) the printed text has "doeth" and the manuscript "does," suggesting a common source in which the "oe" was clear but not the inflection. At 157-58 both texts have "thou viewest ... surveyest" but "thou perceive" at 163.

There are many spelling differences and the manuscript is less consistent than the printed text, but it is impossible to tell which text is closer to Ford's original manuscript or whether the manuscript reflects Ford's own inconsistencies.

The punctuation of the two texts is sufficiently similar to suggest that they derive directly from a common source. In the main, they probably give us Ford's own pointing. They are identical in about sixty percent of cases, and they agree in the presence of some punctuation mark about three times out of four. If we exclude passages omitted or revised, the two texts use identical parentheses forty-three times and they differ twice in the position of one of the two round brackets. In six more cases there are parentheses in the manuscript but not in the printed text; the reverse occurs seven times. The main differences are a more liberal insertion of commas in the printed text and the scribe's use of virgules before periods (less often before question marks) and occasionally of a double period with a medial virgule (./.). Sometimes one of the texts is better punctuated, but their identical pointing is only once really in need of emendation (753).

The thirteen differences in paragraph division indicate either that the compositor or the copyist was unfaithful to his source or that Ford modified his paragraphs when revising the copy for one of the texts. But as the paragraph divisions of both texts are all acceptable, one cannot say that one

---

[26] For Oliver, there is not "any doubt" that the two manuscripts are in "the same hand, ... the writer has a peculiar way of using two forms of the letter 'r' and two of 'h' that alone would allow one to make the identification" (18). But these forms were in fact very usual.

of the texts is better than the other in this respect and therefore, presumably, revised.

The two texts, however, are seriously at variance as regards italicization; the scribe restricted his use of the Italian hand to the bare minimum. Both texts use italics for proper names (sometimes small capitals in the printed text) and for Latin. In other cases, when the Italian hand is used in the manuscript there are italics (or small capitals) in the printed text,[27] but the reverse is not true; the printed text uses italics (or small capitals) much more frequently. They occur for important words ("*Philosophie* ... *Action* ... *reason* ... *perseverance* ... *Divinitie* ... *sufferance*," 27–31) or expressions ("*The line of life, The middle naturall line,*" 68). For such words, the scribe uses italic several times up to folio 6, but very seldom afterwards, whereas the printed text uses italics (or small capitals) repeatedly throughout the whole of *A Line of Life*. It also carefully indicates all quotations and sentences, whereas the scribe indicates only one, with marginal quotation marks (341–44; fol. 16ʳ). The manuscript does not, for instance, italicize the two long Senecan quotations at 356–60 and 633–40. Moreover, the printed text often draws the reader's attention to contrasted or parallel words: "*speake well* ... *doe well*" (196–97), "*Vanity* ... *Vertue and Moderation*" (261–63), "*The first* ... *The latter*" (418–20), "*two first* ... *two last*" (441, 443), "*mans whore* ... *womans knave*" (495–96). This occurs only once in the manuscript.[28] It is unlikely that the compositor introduced italics (and small capitals) so frequently on his own initiative.[29] The scribe evidently found it more convenient (and perhaps quicker) to stick to secretary after folio 6. In respect of italicization, the printed text is apparently closer to Ford's original than the manuscript.

Although the two derive from a common source, there are important differences in their substantives. (a) The prefatory matter is wholly different in each, and the Corollary is lacking in the manuscript. (b) There is text found in the printed version lacking in the manuscript, both single words[30] and groups of two to eight words.[31] These omissions (except probably

---

[27] There is one exception; "*a good man*" (43; fol. 2ᵛ) is not italicized in the printed text.

[28] "*The multitude of offenders, and the libertie of offending*" (271–72).

[29] There is a similar use of italics in GM: "*selfe-unworthinesse* ... *selfe-reformation*" (529–30), "from *evill to good* ... from *temperance to libertie*" (542). GM was printed by H. Lownes and LL by W. Stansby.

[30] See 20, 31, 91, 107, 118, 144, 155, 177, 183 marg., 190, 373 marg., 376 marg., 395, 522, 628, 634, 640, 641, 663, 683, 728, 747 marg., 753, 769, 774, and 797.

[31] See 27–28 marg. (one word and one numeral), 67 (two words), 400–401 marg. (five

730) seem to be slips of the copyist. As over half of the missing words (single or in groups) have been omitted from the last fifth of the manuscript, their omission seems due to the copyist's flagging attention towards to end of his task. On the other hand, there is material in the manuscript not found in the printed text, twenty single words[32] and seventeen groups of from two to ninety-five words.[33] There are nine variants in word order,[34] thirteen homomorphic variants (that is, different words with forms that look alike),[35] where one of the two is presumably a misreading of the other, forty-two other single-word variants,[36] and in twenty-four instances different forms of the same word.[37] Single paragraphs in the printed text have been divided five times in the manuscript; the reverse occurs eight times.[38]

The simplest way to determine the relative accuracy of the two versions is to see which text contains more mistakes. All mistakes, however, are not as evident as "to to" at 218 (1620) or "in in" at 298 (MS). The many borderline cases have made it necessary to record all substantive variants in the textual notes, even obvious errors.

On balance, the printed text is more accurate for the text it prints.[39] Its

---

words), 684 (three words), 689 (eight words), 730 (three words), 771-72 marg. (three words and one numeral), and 830-31 (eight words).

[32] See 41, 107, 134, 180, 192-93, 309, 321, 335, 363 marg., 376 marg., 436, 468 marg., 494, 578, 579, 586, 605, 789, and 829.

[33] See 74 (three words), 194 (two words), 298 (three words), 311 (two words), 322-28 (seventy-three words instead of nine in the printed text), 357 (two words), 358-59 (four words), 403 (three words), 450-56 (seventy-four words), 469 (two words), 502 (two words), 509-10 (fifteen words), 511-12 (seven words), 515-16 (fourteen words), 553 (three words), 554 (three words), and 836-44 (ninety-five words).

[34] See 140-41, 175, 203, 277-78, 315-16, 415, 567, 631, and 646-47 marg.

[35] The printed text is listed first, and the reading adopted in this edition is followed by an asterisk. Words which could be abbreviated (which, what, etc.) have been omitted. See power/houre* (72), sucke*/seeke (260), profit*/praise (263), chusing*/vsing (296), reproch*/reproofe (370), Collections*/allegacions (394), driving*/drawing (428), vipers*/vysars (495), loyes/lives* (589), gratfully*/gracefully (665), peculiar/particular* (700), confirmed*/confined (734), and inlarging/in leaging* (761).

[36] See (printed text first): 19 (to/unto), 66 (as/and), 78 (then/the), 95 (those/theis), 121 (as/or), etc., 201, 255, 304, 313, 394, 397, 415, 424, 443, 445, 459, 474, 492, 498, 498, 545, 591, 608, 609, 636, 652, 654, 670, 711, 712, 715, 715-16, 720, 723-24, 735, 742, 751, 753 marg., 755, 764, 772, and 815.

[37] See 36 (sitteth/sitts), 38 (on-wardes/onward), 115 (an/a), etc., 210, 219, 230, 311, 322, 370, 378, 416, 426, 465, 466, 494, 504, 643, 653, 672, 674, 681, 687, 758, and 799.

[38] See 76, 123, 429, 461, 827; 283, 329, 368, 372, 579, 701, 712, and 770.

[39] Colin Norman agreed; see 402.

list of obvious errors is short (134, 218, 631, 764, 799), although there seem to be problems at 118 and 175, and inadvertent omissions at 358–59 and 469.[40] The same list in the manuscript is longer (twenty-six).[41] For the homomorphic variants, the reading of the printed text appears correct in nine cases out of thirteen.

The longer passages missing from the printed edition were omitted either by Ford or by the compositor. Ford excised a series a passages so as not to offend the king. He complains in his epistle that "*whatsoever is at all times honestly intended, oftentimes is too largely construed. Generall collections meet (not seldome) with particular applications, and those so dangerous, that it is more safe, more wise, to professe a free silence, then a necessarie industrie.*" And in the Corollary he justifies his "boldnes" by saying that it is "a presumption of love, not love of presumption," adding that his argument is "free from any particularity." As there were many "GREAT ONES" it could always be contended that some "particular application" was unwarranted, but there was only one sovereign in England. This is why Ford dropped a reference to "any unseemely defecte in their prince himselfe" (fol. 21ʳ), and another to "the credulous confidence of misinformed majestie" (fol. 37ᵛ). The "dronkennesse" of Epaminondas (fol. 14ʳ) is most probably omitted "because it invited the obvious comparison" with James's own revels.[42] The word "favourite" is only used in the manuscript (fols. 21ʳ, 21ᵛ, 23ᵛ), never in the printed edition.

---

[40] There are three press-variants. The inner forme of D is uncorrected in the Bodley copy (D2ʳ, 362 marg.: secoud) and the inner forme of E in the British Library copy (E9ᵛ, 641: hononurable; E11ᵛ, 674, catchword: *Truh*). Two misprints occur in both copies (see textual notes at 356 marg. and 755).

[41] See 66, 78, 298, 304, 313, 663, 672, 735, 739, 753 marg., 753, 769, and 772. At 553 there is an erroneous repetition of the "misery of"; the addition of "and the law" (554) is probably a mistake. There is an eye skip from "his friends" to "his friends" at 830, omitting eight words. There are several other suspicious omissions of groups of words (67, 684, 689) and of single words (31, 177, 774). The addition of "their" in front of "love" (487) "shows that the writer of the manuscript did not understand what he was copying" (Oliver, 20). Two more readings (498, 715) seem to be meaningless.

[42] Norman, 405. According to Sir Anthony Weldon, in James's "old age, Buckingham's joviall suppers ... made him sometimes overtaken, which he would the very next day remember and repent with tears"; quoted in Robert Ashton, *James I by His Contemporaries* (London, 1969), 12–13; see also Willson, *King James VI and I*, 378–79, 388–89. And in the presentation copy of his epigrams that he prepared for Prince Henry, Sir John Harington omitted two epigrams on drunkenness which may "have come too close to the royal conscience"; see R. H. Miller, "Unpublished Poems by Sir John Harington," *English Literary Renaissance* 14 (1984): 150 n. 9.

Ford's prudence cannot, however, account for two long omissions. The first (322-28) is a eulogy of the second Baron Harington of Exton that could hardly give offense to anyone. The second (really three omissions from 509 to 516) is no different from several other passages of *A Line of Life* (for example, 368-71) and contains nothing derogatory to James I. Rather, the compositor shortened his text because he had too much copy for sheets C and D. These omissions each occur at the end of a sheet, the first on C12^r and the second on D12$^{r\cdot v}$. The omitted material is equivalent to about a page plus four lines of printed text and could, admittedly, have been included; the Corollary would have ended on G6^r instead of G5^r. But this shows that there was not much room for error in casting off if the six folios of signature A (which contains the preliminaries) were to be printed on the same sheet as the six folios of signature G (with the end of the text and the Corollary).[43] Even if this combined sheet was set last, as was usual, it would be necessary to cast off the copy between sheets B to F in order to ensure that there was not too much copy for G. But a prose manuscript was much more difficult to cast off accurately than verse; when too much copy had been assigned to a sheet there was no possibility of resorting to the devices used for compressing the text of a verse play (smaller scene boxes, shortened headings, "turning up" a line instead of turning it over, etc.). Morever, there seem to be other signs of compression on sheets C and D. On C10^v and D8^r the compositor has set an extra (twenty-first) line with a single word (ending a paragraph) on the left and the catchword on the right to avoid a widow at the top of the next page. He could have spaced out the type a little on C10^v and D8^r and set a line of two words and a half (as on B7^v) or three words (D3^r, F7^r), but then he would have used an extra type-line.[44] If the compositor had to shorten his text when he reached the end of sheet C, he would naturally prefer to

---

[43] For the combined sheet A/G, see Norman (397-98), who makes a detailed study of the printing of *GM* 1613 and *LL* 1620. For *LL*, he thinks two skeleton formes were used "for the printing of sheets B-F, Skeleton I imposing all the outer formes, and inner formes being imposed by Skeleton II. It is also probable that these sheets were set *seriatim* rather than by formes" (395). But the printing of *LL* does not seem to have been perfectly straightforward. The recurrence of some slightly defective letters in the running title shows indeed that two skeleton formes were used for sheets C-F. But the recurrence of four letters also shows that the skeleton for the outer forme of C-F (or at least part of it) had been used for the inner forme of B, and vice versa.

[44] Once, on E9^r, the compositor set twenty-one lines (instead of twenty) without the catchword.

omit a few lines about Harington than anything about Ralegh, whose character comes next. The shortening was clumsy as "the religious learned Divine" is given undue importance at the end of a paragraph, whereas the manuscript only mentions him in a parenthesis. The shortening on D12 was neater: there are simply three excisions (15 words, 7 words, 14 words).

In addition, there is evidence that the scribe's copy had been revised and annotated by the author. First of all, we find some passages where the scribe's hesitations and corrections suggest that he was working from a revised version of the same copy that had been used for the printed text, in which the revisions were not always perfectly clear. At 605 "and," not in the printed text, has been added above the line, as if the copyist had first missed a correction. At 712 the reading of the printed text is crossed out and another word has been substituted: "Fynally try in all his desires" (fol. 32^r).

The revisions seem to have been sometimes misleading or hasty. At 400–404 the printed text is perfectly satisfactory:

> First, of publique men there are two generall sorts; The one, such as by the speciall favour of their Prince (which favour cannot ordinarily be conferred without some mayne and evident note of desert) have beene raised, to a supereminent ranck of honour, ... (D4^v-5^r)

The manuscript has:

> First of publique men, there are twoe generall sortes; The one such as by the speciall favour of their prince (wch favour cannot ordynarily be conferred without some mayne and evident note of deseart) by wch they) have been raised to a supereminent rancke of honor, ... (fol. 19^r)

It is unclear why the scribe introduced "by wch they," and the reading of the manuscript seems to be due to a hasty revision which disrupted the syntax; the correction cannot have been very clear as the scribe first put a parenthesis after "deseart" and then crossed it out and put it after "they." At 435–36 the printed version is "The eloquentest and gravest Divine of all the Ancients" (D7^v), whereas the manuscript has "The eloquentest and gravest divine of all the auncyent divines" (fol. 20^v), with the clumsy repetition of the noun. Perhaps the scribe did not see that "divine" had been, or should have been, crossed out and that Ford had revised his text to "The eloquentest and gravest divine of all the auncyent divines," the reading adopted in this edition.

Moreover, there are passages where the manuscript gives a better text, without any material evidence of revision in the form of scribal corrections.

At 20 "notwithstanding" is found in the printed text but not in the manuscript; the repetition of an adverb used a little earlier is the sort of thing an author would wish to correct when revising his text. The word is too long to be a scribal omission. There is a repetition of "yet" at 579 which is not in the printed text, but here the word is probably repeated for emphasis. At 640–41 the printed text is "But hee, he who directs all his whole private life" (E9^v). The manuscript ("But hee who directs his whole private life," fol. 29^v) avoids the pleonastic "all his whole," which was, however, not unusual in the seventeenth century. At 607–10 Ford says that a virtuous public man "cannot chuse in his own lifetime, but build a monument, to which the Triumph and Trophies of his memorie, shall give a longer life then the perpetuitie of stone, Marble or Brasse can preserve" E7^{r-v}. Instead of "to which ... give" the manuscript has "where ... gayne" (fol. 28^r), a clearly authorial revision.[45]

Sometimes a mere change in the word order seems to be the evidence of authorial revision, as in the following:

140–42: so consequently, without question, the frame of our humane composition, must preposterously sinke under its owne burthen, (B11^r)
 so must consequently wthout question, the frame of our humane composition, preposterously syncke under its owne burthen, (fol. 7^v).

315–16: for then indeed it were miraculous, (C11^v) for then it were indeed miraculous, (fol. 15^r)

414–15: there are *two capitall and deadly opposites* (if it were possible) to becharme their resolutions, (D5^v–6^r)
 there are twoe capitall and deadly opposites, to (if it be possible) becharme their resolutions, (fol. 19^v). (There is also a correction from "were" to "be.")

566–67: (whose ashes are scarce yet colde) (E4^r) (whose ashes are yett scarce cold) (fol. 26^v)

There are other variants or minor additions that suggest revision; for instance, the addition of "in their deceiptes" (74; fol. 4^v), or the change from "in his action" (321–22; C12^r) to "in all his actions" (fol. 15^r). The conjunction "and" has been added several times in the manuscript (41,

---

[45] Compare "gayning them the truest honour *A deserved fame*" (125–26).

309, 335, 494, 605), and its introduction is usually felicitous. In one instance, an omission in the manuscript may be authorial. The printed text is "*Flatterie and envie* are not a more pestilent broode set in armes against a *publique man*, then those two miscreant monsters are against a *good man*" (730-31; F3ᵛ). The words "set in armes," omitted in the manuscript, add nothing to the sense and upset the parallelism of the clauses.

We have, then, two authoritative texts, each a witness to the authorial original. The manuscript gives a more complete and occasionally revised version of the text proper, but the printed text is longer because of the dedicatory epistles and the Corollary. The compositor seems to be the more reliable witness, perhaps simply because a mistake caught in proofing was easier for him to rectify.

As to the exact relation of the two surviving witnesses to the lost original, there are three possibilities:

1. The same authorial manuscript was used first by the scribe and then by the compositor, after Ford had deleted the material he did not want to publish. But it is difficult to see why he or the compositor would have added "notwithstanding" (20) or changed "his whole" to "all his whole" (641), unless of course these had been mistakenly omitted by the scribe.

2. Ford may have prepared two manuscripts, one for the printer and one for the scribe, making some revisions in the latter after giving the first to the printer. But would an author want to prepare two manuscripts when the differences are so small?

3. After his manuscript had been returned by the printer Ford revised his text, added the passages he had not considered it prudent to publish, and gave it to a professional scribe.

Of the three, the third is the most likely.

This Edition

We have two texts, both of them authoritative in spite of their blemishes. The manuscript gives a more complete and occasionally revised version of the text proper, but the printed text is longer if one takes into account the epistles and the Corollary. The printed text is, in the main, more accurate and has fewer obvious errors than the manuscript; it seems, moreover, to be much more faithful to Ford's original in respect of italicization. The 1620 edition has

A LINE OF LIFE 297

therefore been chosen as copy-text and its accidentals adopted, including paragraphing, unless otherwise indicated in the textual notes.

When the manuscript's substantives are different from the copy-text, the editor must try to discriminate between scribal error and authorial revision; a single word lacking in the manuscript might be an involuntary scribal omission or an authorial deletion. Each variant, addition, or omission must be judged on its own merits; decisions are often difficult to make, but they never affect Ford's argument. The following rules have guided editorial choices in respect of substantives. Copy-text has been retained for (1) single words present only in the copy-text (ten exceptions), (2) single-word variants (twenty-two exceptions), (3) groups of two words or more present only in the copy-text (one exception). Manuscript readings have been adopted for (1) single words lacking in the copy-text (five exceptions), (2) variants involving two words, (3) groups of two words or more lacking in the copy-text (four exceptions), (4) differences in word order (one exception). All substantive readings from the manuscript have been placed in brackets. These have not been used for accidentals (punctuation, italics) adopted from the manuscript, but all such emendations have been recorded in the textual notes.

A Line of Life was edited, rather carelessly, by the Shakespeare Society in 1843. There is not only a gap in the text because the imperfect British Library copy was used, but the editor also omitted single words here and there, added a few words, and misread or changed many.[46] There was little attempt at emendation.[47] In 1869 Alexander Dyce added A Line of Life to his revision of William Gifford's edition of Ford's works, but he was "acquainted with [A Line of Life] only as reprinted in 1843 for the Shakespeare Society," as he said himself, and he perpetuated most of the errors of the 1843 edition, which survived into A. H. Bullen's re-issue of 1895. There have been at least four unpublished editions, prepared as Ph.D. dissertations, since 1965 (see 217 n. 1, above).

---

[46] (1) Words omitted: against (Reader 23), sleepe (19), else (20), owne (142), 301 marginal note, most (398), the (401), their (459), ²a (596), even (619), be (779), a (Cor. 26). The figure "1" has been omitted at 27 marginal note. (2) Words added: but (384), and (692), more (734). (3) Words misread or changed (1620/1843): at/out (title page 5), those/these (7), warie/warre (142), mist/trust (270), impietie/pietie (481), imployment/imploiments (489), effect/affect (489), casualty/causality (585), case/ease (621), an/a (653), the rewarder/there warder (656), whom/who (673), those/these (731), complots/exploits (736–37), hostilitie/hostilities (760), Empire/Europe (792), realitie/realities (795), injurie/injuries (803–4). At 375 marg. "5" has been changed to "7."

[47] See the textual notes at 118, 182 marg., 631, 711, 764, and 799.

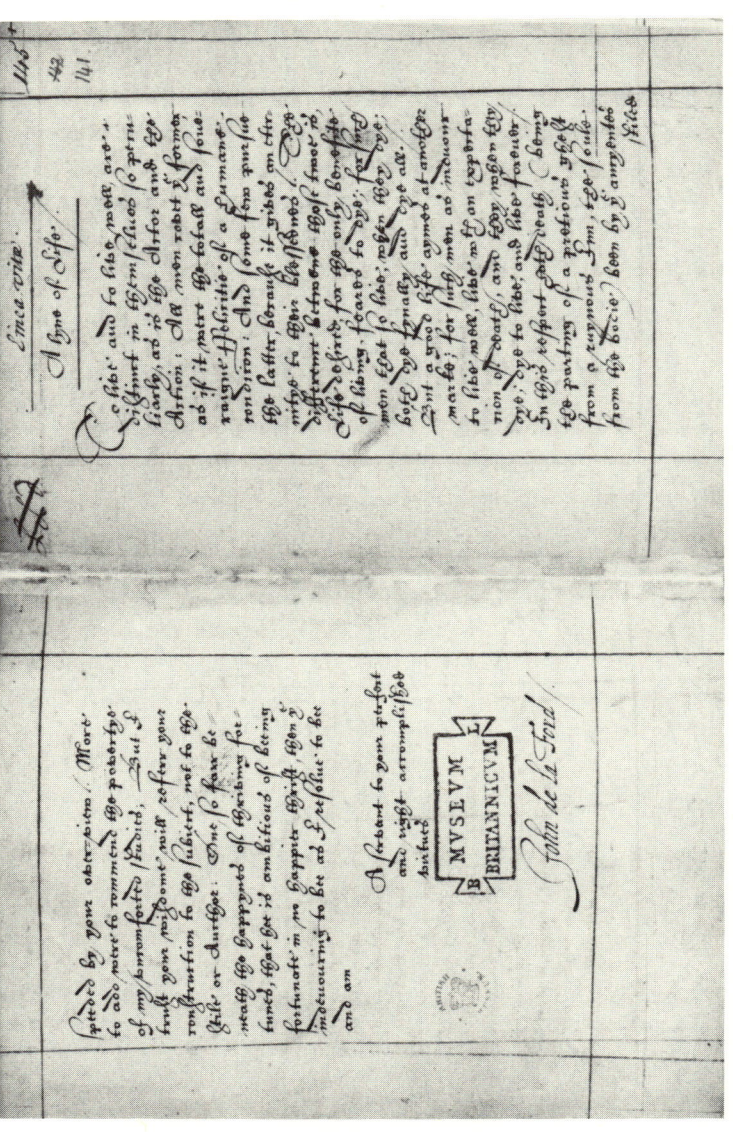

The British Library, Lansdowne MS. 350, fols. *4v-1r. By permission.

A LINE OF LIFE.

Pointing at the *Immortalitie* of a Vertuous NAME.

Printed by *W. S.* for *N. Butter,* and are to be sold at his shop neere Saint *Austens* gate.

1 6 2 0.

WISE, and therein NOBLE.

A2ʳ

Ambition beeing sooner discovered by acting then plotting, can rarely personate practise in studie, unlesse the Arts themselves, which in themselves are liberall, should be too curiously censured, too inquisitively confined. | A2ᵛ *It is an easie vanity, in these dayes of libertie, to be a conceited Interpreter, but a difficult commendation to bee a serious Author: for whatsoever is at all times honestly intended, oftentimes is too largely construed. Generall collections meet (not seldome) with particular applications, and those so dangerous, that it is more safe, more wise, to professe a free silence, then a necessarie industrie. Here in this (scarce an) handfull of discourse, is deciphered, not what any | personally is, but what any personally may be: to the intent,* A3ʳ *that by the view of others wounds, we might provide playsters and cures for our owne, if occasion impose them. It is true, that all men are not borne in one, the same, or the like puritie of qualitie or condition; for in some, Custome is so become another Nature, that Reason, is not the mistresse, but the servant, not the directresse but the foyle to their passions. Folly is a sale-able merchandise, whose factour, youth is* | *not so allowedly profest* A3ᵛ *in young men, as pleasure in men of any age: yet are the ruines, the calamities, the wofull experiences of sundrie presidents and samplars of indiscretion and weakenesse (even in noted, and sometimes in great ones) so apparent, so daily, that no Antidote against the infection, disease, leprosie of so increasing an evill, can be reputed superfluous. For my part, I ingeniously acknowledge, that hitherto (how ever the course hath proved a barre to my thrift, yet) I* | *never fawned upon any mans Fortunes, whose person and* A4ʳ *merit I preferred not. Neither hath any court-ship of applause, set me in a higher straine, a higher pinnacle of opinion, then severest Approbation might make warrantable. Howbeit even in these few lines that follow, my* ayme hath not beene so grossely levelled, that I meant to chuse every Reader for my Patron: considering that none can challenge any interest herein from me (unlesse he challenge it | by way of an usurped impropriation) whom A4ᵛ I my selfe doe not out of some certaine knowledge and allowance of Desert, as it were poynt out and at, with my finger, and confesse that Hic est, it is this one and onely. By which marke, I can deny no man (not guiltie to himselfe of a selfe-unworthinesse) to call it his owne: at least, none of those, who freely returne the defects to their proper owner, and the benefit (if any may be) of this little worke to their own use and themselves. So | much A5ʳ it is to bee presumed, the verie taliarie Law may require and obtaine. In all things, no one thing can more requisitely bee observed to be practised, then *The Golden Meane: The exemplification whereof, however heretofore attributed, I dare not so poorely under-value my selfe and labours, as not to call mine. But if I should farther exceede, I might exceede that meane, which I have endevoured to commend. Let him that is wise, and therein noble, assume | properly to himselfe this interest, that I cannot distrust the* A5ᵛ *successefull acceptation, where the sacrifice is a thriftie love; the Patron a great man good (for to be truly good is to be great) And the Presentor, a feodarie to such as are maisters not more of their own Fortunes then their owne affections.*

Æstatis occasum haùd ægrè tulit unquám A6ʳ
Temperata Hyems.

JO. FORD.

[*To the right worthye of all honours, of
all Love, Sir James Haye knight,
Lord Haye, viscount Doncaster,
Baron of Salye, one of his
Majesties most honorable
privie Councell. &c.*

Great sir.

It is a pardonable presumption that I (though meerely an unknowne stranger to you) amongst all those, who truely serve you, in truely honouring you, offer to your leisurable houres and protection, this pawne of a greater debt. Your virtue and noblenes hath alreadie chronicled your desearts in every gratefull memory, that henceforth you cannott but live (even after life) in the remembrance of your owne goodnes; A much more lasting Register then the fullnes of a story can compile. For the Argument I present (I may justifie without partiallitie) it is worthy your survey; I dare bee playner, without affectation, that your graver imploymentes can be no way intermytted, but rather | speeded by your over-view. More to add were to commend the povertye of my uncomforted studies; But I trust your wisdome will referr your construction to the subject, not to the stile or Aucthor: One, so farr beneath the happynes of thriving fortunes, that hee is ambitious of beeing fortunate in no happier thrift, then the indevouring to bee as I resolve to bee and am

A servant to your perfect and right
accomplished virtues
John de la Ford.]

LINEA VITÆ:
A Line of Life.

To live, and to live well, are distinct in themselves, so peculiarly as is the ACTOR and the ACTION. All men covet the former, as if it were the totall | and sovereigne felicitie of a humane condition: And some few pursue the latter, because it gives an eternity to their blessednesse. The difference between those two is, *Life* desired for the only benefit of living, feares to dye; for such men that so live, when they dye, both dye finally and dye all: But a *good Life* aymes at another mark; for such men as indeavour to live well, live with an expectation of death, and they when they dye, dye to live, | and live for ever. In this respect hath death (being the parting of a precious Ghest from a ruinous Inne, the soule from the bodie) beene by the Ancients, | styled a Haven of safetie, a finishing of Pilgrimages, a resting from travaile, a passage to glorie. Everie man that most shuns it (and he most shunnes it that most feares it) runnes notwithstanding wilfully to meet it, even then posting to it, when hee abhorres it: for (the comparison is lively and remarkeable) as he who | in a Shippe, directs his course to some Port; whether he stand, walk, revell, sleepe, lie downe, or any way else dispose himself, [is alwaies] driven on to the period of his voyage: So in this Ship of our mortalitie, howsoever wee limit our courses, or are suited in any fortune of prosperitie or lownesse, in this great Sea of the World; | yet by the violence and perpetuall motion of time, are we compeld to pace onward to the last and long home of our | graves, and then the victorie of Life is concluded in the victory of our ends.

It is granted in *Philosophie*, that *Action* is the Crowne of Vertue. It cannot in *reason* (the light of Philosophie) be denied, that *perseverance* is the Crowne of Action: and then *Divinitie* (the Queene of Nature) will confirme, that *sufferance* is the Crowne of perseverance. For to be vertuous without the testimonie of imployment, is as a rich Minerall

Arist. in 1. *Ethic.*
Cicer. in off.

in the heart of the | Earth, un-useful because unknowne; yet to bee vertuously imployed, and not to continue, is like a swift runner | for a Prize, who can with ease gaine it from others, but slothfully sitteth downe in the middle way; but to persevere in well-doing without a sence of a dutie, only with hope of reward, is like an Indian Dromedarie, that gallops to his common Inne, prickt on-wardes with the desire of Provender. *It is beast-like not to differ from beasts,* aswell in the abuse of reason, | *as it would bee in the defect.*

ACTION, PERSEVERANCE IN ACTION [AND] SUFFERANCE IN PERSEVERANCE, are the three golden linkes that furnish up the richest Chain wherwith a *good man* can bee adorned; They are a tripartite counter-pawne, wherby wee hold | the possession of life, whose Charter or Poll Deed (as they terme it) are youth till twentie, manhood till fortie, olde age till our end. And hee who beginnes not in the spring | of his minoritie to bud forth fruits of vertuous hopes, or hopefull deserts, which may ripen in the Summer of confirmed manhood; rarely or never yeelds the crop of a plentifull memory in his age, but prevents the winter of his last houre, in the barren Autume of his worst houre, by making an even reckoning with time misspent, dying without any *Issue* to inherit his remembrance or commendation.

Heere is then a preparation made to the | ground-worke and foundation wheron the structure | and faire building of a minde nobly furnisht must stand: which for the perpetuitie and glorie of so lasting a monument, cannot altogether unfitly bee applyed to a LINE OF LIFE. For whosoever shall levell and square his whole course by this just proportion, shall (as by a line) bee led not only to unwinde himselfe from out the Labyrinth and Maze of this naturall and troublesome Race of frailtie, but to flie up in | the middle path, the *via lactea* of immortalitie in his name on Earth, to the Throne of life, and perfection in his whole man, and to an immortalitie that cannot bee changed.

Deceiving and deceiveable *Palmesters*, who will undertake | by the view of the hand, to bee as expert in foretelling the course of life to come to others, as they are ignorant of their own in themselves, have framed and found out three chiefe lines in the hand, wherby to divine | future events; *The line of life, The middle naturall line, and the table line*. According to the fresh colour or palenes, length or shortnesse, bredth or narrownesse, straitnesse or obliquitie, continuance or intermission of either of these, they presume to censure the manners, the infirmities, the qualities, the verie [houre] of Life or Death of the person. But the *line of life* is the eminent mark they must be directed by, to the perfection of their Masterpiece | [in their deceiptes]. All which, are as | far from truth as wonder; onely it is true and wonderfull, that any ignorance can be so deluded. Another *line of life* is the most certaine and infallible rule, which wee as we are men, and more then men; Christians, and more then Christians, the image of our maker; must take our level by. Neither is judgement to be given by the ordinary lineaments of the furniture of Nature, but by the noble indowments of the mind, whose ornaments or ruines are then most apparently | goodly or miserable, when as the actions we doe, are the evidences of a primitive puritie; or a derivative depravation. | Here is a great labour to indure, a great strength in that labour to conquer, a great Resolution in that strength to triumph, requisite, before wee can climbe the almost impregnable and inaccessible toppe of glorie; which they that have attempted have found, and they that have found have enjoyed to their own happines and wonder | of imitation.

RESOLUTION is the plotter and the Actor, nay, it is both the plot and the Act it selfe that must prompt us how to doe, aswell as it must point us out what to do before wee can as much as take into the hands of our purposed constancie, this *line* which must direct us to life, and make us to live.

Whatsoever therefore in those briefe ensuing collections is inserted, | to patterne and personate an excellent man, must be concluded and | understood for methods sake in this one only attribute, RESOLUTION. For by it are exemplified the perfections of the minde, consisting in the whole furniture of an enriched soule; and to it are referred the noblest actions, which are the externall arguments and proofes of the treasure within: For as it is a State Maxime in Policie, that *Force abroad in Warre is of no force, but rather Rashnesse then Souldierie, unlesse there bee counsell peaceably at home to direct for expedition:* | so are all actions of Resolution in the *Oeconomie* and household government of a mans owne particular private wealth, but shining follies, unlesse there bee | a consultation first held within him for determining [of] the [commoditie, conveniencie] and commendation of such actions, aswell in doing, as when they are done.

 Order in everie taske is for conceipt easiest, for demonstration play-
110 nest, for Imitation surest. Let us then take | into our consideration B9^r
this *Line of Life*, and trace the way wherein wee are to travaile, keep-
ing our eye on the Compasse whereby we may runne to the Paradise
of memorable happinesse. And first it is to be observed, That *Resolu-
tion* hath three branches; The one concerns a mans owne particular
115 person for the carriage of himselfe in his proper dutie, and such an
one is knowne by none other note, then in beeing A MAN: Another | 6^v
concernes a mans imployment | in affaires for his Countrey, Prince, B9^v
and Common-wealth, and such a [one is] knowne by the generall
name of A PUBLIKE MAN. The last concernes a mans voluntarie
120 traffique in civill causes without the imposition of authoritie, only
urged on to performe the offices of a friend, as a private Statist to
severall ends, all tending to goodnes and vertue; and such a one is
ever to be call'd a GOOD MAN. In everie one of those there is a plen-
tifull imployment | presenting it selfe to the liberall choyce for enno- B10^r
125 bling themselves with publique honors, or gayning them the truest
honour *A deserved fame*, which is one (if worthie) of the best and
highest rewards of vertue. 7^r

 Superfluous it were and unnecessarie, to enter into   Of the
the contentious lists of divided Philosophers, or un-   first,
130 reconciled Schoolemen, for the absolute and punc-   a man.
tuall definition of man; Since, it sufficeth us to be assured that he
| is mainely and yet pithily distinguish't from all other created sub- B10^v
stances in the only possession of a *reasonable soule*. This royall preroga-
tive alone poynts him to be [the] noblest of creatures; and to speak
135 truth, in an assertion not to be gain-said, he containes the summary
of all the *great world*, in the *little world* of himselfe. As then the
Fabricke of the globe of the earth would of necessitie runne to the
confusion out of which it was first refined, if | there were not a B11^r
great and watchfull providence, to measure it in the just | ballance 7^v
140 of preserving and sustayning; so [must] consequently, without
question, the frame of our humane [composition, preposterously]
sinke under its owne burthen, if warie and prudent direction, as well

in manners as in deedes, restraine it not from the dissolution and wracke, the proclivitie of corrupted Nature doth hourely slide into.

A mans minde is the | *man himselfe* (said the Romane Orator) and the chiefest of the Grecian Naturalists, was confident to averre, that *the temperature of the minde followed the temperature of the body.* It were a Lesson worthie to bee cond, if eyther of those rules may be positively received: For out of the first, as any man feeles his inclinations and affections, thereafter let him judge himselfe | to bee such a man. Out of the latter it may be gathered, how easie it | were, for everie man to be his owne Schoolemaster, in the conformation or reformation of his life, without other tutour then himselfe.

Socrates his speech of the use of mirrours or looking glasses, concludes whatsoever can bee ranged in many wordes of this subject, and is therefore notoriously usefull, and usefully notable; When thou viewest thy selfe in a mirrour, (said that wise man) surveyest thy complexion, thy proportion, | if thy face be more faire, lovely, and sweeter then others, thy bodie straighter, thy lineaments perfecter; consider how much more thou art bound by that, to match those blessings of Nature, with the | accomplishment of more noble qualities, then others of a courser mould. If on the other side, thou perceive thy face deformed, thy body crooked, thy outward constitution unsightly or mishapen; by so much the more hast thou reason | to live a good life, that thereby concord of vertuous conditions, may supply the defects of Nature, and make thee more beautifull inwardly to the eye of judgement, then outwardly thou couldst have beene to the eyes of popular delight.

In short, to be a *man*, the first branch of resolution is to know, feele, and moderate affections, which like traitors, and disturbers of peace, rise up to alter and quite change the Lawes of reason, by working in | the feeble, and oftentimes | the sounder parts, an innovation of folly. Hee can seldome be a flourishing member of a bodie politique, and so a [*deserving publique*] *man*; but more rarely, scantly ever, a reconciler of divisions, and so a civill *good man* for others, that begins not betimes to discharge his owne dutie to himselfe. The old Proverbe was, (and it is lamentable, to speake with truth, and say

it is) that *A man is a beast to a man*; but it must
be of necessitie | granted, when a man to himselfe *Homo homini lupus.* C2ʳ
is a *Monster*, or more proverbially, *a Devill*.

It is said of CAIUS CURIO, that hee was a man [*Velleius*]
most *wittily wicked*, and most *singularly eloquent* in Paterc.
mischiefe against the Common-wealth. What rar- lib. 2.
ities were here lost? (like a Diamond set in a rushen ring:) How much
better had it been for him, to have | had a *duller braine*, if better im- 9ᵛ
ployed, and a *slower tongue*, if availeable for the publique good? Every
| man should in his owne person, endevour and *Fab.* [*inst.*] C2ᵛ
strive to be like *Catoes Orator, a good man, and ex-* *orat.* lib. 12.
pert in pleading, First *good,* then *expert*; For of so cap. 1.
much richer price is *vertue* then *Art*. *Art* without Plin.
vertue being like the *Cantharides*, whose wings [bee- lib. 11.
ing] puld off, they have prettie colours to please the cap. 35.
eye, but poisonous substances to be received into the stomack. How
easie it is to guild a rotten post, to paint a Sepulcher, to varnish an
ill meaning, is soone resolved: | Many men can *speake well*, few men C3ʳ
will *doe well*; The reason, for that we covet to be thought what wee
are not, and yet continue to be what wee are ashamed to be thought.

The excellency of goodnesse is apparent mainly in this one poynt, 10ʳ
that even those who least practise it in outward appearance, cunningly
labour to make it the marke whereto all their actions (how foule
soever in the issue) levell at. It was truely observed by a | grave Author, C3ᵛ
That there [never was] any publique mischiefe attempted in a State
by even Atheists, or very incarnate Devils, but Religion was their
colour to effect it; at least a shew of some false zeale in as false a
worship. For there must be an intention of vertue in the worst ac-
tions, otherwise they could never have passage by any publique ap-
probation; Insomuch, that hypocrisie is reputed the surest and the
safest ground of pollicie.

By this appeareth the richnesse of vertue, that even such as most C4ʳ
| oppose it, must and are compelled to acknowledge it for best. In 10ᵛ
like manner, every man in his particular to distinguish his actions,
is in his knowledge guiltie and conscious of what he doth or should
doe. We were not borne to feed, sleepe, and spinne out our webbe
of life in the delicate softnesse of vanitie, or sloath; wee were not
borne to traffique in follies, and to make merchandize of | our sen- C4ᵛ

sualities; wee were not borne to revel in the apishnesse of ridiculous expence of time; wee were not borne to be Panders to that great Whore of a declyning Reason, *bewitching pleasure*: we were not borne
220 to laugh at our owne securitie, but to bewayle it; we were not borne to live for our selves, but to our selves; as we were not on the other side borne to dye to our selves, | but for our selves. We must learne 11ʳ to rejoyce in true goodnesse, | not vain delights: For as we cannot c5ʳ judge him to have a light heart alwaies, that somtimes laughes (for
225 even in laughter there is a sadnesse,) so wee must not imitate by any outward demeanor, to bewray the minoritie of our Resolution, except we would be as childish in understanding as in action.

What infinite inticers hath a man as he is a meere man, to withdraw him from an erected heart? As the temptation of a reputed | c5ᵛ
230 beautie, the invitement of [presented honors], the bewitching of an inforced wealth, the Lethargie and disease of an infectious Courtgrace; yet all and everie one of these (with what other appendances soever belonging unto them) are (if not wisely | made use of) but 11ᵛ glorious snares, dangerous baites, golden poysons, dreaming distruc-
235 tions, snares to intrappe the mightinesse of constancie; Baites to deceive the constancie of manhood, | poysons to corrupt the manhood c6ʳ of Resolution; destruction to quite cast away the Resolution of a just desert.

Now for a mans carriage in his particular dutie, what can hee de-
240 termine of, since he hath not more himselfe, and his own affections to assault and batter his Resolution in the path of Vertue, then a world of presidents, of partners, of helpers, to perswade and draw him on to the full measure of an unworthy life? It is a labor | wel worthy c6ᵛ a Chronicle | (and chronicled will bee in a perpetuall memorie) to 12ʳ
245 withstand the severe assault of Folly, pressing on with so infinite an Armie of followers and admirers as shee is accompanyed with: what can one *private man* do against such a multitude of temptations? Either hee must consent to doe as they doe; or dissent and hate them: if consent, hee is mischievous with many; if dissent, vertuous by him-
250 selfe; and the last is without controversie | the best. Since never to c7ʳ have seene evill is no praise to well doing; but where the Actours of Mischiefe are a Nation, there and amongst them to live well is a Crowne of immortall commendation.

A Golden Axiome there was registred amongst the Civilians | in 12ᵛ the daies of *Justinian*: *That it was not convenient for any man to pry,* [*nay*] *looke after what was done at Rome, but to examine justly what ought there to bee done.* *Rome* was then the Mart of | the World, all sorts of every people came thither, from thence to receive the Oracles of life (as they might bee termed:) yet doth it not follow that any one man with the multitude, should runne to *Rome*, to sucke the infection of dissolute intemperance. *Vanity* most commonly rides coach't in the high way, the beaten way, the common way; But *Vertue and Moderation* walkes alone. It may be said, what profit can redound, what commendation, what reward, for | one man to bee singular against many? O the profit is infinite, the commendation memorable, the reward | immortall. It is true the olde Greeke Proverbe concluded, that *one man was no man*; yet with their most approved Authours, by the verie word MANY, were the worst sort of people understood, and by FEW the best. For certainely there is not any allurement could lull men in the mist of their misdeeds, so much as those two pestilent yoke-fellowes | and twinnes of confusion, *The multitude of offenders, and the libertie of offending.* They are both Examples and Schoolemasters, to teach even the very ignorant (whose simplicitie else might be their excuse) to do what (if others did not) they might accidentally slide into, but not so eagerly pursue.

To conclude this point, it may somewhat too truly be said, though not by way of discouragement, yet | of caveat, what by the [*pronenesse* | *and proclivitie*] of our frailtie is warrantable; *Let no man bee too confident of his owne merit, The best doe erre: Let no man relye too much on his owne Judgement, the wisest are deceived:* yet let every man so conceive of himselfe, that he may indevour to bee such a one, as distrust shal not make him carelesse, or confidence secure.

It followes that the very consideration of being men, should somwhat rectifie our crooked inclinations, and | ennoble our actions to keepe us worthy of the priviledge wee have above beasts: otherwise only to be a man in substance and name, is no more glorie then to bee knowne and distinguished from a very beast in nature.

Presidents from Antiquitie may | plentifully be borrowed, to set before us what some men have beene, not as they were Commanders, or employed for the Commonwealth; but as they were Commanders of their owne infirmities, | and employed for the Commonwealth of their own particular persons. *Epaminondas* amongst the *Thebanes*, is worthy of note and memorie even to our Ages, and those that shall succeed us; Hee (as the Philosopher recordeth) chose rather to bee moderate alone, then madde with the multitude; chusing at all times to consult with himselfe in excellent things, not with his Countreymen to give Lust, Dalliance, [and Dronkennesse or] Effeminate softnes a Regiment in the Kingdome of his | thoughts; no not of his thoughts, much lesse of his Actions. *Phocion* among the *Athenians*, *Brutus* among the | *Romanes*, are for their particular cariage of themselves as they were only men, well worthy of all remembrance: And the sententious *Seneca* is bold to say, that all Ages will ever hatch and bring forth many such as *Clodius*, (a man bent to mischiefe) but rarely any Age another *Cato*, a man so sincere, so free from corruption, and so severe a Censurer of himselfe.

Plutarch. in Apotheg.

Cicero de leg. lib. 3.

Juvenal. Sat. 14.

Epist. 98.

But what need we to search histories of other times, or the deserts of another Nation, when in our owne Land, [and] in our owne dayes, wee might easily patterne what a man should bee or not bee, by what others have bin? Among many, two of late times are justly [to be] examined; not as they were different in fortune, in | yeares, in degree, but as they differed in the use of the gifts of their mind. The first was JOHN, the last and yongest Lord HARRINGTON, whose rare | and admirable course of life (not as he was a Noble man, for then [it were indeed] miraculous, but as a man,) deserves all prayse and imitation from all. Of whome it may without flatterie (for what benefit can accrue to flatter the dead?) or affection bee said, That He amongst a World of men attayned even in his youth, not only to gravitie in his behaviour, to wisedome in his understanding, to ripenesse in his carriage, to discretion in his discourse, but to perfection | in [all his actions]: A man [in himself so absolute (if the testimony of a most religious learned divine bee of Credite) | that there could not bee more attributed to any living; noe such exquisite rarities to furnishe or sett out a samplarr of wonder and fullnes could bee, which in him were not. In somuch as hee exceeded any whome former Chronicles have mencioned, and may equall any that tyme heereafter can Callender in the monumentes of perpetuitie.]

But for that his owne merit is his best commendation, and questionlesse his surest reward for morall gifts: let him rest in his peace whilest the next is to bee observed.

Sir Waltir Rauleigh may be a second President, a man known, and wel-deserving to be knowne; A man endued not with common endowments, being stored with the best of Natures | furniture, | taught much by much experience, [and] experienc'd in both fortunes so feelingly and apparently, that it may truly bee controverted whether hee were more happie or miserable; yet beholde in him the strange Character of a *meere man*, a man subject to as many changes of *resolution*, as *resolute* to bee the instrument of change: *Politique*, and yet in *Policie* so unsteddie, that his too much apprehension was the foile of his judgement. *For what man soever | leanes too credulously to his owne strength, not supported by the firme Pillars of Constancy and Vertue, that man cannot choose but fall under the weight of his owne burthen*: And so did he, being faulty in nothing more, then not applying himselfe to the trust of | such friends as laboured to doe him service, in honest and honourable Designes. In a word, his *Wisdome* and *Courage* appeared (late enough, though not too late) in his last demeanour; for that *not making | himselfe lesse when he was great, he strove to be so great in his resolution when he came to bee nothing*. I speake of his end, at his end. So heere may this point bee fitly closed up, that a mans particular carriage in his proper dutie, is a sweet and readie preparation for enabling him to undergoe the second branch of a noble Resolution in publique imployment, by beeing made for his Prince and Countrey A Publike Man: which to doe, these few lines comprehend | all what the former Discourse hath amplified; |
Namely that *the only felicitie of a good life, depends in doing all things freely, [and with] beeing content with what wee have* (for wee speake of a morall man.) *This is [to live, this is] to remember that we are mortall, that our dayes passe on, and our life slides away without recoverie.*

        Seneca Epist. 123.

Great is the taske, the labour painfull, the discharge full of danger, and the dangers full of Envy, that he must of necessitie undergoe, that like a | blaze upon a Mountain, stands neerest in grace to his Prince: or like a vigilant Sentinell in a Watch-tower, busies and weakens his owne

    Of the second branch, A Publike man.

naturall and vitall spirits, to administer Equalitie and Justice to all, according to the requisition of his | office.

It is lamentable and much to bee pittyed, when places of Authority in a Commonwealth, are disposed of to some, whose unworthinesse or disabilitie brings a scandall, a scorne, and a reproch to both the place | and the Minister.

The best Law-makers amongst the Ancients, were so curious in their choice of men in Office in the Commonwealth, that precisely and peremptorily, they reputed that STATE plagued, whipped, tormented, wounded, yea wounded to death, where the subordinate Governours were not aswell unblemished in their lives and actions, as in their names and [reputations]. *Plato 3. 6. et 12. de leg. et 7. de Repub. Arist. 5. et 6. Polit. Isocrat. in Pan.*

A PUBLIKE MAN hath not more | neede to be *Bonus Civis*, a good | *Statist*, then *Bonus Vir*, good in himselfe; a very faire and large *Line* is limmed out, to square by it a direct path that leades to a vertuous Name, if a man acquite himselfe nobly, justly, and wisely, in well steering the Helme of State that he sits at; otherwise his Honours are a burthen, his Height a Curse; his Favours a Destruction, his Life a Death, and his Death a Misery: A Misery in respect of his after Defamation, aswell as of his after accompt.

Far from the present purpose it is to dive into the depth of *Policie*, or to set downe any positive rules, what a right *Statesman* should be; for that | were with *Phormio* the Philosopher to read a Lecture of Souldierie to *Hannibal* the most cunningest Warriour of his time; and consequently as *Phormio* was by *Hannibal* to be justly laughed at, so aswell might *Seneca* have written to *Nero* the Art of Crueltie; or *Cicero* to his brother *Quintus* the Commendation of Anger. | The summe of these briefe Collections, is intended to recreate the minde, not to informe Knowledge in practice; but to conforme Practice to Knowledge: Whereto no indeavor can bee found more requisite, more availeable, then [the] undeceiving lesson of an impartiall observation; wherin if our studies erre not with many and those most approved, thus we have observed.

First, of publique men there are two generall sorts; The one, | such as by the speciall favour of their Prince (which favour cannot ordinarily be con- *Two sorts of publike men.*

ferred without some mayne and evident note of desert) have beene raised, to a supereminent ranck of honour, and so by degrees (as it for the most part alwayes happens) to speciall places of weightie imployment in the common wealth. *The other* sort are such as the Prince according to his judgement, hath out of their owne sufficiencie, advaunced to particular | offices, whether for administration of justice, for execution of Law, for necessitie of service, and the like, being according to their education and studie, enabled for | the discharge of those places of authoritie; and *these two* are the onely chiefe and principall members of imploiment under that head, of whose politike bodie they are the most usefull and stirring members.

Against both those publique persons, there are *two capitall and | deadly opposites*, [to (if it be possible) becharme] their resolutions, and blot out their [names] from the LINE OF LIFE, by which they should bee led to the endlesse immortalitie of an immortalitie, in an ever-flourishing commendation. *The first* are poysoners of vertue, the betrayers of goodnesse, the bloud-suckers of innocencie: *The latter*, the close deaths-men of merit, the plotters against honestie, and the executioners of honors; They | are in two words discovered, *Blandientes et Sævientes*, Flatterers, and privie Murtherers. It is a disputable question, and well worthie a canvase and discussion in the schools, to decide which of the two doe the greatest injurie to noble personages. How be it most apparent it is, that envie, the inseparable companion that accompanies the vertuous, doeth not worke more mischiefe for the finall overthrow of a noble and deserving man, then Flattery doth, | for driving that noble and deserving man into the snares of envie. No man can be, or should be reputed a God; and then how easie it is for any man of the choycest temper, of the soundest apprehension, of the gracefullest education, | of the sincerest austeritie of life; how easie it is for him to fall into many errours, into many unbecomming follies, into many passions, and affections: his onely being *a man* is both sufficient proofe, and yet sufficient excuse. | The eloquentest and [gravest of all the ancient Divines], confest out of his owne experience,

Augustine.

Non est mihi vicinior hostis memet ipso: that he had not a more neere enemie to him then himselfe. For he that hath about him his frailtie to corrupt him, a World to besot him, an adversarie to terrifie him;

440 and lastly, a death to devoure him: how should hee but bee inveigled with the inticements of the *two first*, and so consequently consent to the unsteadinesse | of his temptation before he be drawne to a serious | consideration of the danger of the *two [latter]*? Especially as wee are men, being not onely subject to the lapses and vanities of
445 men, but as we are eminent men, in grace, [in] favour, in prioritie of titles, of place, and of command; having men to sooth us up in the maintenance and countenancing of those evils, which else doubtlesse, could not at one time or other, but appeare before us in their own uglinesse and deformitie.

450   [Certeine it is (and lamentable it is that it should bee so certeine) that the favourites of a prince, doe not by many degrees so much labour and indevour for upholding their owne estymation, to pallyate and sodder any unseemely defecte in their prince himselfe, as those grosse and subordinate tyme pleasers | of a lower rancke, stryve and
455 endevour to glorifie that favorite in all his courses, whether they tende to virtue or dishonour.]

   A Flatterer is the onely pestilent bawd to great mens shames; the nurse to their wantonnesse; the fuell to their lusts; and with his poyson of artificiall villanie, most times doth set an edge unto their ryot,
460 which otherwise would be blunted and rebated in the detestation of their owne violent posting to a violent confusion. Not unwisely did a wise man compare a *flattering Language to a silken halter*, which is *soft* because *silken*, but *strangling* | because a *halter*. The words wherewith those   *Diog. Laert.* / *in vita* / *Diog.*
465 *Panders of Vice* doe perswade, | are not so lovely, as the [matter] they dawbe over with their adulations, [is] abhominable. That is a bitter sweetnesse which is onely delicious to the pallate,   *Plin. hist.* and to the stomacke deadly. It is reported, that all   *[nat.] lib.* [sortes of] beasts are wonderfully delighted with   *8. cap. 17.*
470 the sent of the breath of the Panther, a beast fierce and cruell by nature; but that they are else afrighted with the sternenesse of | his lookes: For which cause, the Panther when he hunts his prey, hiding his grimme visage, with the sweetnesse of his breath, allures the other beastes unto him, who being come within his reach, hee rends and
475 cruelly doth dilaniate them. Even so, those Patrons and *minions of false pleasures, the* | *Flatterers*, that they may prey upon the credulitie

of the abused GREAT ONES, imitate the Panthers, extenuating, and as much as in them lyes, | hiding the grossenesse, the uglinesse, the deformitie of those follyes they perswade unto; and with a false glosse, varnishing and setting out the Paradise of uncontrolled pleasures, to the ruine oft times of the informed, and glorie of their owne impietie.

Is such a MIGHTIE MAN inticed to overrule his Reason, nay overbeare it, by giving scope to his licentious eye, first to see, then to delight in, lastly, to covet a chaste beauty? Alasse, | how many swarms of dependants, being | creatures to his greatnesse, will not onely tell him, mocke him, and harden him in a readie and pregnant deceipt, that love is courtly, and women were in their creation ordained to be wooed, and to be won; but also what numbers of them, will thrust themselves into imploiment and servile action, to effect the lewdnesse of desire, to corrupt with promises, with guifts, with perswasions, with threatnings, | with intreaties, to force a Rape on Vertue, [to] adulterate the chaste bosome of spotlesse simplicitie? A folly is commited, how sleight are they ready to prove it, how sedulous to sleighten, [and] how damnably disposed to make it | nothing? Insomuch as those vipers of humanitie, are fitly to be termed, the *mans whore*, and the *womans knave*. Is such a mightie one affected to such a suite, as the graunt and possession of it will draw a curse upon his head by | a generall voyce, of a generall smart and detriment to the Commonwealth? How suddenly will those wilde beasts, labour to assure him, that the multitudes love is wonne by keeping them in awe; not by giving way to their giddinesse by any affabilitie? Will another [gracious favorite] advaunce an unworthy *Court-Ape*, and oppresse a desertfull hope? It were too tedious to recite, what incessant approbations will bee repeated by these *Anthropophagi*, Those | meneaters, to make a *golden calfe* an Idoll, and a *neglected merite* a laughter. That such a | kinde of monsters, may appeare in their likenesse, as monstrous as in effect they are; It is worthie observation, to see how when any man, who whiles hee stood chiefe in the Princes favour, they honoured as an earthly God, yet being [by calumnye, through defect of judgment, errour of youthe, or very casuallye as a man,] declyned from his Princes estimation, [and any other rising in his seate,] it is worthie to be noted, how speedily, how swiftly, how maliciously those cankers | of a State will not onely fall off, will not onely dispise, will not onely deride, but also oppose themselves against the partie distasted, [incense the new master of the tymes, against the olde subject of their insinuation.]

As many subtill practizers | of infamie, have other subordinate ministers of publique office and imployment in a Common-wealth, to betray them to their ruine; yet ever and anon, they like inchanted glasses, set them on fire with the false light of concealement and extenuation. Let it be | spoken with some authority, borrowed from experience [of elder] times, that men in high places, are like some hopelesse marriners, set to sea in a leaking vessel: there is no safetie, no securitie, no comfort, no content in greatnesse, unlesse it be most constantly armed in the defensive armor of a selfe-worthie resolution; especially when their places they hold, are hourely subject to innovation, as their names (if they prevent not their dangers by | leaving them, and their lives at once) | are to reproach, and the libertie of malice.

Flatterie to either publique persons, is not more inductious on the one side, then envie on the other is vigilant. Great men are by great men (not good men by good men) narrowly sifted; their lives, their actions, their demeanors examined; for that their places and honours are hunted after, as the *Beazar* for his preservatives; And then the least blemish, | the least slide, the least error, the least offence, is exasperated, made capitall; the dangers ensuing ever proove (like the wound of an enemies sword) mortall, and many times deadly. Now in this case, when the eye of judgement is awakened, *Flatterie* is discovered to be but an Inmate to *Envie*; an Inmate, at least, consulting together though not dwelling together, the one, being Caterer to the others bloudie banquet; And some wise | men | have been perswaded, that the pestilence, the rigour of Law, Famine, Sicknes, or War, have not devour'd more great ones then *Flattery and Envie*.

Much amisse, and from the purpose it cannot bee, to give instance in [the] publike Presidents of three famous Nations; all chancing within the compasse of twentie yeares. In *England* not long agoe, a man supereminent in Honours, desertfull in many Services, indeared to a vertuous and | a wise Queene, ELIZABETH *of glorious memorie, and eternall happinesse*: A man too publikely beloved, and too confident of the love he held, ROBERT EARLE OF ESSEX, and Earle Marshall

of the Kingdome; He, even he that was thought too high to fall, and
too fixed to bee removed; in a verie handfull of time, felt the misery
| of Greatnesse, by relying on such as flattered and envyed his Great-
nesse. His end was their end, and the execution of Law, is a witnesse
| in him to Posteritie, how a publike person is not at any time longer
happie, then hee preserves his happinesse with a Resolution that de-
pends upon the guard of innocencie and goodnes.

    CHARLES DUKE OF BYRON in *France*, not long after him, ranne
the same Fate; A Prince that was reputed the invicible Fortresse to
his King and Countrey: great in desert, and too great in his Great-
nesse; not managing the fiery chariot of his guiding the Sunne of
that Climate | with moderation; gave testimonie by an imposed and
inexpected end, how a publike man in Authoritie, sits but in Com-
mission on his own Delinquencie, | longer then *Resolution* in noble
actions levels at the immortalitie of *A Line of life*.

    Lastly, SIR JOHN VANOLDEN BARNEVELT in the *Netherlands*, (whose
ashes are [yet scarce] colde) is and will bee a lively president of the
mutabilitie of Greatnesse. Hee was the only one that traffiqued | in
the Counsels of forreine Princes, had factors in all Courts, Intelligencers
amongst all Christian nations; stood as the ORACLE of the Provinces,
and was even the Moderator of Policies of all sorts: was reputed to
bee second to none on Earth for soundnesse of Designes; was indeed
his Countreyes both Mynion, Mirror, and Wonder; yet enforcing his
publike Authoritie, too much to bee servant to his private Ambi-
tion; hee left the Tongue of | *Justice* to proclayme that *long life*,
and a | *peacefull death* are not granted or held by the Charter of
Honours, except vertuous RESOLUTION renew the Patent, at a daily
expence of proficiencie in goodnesse.

    Others [yet] fresh in memorie might bee inserted, but these are
yet bleeding in the wounds which they have given themselves, and
some now living to this day; who both have had, and doe enjoy as
great Honours, and are therefore | as incident to as many wofull
changes, but that they wisely provide to proppe their greatnesse with
many greater deserts.

    Here is in Text Letters layd before us, the hazard, perill and casualty
of A PUBLIKE [GREAT] MAN: the possibilitie what Miserie, Calamity,
Ruine, Greatnesse and Popularitie may winde him into. Heere is

decyphered the unavoydable and incessant Persecutors of their | Honors and [Lives]: *Flatterie and Envie two ancient | Courtiers*. It comes now to conclusion, that it cannot be denied, but those *publike men* have (notwithstanding these) chiefe and immediate meanes in their owne powers, if they well and nobly order their courses to make their Countrey their Debtors, and to enroll their names in the glorious Register of an ever-memorable Glorie: especially if they be not too partially doting on every commendable Vertue, which in private men is reputed as it is, a Vertue; but in | them a Miracle. Certainly (without disparagement to desert in great men) there are many particular persons, fit for publike imployments, whose ablenesse and sufficiencie, is no way inferiour to the prayses of the mightiest, but that they are clouded in their lownesse, and obscured in their privatnesse, but else would and could | give testimony to the World, that all fulnesse and perfection is not confined to Eminence and Authoritie.

A PUBLIKE MAN, | therefore, shunning the Adulation of a Parasite (which hee may easily discover, if hee wisely examine his merit with their Hyperbolical insinuations,) [and] then keeping an even course in the processe of lawfull and just actions, avoyding the toyles, snares and trappes of the envious, cannot chuse in his own lifetime, but build a monument, [where] the Triumph and Trophies of his memorie, shall [gayne] a longer life then the perpetuitie of stone, Marble or Brasse can | preserve. Otherwise if they stand not on the guard of their owne Pietie and Wisedome, they will upon trifles sometime or other bee quarrelled against and evicted. Neyther may they imagine that any one taint (howsoever they would bee | contented to winke at it in themselves, supposing it to be (as perhaps it is) little, and not worthy reprehension) can escape unespyed. For the Morall of the Poets Fiction is a goodly Lesson for their instruction. It | is said that *Thetis* the Mother of *Achilles,* drencht him being an Infant in the *Stygian* Waters, that thereby, his whole bodie might bee made invulnerable: but see the severitie of Fate, for even in that part of the heele that his Mother held him by, was hee shot by the Arrow of *Paris,* of which wound he dyed. In like case, may every Statesman bee like *Achilles* in the generall body of his Actions, impassible and secure from any assault of wilfull and grosse ennormitie: | yet if he give way to *but one* handfull (as it may be termed) of Folly, not

becomming the gravity and greatnes of his Calling; hee shall | soone 29ʳ
meete with some watchfull *Paris,* some industrious Flatterer, or over-
busie envious Competitour, that will take advantage of his weaknesse,
and wound his infirmitie to the ruine of his Honours, if [not the]
jeopardy of his life.

The period of all shal be knit up, with the advise of a famous
[and learned] Philosopher: and as he | wrote to his   E9ʳ
familiar friend, let us transcribe to men in   *Sen. Epi.* 23
Authoritie; *Let a publike man rejoyce in the true pleas-*
ures of a constant Resolution, [*not the*] *deceivable pleasures of vanitie and*
fondnesse. By a good conscience, honest counsells, and just actions, the true
good is acquired. Other momentany delights only supple the forehead, not
unburthen and solace the heart. They are nothing, alasse they are nothing,
it is the minde must be well disposed, it is the | minde must bee confident: 29ᵛ
it is the mind above all things | must be rectified; and the true comfort is E9ᵛ
not easily attayned, and yet with more difficulty retayned. But [hee who
directs his] whole private life in honourable projections, cannot any
way misse our LINE OF LIFE, which points at the immortalitie of
a vertuous name by profitably discharging the burthen of such im-
ployments as are usually imposed upon those, whom their callings
have entitled *Publike men.*

A GOOD MAN is the last branch of *Resolution,*   Of the 3
| and by him is meant (as is said before) such a man,   branch, A   E10ʳ
as doth (beside the care he hath of himselfe in par-   good Man.
ticular) attend all his drifts and actions, to bee a servant for others,
for the good of others, as if it were his owne. School-boyes newly
trayned up in the Principles of | Grammer can resolve what a good 30ʳ
man is, [and] who: Who? *Qui consulta patrum, qui leges iuraque servat.*
Such an one, as not indeed singly observes what he should doe, but
doth even that which | hee observes hee should doe. This man not E10ᵛ
only lives, but lives well, remembring alwayes the old adage; that
God is the rewarder of Adverbes not of Nownes. His intents are
without the hypocrisie of applause, his deedes without the merce-
nary expectation of reward, the issue of both is, all his workes are
crown'd in themselves, and yet crowne not him, for that hee loves
Vertue for it selfe. *This man* never flatters Folly in greatnesse, but rather
pitties, | and in pittie strives to redresse the greatnesse of Folly. *This* E11ʳ

man never envies the eminence of Authoritie, nor feares the Envious: His reprehensions are balms, his Prayses | Glories, and he is as thankfull to bee rebuked, as to bee cherished. From such *a Man* all things are to be gratfully accepted: His desire to doe good to all, hath not a like successe to all (notwithstanding in *him to will* is commendable, and not to be able *to doe,* pardonable.) For it is not only the | propertie of true Vertue, but also of true Friendship, as well to admonish, as to bee admonished: For amongst *good men* those things are ever well taken that are well meant; yet even *this man* (that un-compeld, un-required, not exacted, interposes himselfe to set at unitie the disorders of others not so inclinable to goodnesse, is not free from enmity, with those whom in a general care, he labours to deserve as friends. The Reason, *Flattery procures friends,* | *Truth hatred.* | How? Truth Hatred? Yes, for from Truth is Hatred borne, which is the poyson of Friendship, as *Lælius* wel observed: But what ensues? Hee whose eares are so fortified, and barrocaded against the admitment of Truth, that from his Friend he wil not heare the Truth, this mans safetie is desperat: wherfore if any one will only relish *words of Downe and Honey,* as if wee loved to speake nothing but *pure Roses* (as the Proverbe is:) let such a | one learn from the skilfull Artists of Nature, [that Bees] doe anoint their Hives with the juyce of the bitterest Weeds, against the greedinesse of other Beasts. Let him learne from the skilfullest Phisicians, that the healthfullest Medicines smart most in the Wound. Let him learne from the Prince of Philosophie, that Anger | was given to men by Nature, (as hee writes) as a Whetstone of Valour; and then he cannot but consider, that any paines which a *good* | *Man* undergoes for reconciliation, be they either by way of admonition or reprehension, tend both to one end, that hee may make all like unto himselfe, that is, *Good Men.*

This very word (GOOD) implyes a description in it selfe, more pithy, more patheticall, then by any familiar exemplification can bee made manifest: Such a man, as makes the generall commoditie, his particular benefit, may not unfitly bee stiled a PRIVATE STATES-MAN: | His endevours are publike, the use publike, the profit publike, the commendation publike: But the person private; the Resolution private, the end private, and the reward [particular].

It is impossible, | that the wretched and avaricious banking up of wealth, can draw him into a conceipt, that hee can ever make friends of mony, after his death; considering that the World was created for the use of men, and men created into the World | *to use it, not to enjoy it*. This mans bounty is giving, not lending; and his giving, is free, not reserved: He cherisheth Learning in the Learned, and incourageth the Learned to the love of Learning by cherishing them; He heartneth the upright in Justice, and ratifies Justice in the upright; He helps the distressed with counsell, and approoves the proceedings of wise Counsellors. He is a patterne to all what they should bee, as to himselfe what he is. |

Finally, [in] all his desires, his actions are the | seasoners of his speeches, as his profession is of his actions. Hee is a Physitian to other mens affections as to his own, by comprimitting such passions as runne into an insurrection, by strengthening such as decline, by suppling such as are inflamed, by restrayning such as would runne out, by purging such as over-abound. His Ambition climbes to none other cure then to heale the wounded, not to wound | the whole; beeing neither so unwise to doe any thing that he ought not to doe, nor so unhappy to doe any thing [which] hee does not.

His singular misfortune is, that (with *Drusus* an excellent man) he attempts many times with a more honest and good mind, then good fortune and successe; insomuch, as it often comes to passe, that other | mens mischiefes are preferred before his Vertues: yet still as he is *a good Man*, injuries can no more discourage him, then applause | can over-weene him.

Velleius hist. Rom. lib. 2.

Even this man hath his particular adversaries to threaten him, and (if it could be possible) to [terrifie and] deter him from the soliditie of his temper: *Scandal* to defame him, and *imposture* to traduce him: *Flatterie and envie* are not a more pestilent [broode against] a *publique man*, then those two miscreant monsters are against a *good man*. But is his resolution any way infracted, for that | some refractaries are (like Knights of the post) hired to witnesse against him? Doubtlesse no, but much the rather confirmed to run by a LINE OF LIFE, to the *Goale of Life*. His owne solace is to him, as | an inexpugnable castle of strength, against all the forcible assaults of divellish com-

plots, built onely upon this foundation, that he is conscious to him-
selfe of an unforced sinceritie: With the Poet he
can resolve: *Hic murus aheneus esto, nil conscire | sibi,*   *Horat. lib.* F4ᵛ
740   his integritie to him is a Brazen wall; And with   *1. Epist. 1.*
the Orator, he assures himselfe, that *nullum theatrum virtuti maius con-
scientiâ,* Vertue hath [no] more illustrious and emi-
nent Theatre to act on, then her owne conscience.   *Cicer.*
Socrates (a good man, if a meere morrall man may   *quæst. Tusc.*
745   be termed so) beeing scurrilously by *Aristophanes* the Poet, derided   *lib. 2.*
before the people; and by *Anytus* and *Melytus* un-
justly accused before the Judges, as a trifler, | a   *In Comœd.*
master of follies, a corrupter of youth, a sower of   Νεφέλαις F5ʳ
impieties, answered; *If their alledged imputations be*   *Plat. apol.*
750   *true, | we will amend them; if false, they pertaine not to us.* It was a noble   *Socrat.* 34ʳ
constancie and resolution of a wise man, [And if]
he (inlightned with the only beames of nature) was   *Diog. Laert.*
so moderate and discreet, the good man here per-   *in vita*
sonated (inspired with a farre richer and diviner knowledge then   *Socrat.*
755   humanitie) cannot but asmuch exceede *Socrates* in those | vertues of   F5ᵛ
resolution, as *Socrates* did his adversaries in modestie and moderation.

    Kings and mightie Monarches, as they are first movers to all subor-
dinate ministers, of what ranke or [imploiment] soever, within their
proper dominions, are indeed *publike persons*; But as one king traffiques
760   with another, another, and another, either for repressing of hostilitie,
[inleaging] a confederacie, confirming an Amitie, setling a peace, sup-
planting | an heresie, and such like, | not immediately concerning   F6ʳ; 34ᵛ
his owne particular, or his peoples; but for moderating the differ-
ences betweene other Princes: In this respect even *Kings* [are] *private*
765   *men,* and so their actions belong wholly and onely to themselves;
printing the royalty of their goodnes, in an immortalitie of a vertu-
ous and everlasting name, by which they justly lay a claime to the
Style *of good men*: which attribute doth more glorifie | their desert,   F6ᵛ
then the mightinesse of their thrones can their glories.

770   In which respect, our SOVERAIGNE LORD AND
KING that now is, hath worthily chronicled his   Βασιλ.
Grand-fathers remembrance, which was (as hee best   Δῶρον *lib 2.*
witnesseth) called *The poore mans King.* A title of so inestimable a
wealth, that the riches of many Kingdomes are of too low and | meane   35ʳ

a value, to purchase the dignitie and honour of this onely Style, *The | poore mans King.*

  The famous and most excellent commendation of A GOOD MAN, cannot be more expressly exemplified in any president or myrrour, by all the instances of former times, nor shall be ever (farre, farre bee servilitie or insinuation) over-paralleled by any age succeeding, then in the person of JAMES the King of great *Britaine* presently here reigning over us. *A good man,* so well deserving (from all gratefull memorie) service | and honour, that not to doe him service is an ingratitude to the *greatnesse of his goodnesse*; and not to doe him all honour, an ingratitude to the *goodnesse of his greatnesse. A good man,* that even with his entrance to the Crowne, did | not more bring *peace* to all Christian nations, yea almost to all Nations of the Westerne World, then since the whole course of his glorious reigne, hath preserved [that] *peace* amongst them. *A Good man,* who hath | thus long sought as an equall and upright moderatour to decide, discusse, conclude, and determine all differences between his neighbouring Princes and fellowes in Empire. *A good man,* of whom it may be verified, that he is BONORUM MAXIMUS, and MAGNORUM OPTIMUS. *A good man,* that loves not *vertue* for the name of vertue onely, but for the substance and realitie. *A good man,* whom neither scandal can any way impeach of Injustice, | tyrannie, ignorance; nor imposture traduce, [to neglect] of merite in the desertfull, to levitie in affections, to | surquedrie in passions, to intention of inclyning to folly, or declyning from reall worth; which as an hereditarie inheritance, and a fee simple by nature and education, hee retaynes in himselfe, to the wonder and admiration of all, that may emulously imitate him, never perfectly equall him. Questionlesse, the Chronicles, that | shall hereafter report the Annalls of his life and Actions, shall doe infinite injurie to the incomparable monuments of his name, if they Style him, as some would wish, JAMES THE GREAT, or as others indevour, JAMES THE PEACEABLE, or as not a few hope, JAMES THE LEARNED. For to those titles have the Greekes in *Alexander,* the Romans in *Augustus,* the Germans in *Charles the Fift,* the French men in *Charlemaine,* and | *Henrie the Fourth,* Father to their present King, attayned: | But if he shall be reported in his Style to be, as in his owne worthinesse hee may justly challenge; he must then be styled, as by the approbation of all that truely know him, he is knowne to be, JAMES THE

GOOD. Let the summe of this branch of *Resolution*, which is indeed *Corona operis*, the summe of the whole sum, bee concluded: That *this onely patterne*, as he is onely inferior on earth | to God, who is BONUM SUMMUM, the chiefe and soveraigne good; so the distinction betweene his great Master and him (whose Vicegerent he is) consists in this (with reverence to the divine Majestie be it spoken) That as God (whom to call *good* is but an improprietie of description) is not singly *bonus* good, but *Bonitas* goodnesse, *in abstracto*, (as the Schoole-men speake:) So under the great KING OF KINGS, this King of | men is substitute to his King, with this | up-shut; The one is forever the *King of goodnesse*; and our King on earth, not onely a *good King*, but a *good man*; Such a *good man* as doth himselfe run, and teacheth by his example, others securely and readily to runne, by his *Line of Life*, to the immortalitie of a vertuous name.

A private man, A publique man, A good man, have beene here particularly deciphered and discoursed. It comes to conclusion, that hee, | who desires either in his owne person to be renowned; [or] for the generall prosperitie of the Common-wealth, to be eternized; or for the communitie of his friends, or any whom hee will make his friends, remembred in the Diaries of posteritie, must first lay the foundation of a willingnesse, from thence proceed to a desire, from thence to a delight, from a delight to practise, from practise to a constant perseverance in noble actions. And then such a man, howsoever | he live, | [sequestred from commerce by the injustice of a prevayling enimye, or shutt upp in prison by the suggestion of nimble information, or disgraced by the credulous confidence of misinformed majestie, or dispised by the many tongu'd malice of the abused multitude, or impoverished by the oppression of an ever-begging, but a never satisfied flatterie, or defamed by the gracelesse rumour of scandale, or traduced by the Juggling deceipte and snare of smoothe imposture, or (which is the finishing of mischeifes and miseryes) putt to death by the importunitie of the faultie; Yett such a man] shall never misse to end his dayes, before his honors and the honours of his name can end, for they shal know no end; and yet even in death, and after death, over-live all his | enemies, in the immortall spring of a most glorious memorie; which is the most precious Crowne and reward of *A* most precious *Line of Life*.

The Corollarie.

In the view of the precedent Argument, somewhat (perhaps) too lamely hath the Progresse of a Mans Life (in any Fate) been traced; wherein still the course, like a Pilot sayling for his safetie and welfare, hath alwayes had an eie, to the North-Starre of Vertue: without which, men cannot but suffer shipwrack on the Land, aswell as Mariners on the Sea. Such as have proofes in their owne persons and experiences of both fortunes, have past through their dangers of their beeing MEN, as they were first privat; before they entred: and from their entrance waded, into the Labyrinth of Greatnesse and Imployment, from whence they becam *Publike men.* Now then somwhat boldly (yet the boldnes is a presumption of love, not love of presumption) may bee intimated; that howsoever, any great or popular person, (for to such doth this application properly appertaine, howbeit free from any particularity except particularly challenged) in a peculiar examination of himselfe cannot chuse, but find, that he hath encountred many Oppositions of Youth, (even in grave yeares) and frailtie (in grave actions:) yet having at any time, by any casualtie, a happinesse (danger it selfe is a happinesse if rightly made use of, otherwise a miserie) to account with his expence of time: hee cannot upon indifferent and even reckoning, in stead of impayring his Honours but advance them: he cannot, if hee account faithfully, instead of making the World his Confessour, but confesse his owne Noblenesse; and thereupon He will find, that the toyle in common affaires, is but trash and bondage, compared to the sweete repose of the minde, and the goodly Contemplation of a mans peace with Himselfe. All glory whether it consist of profits or preferments, is WITHOUT, and therefore makes nothing to the essence of true happinesse: But the feeling of a resolved constancie is WITHIN, and ever keepes a Feast in a mans soundest content. One pregnant and notable Samplar deserves an eye of Judgement to be fixed on it. *Demosthenes* after a long government at his pleasure in the Common-wealth (upon what consideration, He Himselfe knew best, and States-men may easily guesse at,) is reported to confesse to his friends, who came to visit him: That if at the Beginning, *Two Waies* had bin proposed before him; *the one* leading to the Tribunall

Plutarch. in vit. Demost.

of Authoritie, *the other* to his Grave; If Hee could by inspiration, have fore-knowne the Evils, the Terrors, the Calumnies, the Envies, the Contentions, the Dangers, that men in such places, must customarily meet with; that Hee would much rather with alacritie, have posted on to his Sepulcher then to his Greatnesse. | *Brutus* when Hee determined his owne end, cried out with Hercules: *O wretched and miserable power of man, thou wert nothing but a name, yet I imbraced thee as a glorious worke, but thou wert a Bond-slave to Fortune.*

   Dion. hist.
   Rom. lib. 47.

 It is superfluous to inlarge (or comment upon) the Sufferings of those famous Men: Every mans owne talent of Wisdome, and share of tryall, may with not much difficultie, conster the sence of their meanings. *A good Man* is | the man, that even the greatest or lowest should both *bee,* and resolve *to be*. And this much may be confidently averred; That men of eminent commands, are not in generall more feared in the tyde of their greatnesse, then beloved, in the ebbe of that greatnesse, if they beare it with moderation. Statists honoured or favoured, (for favour and honour are for the most part inseparable) have the eyes of the World upon their carriage, in the carriage eyther of | their glories or dejections: It is not to bee doubted (which is a singular comfort) but any sequestration from a woonted height, is only but a tryall; for beeing managed with humblenesse and gratitude, it may ennoble the Patients (for their owne particulars) to demeane themselves excellently, in the places they had before (may bee) somewhat too neglectfully discharged. Always there is a Rule in observation, positive and memorable; that an interposition | or eclipse of eminence, must not so make a man undervalue his owne Desert, but that a *Noble Resolution,* should still uphold its owne worth, in deserving well; if wee ayme and intend to repute and use Honours, but as instrumentall causes of vertuous effects in Actions. To all such as so doe, (and all should so doe that are worthy to bee such,) a service not to be neglected is a proper debt: especially from inferiour Ministers to those, whose Creation, | hath not more given them the prerogatives of *being men,* then the vertuous *Resolution,* leading them by A LINE OF LIFE, hath adorned them, with the just, knowne and glorious Titles of beeing *Good Men.*

    VADUM *non transeat excors.*
     F I N I S.

Shorter Pieces

Shorter Pieces

There are a number of problems involved in attempting to identify Ford's shorter works. Most are complimentary verses too short to suggest a distinctive Fordian quality in the lines themselves. Nor does the name "John Ford" give us much certainty; the name was, and is, a very common one. We know, for example, that the dramatist's cousin and friend was also a John Ford, and that there are also variant spellings, including the abbreviated "Jo: Fo:." When we consider initials only, the field of possible authorship widens to include other writers who share them, to whom works now regarded as Ford's were long attributed.

Given these uncertainties, it has been decided to err on the side of inclusiveness and, at the end of an already large volume, to include some works of uncertain authenticity that have been suggested by Ford scholars as possibly being his. For example, two short prose "characters" have been included with the Overbury poems which Davril argued have significant parallels to *The Golden Meane* and *A Line of Life*. And the recent studies of P. J. Finkelpearl and Martin Butler have strengthened the case for the dramatist's authorship of the verses commending the plays of others.[1] Butler concludes that Ford was one of "a large yet intimate circle of friends, lawyers, playwrights, gentlemen and wits focused principally on the Inns of Court but also on the indoor 'private' playhouses."[2] Certainly, given his friendship with Massinger, Shirley, and Webster, the burden of proof would seem to lie with those who would deny Ford's authorship.

Each of the following pieces is preceded by a brief introduction discussing the occasion of its composition, date, text, and the strength of the available evidence attributing it to Ford.

---

[1] P. J. Finkelpearl, *John Marston of the Middle Temple* (Cambridge, Mass., 1969), esp. chaps. 1–6. Martin Butler, "Love's Sacrifice," in *Ford Re-Visited*, ed. Michael Neill (Cambridge, 1988), 201–5, and "The Connection between Donne, Clarendon, and Ford" in *N & Q* 34 (1987): 309–10.

[2] Martin Butler, "Love's Sacrifice," 204.

SHORTER PIECES

   I. *Foure Bookes of Offices* (1606)

  II. *Funeral Teares* (1606)

 III. *The Wife*

   (a) "Encomium" (1614)
   (b) Two Characters (1614)
   (c) "Memoriall" (1616)

  IV. *The Dutchesse of Malfy* (1623)

   V. *The English Dictionarie* (1623)

  VI. *The Wedding* (1629)

 VII. *The Roman Actor* (1629)

VIII. *The Northern Lasse* (1632)

  IX. *Philocothonista* (1635)

   X. *The Great Duke of Florence* (1636)

  XI. *The Navigator* (1636)

 XII. *Ionsonus Virbius* (1638)

XIII. *A Contract of Love and Trueth* (before 1645)

 XIV. *Dia Poemata* (1655)

I

The *Foure Bookes of Offices* (1606; STC 1468) by Barnabe Barnes was published the same year as *Fames Memoriall*, and the two authors exchanged complimentary verses. Sixteen years older than Ford, Barnes had considerable influence on the younger poet's style. Still, his being set up in the poem as a "president for youth" is hard to understand, considering Barnes's criminal record.[3]

There is no reason to attribute Ford's poem to his cousin of Gray's Inn, as Dyce did after having printed it: the friendly relationship of Barnes and the future dramatist is clear from the exchange. Other supposed influences, such as Ford's taking the name of Parthenophil in *The Lover's Melancholy* from Barnes's sonnet cycle or the mechanical chair in *The Broken Heart* from his *Divils Charter*,[4] could equally well suggest simply Ford's acquaintance with current literature on the classics (G-D, 1:ix). Except for Dyce's repudiated acceptance, Ford's verses appear in none of the collected editions.

Copy text: Bodleian
Copies collated: Cambridge; Folger.

---

[3] See Mark Eccles, "Barnabe Barnes," in *Thomas Lodge and Other Elizabethans*, ed. Charles J. Sisson (Cambridge, Mass., 1933), 167-241, esp. 175-91.

[4] For examples of the trick-chair, see Spencer, Append. B, 224-28.

John Forde in commendation of his very good friend the Author.

Not to adorne, but to commend this Frame,
Drawne by the curious hand of judgements art;
Nor to commend, for this commends the same;
But solace to thy labours to impart:
    A worke of thankes, out living terme of fate,
    In briefe prescriptions of a formall State.

Great were thy paines, but greater is thy fame,
Lock't in the Jewel-house of precious treasure;
Which doth by Counsailes wisedome reare thy name,
In equall Justice of well-ballac'd measure;
    Thou teachest souldiers discipline of fight,
    And they againe defend thy merits right.

Write on rare Myrrour of these abject dayes;
Thy good example others will advise:
Thy subject values love, thy Studies praise,
A president to youth, life to the wise:
    So ever shall (while times and Empires last)
    Thy workes by thee, thou by thy works be grac't.

    Verba, decor, methodus, confirmant, denotat, ornat,
    Authorem lepidum, re, gravitate, manu.

                      Iohannes Forda Encomiastes.

II

Like *Fames Memoriall, Funeral Teares* was published in 1606 as a tribute to the recently deceased Earl of Devonshire with music by the English composer John Cooper (or Cowper), who, after a stay in Italy, was generally known as Coprario (as here on the title page) or Coperario. No author is named for the texts set to music (six solo songs and a duet) nor for the long poem of eighty lines in praise of the dead nobleman. No one associated Ford with the work except the antiquarian Joseph Hunter, who ascribed the poem to him.[5] The first Ford scholar to accept (or perhaps to be aware) of this attribution was Davril, who comments "Le style artificiel rappelle celui de *Fame's Memorial*" (68). The poem is accepted as being Ford's by Leech and, more recently, by Colin Gibson.[6]

In an article concerned chiefly with the music of *Funeral Teares*, Richard McGrady says it seems possible that the work was "the result of collaboration with a single poet," but adds that it is also possible the composer himself wrote the words.[7] Richard Charteris in his work on the composer feels the poem is "probably the work of Coprario" but gives no reason for his statement.[8] Coprario collaborated on several occasions with Thomas Campion, most notably in the set of songs lamenting the death of Prince Henry (*Songs of Mourning*, 1613), but there is no reason to believe that Campion was involved in *Funeral Teares*.

The case for Ford, however, is a strong one. Not only the style but also the content is clearly reminiscent of *Fames Memoriall*. Both works vigorously defend Devonshire's relationship with Penelope, Lady Rich, whose divorce and subsequent marriage to the Earl was the source of much criticism (see above, 69-70, 79-80).

Copy text: British Library
Copy collated: Folger

---

[5] Joseph Hunter, *Chorus Vatum* 3:195; renumbered in pencil 112 in British Library (Add. MS. 24489). The STC lists the work under John Cooper, composer; 5679.

[6] Leech, 124; Colin Gibson, "The Stage of My Mortality," in *John Ford: Critical Re-Visions*, ed. Michael Neill (Cambridge, 1988), 55.

[7] Richard McGrady, "Coperario's *Funeral Teares*" in *The Music Review* 38.3 (1977): 167n.

[8] Richard Charteris, *John Coprario* (New York, 1977), 10.

In honorable memory of the Right noble the Earle of Devonshire *late deceased.*

NOE sooner had the Fates pale Minister
    At th'high commaund of sterne Necessitie
Seazd the terrestriall part of Devonshire,
    And rendred his free Soule t'Eternitie:
But loe th'imperfect broode of fruitfull Fame
    (That swarming thicke as atomes buze in th' ayre)
Light winged Rumours in right of their Dame
    Claimed great Mountjoyes name, with swift repaire
Heaving it up to Fames high Consistorie,
    Where she with doome impartiall register
All names t'Eternall fame, or infamie,
    And in her finall judgement never errs.
You sacred seede of Mnemosine pardon me
    If in this suddaine rapture I reveale
Mist'ries which only ravisht sprights can see,
    And envious time did till this houre conceale.
In Christal chaire when starre-like shining Fame
    Her state had plac't, strait with confused noyse
The thronging miscreates brought in Dev'nshires name,
    Some figuring lamentations, others joyes:
Some wept, some sobd, some howld, some laught, some smild,
    And as their passions strange, and different were,
So were their shapes, such heapes were never pil'd
    Of Monstrous heades as now consorted here.
For some like Apes peere out, like foxes some,
    Many like Asses, Wolfes, and Oxen seem'd,
Like hissing Serpents, and fell Hydras some,
    Rhinoceroes some by their arm'd snowtes I deem'd,
Others like Crocodiles hang their slie heads downe:
    But infinite of humane forme appeare
Whose simple lookes were voide of smile or frowne,
    Yet somewhat sad they shewd like skies uncleare:

	In this confusion the great Registresse
	Commaunding silence sev'rallie gave leave
35	To all reportes, and with milde sobernesse
	Both partiall, and impartiall did receive.
	First as accusers spake the busie Ape,
	The envious bould Wolfe, and the spitefull snake,
	And divers in the braying Asses shape,
40	But all their malice did one period make.
	Dev'nshire did love, love was his errour made,
	That only gainst his vertues was oppos'd,
	As if for that his honoured name should fade,
	Whose brest both vertue, and true love enclos'd.
45	But now rise high my spright, while I unfould
	What th'humane speakers in defence replyed:
	To latter ages let this tale be told
	Which is by fame for ever verified.
	Did Mountjoy love? and did not Hercules
50	Feele beauties flame, and couch him underneath
	The winges of Cupid? or did ere the lesse
	His sacred browes deserve a victours wreath?
	Did not he free the trembling world from feare,
	And dire confusion? who else could subdue
55	Monsters that innocents did spoyle, and teare,
	Or Saturnes auncient goulden peace renue?
	Did Mountjoy love? and did not Mountjoyes sword
	When he marcht arm'd with Pallace dreadfull helme
	The rough unquiet Irish rebels curbe?
60	And the invading Spaniard overwhelme?
	Lov'd he? and did not he nathlesse assist
	Great Brittaines counsils, and in secret cells
	The Muses visite? and alone untwist
	The riddles of deepe Philosophick spels?
65	Did Dev'nshire love? and lov'd not Dev'nshire so
	As if all beautie had for him beene fram'd?
	For beautie more adorn'd no age shall know
	Then hers whom he his owne for ever nam'd.
	Let then base envie breake, fond rumour sleepe,

    Blacke malice turne to dove-white charitie,
Let Dev'nshire triumph, and his honor keepe
    Immune, and cleare from darke mortalitie.
This spoken, Fame charg'd Zepherus to sound
    His goulden trumpet, after whose smooth blast
These words she made from earth to heav'n rebound,
    Brave Mountjoyes glory shall for ever last.
Then forth was brought a boss't booke destined
    For Kings, and Heroes, where with liquid gould
Deceased Dev'nshires name she registred
    In charmed letters that can nere grow old.

Omnia vincit Amor, et nos cedamus Amori,
    Scripsit; cuius erant nescia scripta mori.
Annuit huic fortis Mountioius, victus Amori
    Ceßit; cuius erunt nescia facta mori.

III

The ill-fated Sir Thomas Overbury (1581–1613) was five years older than Ford and appeared at the Inns of Court somewhat earlier. His name appears on the register of the Middle Temple in 1597, where Ford's admission is recorded for November 1602. The two men knew each other and moved in the same social and literary circles.

Four works may be taken to show, with varying degrees of certainty, Ford's relationship with Overbury. When the first edition of Overbury's *A Wife* appeared early in 1614, its author was already dead, having been slowly poisoned in the Tower and expiring on 14 September 1613. The work had been entered on 13 December 1613, and although the title page (*A Wife, now a Widowe*) and headings take note of Overbury's death, the first of the commendatory poems, signed "I. F.", does not. It is a lighthearted piece on the usefulness of Overbury's poem on the choice of a wife, clearly written before the author's death. It may or may not be by Ford, and its attribution has been neither attacked nor defended by the leading Ford scholars.

A Wife became very popular and went through nine editions by late 1616 and ten more by 1664. The scandal and trial for murder following Overbury's death undoubtedly contributed much to the success of the rather modest poem, as did the inclusion of Theophrastan characters in the second and subsequent editions. Only the earliest of these could have been by Overbury, but, as edition followed edition, the number of characters continually expanded and were clearly the work of many hands.[9]

The possibility of Ford's being among the contributors was first advanced by Davril, who pointed out similarities between two of the characters in this work, "A Wise-man" and "A noble Spirit," and those in works definitely ascribed to Ford, buttressing the textual evidence with the relationship between Overbury and Ford, and Ford's other tribute to a man "qu'il estimait et qui fut peut-être son ami."[10]

---

[9] On the possible authors, see *The Overburian Characters*, ed. W. J. Paylor (Oxford, 1936), which stresses the influence of Joseph Hall's *Characters of Virtue and Vices* (1608) in introducing virtuous characters as well as satiric ones, especially in the two pieces thought to be by Ford (viii–ix, 114–15).

[10] See Davril, 90–97, and his "John Ford et les *Caractères Overburiens*" in *Études*

Ford's last tributes are not in dispute. On 25 November 1615 the Stationers' Register lists "Sir Thomas Overburyes Ghost, contayneinge the history of his life and untimely death by John Ford, gent." The work is lost, and although its nature has been questioned, its authorship has not.[11]

Ford's final tribute to Overbury is in the eighth edition of *A Wife* (1616), which, the title page announces, contains "NEW ELEGIES upon his (now knowne) *untimely death*." Ford's "Memoriall" alludes to the well-known facts of the case: how Overbury tried to dissuade his friend Carr (made earl of Somerset) from marrying Frances Howard, how friendship turned to hatred, and how Overbury was imprisoned in the Tower and killed by poison. This poem was reprinted by Dyce and has been accepted by Ford scholars (Sargeaunt, 12; Leech, 125).

Each work is taken from the first edition of *A Wife* in which it appeared.

(a) "Encomium"
   Copy text: First edition (1614), Bodleian
   Copy collated: Trinity College, Cambridge
(b) Two Characters
   Copy text: Second edition (1614), British Library
   Copies collated: Bodleian; Folger.
(c) "Memoriall"
   Copy text: Eighth edition (1616), Folger
   Copy collated: Bodleian

Anglaises 6 (1953): 122–26. Leech considers the attribution "very possibly correct, but the evidence does not compel belief" (125). Paylor notes a change of character and style: "It is possible that these two sketches may have come from the same hand, and a different one from the contributor or contributors of the former Characters" (114).

[11] Sargeaunt speculates that it may have been an elegy like FM (12); Davril thinks it a prose piece (90), as does Oliver, who suggests it may have been a pamphlet (8).

Enco: of the wife a widow.

I AM glad yet ere I die, I have found occasion
Honest and just; without the worlds perswasion
Or flattery or bribery to commend
A woman for her goodnesse: and God send
I may find many more: I wish them well,
They are pretty things to play with: when *Eve* fell
She tooke a care that all the wo-menkind
That were to follow her, should be as blind
As she was wilfull; and till this good wife
This peece of vertue that nere tooke her life
From a frayle mothers labor: Those stand still
As marginalls to poynt us to our ill
Came to the world, as other creatures doe
That know no God but will; we learnt to woe,
And if she were but faire and could but kisse,
Twenty to one we could not chuse amisse.
And as we Judge of trees if straight and tall
That may be sound, yet never till the fall
Find how the raine hath drilld them; So till now
We only knew we must love; but not how.
But heere we have example, and so rare,
That if we hold but common sense and care,
And steere by this card; he that goes awry
Ile boldly say at his nativity,
That man was sealde a foole: yet all this good
Given as it is, not cloathd in flesh and blood
Some may aver and strongly twas meere ment
In way of practise, but not president;
Either will make us happy men; for he
That marrieth any way this misterie,
Or any parcell of that benefit,
Though he take hold of nothing but the wit,
Hath got himselfe a partner for his life,
More then a woman, better then a wife.

Eiusdem in Eadem.

As from a man the first fraile woman came,
The first that ever made us know our shame,
And find the curse of labor; so againe
Goodnes and understanding found a man
To take this shame away; and from him sprung
A peece of excellence without a Tongue
Because it should not wrong us; yet the life
Makes it appeare a woman and a wife.
And this is she, if ever woman shall
Doe good hereafter; borne to blesse our fall.

J. F.

A *Wise-man*

Is the truth of the true definition of man, that is, a reasonable creature. His disposition alters, alters not. He hides himselfe with the attire of the vulgar; and in indifferent things is content to be governed by them. He lookes according to nature, so goes his behaviour. His mind enjoyes a continuall smoothnesse, so cometh it, that his consideration is alwaies at home. Hee endures the faults of all men silently, except his friends, and to them hee is the mirrour of their actions; by this meanes his peace commeth not from fortune, but himselfe. He is cunning in men, not to surprise but keepe his owne, and beats off their ill affected humours, no otherwise then if they were flies. Hee chooseth not friends by the subsidie booke, and is not luxurious after acquaintance. Hee maintaines the strength of his body, not by delicacies, but temperance; and his minde by giving it preheminence over his body. Hee understands things not by their forme, but qualities; and his comparisons intend not to excuse, but to provoke him higher. | Hee is not subject to casualties, for fortune hath nothing to doe with the minde, except those drowned in the body: but he hath divided his soule, from the case of his soule, whose weaknesse he assists no otherwise than commiseratively, not that it is his, but that it is. Hee is thus, and will be thus: and lives subject neither to time nor his frailties; the servant of vertue, and by vertue the friend of the highest.

A noble Spirit

HATH surveyed and fortified his disposition, and converts all occurrents into experience, between which experience and his reason, there is a mariage; the issue are his actions. He circuits his intents, and seeth the end before he shoot. Men are the instruments of his Art, and there is no man without his use: occasion encites him, none enticeth him; and hee mooves by affection, not for affection; hee loves glory, skornes shame, and governeth and obeyeth with one countenance; for it comes from one consideration. He calls not the varietie of the world chances, for his meditation hath travailed over them; and his eye mounted upon his understanding seeth them as things underneath. Hee covers not his bodie with delicacies, nor excuseth these delicacies by his bodie, but teacheth it, since it is not able to defend it's owne imbecilitie to shew or suffer. He licenseth not his weaknes, to weare fate, but knowing reason to be no idle gift of nature, he is the Steeres-man | of his owne destinie. Truth is his Goddesse, and hee takes pains to get her, not to looke like hir. He knowes the condition of the world, that he must act one thing by another, and then another. To these he carries his desires, not his desires him; and stickes not fast by the way (for that contentment is repentance) but knowing the circle of all courses, of all intents, of all things, to have but one center or period, without all distraction he hasteth thither and ends there, as his true and naturall element. Hee doth not contemne fortune, but not confesse her. He is no Gamster of the world (which onely complaine and praise her) but being only sensible of the honestie of actions, contemnes a particular profit as the excrement or skum. Unto the societie of men hee is a *Sunne*, whose clearenesse directs their steps in a regular motion: when he is more particular, hee is the wise-mans freind, the example of the indifferent, the medicine of the vicious. Thus time goeth not from him, but with him: and he feeles age more by the strength of his soule, than the weaknesse of his body: thus feeles he not paine, but

55 esteemes all such things as frends that desire to file off his fetters,
and helpe him out of prison.

A Memoriall,
Offered to that man of virtue,
Sir *Thomas Overburie*.

Once dead and twice alive; Death could not frame
A death, whose sting could kil him in his fame.
He might have liv'd, had not the life, which gave
Life to his life, betraid him to his grave.
5 If greatnes could consist in being Good,
His Goodnes did adde titles to his blood.
Only unhappy in his lives last fate,
In that he liv'd so soone, to die so late.
Alas whereto shall men oppressed trust,
10 When Innocence cannot protect the just?
His error was his fault, his truth his end,
No enemie his ruine, but his friend.
Cold friendship, where hot vowes are but a breath,
To guerdon poore simplicitie with Death:
15 Was never man that felt the sense of griefe
So Over-bury'de in a safe beliefe:
Beliefe? ô cruell slaughter? times unbred,
Will say, who dies that is untimely dead,
By treacherie, of lust, or by disgrace.
20 In friendship, 'twas but *Overburies* case;
Which shal not more commend his truth, then prove
Their guilt, who were his opposites in love.
Rest happy Man; and in thy spheare of Awe
Behold how Justice swaies the sword of Law,
25 To weed out those, whose hands imbrew'd in blood,
Cropt of thy youth, and flower in the bud.
    Sleep in thy Peace: thus happie hast thou prov'd,
    Thou mighst have dy'de more knowne, not more belov'd.

Jo: *Fo*:

IV

Ford's verses were prefixed, together with other commendatory verses by Middleton and Rowley, to *The Dutchesse of Malfy*'s first edition in 1623 (STC 25176). They were dropped from the subsequent 1640 edition.

The relationship between Ford and Webster seems to have been one of friendship and collaboration. If they did not meet earlier (perhaps at the Middle Temple), they certainly worked together in the theater. In 1624 they collaborated with Rowley and Dekker in the lost *A Late Murther of the Sonn upon the Mother*.

The verses appear in none of the collected editions of Ford. Although Dyce had included them in his edition of Webster's works in 1830, he overlooked them when he edited Ford almost forty years later. All modern authors have accepted them as the work of the dramatist: Sargeaunt (32-34), Oliver (41-42), and Leech (125).

Copy text: Bodleian

Copies collated: British Library; Dyce Collection, Victoria and Albert Museum.

To the Reader of the Authour, and his Dutchesse of *Malfy*.

CROWNE *Him a Poet, whom nor* Rome, *nor* Greece,
Transcend in all their's, for a Master-peece:
In which, whiles words and matter change, and Men,
Act one another; Hee, from whose cleare Pen
   They All tooke life, To Memory hath lent
A lasting Fame, to raise his Monument.

JOHN FORD.

V

When Henry Cockeram's *The English Dictionarie: or, An Interpreter of hard English Words* was published in 1623 (STC 5461), seven of his friends praised its appearance with verses. Ford is the only one of these to use the spelling "Cockram." Subsequent editions drop the commendatory verses. They are not included in any of the collections of Ford's work.

The reference to Cockeram's birth and residence in the West Country and to his being a *"Countryman"* (lines 1, 16) recalls Ford's own roots in Devon.

Copy text: Bodleian
Copy collated: Folger

To my industrious friend, the Author of this English Dictionarie, Mr. Henry Cockram of Exeter.

BORNE *in the West? live there? so far from Court?*
From Oxford, Cambridge, London? yet report
(Now in these daies of Eloquence) such change
Of words? unknown? untaught? tis new and strange.
5 *Let Gallants therefore skip no more from hence*
To Italie, France, Spaine, *and with expence*
Waste time and faire estates, to learne new fashions
Of complementall phrases, smooth temptations
To glorious beggary: Here let them hand
10 *This Booke; here studie, reade, and understand:*
Then shall they finde varietie at Home,
As curious as at Paris, *or at* Rome.
For my part I confesse, hadst not thou writ,
I had not beene acquainted with more wit
15 *Than our old English taught; but now I can*
Be proud to know I have a Countryman
Hath strugled for a fame, and what is more,
Gain'd it by paths of Art, untrod before.
The benefit is generall; the crowne
20 *Of praise particular, and thats* thine owne.
What should I say? Thine owne deserts inspire thee,
Twere base to envie, I must then admire thee.

A friend and lover of thy paines,

JOHN FORD.

VI

The *Wedding*, by James Shirley, was published in 1629 with five complimentary poems in English and one in Latin (STC 22460). Among the former was the poem here printed. These verses were dropped from subsequent editions in 1633 and 1660.

Shirley reciprocated by writing verses for Ford's *Love's Sacrifice* (1633). Both wrote for the Phoenix playhouse. The only editor of a Ford collected edition to include the poem was Dyce.

Copy text: Bodleian

Copies collated: British Library; Dyce Collection, Victoria and Albert Museum; Folger.

Of this Ingenious Comedy the *Wedding*. To Mr. James Shirley *the Author*.

THE Bonds are equall, and the Marriage fit,
Where judgement is the *Bride*, the *Husband* wit;
Wit hath begot, and judgement hath brought forth
A noble issue, of delight, and worth,
5   Growne in this Comedy to such a strength
Of sweete perfection, as that not the length
Of dayes, nor rage of mallice, can have force
To sue a nullity, or worke divorce
Betweene this well trim'd *Wedding*, and loud Fame,
10   Which shall in every age, renew thy Name.

John Ford.

VII

Among the six commendatory poems prefixed to Massinger's *The Roman Actor* in 1629 (STC 17642) was one signed "John Foorde." Although it has been reprinted in several editions of Massinger's works, and the Hartley Coleridge volume of Massinger and Ford plays, it has not been reprinted in Ford collections. The most recent edition of Massinger (1976) by Philip Edwards and Colin Gibson accepts the poem as "probably" by the dramatist.[12]

The Harbord copy in The Folger Shakespeare Library has a number of manuscript corrections believed to be Massinger's. One of them is in Ford's poem.[13]

Copy text: Bodleian
Copies collated: British Library; Folger.

---

[12] *The Plays and Poems of Philip Massinger* (Oxford, 1976), 3:7, 5:181.

[13] Ford may have collaborated with Massinger and perhaps Fletcher and Webster in *The Faire Maide of the Inne* (1625), although the play was licensed as by Fletcher and only published in the Beaumont and Fletcher Folio of 1647. Critical opinion is divided both on the authorship and the attribution of individual scenes; see Sargeaunt (63–66) and Oliver (43–46). F. L. Lucas discusses the shares of the probable co-authors in some detail and increases Ford's probable share; see *The Complete Works of John Webster* (London, 1927), 4:148–52.

Upon Mr. MASSINGER His Roman Actor.

    To write, is growne so common in our Time
        That every one, who can but frame a Rime
    However monstrous, gives Himselfe that praise
        Which onely Hee should claime, that may weare Bayes
5   By their Applause whose judgements apprehend
        The weight, and truth, of what they dare commend.
    In this besotted Age (friend) 'tis thy glory
        That Heere thou hast out-done the Roman story.
    Domitians pride; his wive's lust unabated
10   In death; with *Paris*, meerly were related
    Without a Soule, Untill thy abler Pen
        Spoke them, and made them speake, nay Act agen
    In such a height, that Heere to know their Deeds
        Hee may become an Actor that but Reades.

                        John Foorde.

VIII

The John Ford who wrote verses for Richard Brome's *The Northern Lasse* (1632; STC 3819) identifies himself as "The Authors very Friend." That this friend was the dramatist was accepted by Dyce, who belatedly included the poem in his revision of Gifford, and by Sargeaunt (25). The doubts expressed by Arthur M. Clark regarding the verses to Thomas Heywood extend to those to Brome as well, although no proof is given for attributing them to the John Ford of Gray's Inn (see *SP*, IX). Both Davril (54n) and Leech (126) list the dramatist as author while taking note of Clark's doubts.

The verses were reprinted in the edition of 1663 and then dropped from subsequent individual editions. They were reprinted in Pearson's edition of Brome's plays (London, 1873; 3:xi).

Copy text: Dyce Collection, Victoria and Albert Museum
Copies collated: Bodleian; British Library; Folger.

Of Mr. RICHARD BROME his ingenious Comedy, the *Northern Lasse*, To the Reader.

A3ᵛ

POETS *and* PAYNTERS *curiously compar'd*
Give life to Fancie; and atchieve Reward
By Immortality of Name: So thrives
Art's Glory, *that* All, *what it breathes on, lives.*
5 *Witnesse this* Northern Piece. *The Court affords*
No newer fashion, or for Wit, or Words.
The Body of the Plot is drawne so faire,
That the Soules language quickens, with fresh ayre,
  This well-limb'd Poëm, *by no Rate, or Thought*
10 *Too dearely priz'd, being or sold, or bought.*

JOHN FORD
The *Authors* very Friend.

IX

Philocothonista, or, the Drunkard, Opened, Dissected, and Anatomized by Thomas Heywood was printed in 1635 (STC 13356). Arthur M. Clark suggested in 1931 that this tract, which he calls a pot-boiling mixture of puritanism, pedantry, and ribaldry, "had commendatory verses by two of Heywood's friends, George Donne, the second son of the Dean,... and John Ford, the dramatist's cousin." In the same place, however, he admits "Heywood appears to have known the dramatist as well."[14]

The reference to support the latter is a line on another of Heywood's works, *The Hierarchie of the blessed Angels* (1635; STC 13327) in which a catalogue of dramatists is given whose Christian names have been "curtal'd," going back to Greene and Marlowe. The line on Ford reads "And hee's now but Jacke Foord, that once were John" (206). As Clark suggests no reason for his attribution, and it is hard to see why Heywood could not have been a friend of both cousins, it seems impossible to attribute this work with certainty to either.[15] It is reprinted here for the first time.

The title comes from the Greek φιλοκωθωνιστής (fond of tippling) which is translated in Heywood's title. Ford picks up the Greek by calling Heywood "*the Author*, NEPHALIOPHILUS," or lover of sobriety (from νηφάλοις, sober). It is perhaps worth noting that both the verses to Heywood and Heywood's line in *The Hierarchie* use the spelling "Foord."

Copy-text: British Library

Copies collated: Bodleian; Dyce Collection, Victoria and Albert Museum.

---

[14] *Thomas Heywood* (Oxford, 1931), 150n. He also suggests Ford's cousin as possibly the author of the verses to Barnes and certainly of those to Brome (128, 150n).

[15] Martin Butler, more recently, accepts the poem as Ford's; see "The Connection between Donne, Clarendon, and Ford," *Notes and Queries* 34 (1987): 310.

OF
Philocothonista,
The Reader:
To the Author, Nephaliophilus.

Thou *hast (my learned friend) with happy fate,*
Shew'n to the world A Monster, *(at cheape rate:)*
Much more A Prodegy, *then all the Toyes*
Set out to cozen Women, Fooles, and Boyes
5   *At Fayres and Markets. In the* Gulph *of drinke,*
Where giddy vessells reele, and lastly sinke;
The Quick-sands, Whirle-pooles, the Rockes, the Shelves,
Are so describ'd; that they must read Themselves
Guilty of wilfull Shipwracke, who ore-looke
10 *Thy paines, yet then be saved by* thy Booke.
Hang Bookes! Let it goe round! Follow your Leader!
Pardon; I'm but Interpreter to th' Reader.

John Foord.

X

Massinger's *The Great Duke of Florence* was published in 1636 (STC 17637) with verses by George Donne and Ford. Despite the date of publication, it may well have been composed as early as 1627,[16] thus placing it shortly after *The Roman Actor*, for which Ford also wrote verses, and the possible collaboration of the two men in *The Faire Maide of the Inne*, already discussed in SP, VII.

Although Ford's verses for *The Great Duke* have occasionally been reprinted in editions of the play, they appear in no collected Ford edition. There has been no suggestion that they are not by the dramatist.

Copy text: Bodleian

Copies collated: British Library; Dyce Collection, Victoria and Albert Museum.

To the deserving memory, of this worthy Worke, and the Author, M.ʳ PHILIP MASSINGER.

A

ACTION *gives many Poems right to live,*
This Piece *gave life to* Action; *and will give*
For state, and language, in each change of Age,
To Time, delight; and honour to the stage.
5 *Should late prescription faile which fames that Seat,*
This Pen, might style The Duke of Florence Great.
Let many Write; Let much be Printed; read,
And censur'd; Toyes; no sooner-hatch't, then dead.
Here, without blush to Truth of commendation,
10 *Is prov'd, how Art hath out-gone Imitation.*

JOHN FORD.

---

[16] *The Plays and Poems of Philip Massinger*, ed. Philip Edwards and Colin Gibson (Oxford, 1976), 3:95.

XI

Captain Charles Saltonstall's *The Navigator* was published in 1636 (STC 21640) as a work explaining both the theoretical and practical aspects of "the famous Art of Navigation," with verses by Ford and five others. A second edition in 1642 omits four of these verses, including Ford's, and the third (1658) contains none at all. It is not listed among Ford's works by either Sargeaunt or Leech but is accepted by Colin Gibson.[17]

Little is known of Charles Saltonstall, despite the importance of his book. It is generally accepted that he was the son of Sir Samuel Saltonstall and thus grandson of Sir Richard Saltonstall, Lord Mayor of London. If this is true, then he was the brother of the poet and translator, Wye Saltonstall. There may be another Inns of Court connection here, as Wye is believed to have studied law at Gray's Inn in the early 1620s.[18] The verses of Wye and Ford are the only ones to appear in both Latin and English.

Copy text: British Library

---

[17] *The Selected Plays of John Ford* (Cambridge, 1986), xi.
[18] DNB 17:711–14; Anthony Wood, *Athenæ Oxoniensis* (London, 1815), 2:676–80.

In laudem CAROLI SALTONSTALL, *et Navigatoris sui,* Ογδοάστιχον.

DIFFICILE *est aliquem subitò prodire Poetam,*
 Me vestram in laudem scribere jussit Amor.
Obsequium indignos laudet cùm divite vena,
 At laudem ex scriptis te meruisse liquet.
5 *Omnia sal sapit, et super omnia spargitur hìc Sal,*
 Artem et Judicium pagina quaque sapit.
Hinc Saltonstalli *nomen tibi convenit, Artis*
 Spargitur, eccè tuo, sal super omne, libro.

I. F.

In Praise of Captaine Charles Saltonstall, *and his* Navigator, an *Ogdoastick*.

'Tis hard for any straight way to come forth
A Poet, yet Love bids me praise your worth;
Flattery may praise those that unworthy are
Of praise, but your Worke doth your praise declare.
5 Salt savours all, heere Salt on all is cast,
Each leafe of Art and Judgement too doth tast,
For you have sprinkled Arts *Salt-on-all*,
And so deserv'd the Name of *Saltonstall*.

J. F.

XII

Bishop Brian Duppa's collection of tributes to Ben Jonson was published under the title *Ionsonus Virbius* in 1638. Among the forty-six contributions in English, Latin, and Greek was one signed John Ford, which has always been accepted as being by the dramatist. It was included in Gifford's edition and Dyce's revision. Gifford surmises that Ford was not a friend of Jonson, "though he might perhaps have known and been known to him; since Ben had, as he says, from his first entrance into life, cultivated an acquaintance with the most celebrated professors of the law." He doubts a dramatic connection, as Jonson "had, in some measure withdrawn from the stage many years before Ford's first published piece appeared on it" (Gifford, 2:611; G-D, 3:330). However, in the light of modern studies of Stuart theater, these arguments are not compelling.

Copy text: British Library
Copies collated: Bodleian; King's College, Cambridge; Folger.

On the best of English *Poets*, BEN: JONSON, *Deceased*.

So seemes a *Starre* to shoot; when from our sight
Falls the deceit, not from *its* losse of *light*;
We want use of a *Soule*, who meerely know
What to our *passion*, or our *sense* we owe:
5 By such a *hollow glasse*, our *cozen'd eye*
Concludes alike, *All dead*, whom it sees *die*.
Nature is *knowledge* here, but un-refin'd,
Both differing, as the *Body* from the *Mind*:
Lawrell and *Cypresse* else, had growne together,
10 And *withered* without *Memory* to either;
Thus undistinguish'd, might in every *part*
The *Sons* of *Earth* vie with the *Sons* of *Art*.
Forbid it, (holy Reverence) to *his* NAME,

Whose *Glory* hath fil'd up the *Booke* of *Fame*!
Where in faire *Capitals*, free, uncontrould,
JOHNSON, a worke of *Honour* lives inroul'd:
Creates that *Booke* a *Worke*; adds this farre more,
'Tis finish'd what unperfect was before.
The *Muses*, first in *Greece* begot, in *Rome*
Brought forth, our *best* of *Poets* hath cald home,
Nurst, taught, and planted here; that *Thames* now sings
The *Delphian Altars*, and the sacred *Springs*.
By Influence of this *Soveraigne*, like the *Spheres*,
Mov'd each by other, the most low (in *yeares*)
[Consented] in their *harmony*; though some
Malignantly aspected, overcome
With popular opinion, aym'd at *Name*
More then *desert*: yet in despight of shame
Ev'n they though foyl'd by *his* contempt of wrongs,
Made *musique* to the harshnes of their *songs*.
Drawne to the life of every *line* and *limbe*,
Hee (in *his* truth of *Art*, and that in *him*)
Lives yet, and will, whiles *letters* can be read.
The losse is ours; now hope of *life* is dead.
Great men, and worthy of *Report*, must fall
Into their earth, and sleeping there sleepe *all*:
Since *He*, whose *Pen* in every *straine* did use
To drop a *Verse*, and every *Verse* a *Muse*,
Is vow'd to *heaven*; as having with faire *glory*,
Sung thankes of *Honour*, or some nobler *Story*.
The *Court*, the *Universitie*, the heat
Of *Theaters*, with what can else beget
Beliefe, and admiration, cleerely prove
Our POET [first] in *merit*, as in *love*:
    Yet if *He* doe not at *his* full appeare,
    Survey *him* in *his* WORKES, and know *him* there.

JOHN FORD.

XIII

The first reference to "A Contract of Love and Trueth" dates from 1925 when Bertram Lloyd came across it in a manuscript of poetical miscellany dating from the second quarter of the seventeenth century.[19] He printed the poem with his reasons for attributing it to Ford in 1925, and the poem was accepted as being Ford's "with great probability" by Sargeaunt (29) and so listed by Leech (126).[20] It is printed here for the first time in an edition of Ford's works.

There is no clear connection between the dramatist and the couple whose marriage is being celebrated, either in London or Ford's native Devon. The bride was of the Noel family established in Rutlandshire and the groom a knight of Leicestershire. Lloyd's hypothesis that the verses "were probably written by the lawyer-dramatist for one of his clients" (219) rests in turn on the hypothesis that Ford actually worked as a lawyer, which is at least doubtful.

More convincing are internal arguments and the Fordian echoes in many of the verses. Lloyd picked out lines 3-6, 8-9, 16-17, and 24-28 as typical of the poet in sentiment and expression (218). That Ford was fond of anagrams and acrostics is shown by his own "Fide honor" anagram and his acrostic "Penelope, Countess of Devonshire" in *Fames Memoriall* (FM Reader, 89 above). Here he combines both forms.

The poem is in secretary on pages 19 cm by 15 cm. The original numbering places it on pages 283-284, but the British Library has renumbered the manuscript sheets in pencil, so that the pagination becomes 134^v-135^r.

---

[19] British Library Egerton MS. 2725. The catalogue indexes it as "circa 1650," but the large number of pieces written to celebrate events of the early seventeenth century suggests an earlier date.

[20] Bertram Lloyd, "An Unprinted Poem by John Ford?" *The Review of English Studies* 1 (1925): 217-19.

A Contract of Love and Trueth

MARYE NOELL.
Anagramme
Reall Monye.

ERASMUS de la Fountayne
Anagramme.
See al most fayre and new.

Contract.

See reall monye, al most fayre and new.

    Soe gold is priz'd; and being chastly *pure*
    Exceeds all grosser Mettalls that endure
    Experiments with losse: as constant *Trueth*
    Renown'd for perfect tryall, love, birth, youth.
5   **E**xcellent sweetnesse, or aught else transcends
    A common Prayse: whose onelye *Beauty* ends
    Lesser [then] when it first beganne: whiles Worth
    Lowder in sound, then *Fame* can set it forth.
    Makes Memory a Chronicle; whose story
10 **O**f Reall meritt amplifies the Glory.
    New ages shall admire; and for fashion
    Yeild their endeavours to an Imitation.
    Example leads to vertue in this *Payre*,
    As in a mirrour may bee seene how *Fayre*
15 **L**ove (without blemish) of Two equall Hearts
    Makes one: and like choyce Musicke set in parts
    Orders a perfect harmony. Here Measure
    Such Reall Constancy, a *Reall Treasure*.
    Trueth is not to be bought; 'tis to be Trew,
20 *Fayre*, and what makes all beauty fairer, *New*.
    A smooth tongue, soft behaviour, winning face
    Youth in the Spring, courtshippe, delight, wit, grace,
    Rich Plentye, are but meere Deceipts of Art;

A
Contract
of
Love & Trueth

MARYE NOELL. ERASMUS de la Fountayne
Anagramme   Anagramme
Reall Monye   See al most fayre and new

Contract
See reall monye at most fayre and new

S or gold it's wirth and being mostly pure
E xceeds all groser Mottalls that indure
E xperiments with Lesse at tempted Trueth
R enews for perfect tryall, Love born youth
E xcellent freedome is or ought the tradicion
A common Prayse who's onelye Bewty such
L oover when it first beganns, could Trust
M onyes on foundacion Fame can not it forth

M ake I know a Christian, who's story
R ead, it will amplifye the glory
Y ield, of, and some, onlye others
E xample, seavens us in that — Payre
A in a manner may be somewhere Fayre
...
N o witt than name is great and to be seen
D only excels their names among well...
N o by Death but though innocent
E x... in neat Example, defect itself
W as Love, whose Mediator, Trueth in...

Finis [Finis]

"A Contract of Love and Trueth," The British Library, Egerton MS. 2725, fols. 134v–135r. By permission.

Except supported by a Noble Heart.
25 Additions then make all estate and blood
Noble; when to be great is to be Good.
Death sweeps their names away, who onely strive
Not by Desert, but Glory, to survive.
End all in this Example, without strife,
30 Wise *Love* is here the Husband, *Trueth* the Wife.

Finis.

J. Foord.

XIV

Two factors speak against including the verses attached to the *Dia Poemata: Poetick Feet standing upon Holy Ground* (Wing E 667) of Edmund Elys among Ford's works. Its date of 1655 is very late, and the very poor quality of the poetry hardly suggests anything Ford could have written.

However, we know nothing of Ford's life after the late 1630s. Reports are uncertain and conflicting, and the place and date of his death are unknown. The case for inclusion is best put by Sargeaunt on the not unreasonable assumption that Ford retired to his native Devon and lived well into the 1650s. Edmund Elys was born in 1634, the son of the rector of East Allington, only seventeen miles from Ford's own birthplace of Islington. He entered Balliol College, Oxford, in 1651 and took his B. A. in 1655, the year *Dia Poemata* was published. Thus the aspiring student-poet might have come in contact with the elderly Ford while spending vacations with his family during his university years and received these verses for his fledgling effort, though it is hard to imagine Ford encouraging the wretched efforts of Elys. Sargeaunt admits *Dia Poemata* is "written in a highly artificial and often very offensive style" and that Ford "tried not unsuccessfully to imitate Elys's manner in them, so that the fact that they do not particularly resemble in style any known writing of the dramatist's need not weigh as evidence in considering their authorship" (30).

Davril doubts that Ford, even if he had known Elys in his retirement, could have approved of "les idées puritaines" which the work contains (62n). Leech also voices doubt as to Ford's authorship of such bad verse (126).

The poem has never been printed in a collection of Ford's works.
Copy-text: Thomason Collection, British Library
Copy collated: Folger

To the AUTHOR.

DEAR *Friend, I've view'd thy Book, wherein each Page*
  Shews me thy Fancy, antidates thy Age.
Thy Epigrams have such Poetick Heat,
As makes their Feet drop Wit instead of Sweat.
So that the Muses say they'l have no Son
But Thee, th'apparent Heire to Helicon:
And if they chance t'adopt a Ganimede,
Their Drink shall be thy Brains, their Cup thy Head.

Jo: Ford.

Textual Notes

Honor Triumphant

Siglum

06 First Edition ([G. Eld] for F. Burton, 1606), STC 11160.

HT:

65	the]	tbe 06
498	cooled.]	~∧ 06
505	Bewty)]	~∧ 06
527	so obstinate]	to ~ 06
582	Women!]	~. 06
589	Proofe.]	precedes mulieri (line above) in 06
707	conjunction]	conuinction 06 (see Commentary)
726	brier,]	~. 06

MM:

120	Danes)]	~∧ 06
181	lowd,]	~. 06

Fames Memoriall

Sigla

06	First Edition ([R. Bradock] for C. Purset, 1606), STC 11158.
MS	Bodleian MS. Malone 319.
Haslewood	Ed. Joseph Haslewood (Lee Priory, Kent, 1818).
Gifford	*The Dramatic Works*, ed. William Gifford, 2 vols. (London, 1827).
Dyce	*The Works*, ed. Gifford, rev. Alexander Dyce, 3 vols. (London, 1869; reprinted, 1895).

FM:

5	imbrac't,] MS, ~ˏ 06
8	recal'd,"] ~,ˏ Ep. Ded. MS
59	allegory,] MS, ~ˏ 06
72	fames] fame MS
79	Writer,] MS, ~ˏ 06
84	can perfect] MS, perfect can 06
99	produc't] MS, product 06
103	urne] MS, arme 06
107	Ballanc't] MS, Ballac't 06
109	gravd] MS, grave 06
114	*Elixar*] *Elizar* MS
115	discerning,] MS, ~ˏ 06
120	confuteˏ] MS, ~; 06
132	remain,] ~ˏ MS
133	MS *reads:* For nobles none but court should entertain.
148	shalbe] shall be MS
150	name,] MS, ~ˏ 06
159	can,] MS, ~ˏ 06
163	heart-easing] heartseasing MS
168	woo'd] MS, wood 06
169	peace] MS, ~; 06
171	amour's] MS, amours 06, amourous *Haslewood* (*the apostrophe floats above the word in the MS; perhaps the reading should be* am'rous)
177	Becomes] become MS
178	locks of amber] locke of Ambers MS
191	ease;] ~ˏ 06 MS
199	idle] idles MS
202	of] in MS
214	out] MS, but 06
219	horse,] *Haslewood*, ~ˏ 06 MS
223	man] MS, men 06
231	assigns] deseignes MS
242	implies,] *Haslewood*, ~ˏ 06 MS
243	two] to MS
245	earth,] MS, ~ˏ 06
246	heaven] haven *Haslewood, Gifford*
251	too] MS, to 06
268	worth and state,] MS, worth, and state, 06
271	gall:] *Haslewood*, ~ˏ 06 MS
280	ceremonious] Ceremoniall MS
296	hopes,] MS, ~ˏ 06; staffe,] MS, ~ˏ 06
297	and] the MS
298	guerdon'd] guerdons MS; pay] MS, pray 06
305	hath] MS, ~, 06
310	fame,] MS, ~ˏ 06; spirit,] *Haslewood*, ~ˏ 06 MS
312	merit,] *Haslewood*, ~ˏ 06 MS

320	fictions,] *Haslewood*, ~ ͚ 06 MS; sin:] *Haslewood*, ~ ͚ 06 MS
323	deep-moving] deep mourning MS
330	*Lycia*] *Lucia* MS
335	rivall] ryval'd MS
337	No,] *Haslewood*, ~ ͚ 06 MS; change,] *Gifford*, ~ ͚ 06 MS
356	either] MS, ether 06
362	monumented] monumental *Haslewood*
368	monster,] *Haslewood*, ~ ͚ 06 MS
369	witnesseth):] ~) ͚ 06, ~. MS
374	a] *om* MS
381	agayne] a game MS
401	the] theis MS
412	thunder] wonder MS
415	meeknes,] MS, ~ ͚ 06
416	rayne] rein *Haslewood*
424	glore was] glorious MS
434	United,] *Dyce*, ~ ͚ 06 MS
438	peace,] MS, ~ ͚ 06
447	frindship,] MS, ~ ͚ 06
448	striving,] MS, ~ ͚ 06
453	destructions,] MS, ~ ͚ 06
456	penury,] MS, ~ ͚ 06
457	store;] *Haselwood*, ~ ͚ 06 MS
459	endow'd] indu'de MS; lore,] MS, ~ ͚ 06
472	spight ͚] MS, ~: 06
476	dominions,] MS, ~ ͚ 06
480	England;] *Haslewood*, ~ ͚ 06 MS
481	bereaven.] MS, ~ ͚ 06
483	mirror.] MS; ~ ͚ 06
485	Which] that MS
487	season,] *Haslewood*, ~ ͚ 06 MS
489	relate,] *Haslewood*, ~ ͚ 06 MS
490	too] MS, to 06
491	Too] MS, to 06; too] MS, to 06; late,] *Haslewood*, ~ ͚ 06 MS
495	Proclamation] MS, praclamation 06
497	downe.] MS, ~ ͚ 06
499	triumph,] MS, ~ ͚ 06
505	peace,] MS, ~ ͚ 06
510	sate] sought MS
513	her Senator] Senator MS
514	good,] MS, ~ ͚ 06; moderate,] *Haslewood*, ~ ͚ 06 MS
518	himselfe he was] he was himself MS
530	it selfe] MS, itself 06
533	betraiers] bewrayers MS; madnesse!] ~? 06, ~ ͚ MS
535	nicenesse,] MS, ~ ͚ 06
539	blaze.] MS, ~ ͚ 06
540	blind] black *Haslewood*
541	Lett] MS, Lest 06, Least *Haslewood*

542	Scornes] skorne MS
558	waite:] *Haslewood*, ~∧ 06 MS
569	currs] curse MS
570	nobility,] MS, ~: 06
574	lights,] MS, ~∧ 06
586	enhaunce:] *Haslewood*, ~∧ 06 MS
590	resolution-armed] MS, resolution armed 06; Fortitude,] ~∧ 06 MS
592	subdu'de,] MS, ~∧ 06
593	review'd:] *Haslewood*, ~∧ 06 MS
599	pleasure,] *Haslewood*, ~∧ 06 MS
601	decerne] discerne MS
602	confirme.] MS, ~∧ 06
604	essenciall,] *Haslewood*, ~∧ 06, ~? MS
607	paiz'd] plac'd MS; all:] *Haslewood*, ~∧ 06 MS
619	can] to MS
621	blisse,] MS, ~∧ 06
622	Mæcenas] Mecænas MS
625	indeer'd] MS, in deer'd 06
627	backbiters, grudgers,] MS, ~∧ ~∧ 06; fear'd,] *Dyce*, ~∧ 06 MS
628	appeard;] *Dyce*, ~∧ 06 MS
630	breast.] MS, ~∧ 06
635	comforts] MS, comfort' 06; destroyd:] *Haslewood*, ~∧ 06 MS
642	scan'd,] MS, ~∧ 06
646	MS *reads*: in setting nought by vulgar rumors slaunder,
648	MS *reads*: by relishing the scorne of bootelesse anger,
649	MS *reads*: "Resistance in defyance breedeth daunger
650	then,] MS, then∧ to 06
651	meekenesse] patience MS; sorrows sad] spleenes unjust MS
652	A sad] unjust MS
653	nature] venome MS
654	envy,] *Haslewood*, ~∧ 06 MS
655	worldly cares] povertie MS
659–79	*om* 06
659	fame!] ~? MS
660	haplesse!] ~? MS
663	MS *deletes* poison *after* of
678	MS *deletes* to *before* thy
686	blush] blusht MS
689	Nor] not MS
695	posterity] posterities MS
718	this] thy MS
724	Fame,] MS, ~∧ 06
727	frinds,] MS, ~∧ 06
728	Who] that MS
729	thoughtes∧] MS, ~, 06; corruption,] MS, ~∧06
733	by] buy MS
738	resident∧] MS, ~; 06
746	With] and MS

748	th'ons] MS, thon's 06
768	Contempt] MS, conrempt 06
772	excellency] excellence MS
775	hart:] *Haslewood*, ~ˬ 06 MS
779	degree,] MS, ~ˬ 06
781	meanest,] MS, ~ˬ 06; decreeˬ] MS, ~, 06
789	ill:] *Haslewood*, ~ˬ 06 MS
791	hate.] MS, ~ˬ 06
803	force?] *Haslewood*, ~ˬ 06 MS
805	vary?] *Haslewood*, ~. 06 MS
810	revisor:] *Haslewood*, ~ˬ 06, revis MS (*end of line missing*)
820	word] MS, wore 06
824	light] sight MS
832	fortune] fortunes MS
836	wise,] MS, ~ˬ 06
839	memory, the merit] MS, memory the merit, 06
848	Life?] MS, ~ˬ 06; tapers,] MS, ~? 06
849	light,] MS, ~ˬ 06
850	exhalacions] MS, exhulations 06; vapors,] MS, ~ˬ 06
851	sight,] MS, ~? 06
852	night.] MS, ~? 06
853	Ah] MS, A 06; no night] MS, ~ might 06; elfe,] MS, ~? 06
854	Ah] A, MS
862	themˬ] them? MS; baiteˬ] MS, ~, 06
863	rapine!] ~? 06
864	it!] ~? 06
866	extreames!] ~? 06
871	best] left MS; divineˬ] MS, ~; 06
874	times] tyme MS
879	slaunder] MS, sclaunder 06
880	quaint] MS, quaintest 06
882	soule,] MS, ~ˬ 06
904	these,] MS, ~ˬ 06
921	contented] conteyned MS
928	consumeth] MS, consumes 06
938-951, 952-965, 966-978, 979-992] *lines spaced and centered as in MS; see Commentary.*
971	this earthly] the earthie MS
975	eache AGE] the Ages MS; the] om MS
989	was] MS, is 06
990	cropt] MS, crost 06
997	saint,] MS, ~ˬ 06
1025	one] MS, on 06
1026	they] MS, the 06
1029	contain'd.] *Haslewood*, ~ˬ 06 MS
1031	mirrourˬ] MS, ~. 06
1033	error,] *Haslewood*, ~ˬ 06, ~. MS
1037	mudd!] ~? 06

1038   muse!] ~? 06
1039   griefes!] ~? 06
1040   mirth!] ~? 06
1041   sadnesse] gladness Gifford, Dyce; newes!] ~? 06
1043   which] that MS
1045   *Lycia*] *Lucia* MS
1057   lamentation] lamentations *Haslewood*
1061   wisedome,] *Haslewood*, ~ˬ 06 MS; intelligenceˬ] MS, ~, 06
1076   mirth:] *Haslewood*, ~ˬ 06 MS
1081   death?] MS, ~ˬ 06
1083   part:] *Haslewood*, ~ˬ 06, ~, MS
1086   disgrace,] MS, ~ˬ 06
1088   majestie] MS, majestyes 06
1090   Empyre,] MS, ~ˬ 06
1092   fate] MS, fatte 06
1095   false] fatt MS
1096   giddie] idle MS
1097   treasure:] *Haslewood*, ~ˬ 06, ~, MS
1105   task] taxe MS
1109   joyes] toyes MS
1124   ceaseˬ] MS, ~: 06
1125   increase.] MS, ~ˬ 06
1126   pleasure] comfort MS
1132   'tis] it's MS; it,] MS, ~ˬ 06
1141   delights] MS, delight 06; agayne.] MS, ~, 06
1143   heavens] heaven MS
1147   in that spheare] MS, it in that speare 06
1148   this] his *Haslewood*
1153   delectation:] *Haslewood*, ~ˬ 06 MS
1158   counterfeytˬ] ~. 06 MS
1160   write:] *Haslewood*, ~ˬ 06 MS

Christes Bloodie Sweat

Sigla

13   First Edition (R. Blower, 1613), STC 11076.
Grosart *Poems of Joseph Fletcher*, ed. Alexander B. Grosart (1869).
Scott   "A Critical Edition of *Christes Bloodie Sweat*," ed. M.I. Scott, Diss. University of Birmingham, 1967.

CBS:

3   Fathers] Farhers 13
11   bloud,] ~ˬ 13

CHRISTES BLOODIE SWEAT

17	Ah] *Scott,* As *13*
32	thriftlesse] *Grosart,* thirstless *13 (see Commentary)*
34	delight,] *comma a mere speck 13*
61	every] *Grosart,* euer *13*
63	even] enen *13*
71	will] *om 13 (see Commentary)*
93	men˄ a man,] *Scott,* ~, ~~˄ *13*
117	marg 21.5.] *Scott,* 2.5. *13*
133	on] one *Grosart*
136	assail'd;] ~˄ *13*
141	Appeares,] ~˄ *13*
155	wombe˄] *Grosart,* ~. *13*
163	far] far off *Scott*
167	[they]] *Scott, om 13 (see Commentary)*
171	marg 22.40.] *Scott,* 22.4 *13*
179	marg 26.38.] *Scott,* 26.28 *13*
181	marg 53.4.7.] *Scott,* 52.4.7. *13*
189	judgment,] *comma a speck 13*
198	Which] which *13*
208	thy˄] *Grosart,* ~, *13*
209	it let] let it *Scott*
210	thy] thy, thy *13*
243	marg 9.2.3.] 8.2.3. *13*
254	us'd] vs d *13*
294	marg 10.22.] 19.22. *13,* 9.22. *Scott*
302	gods] God's *13,* Gods *Scott (see Commentary)*
335	so] *Grosart,* to *13*
340	hate,] ~˄ *13*
365	marg 7.25.] *Scott,* 4.25. *13*
366	marg 11.8.] *Scott,* 11.7. *13*
369	marg 5.26] 15.26 *13*
394	earth] earrh *13*
396	marg Job.] 1.Job. *13*
405	features.] ~. *13*
412	only] *Scott,* only; only *13*
414	most] *Grosart,* not *13 (see Commentary)*
415	ar] or *13,* are *Grosart,*
416	marg 7.28.] *Scott,* 5.7.28. *13 (see Commentary)*
418	[un-]even] *Scott,* euen *13*
425	That] Their *Grosart*
438	list;] ~. *13*
490	warming] *Scott,* warning *13*
491	rotten;] *Scott,* ~, *13*
495	leave] *Scott,* haue *13*
497	other] others *Grosart (see Commentary)*
505	mildly˄] ~, *13*
513	marg Kin.] kin. *13*
516	hath] *Grosart, om 13*

518	to]	*Grosart,* do 13
525	Wash,]	~ˍ 13
542	marg Kin.]	kin. 13
546	he]	we *Scott*
552	recover.ˍ]	~,. 13
592	th'unjust]	th'v niust 13
593	marg 4.7.]	*Scott,* 4.6. 13
595	men,]	*Scott,* ~. 13
597	thenˍ]	*Grosart,* ~: 13
600	Knight,]	*Scott,* ~. 13 (see Commentary)
602	fame:]	*Scott,* ~, 13 (see Commentary)
606	sinnes, denoting]	*Grosart,* sinnesˍ deuoting 13 (see Commentary)
610	sword;]	~ˍ 13
615	thoughts,]	~ˍ 13
623	brest,]	~. 13
629	retreat,]	~ˍ 13
640	Eating]	Eeating 13
648	marg Kin.]	kin. 13; 22.27.] *Scott,* 22.21. 13
654	marg 80.5]	*Scott,* 80.6 13
683	cald]	clad 13, call'd *Grosart*
694	mean]	man 13, means *Grosart* (see Commentary)
699	marg 8.21.]	*Scott,* 8.22. 13
706	savourˍ]	*Scott,* ~: 13
716	ease,]	~ˍ 13
717	selfe-neglect,]	~ˍ 13
718	despight;]	~, 13
724	sacietie]	societie *Scott*
736	A]	rom *Scott,* ital 13
744	marg 7.21.]	1.2. 13, 1.21 *Scott*
749	marg 25.41.]	*Scott,* 25.4.13
751	cryes]	eyes *Grosart*
764	stabbes]	*Grosart,* stables 13
771	brimstone]	brimstome 13
784	cease]	*Grosart,* ceast 13
787	Loe]	see *Scott*
822	fail]	*Grosart conj,* fall 13
828	marg 2.30.]	2.34. 13, 2.3.4. *Scott*
829	marg 16.23]	*Scott,* 13.23. 13
852	marg 1. Cor.]	*Scott,* 2.Cor. 13
878	the]	his *Grosart*
886	death,]	~ˍ 13; agonie?] *Grosart,* ~ˍ 13
888	soule,]	~ˍ 13 (see Commentary)
940	that]	their *Grosart*
950	hearte]	*Grosart,* hearts 13
956	mind,]	~. 13
961	receits,]	~. 13
967	gifts,]	~ˍ 13
979	womane,]	*Grosart,* womansˍ 13

CHRISTES BLOODIE SWEAT

991	marg 3.19.] 2.7. *Scott*
1006	more,] ~; *13*
1026	die;] ~. *13*
1041	marg 7.37.38] *Scott*, 7.31.38 *13*
1071	lust$_\wedge$] *Grosart*, ~, *13*; novelties,] ~; *13*
1085	blood,] *Scott*, ~$_\wedge$ *13*
1090	alike] a like *13*
1100	deede] *Scott*, deeds *13*
1103	commend] condemnd *13*, condemne *Grosart* (*see Commentary*)
1116	comes to woe him.] coms to wo him$_\wedge$ *13* (*see Commentary*)
1119	care] eare *Grosart*
1121	behave] betake *Grosart* (*see Commentary*)
1130	the] rhe *13*
1155	such] such such *13*
1157	grace] *Scott*, griefe *13* (*see Commentary*)
1158	marg 23.26.] *Scott*, 22.23.26. *13*
1164	mine.] ~. *13*
1188	to life intire] *Scott*, in life to tire *13* (*see Commentary*)
1196	marg 7.3.] *Scott*, 8.3.*13*
1204	who] which *Grosart*
1209	marg 9.13.14.] *Scott*, 9:13:18: *13*
1217	is] *Grosart*, *om 13*
1237	furrow-crowned] furrow-drowned *13*, sorrow-drownèd *Grosart* (*see Commentary*)
1246	sums] *Grosart*, sinnes *13* (*see Commentary*)
1256	dilliance] *13*, dalliance *Scott*
1259	implore$_\wedge$] *Scott*, ~, *13*
1312	alone] a lone *13*
1314	young,] ~$_\wedge$ *13*
1324	thy] *Grosart*, they *13*
1338	pride] prid *13*
1350	then] that *Grosart*
1373	conscience,] *Scott*, ~$_\wedge$ *13*
1374	hastes] hastes oh! hastes *Grosart*, hastens her *Scott*
1375	$_\wedge$O God (she cries)] *Scott*, (~ ~$_\wedge$ ~ ~) *13*
1392	angry$_\wedge$] *Scott*, anger, *13* angry, *Grosart* (*see Commentary*)
1396	marg 46.2.] 45.2. *13*
1408	forgiven] for given *13*
1429	soule] *Grosart*, oule *13*
1438	marg 20.11.] *Scott*, 20.2. *13*
1450	marg 1.4.] 2.1. *13*, *Scott*
1485	selfe-accusing$_\wedge$ conscience] *Grosart*, ~$_\wedge$ ~-~ *13*
1491	to] unto *Scott*
1494	Christs] Chists *13*
1508	marg 1.18.] *Scott*, 2.18. *13*
1565	Was ever man as] *ital Scott*, *rom 13*
1565	marg Lamen.] La nen. *13*
1571–72	dye, dye content, / I die content] *rom 13* (*see Commentary*)

374   TEXTUAL NOTES

1574   marg 16.4.] Scott, 6.4. 13
1625   disguise] diguise 13
1631   simple] simpe 13
1633   Spirit,] ~. 13
1657   For] Fos 13
1675   th'ntollerable] th'intollerable Scott
1689   marg 9.13.] Scott, 9.3. 13
1698   endlesse] enlesse 13
1723   light] ligh 13
1770   whats'ever] whats'uer 13, whatsoe'er Scott
1775   marg 12.23.] 8.23. 13, 8.2.3. Scott (see Commentary)
1780   the] tht 13
1805   wreath] Scott, wrath 13, (see Commentary)
1811   Water,] ~. 13
1819   marg 25.7] Scott, 55.7. 13
1824   mee from] from mee Scott (see Commentary)
1870   marg 12.43.] Scott, 22.43. 13
1893   marg 2.12.] Scott, 2. 13
1907   habit] babit 13

The Golden Meane

Sigla

13   First Edition ([H. Lownes] for J. Chorlton, 1613), STC 17757.
14   Second Edition (1614), STC 17758
38   Third Edition (J. H[aviland] for J. Benson, 1638), STC 17759.

These textual notes record: (1) all departures from copy text (14); (2) for 13, all substantive and punctuation variants; (3) 38 substantives when they differ from 14, and punctuation when it agrees with 13 against 14. 13+ indicates agreement of all three texts.

GM:

Ep. Ded. 2   onely best worthie] BEST WORthy Reader 13, RIGHT HONOURABLE
              the Earle of Northumberland 38
Ep. Ded. 6-7 one day] once 13
Ep. Ded. 7   selfe,] ~ˌ 13
Ep. Ded. 15-17   Benè ... publico.] om 13
11-12   that is,] om 13
13   themselves] om 13
15   Vertueˌ] ~, 13 38
50   and] or 13+ (see Commentary)
61   is as] 13, as 14, is 38

THE GOLDEN MEANE

64	Nobly-minded]	Noble minded 13
76	resolution,]	~∧ 13
77	come,]	~∧ 13
80	vertue,]	~∧ 13
84	may]	om 13
91	unimited]	unimitated 38 (see Commentary)
91	conformable,]	~∧ 13
129-54	Such ... of.]	om 13
135	him,]	38, ~; 14
142	doth,]	~) 38 (see Commentary)
167	Wisedome∧]	~, 13
176-200	Can ... wisedome.]	om 13
181	them?]	38, ~. 14
205	delight]	delights 13
212	into∧]	13, ~, 14
220	Empyrie]	Empyre 13 (see Commentary)
230	him,]	~∧ 13
231	²one∧]	~, 13
252	approved]	38, apporved 13 14
252	certainty;]	~, 13
256	ravine;]	~, 13
257	and,]	~∧ 13
257	adventures,]	~; 13
260	treacherous,]	~∧ 13
279	affections,]	~∧ 13
285	conscience,]	consciences∧ 13
297-314	For ... late.]	om 13
317	vertues∧]	~, 13 38
321	pittie]	13, pietie 14 (see Commentary)
327	paths]	parts 13+ (see Commentary)
328-47	If ... sake.]	om 13
354	living,]	~∧ 13
358	their]	13, the 14
365	grew]	grow 13
368	deprivation]	deprevation 13 (see Commentary)
368	ever;]	~∧ 13
372	infirmity]	firmitie 13 (see Commentary)
379-94	It ... proposed.]	om 13
381	an]	a 38 (see Commentary)
388	A]	38, A 14
393	good. Not]	~, not 14
406	extremitie:]	~. 13
409-28	But ... those.]	om 13
430	usually∧]	~, 13
438	will,]	~∧ 13
440-55	Disfavour ... content.]	om 13
442	reputeth,]	~) 38 (see Commentary)
446	much]	more 38

464	marg *Disfavour*] rom 13+
471	commendations$_\wedge$] ~, 13
471	cleerenesse$_\wedge$] ~, 13
473-89	Hee ... death.] om 13
474-75	all$_\wedge$ it's cunning and dishonestie to lay a] all; it is cunning and dishonestie to a 38
480	there he is] there is 14, om 38 (see Commentary)
495	despection] dispertion 13, despertion 14, desperation 38 (see Commentary)
499	Monopolies$_\wedge$] ~, 13
508	danger$_\wedge$] ~, 13
512	acted.] ~: 13
516	is,] ~$_\wedge$ 13
541-55	In ... merite.] om 13
543	ever] still 38
567	greatnesse,] 13, ~$_\wedge$ 14
582	generous] and generous 13 38 (see Commentary)
585	envious?] ~. 13
593	pittied,] ~: 13
594	miserable;] ~: 13 38
595	vertuous.] ~: 13 38
622-23	(or never surely)] surely 13
623	unhappinesse] unhappinesses 13
629	dissignes:] ~, 13
630	wilfull] a wilfull 13; distraction] detraction 13+ (see Commentary)
632	grace$_\wedge$] ~, 13
640	madnesses,] 38, ~$_\wedge$ 13, madnesse, 14
655-84	One ... yoke?] om 13
667	smother] smoother 38 (see Commentary)
685	miseries,] ~$_\wedge$ 13
693	discerning] decerning 13 (see Commentary)
704	judgement$_\wedge$] ~, 13
705	an] a 13
708	by] om 13+ (see Commentary)
712	differs$_\wedge$ in this$_\wedge$] ~, in ~, 13
718	*umbras*] 38, *umbres* 13 14
721-42	Not ... Accusation.] om 13
731	determination] detemination 14
732	time] times 38 (see Commentary)
746	eminent] 38, iminent 13, imminent 14 (see Commentary)
748	give, let] ~. Let 13+, new ¶ 14 38
753	world$_\wedge$] ~, 13
775	much, or more,] ~$_\wedge$ or ~$_\wedge$ 13
785	is] om 13+
787	Abdo-lominus] Abdo-hominus 13
795-805	The ... corruptible.] om 13
809	gifts,] ~$_\wedge$ 13
809	body,] ~$_\wedge$ 13
812	merit$_\wedge$] ~, 13

THE GOLDEN MEANE 377

816	inheritance₍∧₎] ~, 13	
837-51	In ... Comfort.] om 13	
845	as] om 14 (see Commentary)	
846	burie] burne 14 (see Commentary)	
862	mine] of mine 13	
868	later] latter 13	
869-70	it is] is it 13	
872	bloud;] 14 cor, ~, 13 14 uncor 38	
883	be,] ~₍∧₎ 13	
884	possession?] ~. 13	
898	point,] ~₍∧₎ 13	
913	be the] 13 14 cor, by the 14 uncor 38	
917	this] these 38 (see Commentary at 307)	
920	vaine,] ~; 13	
922	Act] art 13	
928	occasions,] ~₍∧₎ 13	
932	respect,] ~₍∧₎ 13	
935-52	The ... freely.] om 13	
942	word] 14 cor, world 14 uncor 38	
942	selfe?] 38 cor, ~. 14 38 uncor	
948	compultion:] 38, ~? 14	
953	Countries₍∧₎] ~, 13 38	
955	¹of] om 13	
967	action,] ~₍∧₎ 13	
974	or] 13 14BDE 38, no 14AC (see press variants)	
975	manner,] ~₍∧₎ 13	
996	Norffolk₍∧₎] ~, 13	
1011	banished;] om 13+ (see Commentary)	
1026	impatiencie] 13, impatience 14 (see Commentary)	
1029	Meane,] ~₍∧₎ 13	
1035	marg Of Imprisonment.] om 13+	
1035	qualitie₍∧₎] ~, 13	
1045	Morall,] ~₍∧₎ 13	
1046	sonne,] ~₍∧₎ 13	
1047	minde, both which₍∧₎] ~: both ~₍∧₎ 13	
1048	imprisoned,] ~; 13	
1049	in] into 13+	
1051	it,] ~₍∧₎ 13	
1051	iter;] ~: 13	
1056	commendation,] ~₍∧₎ 13	
1058-72	What ... immortalitie.] om 13	
1079	busied,] ~₍∧₎ 13	
1090	chamber,] ~₍∧₎ 13	
1102	recreations] recreation 38	
1107	Massinissa,] ~₍∧₎ 13	
1108	him₍∧₎] ~, 13 38	
1110	mercy,] ~₍∧₎ 13	
1116	are,] ~₍∧₎ 13	

1122   desirer] desire 13
1126   ²love] loves 13+
1145-54   More ... prison.] om 13
1162   exercise,] ~ ₐ 13
1177   man,] ~ ₐ 13
1180   threatnedₐ] ~, 13
1186-1206   But ... men.] om 13
1206   ²men,] 38, ~ ₐ 14
1214   itₐ comes,] ~, ~ ₐ 13
1220   death,] ~ ₐ 13
1226   certaineₐ] ~, 13 38
1226   more] om 13
1227   doubtₐ] ~, 13
1230   neere] neerer 13
1238   Inneₐ] ~, 13 38
1239   wearinesseₐ] ~, 13 38
1254   so,] ~ ₐ 13
1255   one,] ~ ₐ 13
1258-77   After ... reference.] om 13
1285-1324   To ... Noblenesse.] om 13
1325   actions:] ~; 13
1327   in resolved steadinesse to] to resolve steadinesse in 13

A Line of Life

Sigla

20   First Edition (W. S[tansby] for N. Butter, 1620), STC 11162.
MS   British Library, Lansdowne MS. 350, Item 3.
Gifford-Dyce   The Works, ed. Gifford, rev. Alexander Dyce, 3 vols. (London, 1869; reprinted, 1895).
SS+   Shakespeare Association Edition (1843), followed by Gifford-Dyce.

These textual notes record all substantive differences between 20 and MS. Adopted MS readings have been made to conform with the accidentals of the host text. Abbreviations have been expanded and i/j, u/v modernized, even in rejected readings. SS+ readings have been recorded only when they are genuine emendations or when they agree with MS against 20 (see Introduction, notes 46 and 47, above.)

LL:

Title page 1-7   A ... NAME.] Linea vitae. / A line of life. / Pointing att the immortallity of / a virtuous name. MS
Reader   WISE ... FORD.] om MS
Ep. Ded.   To ... Ford.] om 20
Ep. Ded. 11   debt. Your] debtₐ your MS

Ep. Ded. 17   intermytted] imtermytted MS
Text 19   to] unto MS
20   is] MS, is notwithstanding 20 (see Commentary)
27-28   marg in 1. Ethic.] in 1. Ethic. 1. 20, 1 Eth: MS
30   (the ... Nature)] MS, ˄~˄ 20
31   the] om MS
36   sitteth] sitts MS (see Commentary)
38   on-wardes] onward MS
41   AND] MS, om 20
43   good man] MS, good man 20
66   as] and MS
67   framed and] om MS
72   houre] MS, power 20 (see Commentary)
74   in their deceiptes] MS, om 20
76   Another ...] new ¶ MS
78   ²then] the MS
83-84   depravation] deprivation Gifford-Dyce
91   the] om MS
95   those] theis MS (see Commentary)
107   ¹of] MS, om 20 (see Commentary)
107   conveniencie] MS, the conveniencie 20
115   an] a MS (see Commentary)
118   is] MS, SS+, as is 20
121   as] or MS (see Commentary)
123   In ...] new ¶ MS
134   the] MS, om 20
140-41   so must consequently ... preposterously] MS, so consequently ... must preposterously 20
144   corrupted] om MS (see Commentary)
155   his] om MS
175   deserving publique] MS, publique deserving 20
177   old] om MS
180   of] of a MS (see Commentary)
182   marg Velleius] SS+, Villeius 20, velleus MS
183   marg Paterc.] om MS
188   marg Fab. inst.] ~: ~: MS, Fabius, 20
190   so] om MS
192-93   beeing] MS, om 20
194   substances] in their substance MS (see Commentary at 191-94)
201   whereto] whereunto MS
203   never was] MS, was never 20
210   appeareth] appeeres MS
218   ²to] MS, to to 20
219   pleasure] pleasures MS
225   imitate] intimate Gifford-Dyce conj (see Commentary)
230   presented honors] MS, a presented honour 20
243   life?] MS, ~. 20
255   pry, nay] MS, pry˄ and 20 (see Commentary)

260	sucke] seeke, MS (see Commentary)	
263	walkes] walk Gifford-Dyce	
263	profit] praise MS	
277–78	pronenesse and proclivitie] MS, proclivitie and pronenesse 20	
283	It …] same ¶ MS	
296	chusing] using MS	
298	and Dronkennesse or] MS, om 20 (see Introduction, 292)	
298	in] in in MS	
304	bold] cal'd MS	
306	marg 98] see Commentary	
309	and] MS, om 20	
311	Among] Amongst MS	
311	to be] MS, om 20	
313	they] the MS	
315–16	it were indeed] MS, indeed it were 20	
321–22	all his actions] MS, his action 20	
322–28	in … perpetuitie.] MS, wel-deserving even the testimonie of a religious learned Divine. 20 (see Introduction, 294)	
324	noe] MS not clear, perhaps nor or not	
329	But …] same ¶ MS	
335	and] MS, om 20	
349	nothing.] MS, ~, 20	
356	marg Seneca] Senea 20, Senec MS	
357	marg 123] 128 20, MS	
357	and with] MS, by 20	
358	for … man] ital 20, secretary in secretary context MS (see Commentary)	
358–59	to live, this is] MS, om 20	
363	marg A] of a MS	
368	It …] same ¶ MS	
370	brings] bring MS	
370	reproch] reproofe MS (see Commentary)	
372	The …] same ¶ MS	
373	marg et 12.] 12. MS	
375–76	marg et 6.] 6 de MS	
377	marg Pan.] pany. MS	
378	reputations] MS, reputation 20	
381	out, … it$_\wedge$] MS, ~$_\wedge$ … ~, 20	
394	these] those MS (see Commentary at 95)	
394	Collections] allegacions MS	
395	[1]to] om MS	
397	the] MS, an 20	
400–401	marg Two … men.] om MS	
403	desert) have] deseart by which they) have MS (parens after deseart probably crossed out)	
412	imploiment$_\wedge$ … head,] MS, ~, … ~$_\wedge$ 20	
415	opposites, to (if it be possible)] MS, ~$_\wedge$ (if it were possible) to 20	
416	names] MS, name 20 (see Commentary)	
424	[1]the] those MS	

A LINE OF LIFE   381

426   doeth] does MS
428   driving] drawing MS (see Commentary)
429   No ...] new ¶ MS
435-36   gravest of all the ancient Divines] gravest divine of all the auncyent
         divines MS, gravest Divine of all the Ancients 20 (see Commentary)
437   vicinior] see Commentary
443   latter] MS, last 20 (see Commentary)
445   grace, in] MS, ~˰ and 20
450-56   Certeine ... dishonour.] MS, om 20 (see Introduction, 292)
459   unto] to MS
461   Not ...] new ¶ MS
465-66   matter ... is] MS, matters ... are 20
468   marg. nat.] MS, om 20
469   sortes of] MS, om 20
474   rends] rentes MS
476   Flatterers,] MS, ~˰ 20
487   love] their love MS
492   to] MS, and 20
494   and] MS, om 20
494   damnably] dampnable MS (see Commentary)
495   vipers] vysars MS (see Commentary)
498   of] by MS
498   to] unto MS
502   gracious favorite] MS, om 20
504   approbations] approbacion MS
505-6   laughter.] MS, ~? 20
509-10   by ... man,] MS, om 20 (see Introduction, 292)
511-12   and ... seate,] MS, om 20 (see Introduction, 292)
515   distasted,] MS, ~. 20
515-16   incense ... insinuation.] MS, om 20 (see Introduction, 292)
522   of elder] MS, of the elder 20 (see Commentary)
545   the ... Presidents˰] MS, three ... Presidents, 20
553   on such] on the misery of such MS (see Commentary)
554   end, and] end, and the law and MS
567   yet scarce] MS, scarce yet 20
578   of] of a MS
579   Others ...] same ¶ MS
579   yet] MS, om 20
586   GREAT] MS, om 20 (see Commentary)
589   Lives] MS, loyes 20 (see Commentary)
591   (notwithstanding these)] ˰not withstanding the˰ MS
605   and] MS, om 20
605   then] in MS their has been altered to then or vise versa
608-9   where ... gayne] MS, to which ... give 20
628   not] MS, not to 20
631   and learned] MS, learned and 20, learned [man] and SS+
634   not] MS, not in 20
636   momentany] momentary MS

640-41	hee who directs his] MS, hee, he who directs all his 20
643	profitably] profitable MS (*see Commentary at 494*)
646-47	marg Of the 3 branch, A] the. 3 branch of a MS
652	and who:] MS, or who? 20
653	an] a MS, SS+ (*see Commentary at 115*)
654	which] what MS
663	is] *om* MS
665	gratfully] gracefully MS
670	that] which MS
670	(that] ˄~MS (*see Commentary*)
672	inclinable] unclynables MS
674	*procures*] procureth MS
681	loved] love MS
683	Bees] MS, the Bees 20 (*see Commentary at 683-89*)
684	the juyce of] *om* MS
687	smart] smarts MS
689	(as ... Valour;] *om* MS
700	particular] MS, peculiar 20
701	It ...] *same* ¶ MS
711	as] and MS, as he is SS+
712	Finally ...] *same* ¶ MS
712	in] MS (try *crossed out*), try 20
715	into] with MS
715-16	suppling] supplyeing MS (*see Commentary*)
720	marg *Velleius*] *Velleus* MS
720	which] MS, what 20
723-24	insomuch, as] for somuch MS (*see Commentary*)
728	terrifie] MS, terrifie him, 20
730	broode˄ against] MS, broode, set in armes against 20 (*see Commentary*)
734	confirmed] confined MS (*see Commentary*)
735	inexpugnable] expugnable MS (*see Commentary*)
739	*aheneus*] *alieneus* MS (*see Commentary*)
742	no] MS, not a 20
747	marg Νεφέλαις] Gifford-Dyce, Νεφαλαις 20, *om* MS
751	And if] MS, that 20 (*see Commentary*)
753	marg *Socrat.*] *Diog* MS
753	discreet, the] ~. The 20, MS
753	man] *om* MS
755	Socrates] MS, Soerates 20
755	those] the MS
758	imploiment] MS, imploiments 20
761	inleaging] MS (in leaging), inlarging 20 (*see Commentary*)
764	are] MS, SS+, and 20
769	then] *om* MS
770	In ...] *same* ¶ MS
771-72	marg *note om* MS
772	marg Δῶρον] Gifford-Dyce, Δωρον 20
772	hee] the MS

774	²of] *om* MS	
789	that] MS, *om* 20	
797	to neglect] MS, to a neglect 20	
799	an] a MS (*see Commentary*)	
799	hereditarie] MS, SS+, heditarie 20	
812	be,] MS, be_∧ 20	
815	who] which MS	
827	A ...] MS, *same* ¶ 20	
829	or] MS, *om* 20	
830–31	or ... friends,] *om* MS	
832	remembred_∧] MS, ~; 20	
835	howsoever_∧] MS, ~, 20	
836–44	sequestred ... man] *om* 20 (*see Introduction*, 292)	
Cor 1–74	The ... FINIS.] *om* MS	

Shorter Pieces

SP, I	19	methodus] gravitas *some edns*; confirmat] confirmant *some edns*
SP, II	37	the] *this edn*; ths 06
	58	Pallace] *this edn*, pallace 06
SP, IV	4	Pen_∧] *this edn*, ~. 23
SP, VII	9	wive's] *Massinger's correction*, wives 29
SP, XII	25	Consented] *Gifford*, contented 38
	33	read.] *Herford and Simpson*, ~_∧ 38
	44	first] *Gifford*, fit 38
SP, XIII	7	then] *B. Lloyd's addition*, Lesser when MS

Commentary

Honor Triumphant

Title page

Faire Lady ... false]   Compare "Fair without but foul within" (Tilley, F.29) and "Beauty and chastity (honesty) seldom meet" (Tilley, B.163).

Perfect Lovers ... wise]   The proposition plays on Publilius Syrus's dictum "Amare et sapere vix Deo conceditur," rendered by Spenser "To be wise and eke to love, / Is graunted scarce to God above" (SC March Emblem). See Tilley, L558; ODEP, 488.

Tam Mercurio, quam Marti]   As much of Mercury as of Mars. Ford gives pre-eminence to the poetic rather than the martial claims of this double ideal. On the reverse order *Tam Marti quam Mercurio* McKerrow comments "I do not know the origin of the phrase, which was in common use at the time. It was G. Gascoigne's motto" (Nashe, 4:98). Nashe uses it in both forms (in *Pierce Penilesse, Strange Newes*, and the preface to *Menaphon*). Gascoigne uses it frequently, for example on the title page of *The Posies* and at the conclusion of *The Steele Glas*. See also J. B. Leishman's note, *The Three Parnassus Plays* (London, 1949), 180. See FM, 738 and n., and 1058–60.

Epistle Dedicatory

the Duke of *Lennox*]   Ludovick Stuart, second duke of Lennox (1574–1624). Cousin, onetime successor to, and long-standing favorite of James VI and I, he accompanied James to England in 1603 and was naturalized an Englishman. Together with the Herbert brothers, he was noted for his prowess in tournaments in the early years of the reign. "They were known as the Knights Errant, and were constantly issuing challenges to their fellow nobles." (Sir Tresham Lever, *The Herberts of Wilton* [London, 1967], 81). He was created earl of Newcastle and duke of Richmond in 1623.

the Earl of *Arundel*]   Thomas Howard, second earl of Arundel (1586–1646). Known by the courtesy title of Lord Maltravers after his father's attainder and death in the Tower in 1595, he was restored to his titles (though not to his property) by James in 1603, and introduced to court in 1605. He restored his fortunes by marrying Alathea, third daughter and coheir of Gilbert Talbot, seventh earl of Shrewsbury, on 30 September 1606. The *DNB* states "the earl led a gay life at court, and his name constantly appears among the performers in masques and jousts." Clarendon comments devastatingly, "He resorted sometimes to the court, because there was a greater man than himself; and went thither the seldomer because there was a greater man than himself" (*History* [Oxford, 1826], 1:98). He later became a noted art collector.

the Earle of *Pembrooke*]   William Herbert, third earl of Pembroke (1580–1630). His mother Mary, countess of Pembroke, Sir Philip Sidney's sister, was herself a poet and great patroness. William and his brother Philip are the "most noble and incomparable paire of brethren" to whom the Shakespeare First Folio is dedicated. Among the learned to whom he was a Mæcenas were his former tutor Samuel Daniel, George Herbert, William Browne, Philip Massinger, Ben Jonson, and Inigo Jones. On 4 November 1604 he married Mary, daughter and coheir of the earl of Shrewsbury. He and Philip were both famed for their activities in tournaments and masques.

the Earle of *Mountgomery*]   Philip Herbert, earl of Montgomery and fourth earl of Pembroke (1584-1650); probably named after his famous uncle. A handsome sportsman, he rapidly became a great favorite with James, who created him Baron Herbert of Shurland and earl of Montgomery in 1605. In October 1604 he was secretly contracted to Susan de Vere, daughter of the earl of Oxford (granddaughter of Lord Burghley; niece of Robert Cecil, after 1605 earl of Salisbury), and very publicly married to her in December 1604. Both brothers had a reputation as amorists.

2-3. *the Countesse* of *Pembrooke*]   Lady Mary Talbot, oldest daughter and coheir of the seventh earl of Shrewsbury (d. 1649), married William 4 November 1604. A. L. Rowse (*Shakespeare's Southampton* [London, 1965], 206) calls her "dwarfish and unattractive," and quotes Clarendon's comment that Pembroke "paid much too dear for his wife's fortune by taking her person into the bargain." One wonders how she responded to Ford's arguments about beauty, virtue, deformity, and vice.

3-4. the Countesse of *Mountgomerie*]   Lady Susan de Vere (1587-1629), third surviving daughter of Edward, seventeenth earl of Oxford, married Philip 27 December 1604. Her cultivated mother, Anne Cecil, and her learned grandmother, Mildred Cooke, had died in her infancy, but perhaps she inherited some of their capacity.

8. gravelled in]   Puzzled, perplexed, with something of the metaphoric sense of "beached" or "stranded."

9. distast]   Regard with displeasure. Cockeram: "to Distast. *Disgust*." Compare *TP* 2.2.43.

16. trueth ... no lustre]   Compare "Truth needs no colours," Tilley, T.585; *ODEP*, 844-45.

17-18. I affect ... the other]   It is hard to choose meanings of "singularity" and "affectation" that will make sense with Ford's verbs. Perhaps "I do not aspire to be specially favored; I do not boast of a special fondness." Then he could hope to avoid being frozen for his ambition in addressing the work to the ladies through being warmed by a decorous devotion to them.

25-26. Mercury ... Mars]   See n. on *Tam Mercurio, quam Marti* above.

Reader

7-8. *I write not ... spirits*]   A sentiment frequently repeated by Ford. See *HT*, 760-61; *LL*, Reader, 29-31; *FM*, Reader, 10-14; *BH*, Epilogue; *LM*, Ep. Ded.

19. *Meritum rependant venustæ*]   "May the fair reward my just due."

Text

10. *everie man ... himselfe*]   Plato's dictum had achieved proverbial status (Tilley, B.141; *ODEP*, 75). Cicero's version, "non nobis solum nati sumus" (*De officiis* 1.7.22), was given wide currency in the popular schoolbook *Ciceronis sententiae* of P. Lagnerius; in the Lugduni [Lyons], 1547 edition it appears as Sententia 129 and Apophthegmatum 11.

13. *Neoterickes*]   A modern; especially a modern writer or author. According to the *OED*, very common in the seventeenth century. Cockeram defines as "One of late time."

18-19. *the chiefest creation ... a woman*]   In *LM* when Menaphon is accepted as Thamasta's servant, he calls it his "first step to honour" and vows service whose neglect would cast him lower than shame (1.3.63-65).

22. *Man be the little world*]   A commonplace to which Ford frequently refers: see *LL*, 136 and 148; *GM*, 564 and 1300.

23. *Women ... earth's Paradise*]   Compare *PW* 1.2.167, 5.3.122, 128-31; *LM* 1.3.28.

27. *undertake ... remisnesse*]   "The obscure phrase 'to undertake any occasion of remissness' means 'to become involved in a matter which leads to the neglect of his lady'" (Merchant, 65).

30-31. *captived happinesse ... bondage of beautie*]   See Spenser, *An Hymne in Honour of Beautie*, 274-78.

33-36. *may hee not be desperate ... blessing?*]   Compare *PW* 1.2.71-77.

34. *abject*]   An outcast, a degraded person. Cockeram: "A cast-away, vile, base." Compare *PW* 3.1.23.

38. *indeered*]   Endeared, bound by obligations of gratitude. The first example of this sense recorded in *OED* is 1607, *Tim* 3.2.32. See also *Tim* 1.2.229.

41-42. *Mars ... Venus leads him captive*]   Compare Shakespeare, *Ven* 103-10; a favorite Renaissance commonplace: see E. Wind, *Pagan Mysteries in the Renaissance* (London, 1958), 82-83.

49-50. *foolish hardinesse ... securitie*]   Cooper cites Cicero on "Temeritas et audacia stultorum."

75-76. *whole pamphlets ... female sex*]   See Introduction, 16.

77-78. *a woman ... weak-ballac't soules*]   See Castiglione, 202-3, for argument and counter-argument about Eve and the Virgin Mary.

86-87. *Ne ii sunt ... amor*]   "Nor are they worthy of love whom love rejects as unworthy" (Merchant).

104. *Apostataes*]   Apostates; *OED* notes "The L. *apostata* was by far the commoner form from 1350-1650, with pl. *apostata(e)s*."

113. *the Poet*]   Ovid. Ford appears to be joking about the familiarity of his source, *Ars Amatoria* 2.13.

114. *Non minor ... tueri*]   "Nor is there less prowess in guarding what is won than in seeking" (Ovid, *Ars Amatoria* 2.13).

122. *chuffes*]   Boors, churls. See *PW* 4.2.58.

126. *like swine touze pearle*]   Matt. 7:6. Tilley, P.165.

130. *fruition*]   Enjoyment, pleasurable possession. Compare *BH* 3.2.165, where there is a strong sexual connotation.

130. *imparadised*]   Rapturous. The first recorded example in *OED* is *Arcadia*, the second *HT*. Cockeram gives "*Imparadiẓ'd*. To enjoy all true content." Compare *BH* 4.3.128.

134. *who can serve two Masters*]   Matt. 6:24; Luke 16:13.

138-39. *a true lover ... worthiness*]   Compare *PW*, 1.2.148-57.

144. *Non amare ... præstat*]   "It is not fitting to love; rather it is preferable to be loved."

145. *sensualitie*]   The part of the nature of man that is concerned with the senses;

chiefly, the animal instincts and appetites; the lower nature as distinguished from the reason. Cockeram: "Brutishnesse, bodily pleasure."

150. *Paris* defended *Hellen*] Paris defended Helen in combat against Menelaus and refused to surrender her to the Greeks (*Iliad* 3, 7), but his death is not closely associated with his love for her. Estienne (*Dictionarium historicum, geographicum, poeticum*, 1596) states that he was killed by Pyrrhus or Philoctetes in the course of the stratagem by which Paris killed Achilles. Other traditions have him wounded at this time and dying because Oenone refuses to heal him. Compare Shakespeare, *Tro* 2.2, especially 130-62.

150-51. *Troylus* ... for *Cresseida*] Compare Chaucer, *T&C* 1.1074, 2.1772-78, 5.43-49; and more ambiguously, Shakespeare, *Tro* 1.2.220-31 and 5.2.161-74.

151. *Æneas* wonne *Lavinia*] Weapons clash and blood streams over Lavinia in the second half of the *Aeneid* , particularly in bk7.

152. *Pælops* ... for *Hippodamia*] Pelops obviated the risk of joining Hippodamia's thirteen earlier suitors in death by depending on bribery and trickery. The outcome of the marriage was the birth of Atreus and Thyestes. Stavig sees the references to Paris, Troilus, and Pelops as ironic, but is puzzled to understand why Ford should link with them the admired Penelope and Mountjoy (Stavig, 10, 201, and n. 18).

154-56. our english *Hector* ... *Ulisses*] Mountjoy, the earl of Devonshire, and his wife Penelope; the name Opia is punningly derived from Ops, opes, wealth or riches. Lady Rich was accustomed to puns on her earlier married name at least since the writing of *Astrophel and Stella*. The likening of this longstanding but irregular relationship to the perfect marriage of Penelope and Ulysses strains belief but seems sincere. See *FM* Introduction, 69-70.

155. gust] Outburst. Cockeram gives "sometimes a great puffe of winde."

159-60. But examples ... convenient] Compare *GM*, 84.

166-69. *Lentulus* ... *Terentia* ... *Non bellum, non fortuna*] See Robert Greene's *Ciceronis Amor: Tullies Love* (1589 and frequently reprinted). Lentulus first sees Terentia at her father's banquet, and "letting fall his knyfe on his trencher saide aloude, *Non fortuna non bellum* meaning that neither the highest state of fortune nor the fatall intent of warre could conquer that hart that her beautie hath made subject." Lentulus proceeds to tell a brief tragic tale of married love and constancy in which the phrase *Non fortuna, non bellum* is twice repeated. (Ed. C. H. Larson [Salzburg: Universität Salzburg, 1974], 21-24).

183. dallie] See Introduction, 22, and compare *HT*, 402.

191-92. in knowen verities ... needlesse] Compare such proverbial sayings as "Truth has no need of rhetoric" and "In too much Dispute, truth is lost" (Tilley, T.575 and D.384; *ODEP*, 843-45).

193-94. her will ... irrefragable] Merchant cites *BH* 3.3.42-43.

197-98. from *the faire* ... *faire*] Compare Tasso, quoted above, 15; Tilley, F.1 and F.5, and *ODEP*, 239; and Castiglione, 308-9.

203-5. horror befits not ... warre] Compare *PW* 3.2.148-50.

223. senceably] So as to be easily understood or to impress the feelings; clearly, strikingly. This spelling is not recorded in OED. Compare *PW* 5.3.205.

224-25. *Et domi, et foris*] Merchant translates, "Both at home and at large (out of doors)," and notes that while the phrase was common, "Two famous passages, widely read in the Renaissance, Cicero's *Second Philippic* against Antony (2.11.26) and Sallust's *Catiline* (52.21) both use it prominently" (80).

230-31. *Plutarch* ... *the Sabines* ladies]   Plutarch, *Lives*, "Romulus," 28-33.
234. *Kissing* had his first originall]   There are no kisses in Plutarch's version. Heywood tells the story of the Trojan women burning the ships after landing in Italy, and greeting their husbands with kisses to turn aside their anger, as the origin of the custom of Roman women kissing their kinsmen at salutations (*Gunaikeion*, 144-45). In Castiglione the same story is immediately followed by the story of the Sabine women (211-12).
235. earnest-peny]   A small sum of money, probably originally a literal penny, paid as earnest to secure a bargain. *OED* notes that in the sixteenth and seventeenth centuries the figurative sense was frequent in religious use.
237-42. *Kissing* seems ... heaven]   The progression of these lines might well make Caraffa in *LS* doubt the restraint of his friend and his wife. Although Fernando protests he never reaped "the benefit of any favour from her, save a kisse" (2562-63), the two kissing scenes (2.4 and 5.1) give prominent dramatic importance to the act. On the meaning and consequences of kissing, see Castiglione, 315-16.
249-50. proverbe ... to *sleepe in a whole skinne*]   Tilley, S.530; *ODEP*, 742. Compare Castiglione, 36, "where they suppose that without missing they may convey themselves from danger, how they are willing inough to sleepe in a whole skinne" ("volentier si lasciano acconciare al sicuro," trilingual edition, 1588).
252. conceited]   Apprehended, imagined. Compare *PW* 3.4.31.
254. provocation]   An invitation or summons; an incitement. Cockeram: "A Challenging."
256-58. the greedy eye of desire ... possession]   Compare Castiglione, 303-4.
259. Cardinall-vertue of invincible *fortitude*]   The four cardinal or "hinge" virtues on which all other moral virtues depend (the other three being prudence, temperance, and justice) were taken over by Christian moral theologians from Aristotle and Plato (*Republic* 4.427). Compare Shakespeare, *H8* 3.1.103, and note in the Arden edition (1964; reprint. 1968), 95.
264. *Beautie!* which prickes on the slowest]   Ford attributes to beauty much the same effects that Castiglione gives to women in *The Courtier*, bk. 3, especially 188.
268. the *Via lactea* to felicitie]   Compare *LL*, 60-61.
269-72. *Achilles* ... *Trophey*]   The trophy, like Achilles' shield and the Golden Fleece, represents a longed-for prize. Peter Blayney suggests Plutarch's *Moralia* for Philip urging Alexander to run in the Olympic Games (*Moralia* 179D). In Plutarch's *Life* of Alexander it is not his father who does the urging. In neither case is a trophy mentioned, but Holland's translation of the "Apophthegmes ... of Kings" reads: "He was wonderfully nimble and deliver of bodie, but in footmanship especially he excelled; insomuch as his father was in hand with him one time to runne a course in the race, for the prize in the Olympick games" (*Morals*, 411).
277-91. Does not the marchant ... acceptable]   Merchant cites *BH* 1.2.115-43 as an example of the theme of beauty inspiring military prowess.
292-93. *Through streames of blood* ... *breath*]   Compare *PW* 1.2.148-57.
326. *Pallas* ... *Bellona*]   Bellona, goddess of war, was frequently identified with Pallas or Minerva, goddess of wisdom, war, and liberal arts.
337. *Audentes forma cogit audaces*]   "Beauty makes bold those who dare." A variant on a familiar idea. Langius's *Loci Communes* (Argentorati [Strassburg], 1598) gives, among others, Vergil "Audentes Forma iuvat," Ovid "Audentes Forsque, Venusque iuvat" (*Fasti* 2), and Tibullus 1.2. "Audendum est fortes adiuvat ipsa Venus."

345-46. *Hercules ... Deianeira*]   The two watery exploits of Hercules connected with Deianeira are his contest with Achelous and the encounter with Nessus (Ovid, *Met.* 9.1-133; *Her.* 9.138-42), but both concern rivers rather than the sea, and their purpose is not specifically to rouse Deianeira's wonder.

350. braverie]   Valour, bravado, in which sense compare *BH*, 3.2.103 and 4.4.48, with a pun on ostentation, finery, fine clothes.

359. corrivall-shipp]   The position of a corrival, mutual rivalry. Cockeram gives "*Corrivall*. Hee which is a suitor with another for marriage to a woman."

362. *Chalibs mihi circa pectus*]   "Steel encircles my breast" (Merchant).

370-74. *Tamburlaine ... his tryumph*]   As the title page of the 1590 edition of Marlowe's "two Tragicall Discourses" announces, Tamburlaine "(for his tyranny, and terrour in Warre) was tearmed, The Scourge of God." His devotion of the spoils of war to Zenocrate is emphasized by Marlowe in part 1, 1.2.102-5; 3.3.126 ff.; 5.1.507 ff.

375-76. *Pax ruat ... Amor*]   "Peace rushes to war, and friendly allies to battle; / the just cause submits: on no front is LOVE overcome" (Merchant).

380-82. I have often marvailed ... ladies with them]   For the argument that armies are inspired by the presence of their loves, see Castiglione, 234-35.

384-86. *Cæsar ... Cleopatra*]   Plutarch's account of Caesar's affair with Cleopatra emphasizes the dangers he underwent for the sake of her love (*Lives*, "Julius Caesar," 781-82).

386. twise suffered ... repulse]   Not the story as Roman histories tell it. Holinshed notes "our histories ... affirm ... that Cesar comming the second time, was by the Britains with valiancie and martiall prowesse beaten and repelled, as he was at the first" ("The Historie of England," 3.16; Ellis, ed., 1.475).

395. home-bred poring Academicke]   Compare *TP*, 5.3.13. Merchant cites Drayton, *Her. Ep., Edw.IV to Mrs Shore*, 126: "Poore plodding Schoole-men they are farre too lowe, / Which by probations, rules, and axiomes goe" and *BH* 1.3.113-21.

398. plodder]   Merchant (101) cites Shakespeare, *LLL* 1.1.86.

400-401. *Hanniball* did *Phormio*]   Cicero, *De oratore* 2.18.75-77. See *LL*, 389-92 and n.

405-6. the truth ... prevaileth]   Proverbial. Tilley, T.576, T.579; *ODEP*, 844.

415. THE temperature ... bodie]   See Tilley, D.381; *ODEP*, 755. Compare "Passiones animae variantur secundum variationem seu dispositionem corporis" attributed *Arist.lib.l.de Ani.* in Langius, *Polyanthea* (1613) under Anima. See *LL* 147-48 and n. Compare *TP* 2.5.14-17, as noted by Roper (47), and Leech (52-53).

417-18. arrogant spleen ... envie]   For the withered juicelessness and gnawing evil of envy, compare Spenser, *FQ* 5.12.28 f.

423. curious impostor]   The "curious impostor" presumably pretends to a false argument because of his spleen and envy. Ford's use of "impostor" causes difficulties in *BH* 4.2.67 (see Spencer, ed., 173 textual variants and notes). Ford uses "impostorous," meaning fraudulent, in *PW* 1.1.100 and *LM* 1.2.132. Warbeck is dismissed as "impostor beyond precedent" in *PW* 5.3.208. Cockeram gives "*Impostor*. A deceiver" and "*Curiositie*. More diligence then needs."

423. *Euge hominem*]   Merchant translates "Well done, man!" The *Oxford Latin Dictionary* notes that the interjection is sometimes ironic, as it is here.

429-30. outward shape ... inward vertues]   Compare Castiglione, 309. Merchant (104) comments, "The lines have a theological flavour. As the phrase 'without controversy' is a Pauline echo, equally the expressions 'outward shape' and 'inward virtues' reflect the current definition of a sacrament as 'an outward and visible sign of an inward and spiritual grace' (1549, *The Book of Common Prayer*, Cat.)."

437-38. Beautie is ... guests within] Compare *LL*, 12-13 and n.; and Shakespeare, *R2* 5.1.13.

440-47. *deformitie* ... *fowlest formes*] Compare the position on physical ugliness taken in *GM*, 510-515. Merchant cites *BH* 2.1.3-7 on the link between physical deformity and moral turpitude.

441. the curse ... child] Merchant cites John 9:2, Exod. 20:56, Rom. 5:12-14.

447-48. *firmest vertues* ... *complexions*] See Spenser, *An Hymne in Honour of Beautie*, 132-40.

452. adulterate] Spurious; corrupted by base intermixture. Compare the first example recorded in OED, Daniel's *Complaint of Rosamund* (1592): "Th'adulterate Beauty of a false Cheek, Vile stain to Honour and to Women eke."

478-82. old writers ... inchantment] Compare Chaucer, "The Wife of Bath's Prologue," 707-10.

490-91. *Scire tuum* ... *alter*] Adapted from Persius, 26-27: "o mores, usque adeone / scire tuum nihil est, nisi te scire hoc sciat alter?" ("Good heavens! Is all your knowledge to go so utterly for nothing unless other people know that you possess it?"). Used also by Nashe, *Anatomie of Absurditie* (1.21.5-6) and Coluander, *Sententiae* (?1552), H5ʳ.

491. a hidden minerall] See *LL*, 32-33.

502. *Theseus* ... *Ariadne*] Ford bends tradition in claiming that Theseus's efforts against the Minotaur were designed to win Ariadne, although his words to her in Ovid, *Her.* 10.73-74, suggest that he pledges his dangers to her devotion. His protestations are more extravagant in Chaucer, *LGW* 2029 ff.

504. inderely] Dearly, earnestly, deeply. Compare *HT* 38 indeered. Indearly (or endearly) is not recorded in OED. Merchant modernizes to endearedly citing Heywood's *Gunaikeion* from OED.

504-5. *Portia* ... swallow coles] Portia reverenced her father Cato, but the main tradition states that she swallowed burning coals upon hearing of her husband Brutus's death. See Shakespeare, *JC*. Ford may have been influenced by Valerius Maximus's comment on her death: "muliebri spiritu virilem patris exitum imitata" (*Factorum et dictorum memorabilium*, Lib. 4, cap. 6, 5. p. 199), or by Robert Greene's tangled examples in *Mamillia*: "we shall never finde anie man so faithfull which hath surpassed women in constancie ... let them tel me if ever any of their bravest champions offered to die for his wife as *Admeta* did for her husband *Alcest*? What man ever swallowed burning coales as *Portia* did for *Cato*?" (*Works*, ed. A. B. Grosart [1881-86; reprint New York, 1964], 2:157.

505. *Alcest* wold die for *Admetus*] One version of Alcestis's sacrifice of herself in place of her husband was popularized by George Pettie's *A petite Pallace of Pettie. his pleasure* (1576 etc.). Heywood tells her story as a stellar example of manly courage, noble resolution, and conjugal love, "with which shee writ herself a character of honour, to outlast all antiquitie" (*Gunaikeion*, 120).

505-6. *Alcest* ... *Penelope*] Compare Katharine, "Unequalled pattern of a matchless wife" *PW* 4.5.11.

505-7. *Penelope* ... *Ulisses*] Penelope is more often praised as "most chaste, wyse, and constant above all the women of hir tyme" (Cooper) than for her beauty, which in the *Odyssey* needs furbishing by Venus (bk. 18). However, Heywood begins her story, "The beauty of *Penelope* attracted a number of suitors" (*Gunaikeion*, 276)

512-13. *rara præclara* ... estemed]   Cited Tilley, T.145, and *ODEP*, 812. The phrase is Sententia 157 in P. Lagnerius, M. *Tull. Ciceronis sententiae* (Lugduni [Lyons], 1547), with the most familiar quotation being from *De amicitia* 21.79. Ford is arguing against the common saying "Castitas et pulchritudo raro cohabitant" (see L. Coluander, *Sententiae* [?1552], K8^r, and Juvenal *Sat.* 10.297-98). See *PW* 5.3.89-97, 121-31, and compare *HT*, 576-603 and n.

517. *fronti nulla fides*]   "There's no trusting a face" (Merchant). See Juvenal, *Sat.* 2.8. The phrase was widely popular: see, for example, Whitney's *A Choice of Emblemes* (1586, ed. H. Green, 1866), 100, and *A Paradise of Dainty Devices*, ed. H. E. Rollins (Cambridge, Mass., 1927), 204. See also Walther, *Proverbia* (Göttingen, 1963-67), 2:2, entries 10015-16.

518. *Cresseida ... Lais*]   Cresseida may be a poetic invention, but the courtesan Lais's well documented career, though legendary, is not fictional.

525-29. *Lucrece ... death*]   Celebrated by untold numbers of writers besides Shakespeare for her reaction to Tarquin's rape. Heywood begins the section "Of divers Ladies famous for their Modestie" with her story (*Gunaikeion*, 125-26).

526. the mirror of those daies]   Merchant cites *BH* 4.1.81-82. Compare also Spenser, *CCCHA* 513, *SC* October 93, and *FQ* 1 Pr 4.2.

534. *Constantia ... individua*]   "Constancy is beauty's inseparable twin" (Merchant). See 668-70 and n.

541. *forma bonum*]   Ovid, *Ars Amatoria* 2.13: "Forma bonum fragile est," ("A frail advantage is beauty"). The tag's wide popularity is attested by its position as the first of the "Poeticae sententiae" under Forma in Langius's *Polyanthea* (1613). See Walther, *Proverbia* (Göttingen, 1963-67), 2:2, entries 9741-42.

547-51. many there are ... passe for *Beauty*]   Compare Castiglione, 311.

571-72. doves ... spleene]   Compare *TP*, 1.2.58.

577 ff. Angels on earth]   For angelic virtue, beauty, constancy, and love, compare Warbeck's praises of Katharine, *PW* 3.2.155-58, 170; 5.3.89-94, 121-31.

584-85. *faint hearted ... disdaine*]   Compare *LM* 3.2.196-200.

588. *Mulieri ... mortuæ quidem*]   "Don't trust a woman, even a dead one." A favorite maxim: see, for example, Erasmus, *Adagia* 2.10.21.

597. *mans perfection*]   The usual reversal of this phrase, that imperfect woman is perfected by association with man, is set out and debated in Castiglione, 199-202.

598. *Diis compares fœminae*]   "Women equal to the gods" (Merchant).

613-14. PERSPICAX ... *convenientibus*]   "It's smart, the watchful little eye of a lover; it anticipates danger, it looks out for timely opportunities" (Merchant).

614-15. A perfect lover ... imployed]   Compare *GM*, 1078-80.

653-72. being overcome ... *Architecture*]   Compare *TP* 2.5.49-50 (noted by Roper, 49). See Introduction, 14-15. Merchant cites *BH* 2.2.86-90, where "Ford achieves the same synthesis of religious and neoplatonic concepts which is adumbrated in the present passage."

683. discursion]   The action of running away, or wandering, with an implied suggestion of irregularity. Cooper: "Discursus, ... A runnyng hither and thither: and wandryng." This sense is not fully covered in *OED*, but see Discursion, especially the etymology and 1, and Discursive, 1.

704-7. Love is ... authorities confirm]   Compare Castiglione, 303-6.

707. *entire* [*conjunction*] *of soules together*] Huebert takes this statement as representative of Ford's search for love as "an ideal relationship between two souls," and "a force that 'traffiques' between the miraculous and the sensual." He cites *LS* 5.1.2356, "Can there be sinne in unity?" and *TP* 1.1.34, "One soul, one flesh, one love." The reading of all three surviving copies, "*convinction*" ("*conuinction*"), is enticing: although the word is not recorded, it would mean "a binding together" (from con- + vincire vinxi vinctum) and would be appropriate to the context. However, Ford's use of "*conjunction*" at *MM* 150 makes a new coinage unlikely.

708-13. *Mutua sors ... Venus*] "The reciprocal destiny of the soul, the holy exchange of mind, Love is a faithful pledge in a faithful breast. What could be more tranquil? Nothing is more propitious than this; a joyful peace, a noble hand, a safe quietness. Venus shines in goldenhaired beauty with gleaming strength: being bright herself, she rejoices in Love."

726. *prick*] With sexual quibble, as frequently in Shakespeare: for example, *Rom* 1.4.25-28; *AWW* 4.2.18-20.

739. *vulgar*] Public, open. This sense does not appear in OED, but cf. OED 6, which quotes *Err* 3.1.100, glossed by Onions as "public."

748. *singular*] Eminent, above the ordinary in worth or value. Cockeram gives "Fine, excellent." Compare *BH*, 1.2.62.

750. *frigescere ad ignem*] "To freeze in the fire."

760-61. *Non omnibus ... malevolis*] "I care not for all: not for the malicious" (Merchant). See *FM*, Reader, 13-14.

The Monarchs Meeting

20. *A Christian King*] Christian IV of Denmark (1577-1648) was the younger brother of James's queen Anne (1574-1619). He acceded to the throne in 1588 and attained his majority in 1596. He was more noted for his personal courage, energy, and passion, and for his aggressive foreign policy, than for religious behavior.

104. *Seaven Kingdomes*] Merchant suggests Ford "may possibly refer to the four British 'Kingdoms' (England, Wales, Scotland and Ireland), and the three Danish Provinces, Jutland, North Schleswig and The Islands (Funen, Zealand and Laaland)." However, the kingdom of France is more appropriately referred to than the principality of Wales. The royal coat of arms of the House of Stuart (1603-1707) carried the emblems of England, Scotland, Ireland, and France. See also *LS* 1.1.131-32 and *PW* 1.1.112-13.

124. *subtile* French] Merchant cites *BH* 2.3.124-25.

134. *emulating*] Jealous of, envious. The first recorded example in OED is of 1610, in Healey's translation of Augustine's *Citie of God*.

135-36. *we ever chose ... infamy*] Compare "Mors honesta ignominiosae vitae preferenda" (G. Whetstone, *Sir Phillip Sidney, his honorable life, his valiant death etc.* [1587?], C2ᵛ).

178 ff. *Our King himselfe*] For the general rejoicing, Merchant compares *BH* 3.3.70-74.

197. *Cantibus et carmine*] "With songs and verse" (Merchant).

Fames Memorial

Title page of quarto

8-10. *quis talia ... lachrimis?*] Vergil, *Aeneid* 2.6-8: "What Myrmidon or Dolopian, or soldier of stern Ulysses, could in such a tale restrain his tears?"

{Arms}] The arms of the Blount family: Barry nebulee of six or and sable. For a detailed account, see Sir Alexander Croke, *The Geneological History of the Croke Family originally named le Blount* (Oxford, 1823), 1:393-95.

Title page of quarto verso

{Crest}] The crest of the Blount family: the sun in glory charged on the center with an eye issuing tears, all proper. The motto (Inter lachrymas micat) is missing. See Sir Bernard Burke, *The General Armory of England, Scotland, Ireland, and Wales* (London, 1884).

Epistle Dedicatory Q6

2-3. Penelope, Countesse of *Devonshire*] See Introduction, 79.

8. Fate ... recalled] See Tilley, F.83; also T.203.

20-21. being ... you] See LL, Ep. Ded.: "though meerely an unknowne stranger to you" (8-9).

Epistle Dedicatory MS

17-18. for fame ... Minerall] See LL, 32-33.

Reader

This acrostic, lacking in the MS, Gifford (2:566) suggests "may be fairly set down as the worst that ever passed the press."

13-14. *Non omnibus ... malevolis*] "I care not for all: not for the malicious." The same quotation closes *HT* (760-61). See n. to LL, Reader, 30.

To ... Madrigall

15-16. Middle Temple] Ford was admitted to the Middle Temple on 16 November 1602.

22. spightfull plants] Mountjoy's enemies and detractors, to whom Ford repeatedly refers in *FM*.

29. *Castaly*] Castalia or Castalie. Spring on Mount Parnassus sacred to the Muses.

33. Barnabe Barnes seems to have offered friendship and encouragement to the young Ford and strongly influenced his early style. The year 1606 also saw the publication of Barnes's *Foure Bookes of Offices* to which Ford contributed verses. See SP, I.

34-38. *In eundem ... ope*] "To the same. He lives, and for eternity shall live, the general renowned in arms, Mountjoy: your poem, Forde, shall also live, each of you greater, by his own genius. Like the hero of the poem, the noble author is fortunate in the copiousness of his material."

39. T. P.] Burelbach suggests "Probably by T. Proctor, author of *A Gorgeous Gallery of Gallant Inventions*" (66).

Text

42. worthy to the nine] The Nine Worthies (or Nine Nobles) of ancient and medieval history.

94. soules-united *Essex*] For Mountjoy's relationship with Essex, see Introduction, 68-69.

125. Aristotle]   Nicomachean Ethics 1.3; 1095a. See Tro 2.2.162-67: "Young men whom Aristotle thought / Unfit to hear moral philosophy."
160. deity]   Queen Elizabeth.
168. How ... woon]   For other uses by Ford of this proverbial saying, see n. on LL, 488.
260. knightly youth]   Most likely Sir William Godolphin (d. 1613) a Cornishman, knighted for gallantry by Essex in 1599. He was a close friend and confidant of Mountjoy and served under him in important positions. He was probably the "faithful friend" at Mountjoy's deathbed and was definitely one of the three trustees of his estate. In 1607 his daughter was christened Penelope. (See Falls, 121, 235-36; J. Burke, *Extinct and Dormant Baronetcies*, second edition [London, 1844], 221; F. G. Marsh, *The Godolphins*, privately printed 1930.) A possible difficulty is Godolphin's age. The exact date of his birth is unknown, but his Cambridge matriculation was in the Lent term of 1584-85. Though younger than Mountjoy he would hardly be a "youth" in 1606.
268. Great Peer]   Henry Wriothesley, third earl of Southampton (1573-1624). Leader with Mountjoy of the Essex faction in the late 1590s. Involved in the rebellion and condemned to death, but the sentence was not carried out. He was released and restored to favor by James I. Of him Mountjoy said, "I can name no man that I love better than the Earl of Southampton" (*Cal. of State Papers, Ireland* [1600], 233). The close friendship of the two men continued till Mountjoy's death. Southampton was chief mourner at the funeral and seems to have looked after the interests of the children after Penelope's death. (See Akrigg, esp. 150.)
274. grave patron]   Thomas Sackville, first earl of Dorset (1530-1608). Dorset was made Lord Treasurer in May 1599 by Queen Elizabeth and confirmed for life in the post by King James. He was thus in close contact with Mountjoy during the Irish campaign, and later when "in Robes of peace" the newly-created Devonshire supervised Irish affairs from England. Both men served as negotiators for the peace with Spain in 1604.
290. honied speeches]   See LL, 680 and n.
309. ye wars of Belgia]   In August 1585, Queen Elizabeth concluded a treaty with the Dutch. One of the first four companies sent to their aid was under Charles Blount's command. Although his company was used to garrison Ostend, he served as a volunteer in an attack on the fort of Isselcourt in October of that year and was wounded in the thigh. He was cited for bravery and probably spent some time in England recuperating. In September 1586 Blount was present at the skirmish that cost Sidney his life. Ordered home in October 1587 by the queen, he was knighted before his departure by Leicester.
321. Time cannot wrong]   See similar sentiment in GM, 485-88 and n.
330. Lycia]   There is no reason to believe that Lycia (or Lucia in MS) was a real person. Compare "Delia" in Daniel's *Complaint of Rosamund*, and see Sargeaunt, 7.
338. Angell]   Penelope.
340. frontyres of hir brows]   Her forehead.
348. fowle envies hate]   In GM Essex is "cast downe by envie" (122). In LL, 549-57 the fall of Essex is attributed to over-confidence. See notes to these lines and Introduction, 65, 70-71.
349. cal'd ... home]   Far from the fact. Among the charges of which the Privy

Council found Essex guilty the day after his return (29 September 1599) were: "(1) His contemptuous disobedience to Her Majesty's instructions in returning to England; ... (3) His rash manner of coming away from Ireland" (quoted in Akrigg, 95–96).

363. Vowing revenge] The picture of Mountjoy in this and the two following stanzas is completely unhistorical. But see Introduction, 73–74.

375. half-conquered] Perhaps in compliment to Essex. In fact, English fortunes were at an extreme low point when Mountjoy assumed command.

500. with Tyrone] Mountjoy landed with Tyrone in Wales on 30 May 1603 and rode with him to London and to his house at Wanstead.

504. *Devonshieres* ennobled Earle] At Hampton Court, 21 July 1603.

506. Counsayllour] While Mountjoy was still in Ireland, King James made him a Privy Councillor, with the stipulation that the appointment take effect immediately, rather than after the ceremony of taking the oath, (Jones, 176).

520. Save some] For example, a disappointed petitioner who claimed to have saved his life during the Irish campaign and "published a violent tirade against him in the autumn of 1603" (Jones, 177).

550. cancelling] Here presumably by annulling or rendering void in the interest of justice.

577. prudence] On this and the following four stanzas, see Introduction, 74.

617. Thou ... poesy] Reference uncertain; perhaps Samuel Daniel.

632. Unjustly term'd disgracefull] A defence of the validity of Mountjoy's marriage. See Introduction, 69–70.

638. starre] Stella.

645. wisely discreete] Historically, Penelope was rash and impetuous.

697. times yet breeding] Times to come; the future.

701. *James ... peace*] For an appreciation of James's role as peacemaker in later years, see *LL*, 786–92 and n. In *FM* the reference is to the king's ending the long war with Spain and his oft-proclaimed pacific intentions.

708. A worke of thankes] This phrase re-appears in Ford's commendatory verses for Barnabe Barnes's *Foure Bookes of Offices*, also published in 1606. See *SP*, I.5.

708–14. Besides the general recollection of *R2* 2.1.43–49, this stanza reflects the Proclamation of Union (1603) which speaks of "a little world within itself." Mountjoy's reconquest of Ireland completed the union of 1603.

722. *Phœnix ... rare*] There was never more than one phoenix at a time. See *CBS*, 277.

733. *preconion's*] Of a crier or herald; from Lat. praeco, "herald." The OED gives only the adjective "preconious" with a single citation from 1656.

738. *Mercury* and *Mars*] Mercury, in his identification with Hermes, is taken as the god of eloquence. Mercury's further reputation as the god of prudence, and his connection with the concluding of treaties and the maintaining of peace could also refer to Mountjoy. The Mars-Mercury reference is repeated in 1058–60. See *HT*, title page and n.

776. Pharaos tower] The tower built on an island off Alexandria by Ptolemy Phildalphus. It served as a lighthouse and counted as one of the seven wonders of the ancient world.

785. *Heraclitus*] Heraclitus of Ephesus (ca. 535–475 BC), the "weeping philosopher" of the ancients, in contrast to Democritus. See Juvenal, 10.28–53.

818. Floraes] Of Flora, goddess of spring and of flowers.

819. Ere shee ... died] Devonshire died on 3 April 1606. The festivals of Flora among the ancients began on 28 April.
848. Life? ah no life ...] This stanza is based on Kyd's "O eyes, no eyes ..." (*Spanish Tragedy*, 3.2.1-4) which was parodied as an example of old-fashioned rhetoric long before 1606. The figure is *correctio* or *epanorthosis*. (See, for example, Jonson's *Every Man in his Humour*, 1.5.56-63.) Ford still regards it as a worthy model.
938-65. These two epitaphs were written with stanzas of varying line lengths to suggest the form of urns. In the MS this is quite clear, and the scribe drew the outline of urns inside oblong rules. The compositor of 06 made no attempt to set the urn shape and set the lines very irregularly, running the second and third stanzas together (942-49). (The typesetting software for this edition is able to mimic these shapes only approximately.)
966-92. These two epitaphs achieve pyramid shape by breaking up the first two lines in each. This corresponds exactly to their shape in the MS. (But see n. preceding.)
1045. *Lycia*] See n. at 330.
1058-60. *Mars ... Mercury*] See 733-40 and n. at 738.
1061. *Numas* grave intelligence] Numa Pompilius, the second of Rome's kings, was renowned for his wisdom and piety.
1062. *Affrican's* stout eminence] Publius Cornelius Scipio Africanus Major (236-184/3 BC). Ford refers to him in GM as an example of banishment. See GM, 1024 and n.
1065. *Charles* the greate] See JAMES THE GREAT and reference to Charlemaine in LL, 805-08.
1114-20. Compare 519-46 and n. at 520.
Anagramma] The anagram plays on the sun in the Blount family crest.
13-14. *Dignum ... mori*] "A man worthy of praise the Muse does not allow to die" (Horace, *Odes* 4.8.28).

Christes Bloodie Sweat

Title
The spelling of the title page, rather than that of the head title (*Christes Bloudy Sweat*) is adopted, even though the latter may be authorial, as it is by the former that the poem is known in the STC and Ford scholarship.

Epistle Dedicatory
Ep. Ded.] On Pembroke, see Introduction, 136 above, and HT, Ep. Ded., n.

Text
10. Then selfe ... unfolde] Than the treasure of creation itself can disclose (because the "creature's good" comes not from the creation but from the Creator).
11-12. Deare ransome ... underproppes] The ransom is purchased at the cost of Christ's life, yet the life Christ gives is upheld by his death.
14-16. All *Frailty* ... Hell alone] All of humankind ("*Frailty*") are given life by the death of one who, uniting himself with the human race, freely cancelled their debit account, thereby cancelling the effects of hell. "Freely" means both "generous-

ly" and "of his free will"; "crost" means both "cancelled" and "made the sign of the cross over."

21. An Heyre of *promise*]   Echoes "heires of promes" (Heb. 6:17).

27. *Arke*, and mercie-seat]   The mercy seat was that from which God spoke. See Exod. 25:21-22.

32. thriftlesse]   The emendation is justified by considerations of paleography and of sense. Compare *TP* 5.1.1-2: "Pleasures farewell, and all ye thriftless minutes / Wherein false joys have spun a weary life."

45-46. which sighes ... affliction beares]   The sighs reveal what a rock of torment is endured by Christ in his affliction.

67-72. The cause of Christ's suffering is above all his Father's will (see Matt. 26:42); and, as a cause, his Father's will is above (over) all the rest. The interpolation of "will" in 71 is justified by the continuous sharpening of the point in the stanza, which climaxes in the idea that his Father's will called him to endure such vile treatment, and by the presence of "will" in 70, which makes it more likely that the compositor omitted the word in 71.

73. whose]   The Father's.

99-100. choyce ... releast]   The Son's choice (or will—see Matt. 26:42) was not about to be freed from obligation to the Father's command. See 109-14.

109-10. The holy ... unchaunging wisdome]   In GM, Ford refers to the necessity of death as being "commanded by an unchangeable decree from Heaven" (989).

130-32. speake ... wept]   Christ spoke in measure (moderately); and his words kept such measure (were so commensurate) with his grief, that his speech took the form of sighs accompanied by weeping.

141-43. as an *Artist's* ... Untrim'd]   Like an artist's masterpiece that is nevertheless considered barely worth looking at, his hair, unadorned, covers his head.

145-50. The stanza continues the theme of Christ's beauty altered by sorrow and follows that of the cited passage, Isa. 53:2 (and 3). The AV "there is no beauty that we should desire him" is rendered "there shalbe no forme ..." in the GB and "Ther is not shap" in Wycliffe's translation. Compare 145-46 to Giovanni's statement to Annabella: "The lily and the rose, most sweetly strange, / Upon your dimpled cheeks do strive for change" (*TP* 1.2.200-201); and "the ruins of a face" (148) to Penthea's description of Orgilus in *BH* 2.3.129-30: " 'A looked not like the ruins of his youth, / But like the ruins of those ruins."

167. whereto [they] say]   The preceding word, *Gethsemane*, may well have been pronounced Gĕth´-sĕ-mān. The emendation would accordingly support metre as well as sense.

209-10. though death ... flesh]   Although death has already pillaged my physical body.

257. His voyce un-fee'd, spoke]   No paid mouthpiece, he spoke; *or*, unremunerated, he spoke.

271-76. Compare the *Bestiary*, 132-33: "PELICANUS the Pelican ... is excessively devoted to its children. But when these have been born and begin to grow up, they flap their parents in the face with their wings, and the parents, striking back, kill them. Three days afterward the mother pierces her breast, opens her side, and lays herself across her young, pouring out her blood over the dead bodies. This brings them to life again.

"In the same way, Our Lord Jesus Christ, who is the originator and maker of all created things, begets us and calls us into being out of nothing. We, on the contrary, strike him in the face....

"That was why he ascended into the height of the cross, and, his side having been pierced, there came from it blood and water for our salvation and eternal life."

277-82. This description of the Phoenix and its application to Christ are traditional. See for example *Bestiary*, 125-26: "FENIX the Bird of Arabia ... builds itself a funeral pyre, ... and on this, turning its body toward the rays of the sun and flapping its wings, it sets fire to itself of its own accord until it burns itself up. Then verily, on the ninth day afterward, it rises from its own ashes!

"Now Our Lord Jesus Christ exhibits the character of this bird, who says: 'I have the power to lay down my life and to take it up again' ... and who offered himself on the altar of the cross to suffer for us and on the third day rise again."

Compare also Robert Southwell's poem entitled "Christs bloody sweat," stanza two:

> He Pelicans, he Phenix fate doth prove,
> Whom flames consume, whom streames enforce to die,
> How burneth bloud, how bleedeth burning love?
> Can one in flame and streame both bathe and frie?
> How could he joine a Phenix fiery paines
> In fainting Pelicans still bleeding vaines?

See Introduction, above, 137, n. 7. See also *FM*, 722.

237. so ... accurst]   Accurst mortality is so prone to sin.

299. Graceing the gracelesse]   The implied subject is "he" (Christ), not "Princes."

302. gods]   That this, and not "God's," is the intended reading is clear from the marginal reference to Ps. 82:6: "Ye are gods, and ye all are children of the most High."

302-5. prophane ... royalty]   The object of the verb "prophane" (302) is "the law" (304).

313. *Moses* chayre]   The place of the one who transcribes the religious law (Moses being the reputed author of the Pentateuch).

317. *Levits* power]   The priestly authority (Levites being the priestly class—see Deut. 10:8-9).

319. Those whom ... inspir'd]   The prophets.

335-36. For those ... condemn'd]   The same thought and text (Matt. 7:1-2) underlie Shakespeare's *Meas.*

386-88. in extremityes ... garners]   In their extravagance retiring ... to their full garners; *or*, retiring, as they pretend, in great need and for the good of their health, to their full garners.

400-402. gayning ... repented]   Of usurers charging twenty per cent (who would not be satisfied with a thousand per cent), fewer than ten per cent repented.

414. [most]   deni'd] The emendation seems to be required by the sense and to be paleographically explicable.

416 marg. Eccle.7.28.]   This verse appears in the Authorized Version as Eccles. 7:26.

416-18. whereto ... Abus'd]   These things which God intended as blessings are abused and made into bonds of sin.

421-23. all in all ... comfort]   Everyone, of whatever kind or rank, derived comfort.

427-28. The tide ... ebb]   In GM, also in the context of a discussion of sin and death, Ford uses the expression "the high tide of acting unlawfull pleasures or abuses" (1231-32). Compare Q 2.2.1185-86: "the tyde / Of thy luxurious blood is at the full."

433-50. These three stanzas properly form a single sentence, an extended double simile: "even as a man ... ; Or as some *Christian* Marchant ... : So men, ..."

452-53. but he abates / His policy] But the Lord abates (literally, "beats down") the devil's strategem.

457. Captivitie, led Captive] This phrase occurs in Judg. 5:12, Ps. 68:18, and Eph. 4:8. The GB's marginal note on the latter verse reads in part: "The Messias came downe from heaven into the earth, to triumph over Satan, death and sinne, and led them as prisoners and sclaves, which before were conquerers, and kept all in subjection."

457-58. un-maske / The hideous visor] Compare GM: "To unmaske the vizour that hides the deformitie ... " (360-61).

465. such ... hath] For which there is no antidote.

469. All those ... layd open] Christ's dear bloody sweat has exposed (or brought under control) all those consumptions; *or*, Christ's ... sweat has revealed the true restoratives and cordials (namely, the nourishing elements of his flesh and his blood).

481. This did the *Leacher*] Here and in the following stanzas, the opening clause is hypothetical subjunctive: "If the lecher ... would but."

494. such gain is losse] Compare the Friar's advice to Giovanni in TP 1.1.63: "in such [lustful] games as those they lose that win." The surface paradox is reversed in GM 654: "there is much gaine in such a losse."

497. other] "Other" can function as either singular or plural.

502. *Shees*] Women. See Shakespeare's Sonnet 130: "I think my love as rare / As any she."

532. woe] Alternative spelling of "woo."

535. in secure content] In secure (or careless) contentment; *or*, in the contentment of your (false) security. See 1348 and n.

539. that un-hopefull state] The state of the unrepentant person after the Judgement (unhopeful because beyond hope).

600-602. Knight, ... fame:] A comma rather than a period is required after *Knight* because the sense continues into the next stanza, where the construction is completed.

605-6. By Christian combat ... lust] The emendation, involving the addition of but one comma and the altering of but one letter (u becomes n in "denoting", or "devouring"), corrects the *a fortiori* sense of the stanza: What an honor it is then if one sheds blood in Christ's service, and in his name levels in the dust the sins of the world that aspire (upwards), denoting (mere) lust (=pleasure generally, roughly appositive). A difficult line in a muddy stanza.

607-12. Compare GM, 1084-86. See also Milton, *Paradise Regained* 2.466-68: "he who reigns within himself, and rules / Passions, desires, and fears is more a king ...."

641-42. Then all ... free him] A typological statement: see 1 Cor. 15:22 and 45.

644. Achab ... Michaiah] See 1 Kings 22 and 2 Chron. 18.

651-52. when doubting ... Churches smart] These lines and the rest of the stanza rely heavily on the language of Ps. 80:1-5 and on the interpretation indicated by the GB, whose headnote to the chapter begins: "A lamentable praier to God to helpe the miseries of his Church."

656. *Esay*] Isaiah (here and throughout CBS).

659. be sweated so]   Produced with such labor.
694. mean]   The emendation is suggested by the biblical context (see Mark 10:17) and by the sense: It can denote "way" or, just as appropriately, "mediator."
706-7. the precious ... to life]   The precious smell *of* life, which also leads *to* life.
736. *miserere mei*]   "Have mercy upon me" (Ps. 50:1; Vulgate).
751-74. Compare the Friar's account of hell, recited to induce Annabella's repentance, in *TP* 3.6.8-23.
757. for]   Instead of (resting on).
770-71. lead ... brimstone]   Lead here functions as an ironic opposite of gold (with alchemical overtones). A "spruce" is probably a dandy.
808. Hungry, cold, naked, thirstie]   Echoes the language of Matt. 25:35-40.
817-22. The stanza echoes the language of Matt. 5:3-13.
829. *Dives*]   Traditional name for the rich man in Luke 16:19 ff. (from Vulgate).
850. heires of promise]   The phrase (but not the pun) is from Heb. 6:17.
887-88. That ... finisht]   The added comma clarifies the sense: Just as the bloody sweat before Christ's death mitigated the death of the soul, so the gush of blood and water completed the killing of death.
903-4. still ... chose]   Continually suppressed those whom Christ in mercy elected (that is, the Church).
906. How love ... lovers]   Compare GM, 1129-30.
915. Jesus did purchase]   Jesus purchased them.
925-28. The ever ... keepe]   His blood has rendered empty and vain the empty pit of the grave and the bottomless confusion of the abyss; and this action frees from dangers those whom dangers imprison daily.
934. so much his care mistakes]   His care is so in error; *or*, he is so mistaken in that about which he concerns himself.
949-54. Although this stanza plays on the traditional association of the sun with the Son, all personal pronouns in it refer to "a sinner" (931).
974. *Achab, Eserod*]   Ahab (see n. to 644, above) and Esar-haddon (see Ezra 4:2).
983-84. had she ... liv'd]   If she had seen Christ's bloody sweat revealed or prefigured (?) in the grief of Elijah his prophet, then she might have lived.
1025-26. Whiles ... sayes]   And if ... someone informs him ....
1056. That use ... begot]   Which disease the practice of sin nourishes, just as sin produced it in the first place.
1103. commend]   The emendation, suggested by G. D. Monsarrat, is supported by the sense (see Glossary).
1112-16. Here and in subsequent stanzas the change of speaker from angels to souls must be inferred from the alternating sentences.
1116. comes to woe him]   The tightness of the typed in line in 13 explains the shortened spellings.
1118. truth]   Troth, or faithfulness. These lines echo the teaching of James 2:20 that faith (1116) without works (1118) is dead.
1121. behave]   Older uses perhaps justify the sense of literally bearing or conducting oneself.
1126. those have overthrowne it]   Those sins have negated the effects of the bloody sweat for you.
1135-37. Never ... botled up]   See Ps. 56:8: "Thou hast ... put my teares into thy bottel." Compare Annabella's repentance in *TP* 5.1.1-42.

1157. grace] The emendation is supported by the logic of the stanza combined with the use of "grace" in 1156 and 1162.

1174. he lives still in extreame] He continuously lives at full tilt. There may be an echo of the Latin *in extremo*, "in mortal danger."

1187-88. Thus then ... intire] Thus wordly desire promises nothing other than to carry the living unto death, and then itself to die entirely unto life. Compare Annabella's repentance, her "leaving of that life / I long have died in" (TP 5.1.36-37). See also GM, 212-22.

1206. His justice ... prove] This (the turning of water to blood) proved his justice; that (the blood turned to water) proved his mercy. Logically, "this" and "that" ought to be reversed.

1207-10. By blood ... stiled] In the written (OT) law, offences were expiated by the shedding of blood. Offences must be atoned by means of blood and from blood. That process of redemption through the shedding of blood is now refashioned in the Gospel.

1213-18. A surety ... at least] One who for a friend acts as a surety—makes himself liable for the default of another—and who in this capacity is arrested ... and suffers hunger ... and the vicissitudes of inward griefs and outward pains, deserves at least thanks, if not a full reward, from that friend for whom he is penalized.

1217. asseast] Fined; see *OED* assess.

1221. his quarrell] The friend's quarrel.

1224. the tribute of his eyes] His friend's tears.

1237. furrow-crowned] This emendation, unlike Grosart's "sorow-drowned," saves "sorrowes" in 1238 from redundancy and accords with "stampe" in the same line, in that both furrows and stamps involve the etching or impressing of a pattern upon something, in this case the brow of Christ.

1241-42. In GM, Ford refers to ingratitude as "a sinne hatefull in all men, but in Kings, estates, or governours horrible" (694-95).

1246. sums] The emendation is required by rhyme and the sense (sums = quantities).

1264-66. troth ... plighted promise] The language echoes the form for the solemnization of matrimony: "thereto I plight thee my troth" (*Common Prayer*, 292).

1271. Faire daughter] This begins the speech spoken by "Old sin" to "simplicitie," which continues to 1308.

1275. Beauty ... priz'd] Beauty is prized only when fertile, or only when ripe for picking.

1292. standing ... text] Basing yourself upon some (biblical) text that warns against (worldly) pleasure.

1305-6. seeke not ... weare] Do not seek to commit or promise your best means of enjoyment (to God) until after they are worn out.

1330. Whose only surfeit] The very excess of which.

1348. Bee not secure] Do not be too sure. Security also carries the implication of spiritual carelessness. See Webster's *The Dutchess of Malfi* 5.2.372-73: "Securitie some men call the Suburbs of Hell, / Onely a dead wall betweene"; and Shakespeare, *Macbeth* 3.5.32-33: "security / Is mortals' chiefest enemy." See also CBS, 535, 1644, and 1897-98.

1364-65. Christes love ... confirm'd] Christ's love is willing, the sick soul wilful and avoiding its own spiritual restoration. "This" and "that" should logically be reversed.

1392. angry]   The emendation is supported by the sense of 1393: "be not mov'd" = "do not be angry." The angry God is Christ himself, now assuming his role as judge. In TP 2.5.9, Giovanni is warned by the Friar that "Heaven is angry."

1402. to his onlie blood]   To his blood which alone.

1411-16. In TP 2.5.64-69, the Friar implores Giovanni (as he does Annabella in 3.6.34) to think on God's mercy. Giovanni's response embodies the presumption and boldness of which Ford in this stanza speaks.

1453-58. The poor widow (Mark 12:41-44, Luke 21:1-4) is commended because she gave all she had. Here the repentant one has only the expression of his sorrow to give.

1465-82. These three stanzas employ parallels between the "machinery" of Roman Catholicism and the means, in Ford's Protestant view, of genuine repentance, which centers directly on the unmediated relationship between Christ and the repentant individual. The parallels thus give concreteness to Ford's picture of repentance and at the same time satirize the machinery: the cloister (1465), the rosary beads (1467), the candle (1469), the missal (1471), the incense (1472), the penance and confession (1473), the confessor (1475), the absolution (or shrift) given in exchange for a payment (1475-76), the altar (1477), the oblation (1478), the dispensation (1479), the holy water (1481), and the burnt offering (1482), this last more obviously Jewish than Roman Catholic in reference.

1489-94. This stanza reveals a common (especially Puritan) emphasis: "to make your calling and election sure" (2 Pet. 1:10; see the GB's marginal note).

1535. it]   The doom or judgment, which Christ saw in his descent into hell.

1565. *Was ever man as I am?*]   For *I am* as a name of God, see Exod. 3:14; as it is applied to Christ, see John 8:58.

1571-72. dye ... content]   The emendation renders these lines consistent with the rest of this and the preceding stanza, in that "lines" spoken by the heart and by the eyes are indicated by italics in place of quotation marks.

1587-88. As for ... committed]   He groaned for his own friends, just as he did for his enemies, and for the sins of both friends and enemies.

1603-4. Anti-christian throne ... crownes]   The identification of the pope as the Antichrist was a commonplace among English Protestants in the sixteenth and seventeenth centuries. Compare TP 5.6.147-50.

1605. To vassaile Princes rights]   To make vassals of the rights of kings.

1621-26. The reference is to the Jesuits.

1632. *Blinde ... blinde*]   Matt. 15:14; Luke 6:39.

1644. securitie]   See nn. to 1348 and 1897-98.

1651. No measure ... acquaint]   Not at all was his tormented soul acquainted....

1687-88. Yet ... to Hell]   See Introduction, 148. Compare the Friar's description of Giovanni as "sold to Hell" (TP 2.5.37).

1775 marg. Luk.12.23.]   The emendation of chap. 8 to 12 is conjectural. A reference to Luke 3:23 would be plausible if it were aligned with 1771.

1805-6. the wreath / Of life]   Emendation is required by the sense. "Wreath of life" may be a rendering of "crown of life" (James 1:12, Rev. 2:10.). Also possible is "breath of life" (Gen. 7:22.).

1807. sad Patron]   Steadfast founder and source.

1824. wash mee ... sin]   No emendation is necessary. See the text cited, Ps. 51:2: "Wash me throughly from mine iniquitie, and clense me from my sinne."

1826. inventive pleasure]   The adjective may refer to literary invention or more generally to contrived or counterfeit pleasure. See 31-34.
1847. The Plurisies of sin]   Compare Q: "raging plurisie of lust" (2.2.1187).
1849-51. For which ... write]   See 25-30.
1872. accept thy heart]   See 1158-59.
1897-98. be secure ... cares be eas'd]   This faithful security contrasts with the spiritually "careless" security of 535, 1348, and 1644. (Compare 1 Pet. 5:7.)

The Golden Meane

Title Page
8. *Northumberland*]   Henry Percy, ninth earl of Northumberland (1564-1632), known as the "Wizard Earl." He succeeded to the earldom on his father's death in 1585 and served in the Low Countries in 1585-86 and 1600 and against the Armada in 1588. In 1594 he married Dorothy Devereux, widow of Sir Thomas Perrott and sister to the second earl of Essex. In November 1605 he was sent to the Tower for complicity in the Gunpowder Plot. Tried in June 1606, he was sentenced to a fine of £30,000 and life imprisonment. In 1621 he was released to live in retirement until his death, 5 November 1632.

From his youth, the earl showed great interest in art and science, including astrology and alchemy, but "did not have any considerable interests in contemporary drama or literature" (G. R. Batho, *The Library* 5th series, 15 [1960]: 256). His studies and experiments continued in the Tower, where he had a large library and paid assistants. Van Dyck painted his portrait.

1638 Title Page
This page has no equivalent in the editions of 1613 and 1614, although the text in the central field reproduces the text of the 1614 title page with the addition of "late." A work of the prolific William Marshall, it shows Virtus, armed with spear and shield and triumphing over a prostrate Fortuna, shown with crown and coins to the left of this field. To the right, Ratio with a bridle (often an attribute of Temperance) and a rod of command stands over the satyr-like (pointed ears) figure of Violentia holding a club; in G. Wither, *A Collection of Emblems* (1635, p. 169), the golden mean is also represented by a female figure holding a bridle. Above, the hand of God stretches from a cloud holding the crown (reward). On the left is a palm-tree, oppressed by a slab of stone; it illustrates the oppression of virtue by fortune: "Dum premitur erigitur." See Tilley, P.37: "The straighter (higher) grows the Palm the heavier the weight it bears"; see also S. C. Chew, *The Pilgrimage of Life* (New Haven & London, 1962), 117-18. This emblem is also found in Wither (172) where the Latin tag is "Veritas premitur non opprimitur." The emblem on the right is more difficult to interpret. "Ratio ut fulmen" probably because they are both of divine origin. But the tree seems to withstand the thunderbolt unscathed; this suggests that it is a laurel or bay tree (see Pliny, 2.55 and 15.30) which, like Ratio, is immune to the Violentia of the thunderbolt; H. Hawkins, *Partheneia Sacra* (1633, p. 14) speaks of "the *Lawrel* of *Constancie*." If this is correct, the thunderbolt is the emblem both of the divine origin of reason and of the violence which reason overcomes.

Epistle Dedicatory

1-2. TO THE onely best worthie]   As the epistle dedicatory is repeated from the first edition, in which Northumberland is not named, there is no open reference to him.

3. Accidents]   As distinguished from substance.

8. personated in moderation]   Ford's meaning seems closer to the late Latin *personare* (bear the character) than the usual meanings of the word in the early seventeenth century (see OED, 5, 6).

9-11. Bee ... are]   See LL, 710-11.

11. maske]   To hide one's real form or character under an outward show; here used in reference to Ford's publishing his tract anonymously (see above, 6-7: "I may one day open my selfe").

15. *Benè vixit, qui benè latuit*]   See Ovid, *Tristia* 3.4.25: "Crede mihi, bene qui latuit bene vixit" ("Let me tell thee, he who hides well his life, lives well"), and Erasmus, *Adagia* 2.10.50 ("Late vivens").

17. *Honestè ... publico*]   "He who has not submitted to public evil is nobly wise."

Text

4-5. MEN ... dangers]   See Job 14:1: "Man that is borne of woman, is of short continuance [AV: "of few days"], and ful of trouble." Verse 2 adds that "he vanisheth also as a shadow"; and in the next few lines, Ford compares man's glory to his shadow.

5-11. whose ... pitty]   Imitates and expands Seneca, *Ep.* 79.13; see also Tilley, P.541.

17-18. See below, 98-101 and 1019-21.

21. outward actions]   See *PW* 2.2.32: "Than what his outward actions did present."

23-24. doth ... lives]   Adapted from Seneca, *Ep.* 78.6.

27-28. but ... happinesse]   See Tilley, M.1010, and below, 293 ff.

29. so aunciently commended]   By Aristotle, *Nicomachean Ethics* 2.6; Horace, *Odes* 2.10; etc.

32-40. Imitates and expands Seneca, *De providentia* 2.1.

42. nothing ... selfe]   See Seneca, *Ep.* 24.12.

50. and]   The reading "&" is suggested by a manuscript correction in 1614D. "Both ... & ... " is found again at 52. "Both ... or ... " is possible only after "a negative or word implying exclusion" (OED). See also LM 1.1.109 (where Dyce emends "or" to "and").

67. complement]   Probably here "that which goes to 'complete' the character of a gentleman in regard to external appearance or demeanour" (Onions).

70-72. The servile weakenesse ... desert]   Aristotle, *Politics* 3.13.3. For a standard Renaissance treatment, see Mulcaster, *Positions* (1581), 200.

73-74. distasteth ... ease]   See below, 161-633.

75-77. they ... calamitie]   See Seneca, *De tranquillitate animi* 11.6.

83-84. measuring ... them]   See Lipsius, *Of Constancie* (1594), 2.26.

84. not ... examples]   See HT, 159-60.

85. *Isocacius*]   Isocasius (usually so spelt), a native of Cilicia, was a philosopher and quaestor at Antioch; he was accused of being a pagan in 467. The emperor ordered him tried before Pusaeus (Posaeus), pretorian prefect of the East and his former colleague. His "wonderfull noblenesse and constancy" led to his release and baptism. Ford's text is a literal translation of a passage in the *Chronicon Paschale* or *Chronicon Alexandrinum* (Latin translation by M. Raderus, Munich, 1615; see 745, 747),

and in the chronographies of Theophanes and Malalas. The Greek text is found in Joseph Scaliger's *Thesaurus temporum* (Lyons, 1606). Ford's (probably) Latin source has not been traced.

91. unimited] Not in OED; changed to "unimitated" in 1638. The change seems unnecessary as many verbs had two parallel forms, one with the suffix -ate and another without it, in seventeenth-century English (e.g., "facilite" and "facilitate"). However, the meaning itself is not very satisfactory and "unimited" may be a misprint for "unlimited." Though "unlimited" is not applied to a person in any of the OED examples, it is so used by Anthony Stafford: "Unlimited Luther, thou verities chiefe champion" (*Staffords Niobe: or His Age of Teares* [1611], 139).

92-93. plotter ... actor] See LL, Reader 4, and text, 90-91.

101-2. the greatest temporall ... opinion] That is, riches, honor, and political power; the triad recurs regularly in the next few pages; see 104-10, 116-19, 157-58, 201-3, 218.

104-15. As what riches are ... himselfe] Freely translated from Seneca, *De tranquillitate animi* 11.9-10.

116-19. In ... extinguisht] Condensed from *De tranquillitate animi*, 11.10-12, where Seneca gives the examples of Pompey, Ptolemy, and Sejanus. The Pompey mentioned by Seneca was Sextus Pompeius, consul in AD 14; Ford probably confuses him with Gnaeus Pompeius, later called Magnus (106-48 BC), whom he mentions below (501, 1023). The Ptolemy here became king in AD 23. In AD 40 he was summoned to Rome where Caligula had him imprisoned and executed.

120. *Woolsey*] Thomas Wolsey fell in October 1529 because of his failure to obtain the annulment of Henry VIII's first marriage; he died in November of the following year. Shakespeare/Fletcher's H8 was new on the London stage (early 1613) when GM was published.

121-22. ROBERT, Earle of ESSEX] Robert Devereux, second earl of Essex (b. 1567), beheaded 25 February 1601. That Essex was "propt up in honours" is clear from his early rise and titles: General of the Horse and Knight of the Garter at twenty-one, later Earl of Marshal of England, lieutenant and governor general of Ireland. Envy is given as the cause of Essex's fall in FM, 348, and LL, 550. Essex was the brother of the countess of Devonshire, to whom FM is dedicated; his sister Dorothy was the wife of Ford's patron, Northumberland.

130. shrinke ... afflictions] See LL, 341-43 and n.

131-32. stand ... light] See Tilley, L.276.

134-36. This story about Diogenes and Alexander III of Macedon is well known, but in none of the more obvious classical sources nor in Erasmus's *Apophthegms* does Diogenes make the point that Alexander is depriving Diogenes of something he cannot give him. Ford's direct source is probably Lyly's *Campaspe* (1584), 2.2.136-39: "*Alex.* If *Alexander* have any thing that may pleasure *Diogenes*, let me know, and take it. *Diog.* Then take not from me, that you cannot give me, the light of the world" (Lyly, 2:332).

140. enjoy] Used catachrestically with object denoting something *not* pleasurable.

141-42. if ... doth] See Erasmus, *Adagia* 2.8.81; also Tilley, T.301, P.529, and Smith, 121, 234. Compare PW 3.4.79-80: "how misery / Is destitute of friends."

142. doth,] As a comma could close a parenthesis its use here (instead of a round bracket) may be intentional. See 442 and LL, 670.

161-63. he ... will] Close to Seneca, *Ad Marciam* 5.5.

165. uncomforting]   The only OED quotation for "uncomforting" (*ppl. a.*) is dated 1798; "uncomforted" (OED, 1583-1835) is found in LL, Ep. Ded., 19.
167. the . . . Wisedome]   Compare LS 1.1.296: "the nobleness of your wisedome."
168-72. It . . . felicitie]   Translated from Seneca, *Ad Marciam* 5.5. See Erasmus, *Adagia* 4.4.96; Tilley, S.174; Smith, 262.
172-73. Fortune . . . resolution]   From *Ad Marciam* 5.6.
173-74. and such . . . Maste]   Translated from *Ad Marciam* 6.3. Ford's change from "clavus" (rudder) to "Maste" somewhat weakens the simile; he may have been remembering Marina's father who, "clasping to the mast, endur'd a sea / That almost burst the deck" (*Per* 4.1.57-58).
178. winke]   Here probably "to close one's eyes" or perhaps "to shrink or wince."
180. tasting]   See "in tasting any fortune" (*PW* 3.2.177). "lasting" (1614*BDE*) is probably a misprint; but see OED, 3c(b): "to sustain, hold out under or against."
182. conquer by bearing]   See below, 1050-53, where this idea is explicitly developed in relation to the golden mean; also 1173-74.
187-90. to put . . . out of his vaine bias]   To put out, disconcert, confuse (OED, B4). See *LS* 2.1.779-80.
201-2. endowments]   Riches, possessions. See also the nn. 101-2 and 806-7.
207-8. paying . . . death]   Tilley, D.168 ("To pay one's debt to nature") and G.237 ("I owe God a death"). Ford usually speaks of a debt to *nature*; see *BH* 5.2.91; *LS* 1.1.254-55; *Q* 1.1.323-24, 2.2.1182-84, 5.1.3288-90.
212-22. If hee looks . . . death]   See *CBS*, 1183-88.
213-14. it . . . death]   A commonplace; Ford translates from Seneca, *Ad Polybium* 11.2. See below, 269-70; *WE* 4.2.31-32; *BH* 2.3.146-48.
220. Empyrie]   "Empyre" (1613) and "Empyrie" (1614; OED s.v. "empery") are two different words, though their meanings are very close. Ford uses "empery" (MS: "Emperie") in *FM*, 161.
223-25. This saying is attributed to both Anaxagoras and Xenophon. Ford gives no name because Seneca, whom he is here translating, gives none (*Ad Polybium* 11.2).
226-27. whosoever . . . earth]   Adapted from *Ad Polybium* 11.3; see also *Ep.* 99.8.
229-30. to . . . life]   Expands *Ad Polybium* 11.3.
231-34. The . . . for]   Translated from *Ad Polybium* 11.3, except for the expression "keepe measure," which is Ford's own.
232. measure]   The golden mean; see Tilley, M.804.
236-43. All men . . . nature]   Translated, sometimes loosely, from *Ad Polybium* 11.4.
243-44. Hee . . . death]   See Tilley, L.391.
247-61. In this imitation of Seneca, *Ad Marciam* 17.2-5, Ford has substituted Constantinople for Syracuse and replaced the tyrant Dionysius with the Turkish emperor.
266. both fortunes]   "Utraque fortuna" is found in Seneca, *Ep.* 71.37. Ford uses this expression again at 1327; *LL*, 335 and *Corollarie*, 8; *PW* 2.1.23). It is also found in Cornwallis (*Essayes* [1600], ed. D. C. Allen, 8) and in Holland's translation of Plutarch's *Morals* (510). See the iconological tradition of Fortuna Bifrons.
287. a sure . . . die]   See *PW* 5.3.214: "Perkin, we are informed, is armed to die."
290-91. Heere . . . considerations]   See below, 395-97 n.
307. that mischievous flatteries]   For "that" followed by a plural noun (OED, B II 1c), see also *CBS*, 425. For "this" followed by a plural noun (OED, B II 1f), see below, 917; *BH* 5.2.109 (emended to "his" by Spencer); *LM* 4.2.1 (emended to "these" by Weber, Dyce, and Hill).

THE GOLDEN MEANE 407

321. pittie]   At 341-44 Ford says "good men" should "allow any burthen ... to worke miracles (above the capacitie of the vulgar) upon themselves." But here (315-21) Ford stresses that "worthie personages" who have both blood and merit should remain constant (see 329) and neither be "blowne up with the simplicitie of pride" nor "become the miracles of pittie." Constancy preserves them from pity, not piety. Ford often connects "discent" (320) with pity; see 163-65 and 502. Though the expression "miracles of pietie" (14) is more satisfactory than "miracles of pittie" (13), it seems to be a compositorial error. Confusion between the two words was frequent and produced changes in successive editions of the same text (for example, see Lyly 2:18 and 207).

323. preserve]   See 379-80 and LL, 34.

327. the [paths] that leade]   The "path" that "leads" to a desirable station or condition is a frequent metaphor in Ford; see below 576 and 1071; LL, 381; CBS, Reader, 12-13, and text, 1411; PW, 3.2.145.

330. narrownesse]   Difficulty, the opposite of "ease" at 329. This meaning is not given in the OED, but the "narrow" way (Matt.7:14) is the difficult way. See also 341: "straite inconveniences."

350-355. The remainder of this paragraph contains several short passages translated from Seneca, Ep. 23.9-11. At 23.11, Ford's text was "Quidam vivere [Loeb: vero] tunc incipiunt, cum desinendum est" (Opera, ed. C. S. Curio, Basle, 1573).

354. the race of so living]   /   See above, 221: "the full race of their living."

356-57. Most ... carried]   Adapted from Seneca, Ep. 23.8.

360-61. To ... vilenesse]   See HT, 557-58; and CBS, 457-58.

366. numberles in number]   For the combination of "numberless" and "number" see OED, 1b.

368. deprivation]   Though "deprauation" (1613) makes good sense, 1614 is supported by "depriuation of judgement" (620-21).

369-70. for ... reason]   See LL, 278-80 and n.

372. infirmity]   "Firmitie" (1613) is probably a mistake; OED gives this as an aphetic form of "infirmity" but the only quotation is dated 1426. "Infirmity" is used repeatedly in GM and LL.

375-76. which ... place]   Same imagery below, 762-63 and in LL, Corollarie, 5.

379-81. It ... still]   Ford is pointing out the Aristotelian principle of virtue as "habitus."

381. an]   The text is corrupt. 14 "That to see an Noble man" was corrected to "a Noble" in 38, but the corruption may be due to loss of text between "an" and "Noble." Ford always uses "a Noble."

386. Scævola]   Legendary Roman hero who attempted to assassinate Lars Porsena, then besieging Rome. Captured and threatened with torture, he showed his indifference to physical pain by thrusting his right hand into the fire and holding it there until it was consumed. The story is related by Livy (2.12) and was often given as an example of Stoic fortitude.

389. persevers in his sufferances]   See LL, 31 and n. Here, however, "sufferances" is used as a synonym for "sufferings." See also PW 5.1.4.

395-97. Even ... come]   For "building" imagery, see 93-101, 155-57, 290-92, 403-5, and 1028-29; see also LL, 53-57, where the imagery is associated with the Line of Life.

401-2. interaccidents]   Not in OED; perhaps coined under the influence of *accidere* and *intercedere*, both of which mean "to happen"; see also n. at 433-34 below.

403-5. So ... resolution]   Ford is continuing the metaphor introduced in 155-57 above.
408. present]   Affair in hand, question under consideration. The word was almost synonymous with "purpose"; "from the purpose" and "from the present" (Shakespeare, *Ant* 2.6.30) both meant "beside the point."
420. In example]   The only *OED* quotation is dated 1568.
431-32. *Disfavour ... Death*]   These were considered "things indifferent" by the Stoics (see Seneca, *Ep.* 82.10, 14, etc.).
433-34. subserted]   Listed below. Not in *OED*; a coinage from *subsero, subsertus* ("to put or insert under").
436. *selfe-unworthynesse*]   One of Ford's favorite compounds; see below 491, 495, 504, 525; *LL*, Reader, 36; *BH* 1.1.6; *FCN* 2.1.597 (sig. C3ʳ). The only *OED* quotation is *BH*. Ford also uses "self-worthie" (*LL*, 525; not in *OED*) and "selfe-worthinesse" (below, 605; only *OED* quotation dated 1639).
442. reputeth,]   See Commentary at 142.
448. some person]   Should perhaps be "such a person."
458-59. since ... miserie]   But see above, 4-5.
472. pillars]   See *LL*, 342.
479-80. that there [he] is free]   The 1614 text ("that there is free") puzzled the 1638 compositor, who printed "that free." Another possible emendation, "that he is free," is suggested by a manuscript correction in 1614D.
485-88. These lines are probably Ford's own words, and not a quotation; "blemish" and "steddinesse" are both frequent in Ford. Compare "time cannot wrong mee" with *FM*, 321-22.
495. despection]   The change from "dispertion" (1613) to "despertion" (1614) and finally to "desperation" (1638) shows that the compositors were puzzled. Despite the identical -pertion endings (homoioteleuton) of "despertion" and "aspertion," "dispertion" ("scattering," with reference to nations, in all *OED* examples earlier than 1664) does not give a satisfactory meaning. The 1613 compositor may have read "r" instead of "c" as the two letters are similar in secretary hand; see textual note at 922. "Despection" means "despising," synonymous with "Contempt" (500).
498-99. *Monopolies*]   James I's practice of granting these lucrative patents was a source of continuing discontent and scandal. See *LL*, 496-98.
501. *Pompeys* minde]   Pompey the Great; see n. at 116-19.
503. a foolish Flye in the candle]   Tilley, F.394.
512-15. For ... minde]   See *LL*, 163-69 and *FCN* 2.2.732-38; Seneca, *Ep.* 66.2-3.
516. not ... Histories]   See *LL*, 308-9.
518. Earle of SALISBURIE]   Robert Cecil (b. 1563), first earl of Salisbury, principal minister of James I, died in May 1612. How "uneven" his shape was is disputed. The descriptions given by friends of Essex ("wry neck," "crooked back," "splay foot") are exaggerated, but he did suffer from a curvature of the spine and was very short, not much above five feet. Elizabeth called him her "little elf," and James referred to him as a "pygmy" and as his "little beagle." Bacon's essay "Of Deformity" (1612) may be a portrait of his cousin and rival.
520. *Æsope*]   No ancient account of Aesop makes him ugly or deformed. The first reference to his ugliness seems to be a thirteenth-century manuscript Life, prefixed to the collection of fables made by the monk Maximus Planudes in the fourteenth century. Thereafter his deformity is frequently referred to.

521-23. Socrates ... workmanship] Probably from Cicero, *Tusc. Disp.* 4.37.80.
535. Agent, Patient] The speaker and the reformed thief. These terms from scholastic philosophy seem rather odd in this context. See *LL*, *Corollarie*, 59 and n. for a similar use of "patient."
539. Non ... facimus] "We call our own neither the things we did not do ourselves, nor those we do not do ourselves." The "olde Verse" is Ovid, *Metamorphoses* 13.140-41.
543. Marcus Aurelius] Ford's reference to the "disorders" of the youth of Marcus Aurelius probably comes from Guevara's *The Golden Booke of Marcus Aurelius Emperour*: "When I kept the Cantons, I jetted in the streetes, I sang balades, I gased to the wyndowes, I played on instruments, I scaled the walles, I wakened light persons: thinkest thou that I wist what I did in my youth?" (1573 ed., sig. L16^{r-v}). This is not true of the historical Marcus.
544. Nero] "The first five yeares of his Empire, he was so finely handled by *Seneca*, seconded with *Burrus*, that the affaires of peace and warre prospered, every man having great hope of *Nero*, who shewed himselfe lowly, and given to vertue" (Plutarch et al., *Lives*, "Seneca," [by S. Goulart], trans. North, ed. 1603, 2nd part, 105). Ford uses the phrase "Quinquennium Neronis" in a marginal note below (645); it comes from Sextus Aurelius Victor, *De Caesaribus* 5.2.
564. his owne little world] For man as a microcosm, see below, 1300 and *LL*, 135, 291-92.
570-71. that ... Envie] See below, 594-95 and *LL*, 425-26; proverbial (Tilley, E.171, E.171a, E.175).
571. Envie ... Courtier] See *LL*, 589.
582. nobly generous] 1613 and 1638 both read "nobly and generous," which must have been the reading of the uncorrected state of the outer forme of sheet D in the copy of 1614 from which 1638 was set up. In the surviving copies of 1614 the spacing of the type in this line ("generous, and a base-") indicates that "and," the first word of the line in 1613, was taken out when the forme was corrected.
583-85. Whereby ... envious] For envy as a testimony to one's merit, see *Dicta Catonis* 3.28 (*Minor Latin Poets*, 624).
593. It ... pittied] See Tilley, E.177.
615. RICHARD the second] Many sixteenth-century writers describe and comment on Richard's tyranny. Ford knew Richard through Shakespeare's play (see below nn. at 935-37, 996, and 1001-4).
616. NERO] Probably a reference to Seneca's disgrace. See 544, 646, and nn.
616. DIONISIUS] Probably Dionysius the Younger, tyrant of Syracuse, whom Seneca calls "Dionysius illic tyrannus" in *Ad Marciam* 17.5; for Ford's previous imitation of this passage, see above n. at 247-61.
626. the moveable sandes ... favour] Proverbial: see Tilley, C.722, C.726 and *ODEP*, 480.
627-28. a broken vessell] See *LL*, 523.
630. distraction] The reading of all three editions ("detraction") may be correct; the word is used again at 924. An early manuscript correction in 1614D changes it to "destruction," but Ford probably wrote "distraction," repeating the same idea in different words. "Distraction" is used at least thirteen times in the plays. "Folly" and "distraction" are associated in *LM* 3.2.196: "I'll court mine own distraction, dote on folly." For wilfulness associated with distraction, see *CBS*, 1359; *BH*, 2.2.47; *PW*, 5.3.158.

637. good Clarkes]   E.g., Erasmus in *The Praise of Folly*.
646 margin. *Quinquennium Neronis*] Seneca was clearly "neerest in favor" and "in greatest danger," as he was forced to kill himself. See note at 544, above.
655–84. These three paragraphs, added in 1614, reflect a current preoccupation with James's favorites.
664–65. *onely ... made so*]   Probably not a quotation.
667. smother]   This spelling was becoming obsolete, but was still used at the end of the sixteenth century; the 1598 quarto of *1H6* (1.1.66) prints "smothe" (Folio: "smooth"). A double *o* is the usual spelling in Ford's early texts, but as "smother" occurs in a line where the type is generously spaced it may preserve Ford's own spelling.
670–71. were ... governed]   Ford seems to be confusing two idioms, "were better" and "had rather"; but the meaning is clear: "had ... rather be governed."
671. curse]   See Tilley, W.600.
674–75. compact]   A compacted body, structure; "compact" in the sense of "a covenant" is also suggested by the context.
677–78. *Sweet ... sweetenesse*]   If a quotation, not traced.
679. sinewes ... joyntes]   As the sinews (tendons) knit together the bones of the body, so do content and security act as tendons of the good man's life.
693. discerning]   "Discern" and "decern" were not clearly distinguished before the sixteenth century; "decern" was still used with the meaning "discern" or "distinguish" in the seventeenth century (see *OED* s.v "decern" II). *13* and *14* both have "discerning" at 326 and "decerning" at 704.
705–13. For parallel words and ideas, see *BH* 4.2.18–29.
708–9. eate ... labours]   "By," or a similar word, is needed. "Clothe" means "to be clothed."
718. *Amittere carnes, captare umbras*]   This refers to the story of the dog that dropped a piece of meat in order to catch its reflection in the water (*Phaedri fabulae Æsopiae* 1.4: "Canis per fluvium carnem ferens"). See Erasmus, *Adagia* 3.2.98, and Tilley, S.951.
718–19. imbrace ... Centaures]   As Ford says in *BH* 4.1.69–71: "Ixion, aiming / To embrace Juno, bosomed but a cloud / And begat Centaurs." The story is told in N. Comes, *Mythologiae* 6.16. A possible source is the beginning of the lives of Agis and Cleomenes in Plutarch.
722. *a beast with many heads*]   This proverbial metaphor comes from Horace (*Ep.* 1.1.76); see Tilley, M.1029, M.1308, and *LL*, 839.
732. many time]   This form was becoming obsolete; the latest *OED* quotation being 1622. The five occurrences of "many times" in GM first appeared in *13*; the *14* compositor may have been more respectful of Ford's usage in leaving "time."
746. eminent]   According to the evidence in the *OED* it was more usual to use "eminent" as a spelling for "imminent" than the reverse, as in the 1613 and 1614 editions. The 1638 reading has been adopted because "eminence" and "eminent" are used at 101 and 1311.
757. Duke of NORTHUMBERLAND]   In 1551 John Dudley, earl of Warwick and ruler of England during the last years of Edward VI, took the title of duke of Northumberland. Within two years Edward died, and the new duke, having tried and failed to put his daughter-in-law, Lady Jane Grey, on the throne, was forsaken by the lords of the council and executed for high treason by Mary. It is hard to find instances of

his "too much confidence ... in the hearts of the Cominaltie." His treatment by the populace after his fall was rather the result of his continuing unpopularity than of his fickleness.

762-63. A just man ... unmoved]   A common biblical figure, especially in the Psalms (for instance, 112:6-8), here combined with a simile from Ptolemaic astronomy.

767-68. fulnesse of substance]   Worldly wealth.

787-91. Abdolominus ... enjoy]   The story is found in Q. Curtius Rufus, *History of Alexander* 4.1.19-26. But, according to Curtius, Abdolonymus accepted the crown; this is also the version of the story found in Diodorus Siculus, Justin, Plutarch, and Painter (*The Palace of Pleasure*, vol. 1, [1566], 12th novel). Ford's version is found in Lodge, *Paradoxes Against Common Opinion*, 1602, p. 2 ("the good Abdolominus").

795. *The furniture ... himselfe*]   Cicero, *De re publica* 6.24.6. The ODEP's first English citation is 1616 (533). See below, 1100, and *LL*, 145.

798-99. *Abundance ... Servant ... Master*]   See Tilley, M.1055, and Horace, *Ep.* 1.10.47; similar ideas are expressed below, 895ff., and *LL*, 703ff.

803. corruptible]   Compare 1 Pet. 1:18: "corruptible things, as silver and golde."

806-11. *Riches ... Fortune*]   For "bona fortunae" and the tripartite division of gifts, see Aristotle, *Nicomachean Ethics* 1.8 (1098b), and Seneca, *De beneficiis* 5.13.1.

806-7. uncertaine endowments]   See above, 201-2 and n.

820-21. the wise man ... went]   The idea is ascribed by Diogenes Laertius to both Bias (1.88) and Stilpo (2.115). The succinct formulation, "Omnia mea porto mecum," is attributed to Simonides by Phaedrus (*Fabulae* 4.23), to Stilpo by Seneca (*De constantia sapientis* 5.6; *Ep.* 9.18-19), but usually to Bias (Cicero, *Paradoxa* 1.8; Valerius Maximus 7.2.3; Erasmus, quoted in Tilley, M.207; Lipsius, *Of Constancie* 2.8). As Bias was one of the Seven Sages of Greece, he may well be Ford's "wise man of GREECE."

822. *Wisedome, Temperance, Valour, Justice*]   The four cardinal virtues of classical moral philosophy; see, for instance, Cicero, *De officiis* 1.5.15.

833-36. If ... covetousnesse]   Perhaps adapted from Seneca, *Ad Helviam* 10.2. Ford adds "comelinesse."

837. *covet ... poore*]   A commonplace: see Tilley, L.346 and M.1273; Cicero, *Paradoxa* 6; Horace, *Ep.* 1.2.56 and *Odes* 3.16.42-43; Seneca, *Ep.* 2.6; Claudian, *In Rufinum* 1.200.

842-45. *Bountie ... dead*]   Bounty makes the common people grateful, and they remember their benefactors even after their deaths. See Cicero, *De officiis* 2.15.55-17.60. The exact meaning of "strings up" is doubtful. Ford may mean "gives vigour" (OED 3a and 3b, but the first quotation for "strings up" is dated 1845) or "ties up" (see 5, and s.v. "tie," 5d: to bind by favor or service rendered).

845. The emendation ("Such as" instead of "Such") is suggested by an early manuscript correction in 1614D.

846. The emendation ("burie" instead of "burne") is suggested by an early manuscript correction in 1614D.

852. O]   Colin Norman emends to "on," but the exclamation ("ô" in 1613) is supported by the repeated use of "O" (also "ôh" and "oh") in *CBS*, especially at 210 and 1385.

875-76. *Povertie ... imbrace it*]   Epicurus, *Epicurea*: "Honesta res est laeta paupertas" (ed. H. Usener, Leipzig [1887], 303).

876-77. to be content]   See Tilley, C.624.
883-84. care ... care]   Ford plays on two meanings of the word, "charge" and "anxiety." See Horace, Odes 3.16.17.
891-92. plenty ... scarcitie]   Perhaps from Cicero, De officiis 1.8.25.
893-94. considering ... opinion]   Considering how unimportant such a loss is except in opinion. This is the Stoic idea that "it is not the things themselves that disturb men, but their judgements ["opinionibus" in Wolfius's translation] about these things" (Epictetus, Encheiridion 5).
895. It ... much]   The golden mean in relation to wealth.
896. abundance]   Wealth (OED, 3). See 798.
903. God-head]   The distinction "GOD ... God-head" seems to be stylistic rather than theological.
913-17. It ... cured]   Perhaps from Seneca, De tranquillitate animi 2.14-15; but the idea was a commonplace. See Horace (Odes 2.16.19-20; Ep. 1.11.27 and 14.13), Seneca (Ep. 28.1-3; 104.17-20), and Tilley, P.374. See also below, 1140-44 and especially BH 1.1.117-18 and LM 1.1.49-54.
917-21. another ... stickes]   Ford borrows from Stradling's translation of Lipsius, Of Constancie 1.2, who quotes Vergil, Aeneid 4.70-73. Ford uses the same image in CBS, 631-32. For the relationship between the two Ford texts, Lipsius, and Ps. 42, see G. D. Monsarrat, "John Ford's Authorship of Christes Bloodie Sweat," English Language Notes 9 (1971): 23-24.
917. this latter times]   See above, n. at 307.
922. Act]   See above, n. at 495.
930-31. all ... home]   A commonplace; see Tilley, M.426 and Smith, 332. Smith quotes Ovid, Fasti 1.493, and Seneca, Ad Helviam 9.7. See also Lyly, Euphues 1:314.
932. men ... valiant]   See Cicero, Tusc. Disp. 3.7.15.
935-37. The ... places]   Tilley, S.985: "The sun shines upon all alike." In most examples (e.g., Seneca Ep. 47.10, Erasmus Similia, Opera Omnia, p. 607F,) the point is that the sun shines on both rich and poor, or on both good and wicked, whereas Ford is speaking not of different people but of different regions. This is the point made by Bolingbroke in R2 1.3.144-47; see also 1.3.275.
938-39. That ... well]   The saying goes back at least to Aristophanes, Plutus, 1151, and is quoted by Cicero, Tusc. Disp. 5.37.108. See Tilley, M.468, Seneca's De remediis fortuitorum (1547 English translation, sig. B1ᵛ), Erasmus, Adagia 2.2.93, and Kyd, Soliman and Perseda 4.2.7.
942. word]   "Word" not "world" is the correct reading; see below, 976, 1088-89, and Q 5.2.3802-5: "or if you think / The word of banishment too hard to utter." Ford's immediate source is probably Cicero, Tusc. Disp. 5.37.107.
950-51. If a quotation, not traced.
953-59. The distinctions are difficult to appreciate. Ford first distinguishes a class of "voluntary exiles" motivated by "greedy hope of gaine," but then calls them "fugitives and runnagates"; with "exiles" he now classes "travailers." His examples further the confusion. None of the mythical heroes fits the description of greedy motivation and inglorious end. But Ford may be following Christian re-evaluation of classical legend, e.g., St. Augustine, City of God, esp. book 3, for a negative opinion of Romulus and other heroes.
954. voluntary exiles]   See BH 1.1.77, and LM 1.3.14-15.

955. *Romulus*]   The generally-received form of the story of Rome's legendary founder is set out in Livy, 1.3-16 and in Plutarch's *Lives*. Rather than coming to an inglorious end, Romulus, after a successful career, became the god Quirinus.

955. *Aeneas*]   The fall of Troy made Aeneas of necessity a fugitive, but hardly a "voluntary exile," and his wanderings and eventual settlement at Lavinium were held to be according to divine plan. His apotheosis is described in Ovid, *Metamorphoses* 14.581 ff., and is predicted in *Aeneid* 1.258 ff. and 12.794 ff.

956. *Antenor*]   Because he had counselled the return of Helen (*Iliad* 7.347 ff.) Antenor was spared by the Greeks at the fall of Troy. Ford refers to one tradition of his later history, whereby he travelled to the head of the Adriatic and there founded Patavium, the modern Padua (*Aeneid* 1.242-49). Seneca mentions him among other men who left their countries (*Ad Helviam* 7.6). See also Livy 1.1.1-3.

957. *Brute*]   According to Geoffrey of Monmouth, Brut, the grandson of Aeneas, founded New Troy (London). The legend had been rejected by Polydore Vergil but was accepted by Holinshed (*Chronicles*, 1587 ed., vol. 1, part 2, p. 7) and frequently repeated (for example, *Gorboduc* 1.2.270, 3.1.1-10; *The Faerie Queene* 2.10.9-13). Despite the fact that Brut killed his father by accident, he is generally drawn by the chronicle writers as a hero and wise ruler.

960-68. Ford's memory failed him here; he should have written "Sparta," not "Athens." For this action of Lycurgus, see Plutarch, *Lives*, 63-64.

971. for rarities sake]   For the sake of seeing and experiencing rare and unusual things.

972. in complement]   See n. at 67.

990. a severe imposition of man]   Here Ford returns to the idea of banishment as the result of a judicial sentence.

996. THOMAS MOWBRAY]   1366?-1399. Mowbray's death and Richard's motives in banishing him remain disputed. They are rehearsed in Shakespeare, *R2* 1.1-3, whose sources favored the Lancastrians. Ford's eulogy is based on *R2* 4.1.92-100.

999-1000. upon an appeale of Treason]   This phrase is perhaps indebted to Shakespeare's "to appeal each other of high treason" (*R2* 1.1.27). Compare also Ford's "As if we were a mockery-king in state" (*PW* 1.1.4) with "O that I were a mockery king of snow" (*R2* 4.1.260).

1001-4. Mowbray's going on crusade is mentioned in *R2* but, it seems, in no other version of the story. It is doubtful that Mowbray ever fought in the Holy Land. He left England on 19 October 1398 and by February of 1399 had arrived in Venice, where on 18 February he requested of the senate the loan of a galley to take him to Palestine. It is hardly probable that in the few remaining months of his life he could have gone on a crusade, fought, and returned. He died, perhaps of the plague, in Venice on 22 September 1399.

1009. *Henry of Richmond*]   The exaggerated contrast between Richmond and Richard III was put forward by the English chroniclers of the sixteenth century. Ford portrays Henry sympathetically in *PW*, and the epithets applied to Richard in *GM* ("that monster," "that cruell usurper") are echoed by Daubeney's "Richard the tyrant, their unnatural uncle ... the black usurper" (*PW* 1.1.31-35).

1011. banished]   It seems necessary to supply a past participle; for its position and the punctuation, see above, 1000.

1012. such ... Princes]   As the claimant of the defeated Lancastrians, Henry was taken to the Continent for safety in 1471. He remained there, chiefly in Brittany, until his landing at Milford Haven in August 1485.

1017. banishment]   Henry was never ordered to leave England, as was Mowbray. The Yorkist government made repeated efforts to have him returned to England.

1018-21. it is ... misery]   One of the themes of Stoicism (see Seneca, *Ep*. 78.13).

1023. *Pompey* for greatnesse]   For Pompey, whose "banishment" was his final flight from the victorious Caesar, see above n. at 116-19.

1024. *Affricanus*]   Scipio Africanus Major. In the last years of his life the conqueror of Hannibal was charged with keeping back money from the Roman state. He therefore left Rome and retired to Liternum. In North's Plutarch (1173) this is referred to as a "voluntarie banishment." In addition to Plutarch's *Lives*, see Livy, 38.52-56; Seneca, *De Brevitate Vitae* 17.6, and *Ep*. 86.1-3.

1024. *Hannybal*]   Seven years after his defeat at Zama, Hannibal left Carthage and fled to the court of Antiochus III of Syria, when the Romans demanded his surrender. He fled later to Crete and finally sought refuge with Prusias, king of Bithynia. When it appeared certain that Prusias would hand him over to his enemies, he committed suicide. See Livy, 39.51; Cornelius Nepos, *Vita Hannibalis* 7-13.

1024. *Ovid*]   He was banished by Augustus in AD 8, perhaps because of a relationship with the younger Julia, granddaughter of Augustus. Ovid's own guarded explanation was that he had seen too much (*Tristia* 2.102-6). The question is important only because of Ford's concern with guilt or innocence in his definition of misery. Grouping Ovid with victims of fortune (Pompey and Hannibal) and of popular ingratitude (Africanus), Ford seems to have accepted Ovid's explanation.

1026. impatiencie]   Both texts have "impatiencie" at 52-53; *14*'s "impatience" may be a compositor's sophistication.

1032-33. the worlds Citizen]   Diogenes the Cynic (Diogenes Laertius, 6.63) and Socrates (Cicero, *Tusc. Disp.* 5.37.108) both claimed to be citizens of the world.

1034. marg. Of *Imprisonment*]   Imprisonment is one of the "Sixe Miseries that may befall a Noble man" (431-33). Ford devotes a section to each of these "miseries" and there is a marginal title for each section except for imprisonment, which was omitted.

1041-44. *Dædalus*]   The legendary artist and inventor was credited with devising not only the famous wings but the labyrinth in Crete, Pasiphaë's cow, and Ariadne's thread. Minos imprisoned Daedalus because he had helped Pasiphaë, because he wanted to keep the clever inventor for himself, and to prevent the secret of his labyrinth from being revealed.

1042. fayne]   Feign, represent in fiction; the "ancient Poets" include Ovid (see *Metamorphoses* 8.183ff.; *The Art of Love* 2.21-96).

1045-53. The idea that Icarus betokens "the incapacitie of mens bodies" is probably Ford's own interpretation; this is why he writes "may betoken." The usual interpretation of the myth is that man should keep to the middle way and "that everye man should not meddle with things above his compasse" (Th. Wilson, *The Arte of Rhetorique* [1553], fol. 104^v). See Golding's trans. of Ovid's *Metamorphoses* (1567), "The Epistle," sig. a3^v; N. Comes, *Mythologiae* 7.16; F. Bacon, *De sapientia veterum* (1609), "XXVII. Scylla et Icarus, sive via media"; and the quotation from H. Crosse given in the next note.

1051. *Medio tutissimum iter*]   Adapted from Ovid, *Metamorphoses* 2.137: "medio tutissimus ibis." See H. Crosse, *Vertues Common-wealth* (1603), sig. F3^v: "If *Ycoras* had held his *medium tutissimum*, he had not so untimely fallen."

1052. *superat ferendo*] Adapted from Vergil, *Aeneid* 5.710: "quidquid erit, superanda omnis fortuna ferendo est" ("whatever befall, all fortune is to be o'ercome by bearing"). The idea had become proverbial (Tilley, E.136; Smith, 119).

1052-53. triumphs ... minde] See *PW* 5.2.127-28: "Noble thoughts / Meet freedom in captivity."

1077-78. Men ... alone] Ford combines here the two parts of Scipio's saying, as reported by Cicero, *De officiis* 3.1.1: "numquam se minus otiosum esse, quam cum otiosus, nec minus solum, quam cum solus esset" ("he was never less idle than when he had nothing to do and never less lonely than when he was alone"). Quoted by Lipsius in *De Constantia* 2.3, this saying had become proverbial (Tilley, A.228). See *HT*, 614-15.

1084-86. Hee ... conquerour] Prov. 16:32: "He that is slowe unto angre, is better then the mightie man: and he that ruleth his owne minde, is better then he that winneth a citie." Compare Horace, *Odes* 2.2.9-12; Ovid, *Heroides*, Eleg. 3.85, and Seneca, *Ep.* 113.30. See also *CBS*, 607-12.

1101. varietie of bookes] Northumberland had a large library in the Tower; see n. at title page, l. 8.

1107-13. *Massinissa*] There is no record of Masinissa being made captive by Scipio, though he fought against the Romans in Spain (212-206 BC) before changing sides. Scipio did capture Masinissa's nephew, but returned him to his uncle laden with gifts.

1123-24. for he ... discretion] See Tilley, A.42 ("Adversity makes men wise"), and *ODEP*, 4.

1125-28. Hee ... person] For the many variations of the saying that adversity tests friends, see Tilley, F.693-94 and Smith, 2. The Latin, "Amicus certus in re incerta cernitur" (Cicero, *De amicitia* 17.64), is also found in many sixteenth-century writers, for example in Erasmus's *Adagia* 4.5.5. See also Tilley, P.611, and Smith, 244.

1128-30. The saying ... *friendship*] From Seneca, *Ep.* 6.3. The saying is found in Baldwin-Palfreyman, *A Treatise of Morall Philosophie*, ed. 1600, fol. 82^r, and in *Politeuphuia. Wits Commonwealth*, ed. 1608?, 118; it was a favorite with Ford (see the epistles dedicatory of *LS* and *LT*, and *CBS*, 906). See also Aristotle's dictum in *Eudemian Ethics* 7.12 (1245b), rephrased in *Nicomachean Ethics* 9.10.6. Not in Tilley and Smith.

1131-39. it ... miserable] See "A Paradoxe in praise of imprisonment; maintaining, that it is more healthful & profitable to be in Prison, then at libertie" (Th. Milles, *The Treasurie of Auncient and Moderne Times* [1613], 1:612).

1166-67. it is ... misery] For the idea of death as comforter, see, for example, Plutarch (quoting Aeschylus), "Consolation to Apollonius": "How wrongfully have men death in disdaine, / Of many evils the remedie soveraigne" (*Morals*, tr. Holland [1603], 515).

1184. The ... *Death*] See Smith, 53.

1186-95. Probably Socrates, in Plato's *Apology*, 29a-b: "For to fear death, gentlemen, is nothing else than to think one is wise when one is not; for it is thinking one knows what one does not know. For no one knows whether death be not even the greatest of all blessings to man, but they fear it as if they knew that it is the greatest of evils. And is not this the most reprehensible form of ignorance, that of thinking one knows what one does not know?" Quoted by Plutarch in his "Consolation to Apollonius" (*Morals*, 518). Ford calls Socrates "a good man" in *LL*, 744.

1190. a resolution to the doubt]   Perhaps this should read "a resolution of the doubt."

1204. for ever a dying]   See CBS, 745-56; BH 4.3.153; TP 3.6.15.

1207-10. Sleep and Death are the son and daughter of Erebus and Nox; Sleep is therefore Death's brother, and not Death's sister. See N. Comes, *Mythologiae* 3.13 ("De Morte") and 14 ("De Somno"). The "old Poets" referred to are Homer (*Iliad* 14.231 and 16.672, 682) and Vergil (*Aeneid* 6.278). Plutarch, "Consolation to Apollonius" (*Morals*, 517) quotes Homer. See also Tilley, S.526.

1218-36. Plutarch's opinion is the opposite of Ford's: "And verily, I beleeve that nature seeing the uncertainty and shortnesse of our life, would that the end thereof and the prefixed houre of death should be hidden from us, for that shee knew it good & expedient for us so to be; for if it had bene fore-knowen of us, some (no doubt) would have languished and fallen away before, with griefe and sorrow; dead they would have bene before their death came" ("Consolation to Apollonius," *Morals*, 516).

1220-21. the houre of *death* ... is uncertaine]   See Tilley, N.311. For the expression "the houre of death," see *LL*, 72 and n.

1229. dying time]   See TP 5.5.17, "dying time" (Q uncorr.) and "dyning time" (Q corr.)

1237. *Death* is a happie Haven]   See *LL*, 14 and n.

1238. a safe Inne]   See Florio, *Firste Fruites* (1578), fol. 98ʳ: "Death at last is the Inne where our lyfe doth take up his lodgyng." See *LL*, 12-15 and nn.

1239-40. a path to blessednesse]   See *LL*, 60-61: "the *via lactea* of immortalitie."

1243-47. The story of the priestess of Argos and her sons Cleobis and Biton is found in Cicero (*Tusc. Disp.* 1.47.113-14), Plutarch (*Lives*, "Solon" [ed. 1595], 103); Painter (*The Palace of Pleasure* [1566], vol. 1, "Croesus and Solon"); the pseudoplatonic *Axiochus* (367 c-d); and others. In all the sources the prayer is addressed to Juno. Ford's wording is reminiscent of Holland's version in the "Consolation to Apollonius": "she ... praied unto the goddesse, that she would vouchsafe to give them the best gift that could befall to man: and they the same night following, being gone to bedde for to sleepe, never rose againe" (Plutarch, *Morals*, 518).

1252-54. for ... finish it]   In this passage (from the first edition and subsequently repeated) Ford not only contradicts the definition of misery added in the second edition (see 410 ff.), but removes any possibility of misery in human life.

1257. make]   Plural because of the proximity of "extreames."

1258-77. The two additional miseries briefly alluded to would affect courtiers rather than the common man.

1269. before]   See above, 536-40, and n. at 539.

1274. temper himselfe]   Control himself.

1276-77. neyther ... reference]   Nor are they in any way considered suitable (fitting) for inclusion in this work. For this archaic sense of "answerable," see OED, 2b, which gives no example of "answerable" followed by an infinitive.

1293. purchasing dignitie]   The buying of titles during the reign of James I was the source of much discontent.

1300. a little *Common-wealth*]   See above, 564 and n.

1327. both fortunes]   See above, n. at 266.

A Line of Life

Reader

1-3. WISE, and therein NOBLE] That LL builds upon and is a continuation of GM is clear from these words. The concluding section of the latter (1289-1329) develops the connection between wisdom and nobility, ending with the confirmation that one is "perfectly Noble because wise."

4-6. Ambition ... confined.] These lines should perhaps be paraphrased as follows: "As [an author's] ambition is sooner manifested by his works (*"acting"*) than by his thoughts (*"plotting"*), he can seldom describe (*"personate,"* OED, 5) the conduct (*"practise,"* see OED, 1b) [of particular individuals] in his writings (*"studie,"*) lest (*"unlesse,"* OED, 4a) the arts which in themselves are free (*"liberall,"* OED, 1) should be subjected to over-zealous (*"curiously,"* see OED, 1 and 2) criticism and unduly (*"inquisitively,"*) restricted." And Ford points out immediately after (13) that his short *"discourse"* does not show *"what any personally is, but what any personally may be."* (This note is partly indebted to Colin Norman's Ph. D. thesis.)

7. conceited] Contrasted with *"serious"* (8), and meaning "fanciful," "imaginative"; perhaps also "witty, amusing."

9-13. Generall ... may be] Ford means that in what follows he is not referring to a specific individual, and that *"particular applications"* of this nature can be quite risky (*"and those so dangerous"*).

9-10. collections] Ford seems to use the word with the meaning "remarks," and speaks twice of "brief collections" (LL, 95 and 394).

11-12. it is ... industrie] See LS, Ep. Ded., 26-28: "it is more safe, more wise, to be *suspectedly silent*, then *modestly confident* of opinion, herein."

17. Custome ... Nature] See Tilley, C.932; Erasmus (*Adagia* 4.9.25) says nothing is more common than this proverb.

18. foyle] Anything that serves by contrast to set off another thing to advantage, often deceptively. See TP 2.2.30-31: "and shall I / Be now a foil to thy unsated change?"

30. ayme ... levelled] See HT Reader, 7-8 and 760-61; FM Reader, 13-14; BH, "The Epilogue," 10-12; LM Ep. Ded., 9-11.

31-32. none ... impropriation] No one can claim any right herein, unless through illegal appropriation.

36. selfe-unworthinesse] See n. at GM, 436.

39. taliarie Law] This is the only OED quotation for "taliary"; more common forms are "talion law" or simply "talion."

40. requisitely] Necessarily; antedates OED (1656).

41-43. The ... mine] A claim to the authorship of GM.

46. thriftie] Respectable, proper, decent; postdates OED 2a (1596) and 2b (c.1449).

47. good ... great] An echo of GM, where "good" and "great" are said to stand in the relationship of "wise" and "noble" (1285-88).

50-51. Æstatis ... Hyems] If a quotation, not traced. "A temperate winter was never grieved by the end of summer." This probably refers to the seasons of man's life; see CBS, 1346; LL, 46-52; LS 1.2.614.

Epistle Dedicatory

2. Sir James Haye] Hay (c. 1580-1636) was one of James's Scottish favorites: he

was created Lord Hay in 1606, baron of Sawley in 1615, Viscount Doncaster in July 1618, and earl of Carlisle in September 1622.

8-9. though ... you]   See *FM*, Ep. Ded., 06: "being a meere straunger alltogether unknowne unto you" (20-21).

26. *John de la Ford*]   Ford's name never appears in print as "de la Ford." The only other instance of this form of his name is found in an 1858 catalogue of Thomas Kerslake, the nineteenth-century Bristol bookseller; this catalogue is mentioned by Joseph Hunter in his *Chorus vatum anglicanorum*, vol. 3, fol. 328ʳ. The complete entry of the catalogue reads: "3250. The Golden Meane, enlarged by the first Author, as it was formerly written to the Earle of Northumberland, by John de la Ford, 2nd edition, Jeff Chorlton, 1614, 12mo original binding, 9s. This book seems to be totally unrecorded by the Bibliographers." Unfortunately Kerslake's shop was destroyed by fire in 1860 and this copy of GM does not seem to have survived. "John de la Ford" was probably a manuscript addition to the title. If Ford died in Devon, one of his books might easily have found its way to Bristol, and Kerslake may have had Ford's own copy.

Text

3. To ... well]   Proverbial (Tilley, L.378; Smith, 182; Seneca, *Ep.* 70.4). See also below, 654-55.

8-9. when ... all]   The everlasting death of damnation, "A death which both the soule and body kils" (*CBS*, 1017). See also *CBS*, 1183.

11. dye to live]   See Matt. 16:25; John 5:24, 11:25-26.

12-13. being ... bodie]   Seneca says the body is an inn (*Ep.* 120.14), and Cicero compares life itself to an inn (*De senectute* 23.84). The image is used for death in GM, 1238.

12. Ghest]   A seventeenth-century spelling of "guest," which Ford has chosen because of the pun on "ghost," for which the *OED* only gives it as an eighteenth-century spelling.

14. a Haven of safetie]   See Cicero (*Tusc. Disp.* 1.49.118 and 5.40.117; *De senectute* 19.71), Seneca (*Ep.* 70.3). See also GM, 1237, and LM 5.1.8.

14. a finishing of Pilgrimages]   Proverbial: see Erasmus, *Adagia* 4.10.74, and Tilley, L.249. It is found in the Senecan *De remediis fortuitorum* and in Plutarch's "Consolation to Apollonius" (*Morals*, tr. Holland, 517 and 528).

18-25. as he ... graves]   The comparison of life to a sea voyage dates at least to Palladas (Epigram 65, *Greek Anthology*, book 10). Ford borrowed the simile from J. Lipsius, *De constantia* 1.20, and seems to have used Sir John Stradling's 1594 translation: "As it is lawfull for me to walke up and downe in a shippe and to runne about the hatches or seates, but this stirring of mine cannot hinder the sailing of the ship: So in this fatall vessell wherein we all sayle, let our willes wrangle and wrest as they list, they shal not turne her out of her course, nor anie thing hinder the same" (53).

20. is alwaies]   When revising his manuscript, Ford probably deleted "notwithstanding" (20) as it had just been used at 16.

26. victory of our ends]   "Death is swalowed up into victorie" (1 Cor. 15:54).

27-28. *Action ... Vertue*]   Cicero, *De officiis* 1.6.19. For the Aristotelian definition of happiness as activity in conformity with virtue, see *Nicomachean Ethics* (1.7.1098a). Ford is probably indebted to James's *Basilikon Doron* which has the marginal references "Ar. 1. Eth. Cic. in Of." opposite the quotation "Virtutis ... consistit" (1603 ed., 61).

28. *perseverance*]   Cicero's definition of *perseverantia* was generally accepted by medieval and later writers (*De inventione* 2.54.164): "perseverantia est in ratione bene considerata stabilis et perpetua permansio" ("Perseverance is a firm and abiding persistence in a well-considered plan of action").

30–31. *Divinitie ... will confirme*]   Gregory, *Homiliarum in Evangelia libri* 2:35: "Radix omnium custosque virtutum patientia est" ("Patience is the source and guardian of all virtues").

31. *sufferance*]   Patient endurance (OED, 1). See Augustine, *De patientia*, 2, and Cicero, *De inventione* 2.54.163.

32–33. rich ... Earth]   Same metaphor in FM, Ep. Ded. of MS, 17–18; HT, 490–91.

34. not to continue]   Same idea in GM, 323 and 379–80.

36. sitteth]   Copy text has been retained, but "sits" is found in both texts at 383 and 563.

38–39. *It ... defect*]   To use one's reason improperly is as beast-like as to lack reason, the distinguishing mark of the "animal rationale." This is probably not a quotation; similar phrasing appears in GM, 712–13, and BH 4.2.18–28.

43–44. counterpawne]   Less usual than "counterpane"; OED gives Cotgrave (1611), this passage, and PW 3.2.118. The modern form of both is "counterpart," i.e., the opposite part of an indenture.

45. Poll Deed]   Deed poll; a legal document made by one party only, and thus with the parchment "polled" or cut even, as opposed to an indenture.

52. *Issue*]   Deeds to be remembered after a person is dead.

53–57. See n. at GM, 395–97.

56–57. LINE OF LIFE]   Ford takes his metaphors from construction, the thread Ariadne gave Theseus to guide him out of the Cretan labyrinth, and from palmistry. He is also punning on the meaning "rule, canon, precept" of life.

60. middle path]   The "via media" of the golden mean.

60–61. *via lactea*]   The milky way, figuratively and allusively as a way leading to heaven (OED, 2a, although the first example cited of this figurative use is 1649).

67–69. three ... line]   For these lines, see for instance John Indagine (Joannes ab Indagine), *Briefe Introductions, both naturall, pleasant, and delectable unto the arte of Chiromancy*, trans. Fabian Withers (London, 1598). This was first published in 1558 and had gone through at least five editions by 1633. Ford may have seen this book; his enumeration of the lines is identical, both in order and phrasing, with the titles of chap. 2, 3, and 4: "of the line of life, or of the heart" (sig. B7ʳ), "of the middle [1558 ed.: meane] naturall line" (sig. C4ᵛ), "of the Table line" (sig. D1ʳ).

72. houre]   Though the reading "power" gives a satisfactory sense with "Life," it is meaningless with "Death"; see also "the houre of *death*" (GM, 1220).

76. ignorance ... deluded]   For references to palmistry, see Carroll Camden, "Elizabethan Chiromancy," *Modern Language Notes* 62 (1947): 1–7.

80. lineaments ... Nature]   The lines of the hand.

89. wonder of imitation]   So that others have imitated their goodness.

90–91. plotter ... Act]   See above, Reader, 4, and GM, 92–93.

95. those]   Copy text has been retained although "these ... ensuing" is more natural and Reader 29 has "*these few lines that follow.*" The only other these/those

variant in *LL* is at 394 (again before "briefe Collections") where it is reversed ("these," 20; "those," MS).

95. collections] See above, Reader 9-10, and n.

101-3. State ... *expedition*] As Elyot says, "Tully affirmeth in hys boke of offices [1.22.76], armes without the doores be of lyttle importance, if counsayle bee not at home" (*The Governour* 3.28, 1565 ed., fol. 212^v).

106. consultation] The end is to be established and the action controlled by right reason.

107. of] The addition of "of" and the deletion of "the" in MS seem to be part of the same revision.

111. travaile] Both to labor or toil (*OED*, 2) and to journey or travel (*OED*, 5).

115. an] 20 twice has "such an one" where MS has "such a one" (115, 653), which they both have at 118, 122, 281, and 682. For the other a/an variant, see 799.

121. as] The 20 reading has been retained because the good man "may not unfitly bee stiled a PRIVATE STATES-MAN" (697).

126-27. A *deserved* ... vertue] Tilley, V.70.

135. *little world*] See GM, 564 and n.

142. sinke ... burthen] See below, 341-43 and n.

144. corrupted] The omission of this word in MS is perhaps a slip, but Ford may have deleted it as superfluous.

145. A *mans* ... *himselfe*] See n. at GM, 795; also Tilley, M.405.

147-48. *the temperature* ... *body*] A commonplace of Renaissance psychology; see Tilley, D.381; P. de La Primaudaye, *The French Academie* (1594), vol. 2, chap. 39, 230-31; H. Romei, *The Courtiers Academie* (1598), 233; P. Charron, *Of Wisdome* (1607?), 48; R. Nixon, *The Dignitie of Man* (1612), 54; R. Burton, *The Anatomy of Melancholy* (1621), 1.2.5. Ford repeats the dictum in TP 2.5.14 ff. and HT, 415-17, and both in the latter work and LL he attributes it to Aristotle, though it seems, in fact, to come from Galen, "Animi mores corporis temperaturas sequuntur" (*Galeni omnia quae extant opera in Latinum sermonem conversa*, 5th ed., Venice [1576]), 1, fols. 317^r-21^v), where he attributes the doctrine to Aristotle.

155-69. Socrates ... delight] See Diogenes Laertius, 2.33, and Erasmus, *Apophthegmes*, tr. N. Udall (1542), fol. 19^v; also n. at GM, 521-23.

157. usefully] Earliest *OED* quotation 1634, Massinger.

163-69. See GM, 512-15 and n.

180-81 marg. *Homo homini lupus*] From Plautus, *Asinaria* 495, quoted by Erasmus, *Adagia* 1.1.70; see Tilley, M.245.

180. of necessitie] The MS reading ("of a necessitie") has been rejected because "of necessity" is used at 137 and 363 (also GM, 232, 247, 629); "of a necessity" is not in the *OED*.

181. proverbially, *a Devill*] See Lodge, *Wits Miserie* (1596), sig. B1^r: "the old Proverbe ... that *Homo est homini daemon*, Man unto man is a devill"; see also Tilley, M.247.

182 marg. *Velleius Paterc.*] See his *Historia Romana* 2.48.3, which Ford paraphrases.

185. rushen] Made of rushes and therefore impermanent and unsuitable as the setting of a diamond. The simile is the "Art without *vertue*" (191).

189. *Catoes Orator*] Ford here quotes M. Fabius Quintilian's *Institutio oratoria* 12.1.1.

191-94. Art ... stomack]   This sentence was revised ("beeing" and "in their substance" added in MS). The first revision has been adopted but not the second, because this part of the revised text is faulty: "they have pretty cullours to please the eye; but poysonous in their substance to be ... " (MS). Perhaps Ford (intended to) put "but are poysonous."

192. *Cantharides*]   "As for the Cantharides or French greene flies, they be bred of little wormes in Fig-trees, Peare-trees, wild pines or Pitch-trees, the Eglantine brier, and Roses: A venomous vermine this is, howbeit, medicinable in some sort. The wings be they that are good in Physicke: cast them away, and the rest deadly" (Pliny, *The Historie of the World*, tr. Ph. Holland [1601], vol. 1, 11.35, p. 330).

195. rotten post]   The closest in Tilley is P.492: "As good trust to a rotten post"; but see the following note.

195. paint a Sepulcher]   From Christ's invective against the hypocrisy of the pharisees (Matt. 23:27). In several of the examples in Tilley, S.225, the whited sepulchers are said to enclose "rotten bones."

196-97. Many ... well]   See Tilley, D.333, S.119, S.121, W.802.

202. a grave Author]   Not identified. J. Bodin says that "the very Atheists themselves ... are of accord, That there is nothing which doth more uphold and maintaine the estates and Commonweals than religion" (*The Six Bookes of a Commonweale* [1606], 536I). Hooker denounces the "politic use of religion" (*Laws* 5.2.3-4). Machiavelli considered that a prince ought to seem devout.

212. in his particular]   For his part, as far as he is concerned. See below, 763 and Corollarie, 59.

213. guiltie and conscious]   "Guiltie" and "conscious" may have much the same meaning, but "guilty" probably means "bound to the performance of."

214-215. We were not borne to ... sloath]   In Aristotle "softnesse" is one of the vices opposed to perseverance (*Nicomachean Ethics* 7.7). Compare the wording with WE 5.3.73-78.

216. make merchandize]   To traffic, usually in a bad sense.

220-21. we were ... our selves]   Ford's fondness for figures of repetition and antithesis obscures his meaning, which depends entirely on the contrast between "to" and "for." This contrast is not supported by contemporary usage, as is shown by the following example: "As we are not borne of our selves, so we are not borne to or for our selves alone" (J. Racster, *The True Art of Living Well* [1605], 71). Ford himself uses "to live to" where "to live for" would be possible; see TP 2.1.27 and 3.6.38, and LS 1.2.429. Ford's first statement ("we were not borne to live for our selves") echoes the proverbial "nemo sibi nascitur" (Erasmus, *Adagia* 4.6.81); see Tilley, B.141, and Smith, 18. His meaning is therefore: "we were not born to live selfishly for our own pleasure" (see 214-20). Ford's second statement ("we were ... borne to live ... to our selves") contradicts Rom. 14:7: "For none of us liveth to him self ... " Richard Sibbes preached five sermons on Rom. 14:7-8 (*The Christians End*, 1639) and he explains (10-12, 18-21) three different ways in which we should not "live to ourselves." The expression could be used to signify the mere selfishness of a villain (see *A Merry Knack to Know a Knave*, pub. 1594, in Dodsley, 6.519), or isolation, or the self-sufficiency of the wise man in contexts of classical philosophy (see T. Nashe, *The Unfortunate Traveller* 2:237; the anonymous *Remedies Against Discontentment* [1596], sigs. E6^v-E7^r; Montaigne, tr. J. Florio [1603], 1:38; ed. Everyman, 1:256). This last sense may be the one intended by Ford, but he may mean that we are born to fulfil our moral duty towards ourselves (see 176-77).

221-22. we were ... our selves]   Ford's first statement ("we were not ... borne to dye to our selves") parallels Rom. 14:7-8: " ... nether doeth anie dye to him self. For whether we live, we live unto the Lord: or whether we dye, we dye unto the Lord ... " Sibbes (43) comments: "To die to the Lord, is to be willing to give up our selves to him, ... with confidence that he wil receive our soules." This explains Ford's second statement ("we were ... borne to dye ... for our selves"), which means that we die for our own benefit as we are immortal; as he says in GM, 1214-15, death is "the quickening to a better life."

225. laughter]   Prov. 14:13: "Even in laughing the heart is sorowful."

225. imitate]   This has authority as it is in both 20 and MS. It meant "endeavor" and was followed by a to-infinitive (OED, 1d). The emendation suggested by Gifford-Dyce is unnecessary, and "intimate" cannot be followed by a to-infinitive.

226. minoritie]   Ford plays here and in the next line ("childish") on two obsolete meanings of the word: (1) the condition of being inferior; and (2) the state of being minor or under age.

228. meere man]   See below, 338 and 744.

229. erected]   Noble; see Q 5.2.3352 ("an erected heart").

240-41. not more ... then]   Not only ... but also.

254. A Golden Axiome]   Not traced.

255-56. to pry, nay looke after]   Here "to pry" (i.e., look at closely) is either used transitively (OED, 3), or intransitively with "after." The OED gives no instance of "to pry after," but this is found in Lyly: "I began to prye after theyr manners, natures, and lyves, ... " (Lyly, 2:198). For Ford's use of "nay," see 90, 482, and PW 1.1.98.

260. sucke]   This seems more expressive than "seeke," the MS reading. "Suck" is frequently used by Ford; see FM, 559.

266. the olde Greeke Proverbe]   See Erasmus (Adagia 1.5.40, "Unus vir, nullus vir"), who begins by giving the Greek version; see Tilley, M.353.

270. mist]   As clouding or obscuring mental vision.

278-80. Let ... deceived]   If a quotation, not traced. See Erasmus, Adagia 2.4.29; Tilley, M.335; and Smith, 333; same idea in GM, 369-70.

292. Epaminondas]   Ford expands from Plutarch's "Regum et Imperatorum Apophthegmata" (Moralia, 192E).

300. Phocion]   There is a section on Phocion, the Athenian general, in the "Regum et Imperatorum Apophthegmata." Plutarch reports that he refused presents from Alexander and Antipater (Moralia 188C and F) and that he disliked everything the multitude did and said (187F); perhaps echoed by Ford at 295-96. (In both 1620 and the MS the marginal reference to Cicero is placed slightly too high, opposite Phocion).

300-301. Brutus]   The Brutus referred to in Cicero, De legibus 3.9.20 is Decimus Junius Brutus Callaicus, consul in 138 BC, a leader of the Optimates against the Populares; but the Brutus referred to in Juvenal, Satires 14.41-43, is Marcus Junius Brutus, the tyrannicide.

304-7. Ford translates Ep. 97.10. P. Clodius Pulcher, a corrupt politician, was one of Cicero's enemies. Seneca's reference is to Cato Uticensis, but Ford appears to be confusing him with Cato the Censor ("a Censurer of himselfe").

306 margin. *Epist.* 98.]   Ford used an Erasmian edition (or one of those derived from Erasmus, such as C. S. Curio's) in which epistle 48 was divided into two epistles (48 and 49); all subsequent numbers were thus altered. Epistle 98 in Erasmian editions corresponds to 97 in Lipsius or the modern Loeb and Budé editions.

314. JOHN ... HARRINGTON]   John, second Baron Harrington of Exton, was born at Combe Abbey near Coventry in 1592. He was educated at Sidney Sussex College, Cambridge, and became the favorite companion of Henry, prince of Wales. He was much praised by his contemporaries; according to Sir James Whitelock, "he was the most compleat yong gentleman of his age that this kingdom coulde afford for religion, learning, and curteous behaviour" (*Liber Famelicus*, ed. J. Bruce. Camden Society, vol. 70 [1858] 39). A very religious person, he is among the Puritan "saints" included in Samuel Clarke's *The Marrow of Ecclesiastical Historie* (1650). Taken ill during a journey to France and Italy, he returned to England and died on 27 February, 1614 at the home of his sister Lucy Russell, countess of Bedford. He left no heir to inherit his title (thus "last and yongest"). Among the memorial verses were John Donne's "Obsequies to the Lord Harrington."

322–23. a most religious learned divine]   Probably the Puritan minister Richard Stock (1569?–1626), who preached Harrington's funeral sermon (*The Churches Lamentation for the losse of the Godly: Delivered in a Sermon, at the funerals of that truly noble, and most hopefull young Gentleman, John Lord Harington, ... By Richard Stock, Pastor of Alhallowes-Breadstreet in London*, 1614). In his epistle "To the Christian Reader" Stock says that Harrington "was not so eminent in place as he was in grace, for his gifts and graces & power of religion were so excellent and rare, as I never yet knew in any, whom I had occasion to speake of " (sig. a7ʳ). As there are no close parallels between Stock and Ford, Ford might be referring to Abraham Jackson (1589–1646?). Jackson, who became chaplain to the lords Harrington of Exton after 1611, dedicated to Harrington's mother and to his sister Lucy his *Sorrowes Lenitive. Written Upon occasion of the Death of that hopefull and Noble young Gentleman, John Lord Harrington* (1614). As Jackson was the son of a Devonshire clergyman, this may explain an acquaintance with Ford.

332. SIR WALTIR RAULEIGH]   The recent execution of Ralegh (29 october 1618) as well as the "miseries" of his last years were still fresh in men's minds at the time Ford wrote. Ford here weighs with some perception the often contradictory qualities of his character. Ralegh's fellow prisoner in the Tower, Northumberland, describes him well: "I must needs affirm Ralegh's ever allowance of your right, and although I know him insolent, extremely heated, a man that desires to seem to be able to sway all men's courses, a man that out of himself, when your time shall come, will never be able to do you much good or harm, yet must I needs confess what I know, that there is excellent good parts of nature in him ..." (Letters to King James, *Calendar of Salisbury Manuscripts at Hatfield* 14:265).

335. in both fortunes]   See n. at GM, 266.

339–40. *Politique*, and yet in *Policie*]   Both words can be taken in a good or bad sense. The antithesis is best retained by paraphrasing "apt in political manoeuvring, but inconstant in the ends for which he manoeuvred."

340. foile]   Cause of failure (OED, 3, although first citation given is *ante* 1683); also metaphorically from foil, a throw in wrestling (OED, 1).

341–43. *For what ... burthen*]   Ford is expanding Horace, *Odes* 3.4.65. See above, 142, and GM, 472.

346-49. There are many witnesses to Ralegh's courage in the face of death during his last days; see contemporary accounts reproduced in N. L. Williams's *Sir Walter Raleigh* (London, 1962), 254 ff. His courage is "late enough" because he had on previous occasions been willing to beg for his life with less than "resolution."

350-51. that ... dutie]   See above, 114-115.

356-60. *the only felicitie ... recoverie*]   Slightly expanded from Seneca *Ep.* 123.10 (*Opera Omnia* [Basle, 1573], 221; epistle 124 in this edition derived from Erasmus): "Una felicitas est bonae vitae, facere omnia libere, frui patrimonio." The Loeb Library text is different. The omission of "to live, this is" in *20* is probably a compositor's slip due to the repetition of "this is," but Ford seems to have revised his text ("and with" instead of "by" at 357).

358. for ... man.]   *20*'s italic is emended to roman because Ford's parenthesis does not indicate clearly that these words are not part of the quotation.

368-71. Ford is probably thinking of such men as Robert Carr, earl of Somerset, Lord Chamberlain in 1614 but tried and found guilty of the murder of Sir Thomas Overbury in 1616, or Somerset's father-in-law, the earl of Suffolk, appointed Lord Treasurer in 1614 but dismissed in 1618 and found guilty of embezzlement.

370. reproch]   See 526-29.

371. Minister]   The man in the "place of authority."

372-78. The marginal references rather overwhelm the single idea of this short paragraph, and it is very doubtful whether Ford had in mind specific passages from Plato, Aristotle, or Isocrates; he is here conflating two marginal notes in *Basilikon Doron*: "Pl. 6. de leg. Is. in pan. Ar. 5. pol." and "Plat. 7. de Rep. 3. & 12. de L. Arist. 5. & 6. Pol." (1603 ed. 64-65). See above, Introduction, 285.

381-82. direct ... Name]   See n. at *GM*, 327.

383. steering the Helme of State]   See *LM* 1.2.8: "steer the helm of government."

389. Phormio]   A Peripatetic invited to lecture before Hannibal during the latter's banishment at Ephesus. His choosing "a Lecture of Souldierie" was a traditional example of the futile attempts of the theoretician to instruct the man of practical experience. The story is found in Cicero, *De oratore* 2.18.75. Ford also refers to the incident in *HT*, 400-402.

391-92. laughed at]   Hannibal said that he had never seen one madder than Phormio (*De oratore* 2.18.75).

392. Seneca]   His *De clementia* is addressed to Nero. See n. at *GM*, 544.

392. Quintus]   Cicero's younger brother had an ungovernable temper; Marcus reproves Quintus for his anger in the first of his letters to him.

394. Collections]   See note at Reader, 9-10.

395. not to informe Knowledge in practice]   Not to give practical advice, "[not] to set downe ... positive rules" (388); "informe" means "shape," "fashion" (*OED*, 1a). See also *BH* 3.4.5, and *LM* 2.1.24.

412. head]   The Prince. See *GM*, 673 ff. and n. at 674-75.

416. names]   Both texts have "names" at 593.

418. poysoners]   A common figure of a flatterer; see Publilius Syrus, *Sententiae*, 251.

420. close deaths-men]   Hidden or secret executioners.

421-22. *Blandientes et Sævientes*]   Flatterers and fiends; the Latin terms are retained from medieval moral treatises (see below, 423: "a canvase and discussion in the schools").

423. canvase]   Canvass, examination of the "pros and cons."

425. envie] See GM, 570–71 and n.
428. driving] This has been preferred to "drawing" (MS) because flattery and envy are distinct ("consulting together though not dwelling together," 539–40) and therefore flattery, who is "Caterer to the others bloudie banquet" (540–41), drives rather than draws public men "into the snares of envie" (428–29; see also 606–7).
435–36. gravest ... Divines] Ford seems to have revised his manuscript but forgotten to cross out "divine," or not done so clearly.
437. *Non ... ipso*] Not traced as such in St. Augustine. Similar phrases in specifically Christian context occur in Sermon 109.3 (*Patrologia Latina* 38:637), and Sermon 82.2 (ibid., 507).
437. *vicinior*] In MS the reading seems to be "*vicimor*" and there is no dot, though this may have faded. At 304 "*Senica*" looks exactly like "*Semca*" with a dot above the last minim. See also n. at 739.
438–39. his frailtie to corrupt him] See CBS, 991–92.
439. besot] Affect with foolish blinding affection and thus make morally stupid.
439. adversarie] "Satan" means "adversary" in Hebrew; in Ps. 109:6 Geneva has "the adversarie" and AV has "Satan."
443. *latter*] This has been adopted because Ford contrasts "first" with "latter" at 150/52 and 418/419.
453. sodder] A dialectical variant of "solder" (used in LM 1.2.134), meaning "repair," "mend." In Marston, *Sophonisba* 2.1, the reading "sodderd up" (1606, sig. C1ᵛ) became "souldred up" in 1633 (sig. K8ᵛ).
462–63. *flattering Language ... silken halter*] According to Diogenes Laertius (6.51), Diogenes said that flattering words were a honey-sweet halter ("mellitus laqueus" in Th. Aldobrandino's Latin translation; "melleus laqueus" in Ambrogio Traversari's; "an hony brake, or a snare of honey" in Udall's translation of Erasmus's *Apophthegmes*, 1542, fol. 119ʳ). Ford is combining this with the proverb (Tilley, G.19): "To be hanged with a silken halter."
465. *Panders of Vice*] Cicero in *De amicitia* calls flattery the assistant of vice (24.89).
470. breath of the Panther] "It is said, that all four-footed beasts are wonderfully delighted and enticed by the smell of Panthers; but their hideous looke and crabbed countenance which they bewray so soone as they shew their heads, skareth them as much againe: and therefore their manner is, to hide their heads, and when they have trained other beasts within their reach by their sweet savour, they flie upon them and worrie them" (Pliny, *The Historie of the World*, tr. Ph. Holland [1601], vol.1, 8.17, p. 204; in modern editions of the *Naturalis Historia* the reference is 8.23). Lyly had already compared flatterers to "these Panthers, which have a sweete smell but a devouringe minde" (Lyly 1:282). Ford, however, is remarkably close to Pettie (*Pallace*, fol. 34ʳ, quoted by Bond, ibid., 336). Compare 473–75 and "allureth other beastes unto hym, and beyng within his reache, he ravenously devoureth them" (Pettie). See also LM 3.3.113.
481. the informed] Those they have informed. See n. at 395.
488. wooed ... won] For contemporary examples see Tilley, W.681, W.731, and W.408. See FCN 5.3.2653; FM, 168; HT, 494–6; LS 1.1.199; LT 3.1.1140; PW 1.2.60.
494. damnably] Both here and at 643 MS uses the adjectival form as an adverb ("dampnable," "profitable"), whereas 20 uses the normal adverbial form. The OED's only quotation for "profitable" (adv.) is dated 1654.

495. vipers]   A more likely reading than "vysars" (MS) as these flatterers are called "wilde beasts" (499). For "vipers," see BH 2.2.1, LS 3.3.1784, and PW 3.4.34. However, "vysars" is a very Fordian word, and he uses "visor/vizard" figuratively at least five times.

497-98. the graunt ... voyce]   Probably a reference to the Stuart practice of granting monopolies, which resulted in higher prices. See GM, 498-99 and n.

502. *Court-Ape*]   Court-fool, here in the sense of a favorite of no great ability, with the further idea that the favorite imitates his royal master, another form of flattery.

502-3. oppresse a desertfull hope]   Disappoint the hopes of a deserving person.

505. *golden calfe*]   A stupid or doltish rich man, like Bergetto, who is called a "golden calf" (TP 1.2.126).

505. Idoll]   Possibly because they hope to receive rich gifts.

516. olde subject of their insinuation]   The fallen favorite, with whom they formerly tried to ingratiate themselves. See also below, 605.

519. they]   The "subtill practizers of infamie."

519-20. inchanted glasses]   Here a burning glass rather than a mirror.

520. concealement]   Perhaps used in its legal sense: the intentional suppression of truth or fact known.

522. [of elder] times]   The OED gives no example of "elder times" (or "elder days") with a definite article, as in 20.

523. a leaking vessel]   Same image in GM, 627-28.

527. innovation]   In the sense of revolution or overthrow.

528. them]   Their high places.

528. their lives]   Either their lives at court (i.e., livelihood), or their bodily lives.

528-29. libertie of malice]   Freedom taken by the malicious, slander.

530. inductious]   This is the only example in the OED, where the meaning is given as "persuasive, seductive." From Latin *induco* (to persuade, mislead, seduce, deceive).

534. *Beazar*]   Obsolete form of *bezoar*, the wild goat of Persia and one of the sources of the "lapis bezoar orientale" or "bezoar-stone," a calculus or concretion found in its stomach and believed useful as a counterpoison or antidote. See also Th. Lupton, *A Thousand Notable Things of Sundrie Sorts* (1601), 184-87.

537. mortall]   Such as might cause death, as opposed to the certainty of "deadly."

539. Inmate]   Normally the mate or associate of another in the same dwelling; as that is not the case here, Ford explicitly adds "though not dwelling together."

550. ROBERT EARLE OF ESSEX]   See n. at GM, 121-22. Essex was long the favorite of the London mob, which did not, however, support him when he attempted to seize the queen. Thus "too publikely beloved, and too confident of the love he held."

553-54. The readings of the MS seem to be scribal errors rather than revisions.

554. His end was their end]   His death was their purpose.

558. CHARLES DUKE OF BYRON]   Charles de Gontaut, duc de Biron, was born in 1562; his brilliant military career led him, like Essex, to great honors while still young. He was made admiral of France at the age of thirty and marshal two years later. His victorious campaigns were paralleled by a series of intrigues and plots against Henry IV, who eventually had him tried for high treason and sentenced to death. Contemporary accounts immediately took the story of his downfall as an example of the nemesis that attends overweening pride. Biron's fall was dramatized by Chapman in *The Conspiracie and Tragedie of Charles Duke of Byron*; the two

plays were acted and printed in 1608. It was Biron's own view that he was "the invincible Fortresse to his King and Countrey" (see *Conspiracy* 3.2.90–105 and *Tragedy* 3.1.151–55). Ford's source is almost certainly Chapman, and not Jean de Serres (tr. E. Grimeston), *A General Inventorie of the History of France* (1607); in Grimeston the name is either "the Duke Biron" or, more often, "the Duke of Biron," but never, it seems, "Charles Duke of Byron."

558. not long after him]   Essex was executed on 25 February 1601, Biron on 31 July 1602.

561–62. not managing ... moderation]   An application of the story of Phaeton, with Biron as Phaeton and his conspiracies as the dangerous course Phaeton took; see Ovid, *Metamorphoses* 1–2. The unsatisfactory "managing ... guiding" is the reading of both the printed text and the MS.

561–62. Sunne ... Climate]   Henry IV.

563. inexpected]   Unexpected. Byron believed the king would never dare execute him. When he realized on the day appointed that he would indeed die, he fell into despair, refused all ministrations, and died miserably.

563–64. sits but in Commission on]   Sits in the exercise of delegated authority, here in judgment of himself. Compare *LT* 2.2.947–50: "but first / Sit in commission on your owne defects, / Accuse your selfe: be your owne Jury, Judge, / And executioner."

564–65. longer ... levels]   When resolution no longer aims.

566. SIR JOHN VANOLDEN BARNEVELT]   Johan (Jan) van Oldenbarnevelt (1547–1619) was one of the great leaders of the Dutch nation in its struggle against Spain, rising to the post of Land's Advocate of Holland, an office he held for thirty-two years. The years of the Truce (signed 1609) led to increasing difference between Barnevelt and Maurice of Nassau, Stadholder and Captain-General. When Holland, under Barnevelt, attempted an independent policy and raised forces of its own, Maurice arrested Barnevelt and disarmed his soldiers (1618). After a trial before a packed bench, he was found guilty of treason and executed. Modern historians regard Barnevelt as a just and honest man, wrongly condemned. Ford, however, reflects the general feeling then prevalent in England that he was, through ambition, led to plot the overthrow of his country. His *Apology* was translated into English (*Barnevels Apology: or Holland Mysterie*, 1618), as were some of the many scurrilous pamphlets published by his enemies (see STC 15352, 18799–18804). *The Tragedy of Sir John van Olden Barnavelt*, an anonymous play generally attributed to Fletcher and Massinger, was acted in August 1619. In the introduction to her edition of the play (Amsterdam, 1922) W. P. Frijlinck discusses the anti-Barnevelt pamphlets printed in England that served as sources for the play and probably for Ford's sketch of the Dutch leader (see esp. xxiv-lviii and cxxvi-cliv). The play has also been edited by T. H. Howard-Hill (The Malone Society, London, 1980). Ford's wording does not echo the play, but he may have made use of at least one of the pamphlets: "onely he held correspondency with the Embassadors of forraine Princes" (*Barnevelt Displayed: or the Golden Legend of New St John* [1619], 14) is perhaps the source of 568–69.

566–67. whose ashes ... colde]   Barnevelt was beheaded on 13 May 1619, evidence that *LL* was not completed much before its publication.

570. Provinces]   All the United Provinces fighting against Spain, not merely his own Holland.

579. Others yet fresh in memorie] If Ford is referring to men still alive ("yet bleeding"), he might be thinking of Robert Carr, earl of Somerset, condemned in 1616 for the murder of Sir Thomas Overbury and imprisoned in the Tower until 1621, or of the former secretary of state Sir Thomas Lake (condemned to imprisonment and a fine in 1619), or of the former lord high treasurer, Thomas Howard, earl of Suffolk (condemned to imprisonment and a fine in 1619). See GM, 125: "those being freshest in memorie."

586. GREAT] The MS reading ("publique great man") may be a revision. There are two sorts of public men, "GREAT ONES" (477) and "subordinate ministers" (517-18), and Ford has just spoken about three men characterized by their greatness. But he does not use "public great man/men" or "great public man/men" anywhere else in LL.

586. what] Which. See below, 720, and textual note.

589. Lives] The MS reading ("honors and lives") is supported by 628-29: "his Honours, ... his life."

589. *Flatterie ... Courtiers*] See GM, 571.

594-95. too partially doting on] Too prejudiced by self-love in talking about and dwelling on.

605. insinuations] See 516 and n.

608-10. monument ... preserve] A commonplace; e.g., Horace, *Odes* 3.30.1.

612. quarrelled against] Complained against. The *OED* does not give this construction, but see 1b for the similar obsolete construction "quarrel at."

615-16. Morall of the Poets Fiction] The poet Ford has in mind is most probably Homer. Although the story of Achilles being dipped in the Stygian waters does not occur earlier than Statius (AD 45-96) in his *Achilleis* 1.134, it was frequently attributed to Homer. See especially Spenser, *The Shepheardes Calender* (1579), the gloss on March 95-97, and also R. Stephanus, *Dictionarium sive Thesaurus* (1543). Both references are from T. DeWitt Starnes and E. W. Talbert, *Classical Myth and Legend in Renaissance Dictionaries* (Chapel Hill, 1955), 62.

619. the severitie of Fate] Same words in *BH* 1.3.2.

631-32. his familiar friend] Lucilius Junior, to whom Seneca's epistles were written.

633-40. Let ... retayned] This is an adaptation and a conflation of three passages taken from *Ep.* 23.1, 23.7, and 23.3-4.

636. supple] Soothe, mollify; Ford is translating "frontem remittunt."

647. said before] Above, 119-23.

650-52. As the 1843 edition of LL indicates (76 n), Ford takes this definition of a good man from William Lily's Latin grammar ("Concordantia Relativi & Antecedentis"). It comes from Horace, *Epistles* 1.16.40-41.

655. the old adage] Tilley, G.198, has only two quotations besides Ford. One of these (a 1675 edition of W. Camden) can be traced back to *A True and Plaine Declaration of the horrible treasons, practised by William Parry the traitor*, 1585, which gives a letter from William Creichton, the Jesuit, to Sir Francis Walsingham: "And therefore, Dixi, *Deum magis amare adverbia quam nomina: Quia in actionibus magis ei placent bene & legitime, quam bonum*" (sig. D1^r). Holinshed reprints this passage with "Deum magis amare adverbia quam nomina" in a marginal note (1587, vol. 3, p. 1388, col. 1). But the contrast is sometimes between adverb and adjective (see R. Dallington, *Aphorismes* [1613], 87; J. Owen, *Epigrams*, tr. J. Vicars [1618], sig. C8^v; H. Cholmley, *The State of the Now Romane Church*

[1629], sig. A2ᵛ) or between adverb and verb: "... in Morality, the Manner is more commended, then the Action it selfe. Whence it is anciently and truly said: *Wee merit not by Verbes but by Adverbes*" (R. G., *A Characterisme of the Foure Cardinall Vertues* [1630], sig. C6ᵛ).

657. hypocrisie of applause] He does not act hypocritically for the sake of applause.

666. in *him to will*] His good intentions.

667–69. For ... admonished] See above, 342, "A Wise-man" (7–9); also "for flattery / Is monstrous in a true friend," LM 1.1.67–68.

670. (that] The round bracket seems to be used as the equivalent of a comma, and the parenthesis is closed by the comma after "goodnesse." However, as all other parentheses in LL are closed by a round bracket, the second one may have been omitted by mistake.

674. Flattery ... hatred] See Erasmus, *Adagia* 2.9.53, and Tilley, T.562 (also F.349 and T.569). Originally from Terence, *Andria* 68, quoted by Cicero in *De amicitia* 24.89.

675–77. from ... observed] Laelius is the main speaker in Cicero's *De amicitia*. Immediately after quoting Terence he goes on (24.89): "Molesta veritas, siquidem ex ea nascitur odium, quod est venenum amicitiae."

677–79. Hee ... desperat] Translated from *De amicitia* 24.90.

680. *words of Downe and Honey*] Honey is often associated with words, for instance Prov. 16:24 or R3 4.1.80: "his honey words." See also FM, 290. The association of down with words is unusual; Ford equates "down" with "softness" in PW 3.2.144.

681. speake nothing but *pure Roses*] Erasmus, *Adagia* 2.6.42: "rosas loqui," which Erasmus explains as meaning "verba gratissima, & rosarum instar amabilia" ("Very sweet words, and lovable like roses"). Not in Tilley or OED.

683–89. that ... Valour] The omission of "the" in MS may be a revision, but the other changes seem due to scribal negligence. Copy text is therefore retained.

683–85. Bees ... Beasts] Pliny, *The Historie of the World* (11.6), tr. Ph. Holland (1601), 1:312–13: "With these and such like, they plaister all the hive within throughout, as it were with a coat or parget, entermingling with all other juices that are more unsavorie, gathered from the bitterest hearbes they can get: to the end that they might keepe out other little vermines that are greedie of their honnie." In modern editions the reference is 11.5.15.

686–87. the healthfullest ... Wound] The proverbial saying is, "A desperate disease must have a desperate cure" (Tilley, D.357; Smith, 70). Sometimes, as in Ford, the painfulness of the remedy is stressed: "To extream diseases extream and exquisite [painful] remedies are best" (*The Whole Aphorismes of great Hippocrates Prince of Physicians*, tr. S. H. [1610], 6).

687–89. Aristotle himself does not say (in *Nicomachean Ethics* 3) that courage is a whetstone; the expression "cos fortitudinis" is attributed to the Peripatetics by Cicero (*Tusc. Disp.* 4.19.43).

690–91. for reconciliation] In reconciling others.

696–700. the ... particular] See SP, V, 19–20 (347 above).

702. conceipt] Fanciful opinion. See above, Reader, 7 and n.

703–4. the World ... men] See GM, 798: "*Abundance* was created for use."

704–5. *to use ... it*] "To enjoy" probably means "to possess selfishly" (see "avaricious banking up of wealth," 701–2). Ford may be thinking of what Cicero says about "the common right to all things that Nature has produced for the common use of man" (*De officiis* 1.16.51).

710-11. He is ... he is] See GM, Ep. Ded. 9-11.

715-16. suppling] Mollifying, soothing (see above, 636). The MS reading ("supplyeing"; see OED, supply V³) occurs in BH 4.1.117 ("the balsam of a supplying patience").

721. *Drusus*] Marcus Livius Drusus, who became tribune in 91 BC, attempted to return the law courts to the control of the senate and grant citizenship to the Italians. He failed in the first effort and was assassinated while engaged in the second. Ford's words echo Velleius Paterculus, *Historia Romana* 2.13.1.

723-25. insomuch ... Vertues] The printed text "insomuch ... that" (i.e., so that), with the parenthetical "as it often comes to passe," is unobjectionable. But Ford uses "insomuch as" at 494-95 and GM, 1325. If he wrote "insomuch as it often comes to passe, that ...," the compositor may have added an erroneous comma before "as." The meaning could have been "seeing that" or "so that" (OED 2a and b). The MS text ("for somuch it often comes to passe, that other mennes ...") is less satisfactory, as OED gives no example of "for somuch" with ellipsis of "as," though this was possible after "forasmuch."

724-25. mischiefes ... Vertues] *Historia Romana* 2.13.3: "In the end it was the misfortune of Drusus to find that the Senate gave more approval to the evil measures of his colleagues than to his own plans, however excellent."

730. broode against] Ford may have deleted "set in armes" (20) as these words add little and upset the symmetry of his clauses.

731. two miscreant monsters] See LM 3.3.43-44: "Envy is a monster, and I defy the beast."

733. Knights of the post] Perjurers, persons earning their living by giving false evidence; see Tilley, K.164.

734 and 735. MS is clearly erroneous. The good man's resolution is "confirmed," i.e., strengthened, by adversity, not "confined" by it; "an expugnable castle of strength" is meaningless because, if the castle is "expugnable," it lacks strength.

735. *Goale of Life*] Demosthenes, *De corona* 97.

739. *Hic ... sibi*] Horace, *Epistles* 1.1.60-61: "Be this our wall of bronze, to have no guilt at heart." See Erasmus, *Adagia* 2.10.25 ("murus aheneus"). The copyist transcribed "aheneus" as "alieneus," but see commentary at 437.

741-42. *nullum ... conscientiâ*] Cicero, *Tusc. Disp.* 2.26.64.

744. a meere morrall man] Virtuous without being a Christian (see below, 752); see also above, 228, 338.

745. *Aristophanes*] He included Socrates in his attack on the Sophists in the *Clouds*.

746. *Anytus* and *Melytus*] The chief accusers of Socrates. See Plato, *Apology*, passim, and Diogenes Laertius, 2.38-44.

749-50. *If ... to us*] Diogenes Laertius, 2.36.

751-53. man ... the] The printed text is good but MS incorporates a revision which improves it ("And if" instead of "that"). This entails lighter pointing after "discreet"; if Ford made these changes they were probably unclear in the scribe's copy, and he did not make sense of what he was copying, dropping "man" after "The good" at 753.

761. inleaging] Both this and the reading of the printed text ("inlarging") are acceptable. "Inleaging" has been preferred as the more unusual of the two words

(earliest *OED* quotation 1602), less likely to have been mistaken for "inlarging" than the reverse; moreover Ford uses the verb twice in his plays, in *PW* 4.3.23 and *BH* 3.4.12. "League" occurs more than twenty times in Ford. In the MS, "in" is clearly separated from "leaging"; this separation of the prefix "in" also occurs in the MS of *FM* ("In comparable," 311; "in herit," 677).

771-73. his Grand-fathers ... *The poore mans King*]   James V; "and remember of the honourable stile given to my Grand-father of worthy memorie, in being called *the poore mans King*" (*Basilikon Doron* [ed. 1603], 28).

786-92. bring ... in Empire]   James was by inclination and policy a man of peace. At the beginning of his reign he ended the war with Spain, and from that time to the time Ford wrote, maintained peace. That he was an "equall and upright moderatour" in maintaining peace on the continent was one of James's cherished delusions. Clearly in mind at the time of writing was the mission (led by Doncaster, dedicatee of the MS) which set out for central Europe in May of 1619 to mediate in the dispute over the Bohemian crown. See also "the monarch of our peace" (*FM*, 701) and n. at 805-6.

795-96. *A good man ... Injustice*]   Ford was no doubt grateful to James for his attitude in the Overbury scandal. James's "resolve, he told the commissioners, was 'to use all lawful courses that the foulness of this fault be sounded to the depth, that for the discharge of our duty both to God and man, the innocent may be cleared, and the nocent may severely be punished.' To this resolve he adhered throughout the investigations and trials which followed" (D. H. Willson, *King James VI & I*, London, 1966 [1956], p. 353).

799. an]   "A" and "an" were both possible; *20* and MS have "an heresie" (762).

799-800. fee simple]   From the Anglo-Latin law term *feodum simplex* denoting absolute possession without limitation or restriction. See *Q* 1.1.513-14.

805-8. JAMES THE GREAT ... *Charles the Fift* ... *Charlemaine*]   For similar flattery, see *FM*, 1065-66.

805-6. JAMES THE PEACEABLE]   James's motto was "Beati Pacifici." In 1618 a tract appeared entitled *The Peace-Maker: or, Great Brittaines Blessing*; though written by Thomas Middleton, it purported to be from the king's pen. The epistle is addressed "To all Our true-loving, and Peace-embracing subjects," and the tract opens with the following words: "Peace *be to you*; I greete you in the blessing of a God, the salutation of an *Apostle*, and the Motto of a *King*: My Subject hath her being in Heaven, her Theory in holy Writ, and her practique in *England, Insula pacis*. The Land of Peace, under the King of Peace" (sig. A4^r).

809. their present King]   Louis XIII.

813-26. Let ... name]   Ford's fulsome eulogy of James was not unique. In *The Treasure of Tranquillity* (1611), Ep. Ded., sig. A11^r, James Maxwell compared him to Christ.

819. improprietie of description]   An erroneous technical term: in Scholastic philosophy God cannot be spoken of as "good" as man can, that is, by attribution.

822. up-shut]   Dialectical variant of "upshot." This is the earliest *OED* quotation for this spelling. "Star-shut" is used in *Q* 1.1.529.

822. forever]   Spelt as one word in both *1620* and MS; first *OED* quotation for this spelling is 1670.

835-44. And then ... faultie]   These lines provide in summary form the miseries described at length in *GM*.

839. many tongu'd]   Because many-headed. See GM, 722 and n.

Corollary
1. *Corollarie*]   In a double sense: (1) in the still current transferred meaning of something following by deduction from what has gone before, a consequence; and (2) in the obsolete meaning of something added to a work beyond what was originally intended; an appendix or conclusion.
5. North-Starre of Vertue]   See same imagery in GM, 375-76.
8. both fortunes]   See n. at GM, 266.
14. this application]   Formerly the rule or practical lesson itself, as well as the testing of it, which is the modern meaning (see OED, 5); the "application" or corollary is formulated in lines 24 ff.
15. free from any particularity]   Not aimed at any individual.
17. grave yeares]   Years of maturity; years in which a statesman would be regarded as having influence, respect, and importance.
18. grave actions]   Serious, important actions.
23. Confessour ... confesse]   A play on two meanings of confessor: (1) one who hears confession; and (2) one who has been recognized as steadfastly adhering to something, commonly a religion, here nobleness. Thus the verb: reveal by circumstance, manifest (OED, 5, *fig.* and *poet.*; first quotation 1646).
29-30. See CBS, 1896, and Tilley, C.605, ODEP, 318.
35-42. As indicated by the marginal reference, Ford is translating a Latin version of Plutarch's life of Demosthenes. "The Terrors, the Calumnies, the Envies, the Contentions" derives from G. Xylander's "terrores, invidias, calumnias, contentiones" (ed. Heidelberg and Basle [1561], 751).
41-45. *Brutus ... Fortune*]   Translated from Dio Cassius, *Roman History* 47.49.
47. talent of Wisdome]   Mental endowment, gift.
59. ennoble]   Perhaps this should be "enable."
59. Patients]   Ford is playing on two meanings of the word: (1) one who suffers patiently; and (2) a person who undergoes some action. See GM, 535.
59. for their owne particulars]   To their personal (as opposed to the public) advantage; see above, 763.
59-60. demeane themselves]   To comport themselves (OED, v^1 6, 1320-1858). The modern meaning "to lower or humble oneself" is first recorded in 1659 (OED, v^2 2).
61-62. in observation]   That one should observe.
62. interposition]   Seems to mean "temporary interruption," or "obstruction" (see OED, Interpose, *v*, 6, to interrupt, to obstruct).
66. instrumentall causes]   As instruments or means toward accomplishment.
67-68. a service ... debt]   The rendering of a service is not to be neglected by the person receiving it, but must be repaid or rewarded.
74. VADUM *non transeat excors*]   "May the fool not cross (the) FORD!" Capitalization draws attention to the pun.

Shorter Pieces

SP, I

16. president to youth] "Our ignorance of his manner of life since 1598 permits to hope, if not to believe, that he had really become a changed character." Mark Eccles, "Barnabe Barnes" in *Thomas Lodge and other Elizabethans*, ed. C. Sisson (Cambridge, 1933), 231.

19. *Verba ... manu*] "Language, elegance, method, establish, designate, and adorn an author who is agreeable in his matter, dignity, and strength."

SP, II

13. Mnemosine] A Titaness, goddess of memory, and mother of the Muses by Zeus.

49. Hercules] The comparison of Mountjoy to Hercules is as warrior, hero, and lover. Both undergo a sort of apotheosis and serve as models for future ages.

57-62. Mountjoyes sword ... counsils] References to the latter part of Mountjoy's career, treated at more length in FM. See also FM Introduction, 65-68.

62. in secret cells] Mountjoy was a patron of the arts and had a special interest in philosophy and theology. See FM Introduction, 64, 70, 74-75.

73. Zepherus] The west wind that fanned Elysium.

81-84. Omnia vincit ... mori] "'Love conquers all things, and let us too yield to Love,' he wrote; whose writings were immune from death. To this agreed brave Mountjoy, and, conquered, he yielded to Love, he whose deeds will be immune from death," Vergil, *Eclogues* 10.69.

SP, III a

35. Eiusdem in Eadem] "From the same upon the same."

SP, III b.1

14. to weare fate] To serve fate by wearing its livery.

19. stickes ... repentance] Incomplete achievement's content leads to later dissatisfaction.

SP, III c

24. Behold ... Law] The trials of the earl and countess of Somerset took place in May 1616.

SP, IV

1-2. CROWNE ... *Master-peece*] In his edition of Webster (London [1927], 127), F. L. Lucas suggests these lines may be "modelled on Propertius's tribute to Vergil's *Aeneid*" (*Elegies* 2.34.65-66).

3. *whiles ... change*] So long as literature is written.

SP, VII

9-10. *Domitians ... Paris*] The play concerns the marriage of the emperor Domitian to Domitia, and her lust for Paris, the "Roman Actor."

SP, X

1-2. ACTION ... Action] Many plays live only through being acted; this play rather gave life to the acting.

5-6. *Should ... Great*] Ford plays on the controversy surrounding Cosimo I's assumption of the title of grand duke as opposed to that of duke. The new title had been granted by Pius V in 1569, but not recognized by the emperor until 1575, when Francesco I had succeeded his father.

SP, XII
9. *Lawrell* and *Cypresse*] Symbols of poetic distinction and of mourning.

SP, XIV
5-6. *Muses ... Helicon*] The Boeotian mountain was sacred to the Muses.
7. *Ganimede*] The youth whom Zeus made his cup-bearer.

Glossary

Spelling of entry is that of first occurrence, except that inflected forms have been reduced.
    *first recorded example in the OED.
    **used before first recorded example in the OED.
    +only recorded example in the OED.
    n. glossed more fully in Commentary.

abject: an outcast, a degraded person, HT, 34 n.
abundance: wealth, GM, 798, 896.
acquit: requite, CBS, 923.
admitment: admission (not in OED), LL, 678.
adulterate: spurious, corrupted by base intermixture, HT, 452 n.
affection: biased feeling, partiality, LL, 318.
after age: subsequent age, FM, 1031.
after-wit: wisdom after the event, recognition of former folly, GM, 313.
ambrosiack: ambrosial, FM, 30.
ancient: long-established, HT, 156.
+annaloger: analogist, he who argues by analogy, HT, 520.
any thing: in any measure, GM, 588.
apishnesse: silly behavior, LL, 217.
apostataes: apostates, HT, 104 n.
appalled: faded, or terrified, CBS, 1380.
apparently: manifestly, LL, 336.
appendance: appendage, LL, 232.
apprehension: understanding, LL, 340.
**approvement: expression of satisfaction, approval, GM, 672; see LM, 1.3.25.
aptnesse: habitual tendency or predisposition, HT, 43-44.
arrant: errand, CBS, 155.
artificiall: artful, cunning, deceitful, LL, 459.
**artsman: artist, FM, 30.
asseast: assessed (for a penalty or fine), CBS, 1217.
**assign: design, FM, 231.
attend: direct, intend, LL, 649.
attentor (attempter): one who attempts in a criminal sense, FM, 543.
attone (atone): join, unite together, FM, 455.
availeable: beneficial, profitable, LL, 397.

baffaild (baffle): disgrace(d), CBS, 1111.
baite: food generally, FM, 862.
banishment: enforced absence, not as punishment, FM, 467.
banneret: title conferred for deeds done in the king's presence, CBS, 602.
bawd: one who panders to any evil design or vicious practice, GM, 636.
before: until, CBS, 437.

behind: yet to come, CBS, 1016.
bereaven: bereft, stripped, CBS, 1301.
bewraye: expose, render hollow, CBS, 1173.
blaze: proclaim, FM, 539.
bolster out: aid and abet, countenance, HT, 555.
brave: finely-dressed, CBS, 245.
braverie: valor, bravado, with a pun on ostentation, finery, fine clothes, HT, 350 n.
brooke: use, FM, 532.
brunts of defence: "The enduring of severe attacks in defence of a lady," Merchant, 78, HT, 185.

cabinet: private chamber, HT, 403.
card: the circular piece of stiff paper on which the thirty-two points are marked in the mariner's compass, SP, IIIa 23.
casuallye: accidentally, by mischance, GM, 240; LL, 510.
casualty: 1. accident, mishap, GM, 783, LL, Cor. 18; 2. chance, accident, as a state of things, GM, 1137; 3. state of subjection to chance, LL, 585; SP, IIIb 17.
catapotion: pill, hence remedy, FM, 163. From the Greek *katapotion*; not in OED.
censure: estimate, judge, LL, Reader 6, [text] 71.
challenge: lay claim to, LL, 811, Cor. 15.
chargeable: costly, expensive, GM, 255.
chicken: chick, young, CBS, 276.
chuffe: boor, churl, HT, 122 n.
circumvention: getting the better of anyone by craft or artifice, HT, 637.
Civilian: practitioner of Civil Law, LL, 254.
cleerenesse: purity, innocence, GM, 471.
**clownage: the behaviour of a rustic, FM, 208.
coarse (corse): corpse, FM, 293.
cocker: foster, indulge, CBS, 374.
+cohere: unite, HT, 648.
coherence: agreement, GM, 951.
commend: render, or present as, worthy of favorable acceptance, CBS, 870, 1103.
commoditie: 1. expediency, LL, 107. 2. interest, profit, LL, 696.
communitie: commonness, ordinary occurrence, HT, 10-11.
compact: a compacted body, structure, GM, 674-75 n.
complement: 1. formal courtesy, GM, Ep. Ded. 6. 2. "that which goes to 'complete' the character of a gentleman in regard to external appearance or demeanour," (Onions), GM, 67, 972.
comprehend: attain to, HT, 296.
comprimitting: appeasing, or repressing, LL, 714 (see OED, compromit, 3b).
conceipt: action of conceiving, LL, 109.
conceit: *vb.* apprehend, imagine, conceive, HT, 252 n; FM, 560. *sb.* fancy, imagination, GM, 359-60.
conclude: include, comprehend, HT, 132.
condolement: sorrowing, lamentation, HT, 363.
confesse: acknowledge, SP, IIIb 47.
conformable: disposed, willing, GM, 91 (not construed with infinitive in OED).
conformation: adjustment in form or character to a pattern or example, LL, 153.

GLOSSARY 437

consequent, by: in consequence, GM, 452.
conster: construe, LL, Cor. 48.
consumer: in the pejorative sense of wasting, squandering, or destroying, GM, 890.
controvert: discuss, debate, LL, 336.
conveniencie: ethical fitness, LL, 107.
convenient: 1. appropriate, HT, 159-60. 2. ethically suitable, LL, 255.
cordiall: medicine stimulating the heart or the circulation, CBS, 467, 963.
cormorant: insatiably greedy or rapacious person; usurer, HT, 350-51.
coronize: crown, FM, 845.
***corrivall-shipp:** the position of a corrival, mutual rivalry, HT, 359 n.
****cosmographick:** geographic, FM, 1136.
cote: quote, FM, 42, 87.
countermaund: to counteract, frustrate; or to control, keep under command, GM, 265.
countervail: to be equivalent or equal in value, FM, 924.
courser: coarser, LL, 163.
cover: the funeral structure, FM, 336. *See* **hearce**.
cunning: knowledge how to do a thing, GM, 814.
curiosity: probably in the blameable sense of "care or attention carried to excess," GM, 581.
curious: 1. careful, interested, HT, 165. 2. prying, officious, HT, 423. 3. singular, skillfully made, HT, 655. 4. dainty, delicious, CBS, 962. 5. cautious, LL, 373.
curiously: skillfully, subtly, carefully, minutely, CBS, 146, 243, 1107.

dangerous: probably injurious or hurtful, GM, 470.
datelesse: endless, FM, 1161.
deceiveable: perhaps "fallible" at LL, 64, but the word might mean "deceitful," as at 634.
decerning: discerning, GM, 704; see n. at 693.
decipher: describe, LL, Reader 12, [text] 588, 828.
dejection: humiliation, lowering in fortune, condition, quality, LL, Cor. 56.
delatorie: dilatory, slow or tardy, HT, 638.
deliciously: voluptuously, HT, 568-69.
****delinquencie:** guilt, LL, 564.
***dependance:** a body of dependants or subordinates; a retinue, HT, 92; GM, 107.
despection: despising, contempt, GM, 495 n.
devoyre (devoir): endeavor or task, HT, 356; FM, 395.
dilaniate: tear to pieces, LL, 475.
dilliance: dalliance, CBS, 1256.
discursion: the act of running away, or wandering, with an implied suggestion of irregularity, HT, 683 n.
disesteem: despise, MM, 137.
***disposure:** power or right to dispose of, HT, 193.
distast: regard with displeasure, dislike, HT, Ep. Ded. 9 n.; GM, 73, 587-88; LL, 515.
dolour: disease, or sorrow, CBS, 1038.
dow: endow, FM, 884.
drift: purpose, object, HT, 310, 315; LL, 649.
drill: make holes, hollow out, SP, IIIa 19.

earnest-peny: a small sum of money, probably originally a literal penny, paid as earnest to secure a bargain, HT, 235 n.
ease: probably "relief," "alleviation," at GM, 1188, but normally followed by "from" or "of," not "in." See TP, 1.1.42: "ease in these extremes."
efficatie: power, force, HT, 169.
elate: lofty, proud, FM, 96, 134.
emulating: jealous of, envious, MM, 134 n.
enabled: authorized or empowered in the legal sense, LL, 410.
enco: encomium, SP, IIIa 1.
encomiastes: encomiast, one who composes or pronounces an encomium, a eulogizer, SP, I 21.
end: purpose, GM, 957.
****endowments:** riches, possession, GM, 201-02 n.
enormious: extraordinarily wicked, outrageous, monstrous, HT, 558.
estates: used elliptically for "persons of estate," GM, 694.
esteeme: look favorably upon, CBS, 1397.
even: even-handed, just, LL, Cor. 21.
exasperate: exaggerate, magnify, LL, 536.
***extinct:** extinction, HT, 531.

fact: deed, crime, CBS, 1021.
faction: factious spirit or action, with a strong sense of opprobrium, GM, 503.
factour: agent or representative, CBS, 381; LL, Reader 19, [text] 569.
***famoused:** celebrated, HT, 272.
fantasticall: capricious, arbitrary, vain, GM, 583.
fatallie: (hyperbolically) unto death, CBS, 1420.
faultie: guilty, LL, 844.
fautor: patron, FM, 1017.
feodarie: subject, dependent, servant, LL, Reader 48.
filthinesse: moral corruption, GM, 835, 1231.
flote (float): flux or flood of the tide. One of F's favorite words, alone or contrasted with "ebb." See FM, 561; GM, 48, 300; LS, 1.2.450 and 2.3.1225; TP, 1.1.65; The Spanish Gipsy, 1.5.29.
fondling: fond or foolish person, HT, 426.
for: because of, GM, 1202.
forcible: strong, powerful, LL, 736.
fore-cast: foresight of consequences and provision against them; forethought, prudence, CBS, 495; GM, 97.
frankly: freely, CBS, 1054.
free: voluntary, perhaps with the further meaning of noble and honorable, LL, Reader 11.
freely: liberally, CBS, 1150.
front: face, CBS, 1069.
fruition: enjoyment, HT, 130 n; GM, 158, 985.
furniture: intellectual aptitudes or mental cultivation, GM, 795.

ginne: device, trick, CBS, 415.
glore (glory): praise, honor, admiration, FM, 424.

GLOSSARY 439

glosse: deceptive appearance, fair semblance, FM, 1111.
gloze: pretence, FM, 730.
gravelled in: puzzled, perplexed, HT, Ep. Ded. 8 *n.*
grayne (dy'd in): (dyed in) a fast color, thoroughly, CBS, 404, 1510.
grutch: begrudge, CBS, 392.
guerdon: reward, recompense, CBS, 608.
gust: outburst, HT, 155 *n.*

hardly: with hardship or severity, CBS, 510.
hauty (haughty): lofty, eminent in a positive sense, FM, 26.
heale (hele): hide, conceal, CBS, 945.
hearse (hearce): the *castrum doloris* or wooden structure erected over the coffin at royal and noble funerals and decorated with banners, heraldic devices, and candles, FM, 241; CBS, 1458.
heart: the seat of feeling, thought and volition, GM, 164.
heavie: weighed down (with grief or sorrow), CBS, 1634.
hollow glasse: false glass, SP, XII 5.
+honorifie: honor, FM, 699.
hyre (hire): reward, FM, 469.

imbecilitie: feebleness, weakness, HT, 250, 666.
imitate: endeavor, make an attempt to do something, LL, 225, *n.*
imparadised: rapturous, HT, 130 *n.*
impart from: give up, part with, HT, 680.
impawne: be pawned in exchange for, imperil, CBS, 238.
impe: scion of a noble house, FM, 100.
implore: beg for tearfully, CBS, 1259.
impostor: one who imposes on others, a deceiver; one who assumes a false character, HT, 423 *n.*
in proofe: in truth, CBS, 1580.
indeered: endeared, bound by obligations of gratitude, HT, 38 *n.*
inderely: dearly, earnestly, deeply, HT, 504 *n.*
indifferent: impartial, LL, Cor. 21.
indignity: loss of honor, a disgraceful act, HT, 493.
*individuat: undivided, inseparable, HT, 532 (OED meaning: rendered individual).
indubitate: *adv.* indubitately: undoubtedly, unquestionably, HT, 263 (in OED only as *adj.*).
induced: adduced, GM, 124.
indurance (endurance): captivity, imprisonment, CBS, 788; GM, 1091, 1146.
inferre: imply, CBS, 1425.
inform: instruct, teach, GM, 906.
information: in Common Law, a charge or accusation, LL, 837.
infracted: checked, weakened, broken; from Latin *infringo, infractus*, LL, 732. The earliest OED example for "infracted" is 1727, but the adjective "infract" (for the same meaning) is dated 1593.
ingeniously: "Used, by confusion, for ingenuously" (OED, 2), GM, 652, 654; LL, Reader 24.
ingrosse, ingrost (engross): to gain or keep exclusive possession of; Cockeram gives

"*Ingrosse.* To buy all for ones selfe," HT, 469; FM, 283.
inroul'd: enrolled, SP, XII 16.
intemperature: intemperateness of action or passion, with the further idea of disease, LL, 261.
***intermure**: wall in, FM, 713.
intermytted: interrupted, LL, Ep. Ded. 17.
***intimate**: make intimate, familiarize, MM, 47.
invicted: unconquered, FM, 46.
invitement: inducement, allurement, LL, 230; CBS, 1541.
irregular: not conforming or obedient to law or moral principle, GM, 366-67.

jeopard: endanger, jeopardize, HT, 277.
judicially: with sound judgement, judiciously, HT, 648.
****juycelesse (juiceless)**: insipid, devoid of interest, FM, 542.

labour: petition or sue (for a pardon or favor), CBS, 1022.
lacky (lackey): do menial service, FM, 15; see LM, 1.2.33.
lanck (lank): hollow, empty, FM, 528.
largely: generally, LL, Reader 9.
laver: a spiritually cleansing agency, in particular the spiritual "washing" of baptism, CBS, 555.
levell: aim, purpose, HT, 316; FM, 229.
levitie: fickleness, inconstancy, LL, 797.
licorish (lickerish): greedy, or lecherous, CBS, 1354.
limn out: portray (artistically), CBS, 1869.
lineally: in direct line of descent, FM, 313.
livelyhood: liveliness, HT, 254.
lodged: sheltered, CBS, 1328.
los'd: loosed, set free, CBS, 197.
luxurious: passionately desirous (after something), SP, IIIb 13.

maine (mayne): *adj.* very great, GM, 668. *sb.* object, FM, 1140.
malediction: reviling, slander, HT, 418.
marginall: marginal note or reference, SP, IIIa 12.
martialist: military man, warrior, HT, 418.
meagre: thin, emaciated, FM, 865.
meerely: absolutely, GM, 62.
members: branches, LL, 413.
memory: what is remembered of a person; posthumous repute, LL, 49.
mint: coin, CBS, 1387.
mirrour: a model of excellence; a paragon, FM, 1031; HT, 526.
mirth: joy, happiness, CBS, 1601.
misconster: misconstrue, GM, 426.
mis-giving: doubting, apprehensive, CBS, 1468.
mistake: misdirect, misapply, CBS, 934.
moderate: regulate, control, rule, GM, 310; LL, 171.
moderation: avoidance of extremes, self-control, temperance, GM, Ep. Ded. 9.
momentany: momentary, LL, 636.

GLOSSARY 441

***monument:** cause to be perpetually remembered, furnish with a monument, FM, 1027; HT, 528.
motion: inward prompting or impulse; desire and inclination, GM, 129, 1082.
much: *adj.* great, LL, 340.
mungrell (mongrel): mixed, indefinite in a contemptuous sense, FM, 841.

narrownesse: difficulty, GM, 330 n.
neotericke: a modern, especially a modern writer or author, HT, 13 n.
nicenesse: subtlety, over-refinement, HT, 224.
nimble: cleverly contrived, LL, 837.
none: *adj.* no (rare by 1600, but sometimes used later before a vowel, as in GM, 1203).
notoriously: evidently, LL, 157.
nought: wicked, CBS, 1623.
number: rhyme, verse, CBS, 1874.

****objure:** forswear, utter an oath against, CBS, 231.
observance: due respect, dutiful service, GM, Ep. Ded. 6.
occurrent: event, GM, 1032.
often: *adj.* frequent, GM, 1054, 1055.
ogdoastick: variant of octastich, a poem of eight lines, SP, XI.
open: reveal, make known, GM, Ep. Ded. 7.
opinion: in a pejorative sense, GM, Ep. Ded. 7, [text] 359, 741-42; SP, XII 27.
oppugner: assailant, opponent, HT, 95-96.
ought: owed, CBS, 143.
****outlanding:** outlandish, GM, 977.
over passe: pass over, disregard, have no part of, CBS, 723.
+**over-paralleled:** surpassed, LL, 780.
over-view: survey, inspection, LL, Ep. Ded. 18.
over-weene: render presumptuous or arrogant, LL, 726.

paize (peise): weigh, FM, 607.
partage: share, GM, 1293.
partially: unfairly, unjustly, GM, Ep. Ded. 4.
particular: 1. *sb.* personal advantage, profit, LL, 763, Cor. 59; 2. *adj.* not occupying public office; private, LL, 597, 700.
****passable:** transient, ephemeral, GM, 206.
passage: event, act, transaction, GM, 572.
patheticall: moving, stirring, LL, 695.
pelfe: riches, trash, CBS, 693.
penall: punitive, or painful, HT, 194.
perplex: torment, CBS, 776.
personate: represent (a person, etc.) in writing as being of such and such a kind, LL, 96.
pithily: in essence, LL, 132.
pithy: significant, FM, 107.
pitifull: compassionate, merciful, FM, 900.
pitty: pitiable state, sad fate, GM, 11.

plaudite: a round of applause, HT, 735.
portly: stately, dignified, FM, 1093.
pose: interrogate, CBS, 1766.
positively: definitely, with assurance, LL, 149.
practizer: a man of wicked or fraudulent devices, LL, 517.
****precedencie:** precedence, superiority in rank or estimation, HT, 262.
precise: strict, scrupulous, FM, 899; CBS, 1288.
pregnant: compelling, cogent, clear, LL, 486, Cor. 30.
preposterously: in a manner contrary to the order of nature, LL, 141.
preservative: antidote, LL, 534.
president: precedent, FM, 315, 736; CBS, 905; GM, Ep. Ded. 9-10; LL, Reader 21; SP, I 16.
prest: ready for action or use, HT, 320.
***pretexted:** put forward or used as a pretext; pretended, HT, 559.
prevent: 1. forestall, LL, 527. 2. anticipate, LL, 49-50.
prick: with sexual quibble, HT, 726 n.
primer: first in importance, FM, 172.
probable: capable of being proved, demonstrable, HT, 84.
profession: speech, declared intent, LL, 713.
projection: project, scheme, LL, 641.
prophaned: irreverent, blasphemous, HT, 574.
providence: foresight, prudent or wise arrangement, GM, 1282.
provocation: invitation, summons, or incitement, HT, 254 n.
punctual: precise or detailed; the two senses are often mixed, LL, 130.

quaint: skillfully made so as to have a good appearance, FM, 880.
queane: impudent, ill-behaved woman, CBS, 1573.

race: the course of life, FM, 275.
range: move from one thing to another, CBS, 1150.
ranne: *see* **run.**
razed: ruined, FM, 16.
readie: straight, direct, GM, 1071.
rebate: make dull, LL, 460.
receit: receipt, recipe, CBS, 961.
recollect: bring back, FM, 707.
rectify: to guide and direct aright, GM, 1083.
recure: restore, CBS, 1320.
reference: relationship, GM, 1310-11.
regiment: government or control over oneself, one's feelings or actions, LL, 298.
regreete: greeting, MM, 113.
repetition: mention, GM, 1276.
reprehension: reproof, LL, 663.
resonant: resounding, celebrated, renowned, HT, 163.
respective: careful, regardful, FM, 898.
retire: withdraw, GM, 1062.
rightly: precisely, GM, 889.
riot: extravagant, wasteful living, often associated with courtiers and noblemen, FM,

611; GM, 506, 640, 641; see also BH, 2.1.31; FCN, 2.1.582 (sig. C2ᵛ), 5.3.2587; LM, 1.2.2, 2.2.96; PW, 4.4.49.
route: disorderly, disreputable crowd, FM, 388.
run (ranne): meet with, LL, 558.
rusticity: lack of breeding, culture, or refinement, FM, 256.

sacietie: satiety, CBS, 724.
samplar: 1. typical instance, LL, Reader 21; 2. model, pattern, LL, 325, Cor. 31.
sanctimonious: holy, in a positive sense, FM, 770.
scandal: a disgraceful imputation, a slander, LL, 729, 795, 841.
scandalous: shameful, GM, 1217.
scholy (scholium): explanatory note or comment, FM, 41.
+seasoner: something that serves to season, LL, 712.
seat: authority or dignity (from chair of state), FM, 1068.
secretary: confidant, or amanuensis, CBS, 1075.
secure: overconfident, CBS, 535, 1348; GM, 295; LL, 282.
security: an ill-founded absence of anxiety, carelessness, CBS, 1644; GM, 308, 574; LL, 220.
senceably: so as to be easily understood or to impress the feelings; clearly, strikingly, HT, 223 n.
sensualitie: the part of the nature of man that is concerned with the senses, chiefly, the animal instincts and appetites, HT, 145 n.
sententious: full of wisdom, LL, 303.
sequestration: removal from public office or station, LL, Cor. 57.
**severation: separation, GM, 990.
share: shear, cut off, CBS, 258.
short: shortly, very soon, CBS, 1380.
shrike: shriek, cry of terror, CBS, 1058.
sift: subject to close scrutiny and questioning, LL, 532.
silly: deserving of pity, helpless, CBS, 147, 1803.
simplicitie: lack of knowledge or judgment, ignorance, GM, 319.
**singly: merely, LL, 653, 820.
singular: eminent, above the ordinary in worth or value, HT, 748 n.
sleight[en]: slight (adj. and vb.), LL, 493, 494.
+smicker: loose, lax, wanton, FM, 207.
soak: impoverish, CBS, 399.
sooth up: confirm or encourage, LL, 446.
sophye: wise man, sage, HT, 330.
sory (sorry): vb. sorrow, FM, 794, 1127.
sowre: sore, grievous, severely painful, CBS, 873.
splendent: bright, shining, FM, 44.
sportive: characterized by levity, or unfortunate, CBS, 1192.
square: frame, direct, GM, 1326; LL, 57, 381.
stain: throw into the shadow by superior excellence, eclipse, FM, 137.
stale: a prostitute of the lowest class, employed as a decoy by thieves. Often used generically as a term of contempt for an unchaste woman, HT, 464.
statist: statesman, LL, 121, 380.
statue: honor, FM, 47.

steeled: hardened like steel, inflexible, HT, 365.
sternenesse: fierceness, LL, 471.
stile: vb. call, CBS, 1210. sb. stylus, pen, or composition, CBS, 1862.
stoppe: a stopping place, in the journey of life, GM, 1062.
storme: to complain with violent language, to rage, GM, 482.
**strayne (strain): style; stream of ungoverned language, CBS, 352 (for both senses, earlier than OED).
subsidie booke: book recording possessions for purposes of taxation, SP, IIIb 12.
substance: wealth, possessions, GM, 767, 777.
sufferance: patient endurance, long-suffering, GM, 209, 880; CBS, 192, 722, 857.
suggestion: false representation or charge, GM, Ep. Ded. 7.
supplant: root out, uproot, LL, 761-62.
surquedrie: (misused for) excess, LL, 798.
*surveior: one who takes a mental view of something; an examiner, contemplator, HT, 648.
suter: suitor, petitioner, CBS, 260.
sweated: gotten, made, or produced by severe labor, CBS, 659.

*tableture: tablature; a tabular formation or structure bearing an inscription or design, HT, 556.
tallage: taxes, CBS, 687.
testifie: give evidence of, CBS, 1323.
text letters: capital letters, LL, 585.
thrift: prosperity, success, LL, Reader 26, Ep. Ded. 22.
thriftie: respectable, proper, decent, LL, Reader 46.
timely: in time, before it is too late, CBS, 1679.
tincture: brightness, FM, 49 (meaning not in OED).
tipe: type, distinguishing mark or sign, MM, 52.
touze: touse, tousle; tear at, or worry like a dog; also tussle, struggle, HT, 126, 295.
toye: foolish or idle fancy, GM, 676.
traduce: mislead, lead astray, GM, 606; LL, 729, 797, 842.
traine: draw by art or inducement, CBS, 237.
traverse: travel widely, HT, 352.
trim: adorn, make comely, FM, 818.
trophey: monument, memorial, FM, 759.
tumour: inflated pride or conceit, FM, 649.
tyme pleasers: time servers, flatterers, LL, 454.

uncertaine: fickle, GM, 755.
undeceiving: freeing from deception or error, LL, 397.
unfurnished: imperfect, GM, 523.
unhop't: unhoped, unexpected, CBS, 1030.
unnecessarilye: fruitlessly, without meaning, GM, 1309.
unrest: absence of rest, hence activity, FM, 308.
unstaidnesse: instability, GM, 203.
un-useful: useless, LL, 33.
unusuall: unaccustomed, FM, Ep. Ded. 11.

GLOSSARY 445

vanitie: foolish, erroneous opinion, GM, 442.
variablenesse: fickleness, GM, 611.
varnish: to cover with a specious or deceptive appearance: gloss over, disguise, LL, 195.
viewe: examination, survey, GM, 1278; LL, Cor. 2.
volly (volley): to utter (words, etc.) rapidly or impetuously, FM, 250.
+voltage: the action of causing a horse to move in volts (circular movements), FM, 221.

wast: waist, CBS, 244.
weak-ballac't: morally unstable, HT, 78.
weight: importance, value, CBS, 508.
winde: involve by enticing methods, LL, 587.
wrested: afflicted with suffering, subjected to twisting movement, CBS, 1215.

Index

This Index lists proper names in texts, introductions, and commentary; page references to Ford's texts are in boldface; references in parentheses are to the line numbers of Ford's texts in this edition, used to locate the relevant commentary note.

Aaron, **193**
Abdolonymus (Abdolominus in F), 228, 232, **262**, 412 (787)
Achelous, 390 (345)
Achilles, **37, 50, 92,** 284n.13, **319,** 388 (150), 389 (269), 429 (615)
Admetus, **44,** 391 (505)
Aeneas, **33, 43, 266,** 388 (151), 414 (955, 957)
Aesop, **255, 260,** 409 (520), 411 (718)
Africanus. See Scipio
Ahab, **176, 186,** 400 (644), 401 (974)
Ajax, **37**
Alberti, L. B., 14
Alcestis, **44,** 391 (505, 505-6)
Alexander (the Great), **37, 244, 262, 324,** 389 (269), 406 (134)
Amadis de Gaul, 5
Anaxagoras, **247,** 407 (223)
Anderson, Donald K., Jr., 19, 138n.9, 218n.5, 281, 286n.19
Andreas, 13
Andrew, Saint, **178**
Anne (of Denmark), 10-11, 393 (20)
Antenor, **266,** 414 (956)
Antichrist, **205,** 403 (1603)
Antioch, **243**
Anytus, **323,** 431 (746)
Aquinas, Thomas, Saint, 145-46 and n.17
Argonauts, **37**
Ariadne, **44,** 391 (502)
Ariosto, 12
Aristophanes, 284, **323,** 431 (745)
Aristotle, **42, 94,** 222, 284, 285, **303, 307, 313, 321,** 389 (259), 395 (125), 405 (29), 408 (379), 412 (806), 416 (1128), 419 (27), 421 (147), 422 (214), 425 (372), 430 (687)

Arthur (king), 8
Arundel, countess of (Alathea Talbot), 385 (Ep. Ded.)
Arundel, second earl of (Thomas Howard) 4, 6, 11, **26, 36,** 385 (Ep. Ded.)
Ascuper le Huge, 5
Athens, **255, 266**
Atlas, **99**
Aubrey, John, 136
Augustine, Saint, 284, **314,** 420 (31), 426 (437)
Augustus, **324,** 415 (1024)
Aurelius, Marcus, **255,** 410 (543)
Aurelius Victor, Sextus, 410 (544)
Authorized Version. See Bible, translations of
Azores, 65, 68

Bacon, Francis, 75, 281, 409 (518), 415 (1045)
Baker, S. A., 231
Bang, W., xn.2
Barckley, Sir Richard, 224, 281
Barnes, Barnabe, ix, 73, 90, 333, 352n.14, 394 (Reader 33), 396 (708), 434 (SP I 16)
Barnevelt. See Van Oldenbarnevelt
Basilikon Doron. See James I
Bastard, Thomas, 75
Batho, G. R., 219nn.9, 12; 404 (tp 8)
Beaumont, Francis, 349n.13
Belgium, **100,** 395 (309)
Bellona, **39,** 389 (326)
Benson, John, 229, 230, 231
Bethseda, **174**
Beza, Theodore, 148n.21
Bias, **263,** 412 (820)
Bible, 226n.32, 405 (4), 408 (330), 412 (762, 803), 416 (1084), 419 (11),

422 (195, 220), 423 (221, 225), 426 (439), 430 (680); **see also** Index of Biblical Citations, below
Bible, translations of, Authorized Version, 153, 398 (145), 399 (416), 403 (1489)
— Geneva, 153, 398, (145), 400 (457, 651)
— Vulgate, 401 (736, 829)
Biron (Byron), Charles de Gontaut, duc de, 284, **318**, 427 (558), 428 (558, 561, 563)
Biton, **274**, 417 (1243)
Blount, Charles Brooke. **See** Devonshire (first earl of)
Blount (family), 63, 77-78, 394 (quarto tp, quarto tp verso), 397 (Anagram)
Blower, Ralph, 133, 149
Boethius, 224n.29
Book of Common Prayer, 390 (429), 402 (1264)
Breton, Nicholas, 75, 138, 139-41, 223n.24
Brome, Richard, ix, **351**, 352n.14
Browne, William, 386 (Ep. Ded. 11)
Brut(e), **266**, 414 (957)
Brutus, Decimus Junius and Marcus Junius (sometimes confused by F), **311, 327**, 391 (504), 423 (300)
Bullen, A. H., 297
Buoni, Tommaso, 15
Burelbach, Frederick M., Jr., 23, 24, 81, 152, 217n.1, 394 (Reader 39)
Burton, Francis, 1, 20, 25
Butter, Nathaniel, 287
Byron. **See** Biron

Caedron, **162**
Caesar, Julius, **41, 93, 105**, 390 (384)
Calvin, John, 148
Cambridge, **347**, 395 (260)
Camden, William, 65n.2, 66n.3, 72, 78, **131**
Campion, Thomas, 335
Carlisle, earl of (James Hay), 8, 220, 280, **302**, 418 (Ep. Ded. 2), 432 (786)
Carr, Robert. **See** Somerset

Castaly, 89, 394 (Reader 29)
Castiglione, Baldassare, 13, 14, 20, 387 (77), 388 (197), 389 (234, 237, 249, 256, 266), 390 (380, 429), 392 (547, 597, 704)
Cato, "Censorius" and Uticensis (sometimes confused by F), **44, 308, 311**, 391 (504), 423 (304)
Cecil, Robert. **See** Salisbury
Chapman, George, 427-28 (558)
Charlemagne, **128, 324**, 397 (1065)
Charles V (emperor), **324**
Charron, Pierre, 220
Chaucer, Geoffrey, 13, 388 (150), 391 (478, 502)
Chorlton (Charlton), Jeffrey, 215, 228, 230, 239
Christ, Jesus (exclusive of CBS), 283, 422 (195), 432 (813)
Christian IV, 3, 4, 6, 7, 12, 20, **53-59**, 393 (20)
Cicero, Marcus Tullius, 14, 220n.13, 221-22, 284, **303, 307, 311, 313, 321, 323**, 386 (10), 387 (49), 388 (224), 390 (400), 392 (512), 410 (521), 412 (795, 820, 822, 837, 842), 413 (891, 932, 938, 942), 415 (1032), 416 (1077, 1125), 417 (1243), 419 (12, 14, 27), 420 (28, 31), 421 (101), 423 (300, 300-301), 425 (389, 391, 392), 426 (465), 430 (674, 675, 677, 687), 431 (704, 741)
Cicero, Quintus Tullius, **313**, 425 (392)
Circe, **33**
Clarendon, earl of (Edward Hyde), 331n.1, 352n.15, 385 (Ep. Ded. 7), 386 (Ep. Ded. 19)
Cleobis, **274**, 417 (1243)
Cleopatra, **41**, 390 (384)
Clerke, Bartholomew, 14
Clodius Pulcher, Publius, **311**, 423 (304)
Cobham, eighth baron, 219
Cockeram, Henry, 346, **347**, 387 (Ep. Ded. 26; text 13), 387 (130), 388 (145, 155), 389 (254), 390 (359, 423)
Coluander, 391 (490), 392 (512)
Comes, Natalis, 411 (718), 415 (1045),

417 (1207)
Constantinople, 227, **247**
Cooper, Thomas, 392 (683)
Coprario, John, 75, 335
Cornwallis, Sir William, 223n.24, 407 (266)
Cosimo I, 435 (*SP* X 5)
Cressida, **33, 45**, 388 (150), 392 (518)
Crosse, Henry, 415 (1051)
Cupid, **30-31, 43, 51, 337**
Curio, Gaius Scribonius, **308**

Daedalus, **269**, 415 (1041)
Dalilah, **204**
Daniel, Samuel, 74, 75-76, 136, 386 (Ep. Ded. 11), 391 (452), 395 (330), 396 (617)
David, **177**
Davies, John (of Hereford), 8, 10, 11n.11
Davril, Robert, 17, 18, 77, 138n.9, 218n.5, 227, 279n.1, 331, 335, 339, 340n.11, 351, 363
de Champagne, Marie, 13
de la Fountayne, Erasmus, 359, **360-62**
de la Puente, Luis, 142
de Sales, Francis, Saint, 142
de Vere, Edward. See Oxford (seventeenth earl of)
de Vere, Susan. See Montgomery (countess of)
De Vocht, H., xn.2
Deianeira, **40**, 390 (345)
Dekker, Thomas, 16, 280, 345
Delphi, **358**
Democritus, 396 (785)
Demosthenes, 284n.13, **326-27**, 431 (735)
Denmark, 9, 10, **56**, 393 (104)
Devereux, Dorothy (sister of Robert). See Northumberland (countess of)
Devereux, Penelope (sister of Robert). See Devonshire (countess of)
Devereux, Robert. See Essex (second earl of)
Devon, 346, 360, 363
Devonshire, countess of (Penelope Devereux), **33, 44, 50,** 66, 69-71, 72, 73, 75, 76, 78n.19, 79-81, **86-89, 98,** 100, 101, **109-10, 127,** 335, **337**, 360, 388 (152, 154), 391, (505-6, 505-7), 394 (06 Ep. Ded. 2), 395 (268, 330, 338), 396 (638, 645), 397 (1045), 406 (121)
Devonshire, first earl of (Charles Brooke Blount), 14, 17, 63-77, 80, 81n.24, **86-88,** 89-90, **91-131,** 335, **336-38,** 388 (152, 154), 394 (Reader 22, 34; text 94), 395 (260, 268, 274, 309), 396 (363, 375, 500, 504, 506, 520, 632, 708, 738), 397 (819), 434 (*SP* II 49, 57, 62)
Diana, **44**
Dio Cassius, 284, **327**, 433 (cor 41)
Diogenes Laertius, 284, **315, 323,** 412 (820), 415 (1032), 421 (155), 426 (462), 431 (746, 749)
Diogenes the Cynic, 228, **244, 315,** 406 (134), 415 (1032), 426 (462)
Dionysius, **257**, 407 (247), 410 (616)
Dives, **182**, 401 (829)
Domitian, **350**, 434 (*SP* VII 9)
Doncaster, viscount. See Carlisle
Donne, George, 352, 354
Donne, John, 13, 136, 331n.1, 352n.15
Doucel del Phoebus, 5
Dorset, first earl of (Thomas Sackville), **99**, 395 (274)
Drayton, Michael, 390 (395)
Drummond, William (of Hawthornden), 3, 6, 6n.1, 8n.8
Drusus, Marcus Livius, **322**, 431 (721, 724)
Du Vair, Guillaume, 75
Dudley, John. See Northumberland (first duke of)
Duppa, Brian, 357
Dyce, Alexander, ix-x, 24, 73, 76-77, 81, 135, 297, 333, 340, 345, 348, 351, 357, 405 (50), 407 (307), 423 (225)

Edwards, Philip, 349, 354n.16
Egypt, **186, 208**
Elijah, **186**, 401 (983)
Elizabeth I, 64, 65, 67, 68-69, 71, 73,

INDEX 449

104–5, 218, **317**, 395 (160, 274, 309), 409 (518), 427 (550)
Elizabeth II, 8n.9
Elyot, Sir Thomas, 281, 421 (101)
Elys, Edmund, 363, **364**
England, 3, 20, **53, 56, 57, 58**, 65–67, **105, 106, 111, 120, 257, 317, 347**
Epaminondas, 284n.13, 292, **311**
Epictetus, 217n.2, 223, 413 (893)
Epicurus, 412 (875)
Erasmus, Desiderius, 392 (588), 405 (Ep. Ded. 15), 406 (134, 141), 407 (168), 411 (637, 718), 412 (820), 413 (935, 938), 416 (1125), 418 (Reader 17), 421 (155, 180), 422 (220), 423 (266, 278), 424, (306), 425 (356), 426 (462), 430 (674, 681), 431 (739)
Esar-haddon (Eserod in F), **186**, 401 (974)
Essex, countess of (Frances Howard), 11
Essex, second earl of (Robert Devereux), 11, 65–66, 68–69, 70–71, **93, 98–99, 101**, 228, **244**, 284, **317–18**, 394 (94), 395 (260, 268, 348, 349), 396 (375), 404 (tp 8), 406 (121), 409 (518), 427 (550, 558), 428 (558)
Eve, **31**, 387 (77)

Farr, Dorothy M., xn.3, 19
Felltham, Owen, 223n.24, 281
Fletcher, John, 349n.13, 406 (120)
Fletcher, Joseph, 135, 151
Flora, **114**, 396 (818, 819)
Florio, John, 417 (1238)
Ford, John
  The Broken Heart, 19, 81n.24, 286, 333, 386 (Reader 7), 387 (130, 130), 388 (193), 389 (277), 390 (350, 395, 423), 391 (440), 392 (526, 653), 393 (748; MM 124, 178), 398 (145), 407 (207, 213, 307), 409 (436), 410 (630), 411 (705, 718), 413 (913, 954), 417 (1204), 418 (Reader 30), 420 (38), 425 (395), 427 (495), 429 (619), 431 (715), 432 (761)
  The Fancies Chast and Noble, 409 (436, 512), 426 (488)
  The Ladies Triall, 416 (1128), 426 (488), 428 (563)
  The Lovers Melancholy, ix, 280–81, 333, 387 (Reader 7; text 18), 387 (23), 390 (423), 392 (584), 405 (50), 407 (307), 410 (630), 413 (913, 954), 418 (Reader 30), 419 (14), 425 (383, 395), 426 (453, 470), 430 (667), 431 (731)
  Loves Sacrifice, 331n.1, 348, 389 (237), 393 (707), 393 (104), 407 (167, 187, 207), 416 (1128), 418 (Reader 11, 50), 422 (220), 426 (488), 427 (495)
  Perkin Warbeck, 286, 387 (23, 33, 34, 122, 138), 388 (203, 223), 389 (252, 292), 390 (423), 391 (505), 392 (512, 577), 393 (104), 405 (21), 406 (141), 407 (180, 266, 287), 408 (327, 389), 410 (630), 414 (999, 1009), 416 (1052), 420 (43), 423 (255), 426 (488), 427 (495), 430 (680), 432 (761)
  The Queen, 400 (427), 404 (1847), 407 (207), 413 (942), 423 (229), 432 (799)
  'Tis Pitty Shees a Whore, 19, 135, 136n.3, 386 (Ep. Ded. 26), 390 (395, 415), 392 (571, 653), 393 (707), 398 (32), 398 (145), 400 (494), 401 (751, 1135), 402 (1187), 403 (1392, 1411, 1603, 1687), 417 (1204, 1229), 418 (Reader 18), 421 (147), 422 (220), 427 (505)
  The Witch of Edmonton, 280, 407 (213), 422 (214)
Ford, John (cousin of dramatist), 331, 352
France, 5, **56, 318, 347**, 393 (104)

Gainsford, Thomas, 223, 223n.24
Galen, 421 (147)
Ganymede, **364**, 435 (SP XIV 7)
Gascoigne, George, 385 (tp 19)
Geneva Bible. **See** Bible, translations of
Geoffrey of Monmouth, 414 (957)
Germany, **56**
Gethsemane, 145, **163**
Gibson, Colin, 349, 354n.16

Gifford, William, ix, 24, 73, 76–77, 81, 135, 297, 351, 357, 394 (Reader), 423 (225)
Godolphin, Sir William, **98**, 395 (260)
Golding, Arthur, 415 (1045)
Great Britain, 9, 10, **41, 111, 126, 324, 337**, 393 (104)
Greece, **50, 263, 345, 358**, 387 (150)
Greene, Robert, 16, 75, 352, 388 (166), 391 (504)
Gregory the Great, Saint, 420 (30)
Guazzo, Stefano, 14
Guevara, Antonio de, 410 (543)

Hall, Joseph, 223n.24, 339n.9
Hannibal, **41, 268**, 285, **313**, 390 (400), 415 (1024, 1024), 425 (389, 391)
Har(r)ington of Exton, John, second baron, 6, 284, 293, 294, **311–12**, 424 (314, 322)
Har(r)ison, John, 148, 228
Haslewood, Joseph, 76, 81
Haviland, John, 229, 230, 231
Hawkins, Henry, 404 (1638 tp)
Hay, Sir James. See Carlisle
Hector, **33**, 388 (154)
Helen of Troy, **33, 43, 44, 50**, 388 (150)
Helicon, **364**, 435 (*SP* XIV 5)
Henries (kings of England), **244**
Henry (Prince of Wales), 6, 7, 72n.12, 335
Henry IV (of France), **318, 324**, 427 (558), 428 (561, 563)
Henry VII (formerly earl of Richmond), **268**, 414 (1009, 1012), 415 (1017)
Henryson, Robert, 13
Heraclitus, **113**, 396 (785)
Herbert, George, 136, 386 (Ep. Ded. 11)
Herbert, Sir Henry, 230
Herbert, Mary (Sidney). See Pembroke (dowager countess of)
Herbert, Mary (Talbot). See Pembroke (countess of)
Herbert, Philip. See Montgomery (fourth earl of)
Herbert, William. See Pembroke (third earl of)

Hercules, **39–40, 327, 337**, 390 (345), 434 (*SP* II 49)
Hermes, 396 (738)
Heylyn, Peter, 69, 70n.9
Heywood, Thomas, 72n.12, 351, 352, 353, 389 (234), 391 (504, 505), 392 (505–7, 525)
Hill, R. F., 407 (307)
Hippodamia, **33**, 388 (152)
Hoby, Sir Thomas, 14
Holinshed, Raphael, 390 (386)
Holland, Philemon, 389 (269), 407 (266), 416 (1166), 417 (1243), 422 (192), 426 (470), 430 (683)
Homer, **92, 273, 319**, 388 (150), 392 (505), 417 (1207), 429 (615)
Horace, 222n.19, 284, 289, **323**, 397 (Anagram 13), 405 (29), 411 (722), 412 (798, 837), 413 (833, 913), 416 (1084), 424 (341), 429 (608, 650), 431 (739)
Hoskins, John, 14, 17
Howard, Frances. See Essex (countess of)
Howard, Lord Henry. See Northampton (earl of)
Howard, Thomas. See Arundel (second earl of)
Howard, Thomas. See Suffolk (first earl of)
Huebert, Ronald, xn.3, 19, 77, 393 (707)
Humphrey, Lawrence, 222n.19, 222–23
Hunter, Joseph, 135, 217, 335, 419 (Ep. Ded. 26)
Hyde, Edward. See Clarendon
Hydra, **41**

Icarus, **269**, 415 (1045)
Indagine, John, 420 (67)
India, **57**
Inns of Court, 73, **86, 88**, 331, 339, 355
  Gray's Inn, 333, 351, 355
  Lincoln's Inn, 13
  Middle Temple, 12, 73, 89, 331n.1, 339, 345, 394 (Reader 15)
Ireland, **56**, 65–68, 71, 73–74, 76, **99, 101–5, 111, 120, 337**, 395 (274), 396 (506, 520, 708)

INDEX 451

Isaac, **208**
Isaiah (Esay in F), **177**, 400 (656)
Isocasius, 228, **243**, 405 (85)
Isocrates, 284, 285, **313**, 425 (372)
Israel, 148, **193**
Italy, **56, 347**

Jackson, Abraham, **311**, 424 (322)
James, Saint, **178**
James I (VI of Scotland), 3, 7, 10, 11, **53–56**, 58, 67, 68, 70, **105, 111,** 218–19, 280–81, 283, 284, 285, 292, 293, **323–25**, 385 (Ep. Ded. 7), 386 (Ep. Ded. 15), 393 (178), 395 (268, 274), 396 (506, 701), 397 (1065), 409 (518), 411 (655), 417 (1293), 418 (Ep. Ded. 2), 432 (786, 795, 805–8, 805–6, 813)
    Basilikon Doron, 285, **323**, 419 (27), 425 (372), 432 (771)
James V (of Scotland), **323**, 432 (771)
Jason, **37**
Jehu, **186**
Jerusalem, **162**
Jesabel, **186**, 401 (983)
Jesuits, **205**, 403 (1621)
Jews, **161, 163, 177, 205, 210,** 403 (1465)
John, Saint, **178**
Johnson, Robert, 223n.24
Jones, Inigo, 11, 386 (Ep. Ded. 11)
Jonson, Ben, ix, 6, 11, 357, **358–59**, 386 (Ep. Ded. 11), 397 (848)
Jordan (river), 147, **174**
Jove. See Jupiter
Jupiter, **54, 116, 274,** 435 (SP XIV 7)
Justinian I (emperor), **310**
Juvenal, 224, 284, **311**, 392 (512, 517), 396 (785), 423 (300)

Kelso, Ruth, 224 and n.26
Kerslake, Thomas, 217, 419 (Ep. Ded. 26)
Kyd, Thomas, 397 (848)

Laelius, Gaius, **321**
Lais, **45**, 392 (518)
Lake, Sir Thomas, 429 (579)

Lando, Ortensio, 13 and n.15
Langius, Josephus, 389 (337), 390 (415), 392 (541)
Laud, William, 70
Lavinia, **33**, 388 (151)
Lazarus, **182**
Leech, Clifford, xn.3, 17, 19, 218n.5, 285n.17, 286, 335, 339n. 10, 340, 345, 351, 355, 360, 363, 390 (415)
Leicester, first earl of (Robert Sidney), 64, 395 (309)
Lennard, Samson. See Buoni
Lennox, second duke of (Ludovick Stuart), 4, 11, **26, 29**, 385 (Ep. Ded.)
Lentulus, **33**, 388 (166)
Levites, **167**, 399 (317)
Lily, William, 429 (650)
Lipsius, Justus, 217n.2, 222, **265**, 283, 284, 285, 405 (83), 412 (820), 413 (917), 416 (1077), 419 (18)
Lisle, Lawrence, 279
Livy, 408 (386), 413 (955), 415 (956), 415 (1024, 1024)
Lloyd, Bertram, 79, 80, 360
Lodge, Thomas, 412 (787)
London, 7, 8, 11, 67, **347,** 360, 396 (500)
Louis XIII (of France), **324**, 432 (809)
Lownes, Humphrey, 217n.2, 228
Loyola, Ignatius, Saint, 142, 143
Lucilius Junior, Gaius, 429 (631)
Lucrece, **45**, 392 (525)
Luther, Martin, 146
Lycia (Lucia). See Devonshire (countess of)
Lycurgus, **266–67**, 414 (960)
Lyly, John, 228, 406 (134), 408 (321), 413 (930), 423 (255), 426 (470)

Macedon(ia), **262**
Maecenas, **105, 109,** 136, 385 (Ep. Ded. 11)
Malone, Edmond, 79
Malory, Sir Thomas, 12
Marcus Aurelius Antoninus. See Aurelius
Markham, Gervase, 75
Marlowe, Christopher, 19, 352, 390 (370)

Mars, **27, 30, 100, 112, 128,** 385 (tp 19), 386 (Ep. Ded. 42), 387 (41), 396 (738), 397 (1058)
Marshall, William, 229, 404 (*1638* tp)
Marston, John, 7n.5, 11, 331n.1, 426 (453)
Martz, Louis L., 136n.5, 142 and nn.12, 13; 143, 145
Mary (the Virgin), **31,** 387 (77)
Masinissa (Massinissa), **270-72,** 416 (1101)
Massinger, Philip, 331, 349, **350, 354,** 386 (Ep. Ded. 11)
Mathew, David, 218n.6, 219n.9
Matthew, Saint, **178**
Melytus, **323,** 431 (746)
Menelaus, 388 (150)
Merchant, David C., 24, 387 (27, 86), 388 (193, 224), 389 (277), 390 (362, 375, 395, 398, 423, 429), 391 (440, 441, 504), 392 (517, 526, 534, 598, 613, 653), 393 (760; MM 104, 124, 178, 197)
Mercury, **27, 112, 128,** 385 (tp 19), 386 (Ep. Ded. 42), 396 (738), 397 (1058)
Meribath, **174**
Merlin, 4
Michaiah, **176,** 400 (644)
Middleton, Thomas, 345
Miller, R. H., 292n.42
Milles, Thomas, 224, 416 (1131)
Milton, John, 147, 400 (607)
Mnemosyne, **336,** 434 (SP II 13)
Monsarrat, G. D., 79, 135 and n.3, 217nn.1, 2; 218n.5, 286n.19, 401 (1103), 413 (917)
Montgomery, countess of (Susan de Vere), 11, 12, **27,** 386 (Ep. Ded. 15, 20)
Montgomery, fourth earl of (Philip Herbert), 4, 8, 11, **26, 48,** 136, 385 (Ep. Ded.), 386 (Ep. Ded.)
Moryson, Fynes, 63n.1, 63-64, 66n.3, 68
Moses, **167,** 399 (313)
Mount of Olives, **162**
Mountjoy, Lord. **See** Devonshire (first earl of)

Mowbray, Thomas. **See** Norfolk

Naaman, **174**
Nashe, Thomas, 75, 385 (tp 19), 391 (490)
Naunton, Robert, 63n.1, 64, 68n.4
Nepos, Cornelius, 415 (1024)
Nero, **255, 257, 258,** 313, 410 (544, 615), 425 (392)
Nessus, 390 (345)
Netherlands, 64, 71, **318,** 395 (309)
Noel, Mary, 359, **360-62**
Norfolk, first duke of (Thomas Mowbray), 228, **267,** 414 (996, 1001), 415 (1017)
Norman, Colin J., 217n.1, 291n.39, 292, 293n.43, 412 (852), 418 (Reader 4)
North, Sir Thomas, 415 (1024)
Northampton, earl of, 218
Northumberland, countess of (Dorothy Devereux, wife of ninth earl), 404 (tp 8), 406 (121)
Northumberland, first duke of (John Dudley), **261,** 411 (757)
Northumberland, ninth earl of (Henry Percy), 218-20, **239, 240,** 404 (tp 8), 416 (1101), 424 (332)
Numa Pompilius, **128,** 397 (1061)

Oenone, 388 (150)
Oliver, H. J., xn.3, 19, 77, 79, 139, 218n.5, 285n.26, 286n.17, 340n.11, 345, 349n.13
Orbison, Tucker, 286n.19
Olympic Games, **37,** 389 (269)
O'Neill, Hugh. **See** Tyrone
Opia. **See** Devonshire, countess of
Overbury, Sir Thomas, ix, 279-80, 331, 339-40, **344,** 425 (368), 429 (579), 432 (795)
Ovid, **268,** 387 (113, 114), 389 (337), 390 (345), 391 (502), 392 (541), 405 (Ep. Ded. 15), 410 (539), 413 (930), 414 (955), 415 (1024, 1042, 1045, 1051), 416 (1084), 428 (561)
Oxford, **347**
Oxford Dictionary of English Proverbs, 222n.19, 385 (tp 12), 386 (Ep. Ded.

33; text 10), 388 (191, 197), 389 (249), 390 (405, 415), 391 (512), 410 (626), 412 (795), 416 (1123), 433 (cor 28)
Oxford, seventeenth earl of (Edward de Vere), 386 (Ep. Ded.)

Paelops, **33**, 388 (152)
Palestine, **268**
Pallas, **39**, 389 (326)
Palmerin de Oliva, 5
Paradise of Dainty Devices, 392 (517)
Paris (France), 347
Paris (Trojan prince), **33**, **319-20**, 350, 388 (150), 388 (152), 434 (SP VII 9)
Paul, Saint, 390 (429)
Peele, George, 69
Pegasus, 8
Pembroke, countess of (Mary Talbot), 12, **27**, 386 (Ep. Ded.)
Pembroke, dowager countess of (Mary Sidney), 138, 385 (Ep. Ded.)
Pembroke, third earl of (William Herbert), 4, 11, **26**, **42**, 136, **156**, 385 (Ep. Ded.), 385-86 (Ep. Ded.), 397 (Ep. Ded.)
Penelope (Rich). See Devonshire (countess of)
Penelope (wife of Ulysses), 391 (505)
Percy, Henry. See Northumberland (ninth earl of)
Percy, Lucy (daughter of Henry), 220
Percy, Thomas (cousin of Henry), 219
Persius, 391 (490)
Peru, 10, 11
Peter, Saint, **178**, **205**
Pettie, George, 391 (505), 426 (470)
Phaeton, 428 (561)
Pharaoh, **113**, **193**, **208**, 396 (776)
Philip (father of Alexander the Great), **37**, 389 (269)
Phil(l)ip, Saint, **178**
Philoctetes, 388 (150)
Philomela, 58
Phocion, **311**, 423 (300)
Phormio, **41**, 285, **313**, 390 (400), 425 (389, 391)

Plato, 284, 285, **313**, **323**, 386 (10), 389 (259), 416 (1186), 425 (372), 431 (746)
Plautus, 421 (180)
Playfere, Thomas, 8
Pliny (the elder), 284, **308**, **315**, **321**, 404 (1638 tp), 422 (192), 426 (470), 430 (683)
Plutarch, 36, 284
 Lives, **326**, 389 (230, 234), 390 (384), 410 (544), 411 (718), 414 (955, 960), 415 (1024), 417 (1243), 433 (cor 35)
 Moralia, **311**, 389 (269), 407 (266), 416 (1166, 1186), 417 (1207, 1218, 1243), 419 (14), 423 (292, 300)
Pompey, "Magnus" and Sextus (sometimes confused by F), **244**, **254**, **268**, 406 (116), 409 (501), 415 (1023, 1024)
Poole, Rachel, 79, 80
Portia, **44**, 391 (504)
Powel, Gabriel, 20, 223n.24
Pricket, Robert, 71 and n.11
Proverbs. See *Oxford Dictionary of English Proverbs*; Smith, Charles G.; Tilley, Morris P.
Provinces, United, **318**, 428 (570)
Psyche, **30-31**
Ptolemy (king of Mauretania), **244**, 406 (116)
Ptolemy II Philadelphus, 396 (776)
Publilius Syrus, 385 (tp 12), 425 (418)
Purset, Christopher, 61, 78, 85
Pusaeus (Posaeus), **243**, 405 (85)
Pyrrhus, 388 (150)

Quintilianus, Marcus Fabius, 284, **308**, 421 (189)
Quintus Curtius. See Rufus

Ralegh, Sir Walter, 70, 219, 284, 294, **312**, 424 (332), 425 (346)
Red Sea, 147, **208**
Rich, Barnabe, 16, 224
Rich, Lord, 69-70, 81n.24
Rich, Penelope. See Devonshire (countess of)

Richard II, **257, 267,** 410 (615), 414 (996)
Richard III, **268,** 414 (1009)
Richmond, Henry earl of. See Henry VII
Roberts, Henry, 6n.2, 7, 8, 8n.9
Rogers, Thomas, 223
Roman Empire, **36**
Rome, **36, 40–41,** 105, **257,** 310, **345, 347, 358**
Romei, Annibale, 14
Romulus, **266,** 413 (953), 414 (955)
Roper, Derek, 19, 139, 390 (415), 392 (653)
Rowley, William, 280, 345
Rufus, Quintus Curtius, **262,** 412 (787)

Sabines, **36,** 388 (230), 389 (234)
Sackville, Thomas. See Dorset
Salisbury, first earl of (Robert Cecil), 67, 69, 218–19, **255,** 409 (518)
Sallust, 388 (224)
Saltonstall, Captain Charles, 355, **356**
Saltonstall, Wye, 355
Sargeaunt, M. Joan, 76–77, 79, 135, 135n.3, 139, 141, 217–18, 340, 340n.11, 345, 349n.13, 351, 355, 360, 363, 395 (330)
Satan, **171,** 400 (457)
Saturn, **337**
Scaevola, Gaius Mucius, **251,** 408 (386)
Scipio Africanus Major (Affrican), **128, 268, 271,** 397 (1062), 415 (1024, 1024), 416 (1077, 1107)
Scotland, **111**
Scott, M. I., 152
Sejanus, 228, **244,** 406 (116)
Seneca, 217n.2, 220n.13, 221–22, 224, 227, **245,** 284, 290, **311, 312, 313, 320,** 405 (5, 23, 32, 42, 75), 406 (104, 116, 161), 407 (168, 172, 173, 213, 223, 226, 229, 231, 236, 247, 266), 408 (350, 356), 409 (431, 512), 410 (544, 616, 616), 411 (646), 412 (806, 820, 833, 837), 413 (913, 930, 935, 938), 414 (956), 415 (1018, 1024), 416 (1084, 1128), 419 (3, 12, 14, 14), 423 (304, 306), 425 (356, 392), 429 (631, 633)
Shakespeare, William, 138, 386 (Ep. Ded. 11), 393 (726)
All's Well That Ends Well, 393 (726)
Antony and Cleopatra, 409 (408)
Comedy of Errors, 393 (739)
Hamlet, 402 (1348)
1 Henry VI, 411 (667)
Henry VIII, 389 (259), 406 (120)
Julius Caesar, 391 (504)
Love's Labour's Lost, 390 (398)
Measure for Measure, 399 (335)
Othello, 13
Pericles, 407 (173)
The Rape of Lucrece, 392 (525)
Richard II, 228, 391 (437), 396 (708), 410 (615), 413 (935), 414 (996, 999, 1001)
Romeo and Juliet, 393 (726)
Sonnets, 400 (502)
Timon of Athens, 387 (38)
Troilus and Cressida, 388 (150, 150–51), 394 (125)
Venus and Adonis, 387 (41)
Sherman, S. P., 17, 18, 77, 81n.24
Shirley, James, ix, 331, **348**
Shrewsbury, seventh earl of (Gilbert Talbot), 385 (Ep. Ded.), 386 (Ep. Ded.)
Sicily (Sicile), **257**
Sidney, Mary. See Pembroke (dowager countess of)
Sidney, Sir Philip, 16–17, 20, 64, 69, 76, 136, 223n.24, 385 (Ep. Ded.), 388 (154), 395 (309)
Sidney, Robert. See Leicester
Sidon, **262**
Siloam, **174**
Smith, Charles G. (proverbs), 407 (168), 413 (930), 416 (1052, 1125, 1128, 1184), 419 (3), 422 (220), 423 (278), 430 (686)
Smith, G. C. Moore, 217n.2
Socrates, **255, 273,** 283, 284n.13, **307, 323,** 409 (521), 415 (1032), 416 (1186), 431 (745, 746)
Sodomites, **186**
Somerset, countess of, 340, 434 (SP IIIc 24)

INDEX 455

Somerset, earl of (Robert Carr), 279, 340, 425 (368), 429 (579), 434 (SP IIIc 24)
Southampton, third earl of (Henry Wriothesley), 68, 70, **99**, 395 (268)
Southwell, Robert, 136n.5, 137, 399 (277)
Spain, **56**, 64, 65, 66–67, **337, 347**, 395 (274), 396 (701), 428 (570)
Speght, Rachel, 13
Spencer, T. J. B., 407 (307)
Spenser, Edmund, 12, 17, 20, 387 (30), 390 (417), 391 (447), 392 (526)
Stafford, Anthony, 217, 281, 406 (91)
Stansby, William, 277, 287, 299
Stavig, Mark, xn.3, 17, 18, 77, 139n.11, 218n.5, 285n.17, 388 (152)
Stella. See Devonshire (countess of)
Stilpo, **263**, 412 (820)
Stock, L. E., 217n.1
Stock, Richard, **311**, 424 (322)
Stow, John, 6n.2, 219n.10
Stradling, Sir John, 222n.18, 283n.12, 413 (913), 419 (18)
Stuart, Ludovick. See Lennox
Suffolk, countess of, 11
Suffolk, first earl of (Thomas Howard), 425 (368), 429 (579)

Talbot, Alathea. See Arundel (countess of)
Talbot, Gilbert. See Shrewsbury
Talbot, Mary. See Pembroke (countess of)
Tamburlaine, **40**, 390 (370)
Tarquin, 392 (525)
Tasso, Ercole and Torquato, 15, 388 (197)
Terence, 430 (674, 675)
Terentia, **34**, 388 (166)
Thames, **53, 54**, 358
Theseus, **44**, 391 (502)
Thetis, **319**
Thompson, E. N. S., 217n.2
Tibullus, 389 (337)
Tilley, Morris P. (proverbs), 222n.19, 385 (tp 11, 12), 386 (Ep. Ded. 33; text 10), 387 (126), 388 (191, 197), 389 (249), 390 (405, 415), 391 (512), 394 (06 Ep. Ded. 8), 404 (*1638* tp), 405 (5, 27), 406 (131, 141), 407 (168, 207, 232, 243), 409 (503), 410 (570, 593, 626), 411 (671, 718, 722), 412 (798, 820, 837), 413, (876), 413 (913, 930, 935, 938), 416 (1052, 1077, 1123, 1125, 1128), 417 (1207, 1220), 418 (Reader 17), 419 (3, 14), 421 (126, 145, 147, 180, 181), 422 (194, 194, 195, 196, 220), 423 (266, 278), 426 (462, 488), 429 (655), 430 (674, 681, 686), 431 (733), 433 (cor 29)
Troilus, **33**, 388 (150, 152)
Troy, **50**
Turkey, **171**
Tyrone, earl of (Hugh O'Neill), 65–67, **102, 105**, 396 (500)

Ulysses, **33, 37, 44, 50**, 388 (154), 391 (505)

Valerius Maximus, 391 (504)
Van Oldenbarnevelt, Johan (Jan), 284, **318**, 428 (566, 566–67)
Velleius Paterculus, 284, **308, 322**, 421 (182), 431 (721, 724)
Venus, **30, 39, 43–44, 51**, 387 (41), 392 (505), 393 (708)
Vergil (Virgil), **265, 273**, 388 (151), 389 (337), 394 (quarto tp 8), 413 (917), 414 (955, 956), 416 (1052), 417 (1207), 434 (SP II 81, SP IV 1)
Vulgate. See Bible, translations of

Wales, 393 (104), 396 (500)
Walther, Hans, 392 (517, 541)
Weber, Henry, ix, 76, 81, 407 (307)
Webster, John, xn.1, 280, 331, 345, **345**, 349n.13, 402 (1348), 434 (SP IV 1)
Whetstone, George, 393 (135)
Whitney, Geoffrey, 392 (517)
Wilson, Thomas, 415 (1045)
Wither, George, 404 (*1638* tp)
Wolfe, John, 14
Wolsey, Thomas (cardinal), 228, **244**, 406 (120)

Wriothesley, Henry. **See** Southampton
Wycliffe, John, 398 (145)

Xenocrates, **40**, 390 (370)
Xenophon, **247**, 407 (223)

Xylander, Gulielmus, 433 (cor 35)

Zepherus, **338**, 434 (SP II 73)
Zeus. **See** Jupiter

Index of Biblical Citations
in Christes Bloodie Sweat

Old Testament
Genesis, **169, 171, 176, 187**, 403 (1805)
Exodus, **193, 208**, 391 (441), 397 (27), 403 (1565)
Leviticus, **166**
Numbers, **174**
Deuteronomy, **171**, 399 (317)
Judges, **204, 212**, 400 (457)
I Samuel, **177**
I Kings, **169, 177, 186**, 400 (644)
II Kings, **173, 174, 186**
II Chronicles, 400 (644)
Job, **169**, 405 (4)
Psalms, **160, 164, 167, 169, 176, 177, 179, 180, 182, 185, 187, 199, 200, 202, 208, 211**, 399 (302), 400 (457, 651, 736), 401 (1135), 403 (1824), 412 (762), 426 (439)
Proverbs, **167, 168, 169, 170, 185, 192, 199, 206**, 416 (1084), 423 (225), 430 (680)
Ecclesiastes, **168, 170**
Song of Solomon (Canticles), **192, 195**
Isaiah, **159, 162, 163, 164, 174, 177, 202**
Lamentations, **162, 204**
Ezekiel, **167, 169, 196, 197**
Hosea, **169, 171**
Joel, **182**
Micah, **168, 169**
Zecheriah, **161, 203**

New Testament
Matthew, **159, 160, 161, 162, 163, 165, 166, 167, 168, 171, 173, 176, 178, 179, 180, 181, 182, 184, 190, 191, 194, 198, 199, 205, 207, 210**, 387 (126, 134), 398 (67, 99), 399 (335), 401 (808, 817), 403 (1632), 408 (330), 419 (11), 422 (194)
Mark, **161, 163, 164, 165, 167, 168, 171, 176, 178, 180, 190, 213**, 400 (694), 403 (1453)
Luke, **159, 160, 161, 162, 163, 164, 165, 166, 167, 168, 178, 179, 181, 182, 185, 194, 197, 205, 209, 210**, 387 (134), 401 (829), 403 (1453, 1632, 1775)
John, **161, 162, 163, 165, 166, 167, 168, 171, 173, 174, 175, 177, 178, 179, 183, 186, 188, 194, 198, 200, 202, 205**, 226n.32, 391 (441), 419 (11), 403 (1565)
Acts, **161, 166, 167, 168, 173, 190, 205**
Romans, **169, 170, 179, 180, 195, 198, 199**, 391 (441), 422 (220), 423 (221)
I Corinthians, **169, 171, 179, 183, 208**, 400 (641)
Galatians, **162, 168, 171, 200**
Ephesians, **162, 174, 176, 183, 209**, 400 (457)
Philippians, **164, 213**
Colossians, **176, 184**
I Thessalonians, **169, 182**
I Timothy, **168, 207**
II Timothy, **171, 175**
Hebrews, **164, 166, 193, 197**, 397 (21)
James, **168, 169, 175, 213**, 401 (1118), 403 (1805)
I Peter, **164, 175, 179, 187, 201, 203**, 404 (1897), 412 (803)
II Peter, **169**, 403 (1489)
Revelation, **161, 167, 169, 171, 182, 185, 187, 194**, 403 (1805)

The Renaissance English Text Society

Council

PRESIDENT, *Arthur F. Kinney*, University of Massachusetts, Amherst
VICE-PRESIDENT, *A. S. G. Edwards*, University of Victoria
SECRETARY, *Carolyn Kent*, New York City
TREASURER, *Mario A. Di Cesare*, SUNY-Binghamton

Thomas Berger, St. Lawrence University
A. R. Braunmuller, University of California, Los Angeles
David Freeman, Memorial University of Newfoundland
W. Speed Hill, Lehman College and The Graduate Center, CUNY
John N. King, The Ohio State University
Gordon Kipling, University of California, Los Angeles
Janel Mueller, University of Chicago
Josephine A. Roberts, Louisiana State University

International Advisory Council

Dominic Baker-Smith, University of Amsterdam
Richard S. M. Hirsch, Birmingham, England
K. J. Höltgen, University of Erlangen-Nürnberg
M. T. Jones-Davies, University of Paris-Sorbonne
Sergio Rossi, University of Milan
Germaine Warkentin, Center for Reformation and Renaissance Studies, Victoria College, University of Toronto
Henry Woudhuysen, University College, University of London

The Renaissance English Text Society was founded to publish scarce literary texts, chiefly nondramatic, of the period 1475–1660. Subscriptions at $25.00 per year should be sent to Mario A. Di Cesare, Department of English, SUNY, Binghamton, NY 13902-6000, USA. Institutional members are requested to provide, at the time of enrollment, any purchase order numbers or other information required for their billing records; the Society cannot provide multiple invoices or other complex forms.

Copies of volumes X–XII may be purchased direct from Associated University Presses, 440 Forsgate Drive, Cranbury, NJ 08512, USA. Copies of earlier volumes still in print or of volumes XIII on may be ordered from MRTS – LNG-99, SUNY, Binghamton, NY 13902-6000.

FIRST SERIES

Vol. I. *Merie Tales of the Mad Men of Gotam* by A. B., edited by Stanley J. Kahrl, and *The History of Tom Thumbe*, by R. I., edited by Curt F. Buhler, 1965. (o.p.)

Vol. II. Thomas Watson's Latin *Amyntas*, edited by Walter F. Staton, Jr., and Abraham Fraunce's translation *The Lamentations of Amyntas*, edited by Franklin M. Dickey, 1967.

SECOND SERIES

Vol. III. *The dyaloge called Funus*, A Translation of Erasmus's Colloquy (1534), and *A very pleasaunt & fruitful Diologe called The Epicure*, Gerrard's Translation of Erasmus's Colloquy (1545), edited by Robert R. Allen, 1969.

Vol. IV. *Leicester's Ghost* by Thomas Rogers, edited by Franklin B. Williams, Jr., 1972.

THIRD SERIES

Vols. V-VI. *A Collection of Emblemes, Ancient and Moderne*, by George Wither, with introduction by Rosemary Freeman and bibliographical notes by Charles S. Hensley, 1975. (o.p.)

FOURTH SERIES

Vols. VII-VIII. *Tom a Lincolne* by R. I., edited by Richard S. M. Hirsch, 1978.

FIFTH SERIES

Vol. IX. *Metrical Visions* by George Cavendish, edited by A. S. G. Edwards, 1980.

SIXTH SERIES

Vol. X. *Two Early Renaissance Bird Poems*, edited by Malcolm Andrew, 1984.

Vol. XI. *Argalus and Parthenia* by Francis Quarles, edited by David Freeman, 1986.

Vol. XII. Cicero's *De Officiis*, trans. Nicholas Grimald, edited by Gerald O'Gorman, 1987.

Vol. XIII. *The Silkewormes and their Flies* by Thomas Moffet (1599), edited with introduction and commentary by Victor Houliston, 1988.

SEVENTH SERIES

Vol. XIV. John Bale, *The Vocacyon of Johan Bale*, edited by Peter Happé and John N. King, 1989.

Vol. XV. *The Nondramatic Works of John Ford*, edited by L. E. Stock, Gilles D. Monsarrat, Judith M. Kennedy, and Dennis Danielson, with the assistance of Marta Straznicky, 1990.